CHILD CARE & EDUCATION

FOURTH EDITION

Tina Bruce and Carolyn Meggitt

Hodder Arnold

A MEMBER OF THE HODDER HEADLINE GROUP

Dedication

For the quiet but solid support, the feeling of belonging to people who help and empower, and the team spirit between us – thank you to Ian, Hannah and Tom from Tina.

This book is dedicated with love and thanks to Dave, Jonathan, Leo and Laura from Carolyn.

Orders: please contact Bookprint Ltd, 130 Milton Park, Abingdon, Oxon OX14 4SB. Telephone: (44) 01235 827720. Fax: (44) 01235 400454. Lines are open from 9.00–5.00, Monday to Saturday, with a 24 hour message answering service. You can also order through our website www.hoddereducation.co.uk

British Library Cataloguing in Publication Data
A catalogue record for this title is available from the British Library

ISBN-10: 0 340 92539 6
ISBN-13: 978 0340 92539 3

First Published 2006
Impression number   10 9 8 7 6 5 4 3 2 1
Year   2012 2011 2010 2009 2008 2007 2006

Cover photo © Getty Images/Digital Vision
Typeset by Servis Filmsetting Limited, Manchester.
Printed in Italy for Hodder Arnold, an imprint of Hodder Education,
a member of the Hodder Headline Group, 338 Euston Road, London NW1 3BH

Contents

Acknowledgements

We gratefully acknowledge the help of Jessica Walker, author and teacher, for writing the chapter on Observation and Assessment.

We would also like to thank the following people for their contributions: Chris Rice (Clydebank College) for her section on operant conditioning; Ruth Forbes and the parents for the case studies of babies; Martin and Alayne Levy for the biography of their daughter Hannah in Chapter 1; Laura Meggitt for her valuable insights and contributions to case studies in early years settings; Pat Evans for the article about her son Euan in Chapter 1.

The authors and publishers would like to thank the following people for the specially commissioned photographs in this book:

David Meggitt for the photographs in Chapters 1, 4, 5, 8, 11, 13, 14, 15 and 16; all the staff, children and their parents at Bushy Park Nursery; Gabriel and his parents, Augusta and her parents and Liz Allen for photos of Jack.

Tom Bruce for the photography in Chapters 3, 6, 7, 9, 10 and 12; Anne-Louise de Buriane and the staff and families of Langford Extended Primary School; Julian Grenier and the staff and families at Kate Greenaway Maintained Nursery School/Children's Centre; Elizabeth Buck and the staff and families at Newark Playgroup; Conan and his parents, Hope and her parents and Julie for the home-based photographs.

We also want to thank each other for being such excellent team-mates and for being so enjoyable to work with. We owe a great debt of gratitude to our students, past and present, for the insights they provide to our learning.

The authors would like to thank the editorial team at Hodder Education for their help and support.

Other photographs – Barnardo's: p. 375; Corbis: p. 522, 523; FASaware UK: p. 517; Foundation for the Study of Infant Death: p. 376; Science Photo Library: p. 400 © Chris Priest, p. 438 © Simon Fraser RVI. Illustrations: Tony Jones Art Construction, Surrey, UK: p. 112, 115, 183.

Every effort has been made to acknowledge ownership of copyright. The publishers will be pleased to make suitable arrangements with copyright holders whom it has not been possible to contact.

Introduction

The broad aim of this book is to equip readers with a basic knowledge of all aspects of child care and education up to the age of 8 years. Learning does not happen all in one go: it takes both children and adults time to learn new things. It is said that children need to sing a song a thousand times before they know the words, and adults too need time to become familiar with new ideas and words.

This book is designed to help readers understand how children develop and learn. Children, like adults, cannot be rushed in their learning. They need to reflect on what they learn practically, and they do this in their play, talk and representations of all kinds (drawings, models, dances, songs etc.). Adults reflect on and consolidate their learning by reading and writing about their new thinking and knowledge; and as they do this, they organise their ideas, share them and put them into practice.

You will find that this book is unique because whilst it introduces you to different ideas and ways of working with young children and their families, it also has a logical shape. This means that it puts principles of inclusivity and equality first. It looks at children in a holistic way, but never separate from the child's parents or carers, who are placed centrally in the book.

Throughout the book, you will find both *he* and *she* are used in a balanced way. This is because both boys and girls need broad roles and relationships, as children and as they become adults. *Early years practitioner* is the term used to describe anyone who works with children from birth to 8 years of age (except parents). It includes nursery nurses, teachers, childminders, nannies, playleaders, etc. The term *early childhood setting* is used to describe the place where the child/children and early years practitioners spend their time together. For the childminder, this will be the childminder's home. For the nursery nurse, it could be a children's centre, family centre, nursery school or class, hospital, etc. Activities and case studies can be found within the text and at the end of the chapters; there is also a comprehensive glossary at the end of the book.

This book will help students and tutors studying on an early childhood course, because it can be used at different levels of understanding and training. It can be used from an introductory level with a tutor's help, e.g. CCE and NVQ1, right through to the newly established Foundation Degree courses and Early Childhood Studies degree courses. MA students have reported its use when the chapters cause thoughts which can be followed in more depth through the bibliography. Feedback from the bestselling first, second and third editions shows that parents/carers also find a book with this kind of logical shape useful.

This book is particularly recommended for students following the CACHE Diploma in Nursery Nursing; it is also useful for the BTEC National Diploma in Nursery Nursing. At the end of the book there is a convenient grid which shows how the chapters match the Children's Care, Learning and Development (CCLD) Level 3 and 4.

This new full colour edition includes a CD-Rom with a variety of exercises matched to each chapter. The CD-Rom contains blank charts to use when making observations of children and a list of useful websites and suggestions for further reading. We hope you will enjoy using the CD-Rom and that it helps to broaden your learning experience.

1

Anti-discriminatory/ anti-bias practice

Contents

Section 1: Equality of Opportunity

EQUALITY EQUALS QUALITY

There can be no quality in early childhood services unless there is **equality of opportunity**. Equality of opportunity means opening up access for every child and family to full participation in early childhood services. Lack of access causes:

❖ poor self-esteem;

❖ misunderstandings;

❖ stereotyping and discrimination;

❖ lack of inclusion;

❖ lack of respect;

❖ lack of confidence.

It is important for early childhood workers of all kinds to work according to principles of equality and inclusivity. This is at the heart of early childhood work in every kind of setting.

THE RIGHTS OF CHILDREN AND THEIR FAMILIES

What are children's rights?

Children are entitled to basic human rights, such as food, health care, a safe home and protection from abuse. However, children are a special case because they cannot always stand up for themselves. They need a *special* set of rights which take account of their vulnerability and ensure that adults take responsibility for their protection and development.

Guidelines for access to full participation in early childhood services

1   Children and their families need to feel part of things and to develop a sense of belonging.

2   All children and their families, especially if they belong to a minority group, need to feel valued and respected.

3   Children need to build positive images of themselves, helped by those around them. They should not be labelled narrowly as this leads to stereotyping.

4   Most discriminating behaviour is not intended. We need to look at what we do and what we take for granted so that we do not discriminate.

5   Every early years setting needs:

   ❖   a policy on equality of opportunity and inclusivity;

   ❖   a code of practice which puts the policy into action;

   ❖   regular meetings to review policy and practice.

6   Individuals matter, and each of us can influence a group's efforts towards more equality of opportunity.

THE UN CONVENTION ON THE RIGHTS OF THE CHILD

This is an international treaty that applies to all children and young people under the age of 18 years. It spells out the basic human rights of children everywhere. All children – without discrimination – have the right:

   ❖   to survival;

   ❖   to develop to their fullest potential;

   ❖   to protection from harmful influences, abuse and exploitation;

   ❖   to participate fully in family, cultural and social life;

   ❖   to express and have their views taken into account on all matters that affect them;

   ❖   to play, rest and enjoy leisure.

This important treaty has been signed by almost every country in the world.

The balance of rights and responsibilities

Children and young people have **responsibilities** as well as rights. Many have jobs, some care for relatives, a large proportion are school or college students, and they all must respect other people's rights and act within the law. However, these responsibilities do not detract from their human rights, which everybody has from the moment they are born.

A parent is responsible for the care and upbringing of their child. The **Children and Young Persons Act 1933** imposes criminal liability for abandonment, neglect or ill treatment upon any person over the age of 16 years who is responsible for a child under 16 years. Because parental responsibility cannot be surrendered or transferred, parents are liable for neglecting their child if they choose an inadequate babysitter.

The rights embodied by the UN Convention which particularly relate to child care and education are as follows:

* Children have the right to be with their family or with those who will care best for them.

* Children have the right to enough food and clean water for their needs.

* Children have the right to an adequate standard of living.

* Children have the right to health care.

* Children have the right to play.

* Children have the right to be kept safe and not hurt or neglected.

* Disabled children have the right to special care and training.

* Children must not be used as cheap workers or as soldiers.

* Children have the right to free education.

Fig 1.1 Children have the right to play

ACTIVITY: EXPLORING CHILDREN'S RIGHTS

'In the UK it is still both legal and socially acceptable for parents to smack their children.'

After considering the case of a boy who had been beaten regularly by his stepfather with a 3-foot garden cane between the ages of 5 and 8 years, the **European Court of Human Rights** ruled that the British law on corporal punishment in the home failed to protect children's rights. The stepfather had been acquitted – or found innocent – by a British court of causing actual bodily harm. The stepfather had argued that the beating was '*reasonable chastisement*'; this means that parents could use a degree of force in order to discipline their children. Recent changes to the law have removed this defence of 'reasonable chastisement', which dates back to 1860. In an amendment to the Children Bill agreed by peers in 2005, smacking is now outlawed in England and Wales '*if it causes harm such as bruising or mental harm*'.

1   Individually, find out all you can about:

✧   The arguments *against* smacking children – in particular, investigate the work of the Children are Unbeatable! Alliance, whose aims are: to seek legal reform to give children the same protection under the law on assault as adults; and to promote positive, non-violent discipline. (www.childrenareunbeatable.org.uk)

✧   The arguments *for* parents' right to smack their own children – for example, look into the Parents Have Rights campaign, which is against any legislation that interferes with a parent's right to punish their children as they see fit. (www.families-first.org.uk)

2   In two groups, organise a debate on the issue of smacking children.

Group A will argue that: **'The law should be changed so that physical punishment of children is never permitted.'**

Group B will argue that: **'Parents have the right to use whatever method of discipline works best for their children.'**

3   Prepare a **fact-file** on the debate on smacking for the use of future students. Include a list of useful addresses and websites. Ensure you find out about any recent changes to these laws in Scotland and elsewhere in the UK.

THE CAUSES AND EFFECTS OF DISCRIMINATION

What is discrimination?

Discrimination is the denial of equality based on personal characteristics, such as race and colour. Discrimination is usually based on **prejudice** and **stereotypes**.

✧   Prejudice literally means to prejudge people based on assumptions. For example, racial prejudice is the belief that physical or cultural differences (e.g. in skin colour, religious beliefs or dress) are directly linked to differences in the development of intelligence, ability, personality or goodness.

❖ The word 'stereotype' comes from the process of making metal plates for printing. When applied to people, stereotyping refers to forming an instant or fixed picture of a group of people, usually based on false or incomplete information. Stereotypes are often negative.

Discrimination in child care and education

We need to be aware of different forms of discrimination so that we can act to promote equality.

❖ **Racial discrimination**: racism is the belief that some races are superior, based on the false idea that things like skin colour make some people better than others.

Examples: refusing a child a nursery place because they are black; failing to address the needs of children from a minority religious or cultural group, such as children from traveller families; only acknowledging festivals from the mainstream culture, such as Christmas and Easter.

❖ **Institutional racism**: following the Stephen Lawrence Inquiry (February 1999) this has been defined as 'the collective failure of an organisation to provide an appropriate and professional service to people because of their colour, culture or ethnic origin. It can be seen or detected in processes, attitudes and behaviour which amount to discrimination through unwitting prejudice, ignorance, thoughtlessness and racist stereotyping which disadvantage minority ethnic people.' It can be difficult to detect and combat institutional racism as it tends to be

integrated into an organisation's culture and practices as a result of its past history. For this reason, it is vital that all early years settings adhere to an up-to-date **policy of equal opportunities**, and that the policy is monitored regularly.

❖ **Disability discrimination**: children with disabilities or impairments may be denied equality of opportunity with their non-disabled peers.

Examples: failing to provide children with special needs with appropriate facilities and services; organising activities in a nursery setting in a way that ignores the special physical, intellectual and emotional needs of certain children.

❖ **Sex discrimination**: this occurs when people of one gender reinforce the stereotype that they are superior to the other.

Examples: boys are routinely offered more opportunities for rough-and-tumble play than girls; early years workers may encourage girls to perform traditional 'female' tasks such as cooking and washing.

Case study

Sade

Sade (4 years) is British-born Nigerian, but she has never been to Nigeria. Both Sade's parents were born in the UK and grew up there. Sade eats Nigerian food only at the family gatherings that happen a few times a year when relatives visit. She finds it rather hot and spicy compared with the European food that she usually eats at home and at nursery. She does not understand her key worker's question about the spices her mother cooks with at home.

No law can prevent prejudiced attitudes. However, the law can prohibit discriminatory practices and behaviours that flow from prejudice.

The effects of discrimination

Children can experience discrimination in a number of ways. Discrimination can be direct or indirect:

❖ **Direct discrimination** occurs when a child is treated less favourably than another child in the same or similar circumstances.

Example: when a child is bullied, by being ignored, verbally or physically abused or teased (see also page 18 on bullying).

❖ **Indirect discrimination** occurs when a condition is applied that will unfairly affect a particular group of children when compared to others; this may be either deliberate or unintended.

Example: when children from a minority ethnic or religious group (such as Sikh, Muslim or Plymouth Brethren) are required to wear a specific school uniform which causes difficulties within their cultural code.

Case Study

Childminder escapes jail for racial assault on 2-year-old

A childminder who crayoned the word 'nigger' on the forehead of a 2-year-old girl in her care narrowly escaped jail after a judge accepted pleas that she was 'ignorant rather than evil'. The 57-year-old childminder made different excuses during her trial, when a jury found her guilty of aggravated racial assault. She thought up the name-crayoning as a way of entertaining a group of children she was minding at her home. She scrawled the first names of the others, who were all white, on their foreheads, but then wrote 'nigger' on the little girl's.

She first claimed that the word was a private joke between her and the girl, but then changed her story to say that she had meant to write 'Tigger', because the child had been playing the character in a game based on A.A. Milne's *Winnie-the-Pooh*.

The insult was still visible when the child returned home, and police and social workers were called in. The childminder tried to laugh off the incident when first interviewed by officers, claiming that the girl had 'pestered' her to use the word instead of her actual name, which cannot be given for legal reasons.

The recorder told her: 'You abused this girl by demonstrating the clearest hostility to her mixed-race status by writing the word nigger. . . You told the police you only wrote the word because she asked you to and that she often referred to herself as the little black bastard. But where did a young girl get that phrase from? This child was brought up in a climate of neglect, hostility and racial abuse, and it is clear that on this occasion when she was in your care you simply continued the abuse.'

The childminder was not registered with Ofsted as a childminder, but is likely to face a social services ban on looking after children in future.

Adapted from a news story in *The Guardian* (September 2005).

ACTIVITY: THE EFFECTS OF DISCRIMINATION

Read the case study above and discuss the following questions:

1   Was the 2-year-old girl a victim of *direct* or *indirect* discrimination?

2   What are the likely consequences for the child's self-esteem?

The effects of discrimination can be very obvious, such as in the case of a child whose self-esteem is seriously damaged by others' behaviour towards them. However, there can also be more subtle, less personal effects, such as the perpetuation of general misunderstandings and stereotypes. When this happens, different groups in society tend not to treat each other with proper respect.

For example, there is a prevalent stereotype that all arranged marriages are unhappy, and that love marriages are 'better'. In fact, most arranged marriages are in the modern form whereby loving parents take great care in their choice of potential partners and encourage their daughters and sons to meet to see if they like one another before they embark on marriage. The reality is that love marriages are less likely to be sanctioned and subsequently supported by the parents of those getting married, and more than one-third of love marriages end in divorce.

LEGISLATION RELATING TO EQUALITY OF OPPORTUNITY

Our laws deal with the overt discrimination that results from prejudice, especially when combined with power. The person who shows prejudice is unwilling to change their views even when their 'facts' are clearly shown to be wrong. If the prejudiced person has power, they may discriminate against the people towards whom they are prejudiced. This might be in the form of racism or sexism, or being disablist, ageist or homophobic (afraid of and hostile to

ACTIVITY: EXPLORING STEREOTYPES

You could arrange to carry out this activity with a group of children in reception class. The aim is to develop children's understanding of stereotyping.

1   Present children with a choice of two videos: one is in its own bright, colourful cover; the other is a very popular film inside a plain box.

2   Ask children which video they wish to watch. After viewing the selected video for 5 minutes, show the children some of the other video.

3   Repeat with two books, one of which is covered in plain brown paper. Talk to the children about what these examples tell us (i.e. you should not judge a book by its cover).

homosexual people). There are laws which try to deal with all these kinds of discrimination. However, while legal restraints on racism and sexism exist, legal protection against disablism, ageism and sexual prejudice is less well developed.

Table 1.1 Laws relating to discrimination

Sex Discrimination Act (1975 and 1986)	These Acts make it illegal to discriminate against someone on the grounds of their gender – when employing someone, when selling or renting a property to them, in their education or when providing them with goods and services. It also protects people from sexual harassment. The Equal Opportunities Commission was set up in 1975 to enforce the laws relating to sexual discrimination.
Equal Pay Act (1984)	This Act gave women the right to equal pay for equal work.
Education Reform Act (1988)	Local education authorities (LEAs) must provide access to the national curriculum to all children including those with special needs and must identify and assess children's needs.
The Children Act (1989)	This Act states that the needs of children are paramount (i.e. the most important). Local authorities must consider a child's race, culture, religion and languages when making decisions. Childcare services must promote self-esteem and racial identity.
Disability Discrimination Act (1995)	Disabled people are given new rights in the areas of employment, access to goods, facilities and services, and buying or renting property. A National Disability Council (NDC) advises the government on discrimination against disabled people.
The Race Relations Act (1976)	This Act makes it unlawful to discriminate against anyone on grounds of race, colour, nationality (including citizenship), or ethnic or national origins. It applies to jobs, training, housing, education and the provision of goods and services. The Commission for Racial Equality (CRE) was set up to research and investigate cases of alleged racial discrimination.
Special Educational Needs and Disability Act (2001)	The Special Educational Needs and Disability Bill was a part of the government's commitment to a 'significant extension of the rights of children'. It aimed to 'strengthen the right' of a disabled child to be educated in mainstream schools where it is appropriate, although there will still be a 'vital' role for special schools. Local Education Authorities are obliged to provide parents and children with information and advice, and a means of resolving disputes when they arise. For more details of these Acts, see Chapter 14.

PROMOTING EFFECTIVE EQUAL OPPORTUNITIES THROUGH ANTI-DISCRIMINATORY AND ANTI-BIAS PRACTICE

As early years workers we are responsible for ensuring equal opportunities within our settings. There are many ways in which we can promote anti-discriminatory practice:

* promoting a sense of belonging;
* appreciating language and bilingualism;
* valuing cultural diversity and respecting difference;
* giving individual children individual help;
* understanding religions;
* including children with disabilities;
* having an awareness of gender roles;
* avoiding stereotypes.

Promoting a sense of belonging

As children grow up, they need to feel that they belong to the group, whether that group is their family, their culture, the community they live in and experience or their early years setting.

Belonging to a group is the result of either:

* being allocated to a group defined by someone else, for example being British-born;
* deciding to join a group, for example choosing to be a vegetarian, or joining a football club.

Until recently, people tended to be seen as belonging to a particular ethnic group if they shared a culture, language, physical features (e.g. skin colour) or religion. This way of grouping people is no longer thought to be useful. Increasingly, people choose the groups they want to be identified with. The early childhood setting is often the first group outside the family and its friendship network that the child joins. It is important when welcoming families to a setting that they feel a sense of belonging.

Taking a multicultural approach

In the UK we live in a diverse and multicultural society. This means that it is important to appreciate, understand and respect different cultural and religious ideas. The whole environment of the early childhood setting needs to reflect a multicultural and multilingual approach. For example, the home area, like every other area of the environment, should include objects which are familiar to children and link with their homes and culture. These are often called **cultural artefacts**.

Using everyday activities to explore different cultures

It is particularly important to introduce children to different cultures through the activities of daily life, such as preparing food and cooking. This is because they can relate to these events most easily.

For example, for those children who have not met Chinese people or who have not experienced Chinese food, it might be possible to invite someone to the nursery to demonstrate and introduce the children to another culture. Remember that it is important not to stereotype your visitor. For instance, not all people of Chinese background will use chopsticks at home: some families may be using knives and forks. Sets of cultural artefacts should not be mixed up in one home area, as this confuses everyone. It also makes it difficult for the children to value the area and take pride in keeping it looking attractive.

There are opportunities for mathematical learning in sorting out chopsticks from spoons, knives and forks, and Chinese soup spoons, or sets of utensils relating to Chinese life, African, Indian or Asian cooking, and European culture.

Encouraging children to use what they know

Children gain by using their own cultural experience and knowledge in an open way. For example, the advantage of play dough, rather than pre-structured plastic food, is that children can bring their own experiences to it. They can make it into roti, pancakes, pasties or pies, depending on their own past experiences. All experiences can be valued, not just those that a toy manufacturer has set in plastic.

Introducing cultural artefacts

A home area needs to reflect familiar aspects of each child's home. It needs to build on all the children's prior experiences. This means that it should have crockery, cutlery and cooking utensils in the West European style. If, for example, there are children from Chinese backgrounds in the group, it would

Fig 1.2 Playing with Gloop

be particularly important also to have chopsticks, bowls, woks, and so on, to reflect their home culture. These would need to be available all the time.

But many children will not know about Chinese woks because they do not meet anyone who cooks with one. These children will need extra help in understanding cultures other than their own. It is very important to include activities that introduce them to the purpose and function of Chinese ways of cooking, for example. So it is important not only that Chinese children see their own culture reflected, but also that other children have the opportunity to learn about different cultures in ways which hold meaning for them and therefore are not tokenist (see below).

A child who has never seen a wok before will need to do *real* cookery with it, and be introduced to this by an adult. *Remember, children learn through real, first-hand experiences.* It is no good simply putting a wok in the home area and hoping the children will then know about Chinese cooking. That would be tokenist.

Giving individual children individual help

There may be children with special educational needs using the home area, for example, and they may require special arrangements to allow them access. A child in a wheelchair will need a lower table so that a mixing bowl can be stirred; it might be necessary to make a toy cooker of an appropriate height. This could be done quite simply, using a cardboard box. Children love to construct their own play props and allowing them to do so makes for a much more culturally diverse selection, because

they can say what they need in order to make a play setting like their homes.

Sharing books, stories, poems, songs, action songs and games

These are useful in linking children with their previous experiences. For example, stories are available about children with disabilities and about children from different cultures. There are stories which look at gender issues. In the last 20 years authors have been recognising the need for children's books to link with the huge range of experiences that different children have.

Understanding religions

Children do not choose their religion. They are born into it. As they grow up they will either accept the belief structure or not. This is also true for children who are born into families who are atheist, agnostic or humanist. Atheists do not believe in a god, gods or God. Agnostics think that we cannot know whether a god, gods or God exist. Humanists believe that people can be good without believing in a god, gods or God. They think that the world can be understood through science and research.

Some children are taught **monotheistic** revelatory religious beliefs (one god). Others learn **polytheistic** revelatory beliefs (more than one god). A revelatory god is a supernatural being who is believed to have created the world and who intervenes. Buddhists have beliefs which are not revelatory of a god. They believe in a god, gods or God who created the world but who does not intervene.

In order that every child feels accepted beyond their home, those working with young children and their families need to learn about belief structures other than their own. It is also important to remember that being a good person and leading a good life has nothing to do with belief in any god or gods. There are many people who lead good lives who are humanists, agnostics or atheists.

Some children are brought up in families which follow more than one religion. For example, there might be a Roman Catholic Christian father and a Jewish mother, or an atheist father and a Quaker Christian mother.

PROMOTING A CHILD'S SENSE OF SELF-WORTH

Children need to feel a sense of their own worth. This comes from:

❖ feeling that they matter to other people;

❖ feeling able to take an active part in things;

❖ feeling competent and skilled enough to do so.

Valuing language and culture

A feeling of belonging obviously contributes to a sense of worth, and language is of deep importance to both. In the last section the importance of including cultural artefacts that are familiar from the child's home was stressed. The same goes for language. If a child's first language is not reflected in settings beyond the home, a large part of the child's previous experiences is being ignored or even actively rejected. Some linguistic experts argue that 'language is power': the dominant language of the culture gives those who speak it the power to discriminate against those who do not.

Ideas for promoting a sense of belonging through equality of opportunity

1   Be willing to find out about different religions and to respect them. Every religion has variety within it. For example, there are Orthodox and Reformed Jews; Roman Catholic Christians, Church of England Christians, Methodist Christians, Quaker Christians, Jehovah's Witness Christians and Mormon Christians. Ask religious leaders and parents for information.

2   Find out about different disabilities. Ask parents and voluntary organisations (e.g. SCOPE, RNIB, RNID) to help you.

3   Do not be afraid to say that you do not know something and that you want to find out and learn. Remember that minority groups of all kinds are as important as the majority groups and are included as part of the whole group.

4   Respect and value the child's home language. Think how you can make yourself understood using body

Fig 1.3 Making sense of what you are saying by using a 'prop'

language, gestures and facial expression; by pointing; by using pictures; by using actions with your words. Try asking children if they would like a drink using one of these strategies. You could use objects as props. It is important to be warm towards children. Remember to smile and to show that you enjoy interacting with them. Make sure that you are giving comprehensible language input.

5   Create opportunities for children to talk with other children and adults who are already fluent in English. Try to accompany a child's actions with language by describing what is happening. For example, talk with the child and describe what they are doing when they cook or use clay. When telling stories you could:

❖ use puppets and props, flannel boards, magnet boards, and so on;

❖ invite children to act out pictures as you go through the story;

❖ use facial expressions, eye contact and body language to 'tell' a story and make it meaningful for the children.

6   Use books in different languages and tell stories in different languages. Remember that there can be problems with dual-language textbooks because although a language like English reads from left to right, a language like Urdu reads from right to left.

7   Invite someone who speaks the child's language to come and tell stories. For example, ask a Hindi speaker to tell a story such as *Where's Spot?* in Hindi, using the book in that language but in a session that is for all the children in a story group. Then tell the story and use

the book in English at the next session, again with all the children in the story group. Remember that grandparents are often particularly concerned that children are losing their home language as they become more fluent in English (transitional bilingualism). They may enjoy coming into the group and helping in this way.

Standard English is the usual way of communicating in English in public, educational, professional and commercial aspects of life. However, young children need to be confident in talking, reading and writing in their home language and to be supported in this in the early childhood setting. This actually helps children to develop fluency and literacy in English. So it is very important that the child's own language is valued and that efforts are made to develop balanced bilingualism (see page 292).

Including children with disabilities

Inclusion is about access for disabled people in its widest sense: not just about physical access to buildings, vehicles, education, health care, leisure facilities and employment, but being part of the community as a whole. To develop their own self-worth, disabled people need to have the same opportunities, services and facilities that are available to other people. Excluding disabled children from everyday experiences which are the norm for most children can lead to a lifetime of segregation. In addition, lack of contact with disabled people can lead to fear and ignorance (in the non-disabled) of those who seem 'different'.

It is necessary to make sure that both indoor and outdoor areas of the early childhood setting are arranged so that children with disabilities can take a full part in activities. This might involve:

❖ providing ramps for wheelchairs;

❖ making sure the light falls on the adult's face, so that a child wearing a hearing aid is able to lip-read and a child with a visual impairment can use any residual eyesight to see facial expressions;

❖ having a tray on the table so that objects stay on the table and a child with a visual impairment does not 'lose' objects that fall off;

❖ having the opportunity to learn sign languages (e.g. British Sign Language and Makaton).

Awareness of gender roles

Creating an environment where girls and boys are respected and cared for equally in early childhood is the first step towards breaking cycles of discrimination and disadvantage, and to promoting a child's sense of self-worth as it relates to their gender.

It is important to remember that some children will have learnt narrow gender roles. In the traditional home situation mothers usually do housework and fathers mend cars. Children need to see adults taking on broader gender roles, and to learn about alternative ways for men and women to behave as men and women.

Sometimes staff think there should be 'girls only' sessions on bicycles or with block play and 'boys only' sessions in the home area, when cooking, or with the dolls. This introduces children to experiences which broaden ideas of gender roles away from traditional stereotypes. It helps to dispel the idea that 'boys will be boys' or that girls are born to be mothers. However, such single-sex sessions do not help girls and boys to

learn about negotiating with each other, helped and supported by adults. Many researchers and educators now think this is very important, and Dunn (1988) says that relationships *between* boys and girls matter as much as what boys do or what girls do.

The way that fathers and mothers work together in bringing up children is an area of great interest for researchers. Children often see their fathers at times when children and parents relax and have fun together, but spend more time with their mothers doing the chores and tasks of daily life. Research is showing that fathers and mothers want to redefine the roles they play in the family, so that both parents are involved in daily life tasks, and both have leisure time to enjoy with their children. This is the case whether

Fig 1.4 Boys like to play with dolls too

family members live apart from or with their children. In countries like Sweden, where there is paternity and maternity leave after children are born, these issues are being actively explored.

AVOIDING STEREOTYPES

Choosing how you want to be described

When adults fill in forms they decide whether to be described as Mr, Ms, Mrs or Miss, and whether they wish to describe themselves according to different ethnic categories. An adult can choose whether to be described as deaf, hearing-impaired or aurally challenged. Children need to be given as much choice as possible about these aspects of their lives. If adults describe a child as 'the one with glasses', or comment 'what a pretty dress', or talk about 'the Afro-Caribbean child', they are stereotyping these children and seeing them narrowly rather than as whole people.

Children need positive images of themselves and of other people. Hazareesingh (1989) suggests that the cultural identity of a child is 'whatever children hold to be emotionally

Guidelines for helping children to have a sense of their own worth

❖ Provide familiar objects for every child in the different areas of the room. These artefacts of their culture might be cooking utensils, clothes or fabrics.

❖ Positive images of different children in different cultures are important. Remember that the important thing about a child is not how they look or the extent of their learning impairment, but that they are a person. The way you behave and talk will give messages about your mental image of each child.

❖ Make sure you tell stories and make displays and interest tables with positive images of children with disabilities and children from different cultures. These stories should also be in the book area.

❖ Make sure that children meet adults with broad gender roles, to show them that men and women are not restricted respectively to a narrow range of activities.

❖ Encourage children to speak to other children and adults within the early childhood setting. Remember that children might feel powerless if they cannot speak to other people.

❖ Use stories from different cultures to introduce children to myths, legends and folk tales. The same themes crop up over and over again in different stories across the world. Find some of these universal themes in the stories you look at from different cultures (e.g. the wicked stepmother, the greedy rich person, good deeds being rewarded after suffering).

❖ Make sure the indoor and outdoor areas offer full access to activities for children with disabilities.

❖ Do not forget that you need to have a sense of your own worth too. What did you do today that made you feel that you had a worthwhile day?

meaningful and significant, both about themselves and in their lives'.

The restricting effect of stereotypes

The most important thing about working with 'the child with glasses' might be the fact that he loves music. The most important thing about 'the Afro-Caribbean child' might be that she loves mathematics and can remember all the sequences and measurements of cooking, even at 3 years of age. The most important thing about the girl 'in the pretty dress' might be that she is worried about getting it dirty and so never plays with clay. Gender stereotypes are also restricting because behaviour is seen as 'what boys do' and 'what girls do'. Through encouraging boys and girls alike to be active and to explore, to be gentle and nurturing, all children are enabled to lead fuller lives with broader roles. It equips them much better for the future.

Adults working with children need to empower them rather than to stereotype them. To focus on one feature of the child is much too narrow. It is important not to stereotype children through labels. Children are people and they have names, not labels!

INSPECTING OUR OWN ATTITUDES AND VALUES

In the UK there is now legislation on race, gender and disability discrimination, which helps teams of people working together to have an impact on racism, sexism and disablist attitudes and work practices, however unconscious these may be. In addition, it is important that each of us inspects what we do so that we become aware of our attitudes and values. Only then can we act on the unwittingly discriminatory behaviour that we will almost inevitably find. Discriminatory behaviour

occurs when, usually without meaning it, we are sexist, racist or disablist. For example, an early childhood worker might ask for a strong boy to lift the chair. We need to look to see whether what we say we believe matches what we actually do. It doesn't usually! So then we have to do something about it.

Each of us has to work at this all the time, throughout our lives. It is not useful to feel guilty and dislike yourself if you find you are discriminating against someone. It *is* useful to do something about it.

The process of inspecting our basic thinking needs to be done on three levels:

1   within the legal framework;

2   in the work setting as part of a team;

3   as individuals.

Cultural and gender identity, and self-labelling

The following all play their part in **cultural identity** and the way children build images of themselves:

❖   disability;

❖   language (spoken or sign);

❖   gender;

❖   skin colour;

❖   food and dress;

❖   music and songs;

❖   heritage, myths and legends;

❖   culturally specific home objects (artefacts);

❖   family relationships and occupations.

It is important to remember that children are people, and every person in the world is of worth. When we stereotype children, we limit them to our image of what we think they can do. This means that we hold them back in their development.

Working as a team

It is important to pause at regular intervals and examine what happens in every work setting. Does what the team members say they believe in match what they actually do? Identifying problems in the way adults work with children and in the way children and adults relate to each other is essential before positive action can be taken by the whole team. It helps to work as a team when doing this because it is hard for individual team members to inspect their own thinking in isolation from other people. It helps to share and discuss things with colleagues. The team should devise a **policy of equality of opportunity** and a **code of practice** and then, as a team, review them regularly:

* The policy states the values of the team and the aims of its work.

* The code of practice sets out how the team will put the policy into practice.

* The review process covers all aspects of the team's work in relation to its policy and code of practice.

USING THE AGE RANGE OF THE TEAM

It is ideal if every team of staff has a good spread of ages among its members. This means that there are some people who have many years of life experience to bring to the team, and others who are at the beginning of their work with children and families; those who have done other things before training to work with children and those who will go on to other kinds of work. It is important that young children and their families are with people:

* who value each other and learn from one another;

* who are trained and informed about children;

* who are sensitive to the needs and concerns of others, especially parents.

It is important that staff learn to make constructive criticisms of each other, to trust and respect each other and to build on each other's strengths.

THE ROLE OF THE INDIVIDUAL MEMBER OF STAFF

Each individual worker needs to be committed and empowered to carry out the team's policy using the code of practice. At the end of this section there are many examples of different ways in which individual staff members can play a very important part in promoting the aims and values of the team in their work. You can make a difference to the lives of the children and families you work with. You can make a difference in your work setting.

Making a difference

One person can have a great impact. Remember, *you* matter and *you* can have an influence on combating discriminatory behaviour:

* *By challenging discriminatory behaviour.* It is important to be assertive and not aggressive. Being assertive means talking clearly and politely about how you feel. This is very different from being rude and angry. For example, you might say: 'I felt very uncomfortable when you asked me to give a drink to the girl with a hearing aid. I felt I needed to know her name, because I am worried that I might stop seeing her as a person if I just think of her as "the girl with a hearing aid".'

* *By challenging situations.* If you see a child hurt or insult someone, explain that such

behaviour is not acceptable. Criticise the behaviour rather than the child.

❧ *By being aware of discrimination in children's resources.* Books which are discriminatory can be discussed with other early childhood workers, removed and replaced with others (chosen as a team) containing positive images of people with disabilities, from different cultures and of different genders.

❧ *By learning from experience.* From time to time you will make mistakes. You will say and do things you regret. For example, someone who had lived in Dorset all her life came to London and laughed at the idea of people eating goat meat. She quickly realised how insulting this was to her new friends and apologised, explaining that it was simply a new idea to her.

❧ *By learning about other cultures and respecting the differences.* It is very important to try to pronounce and spell names correctly, and to try to understand the different systems that different cultures use when choosing names for people. It is also very important to learn about the different clothes people wear in different cultures and to try to learn what garments are called.

Assertiveness training

We have seen that being assertive is important for staff, but it is also vital for children. Reference needs to be made in the team's code of practice to the promotion of children's assertiveness to combat aggression through bullying. Children need to feel protected from aggression and to be able to assert themselves sufficiently to take a full part in the activities provided. In some early childhood settings children are helped to learn to be assertive. For example, in some settings children act out what to do after visits to their new school a few weeks before they leave the nursery.

Both the bully *and* the victim need help to be assertive: one needs help with aggression and the other with timidity. Visualisation techniques can help children to use positive images (seeing themselves as assertive) rather than negative images (being the bully or victim).

Aggression is not always physical. Being pushed by adults to be highly academic at the expense of taking part in childhood pursuits is also a very important issue. Moore and Klauss (1995) have identified four

Guidelines to help you inspect your own feelings and attitudes

❧ Know the legislation on discriminatory behaviour.

❧ Work within the team to construct a policy on equality of opportunities.

❧ Use the code of practice drawn up by the staff in the work setting.

❧ Make sure your team reviews the code of practice together regularly.

❧ Be assertive (not aggressive) and try to work towards greater equality of opportunity in your work setting.

categories of 'hurrying' children out of childhood in the USA and the UK:

1 academic hurrying;

2 over-scheduling children's lives, leaving no time for children to have personal space;

3 expecting children to excel all the time;

4 expecting children to assume adult responsibilities.

The need for assertiveness rather than aggression or an over-dominant manner in relation to early childhood workers is covered in Chapter 15.

Examining our attitudes to strangers

Humans are not very good at dealing with new situations or meeting new people. They feel more comfortable with the people they know and situations they are very familiar with. Meeting people who are in some way different can sometimes cause a reaction called 'stranger fear'. Rather than deal with our feelings, we might ignore or avoid the person or situation. But this is discriminatory and we must confront our own feelings before we can help children with theirs.

It is very important that children are helped to meet a wide range of different people. Positive images help children towards positive experiences.

Valuing cultural diversity and respecting difference

Much can be gained from respecting different ways of bringing up children. For example, the Indian tradition of massaging babies is now widely used in British clinics and family centres; so is the way that African mothers traditionally carry their babies in a sling on their backs. It is important to understand and respect what the child has been taught to do at home. For example, in some cultures it is seen as disrespectful for a child to look an adult directly in the eye, whereas in others children are considered rude if they do not look at an adult directly.

Guidelines for helping children to form positive images of people

❖ *Storytelling.* Asking storytellers (e.g. parents) from different ethnic groups to tell stories in their own languages, as well as in English. This helps children to hear different languages, so that the idea becomes familiar that there are many languages in the world.

❖ *Using arts, crafts and artefacts from different cultures* (fabrics, interest tables, books, posters, jigsaws, etc.). This helps children to realise, for example, that not everyone uses a knife, fork or spoon when eating: they might use fingers or chopsticks instead. Children are helped to learn that there are different ways of eating, something which might seem strange to them at first.

❖ *Including music and dances from different cultures,* listening to them, watching them, perhaps joining in a bit. In every culture children love to stand at the edge while people perform. Children often 'echo-dance'. Watch out the next time you go to a fete. If there are morris dancers or folk dancers you are likely to see children watching them and echo-dancing at the sides. Being introduced to different cultures in this way helps children not to reject unfamiliar music. For example, Chinese music has a five-note scale; African music sometimes has five beats in a bar; European music has two, three or four beats, but not usually five. A child who has never seen ballet before or a child who has never seen an Indian dance before might find these strange at first.

❖ *Doing cookery from different cultures.* You might have multi-language, picture-based cookery books that families can borrow (you might need to make these). For example, there could be a copy of a recipe for roti in English, Urdu and French, or for bread in English, Greek and Swahili; the choice of languages would depend on which were used in the early childhood setting.

❖ *Planning the menu carefully.* Make sure that the menu includes food that children will enjoy and which is in some way familiar. One of the things young children worry about when they are away from home is whether they will like the food. Food and eating with others are a very emotional experience.

Helping children to feel that they belong

Ensure that children who look different, because they are from different cultures or because they have a disability, feel at ease and part of the group.

Having an impact on the bigger picture

There are some equal opportunities issues that seem too big for one person to tackle alone. But there are other things that are easier for each and every one of us to do something about. One individual person can have a great impact on the lives of young children and their families.

❖ *Action on children's rights* – working towards children's rights through international cooperation is an important way to make progress towards better quality early childhood services. It might seem that an individual cannot do very much in this respect. However, in every country there are organisations with

which you can link up. In the UK these include the **National Children's Bureau**, **Save the Children**, **the British Association for Early Childhood Education** (BAECE, now called **Early Education**), **UNICEF** and the **Organisation mondiale pour l'éducation pré-scolaire** (OMEP). It is also important to remember that you can get in touch with your MP and your MEP via their local surgeries or by writing.

❖ *Action on poverty* – many children in the world live in poverty. Reports by voluntary organisations estimate that around 1 in 3 children in the UK are living in poverty. There are absolute limits to the lack of food, shelter and clothing which humans can bear. These result in starvation, disease and slow death. However, in the developed world poverty is more often relative. The reports on poverty in the UK show that, in relation to most people living in the UK, an increasing number of families are living below an acceptable minimum level. This creates stress as families struggle to make ends meet, especially when most other people appear to be financially comfortable.

In the early childhood setting it is important not to have expensive outings or activities, and to be sure to invite all parents to take part in the life of the group. No parent or child should be left out because of their economic background. This is an important equality of opportunity issue.

PRINCIPLES OF INCLUSIVITY

As we have already noted, there are many kinds of minority groups, including the disabled and ethnic groups. Minority groups have generally experienced three kinds of treatment from other people: apartheid, assimilation or integration. Recently there has been a move towards principles of inclusivity.

For some children, special schools are appropriate and to their advantage. However, the vast majority of children with special educational needs will be integrated into mainstream settings. The Special Needs and Disability Act (2001) advised keeping a few special schools for children like Kuhldeep and Winnie (see Case studies on page 23).

Guidelines to help individuals promote equality of opportunity

You cannot be trained to know everything. You cannot be an expert in every area, but you *can* be a good networker. This means linking people together who might be useful to each other. Get in touch with people who know about:

- welfare rights and social services;
- health services;
- voluntary organisations and self-help groups.

Remember that you are part of a multi-professional team and that each member has something different to bring to early childhood work.

When you meet children, whether they are in a mainstream school, a special school or an early childhood setting, make sure that your expectations of what each child can do are sufficiently high.

Set children tasks which help them to make decisions and to exercise choice. It is important to let all children make choices and decisions so that they feel a sense of control in their lives. When people feel they have some control over what they do, they learn better. It gives them greater equality of opportunity.

Respect yourself and others alike. Try to think why people have views and customs that are different to yours. Keep thinking about what you do. Think about issues of race, gender, sexual orientation, age, economics, background, disability, assertiveness, culture and special educational needs. Keep changing what you do not like about what you do. Do this without feeling guilt or shame.

Value the things you keep learning about equality of opportunity so that you can look forward with positive images about yourself and other people.

Remember: equality of opportunity is about giving every child full access to the group.

Some useful definitions

APARTHEID

This occurs when, for example, disability, ethnic, gender or age groups live or work separately from others. This almost inevitably means that groups of people become ignorant about each other. For example, children with special needs often used to be placed in residential settings from the age of 2 years. Consequently, people without disability were often ill at ease and showed stranger fear when meeting them. The practice of apartheid was taken to an extreme in South Africa, before 1990, where black Africans lived separately from white Africans. In the UK, children learning English as a second language used to be taken out of the classroom and taught separately, and children who were vegetarians were often made to sit at a separate table during school lunchtimes.

ASSIMILATION

Assimilation occurs when children are expected to conform to the mainstream culture, for example when they are expected to learn English rather than use their first language. Being made to fit in with the majority, with little help or support, is very stressful. Blind children are greatly disadvantaged in a building if doors are left half-open and they bump into them and hurt themselves. Children in wheelchairs are greatly disadvantaged in a building with no ramps.

INTEGRATION

There are different kinds of integration:

❖ The minority of children who attend special schools now spend a great deal of time meeting children in mainstream settings through regular visits, joint projects, and so on.

❖ Locational integration involves two schools or early childhood settings, one mainstream and one special, sharing a site so that children meet at different points in the day. They might play together outside or share music together.

❖ A special unit placed in a mainstream school or early childhood setting enables children to join in the mainstream classes when it is good for them, but to attend the unit for specialist help and equipment.

❖ Sometimes all children are in the same setting, with those who need it given specialist support, sometimes from a **peripatetic** teacher who visits regularly.

INCLUSION

Inclusion (or inclusive education, inclusive schooling or educational inclusion) is a term used within education to describe the process of ensuring equality of learning opportunities for all children and young people, whatever their disabilities or disadvantages. This means that all children have the right to have their needs met in the best way for them. They are seen as being part of the community, even if they need particular help to live a full life within the community.

So, while **integration** is about bringing people together who are different, inclusion is about providing the support that is needed to enable different people to be together in a community.

Despite the moves towards inclusion, there are arguments for keeping a minority of children in special schools. The following case studies will help you to think about the different ways in which children's needs can be met.

Case Study

Winnie

Winnie (6 years) had a range of disabilities, including severe learning difficulties, visual and hearing impairment, and difficulty sitting. Her parents valued joining a parent group run by the staff of the special school. All the parents had similarly disabled children. This gave them support. The equipment in the special school was geared to Winnie's needs. The staff were specialists trained to work with children like Winnie. The children were visited regularly by children from the local primary school, and they would go on outings together. Winnie lived at home, and went to school daily.

Case Study

Kuhldeep

Kuhldeep (15 years) was with his friends in the park. They were attacked by a gang and he became completely blind. He went immediately to a special residential school for visually impaired but highly academic pupils. He became a weekly boarder. This was because both he and his family were in shock and were devastated by what had happened. His family needed help and support of their own, and did not feel able to support him enough in the early stages.

At the school he received regular assessment and counselling from experts about his feelings, his visual impairment and his state of health. He received individual teaching at the pace he needed while he adjusted to not seeing. He learnt Braille and was taught by highly experienced teachers. He learnt mobility using a white cane.

Kuhldeep went home at weekends and so kept in close contact with his family. His family had the opportunity to learn about his new visual impairment and, over time, to adjust in a way which was positive and which helped him.

At school, Kuhldeep was in the company of other visually impaired people of his own age, who understood how he felt and who helped him. He was able to meet his sighted friends at weekends. He took his school exams a year late and did well.

The key elements in Kuhldeep's experiences were:

❖ expert resources;

❖ specialist teaching;

❖ close links with home;

❖ help for his family and help for him while they all adjusted to his new visual impairment.

Comparing mainstream and special schools

In a special school:

❖ Staff need to be careful to concentrate on the child as a whole person and not on their disability alone. When the latter happens it narrows the child's experiences. Concentrating on disability means concentrating on what children find difficult to do, rather than being positive and thinking about all the things that the child *can* do.

❖ The curriculum might become rather rigid and may be based on exercises, instead of equipping the children to make choices and decisions, and to become autonomous learners. For example, special schools for hearing-impaired children used to concentrate on language teaching in a narrow curriculum, with little art, play, dance, science, and so on. All the effort went into getting the children to talk, read and write. In spite of this emphasis on language and literacy (reading and writing), few children reached a reading age of above 9 years. (A reading age of 9 years is needed to read the tabloid newspapers.)

❖ It may be difficult to arrange for the children to meet children from a mainstream school. This can mean that children begin to imitate mannerisms from each other, leading to 'double delay' – the child not only has the disability that he or she was born with, but the added disadvantage of being in a poor context for learning.

In a mainstream school:

❖ You need to consider different problems. For example, a child might be very lonely if he or she is the only child in the school with a hearing impairment. It is very important to help children make friends in this setting and to ensure that they do not feel that they are different to everyone else.

❖ It is also very easy to underestimate what the child can do. It is essential for adults to have high enough expectations of children with special educational needs in mainstream settings.

❖ There might not be any expert teachers who know about the particular disability that the child has. Even if expert teachers do visit, these visits may be irregular and infrequent, which makes it hard to get the information that is needed in order to help the child.

❖ It is very important to know about the **special educational needs code of practice** (see Section 2, page 45) and to bear in mind what most children achieve. Your task is to find ways of helping children with special education needs to move towards this or to do as much as they can.

❖ Sometimes children with disabilities are overprotected and are not expected to manage things which they could do with a little encouragement.

❖ It is very important to establish links with voluntary organisations that may be able to put children with similar disabilities in touch with each other. For example, there are summer camps where children who are diabetic and attend mainstream schools can come together and enjoy each other's company for a week.

ACTIVITY: TO PROMOTE EQUALITY OF OPPORTUNITY AND INCLUSIVITY

The following suggested activities can often be done as a group exercise. Each provides good opportunities for you to develop these important skills:

✣ observing children;

✣ planning to meet each child's needs;

✣ implementing and evaluating the activities.

1 *Plan a multicultural cooking library*. Make six cookery books with simple recipes from a variety of cultures. Find or draw pictures to illustrate the books. Write the text in English, and another language if possible. If you write in Urdu or Chinese, remember you will need to make two separate books, as Urdu and Chinese text runs from right to left. Use the books with groups of children and run a series of cookery sessions.

Observe the way the children use and respond to the cookery books. Evaluate the aim of your plan, the reason for the activity, how the activities were carried out and what you observed in the children's cooking activities.

2 *Storytelling*. Plan a story which you can tell (rather than read from a book). Choose a story you enjoy and make or find suitable props. You could make puppets out of stuffed socks, finger puppets out of gloves, stick puppets or shadow puppets; or use dolls and dressing-up clothes and various other artefacts.

Observe the children listening as you tell the story. Focus on their understanding and their language, especially children whose first language is not English. Evaluate your activity.

3 *Religious festivals*. Plan how you can make the children you work with more aware of religious festivals in a variety of cultures. For example, how could you introduce the children to Diwali in a way which is not tokenist? Remember to offer children meaningful first-hand experiences.

Observe the children and assess how much they understand. Look particularly at the reactions of children who are familiar with the festival you choose, and compare their behaviour to that of children for whom this is a new experience. Evaluate your plans and observations.

4 *Inclusion*. Plan how you would include a child with disabilities in your early childhood setting. Remember your plans will be different according to each child's needs. A child with a hearing impairment will need different help from a child who is a wheelchair user, for example.

Carry out and observe your plan in action. Focus on how you meet the child's individual needs through your plan. Evaluate your plan.

5 *Equality of opportunity*. Read your setting's policy on equality of opportunity and look at actual practices in the daily routine (e.g. mealtimes, books). Does what happens match the policy?

Evaluate your observations.

6   *Musical development.* Plan a series of activities which introduces children to the music of a variety of cultures. You will need to help children to listen to music and make music. Make musical instruments out of cardboard boxes, elastic bands, yoghurt pots, masking tape and other materials.

7   *Booklet.* Plan a booklet which introduces different religious festivals and helps parents to understand different religious perspectives in your early childhood setting.

Make the booklet and use it in your early childhood setting. Evaluate it.

8   *Display.* Plan and make a display using a multicultural theme.

Evaluate it. How did the adults use it? How did the children react?

9   *International book.* Choose one picture, book, story or poem from each of the following continents: Africa, the Americas, Asia, Australasia and Europe. Make the collection into a book which you can use with children aged 3–7 years.

Evaluate the activity.

10 *Multicultural provision.* Plan an area of provision which is multicultural in approach (e.g. the home area). Perhaps you can add more ideas to those suggested in this section.

Implement and evaluate your plan.

Section 2: Children with special needs and their families

WHAT ARE SPECIAL NEEDS?

Children with special needs are not an easily defined group. Some have a very obvious and well-researched disability, such as Down's syndrome or cerebral palsy; others may have specific learning needs, because of dyslexia or giftedness, for example. What defines them as children with special needs is the fact that they need *additional help* in some area of development, compared with other children.

It is important to remember that children are more alike than they are different. *Every* child needs:

- ❧ to feel welcome;
- ❧ to feel safe, both physically and emotionally;
- ❧ to have friends and to feel as if they belong;
- ❧ to be encouraged to live up to their potential;
- ❧ to be celebrated for their uniqueness.

In other words, **children are always children first** – the special need is secondary.

The range of special needs is enormous, from severe to relatively minor, from temporary or short-lived to permanent.

DEFINING TERMS

It matters a great deal how we 'label' people who are different from us. Many years ago,

Fig 1.5 Children listening to a story with props

people who were obviously *different* – that is, they were perhaps unable to walk or talk or they seemed to be less intelligent – were believed to be evil in some way; some were even burnt to death as witches. Now we are much more aware of individual differences and have a great deal more knowledge about diverse needs and abilities, but it is still very important that we do not apply labels to anyone.

What is disability?

The **Disability Discrimination Act 1995** (DDA 1995) defines a person as having a disability 'if he has a physical or mental impairment which has substantial and long-term adverse effect on his ability to carry out normal day-to-day activities'. The **Special Educational Needs and Disability Act 2001** defines a 'disabled pupil' as a school pupil who meets the definition of disabled person under DDA 1995.

The **Children Act 1989** also includes a definition of disability: a child is disabled if 'he [or she] is blind, deaf or dumb or suffers from mental disorder of any kind, or is substantially and permanently handicapped by illness, injury or congenital or other such disability as may be prescribed'.

Any of the categories of special needs described below (see page 29) could be termed a disability.

Handicap

Many people who have a disability now reject the term 'handicap' as it implies a patronising attitude and dependence on charity; the term originates from the notion of 'hand in the cap', that is, begging for money or charity.

Impairment

Impairment is the loss or limitation of physical, mental or sensory function on a long-term or permanent basis. Often children are described as having a hearing impairment, rather than a hearing disability.

Learning disability

People who have a learning disability have difficulties learning and find it particularly hard to understand new and complex information, and to develop new skills. A learning disability is a *lifelong* condition that is usually present from birth, although it may not become apparent until a child fails to reach particular developmental milestones. Learning disability is a relatively new term that has emerged over the last 20 years or so. Previously, people referred to someone as having a 'mental handicap'. The term intellectual disability is also commonly used in some countries.

Learning difficulty

Learning difficulty is a term used to describe any one of a number of barriers to learning that a child may experience. It is a broad term that covers a wide range of needs and problems – including dyslexia and behavioural problems – and the full range of ability. Children with learning difficulties may find activities that involve thinking and understanding particularly difficult, and many need support in their everyday lives as well as at school. According to the **Special Educational Needs and Disability Act 2001**, a child has a learning difficulty if he or she:

❖ has significantly greater difficulty learning than the majority of children of his or her age;

❖ has a disability which prevents or hinders him or her from making use of educational facilities of a kind generally provided for children of his or her age in schools within the area of the local education authority.

Advocacy

Advocacy is when another individual assumes the responsibility of speaking out on behalf of a person to ensure that their views are heard and that they receive all the rights that they are entitled to. In the UK, the Children Act 1989 makes social services departments responsible for providing for children with special needs, according to the definition above. The concept of advocacy is enshrined in the Act. It recognises that children in the category 'disabled' are the least likely to grow up to be able to speak for themselves, that is, to recognise their own needs and to know how to achieve their potential. Therefore, they need an **advocate**. Usually the advocate is an adult care worker who acts as a spokesperson for the person 'in need'.

Empowerment

This concept is closely linked to advocacy. In the case of children with special needs, the adult advocate should undertake activities with the child which will empower (or enable) the child to make his or her own wishes known. This includes helping with communication, giving the child choices and developing the child's decision-making skills.

CATEGORIES OF SPECIAL NEEDS

* **Physical disability:** needs related to problems with mobility or coordination, such as cerebral palsy, spina bifida or muscular dystrophy.

* **Speech or language difficulties:** needs related to communication problems, such as delayed language, difficulties in articulation or stuttering.

* **Specific learning difficulties (SLD):** needs related to problems usually confined to the areas of reading, writing and numeracy; dyslexia is a term often applied to difficulty in developing literacy skills.

* **Chronic illness:** needs related to medical conditions such as cystic fibrosis, diabetes, asthma or epilepsy.

* **Giftedness:** needs related to being highly academically or artistically gifted.

* **Sensory impairment:** needs related to problems with sight or hearing.

* **Complex needs:** needs related to a range of problems which may result from a genetic defect or from an accident or trauma.

* **Behavioural difficulties:** needs related to aggression, challenging behaviour, hyperactivity, attention deficit hyperactivity disorder (ADHD) or antisocial behaviour.

* **Life-threatening illness:** needs related to a serious or terminal illness (e.g. childhood cancer, leukaemia or HIV and AIDS).

* **Emotional difficulties:** needs related to conditions such as anxiety, fear, depression or autistic spectrum disorder (ASD).

DISABILITY AND DISCRIMINATION

Anyone with a disability forms part of a minority group whose particular needs may not be adequately recognised or taken into account. Having a different appearance often leads to disabled people being treated differently and unequally. Of course, not all disabilities are recognisable from a person's external appearance, for example, deafness, epilepsy, autism or diabetes.

The following attitudes are commonly encountered by disabled people from able-bodied people (see box below).

Common attitudes towards disabled people

* **Stereotype:** a term used when certain characteristics of any given group are applied to all the individuals within that group; a common stereotype of children with Down's syndrome, for example, is that they are always cheerful, placid and affectionate.

* **Hostility:** this may take the form of loud comments being made about the disabled person or aggression towards them. It is often a result of people's fear of the unknown.

* **Invasion of privacy:** certain physical characteristics evoke such strong feelings that people often have to express them

in some way. Physical differences can make disabled people's bodies into objects for public comment.

❖ **Dependency:** the assumption of dependency can lead people to try to be helpful without being asked. This invades the privacy of the disabled person's life, for example, helping a blind person across a road they did not want to cross.

❖ **Patronisation:** this describes the humiliation of people talking to the disabled person's able-bodied companions as if the disabled person would not be able to understand what was being said, leading to the famous, patronising phrase, 'Does he take sugar?'

CAUSES OF DISABILITY

There are three main causes of disability:

❖ **congenital** causes – when a faulty gene leads to a disabling condition;

❖ **developmental** causes – something goes wrong when the foetus is growing in the womb;

❖ **illness and accident** – these can affect individuals who are born with no disability.

We will consider the first two types of causes in this section.

Hereditary and congenital disorders

Many genetic disorders can now be diagnosed antenatally, thus enabling parents to decide on a course of action, that is, whether or not to seek a termination of pregnancy. The growth and development of the embryo and foetus (see Chapter 13) are controlled by genes.

Abnormal genes can cause abnormal growth and development (see Table 1.2).

DOMINANT GENE DEFECTS

A parent with a dominant gene defect has a 50 per cent chance of passing the defect on to each of their children. Examples of dominant gene defects are:

❖ tuberous sclerosis (a disorder affecting the skin and nervous system);

❖ achondroplasia (once called dwarfism);

❖ Huntington's chorea (a disorder of the central nervous system).

RECESSIVE GENE DEFECTS

These defects are only inherited if two recessive genes meet. Therefore, if both parents carry a single recessive gene defect, each of their children has a one in four (25 per cent) chance of being affected. Examples of defects transmitted this way are:

❖ cystic fibrosis (detailed in Chapter 11, Section 2);

❖ sickle-cell anaemia (detailed in Chapter 11, Section 2);

❖ phenylketonuria (a defective enzyme disorder);

❖ thalassaemia (a blood disorder);

❖ Tay-Sachs disease (a disorder of the nervous system);

❖ Friedreich's ataxia (a disorder of the spinal cord).

CHROMOSOMAL DEFECTS

These vary considerably in the severity of their effect on the individual. About 1 in every 200 babies born alive has a chromosomal abnormality – that is, the structure or number of chromosomes varies from normal. Among foetuses that have been spontaneously aborted, about 1 in 2 has such an abnormality. This suggests that most chromosomal abnormalities are incompatible with life, and that those seen

Table 1.2   A summary of genetic defects

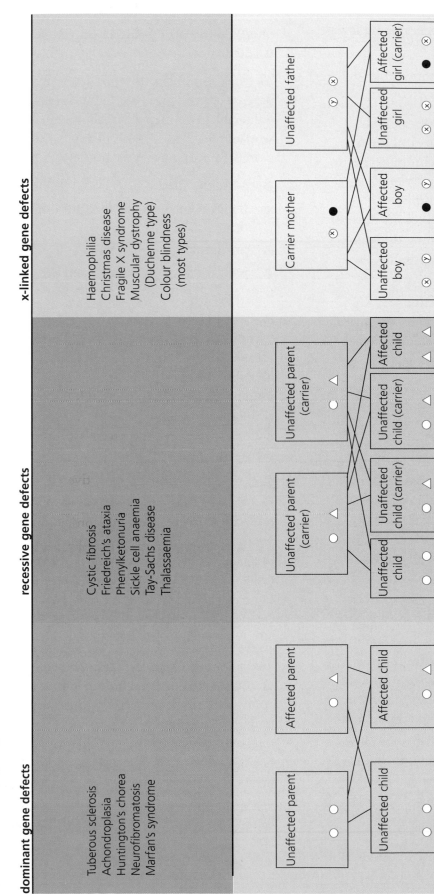

dominant gene defects	recessive gene defects	x-linked gene defects
Tuberous sclerosis Achondroplasia Huntington's chorea Neurofibromatosis Marfan's syndrome	Cystic fibrosis Friedreich's ataxia Phenylketonuria Sickle cell anaemia Tay-Sachs disease Thalassaemia	Haemophilia Christmas disease Fragile X syndrome Muscular dystrophy (Duchenne type) Colour blindness (most types)

in babies born alive are generally the less serious ones.

Examples of defects transmitted this way are:

❖ **Down's syndrome:** Trisomy 21 is the term used for the chromosomal abnormality that results in Down's syndrome. The extra chromosome is number 21; affected individuals have three, instead of two, number 21 chromosomes. This results in short stature, as well as learning difficulties and an increased susceptibility to infection.

❖ **Klinefelter's syndrome:** 47XXY is the term used for the chromosomal abnormality that results in Klinefelter's syndrome. The affected male has one or more extra X chromosomes (normally the pattern is XY). This results in boys who are very tall, with hypogonadism.

❖ **Turner's syndrome:** 45XO is the term used for the chromosomal abnormality which results in Turner's syndrome. Most affected females have only 45 chromosomes instead of 46; having a missing or defective X chromosome. This results in girls with non-functioning ovaries, a webbed neck and a broad chest; they may also have cardiac malfunctions.

❖ **Cri du chat syndrome:** this is a very rare condition in which a portion of one particular chromosome is missing in each of the affected individual's cells.

Genetic counselling is available for anyone with a child or other member of the family with a chromosomal abnormality, and chromosome analysis is offered in early pregnancy.

Developmental factors as causes of disability

The first 3 months (the first trimester) of a pregnancy are when the foetus is particularly vulnerable. The lifestyle of the pregnant woman affects the health of the baby in her womb. Important factors are:

❖ a healthy diet;
❖ the avoidance of alcohol and other drugs;
❖ not smoking;
❖ regular and appropriate exercise.

RUBELLA

Rubella ('German measles') is especially harmful to the developing foetus as it can cause deafness, blindness and learning disability. All girls in the UK are now immunised against rubella before they reach childbearing age, and this measure has drastically reduced the incidence of rubella-damaged babies.

THALIDOMIDE

A drug called Thalidomide was widely prescribed during the late 1950s and early 1960s to alleviate morning sickness in pregnant women. Unfortunately, it was found to cause limb deformities in many of the babies born to women who had used the drug, and was withdrawn in 1961.

TOXOPLASMOSIS

Toxoplasmosis is an infection caused by the protozoan toxoplasma gondii. It may be contracted when pregnant women eat undercooked meat (usually pork) from infected animals, or by poor hygiene after handling cats or their faeces. In about one-third of cases, toxoplasmosis is transmitted to the child and may cause blindness, hydrocephalus or mental retardation.

Infection in late pregnancy usually has no ill effects.

IRRADIATION

If a woman has X-rays in early pregnancy or receives radiotherapy for the treatment of cancer, the embryo may suffer abnormalities. Radiation damage may also result from atomic radiation or radioactive fallout (following a nuclear explosion or a leak from a nuclear reactor). There is also an increased risk of the child's developing leukaemia in later life after exposure to radiation.

CEREBRAL PALSY

This is the general term for disorders of movement and posture resulting from damage to a child's developing brain in the later months of pregnancy, during birth, in the **neonatal** period or in early childhood. The injury does not damage the child's muscles or the nerves that connect them to the spinal cord – only the brain's ability to control the muscles. (Palsy literally means 'paralysis'.)

Cerebral palsy affects 2–3 children in every 1000. In the UK about 1500 babies either are born with or develop the condition each year. It can affect boys and girls, and people from all races and social backgrounds.

TYPES OF CEREBRAL PALSY

Cerebral palsy jumbles messages between the brain and muscles. There are three main types of cerebral palsy which correspond to the different parts of the brain affected:

* **Spastic cerebral palsy.** Children with spastic cerebral palsy find that some muscles become very stiff and weak, especially under effort, which can affect their control of movement. This is the most common type of cerebral palsy and it affects different areas of the body.

* **Athetoid cerebral palsy.** Children with athetoid cerebral palsy have some loss of control of their posture, and tend to make involuntary movements. Their speech can be hard to understand, and hearing problems are also common.

* **Ataxic cerebral palsy.** Children with ataxic cerebral palsy usually have problems with balance. They may also have shaky hand movements and irregular speech.

Often children will have a mixture of the different types of cerebral palsy. In some children the condition is barely noticeable; others will be more severely affected. No two children will be affected in quite the same way.

CAUSES OF CEREBRAL PALSY

Cerebral palsy is most commonly the result of a failure of part of the brain to develop, either before birth or in early childhood. Occasionally it is due to an inherited disorder. It is sometimes possible to identify the cause of cerebral palsy, but not always. Possible causes include:

* **an infection in the mother** during the first weeks of development in the womb (e.g. rubella or a cytomegalovirus);

* **a difficult or pre-term birth**, during which the baby fails to breathe properly (resulting in cerebral hypoxia);

* **toxic injury or poisoning** from drugs or alcohol used by the mother during pregnancy;

* **infections of the child's nervous system**, such as meningitis or encephalitis;

* **cerebral bleed** (haematoma), which particularly affects pre-term babies;

* **bleeding into cavities** inside the brain, which may occur in pre-term babies;
* **head trauma** resulting from a birth injury, fall, car accident or other causes;
* **the baby's brain forming abnormally**, for no apparent reason;
* **a genetic disorder**, which can be inherited even if both parents are completely healthy.

THE EFFECTS OF CEREBRAL PALSY

Cerebral palsy may not be recognised until the child is several months old. A child with cerebral palsy may have some or most of the following features, in varying degrees of severity:

* slow, awkward or jerky movements;
* stiffness of the arms and legs when being picked up;
* delayed sitting or walking;
* feeding difficulties;
* muscle spasms;
* floppiness;
* unwanted (involuntary) movements.

CARE OF CHILDREN WITH CEREBRAL PALSY

There is no cure for cerebral palsy. It is a non-progressive condition, which means that it does not become more severe as the child gets older, but some difficulties may become more noticeable.

Therapy can help children with cerebral palsy. Physiotherapists, occupational therapists and speech therapists often work very closely together to devise a treatment programme that will meet the needs of both the child and the family. As the nature of cerebral palsy varies immensely, the therapy is adapted to the needs of the individual child. These are some of the things that therapists might do:

* **Therapists** work at teaching children with cerebral palsy how to inhibit spasticity (stiffness) in their muscles in order to promote and produce good patterns of movement. They do this through the use of exercise, structured physical activity and, if necessary, the use of splints.

* **Physiotherapists and occupational therapists** look at the best posture, walking pattern and seating for the child. The occupational therapist may try to develop certain physical and learning skills using special play equipment, and will advise on equipment to help mobility, such as tricycles and trolleys. They will also give advice on equipment and aids that may enable the child to achieve greater success with everyday activities of living.

* **Speech and language therapists** may also be involved very early on if a child has feeding, drinking or swallowing problems. If speech is difficult, or if there are any other problems with language, the speech and language therapist will produce programmes. Some children with cerebral palsy have delayed language because they are unable to play and explore like non-disabled children. Speech and language therapists will work with teachers, occupational therapists and parents to encourage suitable learning activities. They may also provide communication devices, which help a child who is having serious problems with language or speech. The use of sign language, symbol speech or a communication aid will often lessen the frustration experienced by not being able to communicate their needs.

OTHER AREAS AFFECTED BY CEREBRAL PALSY

* **Eyesight:** the most common eye problem is a squint that may need

correction with glasses or, in more severe cases, an operation. Some children may have a cortical vision defect, where the part of the brain that is responsible for understanding the images the child sees does not work properly.

❖ **Hearing:** children with athetoid cerebral palsy are more likely to have severe hearing difficulties than other children, but 'glue ear' (see page 386) is as likely to develop in a child with any type of cerebral palsy as it is in unaffected children.

❖ **Learning ability:** some children with cerebral palsy do have learning difficulties, but this is by no means always the case. Some have higher than average intelligence and some have average intelligence. Some children have difficulty learning to do certain tasks (e.g. reading, drawing or arithmetic), because a particular part of the brain is affected; it is termed a 'specific learning difficulty' and should not be confused with the child's general intelligence.

❖ **Spatial perception:** some children with cerebral palsy find it difficult to judge distances or to think spatially (e.g. to visualise a three-dimensional building). This is due to an abnormality in a part of the brain and is not related to intelligence.

❖ **Speech:** speech depends on the ability to control tiny muscles in the mouth, tongue, palate and voice box. Speech difficulties and problems with chewing and swallowing often occur together in children with cerebral palsy.

❖ **Other difficulties:** some children with cerebral palsy may experience the following difficulties:

1 constipation;

2 frustration leading to behavioural difficulties;

3 sleeping problems;

4 not putting on much weight;

5 a tendency to chest infections;

6 epilepsy (an abnormal electrical discharge from the brain, causing seizures, affects about 1 in 3 children with cerebral palsy);

7 difficulty controlling body temperature;

8 negative attitudes of others towards them (people sometimes treat children with cerebral palsy as if they are stupid) – the term 'spastic' became a taunt used by other children for anyone they felt was inferior in any way; the negative way in which children are treated in society can lead to the child feeling isolated and having poor self-esteem.

BLINDNESS AND PARTIAL SIGHT (VISUAL IMPAIRMENT)

The picture of total darkness conjured up by the word 'blindness' is inaccurate: only about 18 per cent of blind people in the UK are affected to this degree; the other 82 per cent all have some remaining sight. In the UK there are just over 1 million blind and partially sighted people, of whom 40 per cent are blind and 60 per cent are partially sighted.

CAUSES OF VISUAL IMPAIRMENT

The main causes of visual impairment in children are:

❖ abnormalities of the eyes from birth, such as **cataracts** (cloudiness of the lens);

❖ **nystagmus** (involuntary jerkiness of the eyes);

- **optic atrophy** (damage to the optic nerve);

- **retinopathy** of prematurity (abnormal development of retinas in premature babies);

- **hereditary** factors such as retinoblastoma, a tumour of the retina which is often inherited.

Childhood glaucoma and diabetic retinopathy are quite rare in children, but are common causes of visual impairment in adults.

TREATMENT OF VISUAL IMPAIRMENT

Some conditions which cause visual impairment are treatable, particularly if detected at an early stage; for example:

- glaucoma can be halted by medical or surgical means;

- a cataract may be cured by removal of the lens;

- laser therapy is now being used to correct various visual defects.

EDUCATION FOR VISUALLY IMPAIRED CHILDREN

More than 55 per cent of visually impaired children in education attend mainstream schools along with sighted children. Most schools will have a **Statement of Special Education Needs** (see page 46), which details the support and special equipment they need.

SETTING OUT

The Royal National Institute of the Blind (RNIB) has produced an excellent booklet, *Setting Out*, for parents of visually impaired children. This offers practical ideas for day-to-day life with a young child with a sight problem. It explains how to create routines and an environment that give the child security and confidence to learn. Play activities suggest fun ways of encouraging children to explore objects and spaces, to learn to communicate and to gain a better understanding of other people and places.

DEAFNESS AND PARTIAL HEARING (HEARING IMPAIRMENT)

Deafness is often called 'the hidden disability' as it may not be outwardly apparent that a person is deaf. As with total blindness, total deafness is rare and is usually congenital (present from birth). Partial deafness is generally the result of an ear disease, injury or degeneration associated with the ageing process.

There are two types of hearing loss:

- **conductive:** when there is faulty transmission of sound from the outer ear to the inner ear;

- **sensori-neural:** when sounds that do reach the inner ear fail to be transmitted to the brain (often referred to as 'nerve' deafness).

CAUSES OF CONDUCTIVE HEARING LOSS

The most common causes of this kind of deafness in children are:

- **otitis media:** infection of the middle ear;

- **glue ear:** a build-up of sticky fluid in the middle ear, usually affecting children under 8 years.

CAUSES OF SENSORI-NEURAL HEARING LOSS

- **heredity:** there may be an inherited fault in a chromosome;

- **birth injury:** causing nerve or brain damage;

- **severe jaundice:** in the newborn baby with severe jaundice there may be damage to the inner ear;

- **rubella:** there may be damage to the developing foetus if the mother is infected with the rubella virus during pregnancy;

- **Ménière's disease:** a rare disorder in which deafness, vertigo and tinnitus result from an accumulation of fluid within the labyrinth in the inner ear;

* **damage to the cochlea or labyrinth (or both):** this can result from an injury, viral infection or prolonged exposure to loud noise;

* **glue ear:** see above.

DIAGNOSIS OF HEARING IMPAIRMENT

Hearing tests are performed as part of a routine assessment of child development (see Chapter 11). The early detection of any hearing defect is vital in order that the best possible help can be offered at the time when development is at its fastest.

TREATMENT OF HEARING IMPAIRMENT

For conductive hearing loss:

* a hearing aid;

* surgical correction of the defect.

For sensori-neural hearing loss:

* a hearing aid;

* special training, for example in language acquisition, speech therapy or perceptual motor training; a bilingual approach using British Sign Language (BSL) and verbal speech is often recommended.

HEARING AIDS

Almost all children with sensori-neural hearing loss will benefit from a hearing aid; and they can also be helpful for children with conductive hearing loss – for example, while they are waiting to be admitted to hospital for corrective surgery.

There are three types of hearing aid (see Figure 1.6):

1 **A body-worn hearing aid:** this is often strapped to the child's waist, with a wire connecting it to the earpiece; this type of aid is used for profound hearing loss as it enables greater amplification of sound than smaller devices.

2 **A post-aural hearing aid:** this fits comfortably behind the ear; it can be used even with small babies.

3 **An in-the-ear hearing aid:** this is generally reserved for use with older children.

The aim of all hearing aids is to amplify sounds. In children whose hearing is not helped by such aids, a cochlear implant may be considered instead.

PROBLEMS ASSOCIATED WITH HEARING IMPAIRMENT

* **Communication:** if possible, children should learn to express themselves through a recognisable

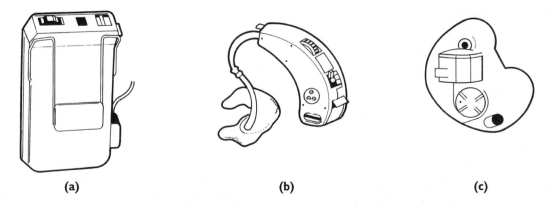

(a) **(b)** **(c)**

Fig 1.6 Hearing aids: (a) Body-worn hearing aid; (b) Post-aural hearing aid; (c) In-the-ear hearing aid

speech pattern (language acquisition). Isolation may result from the deaf child's inability to hear the familiar voices and household noises that a hearing child takes for granted.

❖ **A lack of auditory stimulation:** this may lead to delayed development.

❖ **A potential for injury:** this is related to a failure to detect warning sounds (e.g. traffic or warning shouts).

❖ **Anxiety and coping difficulties:** this is related to reduced social interaction and loneliness.

❖ **Parental anxiety:** this is related to having a child with impaired hearing.

Guidelines for working with children with a hearing impairment

❖ A baby with a hearing impairment may not show the 'startle' reaction to a loud noise; this is evident shortly after birth.

❖ A baby of about 4 months will visibly relax and smile at the sound of their mother's voice, even before they can see her; if the baby does not show this response, there may be some hearing loss.

❖ If babbling starts and then stops after a few weeks, this is often an indication of hearing loss.

❖ Children with hearing loss will be much more observant and visually aware than a hearing child – be aware that they may respond to the ringing of doorbells and telephones by reading the body language of those around them and reacting appropriately.

❖ Toys that make a lot of noise are still popular because children can feel the vibration, even if they cannot hear the sound; dancing to music is also popular for the same reason.

❖ A child with a profound hearing loss may still react quite normally, even turning round in response to someone's approach, since they may be using their other senses to compensate for the loss of hearing (e.g. they may notice a smell of perfume or see the reflection of the person in a window or other reflective surface).

How you can help

❖ Use your well-developed observational skills to detect hearing loss. If you do think there is a problem, refer it to the parent if you are a nanny, or to your line manager or teacher in a nursery or school.

❖ During activities, cut down on background noise (e.g. from the radio or dishwasher). Use carpets, rugs and pillows to absorb excess sound.

❖ Make eye contact before you start to speak. A gentle tap on the shoulder will usually get a child's attention.

❖ Talk in a normal voice – do not shout. Use gestures and facial expressions to clarify your message.

- ❧ Provide headphones for tape recorders or set up a special area where a tape recorder can be played at a higher volume.

- ❧ Teach children to use gestures and sign language (e.g. **Signalong**, **Makaton** or **British Sign Language**).

- ❧ Encourage children to talk about what they are doing. Ask open-ended questions (questions that require a detailed answer), which will encourage children to practise using language.

- ❧ Use stories, songs and finger-play to enhance language development.

- ❧ Encourage dancing to music; children will feel the vibrations and enjoy the chance to express themselves.

- ❧ Provide children with visual cues. For example, label shelves with a picture of toys to make tidying away easier. Use pictures to illustrate the steps of a recipe during cooking activities.

- ❧ Find out how to look after hearing aids and how to protect them from loss or damage within the school or nursery (e.g. sand and dirt can damage hearing aids).

- ❧ Be aware that early diagnosis and treatment can make a significant difference to the language development and learning potential of a child with a hearing impairment.

AUTISM/AUTISTIC SPECTRUM DISORDER

Autism is a disability that disrupts the development of social and communication skills. Many people with autism also have a learning disability, but whatever their level of ability, they share a common difficulty in making sense of the world in the way others do.

CAUSES OF AUTISM

Research suggests there is no single cause, but that there is a physical problem affecting those parts of the brain that integrate language and information from the senses. The condition has a physical cause and is *not* due to emotional problems or emotional deprivation. The onset of autism is almost always before the age of 3 years. It affects four times as many boys as girls.

FEATURES OF AUTISM

The degree to which children with an autistic spectrum disorder are affected varies, but all those affected have what is known as a triad of impairments. This triad affects:

1 **social interaction** (difficulty with social relationships);

2 **social communication** (difficulty with verbal and non-verbal communication);

3 **imagination** (difficulty in the development of play and imagination).

In addition to this triad, repetitive behaviour patterns are a notable feature and a resistance to change in routine is very common.

SUPPORT AND EDUCATION FOR CHILDREN WITH AUTISM

There is no known effective treatment apart from medication to control the associated problems of epilepsy and hyperactivity. The following therapies are often tried:

- ❧ **Holding therapy:** parents group together for long periods of time and

Displays indifference

Joins in only if adult insists and assists

One-sided interaction

Indicates needs by using an adult's hand

Does not play with other children

Talks incessantly about only one topic

Echolalic – copies words like parrot

- Difficulty with social relationships
- Difficulty with verbal communication
- Difficulty with non-verbal communication
- Difficulty in the development of play and imagination
- Resistance to change in routine

Bizarre behaviour

Inappropriate laughing or giggling

Handles or spins objects

No eye contact

Variety is not the spice of life

Lack of creative, pretend play

But some can do some things very well, very quickly; but *not* tasks involving social understanding

Fig 1.7 Some characteristics of a child with autism

try to foster emotional responsiveness by firm holding techniques.

❖ **Behaviour therapy:** with reward and discouragement for acceptable and unacceptable behaviour.

❖ **Daily life therapy:** an educational method based on a programme of physical education and age–appropriate lessons in a residential setting.

❖ **The National Autistic Society's EarlyBird programme:** this combines group training sessions for parents with individual home visits. Video feedback is used to help parents apply what they learn to work with their child.

- **Lovaas method:** developed by Professor Lovaas in California, USA, this offers an intensive programme of therapy using behaviour modification techniques.

A child with severe autism needs constant one-to-one care and requires considerable patience and skill on the part of all family members. Any changes to the child's routine must be planned carefully.

Early years education, for example at a nursery or playgroup, generally helps the family integrate into the community. Most children with severe autism attend local schools for children with severe learning difficulties; others require residential care (e.g. the National Autistic Society runs several schools which offer daily, weekly or termly facilities).

The teaching of **self–help skills** is an essential aspect of education for any child with autism as these can help children to achieve maximum independence and make life easier for the whole family. Because children with autism look 'normal', parents often have difficulty alerting others to the fact that their child has special needs.

ASPERGER SYNDROME

Most children with Asperger syndrome are at the less severe end of the autistic spectrum. Language delay is not as common as in autism, but there are often problems with communication. The child with Asperger syndrome is usually aware of his or her disability. Features of the syndrome are:

- social naivety or simplicity;
- good grammatical language but use of language only for the child's own interests;

- very specialised interests, which are often highly academic or complex (e.g. movement of the planets, railway timetables);
- lack of common sense arising from an unawareness of their environment.

CHILDREN WITH DISABILITIES AND THEIR FAMILIES

Every parent who is expecting a baby hopes that the baby will be perfect. If the baby is disabled in any way, this will have social, psychological and financial implications for the family and affect the way it functions. Each family is unique in the way that it reacts initially and adjusts in the long term. When a mother gives birth to a baby who has a disability, she may experience feelings of guilt – 'It must be because of something I did wrong during pregnancy' – or even of rejection, although this is usually temporary.

Case Study

Mothers' responses to blind babies
Research by Selma Fraiberg (1974–77) showed that blind babies begin to smile at about the same age as sighted babies (roughly 4 weeks), but that they smile less often; the blind infant's smile is also less intense, more fleeting and less frequent than the sighted baby's smile. In addition, blind babies do not enter into a mutual gaze, which is an important factor in the formation of a deep attachment or bond between parents and their baby. Fraiberg's research found that most mothers of blind babies gradually withdrew from their infants. They needed help in learning to 'read' their baby's other signals, such as body movements and gestures. This help led to an improved interaction between mothers and their babies.

Case Study

A mother celebrates the birthday of a very special baby

The following article, which appeared in *The Guardian* (16 December 1992), was written by Pat Evans, whose third child has the chromosomal defect, Down's syndrome. It describes her and her husband's feelings immediately after the birth and later, at the time of the child's first birthday.

My third child was born just before Christmas, a beautiful baby boy with squashy fingers and crinkly ears. I was overjoyed – and relieved. I was 37 and the triple test had given me a slightly worrying result. Carried out in pregnancy, it uses a sample of blood to estimate your chances of having a baby with Down's syndrome. Women scoring 1/250 or less are considered high risk and offered an amniocentesis. I scored 1/260, so had no further tests.

I tried to pick the baby up but the umbilical cord was very short. He was reluctant to feed but after much persuasion took the breast. He lay in my arms, a curiously serene little bundle with a dusting of fine hair. I couldn't wait to get him home but the doctor said they would carry out some routine tests because of his initial refusal to feed. . .

The paediatrician arrived just as we decided to call the baby Euan. He let the baby slip through his fingers, stroking the back of his head with a practised hand. Sitting on the bed, he glanced at John, then back at me. 'Here comes the tricky bit,' he said calmly. 'I think your baby's got Down's syndrome.' He went over the telltale signs – the short umbilical cord, stubby fingers, low-set ears, poor muscle tone. We listened numbly, unable to comprehend that the nightmare had come true: there was something wrong with the baby.

As John leant over the cot and kissed the sleeping child, I realised I was crying, great sheets of tears moving slowly down my face. Inside I felt cold, hard, cruel. The paediatrician kept on talking, as if his words were a charm to keep our suffering at bay.

'. . .There's nothing wrong with this baby, he's just different. He's not suffering, you are. He'll be in touch with things we aren't.' He made it sound as if anyone in their right mind would have Down's syndrome.

'What about intelligence?' I asked sharply.

'Only intelligent people worry about intelligence.' He correctly predicted the emotions we would feel: grief for the child we thought we would have, sorrow for the disastrous human being we thought he would be. . .

John went home to see the children and I was left alone with the baby who didn't belong to me but Mr and Mrs Down's syndrome. He didn't bear our features but theirs, his personality arose from their union, not mine and John's.

They offered to take him into the nursery but I refused, terrified that in his absence I would reject him. I had to keep him close, make him mine once more. Waking in the dead of night, I stared into his sleeping face. He almost frightened me, this tiny alien being wearing a mask which separated him from the rest of humanity. He was branded, set apart and now so was I. Stroking his head, I felt an agony of guilt, pity and fear.

Case Study continued

I had done this to him. I had blighted the flower before it had a chance to bloom. What terrible blackness inside me had afflicted my own child?

Later on they struggled to take blood from a vein in his head and I felt upset in a remote kind of way, the needle made him cry out. He was given a heart scan and I watched, curious about my own reactions. Did I want him to be healthy? Would it be better if he slipped away now? The scan was normal. I took Euan home, just in time for the parties.

Twelve months later, it's nearly Christmas again. . . Euan plays near the foot of the Christmas tree; he has slanted eyes, sticky-out ears and a tongue that pops from his mouth like the label of a collar which refuses to lie flat. He might not go to primary school, let alone university, but every time he smiles – which he does all the time – my heart turns over.

. . .Euan has taught me so many things: that the ability to communicate is more important than IQ and may have nothing to do with it, and that creating love in others is so simple, a child can do it. Try as I might, I can't feel tragic about a baby who shakes with silent laughter as his sister wraps tinsel round his head. Most of all, Euan has made me realise just how much we underestimate our capacity for loving.

Every woman who gives birth to a handicapped child does so in a climate of rejection and fear. Yet even as I struggled to come to terms with Euan's birth, I continued to bond with my baby.

In the end, loving him was easy and – I cannot emphasise this word enough – as natural as falling off a log. Loving Euan, I find I like myself better too. . . When next you see the parents of a handicapped child, don't automatically feel sorry for them, because you have absolutely no idea what they are feeling.

CARING FOR CHILDREN WITH SPECIAL NEEDS

The term 'special needs' is now used to describe children whose development differs from the normal. The important aim is to see the individual child first and then the special need or disability.

The self-concept of children with disabilities

Any child with a disability may have a problem in developing a positive self-concept (see page 13); the problem often results from the reaction of others to the disability.

Common reactions of parents to having a child with disabilities include:

* **A sense of tragedy:** parents who give birth to a child with a disability experience complex emotions. They may grieve for the loss of a 'normal' child, but they have not actually been bereaved. They still have a child with a unique personality and identity of their own. Relatives and friends can be embarrassed if they do not know how to react to the event, and their awkward response can leave parents feeling very isolated at a time which is normally spent celebrating.

* **A fear of making mistakes:** sometimes there is an over-reliance on professional help. If the disability seems like the most important aspect of the child's personality, parents may believe that only a medical expert can advise on the care of their child. The reality is that the parent almost always knows what is required for their child. A great deal of what the child needs is not related to their disability in any case.

* **Being overprotective:** a desire to cocoon the child can be counter-productive. The child needs to be equipped for life and can only learn by making mistakes. In addition, siblings may resent the disabled child who is seen as spoilt or never punished.

* **Exercising control:** parents may take freedom of choice away from the child, so disempowering them. Parents and carers often dictate where and with whom the child plays, thus depriving them of an opportunity for valuable social learning.

The principles of caring for children with disabilities

An early years worker can best promote a child's self-concept by always seeing the child first and the disability second.

Guidelines for caring for children with disabilities

* **Self-empowerment:** always encourage independence. Ask how the child wants to do things – let them make as many choices as possible.

* **Empathy:** try to imagine yourself in the child's situation. How would you like to be helped? (This is not to be confused with unwanted sympathy.)

* **Patience:** always be patient with children, particularly if communication is difficult or time-consuming.

* **Sensitivity:** try to anticipate the child's feelings. Having one's most intimate needs attended to by a stranger can be embarrassing.

* **Respect:** show awareness of a child's personal rights, dignity and privacy; never allow other children to poke fun at a child with a disability.

* **Communication and interpersonal skills:** develop good listening skills. Non-verbal communication is just as important as what you say.

* **Attitude:** an open-minded and non-judgemental attitude is important, as is a warm, friendly manner.

* **Be positive:** praise effort rather than achievement. Provide activities that are appropriate to the child's ability so they have a chance of achieving.

* **Integration and inclusion:** make an effort to involve the child with other children. Integration emphasises the ways in which a child can be brought into the community, whereas inclusion sees the child already as part of the community, but needing additional help within it.

❖ **Set guidelines for behaviour:** these should be the same as for all children: do not make exceptions for the child with a disability.

❖ **Be a good role model:** support the child's carers or parents to enable them to provide a lifestyle that is as normal as possible.

CHILDREN WITH SPECIAL EDUCATIONAL NEEDS

Education is a lifelong process, but in formal terms it involves schooling between the ages of 4 or 5 years and 16 years, with further options of attending colleges and universities, or training schemes with an employer. Until the 1950s in the UK, children born with an obvious disabling condition, such as Down's syndrome or cerebral palsy, would have been cared for within the family for the first few years of life. Then they would be admitted to a large mental handicap hospital where they may have spent the rest of their lives with no contact with mainstream educational institutions. Fortunately this is no longer the case.

What are special educational needs?

The term 'special educational needs', or SEN, has a legal definition. The government's Department for Education and Skills (DfES) defines children with SEN as having 'learning difficulties or disabilities which make it harder for them to learn or access education than most other children of the same age.'

A child with special needs may need extra or different help at school or home because of:

❖ physical difficulties or disability;

❖ communication problems;

❖ a visual or hearing impairment;

❖ emotional, social and behavioural difficulties;

❖ a serious medical condition;

❖ a combination of any of these.

The Children Act 2004 defines learning disability as: 'a state of arrested or incomplete development of mind which induces significant impairment of intelligence and social functioning'.

The SEN Code of Practice

The **SEN Code** (2002) has the following general principles:

❖ a child with special needs should have his or her needs met;

❖ the special needs of children will normally be met in mainstream schools;

❖ the views of children should be sought and taken into account;

❖ parents have a vital role to play in supporting their child's education;

❖ children with special educational needs should be offered full access to a broad, balanced and relevant education, including an appropriate curriculum for the Foundation Stage and the national curriculum (NC);

❖ all early years settings have an **SEN policy** and follow the integrated team approach of the Foundation Stage;

❖ early identification, Early Years Action, Early Years Action Plus and for some children, statutory assessment.

According to the Code, every school must appoint a member of staff who takes responsibility for special education needs – the **special educational needs coordinator** or **SENCO** (see page 55).

Special educational needs policy

A school's SEN policy should include information about:

* how they identify and make provision for children with SEN;

* the facilities they have, including those which increase access for pupils who are disabled, including access to the curriculum;

* how resources are allocated to and among pupils with SEN;

* how they enable pupils with SEN to engage in activities of the school together with pupils who do not have SEN;

* how the governing body evaluates the success of the school's work with pupils with SEN;

* their arrangements for dealing with complaints from parents.

About 17 per cent of all schoolchildren have a special educational need. Most are taught in mainstream schools, where they receive additional help from a range of services. Children with special educational needs but without a statement (see below) will have their needs met through **Early Years Action** or Early Years Action Plus. When children reach school age these are called **School Action** and School Action Plus.

EARLY YEARS ACTION OR SCHOOL ACTION
When a child is identified with special educational needs, the SENCO and practitioners, involving the parent, make additional or different provision, through an **individual education plan**. If the child does not make adequate progress, the situation moves to Early Years Action Plus or School Action Plus. At this point, external support services advise on the individual education plan, which now includes specialist assessments, advice on materials and strategies.

THE ASSESSMENT PROCESS: STATEMENT OF SPECIAL EDUCATIONAL NEEDS

The statement of special educational needs is a legal document produced by local education authorities following multi-professional assessment and contributions from parents or carers. It specifies the precise nature of the pupil's assessed difficulties and educational needs, and the special or additional provision that would be made in order to meet that pupil's needs. Statements must then be reviewed at least annually.

Where a child has severe or complex needs, Early Years Action and Early Years Action Plus will be bypassed. Only about 3 per cent of schoolchildren have a formal statement of special educational needs.

An assessment must take account of the following five factors:

1 **Physical factors:** the child's particular illness or condition.

2 **Psychological and emotional factors:** the child's intellectual ability and levels of anxiety or depression will lead to different needs and priorities (e.g. severe anxiety may adversely affect all daily activities, and its alleviation will therefore assume top priority).

3 **Sociocultural factors:** whether or not the child is part of a family, the family's background and the relationships within the family will all influence needs.

Similarly, the individual's wider community and the social class to which they belong are also influential.

4 **Environmental factors:** a child living in a cold, damp house with an outside toilet will have different needs from someone who is more comfortably housed.

5 **Political and economic factors:** poverty or belonging to a disadvantaged group leads to less choice in day-to-day living.

Case Study

Problems in statementing

Richard is 7 years old and has **muscular dystrophy**. The local education authority (LEA) offered Richard a place at his local mainstream primary school, dependent on the provision of a full-time classroom assistant to help ensure his safety. Richard weighs just 3 stone and is partially sighted. To obtain this provision, the LEA required that Richard be statemented. This process took several months; meanwhile Richard's classmates moved up to a classroom on the first floor for many of their regular activities and Richard, who uses a wheelchair, has been 'profoundly affected emotionally by being separated from his peer group', according to his hospital report. The head teacher has always been very supportive; Richard is an intelligent boy who needs a full education and could obviously receive one if a lift were installed. His parents are fighting the LEA's refusal to fit a lift at the school; they feel that Richard is being marginalised or punished for having a disability.

ACTIVITY: PROBLEMS IN STATEMENTING

1 What can Richard's parents do to ensure that he receives the help he needs?

2 Find out about organisations that fight for the rights of disabled people. Write a report on your findings.

3 Research the range of services available in your own local area for disabled children and their families.

Speech and language impairments

As many as 250,000 children under 5 years of age – and a similar number of school age – have a speech and language impairment. For some, this is a delay – their language is developing, but more slowly than usual. In some cases this may be connected with a hearing impairment, such as glue ear, in early childhood. For others with a language disorder, the difficulty may be more complex. These children do not stammer or lisp. They are not autistic. Their general intelligence is often average or above. Their language impairment is specific or primary – not the result of any other disability. It is sometimes referred to as **dysphasia**.

Children with a speech and language impairment have difficulties with:

❖ talking (expressive language) – this may be due to **dyspraxia**, (difficulty in making the movements which produce speech);

❖ understanding (receptive language);

❖ both of the above.

Some children have other difficulties which affect the development of language. These include:

❖ difficulties with listening and attention skills;

❖ behaviour difficulties, due to the frustration of not understanding or being understood;

❖ difficulties with written language (**dyslexia**);

❖ difficulties understanding abstract ideas, like time, emotions or make-believe – these children have trouble connecting ideas and using language socially;

❖ profound difficulties relating to the outside world – many of these will be described as having 'autistic tendencies'.

Some of these children benefit from learning a sign language, such as Makaton, PECS or British Sign Language/Signed English.

MAKATON

The Makaton vocabulary is a list of over 400 items with corresponding signs and symbols, with an additional resource vocabulary for the UK national curriculum. The signs are based on British Sign Language (BSL), but are used to support spoken English. The Makaton Project publishes a book of illustrations of the Makaton vocabulary (see Figure 1.8). Most signs rely on movement as well as position, so you cannot really learn the signs from the illustrations. Also, in many signs *facial expression* is important. If a child at a school or nursery is learning Makaton, the parents should be invited to learn too. The Makaton Project will support schools and parents in this, as they know that everyone involved with the child must use the same signs.

PICTURE EXCHANGE COMMUNICATION SYSTEM (PECS)

PECS begins with teaching children to exchange a picture of a desired item with a teacher, who immediately honours the request. For example, if they want a drink,

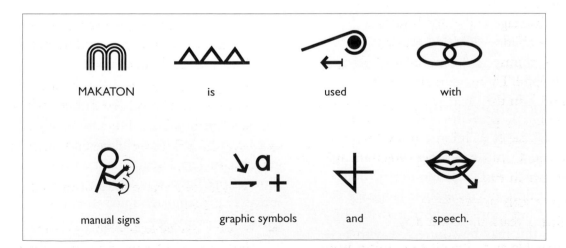

Fig 1.8 Makaton

they will give a picture of 'drink' to an adult, who directly hands them a drink. Verbal prompts are not used, thus encouraging spontaneity and avoiding prompt dependency. The system goes on to teach discrimination of symbols and how to construct simple 'sentences'. Ideas for teaching, commenting and other language structures, such as asking and answering questions, are also incorporated. It has been reported that both children of nursery age and older children have begun to develop speech when using PECS. The system is often used as a communication aid for children and adults who have an autistic spectrum disorder.

DEVELOPMENTAL DYSPRAXIA

Dyspraxia is an immaturity of the brain resulting in messages not being properly transmitted to the body. It affects at least 2 per cent of the population in varying degrees and 70 per cent of those affected are male. Children with dyspraxia can be of average or above intelligence but are often behaviourally immature. They try hard to fit in with the range of socially accepted behaviour when at school, but often throw tantrums when at home. They may find it difficult to understand logic and reason. Dyspraxia is a disability but, as with autism, those affected do not look disabled. This is both an advantage and a disadvantage. Sometimes children with dyspraxia are labelled as 'clumsy' children. Such labelling is very unhelpful. There are many early indications – in the child's first 3 years – that he or she has dyspraxia (see below). Not all of these will apply to every child with dyspraxia, and many of these problems can be overcome in time.

EARLY INDICATIONS OF DYSPRAXIA

In the first 3 years, the child may:

* be irritable and difficult to comfort from birth;

* have delayed early motor skill development – problems sitting unaided, rolling from side to side, and may not crawl;

* be delayed in toilet training;

* have feeding difficulties, including colic, milk allergies, and so on;

* have sleeping difficulties;

* have delayed language development – single words not obvious until aged 3 years;

* avoid simple construction toys, such as jigsaws and Lego;

* constantly move arms and legs;

* be sensitive to loud noises;

* be highly emotional and easily upset.

LATER INDICATIONS OF DYSPRAXIA

Older children are usually very verbally adept and converse well with adults, but they may be ostracised by their own peer group because they do not fit in. They may cleverly avoid doing those tasks that are difficult or even impossible for them.

The child may:

* be clumsy, constantly bumping into objects and falling over;

* often flap their hands when running or jumping;

* be a messy eater – preferring to use fingers to eat and often spilling liquid from the drinking cup;

* be unable to hold a pen or pencil properly and be confused about which hand to use;

* have difficulties throwing and catching a ball;

* be slow to learn to dress or to feed themselves;

* be very excitable, becoming easily distressed and having frequent temper tantrums;

❧ prefer adult company, feeling isolated in their peer group;

❧ have speech problems, being slow to learn to speak, or the speech may be incoherent;

❧ be unable to hop, skip or ride a bike;

❧ have very high levels of motor activity, always swinging and tapping feet when seated, clapping hands and unable to sit still;

❧ be sensitive to touch, finding some clothes uncomfortable;

❧ dislike high levels of noise;

❧ have reading and writing difficulties;

❧ have poor short-term memory, often forgetting tasks learned the previous day;

❧ be unable to answer simple questions, even though they know the answers;

❧ show a lack of imaginative play (e.g. not enjoying dressing up, or playing inappropriately in the home corner);

❧ have phobias or show obsessive behaviour;

❧ have a poor sense of direction;

❧ be intolerant to having hair or teeth brushed, or nails and hair cut;

❧ have no sense of danger (e.g. jumping from an inappropriate height).

ASSESSMENT OF DYSPRAXIA

Assessment involves obtaining a detailed developmental history of the child, and using developmental tests or scales to build up a learning ability profile. Occupational therapists, physiotherapists and extra support at school can all help a child with dyspraxia to cope or to overcome many difficulties.

GIFTEDNESS

Some educationalists make a distinction between 'gifted' and 'talented' children:

❧ **gifted children** being those who are of superior ability over a wide range;

❧ **talented children** being those who have a specific area of expertise, such as musical aptitude or sporting prowess.

There is much debate about whether children who are gifted *do* have special educational needs. Educational approaches include:

❧ **enrichment:** the classroom curriculum is specially adapted to support and extend the child's particular abilities;

❧ **segregation:** the child is placed in a group of other high-ability pupils, who follow a specialised curriculum;

❧ **acceleration:** children are moved up a year in school – this is often the obvious choice, but parents and teachers are now much more aware of the social and emotional effects of separation from the child's peer group.

DYSLEXIA

Dyslexia is a specific learning difficulty characterised by difficulty in coping with written symbols. Some problems encountered by the child with dyslexia are:

❧ language problems;

❧ sequencing difficulties;

❧ short concentration span;

❧ visual perception problems;

❧ poor short-term memory;

❧ stress and fear of failure;

❧ directional confusion;

❧ reversal of letters and numbers.

Dyslexia is a very vague term which tends to be used to cover all kinds of difficulties, ranging from mild problems with spelling to complete illiteracy (inability to read or write). Every child with dyslexia has a different pattern of difficulties. Intelligence is usually unaffected, but the problem may seem more obvious in intelligent children.

Recent research has shown that the brains of people with dyslexia are 'wired' differently from other people's. Microanatomy carried out on dyslexics' brains after death shows that while there is a lack of efficiency in the left brain hemisphere which relates to language ability, there is increased efficiency in the side of the brain which dictates spatial ability. Visual spatial skills seem superior in people with dyslexia; their ability to see the world in a more vivid, three-dimensional way may result in particular artistic talent. Early identification of dyslexia can greatly reduce the difficulties, both for the individual with dyslexia and for their school and family.

TEACHING STRATEGIES FOR CHILDREN WITH DYSLEXIA

❖ Appreciation and regular praise (and more controversially extrinsic reward) – many children with dyslexia have poor self-esteem and see themselves as failures within the school system.

❖ Keeping records of each lesson – so that each lesson builds upon the success of the previous one.

❖ 'Scaffolding' work – structuring the work into a series of small steps, each of which supports the learning.

❖ Specific teaching aids (e.g. special phonic flashcards for letter recognition).

❖ Concrete and visual explanations – presenting instructions in the form of diagrams or essay plans laid out as patterns.

ATTENTION DEFICIT HYPERACTIVITY DISORDER

Attention deficit hyperactivity disorder (ADHD) fits into the category of specific learning difficulty. ADHD is sometimes initially diagnosed as an autistic spectrum disorder as many of the features are common to both. It is estimated that about 50 per cent of children with ADHD also show behavioural problems.

The cause of ADHD is not known, but there is growing evidence to show that a pattern of hyperactivity is inherited. There may also be a biological cause, perhaps due to a slower metabolism of glucose by the brain. Treatment may be by a stimulant medication (usually Ritalin), which often has an immediate improving effect on the child's behaviour but is a controversial treatment; arriving at the correct dosage for the individual, however, takes time and a high degree of cooperation between school and parents. Daily feedback from the child's class teacher is essential for the treatment to be effective in the long term. The classroom may not be appropriate in its expectations of the child.

CHARACTERISTICS OF ADHD

The following are common characteristics found in children with ADHD:

❖ difficulty remaining seated when asked to do so;

❖ difficulty in sharing and taking turns in group situations;

❖ excessive talking;

❖ easily distracted by extraneous stimuli;

❖ appearing not to be listening when being spoken to;

❖ appearing restless, often fidgeting with hands or feet;

❖ difficulty playing quietly;

❖ often losing things necessary for tasks or activities at school or at home (e.g. books, pencils);

❖ difficulty sustaining attention in tasks or play activities;

- interrupting others (e.g. butts into other children's games);
- often engaging in physically dangerous activities without considering possible consequences (e.g. runs across road without looking);
- unable to focus attention on relevant detail at an age when such control is expected.

BEHAVIOURAL, EMOTIONAL AND SOCIAL DIFFICULTY (BESD)

BESD is classed as a special educational need and may be described as any form of behaviour which:

- interferes with children's learning or normal development;
- is harmful to the child, other children or adults;
- puts a child in a high-risk category for later social problems or school failure.

Children with behavioural, emotional and social difficulties cover the full range of ability and a broad scope of severity. Children with relatively mild BESD may have problems associated with:

- social interaction;
- working in a group;
- poor concentration;
- outbursts of temper;
- verbal aggression to their peers and adults.

At the more severe end of the range, children may have problems associated with:

- open defiance;
- physical aggression (biting, scratching, etc.);
- a very short concentration span;
- low self-esteem;
- accepting praise;
- taking responsibility for their behaviour.

Some children display persistent and frequent violent behaviour that requires physical intervention. Others may display similar signs of low esteem, underachievement and inappropriate social interaction, but without outwardly challenging behavioural outbursts. They will be quiet and withdrawn, and find it difficult to communicate. Assessment of need in this area is difficult; before a child is included in this category an educational psychologist will look at both the intensity and the frequency of the child's behaviour. Behaviour that is highly inappropriate in one social context may be quite acceptable in another situation.

CHILDREN WITH SPECIAL NEEDS AND THE ROLE OF PROFESSIONALS

There are many different statutory and voluntary services involved in the care and education of children with special needs. For information about these services, such as **Sure Start**, see Chapter 15.

Parent partnership services

Parent partnership services are statutory services that offer information, impartial advice and support for parents of children and young people with special educational needs. They are also able to put parents in touch with other local organisations. Parent partnership services also have a role in making sure that parents' views are heard and understood and that these views inform local policy and practice.

Early years development and child care partnerships

Early years development and child care partnerships plan local education provision for children below compulsory school age, and plan child care for children aged 0–14 years. There has been one partnership per local education authority area, but this is changing.

Framework for the Assessment of Children in Need and their Families

This Framework provides guidance to local authorities, social services departments and other agencies on the assessment of **children in need** under the Children Act 1989. It describes a systematic approach to information gathering across three areas of a child's life:

❖ the child's developmental needs;

❖ parenting capacity;

❖ family and environmental factors.

Common Assessment Framework

The Common Assessment Framework was introduced in 2005 as an assessment tool that can be used by the whole children's workforce to assess the **additional needs** of children and young people at the first sign of difficulties. An estimated 20–30 per cent of children have additional needs at some point in their childhood, requiring extra support from education, health or social services. This could be for a limited period or on a long-term basis.

The Framework is intended to provide a simple, non-bureaucratic process for a **holistic** assessment of children's needs, taking account of the individual, family and community. Information will follow the child so that a picture builds up over time. It will encourage greater sharing of information between practitioners (where consent is given) and reduce the number and duration of different assessment processes that children and young people historically have had to undergo.

Portage

Portage is a planned approach to home-based preschool education for children with developmental delay, disabilities or other special educational needs. Portage began in the 1970s in Portage, Wisconsin in the USA; there is now an extensive Portage network in the UK, which is overseen by the National Portage Association.

Register of disabled children

Under the Children Act 1989, all local authorities have to keep a register of local disabled children. This is to help the local authority plan services more effectively. Registration is not compulsory and failure to register does not affect a child's right to services.

The role of social service professionals

❖ **Social workers:** most now work in specialised teams dealing with a specific client group (e.g. a Disability and Learning Difficulties Team). They are employed by social services departments ('social work departments' in Scotland) and initially their role is to assess the needs of the child. They may refer the family to other departments, such as the Department of Social Security (DSS), the National Health Service (NHS) or voluntary organisations. A social worker may also act as an advocate on behalf of disabled children, ensuring that they receive all the benefits and services to which they are entitled.

❖ **Technical officers:** usually work with people with specific disorders; for example, audio technicians or audiologists monitor the level of hearing in children as a developmental check,

The following professionals are all involved in the care and education of children with special needs:

❖ Family doctors (GPs): independent professionals who are under contract to the National Health Service, but who are not employed by it. They are the most available of the medical profession, and are also able to refer carers on to specialist doctors and paramedical services.

❖ Health visitors: qualified nurses who have done further training, including midwifery experience. They work exclusively in the community, and can be approached either directly or via the family doctor. They work primarily with children up to the age of 5 years; this obviously includes all children with disabilities, and they carry out a wide range of developmental checks.

❖ Physiotherapists: the majority are employed in hospitals, but some work in special schools or residential facilities. Physiotherapists assess children's motor development and skills, and provide activities and exercises that parents and carers can use to encourage better mobility and coordination.

❖ Occupational therapists (OTs): work in hospitals, schools and other residential establishments. Some OTs specialise in working with children (paediatric occupational therapists) and will assess a child's practical abilities and advise on the most appropriate activities and specialist equipment to encourage independent life skills.

❖ Community nurses: most work closely with family doctors and provide nursing care in the home. They also advise the parent or carer on specialist techniques (e.g. how to lift, catheter care).

❖ School nurses: may visit a number of mainstream schools in their health district to monitor child health and development – by checking weight, height, eyesight and hearing, and by giving advice on common problems such as head lice. They may also be employed in special schools to supervise the routine medical care of disabled children.

❖ Speech therapists: may be employed in schools, hospitals or in the community. They assess a child's speech, tongue and mouth movements, and the effects of these on eating and swallowing. They further provide exercises and activities both to develop all aspects of children's expressive and receptive communication skills and to encourage language development.

❖ Play specialists: employed in hospitals and are often qualified nursery nurses who have additional training. They may prepare a child for hospitalisation and provide play opportunities for children confined to bed or in a hospital playroom.

❖ Play therapists: also work in hospitals and have undertaken specialist training. They use play to enable children with special needs to feel more secure emotionally in potentially threatening situations.

❖ Clinical psychologists: usually work in hospitals. They assess children's emotional, social and intellectual development and advise on appropriate activities to promote development.

❖ Dieticians: most work in hospitals and can advise on a range of special diets (e.g. for diabetics or those with cystic fibrosis or coeliac disease).

and sign–language interpreters translate speech into sign language for deaf and hearing-impaired people.

❖ **Nursery officers:** trained nursery nurses who work in day nurseries and family centres. Such staff are involved in shift work, and they care for children under 5 years when it is not possible for those children to remain at home.

* **Family aids (or home care assistants):** used to be called 'home helps' and provide practical support for families in their own homes – shopping, cooking, looking after children, and so on.

* **Special educational needs coordinators (SENCO):** liaise both with colleagues in special schools and with the parents of children with special needs. They are responsible for coordinating provision for children with special educational needs, for keeping the school's SEN register and for working with external agencies (e.g. educational psychology services, social service departments and voluntary organisations).

* **Educational psychologists:** involved in the educational assessment of children with special needs, and in preparing the statement of special educational needs. They act as advisers to professionals working directly with children with a range of special needs, particularly those with emotional and behavioural difficulties.

* **Portage worker:** Portage is an educational programme for children who have difficulty in learning basic skills due to either physical or behavioural problems. Home Portage advisors are specially trained in understanding child development and come from a variety of professions, ranging from nurses or other health professionals to schoolteachers.

* **Orthoptists:** work with people who have visual problems and abnormal eye movements.

* **Special needs teachers:** qualified teachers with additional training and experience in teaching children with special needs. They are supported by:

special needs support teachers (or specialist teachers), who are often peripatetic, visiting disabled children in different mainstream schools, and sometimes specialising in a particular disorder (e.g. vision or hearing impairment); and by **special needs support assistants,** who may be qualified nursery nurses and who often work with individual statemented children under the direction of the specialist teacher.

* **Educational welfare officers:** as in mainstream education, they will be involved with children whose school attendance is irregular; they may also arrange school transport for disabled children.

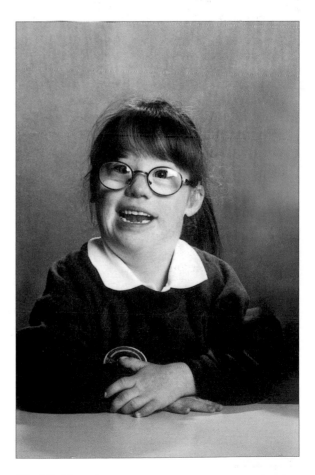

Fig 1.9 Hannah

Case Study

The following case study is a true snapshot biography, written by her parents, of a young girl who has Down's syndrome.

Hannah

When Hannah was born, we suspected straightaway that she had Down's syndrome. Our thoughts were confirmed by the consultant the following morning. Many children with Down's syndrome find it hard to suck, and with Hannah breastfeeding proved very difficult; but with the support of a wonderful nursery nurse at the hospital, we managed it. During this time, a midwife noticed that Hannah appeared to be blue around the face, which suggested that she had a possible heart condition.

At less than a week old, we took Hannah to a London hospital to have a heart scan. She was diagnosed as having an atrio-ventricular septal defect (AVSD). Corrective surgery would involve patching up two holes and reconstructing a heart valve. We were informed by a consultant that, if surgery were not performed, Hannah would probably not live beyond her teens. The consultant suggested that we choose not to follow the surgery option, since the quality of life for a teenager with Down's syndrome was poor. At 1 week old, Hannah was being discriminated against because she was born with Down's syndrome!

At home we were visited by a Portage worker, a home-based early educational intervention service. Hannah was set different tasks each week for which achievable targets were devised. Hannah's babbling and motor skills were developing as one would expect for a child with Down's syndrome. She still had difficulty sucking and eating baby foods. When she was a year old we were visited by a speech therapist and physiotherapist. More tasks were given and Makaton signs were introduced, to aid her communication and eating skills.

Regular visits continued to be made to various hospitals. We decided that Hannah would undergo corrective heart surgery. She was on medication for her heart condition, and her hearing and eyesight were being monitored. Hannah had her open heart surgery at 14 months at a different London children's hospital. The corrective surgery was successful, but she caught two infections during the recovery phase while still in hospital. As a result she became totally floppy again and lost her spontaneous babbling. After five weeks in hospital, Hannah was well enough to return home, even though her muscle tone was very poor. Visits to various hospitals continued and Hannah was gradually weaned off her medicines. With this major hurdle over, we could again begin to concentrate on other areas of her development. For the first time Hannah began to eat real food. Chocolate buttons were an early favourite! We had heard how many children with Down's syndrome tended to be obese, but Hannah was tiny and needed feeding up! We also knew that children with Down's syndrome were 'loving'. Well, Hannah was very affectionate towards some people, but understandably feared any medical staff.

Hannah's verbal and motor skills developed at an extremely slow rate. Her peers who also had Down's syndrome were beginning to walk and talk, but Hannah was not. It was apparent that her level of understanding was developing much more quickly than her expressive skills.

We were very keen that Hannah should go to an integrated nursery. We eventually found a lovely nursery, but would need to find a volunteer to be with Hannah throughout the sessions she attended. Hannah stayed at nursery for several years. Her volunteers changed although on several occasions I had to go in to support her myself. It was not until her final year that the local educational authority began

Case Study continued

to fund nursery support for children with Down's syndrome. She then received regular professional support, and for the first time I did not have to worry if her helper did not turn up.

Hannah was still not walking or talking. She used Makaton to sign her needs and to read simple books. She was able to count up to 5, by pointing to the numbers. She had been allowed to spend an extra year at the nursery, but by the time she was 6 the local authority was keen to place her in a special school or a special unit. We opposed and fought against this. For the following year, Hannah was educated at home. She developed further many of her basic skills. Finally, after numerous meetings, the authority agreed to allow her to go to our local school. Hannah has settled into school life quickly and easily, and has amazed everyone, despite all her difficulties.

Although she can be stubborn, Hannah is also very cooperative. She loves the social aspects of school life, as well as the learning activities. The school, children and other parents hold a wonderfully supportive attitude towards her as an individual. Hannah receives the full-time support that she is entitled to and, as long as she is progressing and happy at school, then we will continue to fight for an integrated education for her.

It could not be said that Hannah is typical of a child who has Down's syndrome (in fact, there is no such thing as a typical child who has Down's syndrome). Hannah's physical and verbal difficulties make everyday life harder for her, but her strong personality, charm and determination are helping her get on with life and have earned her the respect of her parents, teachers, helpers and fellow classmates.

Children in residential care

The Children Act 1989 emphasised that the best place for children to be brought up is within their own families and statistics show that the vast majority of disabled children *are* living at home. Some residential special schools offer weekly or termly boarding facilities; children may be in residential care for medical reasons or because the family cannot manage the care involved. All homes must be registered and inspected by social services departments to safeguard the interests of this particularly vulnerable group.

Foster placements

The Foster Placement (Children) Regulations 1991 apply safeguards to any child in foster care (see Chapter 15). Some voluntary organisations provide specialist training programmes for carers who foster disabled children, and the carer's active involvement in the child's education is encouraged.

Respite care

Ideally, this would be renamed 'natural break' or 'short-stay' care, as 'respite care' implies that carers need relief from an unwanted burden. However, the aim of such care is to provide support and encouragement so that parents and carers are able to continue caring for their child within the family. There are four types of respite care:

1   care in a foster placement;

2   residential care, in a home or sometimes in a hospital unit;

3   holiday schemes (e.g. diabetic camps);

4   care within the child's own home.

The last is often the best provision of care if the right substitute carer can be found.

Provision is patchy and is only worthwhile if the child derives as much benefit from the break as the carers.

ACTIVITY: MORAL VALUES

Read the following poem and then answer the questions below.

Children Learn What They Live

Dorothy Law Nolte

If children live with criticism,

They learn to condemn.

If children live with hostility,

They learn to fight.

If children live with ridicule,

They learn to be shy.

If children live with shame,

They learn to feel guilty.

If children live with encouragement,

They learn confidence.

If children live with tolerance,

They learn to be patient.

If children live with praise,

They learn to appreciate.

If children live with acceptance,

They learn to love.

If children live with approval,

They learn to like themselves.

If children live with honesty,

They learn truthfulness.

If children live with security,

They learn to have faith in themselves and others.

If children live with friendliness,

They learn the world is a nice place in which to live.

This famous poem neatly describes the way in which children learn their moral values – by *example* and by *imitation*. Our **moral values** are our beliefs about what is important in life. Some values refer to how one should act (be honest, altruistic, self-disciplined), while other values refer to what one wants to accomplish or obtain in life (a lot of money, fame, a family, friendships, world peace). Some examples of moral values are: integrity, respect, caring, justice, civic virtue and openness. There are many moral values – these represent only a very few.

1   Working in pairs or small groups, identify and list *three* moral values within the poem above.

2   For each value chosen discuss how this value can be promoted in your early years setting.

ACTIVITY: INVESTIGATING DISABILITY

Choose one of the genetic and chromosomal disorders listed in this chapter – a different one from those chosen by your fellow students – and research it in preparation for a talk which you will present to the rest of your class. Use the following guidelines to help you structure the talk:

❧ Introduce your chosen disorder.

❧ Discuss its causes and incidence (use charts).

❧ Say how it is diagnosed and whether there is genetic screening availability.

❧ Cover its effects.

❧ Discuss treatment and care needs.

Your presentation may be recorded on video, assessed as a verbal presentation or graded as a written assignment (or two or more of these options). Your work could be placed in a fact-file to be used as a class resource.

Your teacher or lecturer may allow 3–4 weeks for preparation of the talk, so that you have time to research via the Internet or write off to specialist groups for relevant information.

ACTIVITY: TESTING AND SCREENING METHODS

Find out all you can about:

1 amniocentesis;

2 the AFP blood test;

3 chorionic villus sampling

4 ultrasound.

For each, answer the following questions:

❧ What is it?

❧ What conditions can be detected?

❧ What are the risks?

The Association of Spina Bifida and Hydrocephalus produces an information sheet on antenatal screening which you may find useful.

Spina bifida is a congenital defect in which one or more vertebrae fail to develop completely, leaving a portion of the spinal cord exposed.

1 Describe the three forms of spinal bifida.

2 What is hydrocephalus, and how is it treated?

Many parents whose children have cerebral palsy seek new ways of furthering their progress through education. Three such programmes are:

❧ **Conductive education:** this has the backing of the charity for people with cerebral palsy (SCOPE).

❧ **Doman-Delacato therapy:** this is based on the theory that the brain, like a muscle, will grow if given regular exercise.

❧ **Bobath therapy:** specialised physiotherapy for children with cerebral palsy.

ACTIVITY: PROGRAMMES FOR CHILDREN WITH CEREBRAL PALSY

1 Find out the principles behind conductive education. Where can parents go to have their child assessed? Which model of disability does it follow?

2 Contact your local Portage group and try to arrange for a speaker to come into college or school to explain its benefits to the disabled child and their family.

3 Find out about the Bobath technique.

ACTIVITY: PROMOTING AN AWARENESS OF VISUAL IMPAIRMENT

Tutors or students – or both – may wish to send away for copies of booklets produced by the RNIB to enable them to carry out the first of the following two activities.

1 A display. Plan and mount a display on 'Children with visual impairment'. Using the booklets as a guide, each small group should plan and mount a display on one of the following topics:

  ❧ developing the senses;

  ❧ establishing routines;

  ❧ movement games;

  ❧ play and toys.

When the displays are up, the groups should **evaluate** each other's displays, using a set of criteria agreed beforehand. Is the information presented in an easy-to-understand format? Does the material used illustrate the points effectively?

Try to contact a local group of parents of visually impaired children and invite them to view the display; health visitors or social services departments may be able to make the first contact for you here.

2 An exercise in empathy. The following exercise cannot give a real experience of blindness, but may help to promote understanding. In pairs:

  ❧ One person ties a blindfold (e.g. a scarf) around their own eyes and the other person then escorts them around the college or neighbourhood. On return, the sighted student offers the 'blind person' a drink and a sandwich.

  ❧ Then swap roles. After the exercise, **evaluate** the activity. How did it feel to be so reliant on someone else? How did it feel to be responsible for someone else?

  ❧ Draw up a list of practical points to help others who are offering guidance and refreshment to someone who is blind.

3 Find out about the aids that are available for those with visual impairment, including the Braille alphabet.

ACTIVITY: CHILDREN WITH HEARING IMPAIRMENTS

1   Make a list of toys and games which are especially suitable for children with hearing impairments.

2   Find out what is involved in the operation for glue ear (myringotomy and the insertion of grommets). How many such operations are carried out in your district health authority each year?

ACTIVITY: FINDING OUT ABOUT AUTISM

1   Find out if there is any special provision for children with autism in your local area.

2   Find out about the work of the National Autistic Society.

3   List the social skills required to participate fully in daily activities in a reception class. Try to describe the difficulties a child with autism may have in integrating.

4   What help and support are available to a family that has a child with autism? What might the effects be on the siblings living with a child with autism?

ACTIVITY: THE PARENTAL RESPONSE TO DISABILITY

Read the extract 'A mother celebrates the birthday of a very special baby' on page 42.

1   Do you think that the paediatrician showed understanding when he told the parents that their newborn baby had Down's syndrome? Give reasons for your answer.

2   Why does the author say that 'every woman who gives birth to a handicapped child does so in a climate of rejection and fear'?

3   Look at Cunningham's model of psychic crisis (Figure 1.11), which outlines the various parental emotions and reactions at the time of finding out about their child's disability. Try to identify the phases which Euan's mother went through.

4   Research the condition of Down's syndrome, including the following points:

❖ the cause;

❖ the incidence in the UK and worldwide;

❖ the characteristics of a child with Down's syndrome;

❖ the prognosis and help available.

SHOCK PHASE:	confusion, denial, irrationality, numbness
↓	
REACTION PHASE:	express sorrow, grief, disappointment, anxiety, aggression, feelings of failure
↓	
ADAPTION PHASE:	realistic appraisal – what can be done? At this point professionals need to be able to give more information
↓	
ORIENTATION PHASE:	begin to organise, seek help and information, and plan for the future

Fig 1.10 Cunningham's model of psychic crisis

ACTIVITY: RESEARCH INTO INCLUSION

1   Find out about the education and support offered to children with Down's syndrome in your area:

   ♣ What is available for children with Down's syndrome of nursery school age, of primary school age and of secondary school age?

   ♣ What are the advantages of inclusive education for children with Down's syndrome, and for their peers?

   ♣ Find out about Makaton as a method of communication.

ACTIVITY: ENABLING THE CHILD WITH A DISABILITY

1   Look at the layout of your own work placement. What physical changes would be necessary to include a child in a wheelchair or a partially sighted child?

2   Try to write a story in which a child with a disability is the hero or heroine, but their heroism does not involve bravely enduring or overcoming their disability.

ACTIVITY: ACCESS TO RESPITE CARE

Think of ways in which parents and carers of able-bodied children get **respite** from full-time care. Why can the same avenues not be opened to all carers? List the possible problems for parents of disabled children in obtaining respite care, and then list their possible solutions.

ACTIVITY: EXTENSION WORK

1   A time sample observation. Observe a child in your work placement whom you or the teacher has identified as being shy or withdrawn. Choose a day when you can observe the child at regular intervals, say every 10 or 15 minutes, and display the information obtained on a prepared chart.

2   Evaluate your observation. Do you think the child has special needs, and if so, what is the nature of those needs? How could you help meet them?

3   A talking/listening game. Plan a talking/listening game that could be adapted to allow full participation by a child with a hearing impairment.

4   Discussion topic.

❖ Are televised charity appeals ('telethons', such as BBC's Children in Need) an ethical way of raising money for children's charities?

❖ Is the image of the child 'suffering bravely' a healthy one?

❖ Has not every child the right to a fulfilled, comfortable life without having to rely on public generosity?

Organise a debate in class, preferably after watching a recent telethon.

2
Observation and assessment

Contents

● Observation and assessment frameworks ● The role of observation and assessment in early years settings ● Limits of professional role and competence ● Sharing of information ● Work settings' policies, rules and procedures ● Rights and involvement of parents/primary carers ● What to observe ● Observational and recording techniques ● The impact of the observer ● Observing and assessing naturally occurring and structured activities ● Using norms ● Methods of observation

OBSERVATION AND ASSESSMENT FRAMEWORKS

For a long time it has been the role of health and medical professionals to carry out regular checks, measurements and assessments on children, initially as foetuses in the womb during pregnancy, through birth and into the early years.

✣ **Health visitors** oversee infant health, referring to paediatricians when necessary. They monitor weight, diet, general growth and development, usually until the child begins school.

✣ **School health services** continue sight and hearing tests, and may administer immunisations or vaccinations (e.g. in cases of hepatitis or meningitis outbreaks).

✣ **Child clinics, family health centres and paediatric wards** in hospitals also carry out health surveillance, which relies on observation and assessment of children.

Why observe and assess children in early childhood settings?

The trend towards babies and infants being cared for in settings other than their own homes has led to the need for parents and other caregivers, including early childhood practitioners, to gather information – formally and informally – and to share it for the benefit of the children. Record keeping and assessment have always been good practice in early years settings, but there is now a **legal requirement** to demonstrate the process.

There is a **registration and inspection framework** for settings providing care and/or education for babies and children. Day care and early education are regulated by **Ofsted** through their Early Years Directorate (established 2001) (see Chapters 9, 13, 14 and 16).

Part of the inspections deals with the methods of reporting to parents and of record-keeping and assessment. Therefore, settings need to establish and maintain their own **framework for observation and assessment** as an integral part of their provision (see below) and to meet the requirements of **Children's Care, Learning and Development** (CCLD).

Methods of record-keeping, assessment and reporting will vary from setting to setting, depending on the setting's main function (i.e. care and/or education), the ages of the children concerned, its size (number of staff and children on the roll), the needs of the parents and main carers, and in response to the needs of the children.

For example, a **day nursery**, caring for babies and young children, may use a framework which includes the following:

❖ a **calendar or cycle** indicating opportunities to report to parents in both formal and informal ways;

❖ a **rota or table** identifying **key workers** (if appropriate) or the staff involved in planning and carrying out observations and assessments;

❖ a **daily record** of the routine aspects of daily care, such as feeding, nappy-changing, sleeping (see Chapter 12);

❖ **regular observations** of a 'new' child throughout the day for the first few attendances;

❖ **observations of every child** as part of planned and ongoing assessment (perhaps on a rotating basis);

❖ regular observations to check **safety aspects**;

❖ **records of responses** to parental concerns or requests;

❖ **responses to changes** noticed in children's health, attitude, etc.;

❖ **observations to check, plan for and review** changes to the provision;

❖ **an outline of observations and assessment practice and methods of record-keeping** (the different practices and methods are covered later in this chapter).

Reporting formats

In settings for younger children and babies, where the child-to-worker ratio is fairly low, recorded observations are likely to be made more regularly and in varied formats. These will be based on observations made using *Birth to Three Matters: A framework to support children in their earliest years* (DfES/Sure Start 2002).

STEPPING STONES

The core reference document for England, *Curriculum Guidance for the Foundation Stage*, for children from 3 years of age until the end of the reception year (in any setting, including childminders), gives examples of '**stepping stones**' within each of the **six areas of learning**. Early childhood practitioners select the stepping stones which are appropriate for individual children to suit their interests and needs. In this way each child makes an individual journey, flexibly using his or her stepping stones, towards the **early learning goals**. Most, but not all, children will reach the goals by the end of the reception year. Staff will use their observations to inform them about which stepping stones are best for particular children.

IN SCHOOLS

A different framework is likely to be in place in schools. With the ratio of pupils to teachers being fairly high (possibly 28:1 or 30:1), reports are usually more formal and are issued perhaps twice a year, in addition to parents' evenings, when a personal discussion of a child's progress is possible. Schools are also required to work within the national framework of assessments. Apart from ongoing assessment, children are assessed at the end of the Foundation Stage (**Foundation Profile** from 2003) and again at the end of Key Stage 1. Observation will inform planning and assessment throughout the Foundation Stage, leading to a summarised set of observations at the end of the reception year, in the Foundation Profile. In England and Northern Ireland there are **Standard Assessment Tasks** at the end of Key Stage 1, but not in Wales and Scotland.

THE ROLE OF OBSERVATION AND ASSESSMENT IN EARLY YEARS SETTINGS

The most important reason for carrying out observations and assessments is to ensure that the needs of individual children are met. What can we learn from observation?

Observing children

Observations provide us with valuable information about **individual children**:

❖ *where* children are in their development and learning;

❖ their progress in the different areas of development;

❖ aspects of their health and wellbeing;

❖ personality, temperament, likes and dislikes;

❖ response to different experiences;

❖ behaviour in a range of contexts, for example in different social and physical environments.

We can also observe **groups of children** to learn about:

❖ differences between individual children, their health and growth, their response to similar situations, their response to adults;

❖ the interaction between individuals;

❖ communication within the group;

❖ the way conflicts arise and children's strategies for dealing with them;

❖ the ways in which children learn from each other in interdependent relationships.

Observing adults

In addition, through making observations and by generally watching what is going on around you, you can also learn a lot about the way adults behave:

❖ the ways in which they communicate with children – using both verbal and non-verbal forms of communication;

❖ how they support children and deal with issues about the ways in which children develop self-discipline;

❖ how they interact with parents, other staff and other professionals;

❖ how they support and extend play.

Observing features of the setting

Observation can tell you a lot about the **work environment**:

❖ how children use and enjoy the equipment and resources provided;

❖ the use of space and the effectiveness of the setting's layout;

❖ the appropriateness of storage of, and access to, equipment;

❖ safety and hygiene issues;

❖ the effectiveness of supervision.

In addition, workers and researchers make use of observations to:

❖ find out more about different aspects of child development;

❖ identify ways in which children learn;

❖ reflect on what providers must do to promote development and learning, and thus further develop good practice.

Observation and assessment inform planning

Figure 2.1 shows how observation and assessment inform the planning process. The cycle is a continuous one and settings adapt their provision to suit the needs of the children and families they are working with at any one time. It is through close observation, monitoring and assessment that staff can ensure that they introduce appropriate changes in their practice to meet the specific needs of individual children, as well as the whole group. This is particularly relevant to identifying children's schemas (see Chapter 6), which can be taken into account when planning.

LIMITS OF PROFESSIONAL ROLE AND COMPETENCE

Even the most experienced early childhood practitioners may find that, although they have observed a child and made efforts to adapt their provision, they need help from outside the setting. This is particularly true if there is a specific medical condition or developmental delay. In these cases the people who best know the child – almost always the parents or main carer – will provide the most valuable suggestions, alongside the advice and guidance of other expert or specialist professionals.

The development of an individual **care plan** or **special educational programme** will take account of evidence gathered from different sources, for example from parents, early childhood practitioners, health visitors,

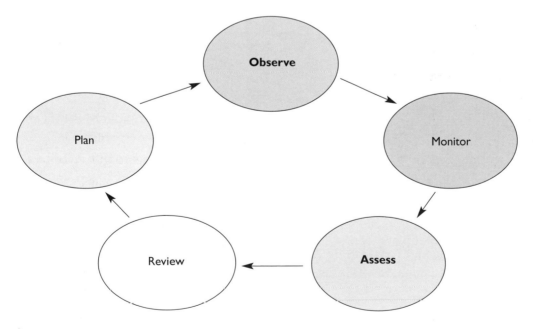

Figure 2.1 The planning cycle

doctors, social services or speech therapists. These provisions can only meet the child's needs when there is cooperation between all the services involved, and those who are competent to do so make accurate assessments.

SHARING OF INFORMATION

Cooperation between professionals requires sharing of information. However, in a work setting observations and records must be kept confidentially and access given only to certain people – these may include the individual child's parents or legal guardian, supervisor, teacher or key worker and other involved professionals (e.g. the health visitor). **Note that any information about a child may only be shared if the parent or legal guardian gives consent.** Where there is a positive partnership between professionals and parents, it will be clearly

understood that ongoing observation and monitoring are part of the setting's role in caring for and educating children. Indeed, parents and main carers are the people who know a child best and they have valuable information which helps us to know the 'whole' child (see Chapter 16). The Children Act 2004 (see also Chapter 16) seeks to provide a legal framework to underpin its programme for changes to children's services. In recognition of the uncertainty some practitioners may feel about their legal position in sharing information and gaining consent, the government offers guidance for cases when a child's welfare may be at risk. 'Cross-government guidance' addresses this issue in relation to different settings and circumstances. The following case study is based on one example concerning a child attending a playgroup.

Case Study

Josh

Josh's parents are both professionals and work full-time (sometimes longer) hours. They employ an au pair who cares for Josh, takes him to the local playgroup three times a week and carries out household tasks. The au pair does not speak much English and her understanding is developing slowly. Josh tends to sit quietly by himself and does not socialise or play with any of the other children. He does not seek adult company or attention and rarely communicates with them at playgroup. Staff are concerned about his lack of communication and are unable to assess his level of social interaction and speech.

Apart from at Josh's initial registration, the playgroup leader has never seen or spoken to either of Josh's parents. She writes to the parents asking them to contact her or come in to discuss how Josh

has settled in. There is no response and the au pair does not seem to understand. The family uses private medical care and is not registered with an NHS doctor.

In this situation the guidance is that the leader should:

- continue attempts to make **contact with the parents** to express her concerns about Josh and why she needs to talk to them;

- make it clear that she would like to **share information** with health practitioners and to do that she would like their consent;

- also make it clear that their **refusal to give consent** would increase her concerns and anxieties, and then she may seek any information available from a health visitor or other agency.

Case Study continued

Hopefully, Josh's parents would respond positively, but if they did not, then the playgroup leader should use her professional judgement to consider the risks to Josh's welfare of not sharing and seeking more information. She could consider referring Josh to 'Social Care for a Child in Need of Assessment' if she believed that, by withholding consent or giving no response, Josh's parents were neglecting his needs.

If information is shared, then any developmental problems may be detected at an early stage and extra treatment and support provided. Should information not be shared, any problems Josh has may go undiagnosed, which would probably result in them being harder to treat at a later stage. The leader should keep accurate records of all correspondence and actions taken.

Confidentiality

Maintaining confidentiality is an important aspect of your role, but it is particularly important when carrying out observations, especially those which are written and recorded. For your own training and assessment purposes, the identity of the child and setting is not important. It must, therefore, be protected (see below). You are developing your observational and record-keeping skills as you learn more about children in general, children as individuals and the various work settings.

Ethical guidelines for maintaining confidentiality in your observations

❖ Ensure you have permission for making an observation – from your supervisor and the parent/main carer (this is confirmed by an authorising signature).

❖ Use codes rather than names to refer to the individuals involved – you should never use a child's first name. An initial or some other form of identification, e.g. Child 1, is sufficient. (You may use 'T' or 'A' for 'teacher' or 'adult'.)

❖ Understand and abide by policies and procedures in the setting.

❖ Remember that photographic and taped evidence can reveal identity and should only be used with appropriate authority.

❖ Take extra care when sharing observations with fellow-students – they may have friends or family involved in a work setting and could easily identify individuals.

❖ Never discuss children or staff from your work setting in a public place (e.g. when sitting on a bus or in a cafe).

❖ Never identify individuals when talking at home about your daily experiences (e.g. they could be neighbours' children).

WORK SETTINGS' POLICIES, RULES AND PROCEDURES

As we have seen, all settings have to monitor individual children's progress and maintain records. There may not be a policy specifically called 'Observation and Assessment', but other policies, such as 'Partnership with Parents' (see Chapter 16), 'Behaviour' and 'Equal Opportunities', will contain relevant information. Such policies provide the framework for rules and procedures; these may relate to safety, hygiene, the management of behaviour and the development of self-discipline, communicating with parents and aspects of security. You will find that some policies vary little from one setting to another as they are based on national legislation (e.g. the Children Act 1989), but others will reflect the setting's nature, function, location and community, and may be quite individual.

Every setting should identify the following:

* the person having overall responsibility for record-keeping (usually the nursery manager, supervisor or head teacher);

* how and where records are to be stored, and who may have access to them;

* who will be responsible for collecting and collating observational and assessment material – including information from home – for particular children or groups of children (e.g. the key worker, room supervisor or teacher);

* procedures for reporting to parents;

* procedures and rules for carrying out observations and making assessments;

* when and how the policy and procedures will be reviewed.

Recording individual progress and development

It is the duty of all work settings to maintain individual and confidential records of a child's progress and development. Such a profile needs to be up-to-date, stored carefully and made available only to those who have authorised access. It should contain relevant information, such as:

* the full name of the child (as on the birth certificate and any other name by which the child is commonly or otherwise known);

* date and place of birth;

* medical details (e.g. problems at birth, medication, hereditary condition);

* child's first language;

* name and home address of the parent(s)/main carer with whom child lives;

* name and address of an absent parent (if appropriate);

* a record of any legal aspects which affect access to information;

* information as to who may, or may not, collect the child;

* observations – in a range of formats and possibly carried out by two or three different members of staff – which track development, skill acquisition, growth, response to different experiences;

* information and contributions from parents/main carers and the child himself;

* regular assessments of the child's development, based on observations and any other relevant information;

* action taken (and any future plans) in response to assessments of the child's changing needs;

records of meetings and discussions with parents/main carers.

In addition, the child's profile should be presented in such a way as to be readily understood by his or her parents or main carers and other professionals. It should record positive achievements and all entries should be accurately dated, with the source identified.

Observations made on student placements

Most settings provide clear guidance about working with children (sometimes in a booklet or sheet written especially for students). As a student, you should also be given information which will help you understand what a particular setting is trying to achieve and how it goes about it. You will always need to gain permission to carry out an observation and your placement supervisor may well wish to read your work. This is not only to check it through, but also out of interest, to find out more about the children, activity or safety aspects that you have observed. Remember that information accurately observed by you can be just as valuable to the setting as that gathered by staff.

At each new placement you will need to settle in as quickly as possible. Problems can arise when:

❖ you fail to communicate your needs to your supervisor;

❖ staff in the setting fail to communicate their needs to you.

Many experienced staff are unaware of many of the more recent changes in child care course requirements. Your study centre should outline what you are expected to achieve during your time on placement, but you also need to be clear about specific tasks and observations that you must complete. Visiting tutors often discover that a student has very different perceptions of a situation from the placement supervisor, as the case study below demonstrates.

Case Study

Student's account
'My supervisor wouldn't let me do my taped observation because she had me down to supervise children on the large apparatus. I had my tape recorder with me. All I needed was some time to get everything ready and to fix up a session with a member of staff and W.'

Supervisor's account
'I have asked G several times whether she has observations to do and she has been very vague. Last week, however, she arrived in the morning and asked if she could carry out a taped observation of one child. I had already planned for her to help supervise outdoor play because she said this was something she needed to do. Also the child she wanted to observe was involved in a structured task which had been specially planned for him and two other children.'

Had student G made thorough preparation and discussed her intention with her supervisor, she would probably have been given some helpful advice and, perhaps, a particular task or activity would have been set up for the purpose. Instead, she feels disgruntled and her supervisor is frustrated as to how best to help her.

Guidelines for maintaining positive working relationships

To help you negotiate your needs and maintain positive working relationships on placements you should:

❖ identify a regular, mutually convenient time when you can discuss your progress and course requirements with your placement supervisor;

❖ check with your tutor what you need to do in each setting and each age range;

❖ plan your tasks at least one week ahead and agree with your supervisor and/or other staff when you will implement them (be prepared to adapt your plans at short notice if emergencies arise);

❖ be well prepared for each placement session;

❖ try to settle quickly into the setting's routine;

❖ ask questions about rotas and duties etc., so your observations can be implemented with the minimum of disruption to routines;

❖ arrive early enough to set up your activity or observation so you do not keep groups of children waiting;

❖ make sure you obtain authorising signatures and show your work to your supervisor if asked;

❖ try to reflect on each day's experiences – some students have to keep a placement journal – and learn from them to improve your own understanding;

❖ share your thoughts and feelings with your supervisors when time allows and try to become part of the team.

RIGHTS AND INVOLVEMENT OF PARENTS/PRIMARY CARERS

Parents' rights and responsibilities were clearly defined in the Children Act 1989 (see Chapter 16), which says they have a right to be involved in decisions affecting their children's care and education. In addition, we have already seen that parents, or whoever is legally responsible for a child, have the right to see their own child's records unless there is a legal restriction which prevents it (e.g. the child is subject to a care order and someone else has 'parental responsibility'). Work settings will explain to parents that attendance at the setting means

their child will be observed within the setting's confidentiality rules and may be asked if the placement supervisor can give authority for student observation of children on the parents' behalf.

Purpose of entry assessment

Initial information is provided by parents on a child's admission to a setting. The amount and type of further information contributed by parents will depend, probably, on the age of the child, his or her stage of development, family events, any particular needs the child may have and the type of setting. Information from other professionals usually comes via the parents unless there is a **child**

protection issue, in which case it may be shared confidentially, between professionals.

Involving parents in the assessment of their child is of central importance, so they can:

❖ share achievements and celebrate success;

❖ look at observational material;

❖ discuss with the setting any concerns which have arisen, perhaps to do with eating problems or behaviour towards a new sibling.

Positive partnership with parents benefits children, their families and the setting. Parents, and anyone involved with children, generally share the aim of helping children to develop healthily and to achieve their own individual potential.

Entry assessments

To be able to track progress it is necessary to identify a starting point. Therefore, in addition to collecting admission information, settings will carry out a range of observations and assessments to plan for further development. In settings for younger children, workers will automatically want to find out:

❖ what individual children can do;

❖ what they understand;

❖ how they respond to different experiences and learning opportunities;

❖ how they express themselves;

❖ their likes and dislikes.

Such entry assessments are used to plan and provide for individual children's needs and, as such, may highlight aspects which need monitoring, for example, physical difficulties or apparent hearing difficulties. The different rates at which children normally develop mean that there can be marked differences between the skills of children of the same age. Regular monitoring can identify a developmental delay outside the usual range which may need the attention of other professionals. Similarly, outstanding ability in any developmental area may indicate the need for specialist provision. For children identified as having a special need, the monitoring of achievements over a period of time is essential to planning and can reassure parents and staff that progress is being made, even if it is rather slow.

As a result of recent early years initiatives, the provision for under-8s and their families is less fragmented and promotes closer liaison between the different sectors and work settings within sectors. In England *Birth to Three Matters: A framework to support children in their earliest years* (DfES/Sure Start 2002) and the introduction of wider nursery provision for 3- and 4-year-olds, alongside a curriculum framework, have required all early childhood practitioners to review their record-keeping and assessment methods and procedures, including ways of reporting to parents.

Good observational skills develop over a period of time and through experience, but are essential for all early childhood practitioners. It is worth **learning and practising these skills** now, as a student, so you have a good foundation for your future work with children. There is a wide range of methods to choose from and you will be given opportunities to try several, if not all. Deciding what to observe and which method best suits your purposes is, in the initial stage, a question of following whatever guidance you are given. The more methods you try for yourself, the better able you will be to make your own selection and to justify it when required to do so.

WHAT TO OBSERVE

You may find it helpful to identify categories of things you can observe, such as those shown in Table 2.1. It is clear, though, that these categories can overlap, so you may be observing a small group of children playing with wooden blocks and decide to focus on their communication or manipulative skills. The range and scope are very wide and the requirements of your course may dictate generally what you should observe. You may be required to carry out an observation which focuses on babies or toddlers using *Birth to Three Matters: A framework to support children in their earliest years*, or an observation which focuses on the Foundation Stage or on Year One or Year Two of Key Stage 1 of the National Curriculum.

In consultation with your tutor and/or placement supervisor, you will need to choose not only what you are going to observe, but also to identify an aim for your observation. You must ensure that what you observe will (or, at least, be likely to) produce the information which will enable you to achieve your identified aim. Potential difficulties with this are highlighted by the following case study.

Case Study

Observation

A student had been asked to observe a group of children aged 5–7 years who were involved in a maths activity, with a view to identifying what aspects of the maths curriculum they were addressing and to find out how the children tackled the work, that is, what maths skills and processes (counting, reasoning, checking, etc.) they used to complete the task.

The student decided to observe a group of children involved in a 'money' activity during the daily mathematics session. It involved selecting appropriate coins to make a given amount of money (e.g. 4 x 2p coins or 1 x 5p plus 3 x 1p coins to make 8p). On the face of it, this would seem an ideal activity to observe as it should provide opportunities to hear and watch children adding, subtracting, counting, counting on, recognising coins and showing their understanding that one coin can represent a multiple (more than one). However, the children were completing a worksheet of written sums and, rather than handling and counting out the coins, they merely filled in their answers on the worksheet. As the children did their reasoning and working out in their heads, all the student could comment on was whether or not they had answered correctly and appeared to enjoy the task.

Table 2.1 Examples of subjects for observation

Aspect of development	Social context	Aspect of behaviour	Health/growth	Aspect of daily routine
Physical skills: e.g. gross and fine motor **Intellectual:** e.g. concept development; problem solving; memory; reasoning; decision making; concentration **Communication and literacy:** e.g. speaking (incl. fluency), listening, reading and writing (incl. early stages of symbol recognition and mark making) **Emotional:** e.g. expression of feelings; self-esteem; feelings for others **Social:** e.g. relationships with other children/adults; independence; self-reliance resolving conflicts	**Individual child:** e.g. alone; with adult (familiar/unfamiliar) **Two children (familiar/unfamiliar):** e.g. same age; different ages; same/different gender; with/without adult(s) (familiar/unfamiliar) **Small group (familiar/unfamiliar/mixed):** e.g. same or mixed ages; same or mixed gender; with/without adult(s) (familiar/unfamiliar) **Large(r) group (familiar/unfamiliar/mixed):** e.g. same or mixed ages; same or mixed gender; with/ without adult(s) (familiar/unfamiliar)	**Aggression** **Being withdrawn** **Habit:** e.g. thumb-sucking, hair-pulling, head-banging **See Chapter ?**	**Physical measurements:** length/height; weight; foot size **General wellbeing:** appetite and diet; sleep; exercise; energy **Record of illness/immunisations**	**At home:** e.g. mealtime; bath-time; bedtime; getting dressed; going out **At work setting:** e.g. arrival; group or story registration (if appropriate); outdoor play; snack; meal; going home

Table 2.1 (continued)

Spontaneous	Structured situation	Special event	Aspect of play	Use of equipment/play area
A child or group of children responding to a new or unexpected experience: e.g. a rainbow, large puddles, snow, hail, bouncy castle **In response to an awareness that a child seems different from usual self:** e.g. unusually loud or withdrawn or tearful **In response to child/ren playing in an original way:** e.g. using crayons and paints cooperatively and linking all the pieces together rather than making individual creations	**A particular activity designed to promote specific learning or skill development:** e.g. water activity for floating and sinking; music activity for loud and soft sounds **A play activity structured through selection of equipment or grouping of children**	**An outing:** perhaps an annual event or one which happens more regularly e.g. to local library, park or shops **Visitor(s):** e.g. theatre company, emergency services **Seasonal festivals:** e.g. Christmas party or play, Diwali celebrations	**Outdoor/adventure:** e.g. building dens, large apparatus **Imaginative:** e.g. dressing up, small world, puppets **Exploratory:** e.g. water, sand, mud, clay, play dough, lentils **Constructional:** e.g. Lego, BRIO **Creative:** e.g. music, dance, painting, modelling, collage **See Chapter 3 and 12**	**Messy:** use of material and utensils provided e.g. hoses and tubes in water or containers with holes in sand or water **Role play:** e.g. use made of 'home' equipment, different types of dressing-up materials **Book/quiet corner:** e.g. monitoring reading behaviour, favourite books, concentration and attention **Small world/construction** ways in which resources are used e.g. for cooperative play and joint projects, monitor children's manipulative and imaginative skills **See Chapter 3 and 12**

OBSERVATIONAL AND RECORDING TECHNIQUES

As a student you will be required to produce a **portfolio** containing several observations of children using a variety of methods. Although you will learn about the planning cycle of observation and assessment shown in Figure 2.1 (page 75), carrying out regular observations in your various placement settings can be problematic, and you may have few opportunities to see the relevance of individual observations in the context of the complete process.

Using a standard format

For the requirements of your course you will be taught to follow a commonly used structure so that each observation comprises the following:

1 **Standard information** (often recorded on a front sheet), including:

  ❖ the aim of your observation;

  ❖ your name;

  ❖ date of observation;

  ❖ start and finish times;

  ❖ location and type of setting (e.g. outdoor play area, educational nursery);

  ❖ number of children in observed group;

  ❖ number of adults present and involved during the observation – do not count yourself unless you are involved in the activity;

  ❖ age(s) of child or children (in months e.g. 7 months, or years and months e.g. 3 years 2 months);

  ❖ identity code for those mentioned in observation, e.g. Child A, Child B, T = teacher;

  ❖ the child or children's gender, if relevant;

  ❖ method or technique used and rationale;

  ❖ authorising signature.

2 **Introduction** to explain the context of your observation.

3 **Actual observation**, presented in an acceptable format.

4 **Evaluation** which **summarises** and **analyses** the information collected and reaches some conclusion about what has been discovered. This section also sets out any implications for the future – with regard to the child or children, the setting and your own development and learning.

5 **Reference and bibliography section** which acknowledges your sources of information.

(Sections 2, 3, 4 and 5 are covered in greater detail later in this chapter.)

Planning your observation

You cannot carry out an observation without planning what you are going to do. Figure 2.2 is a flow chart which outlines the steps you need to take to plan effectively.

DECIDING ON AN AIM

Identifying an aim which is specific and focused makes it easier to plan what sort of information you will need to record. It is also helpful at this stage to think about how, or in what context, you will try to find out what you need to know.

Skilled early childhood practitioners do not need to use an adult-led 'task'. They find out, while a child is exploring the natural material or in a real conversation, whether or not the child understands 'full' and 'empty' or can name colours of pegs or sort socks into pairs.

1 What do I want to find out?

This is the aim of your observation. Your aim might be to find out how children explore natural materials, or to see whether a child can name and sort two different colours in a real-life situation.

2 What should I observe, and whom should I observe?

Is there a particular activity or routine that will give you the best chance of achieving your aim? For example, to find out how children explore natural materials, you might want to observe a free-play situation. To find out whether one child can achieve a colour-sorting task, you will have to structure the play situation.

- ❑ Do you need to plan a particular acitivity or task?
- ❑ Do you need to make sure that certain resources are available to the children?
- ❑ Do you need to ensure that identified children use specific resources?

3 How long should I observe for?

This depends on what you have decided in relation to step 1 and step 2. Your observation of children playing with natural materials might take 10 or 20 minutes, or it could last until the children move naturally on to another activity. You need to find out how much the child knows about water and its properties and any appropriate vocabulary.

4 How will I record what I see and hear?

You must consider what sort of detail you require to be able to achieve your aim. Do you need an exact description of every word and movement? Or can you use a pre-made chart to record what happens?

- ❑ Do you need to observe from outside the activity, or could you make your observation while taking part?
- ❑ Think about whether you need to tell the children what you are doing.

Figure 2.2 Flow chart

Some of the aims presented in the box below sound fine until you try to work out exactly what you need to record – in aim 1 'physical skills' is far too broad a category and it is unlikely that you would be able to observe, on a single occasion, the full range of fine and gross motor skills. Aim 4 is not specific enough. What exactly do you want to find out – what the baby eats or drinks, how much, how quickly, who gives the feed, how often or when? All of these, some of these, something else? Your identified aim will affect what you include in your introduction and what information you record from your actual observation. For example, if you are focusing on communication skills you will need to include all aspects of communication – speech, facial expression, body language, posture and tone of voice as well as actions. Getting your aim right will help you decide on the method of observation best suited to your purpose.

Some examples of aims for observations

1 To find out how good a 3-year-old's physical skills are.

2 To find out what gross motor skills a particular child uses when playing on large apparatus, and to see whether she has good movement control and is confident.

3 To find out how a group of children communicate and cooperate with each other when involved in imaginative role play.

4 To find out about a baby's feeds.

5 To see how a child behaves in the setting.

6 To see how a child uses manipulative skills when playing with Lego.

7 To compare the heights of a large group of children – boys and girls – in relation to their ages, and to consider variations in growth.

RATIONALE FOR SELECTING A PARTICULAR METHOD

This is a brief statement explaining why you have selected a particular type of observation and recording method. Table 2.2 might help you to decide on the advantages and disadvantages of different techniques.

Note that you may improve your grade if you are able to reflect upon the effectiveness of your chosen method and to consider whether any alternatives would have met your identified aims equally well or even better. You would discuss this aspect of your observation in your evaluation section, which is covered later in this chapter.

Examples of rationales for two different methods

Observing the child at regular intervals throughout the day using a **time-sampling** method enables me to see her/him in different situations, with different people and participating in a range of activities. I will be able to prepare a recording chart, in advance, choosing my own headings, and this will help to ensure that I record significant details. It will also provide me with an overview of the child's day.

The **descriptive** method will allow me to record events as they happen, as well as to note small details of movement and communication. It is suitable for my purpose because I am looking at specific skills in a structured activity and am observing a single child for a short period of time.

Introduction

This section explains:

1 The **conditions** under which you are observing.

  ❖ Are you observing from a distance as onlooker (uninvolved)?

  ❖ Are you observing from a distance but retaining some supervisory responsibility?

  ❖ Are you observing as a participant helper/supervisor?

ACTIVITY: AIMS FOR OBSERVATIONS

Using the suggested aims 1–6 in the above box create two lists – one for aims that you think are sufficiently specific and another for those which are too general or vague.

For each aim in the first list, decide what particular skills or competencies you might look for to help you achieve your aim.

For each aim on the second list, choose two more refined aims and then decide on the activity or situation which will be best to observe.

Compare and discuss your lists and suggestions with others in your group.

Table 2.2 Possible suitability of different methods/techniques

	Descriptive	Detailed	Target child	Tape and transcript	Video recordings	Time sample	Event sample	Sociogram	Movement/ flow chart	Graphs, pie and bar charts	Checklists	Longitudinal study
Easy to use/little preparation	✓	✗	✗	✗	✗	✗	✗	✗	✗		✗	✗
Preparation needed	✗	✓	✓	✓	✓	✓	✓	✓		✓	✓	✓
Individual child	✓	✗	✓	✓	✓	✓	✓	✗	✓	✗	✓	✓
Several children or small group	✗	✓	✗	✗	✓	✗	✗	✓	✗	✓	✓	✗
Large group	✗	✗	✗	✗	✓	✗	✗	✗	✗	✓	✗	✗
Short time	✓	✓	✓	✓	✓	✗	✗	✓	✗			✗
Long time	✗	✗	✗	✗		✓	✓	✓	✓			✓
Over a period of time	✗	✗	✗	✗	✓	✓	✓	✓				✓
Lots of detail	✓	✓	✓	✓	✓	✗	✗	✗	✗	✗	✗	✓
Overview	✗	✗	✗	✗		✓	✗	✓	✓	✓	✗	✓
Likelihood of bias	✗	✓	✓	✓	✓	✗	✓	✗	✗	✗		
Data collection	✓	✗	✗	✗	✓			✗	✗	✓	✓	✓
Accurate reproduction				✓	✓			✗				
Several aspects	✓	✓	✓		✓	✓	✗	✗	✗	✗		✓
One-off situation	✓	✓	✓	✓	✓	✗	✗	✗	✗		✗	✗
Changes	✗	✗	✗		✓*	✓	✗			✗	✓	✓
Behaviour	✓	✓	✓	✓	✓	✓	✓		✗	✗	✓	✓

Table 2.2 (continued)

Table 2.2 Possible suitability of different methods/techniques

Developmental progress	✓*	✓	✗	✗	✓*	✓
Particular incidents	✓	✓	✗	✓	✗	✗
'Can-do' achievement	✓	✓	✗	✓	✗	✓
Interaction	✓	✓	✗	✓	✗	✗
Relationships	✓	✓	✓	✗	✗	✗
Structured task	✓	✓	✗	✗	✓	✗
Naturally occurring activity	✓	✓	✓	✗	✓	✓

* Repeated observations made over time can be used to show developmental progress/changes.

2 The **context** – that is, the physical and social background of the activity or routine.

♣ Are you in the book corner, messy area, outdoor play area or baby room?

♣ Whom are you observing? One child playing in a group with two adult supervisors present? Or two children playing at the sand tray with no adult involved?

♣ Did the child choose the activity during a free-play session?

♣ Are you observing a child-chosen activity which is adult-directed?

♣ Is it a structured activity under adult direction and supervision?

♣ What equipment is being used? Computer software? A book? Give a brief description of it and say what is required of the child.

3 Any **relevant information** about the individual child or group of children.

♣ For an observation of gross motor skills you might make reference to a child's physical build.

♣ For an observation about growth you might mention factual knowledge about the child's history, perhaps an illness, medical condition or other aspect which needs to be taken into consideration when reaching your conclusion.

4 Any **particular reason** for observing this particular child/group/activity/ routine.

♣ Are you responding to a request from staff?

♣ Has there been a noticeable change in behaviour, appetite or concentration?

♣ Is your work part of a series of observations which will contribute to a longitudinal study?

♣ Have you noticed a child experiencing difficulty in a particular developmental area?

The record of your observation

It is at this stage in the chapter that you need to familiarise yourself with the wide range of observation types and recording methods available. Further on in this chapter you will find a list (not exhaustive) and descriptions of those most commonly used.

Having recorded your observation (in rough or note form) using one of these methods, you need to write it up in a presentable format. This may mean:

♣ copying out what you have already recorded in the same format, but neatly;

♣ translating your findings into another appropriate format (e.g. presenting measurements of children's heights as a bar chart);

♣ adapting your original record to include further significant information (for example, you might find that your original chart for the 'detailed' method has extra information in the 'other' column which can be given a more specific heading).

Remember, your observation must be clear and accessible to those who read it, while maintaining **confidentiality**.

Objectivity

When you record your observational findings you need to be as objective as possible. This means that you must record factual information – what you actually see and hear – rather than information which you have already begun to interpret.

By including plenty of detail to describe what you see, you are providing yourself (and any reader) with a lot of information for analysis. Observation A (see Activity below) presents a much fuller picture of the situation than Observation B, and may lead you to a different conclusion about G's interest and attention.

It is often difficult to describe facial expressions and actions accurately, which is why many students produce work in the style of Observation B rather than in the style of A.

Preparing for observations

In preparation for your observations, in pairs or small groups, try to compile a comprehensive list of suitable adjectives to describe facial expressions, actions, tones of voice and any other useful vocabulary. The more experienced you become at observing children, the more readily you will use appropriate vocabulary and enrich your work with the necessary detail.

Anti-discriminatory and anti-bias practice

You must be careful not to make assumptions about children's responses based on what you

know of their home lives or their cultural backgrounds. Stereotyping must always be avoided. Read the case study below.

Case Study

Child C

On an outing to a 'live' music event, a class of 28 children was seated in the front rows. They all thoroughly enjoyed the jazz-style pieces and many of them were standing up and swaying or moving in time with the music. Child C was the only mixed-race child present, being Afro-Caribbean and part English. One of the adult helpers, watching the children with pleasure, said, 'I suppose it's because she's black that C has such a good sense of rhythm.'

The comment about Child C was said with admiration rather than malice or criticism, but is based on a stereotypical view. Other observers may have noticed that C was only one of many in the class who showed good rhythmical movement.

We all have biased opinions as a result of our own upbringing and experiences. Being aware of the possibility of bias will help us not to prejudge children.

ACTIVITY: OBSERVATIONS

Read the two brief examples below and identify where the observer has substituted a conclusion or interpretation for what was actually seen.

Observation A
…G is sitting on the floor with her legs crossed and her left hand in her lap. She is twiddling her hair with her right hand and staring at a picture on the wall display behind the teacher's head. She is smiling. The teacher says, 'G, what do you think will

happen to the cat next?' G stops fiddling with her hair and looks at the teacher. 'I think it will hide,' she says and laughs as she turns to N next to her…

Observation B
…G is sitting cross-legged on the floor in front of the teacher. She is fiddling with her hair and looking bored. The teacher asks her a question: 'G, what do you think will happen to the cat next?' G says, 'I think it will hide.'

Case Study

Gender bias

Child R is leaning over Child M and saying, 'I'm going to build a house and I need those red bricks.' R bends down, keeping eyes on M, and picks up four red bricks which M has just laid out on the floor. M pushes R and says, 'No, this is my fence.' R walks off with the bricks and joins S in another part of the area. M watches and then walks to the box and gets out several more red bricks – different shapes and sizes. S comes over to M and says, 'R wants some more bricks,' and begins to pick up some of them. M begins to cry and approaches T, who is supervising snacks.

Children – R, M, S. Teacher – T.

Summary 1: Child M was playing happily and independently when R came over. She had taken some time choosing the bricks she wanted. Child R had just come in from playing outside and he rushed straight over to the construction area. R did not ask if he could have the bricks and watched carefully to see how M would react. M gave R a push, but did not pursue him. R took the bricks away to play elsewhere and with another boy – S. M appeared to be well motivated because she just began to choose her bricks again. S was obviously following R's instructions – he did not ask for the bricks either. M did not seem to know how to cope with this second incident and turned to an adult for support.

Summary 2: Child M was playing on his own, which he quite often does, when R came over. R had just come in from playing outside and she rushed over to M. She was quite bossy because she just demanded the bricks and took them. She was not bothered at all by M's push. M did not challenge R, but went to the box for more bricks. When S came along and said that R needed them, M just let him take them. He did not attempt any physical retaliation but just ran off to the teacher. He is often rather clingy to his mum and she says that he is a bit of a mummy's boy.

The above case study demonstrates how gender bias can lead us to use different language to describe essentially similar behaviour by a boy and a girl. The language used for M as a girl is different from that used for M as a boy. Think carefully about the assumptions you made when you read the observation extract for the first time and whether you showed gender bias.

When writing up an observation you need to describe how your own **anti-discriminatory and anti-bias practice**, and your understanding of **equality of opportunity**, affected what you did and what you have written.

You should also:

- ❖ check there is no cultural, gender or other bias in the vocabulary you use;

- ❖ ensure headings for charts are appropriate for use with all children and do not reflect prejudice or limited expectations;

- ❖ evaluate your findings in light of cultural differences which may affect children's responses or behaviour.

Evaluation

This is the section which usually causes students the most difficulty. If you were clear in identifying your original aim you will find this section easier to complete.

The evaluation can be broken down into subsections as follows:

- ❖ **Summary:** read through your observation section and summarize (recap) the main points, relating your findings back to your aim.

- **Analysis:** look again through the main pieces of information you gathered that relate to what you wanted to find out. Use them to **analyse** (consider or evaluate) what your evidence tells you about the child or children, about the situation, the environment or the equipment that you set out to study.

In your evaluation you will need to refer to **theories** about various aspects of development and growth to put your findings into context. This means doing some **background reading**. For example, given all the information you have, does the child appear to be at the developmental point associated with what is known of developmental sequences (remembering to take into account cultural and health aspects)? If not, what factors may be affecting development? Remember also that a child may be ahead of the 'expected' stage in some aspects.

Your background reading should include not only textbooks, but also journal articles, information leaflets and internet websites if appropriate. You need to get into the habit of noting sources as you use them and copying accurately brief statements or phrases (noting page numbers) that you may wish to quote. Do not write your analysis and then turn to books and articles for quotes to include as an afterthought.

Using quotes in your report

The box below shows an extract from a student's evaluation. The work demonstrates the correct way to embed quotes and theoretical views within the report.

In extract A below the student has selected brief sentences or statements which relate directly to the tasks which were observed –

dressing, eating, washing hands – and has identified that the child lacks confidence.

> **Extract A**
> ...It is clear from the way GD is reluctant to try simple tasks for herself and from her need for adult support that she lacks confidence and is not developing the level of independence which might be expected for a child of her age. Meggitt and Sunderland state that 4-year-olds are likely to be able to 'eat skilfully...wash and dry their hands...undress, and dress themselves', and that they 'like to be independent' (2000: 81). Bruce and Meggitt (2006: 263) suggest there is a clear link between confidence and self-esteem, and that children need to feel good about themselves and their bodies to be able to develop self-confidence...

Extract B, also from an evaluation, uses a quote incorrectly. Here the student has not selected statements which are relevant to her observations, but has quoted a large section 'wholesale'. In addition, she has not checked that the text will make sense. At the beginning of the extract 'should be able to' is followed by 'can', which is clearly incorrect.

> **Extract B**
> Four-year-olds should be able to:
> 'can eat skilfully with a spoon and a fork, can wash and dry their hands, and brush their teeth, can undress and dress themselves, except for laces, ties and back buttons, often show a sense of humour, both in talk and in activities, like to be independent and are strongly self-willed, like to be with other children' (Meggitt and Sunderland, 2000: 81). GD needed help with some of these things so she is not at the right stage of development for her age.

In your evaluation you should also include:

- **Future planning ideas:** here you should show your understanding of what you have observed by indicating what

empty and she is shaking it, turning it around in her hands and fiddling with the 'knob' in the middle of the base. Child A stands up and says, 'Give it here, I can do it.' He gently takes the sifter from Child B in his right hand and tries to prise off the 'holed' top. He then looks at the bottom of the sifter and, using his left hand, holds the knob and twists the base to the right and the left until it moves. He shouts, 'I've done it. It's easy.' He then holds the sifter upside down and starts to scoop sand into it, using a large measuring spoon.

Child B says excitedly, 'Look. It's comin' out there – stop!' pointing to the 'holed' top. Child C picks up another sifter and begins to do what she has seen Child A do. She removes the base and then holds the sifter in her left hand and tips it horizontally as she fills it with sand using a spoon in her left hand. Child B says, 'Yeah, that's how you do it. Give it me an' I'll do it.' She reaches for the sifter from Child A, who turns away and accidentally spills sand on the floor. 'Now look what you've made me do. I'm telling.' He looks around and calls over to the nursery teacher, 'Mrs L., look what B's made me do.'

Detailed observation

This is a very useful method for recording observations of one or more children (perhaps up to four individuals). You record and present your information in a chart, which is best laid out in landscape orientation (see Figure 2.3). Headings for columns might include time, location or activity, social context, actions, language and 'other' – this last one is very useful for noting down unexpected happenings (e.g. the arrival of a visitor or a sudden interruption from outside, such as an ambulance siren). Alternatively, you could have a column for each child if you are observing a group activity, such as registration or story-time. If your observation

takes place in the same location and with the same people present throughout, you could dispense with the 'location/activity' and 'social context' columns, as long as you remember to include the information in your introduction.

Target child

This method is more usually used in nursery settings to focus on one particular child and was originally devised to observe concentration. A chart with four columns – 'activity record', 'language record', 'task' and 'social context' – is needed to present the information. For this method you need to use a pre-selected code for recording regular or repeated aspects, such as: **RP** = role play, **A** = art activities, **SOL** = solitary, **SG** = small group, **LG** = large group.

For these observations to be shared successfully within a setting an agreed common code must be used.

For your portfolio you can devise your own code, which will also be useful for other methods that require a shorthand for speed. A key to the codes being used must always be provided in your final presentation.

Diary description

This is usually kept to monitor learning and development of an individual child (but can also be used for a group) and provides a day-to-day account of significant events. It may include **anecdotal records** (see page 92) and other forms of observation. A diary is time-consuming to keep and you need to be sure that the information gathered is helpful and remains objective, rather than being mundane, repetitive and subjective. This type of observation can help to record the progress of every child in a group over time.

Time	Location/activity	Social context	Actions	Language	Other
9.02 a.m.	Messy area at sand tray	1 adult, 4 children	G picks up blue bucket and snatches yellow spade from J. T holds out green spade to G.	G: 'I need that.' T: 'J was using that spade, G. Here you are, have this one.'	H leaves the sand tray.
9.05 a.m.		1 adult, 3 children	G and J begin to fill a large, empty tub with sand, putting in a spadeful each in turn. J pats the top with her hand when it is full.	T: 'Well done. You've filled it.' J: 'We can't get any more sand in now.'	L arrives and asks J to go for her snack.

Time	Location/activity	Social context	Child1	Child2	Child 3
11.30 a.m.	Book corner/story-time	3 adults, 22 children	Sitting at front of group on bottom, legs crossed, one hand in lap, other hand fiddling with buttons on dress. Looking at storybook.	Sitting at back of group, kneeling with bottom resting on heels. Both hands on knees. Looking at T and book.	In middle of group. Sitting on bottom with knees bent and legs to one side. Holding a piece of Lego in both hands and turning it over. Looking at Lego.
11.35 a.m.			Puts up hand. 'He's under the bed.'	Puts hand up and then down again.	Looks up as children around put hands up. Looks at T and book.

Time	Activity	Language	Facial expression
9.24 a.m.	Puts on apron and sits down at collage table next to T. Picks up scissors in right hand, correct grip, opens and closes them 4 times. Points to piece of Christmas wrapping paper.	T: "Are you coming to make a picture, K?' K: 'What can I have? Can I have some of that?'	D smiles and looks at the trays containing collage materials. Looks at trays, eyes open wide at pieces of wrapping paper – turns to T with hesitant look.

Fig 2.3 Example of a detailed observation

Anecdotal record

This is a brief description of an incident written soon after it has occurred. This is a widely used method of observation and is useful because it is recorded only a short time after the incident. The adult records a significant piece of learning, perhaps a model a child has made (a photograph of the model can be useful as an addition), or an important development in relationships with other children. This method enhances the descriptive, narrative and detailed observations made. Anecdotal observations are often made in a different-coloured pen, to show that they are not 'on-the-spot', but recalled events.

Tape and transcript

This is an ideal method for observing language and interaction. It can be used to assess speech and, to some extent, a child's understanding. It is usual to tape-record a complete conversation or task, but the transcript (the written record of what has been recorded) can be a selected brief section – perhaps 2 minutes.

Several factors need to be taken into account when carrying out a taped observation:

* The children's (and possibly the adult's) awareness of the tape recorder and you, writing notes, could affect their behaviour.
* Children's familiarity with being recorded in this way will affect the extent of the impact on their behaviour.
* Background or surrounding noise can distort the recording.
* The distance of the children from the microphone can be a problem.
* The clarity and volume of the children's voices can be a problem.

* Children may talk over each other when in a group.
* Accents or dialect may make transcription of the recording difficult.
* Interruptions are disruptive.

Video recording

This would seem to be a comprehensive method for recording all aspects of behaviour – actions, speech, tone of voice, facial expression, posture, interaction – as they happen and without having to do a lot of writing. This method conveys information about a child's personality and appearance that can be difficult to describe in written forms.

You need to consider:

* whether you use a hand-held or a fixed camera;
* whether the children are used to being filmed in this way;
* what you are trying to film.

Note that video presents issues of **confidentiality** as anyone filmed can be easily identified.

A fixed camera has very limited scope but can be useful for monitoring safety, access and use, or interest in one area or room. You need to consider carefully where it will be best sited and ensure children are unable to interfere with it. You may need to edit the tape if there are periods when not much is happening. In your report, clarify why any edits were made. An edited recording may not be considered to fit into the 'narrative' category.

A hand-held camera is more flexible, but more intrusive. Remember that if you are carrying out the filming you cannot maintain an overview and may miss interesting events. Also, filming as you are moving along can be unsatisfactory – be careful if walking backwards! Practise a bit first! In many settings

Guidelines for achieving a successful taped observation

❖ Make sure your tape recorder is working properly – check the batteries or the power supply.

❖ Some students use smaller Dictaphones, but you need to check with your tutor that the college has a suitable machine on which to play your tape for assessment purposes.

❖ Check that the tape you are using is undamaged. Wind the tape through the blank 'lead-in' and record your name, PIN, observation number, date, time and setting.

❖ Check that your recording worked. Leave the tape ready for recording your observation. A 20-minute tape (10 minutes each side) is usually sufficient.

❖ In consultation with your supervisor, choose the location for your recording – preferably somewhere quiet, with soft furnishings (they absorb sound and reduce the 'echo' factor), where you are unlikely to be interrupted.

❖ Decide when will be the best time to make your recording – not 5 minutes before snack-time or going home.

❖ Depending on whether you are recording a naturally occurring event or a structured situation, you need to place yourself in a position to note other significant information (e.g. facial expression, actions).

❖ If you are observing interaction, it would be a good idea to draw up a chart (use the detailed method) with headings to help you add important detail. Figure 2.4 shows a suitable chart.

❖ When transcribing, try to write down exactly what you hear rather than the word you know is being attempted (e.g. 'barf' when the child wants to say 'bath', or 'somethink' instead of 'something'). This is especially important if you are trying to identify speech difficulties. You can always write the intended word alongside in brackets.

❖ When you have finished the recording, read quickly through your notes to check they make sense to you.

❖ Listen to the tape at least twice, reading your notes and adding any detail.

❖ Refer back to your aim and decide which portion of the recording will be most useful for analysis. If your machine has a counter on it, make a note of the section you will transcribe.

❖ Play the chosen section a little bit at a time and write down everything that is said. You may need to do this several times, until you are satisfied that you have transcribed it correctly. This first transcription can be very rough.

❖ Using both the transcript and your chart information, write out the spoken language, using a new line for each speaker. Put actions and other information alongside to correspond with the speech. For example:

Child 1: *This is my best story. I like Spot.* (Opens book and points to Spot. Looks up at T, smiling.)

T: *What is he doing in this picture?* (Reaches over to point to right-hand page.)

❖ Check through your work as you listen to the selected section of tape. Ensure you have included all the relevant detail.

❖ Use your information to complete the evaluation and reference or bibliography.

RP = role play, SOL = solitary, SG = small group, LG = large group, TC = target child, C = child, A = adult, BC = book corner, SW = small world, W = waiting

Child initials: JG   Gender: M   Age: 3 yrs 10mths   Date/Time: 1/10/05 2.15 p.m.

ACTIVITY RECORD	LANGUAGE RECORD	TASK	SOCIAL
1 min TC on carpeted area, playing with farm animals and buildings.	TC→C My cow wants to come in your field. C→TC No. You'll have to wait till my tractor has finished.	SW	SG
2 min TC sitting at edge of carpet, looking at wall display.		W	SOL
3 min Now in dressing-up area, putting on a floppy hat and laughing.	C→TC You look funny in that. TC→C Let me see. Where's the mirror?	RP	SG
4 min Sitting in a small chair at a table, holding a knife and fork in his hands.	TC→C Where's my tea? I want my tea. Not fish fingers again!	RP	SG
5 min Standing at 'cooker' and stirring something in a pan.	A→TC What are you cooking? TC→A I'm a good cooker. It's basgetti.	RP	SG
6 min Taking off hat and tidying equipment.		RP	SOL
7 min Sitting in story corner, looking at book.		BC	LG

Fig 2.4 Example of a target child observation

now, practitioners capture a sequence of events with a series of photographs, e.g. showing a child mixing paints and the process involved.

Time sample

This involves making a series of short observations (usually up to 2 minutes each) at regular intervals over a fairly long period. The interval between observations and the overall duration is your decision, depending on exactly what you are observing and why. For example, you may choose to record at 20-minute intervals over the course of a whole day, or every 15 minutes during a half-day session.

Child observed = HR   Teacher = T   Other children = A, B, C, D, E.
LG = large group, SG = small group, P = pair of children
Aim: To find out how well a child, newly arrived from another school, has settled in, looking particularly at interaction with other children.

Time	Setting	Language	Social group	Other
9.00	Registration – sitting on carpeted area.	None	LG	At back of class group, fiddling with shoelaces and looking around the room.
9.20	At a table, playing a language game.	HR: 'It's *not* my turn.'	SG	One parent helper and 3 other children.
9.40	On floor of cloakroom.	HR: 'You splashed me first and my jumper's all wet, look.'	P	Had been to toilet and is washing hands.
10.00	In maths area, carrying out a sorting activity using coloured cubes.	T: 'Can you find some more cubes the same colour, HR?' HR: 'There's only 2 more red ones.'	SG	Concentrating and smiling as he completes the task.
10.20	Playground – HR is standing by a wall, crying.	Sobbing sounds – won't make eye contact with or speak to T on duty.	SOL	Small group of children look on.
10.40	Music activity - playing a tambour to beat the rhythm of his name.	Says his name in 2-syllable beats.	LG	Showing enjoyment by smiling – T praises him.
11.00	Tidying away instruments with another child.	A→HR: 'We have instruments every week. It's good, isn't it?' HR→A: 'Yeh. I liked it.'	P	
11.20	Playing with construction equipment with A and B.	B→HR + A: 'I've got loads of Lego at home.' HR→B + A: 'So have I. I like the technical stuff best.' B→HR: 'What's that like?'	SG	Children working together to build a garage for toy cars.
11.40	HR fetching reading book to read to T.	Humming to himself.	SOL	
12.00	Lining up with other children to go for lunch.		LG	Nudging A, who is standing in front of him. A turns round and grins.

Fig 2.5 Example of a time sample in a Year 1 class

It can be a useful way of finding out how children use particular toys or resources, to monitor how a new child has settled in, or to observe the behaviour of an individual child. When observing an individual child's behaviour, time sampling can raise awareness of positive aspects which may, in the normal run of a busy day, be overlooked. Staff can then make a point of noticing and appreciating the incidents of positive behaviour and encourage these as part of a strategy to reduce unwanted aspects.

The difficulty many students experience is managing to step away at regular intervals from whatever else they are doing to make their record. Negotiation with your supervisor and other staff is essential so that children's safety is not put at risk.

You can choose your own headings for the chart format to match the detail you need to include. Usual headings are 'time', 'setting or location', 'language' and 'social group', but you may want to include 'actions' and 'other'.

Event sample or frequency count

This is similar to a time sample, but instead of recording at regular intervals, you record particular identified events, for example every time the observed child seeks adult help or every time he or she displays aggressive behaviour. This is usually done over a long period of time, depending on the child and the type of event. You may observe over the course of a week or even longer (see Figure 2.6). You might need to record each event for the duration of the incident: every time the child has a temper tantrum you would observe from the time you are first aware of it until the child has calmed down and resumed an activity. If you want to gain a clear picture of how many times a particular event occurs then you may use your record for a frequency count and note down less detail (see Figure 2.7).

Again, you can structure your chart to suit the information you require. This method is more problematic than time sampling because you have no idea when you will need to make your records. Again, it is essential that others in your work setting understand that you are carrying out this type of observation.

Pie charts and bar charts

These are pictorial or diagrammatic ways of representing information you have already recorded using different techniques. Although not appropriate for individual child observation, they are ideal for presenting your findings about groups of children, for example measurements such as

height, foot or shoe size, food likes and dislikes, skill competence such as use of scissors or hopping. You would first gather the data and then present your results in the chosen form. This would take the place of the observation section in your report, but you will still need to complete front-sheet information, and write an introduction, an evaluation and a reference or bibliography.

Flow diagram (or movement chart)

This method allows you to present information about an individual child or a group of children, activities, safety in a work setting or use of equipment. It can be very simple with very basic information (see Figure 2.10) or more detailed to highlight more than one aspect (see Figure 2.11). If you want to track one child from one area or activity to another during the course of a morning session, it might help to have a prepared plan of the room on which to map her or his movement.

From this type of observation you can see:

- ❖ which activities the child visited;
- ❖ the order in which she visited them;
- ❖ how long she spent at each one;
- ❖ which activities she visited on more than one occasion;
- ❖ which activities she did not visit at all.

The more detailed version provides the following additional information:

- ❖ which activities had adult-led tasks;
- ❖ which ones had an adult permanently supervising or helping;
- ❖ which other children were at an activity when the observed child arrived.

From this level of detail you may gain further insight into the child's movements. Repeated observations may enable you to find out if

Child observed = KD Age: 3 years 4 months Teacher = T Other children A, B, C, D, E, etc. NN = nursery nurse
Aim: To monitor the frequency and nature of aggressive outbursts and, where possible, identify 'trigger' factors. Also to record KD's response to adults.

Time	Setting/ context	Social context	Behaviour	Adult/KD response
9.02	By coat pegs	KD and A	A standing in front of KD's peg. KD pulls A's hair. A screams and runs to T.	T explains to KD that she needs to tell A the problem, that A is upset because it hurts to have her hair pulled. KD pats A's head.
9.51	In book area	Small group	KD snatches book from B. A page is torn. B begins to cry.	NN takes book gently from KD and says she must be more careful. Puts arm around B and suggests that they both sit with her and share another story. KD on verge of crying, sits down next to NN.
10.34	Outdoor play area where bikes, prams and pushchairs are available.	Large group	KD and C both holding handle of a pram, arguing. KD pushes C away and runs off, pushing pram.	NN follows KD, telling her she may have a turn, but must then bring it back for C to have a go. Explains that she must not push anyone and that she needs to take turns, or ask an adult to find another pram. KD has a turn and the adult finds C another pram.
10.47	As above	Large group	D takes doll from KD's pram. KD chases her, snatches back doll and pinches D's arm.	T explains to D the doll is being used by KD (who is crying) and it makes her sad when the doll is taken from the pram T helps to find a different doll and encourages D to give back the doll to KD, who returns it to the pram.
11.50	Singing activity –carpet area	Large group	E accidentally treads on KD's fingers as he walks past to sit down. KD pushes him and he falls over onto another child.	T asks NN to check nobody badly hurt. KD is looking anxious and NN takes KD away from group. Explains that E didn't mean to tread on her and that she must not hurt other children, and needs to say 'That hurt me!' to show E how KD feels.

Fig 2.6 Event sample

the child never visits the sand, always heads for an activity with an adult present, or always follows another child.

Sociogram

This is a diagrammatic method used to show an individual child's social relationships within a group, or to find out about friendship patterns between several children within a group (see Figure 2.12). Identifying girls and boys separately can sometimes make it immediately clear whether girls play with girls, and boys with boys, or if they play in mixed gender groups. You should record the ages of the children involved. You may find that an older child habitually plays with a group of much younger children. You will be able to identify any child who always plays

Usual information on front sheet
Child observed = LP   Teacher = T   Nursery Nurse = NN
Aim: To monitor the frequency of acts of aggression and record whether they are provoked or unprovoked

Day	No.	Duration	Provoked/ unprovoked	Comments
Monday	1	3 secs	u.p.	LP pinched mother as she left.
	2	10 secs	p.	LP sat on HJ after he had knocked down his brick tower.
Tuesday	1	4 secs	u.p.	LP pushed KP over as he ran around outdoor area.
	2	5 secs	u.p.	LP pinched GD as they were sitting down for story-time.
Wednesday	0			
Thursday	1	10 secs	u.p.	LP kicked SR several times as she walked past him to go to the toilet.
	2	4 secs	u.p.	LP bit WT's hand because he wanted the truck that WT was playing with.
	3	3 secs	u.p.	LP bit FD's hand (no apparent reason).
	4	2 secs	p	LP pushed RA, who had drawn on his picture.
Friday		absent		

Fig 2.7 Frequency count

alone or who always seeks the company of an adult. There are many factors which will affect the play relationships – friendship of parents, proximity of homes, presence of siblings and, not least, pattern of attendance (see Chapter 9). These factors need to be taken into account when drawing your conclusions.

Growth charts

These can be used to plot the height and/or weight of an individual child over a period of time. (An example of a growth chart is shown in Chapter 8.) Make sure you use one for the correct gender as there are variations between boys and girls. The chart cannot be submitted in isolation but must be accompanied by your analysis of the information which makes reference to percentiles and shows your understanding. You must use the chart to interpret 'your' child's information. This type of chart is

good to include in a longitudinal study. Even if you are studying a child aged 2 years or over, it is quite likely that the parents will have a record of length/height and weight at birth and at some intervening intervals which you can plot.

Checklists

This form of recording has its limitations, including the following:

❖ giving no detail or supporting evidence;

❖ being narrow in focus;

❖ making practitioners feel that they have more information than they really do;

❖ being time-consuming to create.

However, if these limitations are appreciated and the checklist is well thought out, it can be a very straightforward method of recording your observation. It should only be used in addition to other methods.

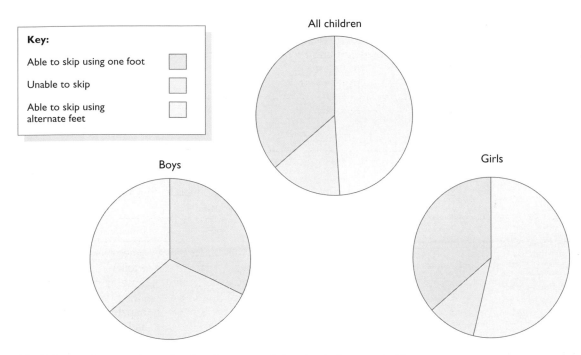

Fig 2.8 Pie chart to show the development of skipping in boys and girls

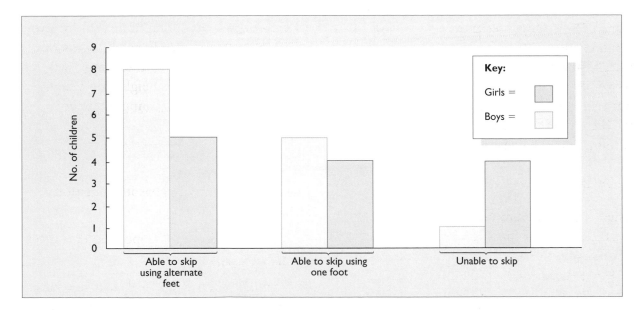

Fig 2.9 Bar chart to show the development of skipping in boys and girls of different ages

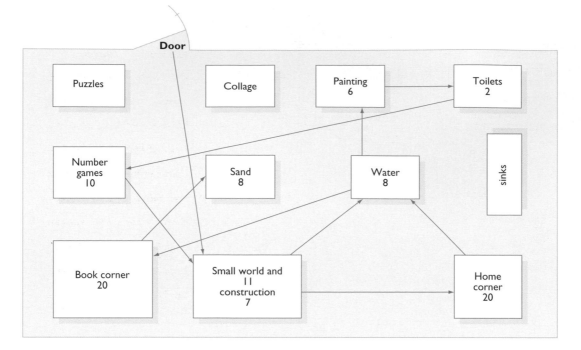

Fig 2.10 Flow chart

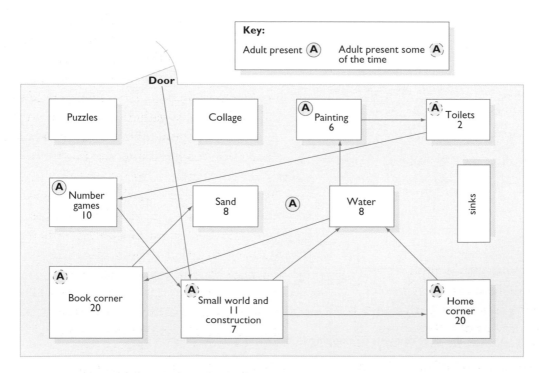

Fig 2.11 Flow chart – with extra detail

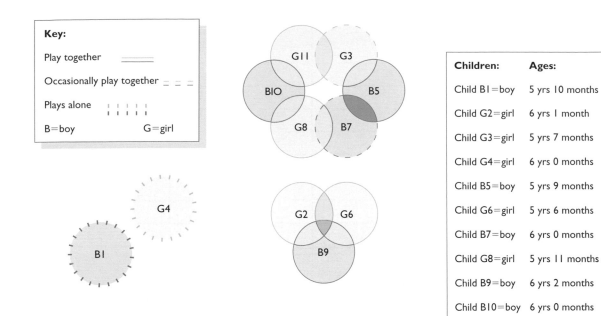

Key:

Play together _____

Occasionally play together _ _ _

Plays alone ¦ ¦ ¦ ¦ ¦

B=boy G=girl

Children:	Ages:
Child B1=boy	5 yrs 10 months
Child G2=girl	6 yrs 1 month
Child G3=girl	5 yrs 7 months
Child G4=girl	6 yrs 0 months
Child B5=boy	5 yrs 9 months
Child G6=girl	5 yrs 6 months
Child B7=boy	6 yrs 0 months
Child G8=girl	5 yrs 11 months
Child B9=boy	6 yrs 2 months
Child B10=boy	6 yrs 0 months

Fig 2.12 Sociogram

It can be used to help:

* monitor developmental progress, of an individual child or several children;

* assess children on a regular basis over a period of time;

* staff plan for children's changing needs;

* consideration of one area of development;

* assess a child's behaviour.

Longitudinal study

As you may imagine, a longitudinal study is not something which can be achieved through a single observation. It consists of a series of observations of different aspects of development, recorded using a variety of techniques over a period of time – a few weeks, months, a year or more. It provides opportunities to look at the 'whole' child by observing and assessing progress in all areas of development. As a student you are most likely to carry out such a study on a child whom you know well or whose family you know well. In this case you may be given permission to include photographs and/or video footage. The initial part of the study will involve gathering background and factual information, followed by observations carried out at agreed intervals (not necessarily regular). You may get the chance to observe special events, such as outings, birthdays, clinic visits, as well as the child's time spent in a setting. When you have recorded all your observations you can collate the information. You might choose to present them in strict chronological order or in groups of observations of different developmental areas. This will depend on the focus of your study and the individual observations.

In work settings a longitudinal study can be useful in planning long-term strategies for a child with special needs.

	CHILD 1 yrs m	CHILD 2 yrs m	CHILD 3 yrs m
1. WALKING			
Looks ahead			
Walks upright			
Avoids objects			
Small steps			
Strides			
Walks heel to toe			
Arms by side			
Arms swinging			
Other observation			
2. BALANCE			
Stands on one foot			
Balances for 3–4 seconds			
Balances for longer			
Leans to one side			
Arms stretched out			
Arms by side			
Arms folded			
Can walk on narrow line			
Other observation			
3. RUNNING			
Runs on tiptoe			
Runs flat-footed			
Swings arms			
Arms by side			
Arms folded			
Able to change speed			
Changes direction			
Runs round corners			
Other observation			

You can add to this chart for other gross motor skills, such as skipping, hopping, climbing, swinging etc., by identifying the important components of the action. The Foundation Profile (2002) requires observation to support the child's journey through the stepping stones and Early Learning Goals achieved at the end of the Foundation Stage. It is important to note that most children in England do not achieve the ELGs for literacy before entering key stage 1.

Fig 2.13 Example of a gross motor skills checklist

Possible use: for monitoring reading skills

Title of book used: *The Birthday Cake* **Date:**

Skill	Child 1	Comment	Child 2	Comment
1. Holds book right way up	✓	Held book correctly in both hands	✓	Took book from me and turned it right way
2. Knows which is the front of a book	✓	Looked at front cover before opening book	✓	Pointed to character on cover picture
3. Follows text/pictures left to right	✓	Followed pictures as story was read	✓	Head movements showed was doing this
4. Knows text 'works' top to bottom	✓	As above	✓	As above
5. Can point to known characters in illustrations	✓	Pointed to Chip and Floppy	✓	Named characters as they appeared in illustrations
6. Can talk about illustrations	✓	Did so when prompted	✓	Pointed to things in pictures which he found funny
7. Can recap the story partway through	✗	Needed prompting and had to turn back through pages	✓	Good recall of what had happened
8. Can suggest what might happen next	✗	Could offer no ideas	✓	Good suggestions with reasons
9. Identifies some individual letters	✓	Named and pointed to 'c', 'd' and 'a'	✓	Named and pointed to 'c', 'd', 'a', 'g', 'h', 'l', 'b', 'n', 'w', 't', 's', 'r', 'y', 'p'
10. Can identify a capital (upper-case) letter	✓	Named and pointed to 'C' – own initial letter	✓	Named and pointed to 'C', 'F', 'B', 'H', 'T', 'R'
11. Can identify a full stop	✗		✗	

Fig 2.14 Example of an expanded checklist showing reading development

3

Working with young children

Contents

PLANNING THE CURRICULUM

It is important to note that there is a shift from making curriculum plans (which are too rigid to meet the needs or develop the interests of individual children) to curriculum **planning, which is flexible and ever-changing**.

The principles set out in the box below have a long tradition and have informed the curriculum frameworks of the four UK countries as they exist today. The principles inform the planning alongside observations of individual children. This means that the emphasis is on **planning within an effective curriculum framework**, rather than making a plan using a rigid and prescribed curriculum syllabus.

The curriculum framework has three parts, which involve:

❖ **child:** processes in the child's development and learning, such as

movement, communication, play and symbolic behaviour, and emotional well-being;

❖ **context:** the access the practitioners create so that the child is helped to learn, and how learning builds on the child's social relationships, and family and cultural experiences;

❖ **content:** what the child learns and understands – the content of the curriculum framework for each of the four UK countries is different (see page 480).

These three aspects of a quality learning environment need to be balanced, or the curriculum framework offered will be of poor quality. In England, Wales, Scotland and Northern Ireland this is about helping children from birth to 6 years develop and learn.

The three Cs of a quality learning environment (often called the curriculum

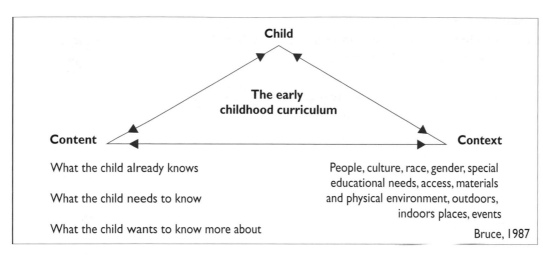

Fig 3.1 Diagram of three Cs

framework) are based on principles which have long and respected traditions, mainly in the Western world.

Principles supporting the early childhood curriculum frameworks in the UK

1 The best way to prepare children for their adult life is to give them what they need as children.

2 Children are whole people who have feelings, ideas, relationships with others, a sense of self and wellbeing, and who need to be physically, morally and spiritually healthy.

3 Children do not learn in neat and tidy compartments. Everything new they learn links with everything they have already learnt.

4 Children learn best when they are respected and helped to be autonomous, active learners.

5 Self-discipline is emphasised as the only kind of discipline worth having. Children need their efforts to be valued in their own right.

6 There are times when children are especially able to learn particular things.

7 What children can do (rather than what they cannot do) is the starting point for a child's learning.

8 There are many different kinds of symbolic behaviour. These show the inner thoughts, feelings and ideas of the child, through the way they draw, paint, make things, dance, sing, talk/sign, enjoy making stories, mark-make or pretend-play. The Italian educator Malaguzzi calls this the 'one hundred languages' of children.

9 Relationships with other people are central to a child's emotional and social well-being.

10 Quality education is about the child, the context in which learning takes place, and the knowledge and understanding which the child develops and learns.

(Bruce 1987, updated 2006)

Curriculum planning begins with the child

In order to plan a quality curriculum framework, the first step is to observe children as individuals. Observation helps adults to tune in to what interests a child, and to see how to support and extend their

children by giving them vocabulary, explaining and engaging with children in shared and sustained conversations during activities and experiences. Extending learning is about helping children to take the next steps in their learning. Next steps can be in a broadening direction or an upward direction.

4 Next steps in planning

* Broadening – doing more of the same, but with a slight difference. Bread is made in every culture across the world, so helping children to understand what it always contains is helpful in developing a concept of 'bread' (e.g. making roti and then making a type of bread typical in the UK, and seeing that both use flour and water as the base, which is then cooked in an oven or on a hot surface).

* Onwards and upwards – introducing something new, to show a contrast with what went before, but which definitely builds on what went before. Making a carrot cake is a bit like making bread, but eggs are also needed, and the mixture is stirred and beaten rather than rolled and pummelled.

PLANNING THE GENERAL LEARNING ENVIRONMENT

Planning begins with the observation of the child as a unique, valued and respected individual, with their own interests and needs. We could say this is all about getting to know the child. But further general planning is also necessary, because there is only so much that children can learn on their own. They need an environment that has been carefully thought through, along with the right help in using that environment. This aspect of planning ensures that the learning environment indoors and outdoors is balanced in what it offers, so that it helps all children in general, but also caters for individual children.

In this way the curriculum:

* is differentiated for individual children;

* is inclusive and embraces diversity;

* offers experiences and activities which are appropriate for most children of the age range, because it considers the social and cultural context, and the biological aspects of children developing in a community of learning;

* links with the requirements of legally framed curriculum documents (which include the first three points).

A curriculum which includes all children – inclusion and diversity

Most children learn in a rather uneven way. They have bursts of learning and then they have plateaux when their learning does not seem to move forward (but really they are consolidating their learning during this time). This is why careful observation and **assessment for learning** of individual children plus a general knowledge of child development are all very important.

Catching the right point for a particular bit of learning during development is a skill. So is recognising the child's pace of learning. Children have their own personalities and moods. They are affected by the weather, the time of day, whether they need food, sleep or the lavatory, the experiences they have, their sense of wellbeing and their social relationships with children and adults.

GIFTED AND TALENTED CHILDREN

People who are talented in music, dance and mathematics tend to show promise early in their lives. The most important thing is that adults provide a rich and stimulating learning environment, indoors and outdoors, which encourages children to develop and extend their thinking, understand and talk about their feelings, and understand themselves and others. It is frustrating for gifted children when they are constrained and held back in their learning.

It is also important to remember that however gifted or talented a child may be in a particular respect, he or she is still a child. They need all the things that any child needs, and should not be put under pressure to behave and learn in advance of their general development.

CHILDREN WITH SPECIAL EDUCATIONAL NEEDS (SEN) AND DISABILITIES

Some children will be challenged in their learning, and those working with children with special educational needs and disabilities will need to be particularly resourceful, imaginative and determined in helping them to learn. Many children with SEN and disabilities are underestimated by the adults working with them. For example, most 6-year-old children can run confidently across a field. In general, visually impaired children in mainstream settings are not expected to try to do this, and so they don't. No one suggests it to them or offers them help to do it. With the right help, the child might manage it, becoming physically more confident and mobile as a result. The experience of running across a field depends on the child's development, personality and mood. Walking hand–in–hand first might be important. Talking as you go helps. The child may need tips about picking up their feet, and eventually perhaps running towards your voice. If the child tumbles he will need reassurance, and not an anxious adult. Saying, 'Can I help you up?' is more helpful than rushing over and asking, 'Are you hurt?'

VALUING AND RESPECTING THE CHILD'S CULTURE AND FAMILY BACKGROUND

Every child needs to be included and to have full access to the curriculum, regardless of their ethnic background, culture, language, gender or economic background. No child should be held back in their learning due to restricted access to learning opportunities.

In order to apply curriculum plans, it is important to work closely in partnership with the child's parents/carers. Practitioners sometimes talk about 'my children', but children belong to their parents. When parents and practitioners work well together, respecting what they each bring to the partnership, in a spirit of respect and trust, with a genuine exchange of information and knowledge, the child gains and so do the parents and staff.

Planning a predictable environment which encourages learning

Children need to feel there is some kind of predictable shape to their day; otherwise they feel confused and insecure. This does not mean keeping to strict and rigid routines – that would constrain learning – but the following points are important:

- **Greetings:** every child and the adult accompanying them should be greeted as they arrive. Otherwise they will not feel welcome, or feel that they matter. Staff need to plan how to bring this about.

- **Anchor activities:** some children need to be with a member of staff when they part from their parent/carer. They benefit from a familiar and comforting activity, with the adult close to them, talking with them and helping them to make the transition from home

into the early childhood setting.
A rocking-horse, sand-play or play
with dough are often used in this
way in the planning of the day.

♣ **Children need to know that they
will be nurtured:** this is especially
important if they are upset or take a
tumble and hurt themselves. Many
settings plan for this through a key
worker system. This means that a member
of staff is assigned to each child as their
advocate and comforter. The child goes to
them for group time, and the adult links
with their family/carer, and ensures
that at curriculum planning meetings
the child's interest and needs are
planned for.

Planning for the child's learning journey (the processes of learning) and not just focusing on the results (products of learning)

It is through other people that children feel
valued or not. When children feel their
efforts are appreciated and celebrated, they
learn more effectively. If adults only praise
and recognise results, children are more
likely to lose heart and become less
motivated to learn. Planning should
therefore emphasise experiences and
activities which focus on process rather than
product. Examples would be finger-painting
rather than handprints, so that children can
freely make their own patterns in the paint.
At the end, the paint is cleared away, with
no pressure on children to produce a
product. However, staff might photograph
the processes involved in finger-painting and
display these on the wall, to remind children
of what they did. Children love to reflect on
their learning journeys, and talk about them
later with interested adults, other children
and their parents/carers.

Fig 3.2 a and b Language develops when adults
take time to sit with children and show sensitive
interest in their thoughts

Process of finger-painting

♣ Mix the powder paint with the water, and
perhaps add a little flour to thicken it.

♣ Tip the paint onto the tabletop.

♣ Make different patterns with the paint.

♣ Wash your hands.

♣ Help to clear up (if appropriate – not
babies and toddlers), usually showing
children each step of the process, helping
them to learn about sequences, which
will be important in learning science,
mathematics, as well as how to
read and write.

Planning a safe and predictable environment

Children need a safe and predictable environment. It is important for staff to work as a team so that different messages are not given by different people. For example, if one adult allows children to sit on tables and another does not, children will push the boundaries to find out what they are. They will push the boundaries because they are confused. They do this because they are trying to work out what they are and are not allowed to do. When children feel safe, they explore and enjoy stimulating provision that has been planned for them.

MAKING RISK ASSESSMENTS

Children are biologically driven to make risk assessments, but only if they are constantly encouraged to use these processes. For example, toddlers can be encouraged to come down the stairs (under supervision) sliding on their tummies, feet first. They will pause and check where they are every few steps, making their own risk assessment. Children who are not supported to make their own risk assessments, by an adult sensitive and helpful to their needs, are more likely to have accidents.

In order to set down neural patterns in the brain, children need to develop their sense of balance (vestibular learning) through spinning, tipping, rolling and tilting. They need rough-and-tumble play, which helps them to have a sense of one part of their body in relation to another. This leads to a sense of identity and embodiment, both central aspects of development and learning. Children who can make risk assessments are more likely to be physically safe. In a predictable environment activities are not controlled by adults all the time, but there is a shape to the day. Children feel safe because they have a sense of what is coming next, such as regular mealtimes and group times for stories, or songs and dances.

PLANNING THE INDOOR AND OUTDOOR LEARNING ENVIRONMENT

It is important to build on the traditions of the UK, which have emerged out of nursery schools and which have been tried and tested for excellence in the EPPE (Effective Provision of Preschool Education) research directed by Kathy Sylva at the University of Oxford.

Remember:

- to make the areas of the building flexible and easy to transform for different uses;
- that the way light shines in a building changes the atmosphere;
- that temperature is important;
- that areas should be uncluttered and beautifully arranged.

There should be nothing in a learning environment, either indoors or outdoors, that has not been carefully thought through and well organised. Many areas are full of clutter, which confuses children, so that they do not know what they are allowed to do, or how to look after the equipment and resources. When children feel insecure, they behave badly. They keep testing the boundaries to find out if there are any, and what they are. Children without boundaries are unhappy.

Children from birth to 3 years enjoy the companionship and stimulation of being with older children, but they also become

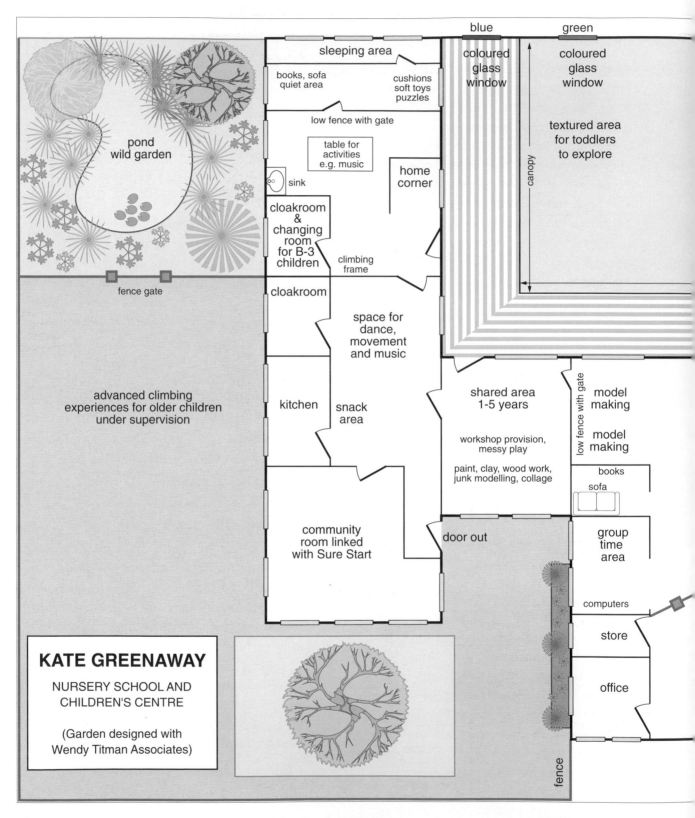

Fig 3.3 Kate Greenaway Maintained Nursery School and Children's Centre (garden designed with Wendy Titman Associates)

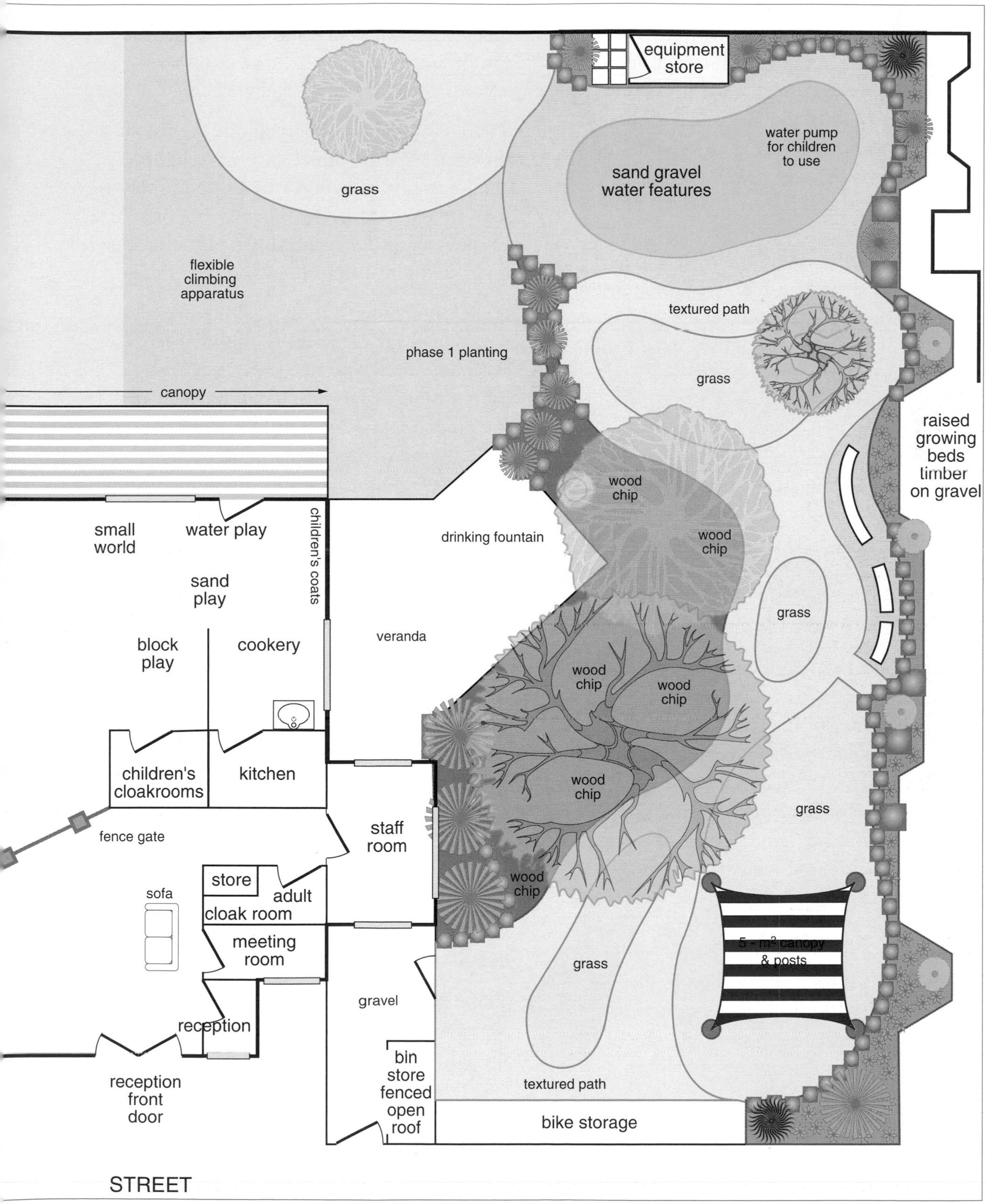

equipment store

water pump for children to use

sand gravel water features

grass

flexible climbing apparatus

textured path

grass

phase 1 planting

raised growing beds timber on gravel

canopy

small world

water play

children's coats

wood chip

drinking fountain

wood chip

sand play

grass

block play

cookery

veranda

wood chip

wood chip

children's cloakrooms

kitchen

wood chip

grass

staff room

fence gate

wood chip

sofa

store

adult cloak room

meeting room

5 - m² canopy & posts

reception

gravel

grass

reception front door

bin store fenced open roof

textured path

bike storage

exhausted if they do not have a safe nest to retreat into, where they can be quiet and calm. The environment indoors and outdoors is planned with this in mind at the Kate Greenaway Maintained Nursery School and Children's Centre, where the children range from 1 to 5 years.

Look at Figure 3.3.

Beginning at the left-hand side of the page, you will see that there is an area for children between the ages of 1 and 3 years to sleep. Children sleep here only if they need to, and their sleep patterns are discussed with parents/carers (see Chapter 4, page 173). The colours are neutral and there is a chair for an adult to sit in, should a child need to be cuddled as they fall asleep. It is important to find out about home sleep patterns. The room is quiet and calm, but the door is left open, so that staff can observe, and children feel near their important adult (key worker) and therefore secure.

This is next to the quiet area, which is also for the children aged 1–3 years. It is fenced-off from the rest of the room. There is a sofa where the practitioner or parents can sit and cuddle a child, and there is a carefully selected range of books next to it. Hanging above the book case are several story/song sacks, which are used regularly at group times. Parents and practitioners often sit with children and share these. Sometimes they sit on the sofa together with children beside them and on their laps. Sometimes they sit on the floor, with their back supported against the sofa. A sofa is probably one of the most important pieces of equipment in a room for children aged 1–3 years.

There are beanbags in soft neutral colours, with soft toys. There are a few jigsaw-type toys on the floor.

Children can see through the fence, and they quickly learn to open the gate, so that they can go into the quiet area or leave it, according to how they feel.

There is a clear boundary about the use of this space. It is for quiet and calm, and if children want or need to be more boisterous, they are encouraged to move to the next area or into the garden, with the explanation that there are more things they will enjoy there.

Sometimes a practitioner will take a child into the area if they feel the toddler is becoming tired and needs some quieter, calmer time. Obviously it is important that the practitioner stays with the child and helps them, perhaps looking at a book together, or hugging a soft toy while sitting on the practitioner's lap.

In the main area for the 1–3-year-olds there is a set of **wooden blocks**, beautifully presented on shelves. Nearby there are shelves with a **wooden Brio train set**. As many materials as possible are of **natural materials**, although plastic is not banned. There is a basket with stones and natural sponges in it for children to hold and manipulate, or make patterns with. Toddlers are often seen quietly lining these up and concentrating deeply.

There is a cupboard with musical instruments in it for group sessions with an adult leading. Near the sink is an area for dough and an area for mark-making.

There is also a domestic play/home corner area. For children of this age group there should always be an area where they can become involved in the beginnings of role play and pretend play. We will see in Chapter 12 that even the youngest children are beginning to understand that they can imitate what adults do in their role play, and

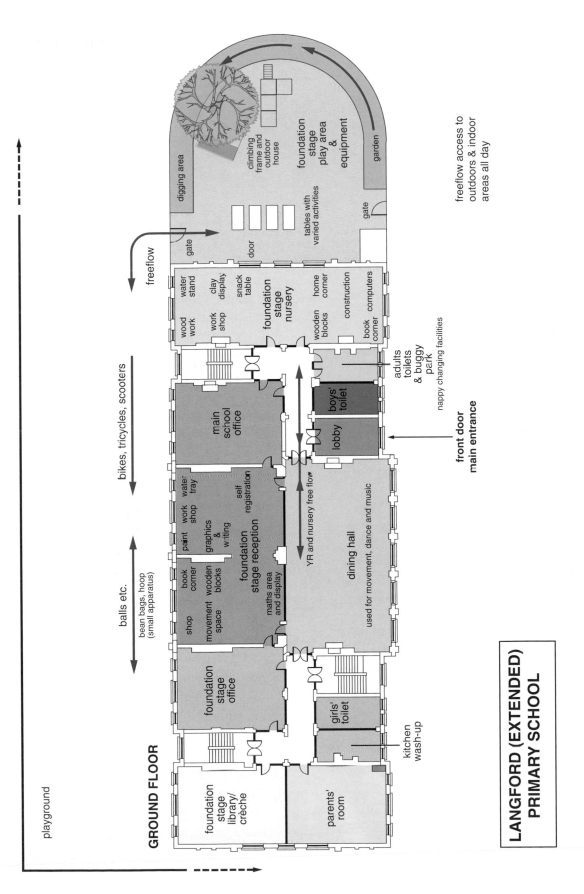

LANGFORD (EXTENDED) PRIMARY SCHOOL

Fig 3.4 Langford (extended) primary school has a Foundation Stage layout with the nursery class and reception class working together. The school received positive feedback from Ofsted inspections.

pretend to eat food. Food preparation play is one of the earliest forms of role play and pretend play in young children throughout the world.

There is an indoor climbing frame, which is very popular when children arrive. The changing area is off this room, and there is a lavatory for children to use as they become toilet trained (see Chapter 4).

Children from the Foundation Stage are welcome to use this area, providing they do not overwhelm the younger children. Often children who are vulnerable, experiencing trauma, developmentally young for their age or who have special needs enjoy this area, as it is appropriate for their needs. However, the staff whose work is with the 1–3-year-olds focus on those children, and treat the older children as visitors. If they begin to take too much of their attention, they are directed, gently and positively, out of this space.

Next door, there is a truly shared space, where children of all ages (1–5 years) can dance and move. A kitchen off this area also provides opportunities for staff to make snacks for children, which can be served to children at a table in this area.

It is next to another shared space, which is the messy area. Here there is double provision. Whatever is available at a more advanced level is also available at a simpler level. This double provision means there is **progression and differentiation**. Children can become involved in the way that is appropriate for them. For example, there is the opportunity for children to mix their own paint colours at a table, but on the floor there are trays of ready-mixed paint which children can use in a large builder's tray on the floor. Toddlers can be dressed appropriately to experience this, and so can

older children if they wish. But the children who want to paint a picture, and choose their colours carefully, can also do so at the table. There is something for everyone. The children aged 1–3 years are only allowed to use this area if their key worker goes with them. This is because they need a great deal of support, and so the mess does not get out of hand, thereby maintaining a safely structured experience which everyone enjoys together. Parents and grandparents also enjoy joining their children here.

There is another reason why it is important to offer young children experiences down on the floor, rather than on the table. This is because (as JABADAO shows) belly-crawling, crawling on knees and floor-based movements lay down essential patterns in the brain for future effective learning, influencing reading, writing, mathematics and wellbeing, for example.

Only one very messy experience/activity is offered per day, so that the mess is controlled carefully and children do not feel insecure and without boundaries. The practitioners in the 1–3-years area and the Foundation Stage plan this space together. What is provided is the result of their observations of children, linked to the two frameworks, *Birth to Three Matters* and *Curriculum Guidance for the Foundation Stage*. There is always **paint, clay and modelling with found/junk materials**, involving a workshop area with glue, sticky tape, scissors and string, For example, while the older children might sit or stand at a table and make a model of a car, a house or a puppet, a young child might prefer to sit at a basket on the floor and manipulate different balls of string and simply find out about string and its properties. The older children often return to these simpler activities when they have finished making a model, and they need the comfort of doing something less challenging after all their effort.

There is a gate in a fenced-off area between the shared messy space and the Foundation Stage area. The children can use this easily once they have been shown how to, or they enjoy working it out themselves from the earliest age. However, the youngest children only go though this gate as they arrive and leave the setting with their parent/carer. They do not use the Foundation Stage area because it is set up with activities and experiences which are for children from 3 years upwards.

There is a graphics area, with carefully structured pencils, felt-tip pens and paper, scissors, masking tape and Sellotape. Everything is labelled with a picture and the word in boxes of wood or baskets. Having natural materials in which to keep equipment, such as wood and baskets, and wooden units, makes the colours neutral and gives the area a feeling of calm and focus.

Planning should fit in with children's natural rhythms. Adults need to bear in mind that it is important not to work to a tight, inflexible routine, which is really for their own convenience rather than serving the needs of the children. There are times when children go at a fast pace, and times when they tire; times when they want to be alone, or have a cuddle and be nurtured; and times when they enjoy working with other children and adults. Different children will need different things at different times of the day. All the children will not need to sleep at the same time. One 2-year-old might need a sleep before lunch and enjoy it once rested, while another will sleep after lunch, relaxed with a comfortable, full stomach.

Kate Greenaway achieved an outstanding Ofsted report in 2006 for her work with children from birth to 3.

A SENSE OF BELONGING TO THE GROUP

A well-planned environment allows children to learn in their own individual way while giving them a **sense of belonging to the community**. Eating together needs careful planning, but helps to bring this about. Planning where children should sit and how the group will be arranged enhances the curriculum through everyday activities of daily living. These are powerful learning opportunities. As adults talk with children, and help them, encouraging them to help each other and be as independent as possible, the children benefit if planning is thorough.

❖ Do children know how to help themselves to vegetables?

❖ Do they clear away their own plates after eating?

Fig 3.5 Helping children to become involved

Using everyday experiences

Some of the richest learning comes from experiences of everyday living. Examples would be getting dressed, choosing what to do, going shopping, using what you have bought in cooking, using a recipe book, washing up, sharing a story or photographs of shared events (visiting the park), laying the table, eating together, sorting the washing, washing clothes. It is a challenge to find ways of making this manageable for children to take part in with independence, but careful planning makes this both possible and enjoyable, and the learning goes deep. For further information, see the case studies on page 123.

PLANNING FROM BIRTH TO 5 YEARS

Children in a group setting need a carefully planned learning environment. It is important, however, that practitioners engage with assessing where a child is in their learning, using observation informed by knowledge of child development, and then planning using the appropriate document.

In England the planning would be linked to the *Birth to Three Matters* framework or the *Curriculum Guidance for the Foundation Stage* (as explored above). There is a useful overlap while the child is 3 years old, since these documents both address the needs of 3-year-olds, and this is very helpful to practitioners. In each country of the UK planning will link into the official curriculum framework (see Chapter 12), but planning is always informed by observation of individual children, especially if the child has special educational needs or disabilities. Even babies 'tell' us things and can be involved in what we plan for them if we observe what interests them.

As we have already seen, if we become skilled observers we can identify what interests babies, toddlers on the cusp of language or children with special needs and disabilities. In this way every child can participate and can influence what we are planning. This is an important part of the government's 'Every Child Matters' agenda.

The award-winning 'Listening to Children' project developed by Penny Lancaster is helpful.

Long-term planning

This focuses on what is known about the general development and learning needs of most children between birth and 5 years of age, and makes general provision for these in what is planned indoors and outdoors. As we have seen throughout this chapter, what a baby of 1 year old is interested in or needs is different from that of a child aged 3, 4 or 5 years. However, we have also seen that children are very diverse, and there are huge differences between what each child does at a particular age. The long-term plan gives a general sense of direction and makes everyone aware of the principles, values and philosophy that support the curriculum (see page 106). The long-term plan may also take a particular emphasis for a time (perhaps for several months), such as the way children and adults communicate non-verbally and use spoken language/sign; how to get the most from the outdoor environment; the settling in of children; creativity; or play.

Medium-term planning

This is the way in which the principles and general framework set by the long-term planning are applied.

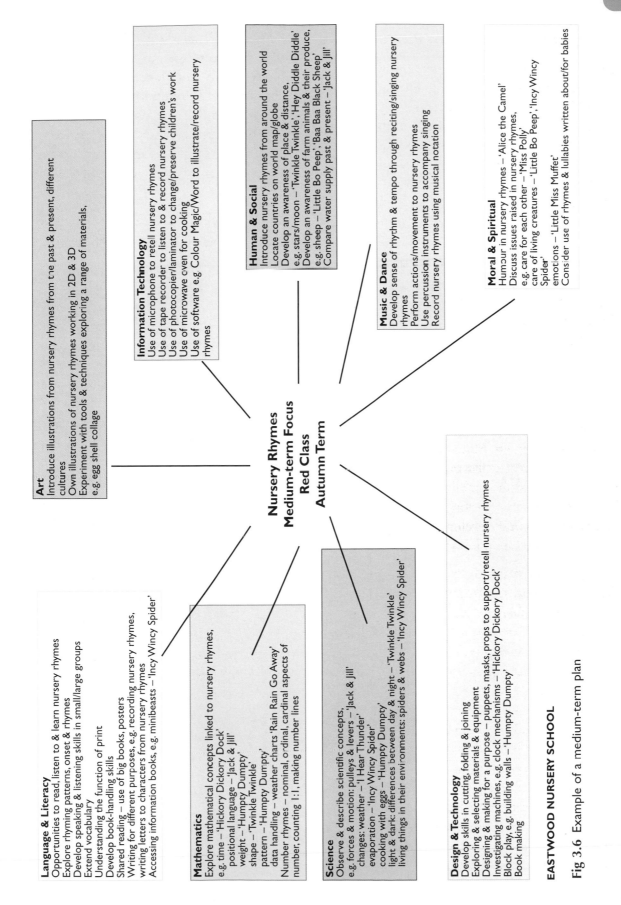

Art
Introduce illustrations from nursery rhymes from the past & present, different cultures
Own illustrations of nursery rhymes working in 2D & 3D
Experiment with tools & techniques exploring a range of materials, e.g. egg shell collage

Information Technology
Use of microphone to retell nursery rhymes
Use of tape recorder to listen to & record nursery rhymes
Use of photocopier/laminator to change/preserve children's work
Use of microwave oven for cooking
Use of software e.g Colour Magic/Word to illustrate/record nursery rhymes

Human & Social
Introduce nursery rhymes from around the world
Locate countries on world map/globe
Develop an awareness of place & distance, e.g. stars/moon – 'Twinkle Twinkle'; 'Hey Diddle Diddle'
Develop an awareness of farm animals & their produce, e.g. sheep – 'Little Bo Peep', 'Baa Baa Black Sheep'
Compare water supply past & present – 'Jack & Jill'

Music & Dance
Develop sense of rhythm & tempo through reciting/singing nursery rhymes
Perform actions/movement to nursery rhymes
Use percussion instruments to accompany singing
Record nursery rhymes using musical notation

Moral & Spiritual
Humour in nursery rhymes – 'Alice the Camel'
Discuss issues raised in nursery rhymes, e.g. care for each other – 'Miss Polly'
care of living creatures – 'Little Bo Peep', 'Incy Wincy Spider'
emotions – 'Little Miss Muffet'
Consider use of rhymes & lullabies written about/for babies

**Nursery Rhymes
Medium-term Focus
Red Class
Autumn Term**

Language & Literacy
Opportunities to read, listen to & learn nursery rhymes
Explore rhyming patterns, onset & rhymes
Develop speaking & listening skills in small/large groups
Extend vocabulary
Understanding the function of print
Develop book-handling skills
Shared reading – use of big books, posters
Writing for different purposes, e.g. recording nursery rhymes, writing letters to characters from nursery rhymes
Accessing information books, e.g. minibeasts – 'Incy Wincy Spider'

Mathematics
Explore mathematical concepts linked to nursery rhymes, e.g. time – 'Hickory Dickory Dock'
positional language – 'Jack & Jill'
weight – 'Humpty Dumpty'
shape – 'Twinkle Twinkle'
pattern – 'Humpty Dumpty'
data handling – weather charts 'Rain Rain Go Away'
Number rhymes – nominal, ordinal, cardinal aspects of number, counting 1:1, making number lines

Science
Observe & describe scientific concepts,
e.g. forces & motion: pulleys & levers – 'Jack & Jill'
changes: weather – 'I Hear Thunder'
evaporation – 'Incy Wincy Spider'
cooking with eggs – 'Humpty Dumpty'
light & dark: difference between day & night – 'Twinkle Twinkle'
living things in their environments: spiders & webs – 'Incy Wincy Spider'

Design & Technology
Develop skills in cutting, folding & joining
Exploring & selecting materials & equipment
Designing & making for a purpose – puppets, masks, props to support/retell nursery rhymes
Investigating machines, e.g. clock mechanisms – 'Hickory Dickory Dock'
Block play, e.g. building walls – 'Humpty Dumpty'
Book making

EASTWOOD NURSERY SCHOOL

Fig 3.6 Example of a medium-term plan

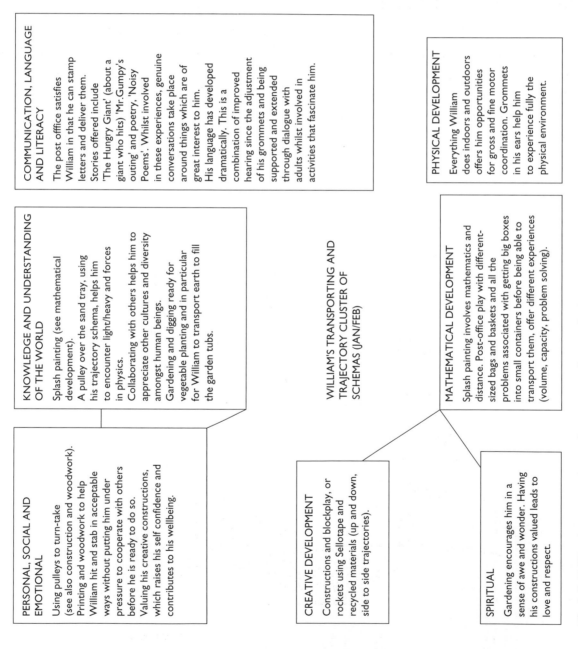

PERSONAL, SOCIAL AND EMOTIONAL

Using pulleys to turn-take (see also construction and woodwork). Printing and woodwork to help William hit and stab in acceptable ways without putting him under pressure to cooperate with others before he is ready to do so. Valuing his creative constructions, which raises his self confidence and contributes to his wellbeing.

KNOWLEDGE AND UNDERSTANDING OF THE WORLD

Splash painting (see mathematical development).
A pulley over the sand tray, using his trajectory schema, helps him to encounter light/heavy and forces in physics.
Collaborating with others helps him to appreciate other cultures and diversity amongst human beings.
Gardening and digging ready for vegetable planting and in particular for William to transport earth to fill the garden tubs.

COMMUNICATION, LANGUAGE AND LITERACY

The post offfice satisfies William in that he can stamp letters and deliver them. Stories offered include 'The Hungry Giant' (about a giant who hits) 'Mr. Gumpy's outing' and poetry, 'Noisy Poems'. Whilst involved in these experiences, genuine conversations take place around things which are of great interest to him.
His language has developed dramatically. This is a combination of improved hearing since the adjustment of his grommets and being supported and extended through dialogue with adults whilst involved in activities that fascinate him.

CREATIVE DEVELOPMENT

Constructions and blockplay, or rockets using Sellotape and recycled materials (up and down, side to side trajectories).

SPIRITUAL

Gardening encourages him in a sense of awe and wonder. Having his constructions valued leads to love and respect.

WILLIAM'S TRANSPORTING AND TRAJECTORY CLUSTER OF SCHEMAS (JAN/FEB)

MATHEMATICAL DEVELOPMENT

Splash painting involves mathematics and distance. Post-office play with different-sized bags and baskets and all the problems associated with getting big boxes into small containers before being able to transport them, offer different experiences (volume, capacity, problem solving).

PHYSICAL DEVELOPMENT

Everything William does indoors and outdoors offers him opportunities for gross and fine motor coordination. Grommets in his ears help him to experience fully the physical environment.

Fig 3.7 William's transporting and trajectory cluster of schemas

The medium-term planning will need to be **adjusted constantly** because it will be influenced by the observations made of individual children. This is why, for children from birth to 3 years, it needs to include reviews of care routines, key worker relationships and the way the day is organised to offer play and experiences, including the materials and physical resources.

The 'Listening to Children' initiative is helping us to involve children more in what we plan for them. In a broad way, It will plan for experiences and activities staff will offer across several weeks. *Birth to Three Matters* is helping staff to plan in this way in England.

New training materials are supporting Scottish practitioners developing the Framework. For children aged 3–5 years it will show planning across key aspects of development and learning in the curriculum documents across the UK.

Short-term planning

This is usually based on observation sheets of individual children's interests and needs. These observations inform the medium-term planning; it is constantly modified so that it is relevant and useful for each child's learning.

Using the observations, practitioners and parents can make assessments for learning

Example of a medium-term plan
Developed from observations of children into a water theme.
(about 3/4 weeks duration usually, depending on the interest in it from the children).

In a medium-term plan, the focus is on creating a learning enviroment:
• which is well-resourced and well-organised
• where adults are clear about how they will work on specific areas at particular times, and make a bridge between long-term plans for the group as a whole, and short-term immediate action plans for particular children.

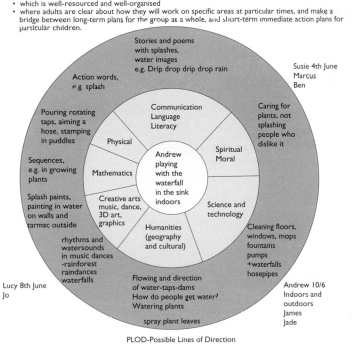

PLOD-Possible Lines of Direction

DAVIDGRAHAM

Fig 3.8 Example of a medium-term plan, in which personal, social and emotional learning occurs throughout

and plan what the child needs next. This will not necessarily mean giving the child something new. More often than not it means deepening what the child has found interesting. For example, planning may arise out of several observations of a baby crawling to grab spherical objects, such as a soft ball or a wooden ball. Rather than deciding that now the baby has experienced spheres, the next shape is a cube, and providing cubes, a more appropriate plan would be to deepen the opportunities for sphere play by providing a range of spheres and placing them everywhere within crawling possibilities for the baby to find and enjoy, and to introduce spherical fruit and vegetables (e.g. apples, oranges and tomatoes) and cut them up for snacks, at the same time talking/signing so that children are offered the names and descriptions and what they are for (function).

Planning to extend learning is often of the deepening kind, rather than introducing new things all the time.

The same is true with children aged 3–5 years. The child might still be exploring spheres! Finding a dandelion clock and comparing its shape with a clover flower found in the garden is exciting, and can lead to a deepening understanding of flowers and why the petals are on the flower in a particular shape, or an exploration of seed dispersal. This sort of deepening of understanding more often than not involves the practitioners in deepening their knowledge too. Just enjoying the plants in the garden and talking about them while doing so would be a good plan. The medium-term plan could be adjusted to include a pretend flower shop, which might support and extend the interests and needs of other children.

One type of plan which is widely used as a medium-term plan, or as a plan for an individual child, is called a PLOD (possible line of direction). This was first conceptualised with staff at Redford House Workplace Nursery at Froebel College in Roehampton, and later developed with staff at Pen Green Children's Centre.

Guidelines for medium-term planning

❖ You will be observing children, getting to know them and their characters. You need to match your observations to your medium-term plans.

❖ The staff, planning together, should look at how they can create a rich learning environment which links the long-term plans to each child as an individual. The medium-term plan must grow gradually and must be flexible, open to changes and moderations.

❖ You will need to look at the observation profiles of all the children.

❖ Many early years settings now target particular children on particular days. This means each child is observed regularly, and the curriculum is planned in a **differentiated** way to cater for the interests and needs of individual children.

Case Study

Observation and planning

In one setting, observations of the target child over a week showed that the waterfall was greatly used. The waterfall consisted of three beakers of graded sizes. When the tap was turned on, a waterfall was created, which led to much glee and discussion. The nursery school's development plan identified science as a major area, with money set aside to buy more equipment. The staff planned to support and extend the learning by introducing cascades of water in many different ways. They developed a project (or medium-term plan) on water, to last for as long as the interest continued.

Guidelines for short-term planning

❖ A short-term plan focuses on target children for one week. In this way each child is observed regularly.

❖ Short-term planning is more specific, but should not be rigid.

❖ Staff will use weekly and daily planning sessions to build particular learning intentions for particular children.

❖ Some activities will be planned to provide opportunities for children to explore and experiment (indirect teaching). Some will be adult-led (direct teaching).

❖ The staff will prepare by deciding what resources are needed, at what time in the day and who will be there at particular points.

Case Study

Andrew

A nursery nurse has observed Andrew (3 years), who spends 20 minutes with the waterfall beakers. He lines them up next to the tap so that the water falls exactly as he wants. He has a bowl of corks under the waterfall. He aims the water at them one by one to make them bob about.

The nursery nurse feeds back this observation of Andrew, who is the target child that day, to a group of staff. They decide to put the waterfall out again. In addition they will provide a bigger version in the outside area, using buckets and old water trays. They plan who will be in which areas and they hope Andrew will learn:

❖ that water flows;

❖ that it splashes;

❖ that it cascades in the outdoor waterfall more than the indoor waterfall;

❖ that it flows downwards if it can;

❖ that it makes a trajectory (which is a moving line);

❖ that it has force to move things in its way.

To extend Andrew's interest, they plan a visit to the local shopping mall where there is a fountain. They also link the short-term plans made for Andrew with the medium-term plan described above.

123

Guidelines for evaluating plans

❖ A medium-term plan can be used to check the balance of the long-term plan. Is science being developed so that it reaches every child? Not all children will learn exactly the same science, but they should all have appropriate opportunities.

❖ How does science link with the official documents? What science are children supposed to have learned about at this stage in their education?

❖ Are the medium-term planning resources working well for this group of children in their learning? Most experts agree that if there are good plans for individual children, the whole group tends to benefit.

❖ Are the adults using observation of children to inform their planning?

❖ Are the adults giving support to individual children's learning as well as to the group?

❖ Are adults able to extend the learning to add knowledge that children did not previously have (e.g. Andrew might be interested in water pumps)?

❖ Are children learning about areas other than science? Is there a good balance in this curriculum?

Quality learning takes place when you are able to match what is offered in the curriculum to the interests and needs of individual children. Good teaching means helping children to learn, so that they make connections with what they already know, and at times are helped to extend this.

PLANNING A QUALITY CURRICULUM

Although it can seem a daunting task to provide a quality learing environment for children from birth to the age of 8 years, remember that the things which matter most are:

❖ your relationship with the children, their families and the other staff;

❖ the provision that you offer;

❖ the conversations that you have with children as they experience the materials – the learning context is crucial.

Bear these factors in mind when you plan – quality is more likely to result. If you can help children to enjoy learning, you will have given them a good start, which they will take with them through their lives. The shaded area in Figure 3.9 shows the importance of operating the curriculum in such a way that both the teacher and the child contribute actively as much as possible.

Staying anchored and available to children at their height or at floor level

It is very difficult for children when adults flit about and do not stay in one place for long enough for children to engage with them in focused ways. It does not encourage children to focus either.

It is a good idea, as part of planning the curriculum framework in the learning environments, indoors and outdoors, to see where there might need to be anchored adults working in depth with children. The following points are important:

* The anchored adult needs to sit at the child's height or on the floor so as to give full attention to a child or children in one area while retaining an overview of the rest of the room.

* The practitioner must be free to focus on what the children in a particular area are doing (e.g. playing with wooden blocks or in the movement corner) and be able to have engaging conversations, listening to what children say and being sensitive to what they do, allowing them plenty of time (e.g. cooking together or planting bulbs in the garden).

* Another adult must be free to help children generally, for example to deal with children's toilet needs, to hang up a painting or comfort a tearful child, or simply respond to children who ask for help.

* If each adult has a clear understanding of their role in the team, it helps each practitioner to focus on children and reduces the temptation to chat with other adults instead of engaging with the children.

It is always useful to move around the environment on your knees in order to see it from a child's-eye view (or crawl to gain a toddler or mobile baby's view). Lying on

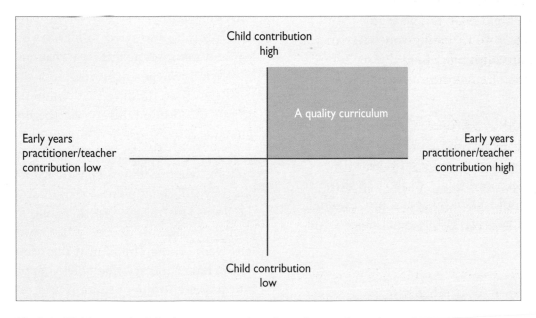

Fig 3.9 Children and adults learning together through interdependent relationships

your back helps to understand a baby's view from a cot. In other words, what would a child see as they move about the learning environment?

LEARNING IN THE FIRST YEAR

Before sitting

It can be very boring to be a baby. This is because babies depend on adults to bring interesting experiences to them, because they cannot move about enough to reach for things when sitting, or crawl or walk to get them.

Bored, unhappy babies cannot learn much, and the important period of babyhood, when so much learning is possible, will then be lost. Studies of child development suggest that the first years of life are of great importance for development and learning, and also that this is the time when the dispositions for future learning are set.

Imagine what it would be like if you spent long periods on your back with only a ceiling to look at, or you were in a pram with a plastic cover hiding your view, or you could hear voices, but could not see who was talking because they were standing behind you.

Babies need to be cuddled, held on your knee so that they can see things, talked to and sung to, and bounced in time with music. They need things to look at, swipe at, grab and hold, chew, suck and mouth, smell, shake and listen to. Babies need objects and people.

Quiet times

Sometimes they need to be quiet, but they still need to feel that people are near. They need times when perhaps they are given the personal space to look at a mobile, with gentle music playing, or to hear the birds singing as they lie in a pram under a tree, looking through the branches at the patterns of the leaves against the sky. Of course, it is important that the sun is not in their eyes, and that they are comfortable in temperature and with a clean nappy.

Babies often love to sit propped in a specially designed chair and watch what is going on. They seem to be especially tuned in to watching other children, and to following with their gaze people whose voices they know because they spend time with them and love them. But this should never be a substitute for cuddles.

Anyone who observes babies finds that they are exploring the environment using their senses and movement. They need plenty of opportunities to be on the floor so that they can do this. When lying on their backs, they can watch mobiles or leaves and branches swaying and fluttering in the trees above their pram, and swipe at objects above them with their arms, or kick at them with their legs. But they also need to feel their arms, legs and tummies against the ground. Experts in physical movement development (like JABADAO) are finding that children often do not spend enough time on the floor. They need to be given opportunities to crawl as well as to sit and lie down. It is exciting when children take their first steps, but they still need plenty of time down on the floor. This means that there should be plenty of spaces to do this when working with very young children in their first year of life. Babies need to be able to explore the learning environment indoors and outdoors, using all their senses and moving their whole bodies.

Babies need time to be on the floor, on their tummies, with interesting natural objects (not plastic all the time) placed in front of them, which they need to reach for. Adults can be very encouraging and help babies to have things in reach, and at the point where the baby is trying to crawl, keeping frustration at bay by making sure there is enough success to keep them trying. It is very difficult for a baby when they are trying to crawl forwards to get something they want, and they find they are moving backwards. Having something to push against can be just the right help at the right time!

Are there objects a baby can put in its mouth, touch and handle, smell, carry about, look at and make sounds with? They will learn more if everything is not made of plastic. The floors will need to be clean, as they will stop to examine every piece of fluff, dropped crumb or spillage. When they crawl outside they will need surfaces such as grass, rather than rough surfaces or gravel, for example, which will hurt their knees or are dangerous to put in their mouth.

Sitting babies

Elinor Goldschmied (one of Europe's acknowledged experts on the management of quality learning experiences for children from birth to three years) has pioneered treasure baskets for sitting babies. These are now widely used in most settings. It is very important that they are presented to babies in the correct way or the baby will not get the full benefit of the learning the treasure basket offers. Make sure the basket is the correct shape, height and size. It is distressing for the baby if it tips as they lean on it, or if they are unable to reach the objects on the other side. It is uncomfortable to sit at a

basket that is too high (like an adult sitting at a table when the chair is too low for the table height).

The baby needs the companionship of an adult who sits near them (usually on a chair that is near to the ground in height), but who does not join in, is simply there as an anchor, smiling when shown objects, but saying nothing. When adults are concentrating (perhaps writing and thinking hard) it would interrupt the flow of thought and the deep focusing to have someone make suggestions or ask questions and try to make conversation with them. Ideally, the treasure basket experience will take place away from the hurly-burly of the main area, perhaps screened-off with a clothes horses draped with material, to signal to other, older, more mobile children that this is a quiet area, set aside for sitting babies to concentrate and learn.

The objects should not be made of plastic, but of natural materials or metals which can be washed and kept clean. This is because plastic does not offer much to the range of senses through which babies learn. As objects become shabby they should be removed, and there should be new objects to keep the interest of the baby who has regular use of the basket. As your observations of a baby build, you will be able to select objects with that baby's interests in mind. The baby who loves to bang and bash objects will choose different ones to the baby who loves to dangle and shake objects. It is deeply satisfying to try to work out what a baby will particularly enjoy exploring, especially when you have analysed your observations accurately.

Babies need sufficient objects to be able to select from, so the basket should be full enough to encourage this. Examples would be: a small wooden brush, a small cardboard box, a loofah, a wooden spoon, a small metal egg whisk, a bath plug and chain, a small bag of lavender, a large feather.

Of course, you will need to make a risk assessment based on your observations of what a baby needs. Never put an object in the treasure basket which makes you anxious about its safety for a baby, and remember that some babies have allergies. Remember also that some babies are less adventurous than others and will need more support and encouragement to enjoy the treasure basket.

Crawlers and toddlers – heuristic play

Becoming mobile changes the life of a baby. Crawling babies love to follow people and to find out about objects wherever they travel. They need stable furniture so that they can pull themselves up and cruise in between.

This is a good time to offer crawling babies and toddlers heuristic play experiences, which were first developed by Elinor Goldschmied. The term 'heuristic' comes from the Greek 'to discover'.

Children need to be comfortable. Rather than a cold, draughty floor, they need a warm, inviting floor place, without lots of clutter which diverts their attention. The space needs to be prepared in advance so that children come upon the carefully spaced piles of objects when they enter the area. All the objects are collected from everyday use, rather than toys.

One pile might include spheres, circular objects and cylinders, such as a cotton reel, a bobble from a hat, a bracelet. Another might be of metal objects, such as tins with smoothed edges, or a metal tea caddy. The

adult sits quietly and provides a calm and concentrating atmosphere that supports the child's explorations without intervening, except to say something like, 'Yes, you have a lovely tin' – but only if the child brings it to them. Otherwise a warm smile is sufficient and the child returns to their explorations.

The session varies in length, but careful observation will signal to the adult when to draw things to a close. Often children stay concentrating for half an hour. A further 10 minutes or so should be taken to clear up with the children, who are encouraged to put the collections into the right type of bag. This is then hung on the wall, with the children watching. As long as children's efforts are valued, they enjoy helping. They do not respond well when nagged or criticised for putting an object in the wrong bag. They need encouragement and positive, sensitive support.

Sleep is important for learning

Getting the right rest is crucial for the learning of babies and young children. Not all babies will need to sleep at the same time, and it is very worrying to find practices where all babies are expected to have their nappies changed at the same time and to sleep at the same time. These are very individual things.

It is important for babies to feel that they are near someone when they sleep. Some babies sleep best on a mat, with a cover to keep them warm, on the floor of a quiet area that is gated. Others sleep better in a darkened room in a cot kept for them. This area should not be too full of stimulation. It is important to relax and let go when falling asleep. Neutral colouring is best, and the room should not be cluttered.

It is also important to keep to the sleep-time rituals that are familiar to the baby at home. Some babies need to have a cuddle, being lowered into their cot as they fall asleep. Others might never go to sleep on a lap, but need to be in a cot, in a quiet room, with their teddy, in order to fall asleep.

Sleep is important for learning. It helps the memory to embed rich learning experiences with people, objects, events and places.

Eating together

The advantage of family groups in early childhood settings is that babies can easily be part of mealtimes. When a whole row of babies all need feeding together, there are often tears and staff become anxious and frustrated because it seems impossible to get each baby fed quickly enough. Meals become times of stress instead of times of deep pleasure.

Babies learn more if they are given finger foods as soon as this is appropriate. A carrot stick is a wonderful learning experience, and makes a good contrast with a metal teaspoon. Observing a baby's learning at mealtimes is fascinating. For example, does the baby pass the spoon from one hand to the other? Is the spoon held with a palmar grip, and does the baby try to pick up the carrot stick with a pincer grip?

It is important to have tables at an appropriate height. Children like to stand or work on the floor. Children need to be free to move, and often they do not want to sit on chairs (although they should be provided). It is important to offer experiences and activities so that children have choice about this.

Children usually like to feel that an adult is nearby. It makes them feel safe and secure, especially when they are trying something new and unfamiliar. The first time glue is used or paint is mixed are good examples of this. It is important not to crowd, overwhelm or invade a child's thinking space, but it is vital to support a child's learning by being there for them, smiling and looking interested, and commenting on what they do from time to time; for example, 'You like red best, I think, because I've noticed that you have used it three times in your painting so far.'

We must never underestimate the importance of early friendships. Children miss their friends when they are away or ill, and find it more difficult to get involved. A supportive adult is important at these times, offering companionship as the child chooses activities and experiences.

LAYOUT OF INDOOR AND OUTDOOR LEARNING ENVIRONMENTS

In an inclusive early childhood setting, which embraces diversity, the layout and presentation of material provision offer a range of experiences and activities across the birth-to-5-years Framework. Increasingly, from the time they can walk, children are integrating with children in the foundation years for parts of the day, which gives a more natural and family-group feeling. Children with special educational needs and disabilities are also included in settings. All of this means that the traditions of wide provision are of central importance.

Indoor learning environment

Given that children from birth to 6 years **learn through the senses**, the layout needs to support and extend this kind of learning. The layouts from Reggio Emilia and Pistoia in Northern Italy have reminded practitioners in the UK of the importance of:

❖ an attractive and welcoming entrance area, where children and families are greeted and can find and share information, and feel part of a community;

❖ natural light;

❖ the feeling of space without clutter;

❖ making spaces beautiful using natural materials.

The environment also needs to support and actively encourage and extend **the symbolic life of the child**, making one thing stand for another (e.g. pretending a leaf is a plate in the outside playhouse). Understanding **cause-and-effect relationships** is also very important and the learning environment needs to promote this (e.g. kicking the ball hard makes it go a long distance, while tapping it with your toes makes it roll only a little way).

The following should be provided every day:

❖ wet sand and dry sand (these are two entirely different learning experiences),with equipment nearby in boxes labelled with words and pictures for children to select;

❖ clean water in a water tray or baby bath, with buckets, guttering, waterwheels, and so on, to make waterfalls, and boxes of equipment labelled with pictures and words;

❖ found and recycled materials in a workshop area, with glue, scissors, masking tape, and so on;

❖ small world – doll's house, train set, garage, cars, farms, zoos, dinosaurs;

❖ paint/graphics materials in a mark-making area, with a variety of paper and different kinds of pencils and pens and chalks (this might be next to the workshop area);

❖ malleable clay or dough;

❖ wooden set of free-standing blocks (not plastic, and not bits and pieces from different sets) – unit blocks, hollow blocks and mini hollow blocks (e.g. Community Playthings);

❖ construction kit (one or two carefully selected types, such as Duplo or Brio);

❖ book area, which is warm, light and cosy;

❖ domestic play area;

❖ dressing-up clothes;

❖ daily cookery with baking materials and equipment;

❖ ICT, digital camera, computer – it is preferable to use computer programmes which encourage children to use their imaginations, rather than responding to computer-led tasks;

❖ nature table, with magnifiers, growing and living things, such as mustard and cress, hyacinths, wormery, fish tank;

❖ interest table with fascinating objects to handle;

❖ sewing table;

❖ woodwork bench;

❖ a range of dolls and soft toys;

❖ music and sounds area with home-made and commercially produced instruments;

❖ story props, poetry and song cards.

Fig 3.10 Adults need to provide small-world props to encourage children to create their own stories and characters

Outdoor learning environment

Children should be able to learn outside for most of the day if they choose to do so. They need appropriate clothes, and so do adults, so that everyone can be outside in all weathers. The idea that learning can only take place indoors is extraordinary when we stop to think about it.

There should be different surfaces – playground surfaces, grass and an earth patch to dig in, a large, drained sandpit, and planted areas with trees as well as wild areas for butterflies. Settings which do not value the importance of the outdoor learning environment are only offering children half a curriculum.

Children need challenging places to climb and swing, and to be taught how to stay safe and be responsible. Children are biologically driven to make risk assessments, but only if this is encouraged. They need places to run, jump, skip and wheel.

Bikes need to be three-wheeled and two-wheeled, with some needing two or three children cooperating in order to make them work. Scooters and carts to push and pull are also important, as are prams and pushchairs.

Hoses for warmer weather, and a water pump, give children opportunities for learning in many ways, from not splashing others to the science of pumping and spraying. Gardening equipment is needed for the planting areas. Buckets, spades, sieves, and so on, are needed in the sand area.

The outdoor learning environment should echo and mirror the indoor area, but each will offer different experiences. Indoors children will use felt-tip pens and pencils, while outdoors they might chalk on the ground and make marks on a larger scale. Indoors they might use paint and brushes on paper, but outdoors they may have buckets of water and large brushes, and paint on walls and the ground.

Indoors there will be a home-corner, and outdoors they will make dens, play in tents and may wear dressing-up clothes indoors or outdoors.

It is very important that great care is taken of equipment in both environments, so that jigsaw pieces do not end up on a flowerbed, for example. Sets (puzzles, crockery from the home corner, sets of zoo animals, wooden blocks) should not be moved from the area where they belong. If children have made a den and want to have a pretend meal in it, then a picnic box can be taken into the garden, full of bits and bobs. This means that children learn to care for equipment.

Double provision

Through double provision the different needs and interests of children from birth to 5 years can be attended to with quality. There might be a workshop area, with carefully selected and presented found materials, such as boxes, tubes, dried flowers, moss, twigs, wool, string, masking tape and glue, scissors and card. Here children could become involved in making models and constructions, and adults can help them to carry out their ideas without losing track of them on the way or becoming frustrated. Children can be helped as they try to join things, and make decisions about whether a string knot would be better than masking tape or glue.

Nearby, on the floor, there might be a beautiful basket full of balls of wool and string, which younger and less experienced children can enjoy unravelling and finding out how these behave. Other children might like to return to this earlier way of using string too.

It is a good idea to try to offer everything at different levels of difficulty, so that there is something for everyone to find absorbing. Absorbed children behave better, on the whole.

Attractive presentation of the learning environment indoors and outdoors

If an area is dirty, shabby and in a muddle, it is less attractive to children. Often a well-used area becomes cluttered and untidy halfway through a morning or afternoon, and the children leave it. It is important that adults do not neglect these abandoned areas. Children can be encouraged to help tidy it, but adults can role-model this mid-session if children are very involved in other areas. At the end of the session everyone needs to tidy up, though, unless there are good reasons for a child not to, such as being upset or unsettled. Children should never be nagged or made to feel bad, but they should be encouraged and given specific but appropriate tasks as members of the learning community. Even a toddler enjoys putting rubbish in the bin. It is a question of finding something suitable for each particular child. The important thing is not to overdo the requests for help in tidying, and to remember that it is discriminatory to expect only a few children to do all the tidying. (Look again at the section on tidying away at the end of the heuristic play session earlier in this chapter, page 128.)

Important play provision for babies, crawlers, toddlers and children at least up to 5 years is on the floor! Making a movement corner is as important as making a book corner for brain development, learning and wellbeing. The floor needs to be clean and carpets should not be scratchy.

Having an interested person, sensitively supporting and mirroring is also important. Mirroring is another vital pattern for late learning, as research by Colwyn Trevarthen at Edinburgh University shows. Adults who make good play companions are a valuable resource as part of the play provision. The rough-and-tumble play traditional in mammals, including human children, just before sleeping, is often engaged in with adults in the family.

Displays and interest tables

Issues of gender, culture and disability need to be thought through when it comes to setting up displays. Positive images and multicultural artefacts need to be discussed and planned by staff as a team.

❖ Displays should respect children's work – do not cut up children's paintings to make an adult's collage. The paintings children do should be mounted and displayed as they are. How would Van Gogh have felt if the famous painting he did of a chair had been cut out and made into a collage of Goldilocks and the Three Bears?

❖ Adults should not draw or write on children's work without their permission. After all, adults do not allow children to draw or write on their records without permission.

❖ Any writing or notes about a painting should be mounted separately underneath the child's painting or drawing. The label should be discussed with the child, who should agree to the wording.

❖ Any lettering should be done carefully on ruled lines so that it looks attractive. Your writing must project a good role model for children.

❖ Writing should not be at 'jaunty angles' on a display, as children are developing their understanding of which direction the print goes when reading. The direction is different in English, Chinese and Urdu. It is best not to display print at angles as this is confusing. Imagine going to a station and trying to read the words on the display of arrivals and departures if they were all at jaunty angles! It would be very confusing.

Wall displays, such as photographs, for crawling babies should be at their eye height along the floor against the wall. Wall displays for older children should also be at their eye height, and not above. Remember not to clutter the walls. Leave some walls blank, and perhaps only put a display on one wall.

Fig 3.11a A display about autumn

Fig 3.11b A display about wood

Having too much on the walls is too exciting and colourful, and children become calmer when the walls are calmer, in natural shades.

In the photographs, you can see examples of interactive displays. Some of these are

A child's questions:

BELONGING: DO YOU KNOW ME?

How do you appreciate and understand my interests and abilities and those of my family?

WELLBEING: CAN I TRUST YOU?

How do you meet my daily needs with care and consideration?

EXPLORATION: DO YOU LET ME FLY?

How do you engage my mind, offer challenges and extend my world?

COMMUNICATION: DO YOU HEAR ME?

How do you invite me to listen and communicate, and respond to my own particular efforts?

CONTRIBUTION: IS THIS THE PLACE FOR US?

How do you encourage and facilitate my endeavours to be part of the group?

Margaret Carr, Teaching Stories

4

Caring for young children – the essential foundations

Contents

Section 1: Promoting a positive, integrated, early childhood environment

● What is a positive, integrated, early childhood environment? ● Hygiene and health ● Safety and security ● Feeling valued ● Providing for children's developmental needs, indoors and ● outdoors ● A sense of belonging ● A comfortable child and a family-friendly environment ● Providing for children's special needs ● Displaying children's work ● Encouraging children to relate to the world around them ● Professional practice in the support of a positive, integrated environment

Section 2: Physical care of children (1–7 years and 11 months)

● Basic physical and health needs of children ● Basic care of children (1–7 years and 11 months) ● The need for rest and sleep ● Signs and symptoms of potential concern ● Clothing for children ● The development of bowel and bladder control

Section 3: Health and safety requirements

● Regulations for early years settings ● Food-handling regulations ● Hygiene routines ● Safe and hygienic practice when caring for animals ● Identifying and reporting hazards ● Adults as positive role models ● Safe management of daily routines ● Safe management of trips and outings

Section 4: Diet, nutrition and food

● The principles of a healthy diet ● Promoting healthy eating ● Multicultural provision and dietary implications ● Vegetarian diets ● Nutritional disorders in children ● Common food allergies ● The effects of illness on a child's appetite ● Economic and social factors affecting diet and nutrition ● Food presentation and children's preferences ● The social and educational role of food and mealtimes ● Special (or therapeutic) diets

Section 1: Promoting a positive, integrated, early childhood environment

WHAT IS A POSITIVE, INTEGRATED, EARLY CHILDHOOD ENVIRONMENT?

The environment in which children grow and develop has a profound influence on all aspects of their lives, including their physical, cultural, emotional, social and spiritual development. In addition, the surroundings in which we all live have an effect on our lifestyle and behaviour.

Difficult environments

In recent years the UK's inner cities have become less pleasant places to live because of the increase in:

* **air pollution** – from car exhausts and industrial effluents, for example;

* **poverty** and **unemployment;**

* **poor living conditions**, often with no access to outdoor play space;

* **social isolation** – there are increasing numbers of one-parent families who have no access to an extended family network;

* **discrimination** on the basis of ethnicity or disability – this is often reinforced by planning decisions, for example lack of access or mobility for people with physical disabilities.

The rural environment also poses problems for families where there is high unemployment or subsistence on low incomes; public transport may be limited and housing may be difficult to obtain.

There is far more to creating a positive environment for children than just meeting their basic needs. Children and families need an integrated environment – that is, one that provides:

* **safety and hygiene** – children and their families need to feel and to be safe;

* **adequate housing**;

* **education and stimulation**;

* **freedom from discrimination**;

* **a caring ethos** – everyone who works with young children should have a caring attitude;

* **access to health and social care services**;

* **equality of opportunity**;

* **a nourishing diet**;

* **opportunities for play** – with peers, indoors and outdoors in gardens.

If any of these needs are not met, the family (and the children) will experience stress.

The integrated early childhood setting must meet all the needs of the child. We will consider these needs under the following headings:

* Hygiene and health;
* Food hygiene;
* Safety and security;
* Feeling valued;
* Providing for children's developmental needs, indoors and outdoors;
* A sense of belonging;
* A comfortable child and a family-friendly environment.

HYGIENE AND HEALTH

Providing a healthy and hygienic environment for children is vital to their development. A balance also has to be struck between a child being allowed to get dirty when playing, but understanding that they will need to wash afterwards. Developing good hygiene routines is important because:

❖ **It helps to prevent infection and the spread of disease.** Children who play closely together for long periods of time are more likely than others to develop an infection – and any infection can spread very quickly from one child to another.

❖ **Being clean increases self-esteem and social acceptance.** Nobody likes to be close to someone who appears dirty or whose clothes smell.

❖ **It helps to prepare children in skills of independence and self-caring.** All children benefit from regular routines in daily care. Obviously parents and carers have their own routines and hygiene practices and these should always be respected. For example, Muslims prefer to wash under running water and Rastafarians wear their hair braided so may not use a comb or brush.

Being a good role model

You need to set a good example by always taking care with your appearance and your

---

Guidelines for personal hygiene: being a good role model

Personal hygiene involves regular and thorough cleaning of your skin, hair, teeth and clothes. The following are particularly important:

❖ The most important defence against the spread of infection is **hand washing**; wash your hands frequently – especially before eating, and before and after touching your mouth or nose. You should not use the kitchen sink to wash your hands.

❖ Parents and carers must wash their hands after they blow the nose or wipe the mouth of a sick child.

❖ Use paper towels to dry your hands if possible; if cloth towels are used, make sure they are washed daily in hot water.

❖ Keep your nails clean and short as long fingernails harbour dirt. Do not wear nail varnish because flakes of varnish *could* chip off into a snack you are preparing.

❖ Avoid jewellery other than a simple wedding ring and a watch.

❖ Avoid contact with the secretions (especially on stray facial tissues) of somebody with a runny nose, sore throat or cough.

❖ Cover any cuts or sores on the hands with a clean, waterproof plaster. Use a new plaster each day.

❖ Do not share utensils or cups with somebody who has a cold, sore throat or upper respiratory tract infection.

❖ Wear disposable gloves when changing nappies or when dealing with blood, urine, faeces or vomit.

❖ Hair should be kept clean, be brushed regularly and be tied back, if long.

own personal hygiene. Often your early years setting will provide you with a uniform – usually sweatshirt and trousers – but if this is not the case, choose your clothing carefully, bearing in mind the sort of activity you are likely to be involved in.

Guidelines for providing a safe and hygienic indoor environment

❖ Adequate **ventilation** is important to disperse bacteria or viruses transmitted through sneezing or coughing. Make sure that windows are opened to let in fresh air to the nursery – but also make sure there are no draughts.

❖ **Cleaning routines:**

1 All surfaces should be damp-dusted daily. Floors, surfaces and the toilet area must be checked on a regular basis for cleanliness.

2 All toys and play equipment should be cleaned regularly – *at least* once a week. This includes dressing-up clothes and soft toys. Use antiseptic solutions such as Savlon to disinfect toys and play equipment regularly; toys used by babies under 1 year should be disinfected daily.

3 Check that sandpits or trays are clean and that toys are removed and cleaned at the end of a play session; if the sandpit is kept outside make sure it is kept covered when not in use. Keep sand trays clean by sieving and washing the sand regularly.

4 Water trays should be emptied daily as germs can multiply quickly in pools of water.

5 The home area often contains dolls, saucepans and plastic food; these need to be included in the checking and regular washing procedures.

6 Apart from routine cleaning, you should always clean up any spills straightaway; both young children and adults often slip on wet surfaces.

❖ Use paper towels and tissues, and dispose of them in covered bins.

❖ Remove from the nursery any toy that has been in contact with a child who has an infectious illness.

❖ Throw out any plastic toys that have cracks or splits in them as these cracks can harbour germs. Particular care should be taken to keep hats, head coverings and hairbrushes clean in order to help prevent the spread of head lice.

❖ Animals visiting the nursery or nursery pets must be free from disease, safe to be with children and must not pose a health risk. Children should *always* be supervised when handling animals and make sure they always wash their hands after touching any pet.

❖ A no smoking policy must be observed by staff and visitors.

Providing a hygienic indoor environment

Children need a clean, warm and hygienic environment in order to stay healthy. Although most large early years settings employ a cleaner, there will be many occasions when you have to take responsibility for ensuring that the environment is kept clean and safe, for example if a child has been sick or has had a toileting accident.

All early years settings should have set **routines** for tidying up and for cleaning the floors, walls, furniture and play equipment; details may be found in the setting's written **policy** for health and hygiene issues.

Providing a hygienic outdoor environment

Children benefit from playing in the fresh air, as long as they are dressed for the weather. All early years settings should be checked regularly to make sure a safe and hygienic environment is being provided.

Policies relating to health and hygiene issues

All early years settings must have a written policy for dealing with health and hygiene issues. The guidelines below include points which are often part of the policy document.

Guidelines for ensuring a hygienic outdoor environment

- ❖ Check the outdoor play area daily for litter, dog excrement and hazards such as broken glass, syringes or rusty cans.
- ❖ Follow the sun safety code; provide floppy hats and use sun cream (SPF15) to prevent sunburn (if parents give their permission).
- ❖ Check all play equipment for splinters, jagged edges, protruding nails and other hazards.
- ❖ Supervise children at all times.
- ❖ Keep sand covered and check regularly for insects, litter and other contamination.
- ❖ Keep gates locked and check that hinges are secure.

Guidelines for addressing health and hygiene issues

- ❖ Always wear disposable gloves when dealing with blood, urine, faeces or vomit.
- ❖ Always wash your hands after dealing with spillages – even if gloves have been worn.
- ❖ Use a dilute bleach (hypochlorite) solution (or product specified by your setting's policy) to mop up any spillages.
- ❖ Make sure paper tissues are available for children to use.

❖ Always cover cuts and open sores with adhesive plasters.

❖ Food must be stored and prepared hygienically.

❖ Ask parents to keep their children at home if they are feeling unwell or they have an infection.

❖ Children who are sent home with vomiting or diarrhoea must remain at home until at least 24 hours have elapsed since the last attack.

❖ Parents must provide written authorisation for early years workers to administer medications to children.

Guidelines for disposing of waste

❖ Staff should *always* wear disposable gloves when handling any bodily waste (i.e. blood, urine, vomit and faeces). Always dispose of the gloves and wash your hands after dealing with such waste, even though gloves have been worn.

❖ A dilute bleach (hypochlorite) solution should be used to mop up any spillages.

❖ Different types of waste should be kept in separate covered bins in designated areas; food waste should be kept well away from toilet waste.

❖ Soiled nappies, dressings, disposable towels and gloves should be placed in a sealed bag before being put in a plastic-lined, covered bin for incineration.

❖ Always cover any cuts and open sores with waterproof adhesive plasters.

Promoting children's hygiene

All children need adult help and supervision to keep their skin, hair and teeth clean. You should not expect children to be forever worrying about personal cleanliness, but by encouraging **hygiene routines** you will help to prevent the spread of infection.

Children are more likely than adults to develop an infection because:

❖ they have immature immune systems;

❖ they are not usually aware of the need for hygiene – they need to be taught and reminded to wash their hands;

❖ they tend to play closely with other children for long periods of time.

Good hygiene routines will help to prevent infection. Children will take their cue from you, so you need to ensure that you are a good role model by setting a high standard for your own personal hygiene.

Food hygiene

Good food hygiene is essential for the prevention of food poisoning; young children are particularly vulnerable to the bacteria which cause gastroenteritis or **food poisoning**.

HOW BACTERIA ENTER FOOD

Bacteria can enter food without causing the food to look, smell or even taste bad. Bacteria thrive in warm, moist foods, especially those rich in protein, such as meat and poultry (both cooked and raw), seafood, gravy, soup, cooked rice, milk, cream and egg dishes. Harmful bacteria multiply rapidly, dividing into 2 every 10–20 minutes, and soon build up a colony of thousands that will cause poisoning. To live and grow, bacteria must have:

* **food** – especially the foods mentioned above;

* **moisture** – fresh foods are more susceptible to bacterial contamination than dried foods;

* **warmth** – bacteria thrive best at body temperature (37°C);

* **time** – bacteria reproduce rapidly in warm, moist food.

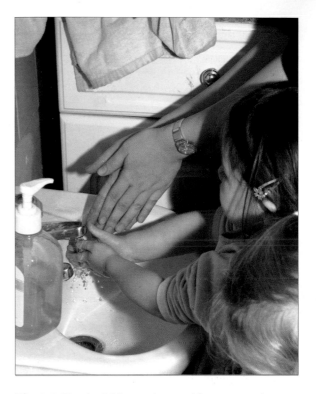

Fig 4.1 Teach children when and how to wash their hands

Guidelines for safe storage of food

* Keep food cold. The fridge should be kept as cold as it will go without actually freezing the food (1–5°C or 34–41°F). To be safe, use a fridge thermometer and open the door as few times as possible.

* Cool food quickly before placing in the fridge.

* Cover or wrap food with food wrap or microwave cling film.

* Store raw foods at the bottom so that juices cannot drip onto cooked food.

* Freezers must be at a low enough temperature (-21°C or 0°F maximum).

* Never refreeze food that has begun to thaw.

* Label each item with the use-by date.

* Thaw frozen meat completely before cooking.

Guidelines for safe preparation and cooking of food

❖ Always wash hands using warm water and soap, and dry on a clean towel. Do this before handling food; after using the toilet; after touching raw food; after coughing into your hands; after using a hankie; and after touching your face or hair.

❖ Never cough or sneeze over food.

❖ Always cover any cuts or boils with a waterproof dressing.

❖ Never smoke in any room that is used for food – apart from being unhygienic, it is illegal.

❖ Keep clean and wear clean, protective clothing that is solely for use in the kitchen.

Cook food thoroughly

❖ Eggs should be cooked so both the yolk and white are firm.

❖ Chicken must be tested to ensure that it is thoroughly cooked.

❖ Joints of meat and mince dishes must be cooked right through.

❖ Avoid cooking chilled foods, which need very careful handling.

❖ Avoid eating leftovers – they are a common cause of food poisoning.

❖ *Do not* reheat food – even if it appears wasteful not to.

❖ *Do not* reheat food using a microwave oven.

❖ *Do not* use a microwave oven to heat babies' bottles.

❖ Always follow instructions for cooking using a microwave oven and include standing time to avoid burns.

❖ Keep the oven clean.

Guidelines for maintaining a safe kitchen

❖ Keep the kitchen clean – the floor, work surfaces, sink, utensils, cloths and waste bins should be cleaned regularly.

❖ Clean tin-openers, graters and mixers thoroughly after use.

❖ Tea towels should be boiled every day, and dishcloths boiled or disinfected.

❖ Keep flies and other insects away – use a fine mesh over open windows.

❖ Keep pets away from the kitchen.

❖ Keep all waste bins covered and empty them regularly.

❖ Stay away from the kitchen if you are suffering from diarrhoea or sickness.

THE PREVENTION OF FOOD POISONING
FOOD-POISONING BACTERIA

Several types of bacteria can cause food poisoning (see Table 4.1, below), including the following:

❖ salmonella;

❖ clostridium botulinum;

❖ staphylococcus;

❖ clostridium welchii;

❖ listeria.

SAFETY AND SECURITY

One of the cornerstones of early childhood care and education is to offer an exciting range of experiences to children, which will stimulate them and extend their skills in all areas of development. As they grow you need to be responsive to their changing **safety needs** at each stage of development.

Close supervision is the most effective way of ensuring children's safety.

Supervising children's safety

The most important thing to remember when caring for children is to treat each child as an individual – with individual needs. Babies' and young children's abilities will differ over time; it may be surprising when they do things for the first time, but you should be able to anticipate, adapt and avoid dangerous situations in order to

Table 4.1 Food poisoning bacteria.

Bacteria	Typically found in	Symptoms	To reduce risk
Salmonella	Meat, poultry, raw eggs, meat pies and pasties, left-over food, unpasteurised milk	Starts suddenly 12 to 14 hours after eating: nausea, vomiting, abdominal pain and headache	Good personal hygiene; cook eggs well; avoid cross-infection from raw to cooked foods; cook food thoroughly
Clostridium welchii	Meat, poultry, meat dishes, left-over food, gravy	Starts 8 to 18 hours after eating: diarrhoea, abdominal pain, but no fever. Lasts 12 to 24 hours	Cook food thoroughly; heat to 100°C
Listeria	Chilled foods, e.g. soft cheeses and meat pâté	Starts 5 to 30 days after eating: 1 in 4 cases fatal; miscarriage, blood poisoning, meningitis. Babies especially at risk	Avoid high-risk foods; avoid storing chilled foods for long periods; ensure proper re-heating
Clostridium botulinum	Canned food not heated properly at time of canning; raw fish	Starts 12 to 36 hours after eating: often fatal; double vision, breathing difficulties	Avoid damaged or 'blown' cans; avoid keeping vacuum-packed fish in warm temperatures
Staphylococcus	Food that needs careful handling; custards and creams, cold desserts, sandwiches, unpasteurised milk	Starts 1 to 6 hours after eating: abdominal cramps, vomiting. Lasts up to 24 hours	Good personal hygiene; avoid coughing and sneezing over food; avoid cross-infection from raw to cooked food; heat to 70°C for 15 minutes

employer will do this on a formal basis, carrying out a **health and safety risk assessment** (see page 179). To ensure children's safety you need to be able to:

❖ **Identify a hazard.** At every stage of a child's life, you must think again about the hazards that are present and what you can do to eliminate them. This could be play equipment left on the floor, obstructing an exit or small items which have been left within reach of a baby.

❖ **Be aware of the child's interaction with the environment.** This means understanding the different stages of child development – for example, babies explore objects with their mouths and run the risk of choking, and young children tend to run everywhere and could trip over toys on the floor.

❖ **Provide adequate supervision.** This will vary according to each child's age, needs and abilities.

❖ **Be a good role model.** You will do this by ensuring that the child's environment is kept safe and that you follow the setting's health and safety guidelines.

❖ **Know how to use the safety equipment provided.** This might include safety gates, window locks, baby harnesses and security intercom systems.

❖ **Teach children about safety.** Encourage children to be aware of their own personal safety and the safety of others.

Knowing why accidents happen and how to prevent them

UNDERSTANDING SAFETY ISSUES

Accidents are the most common cause of death in children aged 1–14 years,

accounting for half of all child deaths in the UK:

❖ Every day 3 children are killed in accidents.

❖ Each year 10,000 children are permanently disabled.

❖ Each year, 1 in 6 children attends an accident and emergency department.

The pattern of accidents tends to vary with age, the child's developmental progress and exposure to new hazards.

WHY DO ACCIDENTS HAPPEN?

Babies are vulnerable to accidents because they have no awareness of danger and cannot control their environment; they are totally dependent on their parents or carers to make their world safe. Children are naturally curious and need to investigate their surroundings. As children get older and their memory develops, they start to realise that certain actions have certain consequences (e.g. touching a hot oven door hurts), and so they begin to learn a measure of self-protection. Carers of young children need to have a sound knowledge of child development in order to anticipate when an accident is likely to happen. Carers also have a duty to make the home, car and early years setting safer places, and should know where to go for advice and equipment.

SITUATIONS WHEN ACCIDENTS ARE MORE LIKELY TO HAPPEN

❖ **Stress**: when adults and children are worried or anxious, they are less alert and less aware of possible dangers.

❖ **Lack of awareness:** parents tend to react to an existing threat of danger, rather than anticipate things that may happen. For example, parents may report that they had not realised their child could even climb onto a stool, so had not thought to remove the dangerous object.

❖ **Overprotection:** a child whose parents are overprotective may become timid and will be less aware of dangers when unsupervised.

❖ **Poor role models:** adults who are always in a hurry may dash across the road instead of crossing in a safe place. Children will imitate their actions, and are less able to judge the speed of traffic.

❖ **Under-protection:** the NSPCC recommends that children under the age of 13 years should only be left alone in a house for short periods, and that no young child should be placed at risk by being left 'home alone', even when they are apparently safely asleep. Children who are under-protected generally have not been made aware of dangers, and their natural curiosity leads to dangerous play activities.

THE PREVENTION OF ACCIDENTS

Parents and child carers can reduce the risks of childhood accidents by following the guidelines set out below.

Guidelines for preventing accidents

1   Be a good role model – set a safe example.

2   Make the home, garden and nursery as accident-proof as possible.

3   Teach children about safety – make them aware of dangers in their environment.

4   Never leave children alone in the house.

5   Always try to buy goods displaying the appropriate safety symbol:

❖ The **kite mark** (see Figure 4.4a) on any product means that the British Standards Institution (BSI) has checked the manufacturer's claim that their product meets specific standards.

❖ The new **safety mark** (see Figure 4.4b) means that a product has been checked to ensure that it meets the requirements of the BSI for safety only.

❖ The **lion mark** (see Figure 4.4c) is only found on British-made toys and means that they have met the safety standards required.

❖ The **age advice safety symbol** (see Figure 4.4d) is a 'warning' not to give the toy to children under 3 years, or allow them to play with it.

NB Toys and games bought from market stalls, and cheap foreign imports may be copies of well-known brand-name toys, but may not meet the safety standards.

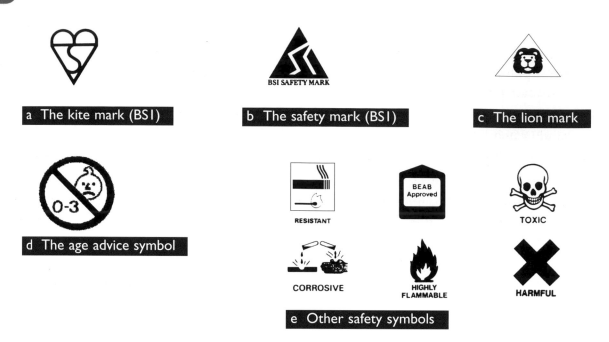

Fig 4.4 (a) The kite mark; (b) BSI safety mark; (c) the lion mark; (d) the age advice symbol; (e) Other safety symbols

Guidelines for preventing choking and suffocation

Choking followed by suffocation is the largest cause of accidental death in babies under 1 year; and older children are also at risk when playing on their own or eating unsupervised.

❖ *Do not* leave rattles, teething rings or squeeze toys in the baby's cot – they can become wedged in the baby's mouth and cause suffocation.

❖ *Do not* use a pillow for babies under 1 year. Baby nests must meet British Standard No. 6595 and have a flat head area. Baby nests should only be used for carrying a baby – not for leaving a sleeping baby unattended.

❖ *Do not* let a baby or young child get hold of tiny items like coins, marbles, dried peas, buttons or Lego – small children explore with their mouths and can easily choke on small objects.

❖ *Do not* leave babies alone with finger foods such as bananas, carrots, cheese, and so on. Always supervise eating and drinking.

❖ *Do not* give peanuts to children under 4 years because they can easily choke on them or inhale them into their lungs, causing infection and lung damage.

❖ *Do not* leave a baby alone, propped up with a bottle – always hold the baby while feeding.

❖ *Do* supervise a baby who is playing with paper, as she may bite off small pieces and choke on them.

❖ *Do* use a firm mattress that meets British Standard No. 1877. For children over 1 year, use a pillow that meets the same standard for allowing air to pass through freely, whatever position the baby is in.

❖ *Do* check that there are no hanging cords – for example, from a window blind – which could catch around a child's neck and strangle them if they fall.

❖ *Do* keep all plastic bags away from babies and children, and teach older children never to put plastic bags on their heads.

❖ *Do* be aware that dummies on long ribbons, and cardigans with ribbons around the neck, can pull tight around a baby's neck if caught on a hook or knob; a dummy must meet safety standards with holes in the flange, in case it is drawn into the back of the throat. Older children have been strangled by tie-cords on anoraks.

❖ *Do* check that any toys given to babies and young children are safe, with no small loose parts or jagged edges.

Guidelines for preventing burns and scalds

As children learn to crawl, climb and walk, the risk of scalds or burns increases.

❖ *Do not* leave burning cigarettes in ashtrays.

❖ *Do not* use tablecloths which young children can pull down on top of themselves.

❖ *Do not* use gas or paraffin heaters in children's bedrooms.

❖ *Do not* leave a hose lying in the sun – water in it can get hot enough to scald a baby.

❖ *Do not* leave a hot iron unattended.

❖ *Do not* iron where children are likely to run past, and try to use a coiled flex.

❖ *Do* keep the water temperature for the house set at about 60°C (140°F) to prevent scalds and burns.

❖ *Do* protect fires with a fixed fine-mesh fireguard. **Note: it is illegal to leave a child under 12 in a room with an open fire.**

❖ *Do* keep matches and lighters well out of reach.

❖ *Do* choose nightclothes and dressing gowns that are flame-resistant.

❖ *Do* install automatic smoke alarms.

❖ *Do* use fire doors in nurseries and schools; and check you know the location of fire extinguishers and fire blankets.

❖ *Do* keep children away from bonfires and fireworks. Attend safe, public displays.

❖ *Do* keep a young child away from your area while you are cooking; always turn pan handles inwards; cooker guards are not a good idea as they can get very hot.

❖ *Do* keep kettles and hot drinks well out of reach; use a coiled kettle flex, and never pass hot drinks over the heads of children.

❖ *Do* test bath water before putting a child in; always put cold water in first and then add the hot water. A special plastic-strip thermometer can be stuck to the side of the bath to check the temperature.

❖ *Do* teach children about the dangers of fire.

Guidelines for preventing falls

All children fall, but there are ways of ensuring that they do not fall too far or too hard.

❖ *Do not* use baby-walkers. Child-safety experts agree that these are dangerous and cause many accidents as babies steer themselves into dangerous situations.

❖ *Do not* place furniture under windows where children may be tempted to climb.

❖ *Do not* leave babies unattended on a table, work surface, bed or sofa – lie them on the floor instead.

❖ *Do* use stair gates at the top and the bottom of stairs and at doors which might be left open.

❖ *Do* fit vertical bars to dangerous windows (note: horizontal bars encourage climbing).

❖ *Do* fit childproof window safety catches on all windows.

❖ *Do* use a safety harness in the high chair, pram, pushchair or supermarket trolley.

❖ *Do* teach children how to use the stairs safely; teach them to come down stairs backwards on all fours.

Guidelines for preventing poisoning

The peak age for accidents with poisons is 1–3 years, when children are highly mobile and inquisitive.

❖ *Do not* store dangerous household chemicals – bleach, disinfectant, white spirit – in the cupboard under the sink. Use a safer, locked cupboard instead.

❖ *Do not* transfer chemicals (e.g. weedkiller) into other containers such as a lemonade bottle, as a child will not know the difference until it is too late.

❖ *Do* keep all medicines in a locked cupboard.

❖ *Do* use childproof containers and ensure that they are closed properly.

❖ *Do* teach children not to eat berries or fungi in the garden or in the park.

- ❖ *Do* keep rubbish and kitchen waste in a tightly covered container or, better still, behind a securely locked door.
- ❖ *Do* make sure that if surma is used on a child's eyes it is a lead-free brand. (Surma or kohl is a preparation used as eyeshadow in some Asian cultures.) Check with a pharmacist.
- ❖ *Do* store children's vitamins in a safe place. Poisoning by an overdose of vitamins is very common.

Guidelines for preventing cuts

Glass presents the biggest safety hazard to young children; every year about 7000 children end up in hospital after being cut by glass.

- ❖ *Do* use special safety glass in doors; this is relatively harmless if it does break, whereas ordinary glass breaks into sharp jagged pieces.
- ❖ *Do* mark large picture windows with coloured strips to make it obvious when they are closed.
- ❖ *Do* use plastic drinking cups and bottles.
- ❖ *Do* keep all knives, scissors and razors out of reach.
- ❖ *Do* teach children never to run with a pencil or lolly stick in their mouth.
- ❖ *Do* use safety scissors when cutting paper and card.
- ❖ *Do* teach children never to play with doors; if possible, fit a device to the top of doors to prevent them from slamming and pinching fingers.

Guidelines for preventing drowning

A baby or toddler can drown in a very shallow amount of water – even a bucket with a few inches of water in it presents a risk. If a small child's face goes underwater, they will automatically breathe in so that they can scream. This action will fill their lungs with water.

- ❖ *Do not* ever leave a child alone in the bath.
- ❖ *Do not* leave an older child looking after a baby or toddler in the bath.
- ❖ *Do* use a non-slip mat in the bath.
- ❖ *Do* always supervise water play.
- ❖ *Do* guard ponds, water butts and ditches.
- ❖ *Do* keep the toilet lid down at all times or fit a locking device; toddlers are fascinated by the swirling water action, and can fall in and drown.

Guidelines for preventing electric shocks

Children may suffer electric shock from poking small objects into sockets or from playing with electric plugs.

- ❧ *Do* fit safety dummy plugs or socket covers to all electric sockets.
- ❧ *Do* check that plugs are correctly wired and safe; when buying Christmas tree lights, check for British Standard No. 4647.
- ❧ *Do* prevent children from pulling at electric cords by installing a cord holder which will make the cord too short to reach over the edge of the table or work surface.

Guidelines for sun safety

- ❧ *Do not* let children run around in only a swimsuit or without any clothes on.
- ❧ *Do not* let children play in the sun between 11 a.m. and 3 p.m. when the sun is highest and most dangerous.
- ❧ *Do* keep babies under the age of 9 months out of the sun altogether.
- ❧ *Do* cover children in loose baggy cotton clothes, such as an oversized T-shirt with sleeves. Some special fabrics have a sun protection factor.
- ❧ *Do* protect a child's shoulders and back of neck when playing, as these are the most common areas for sunburn: let a child wear a 'legionnaire's hat' or a floppy hat with a wide brim that shades the face and neck.
- ❧ *Do* cover exposed parts of the child's skin with a sunscreen, even on cloudy or overcast days. Use one with a minimum sun protection factor (SPF) of 15 and reapply frequently.
- ❧ *Do* use waterproof sunblock if the child is swimming.

Encourage children to be aware of their own safety and the safety of others

Children need a safe environment so that they can explore and learn and grow. As they develop, older children need to learn how to tackle everyday dangers so that they can become safe adults. Children learn some realities of safety the hard way – by banging their heads or grazing their knees. You cannot prevent them from hurting themselves altogether – but you can alert them and keep reminding them. You have an important role – not only in keeping children safe and secure – but also in teaching them to be aware of safety issues. When teaching young children about safety, you will need to find ways to communicate with each child according to their needs; for example, children with hearing difficulties will need both children and adults to face them so that they can see any signs, and to lip-read if the hearing loss is severe.

When teaching young children about safety you must adapt your information and the method in which you present it to the individual child or group of children. You should teach children:

✤ to carry things carefully;

✤ never to run with anything in their mouths, including sweets and other food – something in a child's mouth can choke him;

✤ never to run while carrying a glass, scissors or other pointed objects – if a child falls he can stab himself with something as simple as a pencil.

You need to explain the reasons *behind* the rules you give them, for example by saying:

'You mustn't throw sand because you'll hurt your friend.'

'Never run into the road, because you could be hit by a car.'

'Don't run with a stick in your hand as it would hurt you if you fall.'

For most children, you need to repeat these fundamental safety rules over and over again so that they will remember.

Children under 5 years tend to be absorbed in their play and focus on the here and now. However, young children do tend to avoid any hazard that has been identified for them. It is important that safety issues are talked about at the setting and that learning opportunities are structured into the *everyday* play curriculum. A variety of materials are available to support safety work with children, including books, pictures, posters, plays and puppets. These can support the development of awareness about road safety, water safety and fire safety in children. However, not all teaching needs to be *planned*. You can use any opportunities that arise naturally – such as an accident or a near-miss that has happened to someone the children know.

If children – even very young children – understand *why* the rules have been made they will be more likely to abide by them.

Guidelines for ensuring safety in the early years setting

✤ Children should be **supervised** at all times.

✤ **Premises** must be large enough, and should provide a separate area for the care of babies and toddlers.

✤ The nursery environment and all materials and equipment should be maintained in a safe condition.

✤ Low-level glass (e.g. in doors and cupboards) should be **safety glass** or must be covered with boarding or guards; sharp corners on low-level furniture should be padded.

❖ There must be adequate **first-aid** facilities and staff should be trained in basic first aid.

❖ **Routine safety checks** should be made daily on the premises, both indoors and outdoors.

❖ **Fire drills** should be held twice a term in schools and nurseries and every 6 weeks in day nurseries. **Fire exits** must be left accessible and unlocked at all times.

❖ **Electric sockets** should be covered.

❖ **Floor surfaces** should be clean and free of splinters.

❖ **Access** should be easy for prams, pushchairs and wheelchairs.

❖ **Kitchen facilities** must be adequate in terms of hygiene, storage and safety.

❖ Children should only be allowed home with a parent or authorised adult.

ACTIVITY: SAFETY AND HYGIENE RULES

Find out about safety and hygiene rules in your placement, including guidelines for the hygienic disposal of waste and body fluids.

1   For each safety point, state the principle behind it.

2   As an early years worker, what can you do to prevent infection spreading in the work setting?

ACTIVITY: SAFETY QUIZ

The list below gives activities which children often want to do for fun or to help out in the house. How old does a child have to be to do each activity safely? (Answers on page 215.)

1   Cross a quiet street alone.

2   Make a cup of tea.

3   Have a bath without an adult watching.

4   Have a drink without an adult in the room.

5   Play near water without adults around.

6   Ride a bicycle in a back street.

7   Eat peanuts.

8   Play with plastic bags.

9   Walk downstairs without an adult.

10 Climb trees.

11 Play in the playground with other children and without adults present.

12 Use matches.

(See Chapter 11 for more information on childhood accidents and their prevention.)

FEELING VALUED

Children and their families need to feel that they matter and that they are valued for themselves.

PROVIDING FOR CHILDREN'S DEVELOPMENTAL NEEDS, INDOORS AND OUTDOORS

The early years environment should provide **holistic care and education**, by addressing the range of children's developmental needs (i.e. their physical needs, intellectual and language needs, emotional and social needs).

Guidelines for helping children to feel valued

❖ Establish a good relationship with parents; always be welcoming and listen to them.

❖ Squat down or bend down to the child's level when you are talking with them.

❖ Praise and encourage children.

❖ Be responsive to and interested in children's needs.

❖ Ensure that children experience equality of opportunity and feel included (see Chapter 1).

❖ Use positive images in the setting (see also Chapter 1).

Guidelines for addressing children's developmental needs

The early years setting should:

❖ take account of each **child's individual needs** and provide for them appropriately;

❖ **be stimulating**, offering a wide range of activities which encourage experimentation and problem solving;

❖ provide opportunities for **all types of play**;

❖ provide support for children who may be experiencing **strong feelings**, for example when settling in to a new nursery or when they are angry or jealous;

❖ encourage children who use them to bring in their **comfort objects**, such as a favourite teddy or a piece of blanket;

❖ encourage the development of **self-reliance** and **independence**;

❖ ensure that children who have **special needs** and disabilities are provided with appropriate equipment and support.

ACTIVITY: DEVELOPMENTAL NEEDS OF CHILDREN IN LONE-PARENT FAMILIES

1 Think about the problems for a lone-parent family, living on a very low income, in a poorly maintained block of flats. What particular disadvantages might the children in such a situation have? List these under the headings of the following developmental areas: physical, intellectual, social, emotional and language.

2 How could this young family be helped by:

❖ the statutory services (e.g. a day care centre)?

❖ the voluntary sector (e.g. playgroups, community associations)?

Guidelines for promoting a sense of belonging

You can help by:

❖ **greeting each child** and their parent or carer by name and with a smile when they arrive;

❖ **marking each child's coat peg** with their name and their photograph;

❖ **displaying children's work** with their name alongside it;

❖ ensuring that all children's **cultural backgrounds** are represented in the home corner, in books, displays and interest tables (see Chapter 1 for ideas).

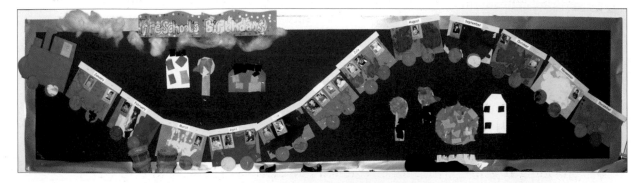

Fig 4.5 An organisation chart helps children to feel that they belong

A SENSE OF BELONGING

Children and their families need an environment that is reassuring and welcoming; children also need to feel that they belong.

A COMFORTABLE CHILD AND A FAMILY-FRIENDLY ENVIRONMENT

'Caring adults count more than resources or equipment.'
(Birth to Three Matters)

You, the early years worker, are the most important resource in any setting; you can make a real difference to the caring environment by showing that you really care and by developing all the skills of empathy and patience that help to create a welcoming and family-friendly environment. Children who are cared for at home, in a childminder's home or in a rural preschool group may not have access to special child-sized equipment or to the range of activities that can be provided in a purpose-built nursery setting. Many preschool groups have to clear away every item of equipment after each session because the hall or room is used by other groups. In purpose-built early years settings and infant schools, there are child-sized chairs, basins, lavatories and low tables. Such provision makes the environment safer and allows children greater independence.

Colour and sound

The way in which colour is used in a setting can have a profound effect both on children and on the staff caring for them. Nursery-age children are particularly responsive to colour, preferring bright, warm colours. However, children and adults can find too many bright primary colours unsettling and overstimulating. Research shows that children play better and show less

Guidelines to creating a comfortable, child-friendly environment

Planning both the **physical layout** and the organisation of **activities** is important. It involves:

❖ considering **health and safety** before anything else; for example, fire exits and doors should be kept clear at all times;

❖ giving children the maximum space and freedom to explore; rooms should be large enough and sufficiently uncluttered to accommodate the number of children;

❖ ensuring that the room temperature is pleasant – neither too hot nor too cold (between 18°C and 21°C);

❖ making maximum use of natural light; rooms should be airy and well-lit;

❖ allowing access to outdoors at all times and in all seasons;

❖ ensuring that displays and interest tables are at child height where possible, and include items which can be handled and explored safely;

❖ providing **routines** for children; children like their environment to be predictable.

hyperactivity when their surroundings reflect the calming colours of nature – soft blues, greens and creams. This does not mean that children's settings should be bland or drab places; the bright primary colours loved by children can be provided by their own artwork, toys and clothes. Sound can also have a marked effect in the early years environment. When sound levels are consistently high, young children often respond by being hyperactive or irritable. Excessive noise can be dampened down by using thick wall-hangings and alternative, less jarring sounds can be provided by using wind chimes near a window.

All children need a **quiet area**, with rest mats, cushions and comfortable seating for both children and adults to enjoy. Children need places where they can simply 'be'. Young children love to make dens – even a large cardboard box can become a cosy house.

The physical layout of the environment

Up to a point, certain fixed features will determine how space is used: for example, the siting of doors, sinks, carpeted areas and electric sockets. Within these constraints you will have some flexibility to organise space to suit your needs. Space should be organised in such a way that children – and adults – can move freely between activities, and so that **children with special needs** can have as much independence as possible. The most important factors in designing the layout of any early years setting are that it should:

1 **Comply with hygiene and safety standards:**

   * furniture should be well-designed to suit its intended purpose; have safe corners (rounded or moulded); be hard-wearing and easily washed or cleaned;

   * electrical equipment, such as computers, televisions, videos and tape recorders must have electric wires secured neatly and be sited close to a wall socket;

   * fire-safety equipment and fire doors should be clearly marked and regularly maintained;

   * a fully equipped first-aid box must be kept in a locked cupboard; also there must be one designated member of staff who is responsible for first aid and for replenishing the box; at least one qualified first-aider must be in the setting at all times;

   * equipment and materials should be available for disinfecting and cleaning surfaces and toys;

   * safety devices for doors and windows, and stair gates; should be in place;

   * safety surfaces should be used in the outdoor area, for example under slides and climbing frames.

2 **Be child-oriented:**

   * furniture should be child-sized and attractive (perhaps made so by the use of natural wood);

   * toys and activities should be provided which are appropriate to the children's level of development – children need a stimulating environment which encourages experimentation and problem solving;

   * a quiet area should be available where children can withdraw from peer play and from the gaze of adults;

❖ an outdoor space with safe equipment is also important.

3 **Provide a safe and pleasant working environment for adults:**

❖ it should allow for adequate supervision by adults at all times;

❖ furniture should be arranged to allow supervision without excessive walking – and should also be easy to rearrange;

❖ materials should be stored conveniently;

❖ equipment should be designed to avoid excessive lifting, for example nappy-changing units with steps, or cots with drop-sides;

❖ seating for adults – special glider chairs, settees and rockers are perfect for bonding with babies; adult chairs should be low, yet scaled to fit adults, so that staff can interact at child level.

4 **Cater for the needs of families** by providing information for them about their children and their activities and other issues of interest about events and organisations in the local community.

5 **Use natural light where possible**

6 **Be at the correct temperature and be well-ventilated.**

Guidelines for organising the physical layout of the setting

Indoors

Rooms should be divided, where possible, into separate areas for:

❖ **sand** (wet and dry): equipment in boxes on shelves nearby, labelled and with a picture of contents;

❖ **water:** activities which require water or hand washing should be near the sink and with aprons close by;

❖ **clay and play dough:** cool, airtight storage, selection of tools for cutting, moulding, and so on;

❖ **a quiet area:** for looking at books and reading stories, doing floor puzzles; ideally carpeted or with rugs and floor cushions;

❖ **puzzles, small blocks and tabletop games;**

❖ **technology:** computer, weighing balance, calculators, tape recorders, and so on;

❖ **cookery:** with measuring equipment, bowls, spoons and baking trays;

❖ **growing and living things:** fish aquarium, wormery, growing mustard and cress, and so on;

❖ **artwork:** with tabards, brushes and paints within easy reach;

❖ **domestic play:** with dolls, cots, kitchen equipment, and so on;

❖ **make-believe play:** box of dressing-up clothes;

❖ **small-world toys:** animals, cars, people, farms, dinosaurs;

- ❖ **construction:** wooden blocks for building, small construction blocks, such as Duplo; a woodwork area;
- ❖ **writing/graphics:** with a variety of paper and different kinds of pencils and pens;
- ❖ **workshop:** with found materials, such as cardboard boxes, egg boxes, glue, scissors and masking tape;
- ❖ **interest table:** with interesting objects for children to handle;
- ❖ **making music:** tape recorders, percussion instruments and song books.

Outdoors

Where possible, the following resources should be provided:

- ❖ **sheltered spaces** from sun, wind and rain, including a covered external play space;
- ❖ **safe equipment** for climbing and swinging, a safety floor surface, wheeled toys, balls and beanbags;
- ❖ **apparatus** that can be used imaginatively, for example tunnels;
- ❖ **plants** and a **growing area**, a wild area to encourage butterflies, a mud patch for digging;
- ❖ **natural features** such as mounds, trees and safe changes in level which can help to promote imaginative play.

ACTIVITY: EVALUATING THE SETTING

In your work placement, investigate points 1 and 2 below.

1   How welcoming is the setting? Describe the factors which help to create a welcoming environment, and list any possible improvements.

2   How safe is the setting? Try to look at the setting from a child's viewpoint and again list any possible improvements.

PROVIDING FOR CHILDREN'S SPECIAL NEEDS

Early years settings may need to adapt their room layout and outdoor areas to improve access, so that all children are included in the opportunities for play and learning; for example, you may need to make changes with children who use wheelchairs or children with visual impairment in mind. You may need to work with parents to find out how a child with special needs can be

---

ACTIVITY: ADAPTING THE ENVIRONMENT FOR A CHILD WITH SPECIAL NEEDS

Look at the layout of your own work placement. What physical changes would be necessary to include:

✤ a child in a wheelchair?

✤ a partially sighted child?

✤ a child who uses elbow crutches?

---

encouraged to participate fully with other children within the nursery. (For more information on working with children with special needs, see Chapter 1.)

DISPLAYING CHILDREN'S WORK

Displays can give a lot of information to children, parents and visitors about the setting's values and ethos, as well as celebrating children's learning. Some displays may be purely for information purposes, for example a parent's noticeboard with named photographs of staff members, menus for the week and other useful things. Other displays are more decorative.

Displays of children's work can take different forms:

✤ **Wall display:** boards of varying shapes and sizes are placed on otherwise plain walls so that displays can be created and changed frequently to provide interest.

✤ **Window display:** pieces of art or craft work can be attached to windows to create a stained-glass effect, but windows should not be covered completely. Children should be able to see out and light should not be restricted.

✤ **Mobile (or hanging) display:** in large rooms, hanging displays can be very

Guidelines for creating displays

DO

✤ Label individual children's work correctly with their name, preferably in the top left-hand corner or underneath.

✤ Let children see you handle their work with respect.

✤ Use appropriate language and symbols in any labels that you add.

✤ Check that work is trimmed and properly aligned.

✤ Make sure that titles and labels are clearly legible.

- ❖ Arrange work at a good viewing height for children.
- ❖ Mount the exhibits, using clean backgrounds and thinking carefully about colours.
- ❖ Allow space and margins around each piece of work; use appropriate lettering for the age and developmental stage of the children.
- ❖ Talk to the children about the display and encourage them to help when choosing work to put up.

DO NOT

- ❖ Use drawing pins (unless instructed to do so by your placement) – they are dangerous and unsightly.
- ❖ Display things where they can be easily damaged, splashed or picked at.
- ❖ Make spelling mistakes.
- ❖ Overcrowd your display space.
- ❖ Waste resources.
- ❖ Leave paper cutters and/or other materials lying around.
- ❖ Cut out parts of the children's drawings or paintings to make them into your own collage. This shows a lack of respect for children's ideas and feelings about their efforts.

attractive. These must be at an appropriate height for the children and should not hinder the movement of adults.

- ❖ **Tabletop display:** these are often called interactive displays as they provide an opportunity for children to handle interesting objects and to use the display as a learning activity. Often a tabletop display is used in conjunction with a wall display.

ENCOURAGING CHILDREN TO RELATE TO THE WORLD AROUND THEM

Young children tend to have a genuine curiosity about the natural world around them. If this interest is encouraged it can result in a lifelong awareness and respect for wildlife and the environment. Outdoor time for children in nursery settings is often limited to a brief period each day in a fenced-in playground with a hard surface, and very few, if any, opportunities for interacting with nature. Most settings can introduce children to a variety of plants and wildlife by taking them outdoors or on trips to a park, children's farm or zoo. Some are fortunate enough to have an area where children can help with simple gardening activities, such as digging, raking and planting seeds and bulbs. Children may visit a real pond and use nets to examine insects and other pond creatures.

In places where it is not possible to take children outdoors as much as one would wish, you need to find ways to *bring nature indoors*. For example:

- Sand, water, pebbles, shells, pine cones, leaves and conkers can be brought in for children's play.

- Children can plant seeds and bulbs and watch them grow.

- An aquarium or water table that contains real pond life could be set up in the indoor setting, or children could play with realistic replicas of frogs and fish in the water table.

- Prepare an interest table with a variety of natural objects and encourage children to touch and smell them and to talk about what they are feeling.

Fig 4.6 Child playing with a treasure basket

ACTIVITY: A NATURAL TREASURE BASKET

Babies learn about their environment using all their senses – touch, smell, taste, sight, hearing – and movement. A treasure basket is a collection of everyday objects chosen to stimulate the different senses. Babies have the chance to decide for themselves what they want to play with, choosing in turn whichever object they want to explore.

1 Choose a sturdy basket or box – one that does not tip over too easily.

2 Fill the basket with lots of natural objects – or objects made from natural materials – so that the baby has plenty to choose from:

   - fir cones;
   - large seashells;
   - large walnuts;
   - pumice stone;
   - fruit (e.g. apple, lemon);
   - brushes;
   - woollen ball;
   - wooden pegs;
   - small baskets;
   - feathers;
   - large pebbles;
   - gourds.

3 Make sure that everything you choose for the basket is clean and safe – remember that babies often want to put everything into their mouths.

Using the treasure basket

❖ Make sure that the baby is seated comfortably and safely, with cushions for support if necessary.

❖ Sit nearby and watch to give the baby confidence. Only talk or intervene if the baby clearly needs attention.

❖ Check the contents of the basket regularly, cleaning objects and removing any damaged items.

Write an **observation** of the activity, noting the following:

❖ the length of time the baby plays with each item;

❖ what he or she does with it;

❖ any facial expressions or sounds made by the baby.

PROFESSIONAL PRACTICE IN THE SUPPORT OF A POSITIVE, INTEGRATED ENVIRONMENT

Early years workers need to ensure that all children feel included, secure and valued – this forms the cornerstone of a positive, integrated environment. As a professional, your practice should include:

❖ developing positive relationships with parents in order to work effectively with them and their children;

❖ understanding the extent of your responsibilities and being answerable to others for your work;

❖ working effectively as part of a team;

❖ knowing the lines of reporting and how to get clarification about your role and duties;

❖ understanding what is meant by confidentiality and your role in the preserving of secret or privileged information that parents or others share with you about their children or themselves.

NB All these issues are covered in depth in Chapter 16.

Section 2: Physical care of children (1–7 years and 11 months)

BASIC PHYSICAL AND HEALTH NEEDS OF CHILDREN

From the moment they are born, all children depend completely on an adult to meet all their needs, but the way in which these needs are met will vary considerably according to family circumstances, culture and the personalities of the child and the caring adult. To achieve and maintain healthy growth and development (i.e. physical, intellectual, emotional and social development) certain basic needs must be fulfilled:

❖ food;

❖ cleanliness;

❖ sleep, rest and activity;

❖ protection from infection and injury;

❖ intellectual stimulation;

❖ relationships and social contacts;

❖ shelter, warmth, clothing;

❖ fresh air and sunlight;

❖ love, and consistent and continuous affection;

- access to health care;
- appreciation, praise and recognition of effort or achievements;
- security and nurture.

It is difficult to separate these basic needs from practical care, as they all contribute to the **holistic** development of a healthy child.

BASIC CARE OF CHILDREN (1–7 YEARS AND 11 MONTHS)

(Care of babies, from birth to 1 year, is covered separately in Chapter 13.)

Care and protection of the skin and hair

As children grow and become involved in more vigorous exercise, especially outside, a daily bath or shower becomes necessary.

Most young children love bath-time, and adding bubble bath to the water adds to the fun of getting clean.

Oral hygiene – caring for children's teeth

During the first year of life, babies eat their first solid food with the help of their primary teeth (or milk teeth). These 20 teeth start to appear at around the age of 6 months (see Figure 4.8).

There are three types of primary teeth:

- **incisors** – tough, chisel-shaped teeth with a sharp edge to help in biting food;
- **canines** – pointed teeth which help to tear food into manageable chunks;
- **molars** – large, strong teeth which grind against each other to crush food.

Guidelines for caring for the skin and hair

- Wash face and hands in the morning.
- Always wash hands after using the toilet and before meals; young children will need supervision.
- Girls should be taught to wipe their bottom from front to back to prevent germs from the anus entering the vagina and urethra.
- Nails should be scrubbed with a soft nailbrush and trimmed regularly by cutting straight across.
- Each child should have their own flannel, comb and brush, which must be cleaned regularly.
- Skin should always be thoroughly dried, taking special care with areas such as between the toes and under the armpits; black skin tends to dryness and may need massaging with special oils or moisturisers.
- Observe skin for any defects, such as rashes, dryness or soreness, and act appropriately.
- Hair usually only needs washing twice a week; children with long or curly hair benefit from the use of a conditioning shampoo which helps to reduce tangles. Hair should always be rinsed thoroughly in clean water and not brushed until it is dry (brushing wet hair damages the hair shafts). A wide-toothed comb is useful for combing wet hair.

❧ Afro-Caribbean hair tends to dryness and may need special oil or moisturisers; if the hair is braided (with or without beads), it may be washed with the braids left intact, unless otherwise advised.

❧ Rastafarian children with hair styled in dreadlocks may not use either combs or shampoo, preferring to brush the dreadlocks gently and secure them with braid; some will wear scarves or caps in the Rastafarian colours of red, gold, green and black.

❧ Devout Sikhs believe that the hair must never be cut or shaved, and young children usually wear a special head covering.

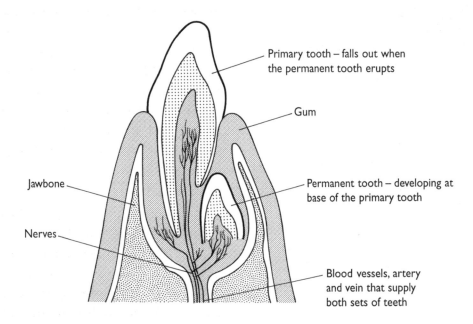

Fig 4.7 Structure of a primary tooth

Teeth need cleaning as soon as they appear. A substance called **plaque** sticks to the teeth and will cause decay if not removed. Caring for the temporary first teeth is important because:

❧ it develops a good hygiene habit which will continue throughout life;

❧ if milk teeth decay, they may need to be extracted; this could lead to crowding in the mouth as the natural gaps for the second teeth to fill will be too small;

❧ painful teeth may prevent chewing and cause eating problems;

❧ clean, white, shining teeth look good.

Use a soft baby toothbrush at first to clean the plaque from the teeth; after their first birthday, children can be taught to brush their own teeth, but will need careful supervision. They should be shown when and how to brush – that is, up and away from the gum when cleaning the lower teeth, and down and away when cleaning the upper teeth. They may need help to clean the back molars.

Rarely, a baby is born with a first tooth and it may have to be removed if it is loose. Most

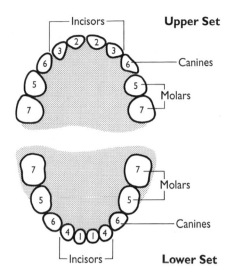

Fig 4.8 The usual order in which primary teeth appear

children have 'cut' all 20 primary teeth by the age of 3 years.

There are 32 **permanent teeth**. These replace the milk teeth and start to come through at about the age of 6 years. The milk teeth that were first to appear become loose first and fall out as the permanent teeth begin to push through the gums.

FLUORIDE

Some toothpastes contain fluoride, which is a mineral that can help prevent dental decay. Some water boards in the UK add fluoride to the water supply; in areas where the fluoride level is low, dentists recommend giving daily fluoride drops to children from 6 months of age until teething is complete (usually by 12 years). If water in your area has added fluoride, do not give drops or tablet supplements as an excess of the mineral can cause mottling of the teeth.

DIET

For healthy teeth we need calcium, fluoride, vitamins A, C and D, and foods that need chewing, such as apples, carrots and wholemeal bread. Sugar causes decay and can damage teeth even before they have come through – 'dinky feeders' and baby bottles filled with sweet drinks are very harmful. It is better to save sweets and sugary snacks for special occasions, or to give them only after meals if teeth are cleaned thoroughly afterwards.

VISITING THE DENTIST

The earlier a child is introduced to the family dentist, the less likely she is to feel nervous about dental inspection and treatment. Regular 6-monthly visits to a dentist from about the age of 3 years will ensure that any necessary advice and treatment are given to combat dental caries (tooth decay). Once the child starts primary school, a visiting dentist will check every child's teeth

ACTIVITY: A DENTAL HYGIENE ROUTINE

Plan a routine for a toddler that will cover all aspects of dental hygiene:

❖ brushing teeth;

❖ dietary advice;

❖ education about teeth/visits to the dentist.

Include examples of books that could be used to help prepare a child for a visit to the dentist. Remember to give a reason for each part of the routine.

and will refer them for treatment if appropriate.

Care of the feet

While a baby is in its mother's womb, a tough, flexible material called cartilage begins to form where harder bones will eventually grow. As the baby grows, cartilage is continually replaced with bone in a process called ossification. This takes place in the shafts (or long sections) and heads (or ends) of all bones. There are 26 bones in the foot (see Figure 4.9).

A child's feet are very soft and supple because the bones are not yet rigid and they are spaced widely apart; as the feet grow they change shape, and often one foot tends to be slightly longer or wider than the other.

Parents and carers should be aware that a child's feet can easily be distorted for life. So foot care must be treated as seriously as dental hygiene.

FOOT PROBLEMS

❖ **Club foot (talipes)** is fairly common and is caused by the foot being fixed in the same position in the womb for a prolonged time. Sometimes the condition rights itself without treatment, but the foot may need gentle manipulation and/or strapping; eventually a surgical operation may be needed.

❖ **Flat feet** are caused by ligaments and muscles that have not developed fully. The condition is very rarely seen in children; parents sometimes misdiagnose flat feet because children's footprints often look completely flat.

❖ **Pigeon toes** is a minor abnormality in which the leg or foot is rotated, forcing the foot and toes to point inwards. It is fairly common in toddlers and generally requires no treatment, correcting itself by the age of about 7 years.

❖ **Chilblains** are red, itchy, swollen areas on toes which can be very painful. They usually heal without treatment, but could be prevented by keeping the feet warm and exercising to improve the circulation.

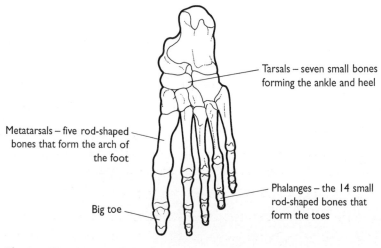

Tarsals – seven small bones forming the ankle and heel

Metatarsals – five rod-shaped bones that form the arch of the foot

Phalanges – the 14 small rod-shaped bones that form the toes

Big toe

Fig 4.9 The bones of the foot

* **Corns** are small areas of thickened skin on a toe caused by pressure from ill-fitting shoes; they are difficult to remove but easy to prevent.
* **Athlete's foot** and **verrucae** are fungal skin conditions of the feet (see Chapter 11).

FOOTWEAR

Parents and carers should always go to a shoe shop where trained children's shoe-fitters can advise on a wide selection of shoes. Second-hand shoes should never be worn as all shoes take on the shape of the wearer's foot.

Guidelines for foot care

* Ensure that bed covers are not tightly tucked in.
* Wash and dry the feet carefully every day.
* Cut toenails straight across; take care not to cut the nails too short. Never dig into the sides of the toenails to remove dirt.
* Allow the child to go barefoot as often as possible.
* Always check that all-in-one stretch suits have plenty of room for the feet to grow.
* Choose socks with a high cotton content so that moisture from the feet can escape.
* Delay buying proper leather shoes until the child is walking and going outdoors regularly; never buy slippers unless they are properly fitted by a reputable shoe-fitter.
* Always check that socks fit properly and do not stretch too tightly over the toes or sag and ruck up around the heels.

Guidelines for choosing the correct footwear for children

* When shoes are fitted, there should be at least 1 cm between the longest toe and the inside of the shoe.
* Both feet should be measured for length, width and girth.
* Shoes must fit snugly around the heel and fasten across the instep to prevent the foot sliding forward.
* The soles of the shoes should be flexible and hard-wearing; non-slip soles are safer.
* Leather is the ideal material for shoes that are to be worn every day as it lets the feet breathe — moisture can escape.
* Padders — soft corduroy shoes — keep a baby's feet warm when crawling or toddling, but should not be worn if the soles become slippery with wear.
* Shoes should never be bought a size too large as they can cause friction and blistering.
* Wellington boots should not be worn routinely because they do not allow the feet to breathe. However, they are very useful for outdoor play, with socks worn underneath.

THE NEED FOR REST AND SLEEP

Children vary in their need for sleep and in the type of sleep they require (see Chapter 13, page 549). Sleep and rest are needed for:

✤ relaxation of the central nervous system (CNS): the brain does not rest completely during sleep; electrical activity – which can be measured by an electroencephalogram (EEG) – continues;

✤ recovery of the muscles and the body's metabolic processes: growth hormone is released during sleep to renew tissues, and produce new bone and red blood cells.

Some children prefer to rest quietly in their cots rather than have a sleep during the day; others will continue to have one or two daytime naps even up to the age of 3 or 4 years.

Establishing a bedtime routine

In the context of modern life in the UK, children benefit from a regular routine at bedtime; it helps to establish good habits and makes children feel more secure. A child will only sleep if actually tired, so it is vital that she has had enough exercise and activity. The stress on parents of a child who will not sleep at night can be severe (about 10–20 per cent of very young children have some sort of sleep problem); establishing a routine that caters for the child's **individual needs** may help parents to prevent such problems developing. Principles involved are:

✤ ensuring the child has had enough exercise during the day;

✤ making sure that the environment is conducive to sleep – a soft night light and non-stimulating toys might help, with no activity going on around bedtime;

Guidelines for a bedtime routine

The following suggestions can be helpful in establishing a bedtime routine:

1 Warn the child that bedtime will be at a certain time (e.g. after a bath and a story).

2 Take a family meal about 1½ to 2 hours before bedtime; this should be a relaxing, social occasion.

3 After the meal, the child can play with other members of the family.

4 Make bath-time a relaxing time to unwind and play gently; this often helps the child to feel drowsy.

5 Give a final bedtime drink, followed by teeth cleaning.

6 Read or tell a story; looking at books together or telling a story enables the child to feel close to the carer.

7 Settle the child in bed, with curtains drawn and night light on if desired. Then say goodnight and leave.

❧ following the precept 'never let the sun go down on a quarrel' – a child who has been in trouble during the day needs to feel reassured that all is forgiven before bedtime;

❧ warning the child that bedtime is approaching and then following the set routine (see guidelines set out below);

❧ reducing anxiety and stress – it is quite natural for a small child to fear being left alone or abandoned; the parents should let the child know they are still around by talking quietly or having the radio on, for example, rather than creeping around silently.

Any care must take into account cultural preferences, such as later bedtimes, and family circumstances: a family living in bed-and-breakfast accommodation may have to share bathroom facilities, or bedtime may be delayed to enable a working parent to be involved in the routine.

ACTIVITY: BEDTIME ROUTINE

Arrange to visit a family with a young child (ideally, your family placement) to talk about the child's bedtime routine. Devise a questionnaire to find out the following:

❧ any problems settling the child to sleep;

❧ any problems with the child waking in the night;

❧ strategies used to address the problems.

Using the answers from the questionnaire to help you, devise a bedtime routine for a 3-year-old girl who has just started nursery school and whose mother has 3-month-old twin boys.

Points to include are:

❧ how to arrange one-to-one care for the 3-year-old;

❧ how to avoid jealousy.

SIGNS AND SYMPTOMS OF POTENTIAL CONCERN

You are in an ideal position to notice when a child has any signs and symptoms of illness. Young children are particularly vulnerable to infection, which can occur within the body (e.g. gastroenteritis) or on the skin (e.g. impetigo). The incidence of the more common infectious diseases, such as chickenpox and measles, rises rapidly in nurseries and schools.

Such illnesses and infections are covered in depth in Chapter 11, but you need to be alert to any of the following signs and symptoms and to respond swiftly when you are concerned:

❧ **Loss of appetite:** the child may not want to eat or drink; this could be because of a sore, painful throat or it may be a sign of a developing infection.

❧ **Lethargy or listlessness:** a child may be drowsy and prefer to sit quietly with a favourite toy or comfort blanket.

❧ **Lacking interest in play:** a child may not want to join in play without being able to explain why.

* **Irritability and fretfulness:** the child may show a change in behaviour, being easily upset and tearful.

* **Abdominal pain:** he or she may rub his or her tummy and say that it hurts – this could be a sign of gastroenteritis.

* **Pallor:** the child may look paler than usual and may have dark shadows under the eyes; a black child may have a paler area around the lips and the conjunctiva may be pale pink instead of the normal dark pink.

* **Raised temperature (fever):** a fever (a temperature above 38°C) is usually an indication of viral or bacterial infection, but can also result from overheating.

* **Rash:** any rash appearing on the child's body should be investigated – a rash is usually a sign of an infectious disease.

* **Diarrhoea and vomiting:** attacks of diarrhoea and/or vomiting are usually a sign of gastroenteritis.

* **Swelling, bruising or bleeding:** any swelling or open wound should be investigated and steps taken to prevent the spread of infection and to relieve any pain.

CLOTHING FOR CHILDREN

The same principles that apply to clothing for babies (see page 555) apply to the selection of clothes for children. Parents and carers should expect children to become dirty as they explore their surroundings and should not show disapproval when clothes become soiled.

Clothes for children should be:

* hard-wearing;

* comfortable;

* easy to put on and take off, especially when going to the toilet;

* washable.

Types of clothes

* **Underwear** should be made of cotton, which is comfortable and sweat-absorbent.

* **Sleepsuits** – all-in-one pyjamas with hard-wearing socks – are useful for children who kick the bedcovers off at night. These must be the correct size to prevent damage to growing feet.

* **Daytime clothes** should be adapted to the stage of mobility and independence of the child; for example a dress will hinder a young girl trying to crawl, and dungarees may prove difficult for a toddler to manage when being toilet-trained. Cotton jersey tracksuits, T-shirts and cotton jumpers are all useful garments which are easy to launder.

* **Outdoor clothes** must be warm and loose enough to fit over clothing and still allow freedom of movement; a showerproof anorak with a hood is ideal as it can be easily washed and dried.

* **Clothes which are appropriate for the weather**. For example, children need to be protected from the sun and should wear wide-brimmed hats with neck shields; they need warm gloves, scarves and woolly or fleece hats in cold, windy weather and waterproof coats and footwear when out in the rain.

Caring for children's clothes

Many nannies have total responsibility for the care of children's clothes and

ACTIVITY: CHILDREN'S CLOTHING

Plan a wardrobe of clothes suitable for a child aged 3 years for an entire year. For each garment, state:

❖ the reason you have chosen it;

❖ how it should be laundered or cleaned;

❖ how it may promote the child's independence.

bed linen. When caring for clothes, you should:

❖ look at the laundry care labels on each garment and make sure that you are familiar with the different symbols;

❖ check and empty all pockets before laundering;

❖ be guided by the parents regarding choice of washing powder – some detergents can cause an adverse skin reaction in some children;

❖ dry clothes thoroughly before putting them away;

❖ label children's clothes with name tapes before they go into group settings.

THE DEVELOPMENT OF BOWEL AND BLADDER CONTROL

Newborn babies pass the waste products of digestion automatically; in other words, although they may go red in the face when passing a stool or motion, they have no conscious control over the action. Parents used to boast with pride that all their children were potty-trained at 9 months, but the reality is that they were lucky in their timing! Up to the age of 18 months, emptying of the bladder and bowel is still a totally automatic reaction – the child's central nervous system is still not sufficiently mature to make the connection between the action and its results.

Toilet-training

There is no point in attempting to start toilet-training until the toddler shows that he or she is ready, and this rarely occurs before the age of 18 months. The usual signs are:

❖ increased interest when passing urine or a motion – the child may pretend-play on the potty with their toys;

❖ they may tell the carer when they have passed urine or a bowel motion, or look very uncomfortable when they have done so;

❖ they may start to be more regular with bowel motions or wet nappies may become rarer.

Toilet-training should be approached in a relaxed, unhurried manner. If the potty is introduced too early or if a child is forced to sit on it for long periods of time, he may rebel and the whole issue of toilet-training becomes a battleground. Toilet-training can be over in a few days or may take some months. Becoming dry at night takes longer, but most children manage this before the age of 5 years.

Guidelines for toilet-training

❖ Before attempting to toilet-train a child, make sure she has shown that she is ready to be trained. Remember that there is, as with all developmental milestones, a wide variation in the age range at which children achieve bowel and bladder control.

❖ Be relaxed about toilet-training and be prepared for accidents.

❖ Have the potty in the home so that the child becomes familiar with it and can include it in her play.

❖ Some children feel insecure when sitting on a potty with no nappy on – try it first still wearing nappy or pants if she shows reluctance.

❖ It is easier to attempt toilet-training in fine weather when the child can run around without a nappy or pants.

❖ It helps if the child sees other children using the toilet or potty.

❖ If you start training when there is a new baby due, be prepared for some accidents. Many children react to a new arrival by regressing to baby behaviour.

❖ Training pants, similar to ordinary pants but with a waterproof covering, are useful in the early stages of training – and having more than one potty in the house makes life easier. Pull-up nappies are a newer version of training pants.

❖ Always praise the child when she succeeds and do not show anger or disapproval if she does not – she may be upset by an accident.

❖ Offer the potty regularly so that the child becomes used to the idea of a routine, and learn to read the signs that a child needs to use it.

❖ Do not show any disgust for the child's faeces. She will regard using the potty as an achievement and will be proud of them. Children have no natural shame about their bodily functions (unless adults make them ashamed).

❖ Some children are frightened when the toilet is flushed; be tactful and sympathetic. You could wait to flush until the child has left the room.

❖ Cover the potty and flush the contents down the toilet. Always wear disposable gloves.

❖ Encourage good hygiene right from the start by washing the child's hands after every use of the potty.

❖ The child may prefer to try the 'big' toilet seat straight away; a toddler seat fixed onto the normal seat makes this easier. Boys need to learn to stand in front of the toilet and aim at the bowl before passing any urine; you could put a piece of toilet paper in the bowl for him to aim at.

Dealing with accidents

Even once a child has become used to using the potty or toilet, there will be occasions when they have an accident, that is, they wet or soil themselves. This happens more often during the early stages of toilet training, as the child may lack the awareness and the control needed to allow enough time to get to the potty. Older children may become so absorbed in their play that they simply forget to go to the toilet.

You can help children when they have an accident by:

❖ not appearing bothered; let the child know that it is not a big problem, just something that happens from time to time;

❖ reassuring the child in a friendly tone of voice and offering a cuddle if they seem distressed;

❖ being discreet; deal with the matter swiftly – wash and change them out of view of others and with the minimum of fuss;

❖ encouraging an older child to manage the incident themselves, if they wish to do so, but always check tactfully afterwards that they have managed;

❖ following safety procedures in the setting, for example wearing disposable gloves and dealing appropriately with soiled clothing and waste.

Enuresis (bedwetting)

Enuresis is a common occurrence; about 1 in 10 children wets the bed at the age of 6 years, and many of these continue to do so until the age of 8 or 9 years. It is more common in boys than in girls and the problem tends to run in families. In the majority of children, enuresis is due to slow maturation of the nervous system functions concerned with control of the bladder; very rarely it occurs because of emotional stress or because of a physical problem such as urinary infection.

Encopresis (soiling)

Encopresis is a type of soiling in which children who have no physical problems with their bowel motions deliberately pass them in their pants or on the floor. It occurs after the age at which bowel control is usually achieved and in children who know the difference between the right and wrong place to go. Fortunately it is a rare condition, but one which needs very sensitive treatment. Encopresis may occur because of emotional problems and stress; if it persists, advice should be sought from the health visitor or doctor.

ACTIVITY: TOILET-TRAINING

Arrange to interview a parent or carer who has recently toilet-trained a child.

1 Try to find out the methods used and any problems encountered.

2 Write a report of the methods used.

3 In class, discuss the problems which can arise in toilet-training and compare the strategies used by different families.

In small groups, make a colourful, eye-catching wall display that provides tips for parents and carers on potty training.

Guidelines for managing bedwetting

❖ Investigate possible physical causes first by taking the child to the doctor.

❖ Protect the mattress with a plastic sheet.

❖ Do not cut down on the amount a child drinks in a day; although a bedtime drink could be given earlier, never let a child go to bed feeling thirsty.

❖ Encourage the child to pass urine just before going to bed; it sometimes helps to 'lift' the child just before adults go to bed, taking her to the toilet. It is important, however, that the child is thoroughly awake when passing urine; this is because she will need to recognise the link between passing urine on the toilet and waking up with a dry bed.

❖ Some parents find that a 'star chart' system of rewards for a dry bed encourages the child to become dry sooner, but there are problems with all reward systems (see Chapter 10). This should only be used if physical problems have been excluded.

❖ If the child continues to wet the bed after the age of 7 years, a special night-time alarm system can be used, with a detector mat placed under the sheet. This triggers a buzzer as soon as it becomes wet; eventually the child will wake before he needs to pass urine (this system is said to succeed in over two-thirds of children).

Section 3: Health and safety requirements

REGULATIONS FOR EARLY YEARS SETTINGS

There are many regulations, laws and guidelines dealing with health and safety. You do not need to know the detail, but you *do* need to know where your responsibilities begin and end. The most relevant laws relating to health and safety in the child care setting are:

❖ Health and Safety at Work Act;

❖ Management of Health and Safety at Work Regulations;

❖ Control of Substances Hazardous to Health (COSHH);

❖ Reporting of Injuries, Diseases and Dangerous Occurrences Regulations (RIDDOR);

❖ Electricity at Work Regulations;

❖ Manual Handling Operations Regulations;

❖ Fire Precautions at Work Regulations;

❖ The Children Act.

Your role and responsibilities

These include:

❖ taking reasonable care for your **own safety** and that of others;

❖ working with your employer in respect of health and safety matters;

❖ knowing about the policies and procedures in your particular place of work – these can all be found in the setting's **health and safety policy**;

❖ not intentionally damaging any **health and safety equipment** or materials provided by the employer;

❖ reporting any **hazards** you come across immediately.

Apart from your legal responsibilities, knowing how to act and being alert and vigilant at all times can prevent accidents, injury, infections and even death – to you, your fellow-workers or the children in your care.

Risk assessment

Risk assessment is a method of preventing accidents and ill health by helping people to think about what could go wrong and devising ways to prevent problems.

❖ Look for the hazards.

❖ Decide who might be harmed and how.

❖ Weigh up the risk – a risk is the likelihood that a hazard will cause harm.

❖ Decide whether existing precautions are adequate.

❖ If not, decide what further precautions are needed to reduce risk.

❖ Record your findings.

Hazards in child care settings

GENERAL SAFETY – SLIPS, TRIPS AND FALLS

You will need to check before, during and after play sessions and remove any items that prevent children – and you – getting from A to B safely. Always be aware of children with special needs, for example those with mobility problems or a visual impairment. Whenever children are playing with or near water – even indoors at the water play area – they must be constantly supervised. Babies

need to be protected from falls – again, close supervision is needed. Everyone who works with children should take a recognised 'baby and child' first-aid course and should take refresher courses periodically.

MOVING AND HANDLING

Lifting and carrying children and moving the equipment used in child care settings could lead to manual handling injuries such as sprains and strains.

If you *do* have to lift something or somebody from the ground, you should follow these rules:

1 Keep your feet apart.

2 Bend your knees and keep your back upright.

3 Use both hands to get a secure hold.

4 Keep your shoulders level, your back upright and slowly straighten your legs.

5 To put the load down, take the weight on the legs by bending your knees.

COSHH – Control of Substances Hazardous to Health Regulations

Safe workplaces depend on the careful use and storage of cleaning materials and other potentially hazardous substances. Every workplace must have a **COSHH file** which lists all the hazardous substances used in the setting. The file should detail:

❖ where they are kept;

❖ how they are labelled;

❖ their effects;

❖ the maximum amount of time it is safe to be exposed to them;

❖ how to deal with an emergency involving one of them.

Never mix products together – they could produce toxic fumes (some bleaches and cleaning products, for example, have this effect).

Infection control

Children who play closely together for long periods of time are more likely than others to develop an infection, and any infection can spread very quickly from one child to another and to adults who care for them. Your setting's **health and safety policy** will establish procedures to reduce the risk of transferring infectious diseases. These include:

❖ providing staff members and parents with **information** on infection control policies and procedures;

❖ stating the **exclusion criteria** that will apply when a child or a staff member is sick;

❖ providing training for staff members so they understand and can use the **infection control** procedures;

❖ providing **adequate supervision** to make sure everyone follows the policies and procedures;

❖ providing adequate supplies of **protective equipment**;

❖ providing **adequate facilities** for hand washing, cleaning and disposing of waste;

❖ providing **safe work practices** for high-risk activities, such as dealing with blood and body fluids, nappy changing and toileting, handling dirty linen and contaminated clothing and preparing and handling food.

Equipment and electrical safety

Children should not be left unsupervised in situations where they may cut electric cords,
spill water onto electric equipment or pull cords and leads out of a power point. You should check cords and leads for nicks, cuts and other damage on a regular basis. Never carry on using damaged equipment – immediately report the damage to your manager or supervisor.

Security issues and violence

Early years settings should be secure environments where children cannot wander off without anyone realising. But they also need to be secure so that strangers cannot enter without a good reason for being there. Occasionally you might encounter a problem with violence – or threats of violence – from a child's parents or carers. Your setting will have a policy that deals with this issue.

Fire safety

In the case of fire or other emergency you need to know what to do to evacuate the children and yourself safely. Follow the rules below for fire safety:

❖ **No smoking** is allowed in any child care setting.

❖ Handbags containing **matches** or **lighters** must be locked securely away out of children's reach.

❖ The **nursery cooker** should not be left unattended when turned on.

❖ **Fire exits** must be clearly marked.

❖ **Fire drills** should be carried out regularly; registers must be kept up-to-date throughout the day.

❖ **Fire exits** and other doors should be free of obstructions on both sides.

❖ **Instructions** about what to do in the event of a fire must be clearly displayed.

ACTIVITY: FIRE AND SAFETY, AND ACCIDENTS

In a practical work placement, research the following information.

1   Fire and safety:

   ❖ What are the instructions in the event of a fire?

   ❖ Where are the fire extinguishers located?

   ❖ Where are the fire exits located?

2   Every workplace is required to maintain an accident report book to keep a record of accidents. Ask for permission to look at the book at your placement.

❖ Present the information in the accident book in the form of a pie chart, using the following (and other) categories of accident: falls, cuts, burns and scalds, choking, stings.

❖ For each category of accident, state how an incident could have been prevented and what treatment should have been given.

❖ Remember to preserve confidentiality – do not use names.

❖ You should know where the **fire extinguishers** are kept and how to use them.

❖ **Electrical equipment** should be regularly checked for any faults.

Reporting illness, injury or accident (RIDDOR)

You have a responsibility to report all accidents, incidents and even near-misses to your manager. As you may be handling food, you should also report any personal incidences of sickness or diarrhoea. Most early years settings keep two separate **accident report books** – one for staff and other adults and one for children. These should always be filled in as soon as possible after the incident (see also Chapter 11, page 432).

FOOD-HANDLING REGULATIONS

Any early years setting that prepares and serves food for children must comply with the food-handling regulations; this means ensuring that all staff members have sufficient training or supervision to ensure a good standard of food hygiene is followed.

You have a duty to:

❖ handle **food safely** and avoid the risk of food poisoning;

❖ keep yourself and your work area **clean**;

❖ wear suitable **protective clothing** – gloves and apron – used for food preparation only;

❖ **protect food from contamination**;

❖ follow **correct temperature controls** during preparation;

❖ tell your employer if you have **food poisoning symptoms** yourself or any infectious disease, illness or infected cuts, and so on;

❖ inform your supervisor or manager if you have concerns about **food hygiene**.

HYGIENE ROUTINES

You have a very important role in reducing the risk of infection. At all times you should wear clean clothes, keep your nails short, cover any open wounds with a waterproof plaster and, if necessary, tie back your hair.

When you have been provided with protective clothing, you *must* wear it. Along with washing hands properly it is a really effective way of preventing cross-infection.

When to wash your hands

Hands are the most obvious way in which a person can contaminate food because they touch utensils, work surfaces and the food itself when being prepared, served or eaten. **Nails** can also harbour dirt and bacteria, and should be kept short and clean at all times.

- ❖ The number of bacteria on fingertips doubles after using the toilet.
- ❖ Bacteria can stay alive on our hands for up to 3 hours.
- ❖ 1000 times as many bacteria spread from damp hands as from dry hands.
- ❖ Even after thorough washing, certain bugs can remain under long fingernails.
- ❖ Right-handed people tend to wash their left hand more thoroughly than their right hand, and vice versa.
- ❖ Millions of bacteria can hide under rings, watches and bracelets.
- ❖ A 1 mm hair follicle can harbour 50,000 bacteria.

Guidelines for washing your hands

You should wash your hands:

Before:

- ❖ starting work – this is particularly important when working in a caring environment;
- ❖ preparing food;
- ❖ eating;
- ❖ putting a plaster on a child or giving medicines, and so on;
- ❖ looking after babies and young children.

Between:

- ❖ handling raw foods (meat, fish, poultry and eggs) and touching any other food or kitchen utensils.

After:

- ❖ handling raw foods, particularly meat, fish and poultry and raw eggs in their shells;
- ❖ going to the toilet;
- ❖ coughing or sneezing (into your hands or a tissue);
- ❖ touching your hair or face;

- ❖ playing outside;
- ❖ touching rubbish/waste bins; cleaning cat litter boxes or using chemical cleansers;
- ❖ changing nappies;
- ❖ caring for someone ill, especially with tummy upsets;
- ❖ handling and stroking pets or farm animals; gardening – even if you wear gloves;
- ❖ smoking.

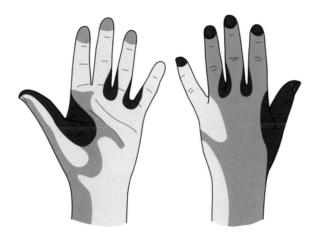

Fig 4.10 Parts commonly missed when washing hands

We all think we know how to wash our hands, but many of us do not do it properly. The picture above shows how we often miss certain parts of our hands when washing them.

A step-by-step guide to effective hand washing

1 Wet your hands thoroughly under warm running water and squirt liquid soap onto the palm of one hand.

2 Rub your hands together to make a lather.

3 Rub the palm of one hand along the back of the other and along the fingers. Then do the same with the other hand.

4 Rub in between each of your fingers on both hands and around your thumbs.

5 Rinse off the soap with clean running water.

6 Dry hands thoroughly on a clean dry towel, paper towel or air dryer.

This should take about 15–20 seconds.

SAFE AND HYGIENIC PRACTICE WHEN CARING FOR ANIMALS

Small pets can help to provide a homely atmosphere in nurseries and schools; they can extend children's knowledge and skills, as well as giving general enjoyment. At home, parents choosing a pet for their children should realise that they are totally responsible for its wellbeing and survival, however keen the children are. A young child cannot judge when an animal has played long enough, whether its diet is suitable or how often its cage needs cleaning.

Guinea pigs

Guinea pigs (or cavies) can be bought from a pet shop at about 6–8 weeks old. They are generally gentle and trusting creatures that are safe for children to handle. It is better to keep two guinea pigs together as they are social animals. They can be kept in a hutch outdoors, but will need to be brought inside if the weather is very cold. About one-third of the hutch should be enclosed as a sleeping area, and this must be raised off the ground, out of the way of draughts and rats. Guinea pigs also need space to exercise in, and a wire-covered run should make up the other two-thirds of the cage. They like to eat corn, oats, fruit, vegetables and dandelion leaves; they also drink a lot of water. The cage should be cleaned daily, and any stale food removed.

Hamsters

Hamsters are solitary animals and may fight if two or more are kept in the same cage. They are nocturnal animals – that is, they sleep during the day and are active at night. They make good pets for children at home, but are not so suitable for nurseries and schools because of their sleeping habits.

Gerbils

Gerbils like to live in company. They breed rapidly, so it is better to keep two of the same sex in a glass tank. Children like to observe their habits of burrowing (supply plenty of empty cardboard rolls and jam jars) and gnawing (supply wood blocks). The advantage of keeping gerbils – rather than mice or rats – is that they are desert animals and so do not pass urine very frequently; they are also easily tamed and appreciate handling.

Dogs and cats

As family pets, dogs and cats are very rewarding animals to keep. They would not, however, be suitable for nurseries and schools.

Fig 4.11 Caring for pet rabbits

The RSPCA view

The RSPCA (Royal Society for the Prevention of Cruelty to Animals) is opposed to the keeping of animals in captivity on school premises *unless* proper provision can be made for their physical and mental well-being. The RSPCA believes that ensuring the welfare of animals is extremely difficult in most nursery classrooms or playgroup spaces, for the following reasons:

❖ **Over-handling:** animals can be exposed to over-handling by large numbers of enthusiastic children.

❖ **Rest:** animals may not receive adequate rest periods during the day.

❖ **Lack of care:** animals may be left unattended for long periods during weekends and holidays.

❖ **Expense:** animals can be expensive to keep.

❖ **Health and safety:** animals can cause both health and safety problems for children.

The RSPCA believes that animal welfare can be taught *without* keeping animals captive, and has produced two booklets that explore the alternatives to keeping a pet in the nursery, while still allowing children valuable first-hand experience of animals and wildlife. The RSPCA suggests the following activities for nursery-age children:

❖ **Personal, social and emotional development:** ask the children to describe what a pet needs to keep it healthy and contented. They could draw their favourite pet with all the things it needs around it.

❖ **Mathematical development:** design a matching game where children have to match the animal to its home or habitat.

❖ **Creative development:** take the children for a sensory walk to the local park to observe animals in their natural habitat.

❖ **Communication, language and literacy:** involve the children in designing a role-play area with a veterinary surgery, farm or kennel as a theme. Ask the children to role-play the animals, their owners, the veterinary surgeon and the animal carers.

❖ **Physical development:** ask the children to make a model animal hospital using plasticine, clay or found materials to form the animals and the hospital.

Guidelines for safe and hygienic practice when caring for animals

❖ **Supervision:** make sure that interaction with animals is supervised.

❖ **Hand washing:** make sure that children wash their hands after handling animals.

❖ **Hygiene:** make sure that children do not play in dirt that may be contaminated by animals; in particular, make sure that children do not place the dirt or dirty hands in their mouths.

❖ **Health:** exclude sick animals from child care settings.

ACTIVITY: A PET FOR THE NURSERY

You have been asked by a day nursery or nursery school to research the possibility of acquiring a pet for the nursery.

1   Prepare an **action plan**, to include:

   ❖ how to choose a pet – what criteria you would use;

   ❖ what preparation would be necessary;

   ❖ the routine care of the pet and how it would be carried out;

   ❖ the benefits to the children of having your chosen pet in the nursery.

2   Write a report for the nursery teacher or manager, including all the above material.

3   Write a plan, following RSPCA guidelines, for a trip to a place where children may enjoy an animal-related experience.

❖ **Knowledge and understanding of the world:** encourage children's natural curiosity about animals. Discuss their habitats and eating habits. Are they birds, mammals, reptiles? What kind of feet, beaks, teeth, fur, feathers, skin do they have?

Health and safety hazards posed by animals

A number of infectious or parasitic diseases may be acquired through contact with animals. Young children are most at risk of becoming infected because of their habit of putting objects into their mouths, and crawling babies may be near to the source of infection.

❖ **Toxocariasis:** This disease is caused by the parasite toxocara (roundworm), found in dog and cat faeces. It is mainly an infection of children who eat dirt or play in areas contaminated by infected dog faeces. It can cause allergic symptoms, such as asthma. Rarely, a larva may lodge in the eye and cause blindness. Prevention is by:

1   preventing parasitic infection in dogs and cats – they should be wormed regularly, according to veterinary instructions;

2   preventing environmental contamination by infective eggs – dog owners should not allow their dogs to foul public places, especially parks and children's play areas;

3   preventing infection through public education – babies and young children should be discouraged from putting objects from the floor near their mouth; dogs should not be allowed to lick people's faces or be allowed to sleep in children's beds (the dog's hair could harbour infected eggs);

4   encouraging children and adults to wash their hands after playing or working outside, or touching dogs, especially before touching food.

❖ **Rabies:** Rabies is a serious viral infection transmitted by a bite from a dog or other animal. The UK is free of rabies, but travellers to countries where rabies exists should treat any dog bite, especially if the dog is a stray, with suspicion.

❖ **Dog bites:** These can cause serious bleeding and shock, and may become infected; fortunately, they are rare, but children should be discouraged from patting dogs they meet outside their home.

❖ **Fleas:** Fleas may transfer from a dog's or cat's fur to humans and can cause irritating bites; the fleas jump onto humans to feed, particularly in the warm weather if the cat or dog is absent.

❖ **Cat-scratch fever:** This is a rare disease that can develop after a scratch or bite by a cat. It is thought to be caused by a small bacterium that has not been identified. The main sign of illness is a swollen lymph node near the scratch, fever and headache. It usually clears up completely within 2 months.

❖ **Psittacosis:** This is a rare illness that is spread from birds to humans. The infection is contracted by inhaling dust contaminated by the droppings of infected birds, usually parrots or pigeons.

❖ **Leptospirosis:** This is also known as Weil's disease. It is a rare disease caused by a type of spirochaete bacterium that is harboured by rats and excreted in their urine. It often affects the kidneys and can also cause liver damage.

❖ **Ringworm (or tinea):** This is a fungal infection of the skin. The most common type is tinea pedis (athlete's foot – see Chapter 11), but tinea can also occur on the body or the scalp. The infection may be passed from animals to people, but more usually is passed from person to person. Treatment is by anti-fungal drugs in the form of lotions, creams or ointments.

❖ **Lyme disease:** This is a disease caused by a bacterium that is transmitted by the bite of a tick that usually lives on deer but can infest dogs. Symptoms are the same as for the flu, but also include some skin changes and joint inflammation. Lyme disease is becoming more common in the UK.

IDENTIFYING AND REPORTING HAZARDS

One of the cornerstones of early years education is to offer an exciting range of experiences to children that will stimulate them and extend their skills in all areas of development. But this must be done safely. Ensuring the children's safety at all times means that staff, preferably in collaboration with parents, should:

❖ identify **potential dangers** in both the indoor and outdoor environment;

❖ develop a **strategy for avoiding these dangers**.

This process results in a set of safety rules that should be displayed in relevant areas, for the benefit of parents and relief staff, and which should be given to all staff working with the children.

Safe disposal of body fluids

Nursery classes, schools and hospitals must have a policy for dealing with body fluids which should be followed at all times. A child may be HIV positive or have hepatitis B without the carers' knowledge, so the policy should be rigorously adhered to. All local authorities issue guidelines on the safe disposal of body fluids, which specify:

❖ wearing disposable latex gloves when dealing with blood, urine, faeces or vomit;

❖ washing the hands after dealing with spillages – even if gloves have been worn;

❖ using a 1 per cent solution of hypochlorite (bleach) to cover any blood spillages; the area should then be wiped over with a gloved hand, using disposable cloths; the cloths must then be discarded into a bag that is sent for incineration;

❖ avoiding sharp instruments that could result in injury;

❖ covering any skin abrasion with a waterproof plaster.

Extra care must be taken if any body fluid comes into contact with the carer's broken skin (e.g. through a puncture wound). The carer should wash the affected area with soap and water, and encourage bleeding to flush out any contamination. An **accident report**

Fig 4.12 Playing outside in a safe environment

form should then be completed and medical advice sought.

Potential hazards in the early years setting

Young children are usually unaware of the extent of dangers in the environment. They are keen to explore everything that they encounter, and this curiosity involves touching and often tasting objects that may be poisonous or unhygienic. A child attending a nursery class for the first time may find that much of the equipment in daily use is unfamiliar and requires them to learn new skills. Potentially dangerous items are:

* climbing frames;
* large blocks;
* scissors;
* hammers and nails at a woodwork bench;
* wheeled toys;
* slides.

Added to this list must be the presence of other children – collisions in the play area are fairly common, especially involving wheeled toys and slides.

ADULTS AS POSITIVE ROLE MODELS

Adults can help children learn about safety issues and become independent by behaving as good role models. To be a good role model for children, you need to:

* **Set a good example** to children and to others. Children unconsciously imitate the adults they are with. If you show a real concern for safety issues,

then children will pick up on this and think about safety as you do. This is indirect teaching.

* **Be vigilant** at all times. When supervising children in a group setting, you need to be aware of their moods and anticipate any problems.

* **Follow safety procedures.** For example, you should learn the **Green Cross Code** (see Chapter 11) and make sure that you always adhere to the rules when you are out with children.

* **Keep the environment as safe and hygienic as possible**; mop up spills straightaway and clear up after activities with children.

SAFE MANAGEMENT OF DAILY ROUTINES

All children benefit from routines in daily care and contribute greatly to the provision of a positive, safe and secure environment. Daily routines include:

* safety at home-times;
* safety at mealtimes and snack-times;
* safety at sleep-times and rest-times;
* hygiene routines.

Safety at home-times

Your setting will have a policy relating to what to do when parents come to collect their child. Many early years settings have door entry phones and a password system for parents and staff to enter the premises. At home-time staff *must* ensure that the child is collected by the appropriate person. If parents know that they will not be able to

Case Study

Problems at home–time

Anna is a 3-year-old child who attends a private nursery group 4 days a week. Her key worker, Jenny, has developed a good professional relationship with Anna's mother and suspects that she and her partner are having problems balancing their home life with their work commitments. Anna's mother, Jane, often arrives late to collect Anna; she is always very flustered and apologetic about it. Anna's father, David, works long hours as a sales rep and is often away from home for weeks at a time. He has only collected Anna on a couple of occasions before – and only when Jane had given prior permission. One Friday afternoon, David arrives at the nursery and explains to Jenny that Jane had rung him to say she was running very late and asked if he could collect Anna on this occasion. When Jenny replies that she must check with the nursery manager before allowing him to take Anna, David becomes very angry and starts to shout about his rights as a father. As Jenny is trying to calm him down, he suddenly pushes his way past her into the nursery room and scoops Anna up, grabbing her coat from her peg as he rushes out. Jane arrives 5 minutes later and becomes very distressed when she hears what has happened. She tells Jenny that she and David had had a massive row that morning and that he had threatened to leave her.

ACTIVITY: PROBLEMS AT HOME-TIME

Discuss this scenario in class and answer the following questions:

1 If you were Jenny, Anna's key worker, what should you do?

2 What are the main issues involved in this case study?

3 How can the nursery ensure each child's safety at home-time?

4 Find out how your setting deals with issues of safety at home-time.

collect their child on a particular occasion, they should notify the setting, giving permission for another named person to collect their child. The child's key worker should, where possible, be responsible for handover at home-times.

Safety at mealtimes and snack-times

Meals and snack-times should be enjoyable occasions for both staff and children. The safety guidelines set out below should be followed to ensure health and safety at these times:

❖ **Hygiene:** wipe all surfaces where food will be served before and after meals and snacks. Make sure that children have washed and dried their hands before eating.

❖ **Serving food:** check that the food you are giving children is appropriate for them; check they have no allergies, for example to milk or wheat. Never give peanuts to children under 4 years as they can easily choke or inhale them into their lungs, causing infection and lung damage. Food should be cut up into manageable pieces and should be served at the correct temperature – not too hot or too cold.

❖ **Seating:** babies should be securely strapped into high chairs, using a 5-point harness.

❖ **Supervision:** supervise children carefully; never leave children unattended with drinks or food in case they choke. Never leave a baby alone eating finger foods. Babies can choke silently when eating soft foods such as pieces of banana. Never leave babies propped up with a bottle or feeding beaker.

❖ Make sure you know what to do if a child is **choking** (see Chapter 11, page 428).

Safety at sleep-times and rest-times

Every setting will have its own routine, providing for the needs of both babies and young children for periods of rest and sleep. You should follow the guidelines set out below.

Hygiene routines

You need to encourage children to become independent by helping them to learn how to take care of themselves. Hand washing is especially important for children who eat with their hands, as infection can be spread in saliva. Make sure that children always wash their hands thoroughly, using soap and water.

Each child in an early years setting should have:

❖ his or her own **flannels**, which are kept exclusively for their own use and washed at the end of the day – unless **disposable cloths** are used; you can use these to

Guidelines for sleep and rest routines

❖ Treat each child uniquely – every child has his or her own needs for sleep and rest.

❖ Be guided by the wishes of the child's parent or carer.

❖ Keep noise to a minimum and darken the room; make sure that children have been to the toilet.

❖ Always put babies on their backs to sleep (see Chapter 13, page 550).

❖ Make sure that the cot or bed is safe and hygienic: no pillows, no small objects within reach and no ribbon fastenings on garments.

❖ Find out all you can about the individual child's preferences; some children like to be patted to sleep; others may need to cuddle their favourite comfort object.

❖ Make sure that someone is always with the child until they fall asleep; reassure them that someone will be there when they wake up.

❖ Provide quiet, relaxing activities for those children who are unable to – or do not want to – sleep, for example reading a book to them, doing a jigsaw puzzle.

Guidelines for supporting hygiene routines

1   Teach children how to wash and dry their hands – using soap and warm water and a paper towel:

- ❖ before eating or drinking;
- ❖ after using the toilet;
- ❖ before and after eating meals or snacks;
- ❖ after handling pets or other animals;
- ❖ after blowing their nose;
- ❖ after being exposed to blood or other body fluids.

2   Provide children with their own combs and brushes, and encourage them to use these every day.

3   Provide a soft toothbrush and teach children how and when to brush their teeth.

4   Ensure that you are a good role model for children – for example, when you cough or sneeze, always cover your mouth.

5   Devise activities which develop an awareness in children of the importance of hygiene routines – for example, you could invite a dental hygienist or dental nurse to the setting to talk to children about daily teeth care.

ACTIVITY: ENCOURAGING CHILDREN TO WASH THEIR HANDS

Plan an activity to do with small groups of nursery-age children that will teach them about the importance of washing their hands. Children should wash their hands by cleaning them with soap for at least 10 seconds under warm, running water. To help the children estimate the right length of time you could get them to sing 'Twinkle Twinkle Little Star', or a similar song, slowly all the way through.

In your write-up you should include:

- ❖ a rationale – a reason for doing your particular activity;

- ❖ an account of how you plan to carry out the activity – when? how many children?

- ❖ an evaluation – how did the activity go? did you achieve your aims?

- ❖ a brief summary of the activity and any ideas for improving it in the future.

Bear in mind that you need to make the activity fun for the children and that you should make sure that you have everything you need before beginning – soap, warm water and paper towels or clean cloth towels.

help a child to wash his or her face after a meal or during the day at any time when they have become sticky and dirty;

✤ his or her own **comb** and/or **brush**; the child should be encouraged to use these every day.

SAFE MANAGEMENT OF TRIPS AND OUTINGS

Any outing away from the children's usual setting – for instance, trips to farms, parks and theatres – must be planned with safety and security issues as top priority.

Guidelines for safety on trips and outings

✤ **Planning:** you may need to visit the place beforehand and to discuss any particular requirements, for example what to do if it rains, or specific lunch arrangements.

✤ **Permission:** the manager or head teacher must give permission for the outing, and a letter should be sent to all parents and guardians of the children.

✤ **Transport:** if a coach is being hired, check whether it has seat belts for children. The law requires all new minibuses and coaches to have seat belts fitted and minibus drivers to have passed a special driving test.

✤ **Help:** usually help is requested from parents so that adequate supervision is ensured.

✤ **First-aid kit and medicines:** staff should carry a bag with a simple first-aid kit, medication such as inhalers, sun cream, nappies, spare clothes, extra drinks, reins and harnesses.

✤ **Inform parents:** tell them about the outing and what the child needs to bring, for example packed meal and waterproof coat – emphasise no glass bottles and no sweets. Advise on spending money if necessary – state the maximum amount.

✤ **Trained staff:** there should always be trained staff on any outing – however local and low-key the trip may seem.

✤ **Child-to-adult ratio:** this should never exceed 4 to 1. If the children are under 2 years or have special needs, then you would expect to have fewer children per adult. The younger the children, the more adults are required, particularly if the trip involves crossing roads, when an adult *must* be available to hold the children's hands.

✤ **Contact information:** you need to have a copy of the children's contact information with you, and you should check the names of the children regularly against the day's attendance list.

✤ **Swimming trips:** these should only be attempted if the ratio is 1 adult to 1 child for children under 5 years.

ACTIVITY: EVALUATING YOUR HEALTH AND SAFETY POLICY

Ask to see the health and safety policy in your workplace.

1 What aspects of care does it cover?

2 Is it reviewed regularly?

3 Is the policy displayed anywhere?

4 Is there anything you could add to the policy?

Section 4: Diet, nutrition and food

THE PRINCIPLES OF A HEALTHY DIET

Good nutrition, or healthy eating, is one of the most important ways we can help ourselves to feel well and be well. We need food:

* to provide **energy** for physical activity and to maintain body temperature;
* to provide material for the **growth** of body cells;
* for the **repair and replacement** of damaged body tissues.

The substances in food that fulfil these functions are called **nutrients**.

Food and energy requirements

Food requirements vary according to age, gender, size, occupation or lifestyle and climate. Food energy is traditionally measured in kilocalories (kcal) or kilojoules (kJ).

Different foods contain different amounts of energy per unit of weight; foods that contain a lot of fat and sugar have high energy values. An excess of calories will result in

weight gain as the surplus energy is stored as fat; an insufficient intake of calories will result in weight loss as the body has to draw on fat reserves to meet energy requirements. Babies and young children have **relatively high energy requirements** in relation to their size.

PROMOTING HEALTHY EATING

During childhood we develop food habits that will affect us for life. By the time we are adults most of us will suffer from some disorder that is related to our diet, for example tooth decay, heart disease or cancer. Establishing healthy eating patterns in children will help to promote normal growth and development, and will protect against later disease. As an early years worker you need to know what constitutes a good diet and how it can be provided (see Table 4.2).

Food groups

Types of food can be arranged into five groups, based on the nutrients they provide. To ensure a balanced, healthy diet, some foods from each group should be included in a child's diet every day (see Figure 4.13). The easiest way to monitor our nutrition is to keep in mind the five food groups; eating a

Table 4.2 Basic food requirements.

Nutrient/food	Use	Source
Carbohydrates Starches Sugars Cellulose Consist of building blocks, called amino acids, which link together to perform required functions. First-class proteins contain all the essential amino acids. Second-class proteins contain some essential amino acids.	Major source of energy for growth, body maintenance and activity. Aid the digestion of other foods.	Bread, cereals, pasta, plantain, potatoes, pulses rice, grains, sugar, honey, fruit, milk.
Proteins Consist of building blocks, called amino acids, which link together to perform required functions. First-class proteins contain all the essential amino acids. Second-class proteins contain some essential amino acids.	Essential for growth and repair of the body. Also produce certain hormones and other active chemicals. Only used as energy as last resort in the absence of other sources.	First-class proteins: meat, poultry, fish, cheese, milk and milk products. Second-class proteins: nuts and seed, soya, pulses (beans and lentils), cereals (rice, oats and cornmeal) and cereal-based foods e.g. pasta, bread, chapatis.
Fats Saturated fats – from animal sources. Unsaturated fats – from vegetable sources.	Provide energy, contain essential vitamins, conserve body heat	Butter, cheese, meat, lard. Nuts, olive oil, vegetable oils, fish oil
Minerals Cannot be manufactured by the body. Major minerals – calcium, sodium, potassium and magnesium, sulphur, other minerals called trace elements or minerals.	Needed for building bones, regulating fluid balance, control of muscles and nerves, energy production.	Found in nearly all foods in varying amounts. Sodium – in table salt, bread, meat and fish. Fluoride – in water, occurring naturally or added to water supply.
Vitamins Cannot be manufactured by the body. Complex chemical substances made by plants and animals. Divided into two groups: Fat-soluble (A, D E and K) Water-soluble (C and the B vitamins).	Vitamin A – vision and healthy skin. Vitamin D – growth of bones and teeth. Vitamin E – protects cells from damage. Vitamin K – helps the blood-clotting process. The B vitamins – blood formation and muscle function. Vitamin C – promotes the healing process.	Fat-soluble – in oily fish, cheese, carrots, tomatoes, egg yolk, liver, green vegetables. Water-soluble – fruits, fruit juices, meat, leafy vegetables, beans, eggs.
Fibre Also known as roughage, fibre cannot be broken down and used by the body.	Adds bulk to food, helps prevent constipation. Some experts believe that fibre reduces the risk of heart disease, and certain types of cancer.	Rolled oats, beans, wholewheat bread, celery, bran, prunes and apples.
Water	Vital component of our diet. Helps in maintaining fluid balance and in elimination of waste products.	Present in all foods.

Fig 4.13 The balance of good health

variety of foods from each of these food groups every day automatically balances our diet.

FOOD GROUP 1: BREAD, OTHER CEREALS AND POTATOES

Foods in group 1 are *high-energy* foods. They also contain vitamins and minerals. Foods in this group include:

* rice;
* bread;
* breakfast cereal;
* potato;
* pasta;
* chapatti;
* couscous;
* yam and green banana.

Wholemeal bread, wholegrain cereals and potatoes in their skins all increase the **fibre** content of the diet. Bran should not be given to children as an extra source of fibre as it can interfere with the absorption of **calcium** and **iron** and may also cause stomach cramps.

All meals throughout the day should include foods from Group 1. For example:

* Breakfast – a breakfast cereal or bread;
* Cooked meals – pasta, rice or potatoes;
* Snack meals – bread or pizza base.

Children require *five servings* from this food group every day. Examples of *one serving* are:

* 1 bowl of breakfast cereal;
* 1 slice of bread;
* 1 small potato;
* 2 tablespoons of cooked rice or pasta.

FOOD GROUP 2: FRUIT AND VEGETABLES

Fruit and vegetables are full of **vitamins**, **minerals** (see Table 4.3) and **fibre**, all of which are needed to maintain good health; they are also very low in fat. A fruit or vegetable that is **high in vitamin C** should be included in children's diets every day. Examples are:

* tomato;
* citrus fruit, such as orange and grapefruit;

Table 4.3 Vitamins and minerals – good food sources.

Vitamins and minerals	Good food sources	Vitamins and minerals	Good food sources
Vitamin A	Liver, milk, cheese, green vegetables	**Folic acid**	Breakfast cereals, green leafy vegetables, offal (mainly liver)
Thiamin (Vitamin B1)	Bread, breakfast cereals	**Copper**	Found generally in all foods, small amounts
Riboflavin (Vitamin B2)	Breakfast cereals, milk and milk products	**Niacin**	Meat, potatoes, bread, breakfast cereals
Biotin	Eggs, wholewheat breakfast cereals. Also found in small amounts in fish, meat and pulses	**Magnesium**	Found generally in all foods in small amounts
Pantothenic acid	Meat, milk, wholewheat breakfast cereals, lentils, beans and pulses	**Iron**	Red meat, offal, pulses eggs, breakfast cereals, green vegetables
Vitamin B6	Breakfast cereals mainly, but also found in small amounts in fruit, meat and vegetables	**Selenium**	Seafood, meat, offal, milk, wholewheat breakfast cereals, flour
Vitamin B12	Eggs, meat, offal (heart, liver, kidney), dairy produce	**Zinc**	Offal (especially liver), seafood, eggs milk, wholegrain cereals
Vitamin C	Citrus fruits, berry fruits, potatoes, green vegetables	**Calcium**	Dairy produce, tinned fish, white bread/flour
Vitamin E	Vegetable oils (especially sunflower oil), eggs, green leafy vegetables	**Iodine**	Milk and milk products, meat, eggs iodized salt

✤ kiwi fruit;

✤ sweet pepper.

Many children will eat slices of raw vegetables or salad in place of cooked vegetables, for example carrots, cucumber, tomato or peppers. Children who are reluctant to eat vegetables should be given fruit or fruit juice instead.

Children require *four servings* from this group every day. Examples of *one serving* are:

✤ 1 glass of fruit juice;

✤ 1 piece of fruit;

✤ sliced tomato in a sandwich;

✤ 2 tablespoons of cooked vegetables;

✤ 1 tablespoon of dried fruit, such as raisins.

Fruit and vegetables are best eaten raw as their vitamin content is easily destroyed by cooking and processing.

FOOD GROUP 3: MILK AND DAIRY FOODS

This group includes:

✤ milk;

✤ yoghurt and fromage frais;

✤ cheese.

Children require about 1 pint (500 ml) of milk each day to ensure an adequate intake of **calcium**. If a child cannot achieve this milk intake, equivalent amounts of calcium can be taken from yoghurt, cheese, fromage frais, and so on. Reduced-fat milks should not generally be given to children under 5 years because of their lower energy and fat-soluble-vitamin content; however, semi-skimmed milk may be introduced from 2 years of age, provided that the child's overall diet is adequate. (Parents on income support can get tokens to exchange for 7 pints of milk a week for each child under 5 years of age).

Children require *three servings* from this food group every day. Examples of *one serving* are:

✤ 1 glass of milk;

✤ 1 pot of yoghurt or fromage frais;

✤ 1 tablespoon of grated cheese, such as cheese on top of a pizza.

FOOD GROUP 4: HIGH-PROTEIN FOODS

These are foods that are high in protein; they include:

✤ lean meat;

✤ fish;

✤ tofu and Quorn;

✤ poultry;

✤ eggs;

✤ pulses – peas, beans (baked beans, kidney beans), lentils, ground nuts and seeds.

Children require *two servings* from this food group every day (see Tables 4.2 and 4.4). Examples of *one serving* are:

✤ a portion of fish fingers;

✤ a portion of baked beans;

✤ a scrambled egg;

✤ a small piece of chicken.

The amount of group-4 food that makes up one serving varies according to the age of the individual child; for example, a 3-year-old may have two fish fingers, while a 7-year-old may have three or four.

FOOD GROUP 5: FATS AND OILS

Fats and oils are found in the foods from the four groups. For instance, meat and cheese contain fat and some vegetables contain oil.

FOODS HIGH IN FAT AND SUGAR

Sweets, cakes, chocolate and crisps are all *high-energy* foods, but they have little other nutritional value. If children eat a lot of these foods, they run the risk of putting on a lot of weight and suffering from tooth decay.

However, children may be offered limited amounts of foods with extra fat or sugar – biscuits, cakes, chocolate, crisps and sweet drinks – as long as these items are not replacing food from the five food groups.

THE DANGERS OF TOO MUCH SALT

Salt (sodium chloride) should be avoided as far as possible in the diets of young children as their kidneys are not mature enough to cope with large amounts. You should be aware that many common foods, such as cheese, manufactured soup, packet meals and bread, are already quite high in added salt. Children will receive sufficient salt for their dietary needs from a normal balanced diet without adding any to food as it is cooked or at the table.

On average children are eating twice the recommended amount of salt. The recommended nutrient intake (RNI) for infants aged 1–3 years is not more than 1.25 g of salt each day; children aged 4–6 years should consume no more than 1.75 g. Many manufactured foods are marketed at children, and some of these can top their daily salt requirement in a single serving – a bag of crisps for example. A small can (200 g) of pasta shapes in tomato sauce contains twice the daily RNI of salt for a child aged 1–3 years and a third more than the daily RNI for a child aged 4–6 years.

Table 4.4 Suitable protein combinations.

Suitable protein combinations	Found in
For vegetarians and vegans:	
beans + cereal	baked beans on toast
lentils + rice	lentil and rice soup
beans + rice	bean casserole with rice
For lacto-vegetarians only:	
cereal + milk	breakfast cereal with milk
egg + bread	scrambled egg on toast
pasta + cheese	macaroni cheese
bread + cheese	cheese sandwich

Guidelines for reducing salt in children's diets

❖ Cut down gradually on the amount of salt you use in cooking so that children become used to less salty foods.

❖ If preparing baby food at home do not add salt, even if it tastes bland. Manufactured baby food is tightly regulated to limit the salt content to a trace.

❖ Try using a low salt substitute, such as LoSalt, Solo or a supermarket's own brand low-sodium salt in cooking or at the table. These products substitute up to 70 per cent of the sodium chloride with potassium chloride.

Providing drinks for children

You must offer children something to drink several times during the day. The best drinks for young children are **water** and **milk**.

❖ Water is a very underrated drink for the whole family. It quenches thirst without spoiling the appetite; if bottled water is preferred it should be still, not carbonated (fizzy) as this is acidic. More water should be given in hot weather in order to prevent **dehydration**.

❖ Research into how the brain develops has found that water is beneficial; many early years settings now make water available for children to help themselves.

❖ Milk is an excellent, nourishing drink which provides valuable **nutrients**.

OTHER DRINKS

All drinks that contain sugar can be harmful to teeth and can also take the edge off children's appetites. Examples are:

❖ flavoured milks;

❖ fruit squashes;

❖ flavoured fizzy drinks;

❖ fruit juices (containing natural sugar).

Unsweetened *diluted* fruit juice is a reasonable option – but not as good as water or milk – for children, but ideally should only be offered at mealtimes. Low-sugar and diet fruit drinks contain artificial sweeteners and are best avoided. Tea and coffee should not be given to children under 5 years as they prevent the absorption of iron from foods. They also tend to fill children up without providing nourishment.

Vitamins and minerals in children's diets

IRON

Iron is essential for children's health. Lack of iron leads to anaemia, which can hold back both physical and mental development. Children who are poor eaters or who are on restricted diets are most at risk.

Iron comes in two forms:

1 in foods derived from animal sources (especially meat) – this form is easily absorbed by the body;

2 in plant foods – iron in this form is not quite so easy for the body to absorb.

If possible, children should be given a portion of meat or fish every day, and kidney or liver once a week. Even a small portion of meat or fish is useful because it also helps the body to absorb iron from other food sources.

CALCIUM AND VITAMIN D

Children need **calcium** for maintaining and repairing bones and teeth. Calcium is:

❖ found in milk, cheese, yoghurt and other dairy products;

❖ only absorbed by the body if it is taken with **vitamin D**.

The skin can make all the vitamin D that a body needs when it is exposed to gentle sunlight. Additional sources of vitamin D include:

❖ milk;

❖ oily fish;

❖ fortified margarine;

❖ tahini paste (tahini is made from sesame seeds, and these may cause an allergic reaction in a small number of children);

❖ fortified breakfast cereals;

❖ meat;

❖ soya mince and soya drinks;

❖ tofu.

VITAMINS A AND C

Vitamin A keeps skin and bones healthy, helps prevent nose and throat infections, and is necessary for vision in dim light. It is found in carrots, fish liver oils and green vegetables.

Vitamin C is important for the immune system and growth. It also helps in the absorption of iron, especially iron from non-meat sources. Vitamin C intake is often low in children who eat little fruit and vegetables.

Young children can be given extra A, C and D vitamins in tablet or drop form. These can be obtained from local health centres and should be given as instructed on the bottle.

VEGETARIAN CHILDREN

NB If children do not eat meat or fish, they must be offered plenty of iron-rich alternatives, such as egg yolks, dried fruit, beans and lentils, and green leafy vegetables. It is also a good idea to give foods or drinks that are high in vitamin C (see page 197) at mealtimes, as this helps the absorption of iron from non-meat sources.

How to promote healthy eating

Our eating habits, tastes and preferences are shaped very early on – in part by the example set to us by our parents and other carers, and by the food offered in infancy. These early influences often mould our attitude towards food and eating throughout school and adult life. Families which lead such busy lives that each member prepares their own meal and then eats it while watching television will have a very different perspective on the role of food and mealtimes to families who regularly sit together at an evening meal. Some children can be choosy about the food they eat. This can be a source of anxiety for parents and for those who work with the children. However, as long as children eat some food from each of the **five food groups** – even if they are same old favourites – there is no cause for worry.

Foods to avoid giving to children

❖ **Salt:** there is no need to add salt to children's food. From the age of 1 to 3 years, children should be having no more than 2 g of salt a day. Even when buying processed food made specifically for children, remember to check the information given on the labels and to choose those with less salt.

❖ **Nuts:** do not give whole or chopped nuts to children under 5 years because of the risk of choking.

❖ **Raw eggs:** avoid food that contains raw or partially cooked eggs because of the risk of **salmonella**, which causes food poisoning. Make sure that eggs are always cooked until both the white and yolk are solid.

❖ **Undiluted fruit juices:** these contain natural sugars which are known to cause tooth decay; they are best given only at mealtimes and should be diluted when given to young children.

❖ **High-fibre foods:** foods like brown rice and wholemeal pasta are too bulky for children under 5 years; too much fibre can also make it more difficult for the body to absorb some essential nutrients, like **calcium** and **iron**.

❖ **Shark, swordfish and marlin:** these fish should not be given to children because they contain relatively high

Table 4.5 An example of a balanced diet.

Meals and snacks	No. of servings in each food group				
	Potato and cereals	Fruit and vegetables	Milk and milk products	High-protein foods	(Extra fat and sugar)
Breakfast					
1 Weetabix	1				
+ milk			1		
1 slice of toast	1				
Mid-morning					
1 packet raisins		1			
1 glass squash					(1)
Lunch					
Chicken pieces				1	
Chips	1				
Peas		1			
Yoghurt			1		
Fruit juice		1			
Mid-afternoon					
Bread and jam	1				
1 glass of milk			1		
Supper					
Baked beans on toast	1			1	
Cucumber slices		1			
Chocolate buttons					(1)
Totals	5	4	3	2	(2)
Recommended daily servings	5	4	3	2	(-)

levels of **mercury**, which might affect a child's developing nervous system.

♣ **Raw shellfish:** these should be avoided to reduce the risk of a child getting food poisoning.

Government schemes

The **School Fruit and Vegetable Scheme (SFVS)** gives children aged 4–6 years a free portion of fruit or vegetables each day. The scheme was set up in response to a government survey which found that, compared to the recommendation of eating at least five portions of fruit and vegetables a day, children eat on average only two.

The **Food in Schools Programme** is a joint Department of Health and Department for Education and Skills programme that provides guidance and resources on the following:

♣ healthier breakfast clubs;

♣ healthier tuck shops;

♣ water provision;

♣ healthier vending machines;

♣ healthier lunchboxes;

♣ dining room environment;

♣ healthier cookery clubs.

The chef Jamie Oliver achieved success in raising awareness about the standard of food served to children in UK schools. When making his TV series *Jamie's School Dinners*, he found that children almost always chose the 'junk-food' option – such as turkey nuggets and chips – which is high in salt and fat.

Jamie Oliver's Feed Me Better Campaign

Jamie Oliver's recent campaign to improve school meals for children aims to redress what he sees as the main problems in children's diets:

'Increasingly, kids are eating an unbalanced diet. Junk food dominates the school meals menu. Kids are not getting the right nutrients to help them grow, concentrate at school and stay healthy in adult life'.

❖ **Obesity:** kids are getting fatter. Of all children under 11 years, 15 per cent are now obese. Fatter children are more likely to stay obese into adulthood, leading to serious health problems. Scientists believe this may be the first generation to live a shorter life than their parents due to ill health.

❖ **Social skills:** more and more of children's daily food intake is snack-based rather than meal-based. Inevitably, this means a diet biased towards unhealthy foods. Many young kids do not know how to lay a table or use a knife and fork.

❖ **Behaviour:** teachers report that bad behaviour peaks around lunchtime, after kids have just eaten processed food high in sugar, salt, fat and a cocktail of other additives. Growing scientific evidence suggests that a junk-food diet has a negative effect on behaviour.

❖ **Lack of food knowledge:** families and young people today simply do not know enough about food and nutrition, making it difficult for them to make better choices about their diet.

Children of school age and their diets

Once children reach primary school age, they have an increasing amount of freedom over food choice, and foods are often eaten outside the home – at friends' houses and at school. Also outside pressures – such as peer pressure and advertising – start to influence food choice. Although growth is slower than in infancy or early childhood, school-aged children still have high nutrient needs, but fairly small appetites. It is therefore important that all meals and snacks provide lots of nutrients, even in a small volume of food.

HEALTHY SNACKS
The following foods have a high concentration of nutrients in a relatively small portion:

❖ breakfast cereal and milk;
❖ toasted crumpet or teacake;
❖ low-fat yoghurt or fromage frais;
❖ glass of milk;
❖ cheese and crackers or oatcakes;
❖ crunchy muesli and yoghurt;
❖ fresh fruit;
❖ nuts, seeds or dried fruit;
❖ fruit smoothies;
❖ slice of fruit loaf or malt loaf.

IDEAS FOR PACKED LUNCHES
Many children take packed lunches to school. There are lots of different types of bread that can be used to add variety. You could offer pitta bread, chapattis, crusty rolls, muffins or bagels with one of these healthy fillings:

❖ peanut butter and banana;
❖ cheese and pickle;
❖ tuna and tomato;
❖ humous and salad;

Fig 4.14 Enjoying a healthy snack

Guidelines for making mealtimes healthy and fun

❖ Offer a wide variety of different foods – give babies and toddlers a chance to try a new food more than once; any refusal on first tasting may be due to dislike of the new rather than of the food itself.

❖ Set an example – children will imitate both what you eat and how you eat it. It will be easier to encourage a child to eat a stick of raw celery if you eat one too! If you show disgust at certain foods, young children will notice and copy you.

❖ Be prepared for messy mealtimes! Present the food in a form that is fairly easy for children to manage by themselves (e.g. not difficult to chew).

❖ Do not use food as a punishment, reward, bribe or threat – for example, do not give sweets or chocolates as a reward for finishing savoury foods. To a child this is like saying, 'Here's something nice after eating those nasty greens.' Give healthy foods as treats, for example raisins and raw carrots, rather than sweets or cakes.

❖ Encourage children to feed themselves – either using a spoon or by offering suitable finger foods.

❖ Introduce new foods in stages – for example, if switching to wholemeal bread, try a soft-grain white bread first. And always involve the children in making choices as far as possible.

❖ Teach children to eat mainly at mealtimes and avoid giving them high-calorie snacks, such as biscuits and sugary drinks, which might take the edge off their appetite for more nutritious food. Most young children need 3 small meals and 3 snacks a day.

❖ Presentation is important – food manufacturers use a variety of techniques to make their children's food products exciting – colours, shapes, themes and characters. Using these tactics can make mealtimes more fun.

❖ Avoid adding salt to any food – too much salt can cause dehydration in babies and may predispose certain people to hypertension (high blood pressure) if taken over a lifetime.

❖ Allow children to follow their own individual appetites when deciding how much they want to eat. If a child rejects food, do not ever force-feed him. Simply remove the food without comment. Give smaller portions next time and praise the child for eating even a little.

❖ Never give a young child whole nuts to eat – particularly peanuts. Children can very easily choke on a small piece of the nut or even inhale it, which can cause a severe type of pneumonia. Rarely, a child may have a serious allergic reaction to nuts.

❖ chicken with a low-fat dressing and salad;

❖ bacon, lettuce and tomato;

❖ salmon and cucumber;

❖ egg with low-fat mayonnaise.

Other ideas for items to supplement a lunchtime sandwich include:

❖ fresh or dried fruit;

❖ sticks of raw vegetables;

❖ cherry tomatoes;

❖ hard-boiled egg;

❖ cheese cubes;

❖ small pot of potato salad;

❖ fruit juice;

❖ pot of yoghurt or a yoghurt drink;

❖ coleslaw;

❖ soup in a flask.

Crisps and other savoury snacks, chocolate or a muesli bar can be added as an occasional treat.

Additives

A food additive is any substance *intentionally* added to food for a specific function (e.g. to preserve or colour it) that is not normally eaten as a food or used as a characteristic ingredient in food. When additives are used in food, they must be declared in the list of ingredients, either by name or **E number**. All food additives must comply with European Union (EU) legislation. They are only allowed to be used if experts decide that they are necessary and safe. However, some people can react to certain additives, just as some people react to certain foods

Fig 4.15 Lunchtime in a nursery

Guidelines for reducing children's intake of additives

To reduce additives in the diet, parents and carers should:

- always look at the labels on food containers and be wary of a long list of E numbers;
- use fresh rather than highly processed food;
- cook their own pies, soups, cakes, and so on.

that most people can eat without any reaction. People who react to additives normally have asthma or other allergies already. Reactions to additives usually bring on an **asthma attack** or cause **nettle rash (urticaria)**.

FOOD ADDITIVES AND BEHAVIOUR

Some people think that certain food additives, especially artificial colours, can cause hyperactivity in children, or make it worse. At the moment there is not enough scientific evidence to say if there is a connection between certain food additives and hyperactivity or ADHD in children. The **Food Standards Agency** has recently funded a new project to investigate if artificial food additives affect the behaviour of children. The results from this study are expected in 2007. Some manufacturers and supermarket chains are now selling additive-free foods, which help parents and carers to avoid additives if they wish to do so.

MULTICULTURAL PROVISION AND DIETARY IMPLICATIONS

The UK is home to a multicultural and multi-ethnic society. The main ethnic minority groups are situated near large cities; many people came from the West Indies and Asia to the UK in response to labour shortages in the 1950s and 1960s. The Asian community represents the largest ethnic minority in the UK – about 1.25 million people. Asian dietary customs are mainly related to the beliefs of the three main religious groups: Muslims, Hindus and Sikhs.

Food and festivals from different cultures

There are particular foods that are associated with certain religious festivals; for example, in the Christian tradition mince pies at Christmas and pancakes on Shrove Tuesday, and in the Hindu tradition poori are eaten at Diwali. Providing foods from different cultures within an early years setting is a very good way of celebrating these festivals. Parents of children from ethnic minority groups are usually very pleased to be asked for advice on how to celebrate festivals with food, and may even be prepared to contribute some samples.

VEGETARIAN DIETS

Children who are on a vegetarian diet need an alternative to meat, fish and chicken as the main sources of **protein**. These could include milk, cheese and eggs, and pulses (lentils and beans).

Table 4.6 Multicultural provision and dietary implications

Muslims	Hindus	Sikhs
Muslims practise the Islamic religion, and their holy book, **The Koran**, provides them with their food laws. **Unlawful** foods (called **haram**) are: pork, all meat which has not been rendered lawful (**halal**), alcohol and fish without scales. Wheat, in the form of chapattis, and rice are the staple foods. The Koran dictates that children should be breastfed up to the age of 2 years. **Fasting:** during the lunar month of **Ramadan** Muslims fast between sunrise and sunset; fasting involves abstinence from all food and drink, so many Muslims rise early to eat before dawn in order to maintain their energy levels. Children under 12 years and the elderly are exempt from fasting.	Wheat is the main staple food eaten by Hindus in the UK; it is used to make types of bread called chapattis, puris and parathas. **Orthodox** Hindus are strict **vegetarians** as they believe in **Ahimsa** – non-violence towards all living beings – and a minority practise veganism. Some will eat dairy products and eggs, while others will refuse eggs on the grounds that they are a potential source of life. Even non-vegetarians do not eat beef as the cow is considered a sacred animal, and it is unusual for pork to be eaten as the pig is considered unclean. Ghee (clarified butter) and vegetable oil are used in cooking. **Fasting:** common for certain festivals, such as Mahshivrati (the birthday of Lord Shiva).	Most Sikhs will not eat pork or beef or any meat that is killed by the **halal** method. Some Sikhs are vegetarian, but many eat chicken, lamb and fish. Wheat and rice are staple foods. **Fasting:** Devout Sikhs will fast once or twice a week, and most will fast on the first day of the Punjabi month or when there is a full moon.

Rastafarians

Dietary practices are based on laws laid down by Moses in the Book of Genesis in the Bible. These laws state that certain types of meat should be avoided. The majority of followers will only eat **Ital** foods, which are foods considered to be in a whole or natural state. Most Rastafarians are **vegetarians** and will not consume processed or preserved foods. No added salt; no coffee.

Afro-Caribbean diets	Jewish diets
The Afro-Caribbean community is the second largest ethnic minority group in the UK. Dietary practices within the community vary widely. Many people include a wide variety of European foods in their diet alongside the traditional foods of cornmeal, coconut, green banana, plantain, okra and yam. Although Afro-Caribbean people are generally Christian, a minority are Rastafarians.	Jewish people observe dietary laws which state that animals and birds must be slaughtered by the Jewish method to render them **kosher** (acceptable). Milk and meat must never be cooked or eaten together, and **pork** in any form is forbidden. Shellfish are not allowed as they are thought to harbour disease. Only fish with fins and scales may be eaten. **Fasting:** The most holy day of the Jewish calendar is Yom Kippur (the Day of Atonement), when Jewish people fast for 25 hours.

Festivals from different cultures

Shichi-go-san (Japanese festival for young children)	November 15
Chinese New Year	Late January/early February
Shrove Tuesday (Mardi Gras)	40 days before Easter
Rosh Hoshanah (Jewish New Year)	Usually September
Holi (Hindu Spring festival)	February or March
Id Al Fitir (major Muslim festival)	At end of Ramadan
Divali (Hindu New Year)	October or November
Rastafarian New Year	January 7

They also need sufficient **iron**. As iron is more difficult to absorb from vegetable sources than from meat, a young child needs to obtain iron from sources such as:

❖ leafy green vegetables (e.g. spinach and watercress);

❖ pulses (beans, lentils and chickpeas);

❖ dried fruit (e.g. apricots, raisins and sultanas);

❖ some breakfast cereals.

As explained above, it is easier to absorb iron from our food if it is eaten *with* foods containing vitamin C, such as fruit and vegetables, or by drinking diluted fruit juices at mealtimes.

The vegan diet

A vegan diet completely excludes all foods of animal origin; that is, animal flesh, milk and milk products, eggs, honey and all additives which may be of animal origin. A vegan diet is based on cereals and cereal products, pulses, fruits, vegetables, nuts and seeds. Human breast milk is acceptable for vegan babies.

NUTRITIONAL DISORDERS IN CHILDREN

Nutritional disorders may be caused by an excess or a deficiency of one or more of the elements of nutrition.

Nutritional excess

Obesity (fatness) results from taking in more energy from the diet than is used up by the body. Some children appear to inherit a tendency to put on weight very easily, and some parents and carers offer more high-calorie food than children need. Some associated problems are:

❖ **changing lifestyles:** fast food is overtaking traditionally prepared meals. Many convenience meals involve coating the food with fatty sauces or batters.

❖ **foods high in sugar and fat:** children eat more sweets and crisps and drink more fizzy drinks – this is partly because of advertising, but also because such foods are more widely available.

❖ **poor fresh fruit and vegetable consumption:** despite fresh fruit and vegetables being more readily available, many children do not eat enough of these, preferring processed varieties that often contain extra sugar and fat.

Obesity can lead to emotional problems as well as to the physical problem of being more prone to infections: an obese child may be taunted by others, and will be unable to participate in the same vigorous play as their peers.

Nutritional deficiency

When particular items in the diet are absent or in short supply, deficiency disorders develop (see Table 4.7).

Failure to thrive

Failure to thrive (FTT), or faltering growth, is a term used when a child does not conform to the usual pattern of weight gain and growth. The first issue to be explored if a baby or child appears to be under-nourished is feeding; often a newly weaned baby will fail to thrive (or gain weight) due to intolerance of a newly introduced food. Once the food is withdrawn from the diet, the baby will usually thrive. There may be other problems associated with feeding a young baby, such as breathing difficulties or a

Table 4.7 A summary of deficiency disorders.

Disorder	Shortage	Effect
Anaemia	Iron or vitamin B12	Fatigue, headaches, weight loss, breathlessness
Rickets	Calcium or vitamin D	Bones do not form properly, resulting in bow legs
Kwashiorkor	Protein or calories	Severe malnutrition, swollen tummy, sparse, brittle hair
Scurvy	Vitamin C	Wounds are slow to heal; gums loose and bleeding
Pellagra	Niacin (a vitamin)	Soreness and cracking of the skin; mental disturbances
Night blindness	Vitamin A	Inability to see in dim light
Beriberi	Thiamine (vitamin B1)	Wasting of the muscles: heart failure
Marasmus	Severe lack of calories and protein	Emaciation, stunted growth and dehydration

poor sucking reflex in a premature baby. A child who is vomiting frequently over a period of time is also unlikely to thrive; vomiting may be the result of pyloric stenosis, gastroenteritis or whooping cough (pertussis).

Failure to thrive can also result from child abuse: physical abuse, emotional abuse, neglect and sexual abuse. This complex subject is discussed in Chapter 15.

Malabsorption of food

❖ **Coeliac disease:** this is a condition in which the lining of the small intestine is damaged by gluten, a protein found in wheat and rye. In babies, it is usually diagnosed about 3 months after weaning onto solids containing gluten, but some children do not show any symptoms until they are older.

❖ **Phenylketonuria:** an affected baby will require a diet which contains limited, measured amounts of phenylalanine, an amino acid which is a basic unit of protein.

❖ **Galactosaemia:** this is a very rare genetic disorder leading to liver disease, eye cataracts and mental handicap; it is caused by an inability to absorb galactose (a nutrient found in milk). Treatment is by a lactose-free diet for life.

COMMON FOOD ALLERGIES

A food allergy is an abnormal response (an allergic reaction) of the immune system to otherwise harmless foods. Up to 5 per cent of children have food allergies. Most children outgrow their allergy, although an allergy to peanuts and some other tree nuts is considered lifelong.

There are eight foods that cause 90 per cent of all food allergic reactions:

❖ peanuts;

❖ soy;

❖ tree nuts (e.g. almonds, walnuts, pecans);

❖ wheat;

❖ milk;

❖ shellfish;

❖ eggs;

❖ fish.

Milk is the most common cause of food allergies in children, but peanuts, nuts, fish and shellfish commonly cause the most severe reactions.

What are the symptoms of an allergic reaction?

Symptoms of an allergic response can include:

* vomiting;
* hives (or urticaria) – an itchy raised rash usually found on the trunk or limbs;
* itching or tightness in the throat;
* diarrhoea;
* eczema;
* difficulty breathing;
* cramps;
* itching or swelling of the lips, tongue or mouth;
* wheezing.

Allergic symptoms can begin within minutes or up to an hour after ingesting the food.

Anaphylaxis

In rare cases of food allergy, just one bite of food can bring on **anaphylaxis**. This is a severe reaction that involves various areas of the body simultaneously. In extreme cases it can cause death.

Anaphylaxis is a sudden and severe, potentially life-threatening allergic reaction. It can be caused by insect stings or medications, as well as by a food allergy. Although potentially any food can cause anaphylaxis, **peanuts**, nuts, **shellfish**, **fish** and **eggs** are foods that most commonly cause this reaction.

Symptoms of anaphylaxis may include all those listed above for food allergies. In addition, the child's breathing is seriously impaired and the pulse rate becomes rapid. Anaphylaxis is fortunately very rare, but is also very dangerous:

* Symptoms can occur in as little as 5–15 minutes.
* As little as half a peanut can cause a fatal reaction in severely allergic individuals.
* Some severely allergic children can have a reaction if milk is splashed on their skin.
* Being kissed by somebody who has eaten peanuts, for example, can cause a reaction in severely allergic individuals.

EMERGENCY TREATMENT OF ANAPHYLAXIS

1 **Summon medical help immediately** – the child will need oxygen and a life-saving injection of adrenaline.

2 **Place the child in a sitting position** to help relieve any breathing difficulty.

3 **Be prepared to resuscitate** if necessary.

In some settings attended by a child or children known to be at risk from anaphylaxis the staff may be trained to give the adrenaline injection.

How can food allergies be managed?

The only way to manage food allergies is strictly to avoid the foods to which the child is allergic. It is important to learn how to interpret ingredients on food labels and how to spot high-risk foods. Many children outgrow earlier food-allergic symptoms as they get older, but parents will need professional support and advice to ensure that their child is receiving a safe, balanced diet.

THE EFFECTS OF ILLNESS ON A CHILD'S APPETITE

Most children with a fever do not want to eat. While you should offer food, you should never force a child to eat.

Certain illnesses may result in failure to thrive; these are usually chronic illnesses or conditions which recur frequently in childhood. Examples include:

❧ congenital heart disease;
❧ severe asthma;
❧ infections;
❧ cystic fibrosis;
❧ urinary tract infections.

(See Chapter 11 for guidelines for encouraging a sick child to eat.)

ECONOMIC AND SOCIAL FACTORS AFFECTING DIET AND NUTRITION

Many families in the UK are on a reduced income as a result of, for example, sickness or unemployment. Surveys have identified four main problems for the many people who receive income support:

1   **Healthy food** is relatively highly priced. Lean meat costs more than fattier cuts, and wholemeal bread can cost 25 per cent more than white bread.

2   **Fuel costs** mean that it can be cheaper to cook chips than jacket potatoes.

3   The siting of **superstores** on the outskirts of towns has meant that shops in inner-city areas are smaller and more expensive, so that healthy foods become less available.

4   Certain **facilities and skills** are required to prepare healthier foods. If a family is living in bed-and-breakfast accommodation, for example, cooking may be impractical.

Ideas for increasing the nutritional quality of the diet that may save money as well are to:

❧ use less meat, adding pulses and lentils to stews and casseroles instead;

❧ use as little oil or fat in cooking as possible;

❧ cut down on meat and fill up on potatoes, rice and starchy vegetables.

FOOD PRESENTATION AND CHILDREN'S PREFERENCES

Many children go through phases of refusing to eat certain foods, or may refuse to eat anything at all. This is particularly common for children up to the age of 5 years, and it is a normal part of growing up and asserting independence. Children will not harm themselves if they do not eat for a short while. Try the following strategies to encourage eating:

❧ Offer regular meals and snacks rather than allowing a child to 'pick.'

❧ Make mealtimes fun. Use brightly coloured plates and present the food in an attractive way.

❧ Remain calm and relaxed.

If the problem shows no sign of improving, seek advice from a health visitor, doctor or dietician.

THE SOCIAL AND EDUCATIONAL ROLE OF FOOD AND MEALTIMES

Eating patterns may be influenced by various factors:

❧ religious beliefs or strong ethical principles;
❧ cultural background and ethnic origin;
❧ the availability of different foods;
❧ time and money constraints;
❧ preferences and tastes that are shaped during early infancy.

Food is part of every child's culture, and eating rituals vary with different cultures. Mealtimes can provide a valuable opportunity to further the child's social development by promoting:

❖ **listening** and other conversation skills;

❖ **independence** in eating and serving food, and in taking responsibility;

❖ **courtesy** towards others and turn-taking;

❖ a **shared experience** which provides a social focus in the child's day;

❖ **self-esteem** – the child's family and cultural background are valued through their mealtime traditions;

❖ **self-confidence –** through learning social skills, taking turns and saying 'please' and 'thank you', the child gains confidence as a valued and unique member of their social situation.

Cognitive development is furthered by mealtimes by:

❖ promoting hand–eye coordination through the use of cutlery and other tools;

❖ stimulating the senses of taste, touch, sight and smell;

❖ enjoyment of interesting conversations;

❖ promoting language development and increasing the vocabulary;

❖ developing the mathematical concepts of shape and size, using foods as examples;

❖ creating opportunities for learning through linked activities – stories about food, origins of food, preparation and cookery;

❖ experiencing cultural variation in foods and mealtime traditions.

As an early years worker, you are ideally placed to ensure that **stereotyping** in

Fig 4.16 Passing a drink helps promote social development

relation to eating habits is not practised. Mealtimes and the choice of food can be used in a positive sense to affirm a feeling of cultural identity.

SPECIAL (OR THERAPEUTIC) DIETS

Most children on special diets are not ill. Often they require a therapeutic diet that replaces or eliminates some particular nutrient to prevent illness.

The diet for diabetes mellitus

Diabetes mellitus occurs in 1 in every 500 children under the age of about 16 years, and results in difficulty in converting carbohydrate into energy due to underproduction of insulin. Insulin is usually given by daily injection, and a diet sheet will be devised by the hospital dietician. It is important that mealtimes be *regular* and that some **carbohydrate** be included at every meal. Children with diabetes should be advised to carry **glucose** sweets whenever they are away from home in case of **hypoglycaemia** (low blood sugar).

The diet for cystic fibrosis

The majority of children with cystic fibrosis (see page 437) have difficulty in absorbing fats; they need to eat 20 per cent more protein and more calories than children without the disease, and so require a diet high in fats and carbohydrates. They are also given daily vitamin supplements and pancreatic enzymes.

The diet for coeliac disease

Treatment for coeliac disease is by gluten-free diet and has to be for the rest of the person's life. All formula milks available in the UK are gluten-free, and many manufactured baby foods are also gluten-free. Any cakes, bread and biscuits should be made from gluten-free flour, and labels on processed foods should be read carefully to ensure that there is no hidden wheat product in the ingredients list.

Commercially available play dough is made from 40 per cent ordinary flour, as is the homemade variety used in nurseries and playgroups. Extra vigilance is needed by staff to stop children with coeliac disease putting it in their mouth; alternatively, dough can be made with gluten-free flour.

The diet for galactosaemia

The child with galactosaemia cannot digest or use galactose, which, together with glucose, forms lactose, the natural sugar of milk. A list of safe foods with a low galactose content will be issued by the dietician, and food labels should be checked for the presence of milk solids and powdered lactose, which contain large quantities of this sugar.

The diet for obesity

A child who is diagnosed as being overweight will usually be prescribed a diet low in fat and sugar; high-fibre carbohydrates are encouraged, for example wholemeal bread and other cereals. The child who has

ACTIVITY: THE BALANCED DAILY DIET

1   Look at the following daily diet:

* Breakfast – a glass of milk, boiled egg, toast;

* Mid-morning – a packet of crisps, a glass of orange squash;

* Lunch – a cheese and egg flan, chips, baked beans; apple fritters and ice cream; apple juice;

* Snack – chocolate mini roll; orange squash;

* Tea – fishfingers; mashed potatoes; peas; strawberry milkshake.

Arrange the servings in five columns, one each for the four food groups and one extra column for extra fat and sugar. Count the number of servings from each food group and assess the nutritional adequacy of the diet.

2   How could you improve the menu to ensure a healthy balanced diet?

to go without crisps, chips and snacks between meals will need a lot of support and encouragement from carers.

The diet for children with difficulties with chewing and swallowing

Children with cerebral palsy can experience difficulties with either or both these aspects of eating. Food has to be liquidised, but this should be done in separate batches so that the end result is not a pool of greyish sludge. Presentation should be imaginative. Try to follow the general principle of making the difference in the meal as unobtrusive as possible.

ACTIVITY: MENU PLANNING

Write up or obtain a copy of an actual weekly menu of a nursery or infant school that you know, and then answer the following questions:

1 Does the menu provide a healthy balance of nutrients?

2 Is there anything that you would change to promote healthy eating? Give reasons for any new foods you may wish to include.

ACTIVITY: THE FOOD QUIZ

Find out the answers to these questions, some of which will require further research. (Answers on page 216.)

1 Which disease linked to diet is the most widespread in the UK and why?

2 What might be the effect on a baby if the mother has suffered from malnutrition during the last 3 months of pregnancy?

3 Fat babies and fat children are often unhealthy. Give two reasons for this and suggest how obesity can be prevented in young children.

4 Why is fibre important in a child's diet?

5 What is meant by a deficiency disorder? Give three examples.

6 What is an E number? Which category of E numbers is linked to behaviour problems in children?

7 What is phenylketonuria? Is it treatable?

8 What is obesity and why is it on the increase among children in the UK?

9 Which foods are most likely to cause an allergic reaction?

10 What sort of diet must be followed by someone with coeliac disease?

ACTIVITY: BUDGETING FOR A HEALTHY DIET

1 Plan a menu for one week, for a family of two adults and three children aged 8, 4 and 2 years, which provides a varied and nutritionally balanced diet for the whole family. Cost the items needed and explain why you have included them.

2 Try to add some practical tips to the ones suggested on page 211 for improving diets with only a limited budget.

ACTIVITY: CULTURAL NEEDS

The nursery school where you are working has 22 white British children and 1 child from Turkey. The nursery teacher says, 'We only offer English food here because we do not have any children from ethnic minorities.' Discuss this statement and decide what your approach would be if you were in charge of the nursery.

ANSWERS TO THE SAFETY QUIZ

These answers are guidelines only. Bear in mind how mature the individual child is.

1 Eight years old. Children cannot judge the speed of cars and cope reliably with heavy traffic until they are 11 or 12 years. An 8-year-old can probably be trusted to wait on the pavement for traffic to clear; they may still dash into the road if they get excited. Children of 2 or 3 years do not have any idea that cars are dangerous.

2 Ten years old. They are strong enough to pick up a kettle and a teapot. They are not clumsy, like a little child, so they can pour the water without getting a scald.

3 Four years old. They are old enough not to slip down and go under the water. You can teach them not to fiddle with the taps. However, someone should be close by to listen out, and the bathroom door should be open and never locked.

4 Eighteen months old. Babies of this age can manage a teacher beaker by themselves. Younger babies can choke on drinks or bottles. Even a toddler can choke on food and an

adult must be present when the child is eating.

5 No age. Toddlers and babies can drown even in a paddling pool or a puddle. Bigger children can drown outdoors.

6 Eleven years old. Secondary school children are safe to use their bikes for school if they have had some cycle training. They need bright reflective clothing and a cycle helmet.

7 Six years old. Peanuts can easily block the lungs because they contain a special oil that makes the lining of the lungs swell up.

8 No age. Plastic bags are not toys. Children can be tempted to use them for dangerous dressing-up games. Children of 6 or 7 years may be given plastic bags to keep things in, as long as they know not to use them for games, and there are no little brothers or sisters around.

9 Three years old. Two-year-olds can be killed by falling downstairs. They need

stair gates to keep them off the stairs and an adult walking with them when they climb stairs.

10 Seven years old. Climbing trees is always dangerous, but you cannot stop children having fun. Seven-year-olds can learn to test branches for strength. They can choose trees over grass, not concrete. They can climb well, unlike little children.

11 It depends on the playground. Toddlers will not be happy unless you are there. Some playgrounds are fine for older children and some are not safe even with an adult around because of broken glass or litter.

12 Seven years old. They are old enough to hold a match properly and to strike it without getting burnt. They can light their own birthday cake candles, but they cannot make a bonfire or light a fire in the hearth. Never leave matches where children can reach them.

ANSWERS TO THE FOOD QUIZ

1 Dental decay – dental services cost the NHS about £450 million every year.

2 The foetus will suffer from the effects of placental insufficiency – the baby may be born prematurely and be light-for-dates (weighing 2.5 kg/5.5 lb or less), with the following problems:

❖ breathing difficulties;

❖ feeding difficulties (poor sucking reflex);

❖ possible poor temperature regulation.

3 Fat babies and children have less resistance to infection, may have mobility problems and may suffer emotional difficulties. Obesity can be avoided by cutting down on foods and

snacks such as chips, biscuits, fizzy drinks and cakes.

4   Fibre helps prevent constipation by encouraging the movement of food through the intestine.

5   A deficiency disorder is one in which particular nutrients in the diet are absent or in short supply. Examples are: rickets (shortage of vitamin D or calcium); anaemia (shortage of iron or vitamin B12); beriberi (shortage of thiamin or vitamin B1); pellagra (shortage of niacin); kwashiorkor (shortage of protein or calories); night blindness (shortage of vitamin A); and marasmus (severe lack of calories and protein).

6   An E number is the code which identifies food additives; colourings are the additives most often linked to behaviour problems in children.

7   Phenylketonuria is a rare metabolic disorder which leads to brain damage and learning difficulties. It is treatable, by a special protein diet.

8   Obesity literally means fatness. It is increasing in the UK because of changes in lifestyle and eating habits.

9   Peanuts, milk and shellfish are the most common causes of food allergy.

10 A gluten-free diet; flour products must be gluten-free.

5

Holistic child development

Contents

WHAT IS CHILD DEVELOPMENT?

It is important to keep in mind that even a tiny baby is a person. People develop physically, but they are whole human beings from the very start.

If different aspects of a child's development are seen as separated strands, isolated from each other, the child comes to be seen as a collection of bits and pieces instead of a whole person. On the other hand, it can be useful to look closely at a particular area of a child's development, whether to check that all is well, to celebrate progress, to see how to help the child with the next step of development and learning, or to give special help where needed. Even when focusing on one aspect of development, however, it is important not to forget that we are looking at a whole person. A person has a physical body, ideas, feelings and relationships – all developing and functioning at the same time.

When we think of the complete child in this way, we are taking a holistic approach.

Child development is a fairly new subject. It is a multidisciplinary subject, drawing on various academic fields, including psychology, neuroscience, sociology, paediatrics, biology and genetics.

Recently, researchers in child development have begun to think about how children develop in different cultures and in different sorts of societies and how children are brought up in different parts of the world. It is very important to find out what people in different cultures do that is the same when they bring up children. It is also equally important to learn about the different ways that children are brought up and yet still turn into stable and successful adults. So researchers are now asking two questions:

1   What is the same about all children?

2   What is different across cultures in the way that children are brought up?

WHY STUDY CHILD DEVELOPMENT?

Child development is an essential subject of study for everyone who works with young children. Looking after other people's children gives you different responsibilities compared to having your own children. So people who work with other people's children need to be trained properly and carefully. They need to be informed about how children develop and learn.

The key to understanding child development is 'wholeness'. Studying holistic child development is a way of seeing children as whole people.

Parents are constantly looking for support and help as they bring up their children. Wanting to know more is part of being a parent. They find it very helpful to watch television and listen to radio programmes. They also read magazines and talk to trained and knowledgeable staff in nurseries as they try to understand their children.

APPROACHES TO STUDYING CHILDREN'S DEVELOPMENT

Integrated development

The whole child may be looked at under six headings. You can remember these as together they make up the acronym **PILESS:**

* Physical development;
* Intellectual development;
* Language development;
* Emotional development;
* Social development;
* Spiritual development.

ADVANTAGES OF PILESS

The advantages of using PILESS in the study of child development are that the approach:

* recognises the important contributions of different disciplines – human biology, psychology, linguistics, sociology, neuroscience, and so on;
* provides a useful framework for students to organise their studies;
* provides a focus for the study of children, for example in the use of observation techniques, case studies and the planning of activities for work with children.

DISADVANTAGES OF PILESS

The disadvantages of using PILESS in the study of child development are that:

* it may be difficult to view the child as a whole person;
* it may be more difficult to contextualise the child if the categories are rigidly prescribed (the contextualised child is discussed below).

The contextualised child

Researchers in the field of child development now realise that when children quarrel, for example, it is almost impossible to say which aspect of their behaviour is:

* emotional (anger);
* physical (stamping with rage);
* intellectual or language (what they say or do).

Researchers now know that, in order to understand what is going on, it is also very important to identify who or what made a particular child angry, starting the quarrel. This is the context of the behaviour. So it is important to contextualise the child when studying child development. By looking at

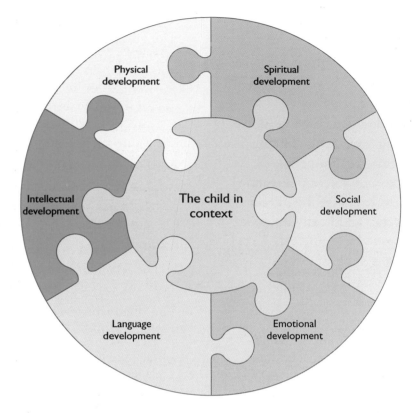

Fig 5.1 We can think of studying integrated development as being like looking at the pieces of a jigsaw

child development in context we recognise that the biological part of development (physical development and genetic factors) is integrated with the cultural part of development (social, cultural, intellectual and linguistic factors).

We now prefer to talk about the contextualised child because:

❖ development is deeply influenced by the child's cultural environment and the people she meets;

❖ the ideas, language, communication, feelings, relationships and other cultural elements which the child experiences have a profound influence on development.

MEASURING DEVELOPMENT

Normative development

A traditional approach to child development study has been to emphasise normative measurement. This is concerned with milestones or stages in a child's development. These show what *most* children can do at a particular age. In reality there is a wide range of normal development, and this will be influenced by genetic, social and cultural factors. Children have been labelled as 'backward' or 'forward' in relation to the so-called 'normal' child, which is not always helpful.

So it is important to be aware that normative measurements can only indicate general *trends* in development in children across the world. They may vary quite a bit according to the culture in which a child lives.

When children do things earlier than the milestones suggest is normal, it does not necessarily mean that they will be outstanding or gifted in any way. Parents sometimes think that because their child speaks early, is potty-trained early or walks early, he or she is gifted in some way. You should handle these situations carefully, as the child may not be gifted at all.

Sequences in a child's development

Children across the world seem to pass through similar sequences of development, but in different ways and at different rates according to their culture. The work of Mary Sheridan on developmental sequences has been invaluable, but she suggests that a child moves through rigidly prescribed stages that are linked to their age: the child sits, then crawls, then stands, then walks. In fact, this is not the case. Not all children *do* crawl. Blind children often do not. Some children (like Mark in the case study below) 'bottom-shuffle', moving along in a sitting position.

Case Study

* Mark moved around by bottom-shuffling and did not walk until he was 2 years old. He went on to run, hop and skip at the normal times. Walking late was not a cause for concern, and he did not suffer from any developmental delay.

* African children living in rural villages estimate volume and capacity earlier than European children who live in towns. This is because they practise measuring out cups of rice into baskets from an early age as part of their daily lives. Learning about volume and capacity early does not mean that children will necessarily go on to become talented mathematicians. Children who learn these concepts later might also become good mathematicians.

Children with special educational needs often seem to 'dance the development ladder': they move through sequences in unusual and very uneven ways. For example, they might walk at the normal age, but they may not talk at the usual age.

As researchers learn more about child development, it is becoming more useful to think of a child's development as a network which becomes increasingly complex as the child matures and becomes more experienced in their culture. So instead of thinking of child development and learning as a ladder, it is probably more useful to think of it as a web.

The following tables summarise normative development.

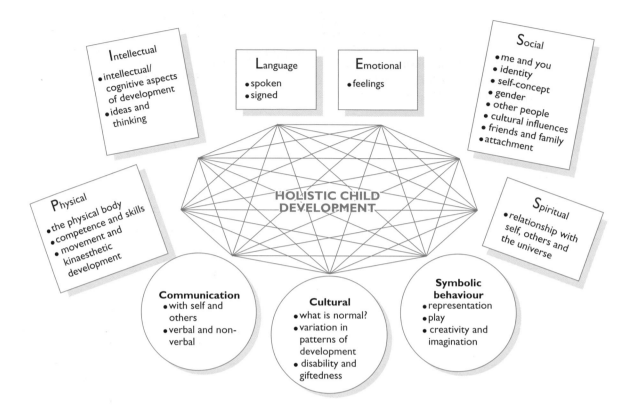

Fig 5.2 Thinking of child development as a web

Table 5.1 Normative physical development, 0–8 years.

Age	Gross motor	Fine motor
Birth to 4 weeks	The baby lies supine (on her back) with head to one side. When placed on her front (the prone position), the baby lies with head turned to one side and by one month can lift the head. If pulled to sitting position, the head will lag, the back curves over and the head falls forward.	The baby turns her head towards the light and stares at bright or shiny objects. The baby is fascinated by human faces and gazes attentively at carer's face when fed or held. The baby's hands are usually tightly closed. The baby reacts to loud sounds but by one month may be soothed by particular music.
4–8 weeks	The baby can now turn from side to back. The baby can lift the head briefly from prone position. Arm and leg movements are jerky and uncontrolled. There is head lag if the baby is pulled to sitting position.	The baby turns her head towards the light and stares at bright or shiny objects. The baby will show interest and excitement by facial expression and will gaze attentively at carer's face whilst being fed. The baby will use his/her hand to grasp the carer's finger.

8–12 weeks	When lying supine, the baby's head is in a central position. The baby can now lift head and chest off bed in prone position, supported on forearms. There is almost no head lag in sitting position. The legs can kick vigorously, both separately and together. The baby can wave her arms and bring hands together over the body.	The baby moves her head to follow adult movements. The baby watches her hands and plays with her fingers. The baby holds a rattle for a brief time before dropping it.
4–5 months (16–20 weeks)	The baby is beginning to use palmar grasp and can transfer objects from hand to hand. The baby is very interested in all activity. Everything is taken to the mouth. The baby moves her head around to follow people and objects.	The baby now has good head control and is beginning to sit with support. The baby rolls over from back to side and is beginning to reach for objects. When supine the baby plays with her own feet. The baby holds the head up when pulled to sitting position.
6–9 months	The baby can roll from front to back. The baby may attempt to crawl but will often end up sliding backwards. The baby may grasp feet and place them in her mouth. The baby can sit without support for longer periods of time. The baby may 'cruise' around furniture and may even stand or walk alone.	The baby is very alert to people and objects. The baby is beginning to use pincer grasp with thumb and index finger. The baby transfers toys from one hand to the other and looks for fallen objects. Everything is explored by putting it in her mouth.
9–12 months	The baby will now be mobile – may be crawling, bear-walking, bottom-shuffling or even walking. The baby can sit up on her own and lean forward to pick things up. The baby may crawl up stairs and onto low items of furniture. The baby may bounce in rhythm to music.	The baby's pincer grasp is now well-developed and she can pick things up and pull them towards her. The baby can poke with one finger and will point to desired objects. The baby can clasp hands and imitate adults' actions. The baby can throw toys deliberately. The baby can manage spoons and finger foods well.
15 months	The baby probably walks alone, with feet wide apart and arms raised to maintain balance. She is likely to fall over and sit down suddenly a lot. The baby can probably manage stairs and steps, but will need supervision. She can get to standing without help from furniture or people and kneels without support.	The baby can build with a few bricks and arrange toys on the floor. She holds a crayon in palmar grasp and turns several pages of a book at once. She can point to desired objects. The baby shows a preference for one hand, but uses either.

18 months	The child walks confidently and is able to stop without falling. The child can kneel, squat, climb and carry things around with her. The child can climb onto an adult chair forwards and then turn round to sit. The child can come downstairs, usually by creeping backwards on her tummy.	The child can thread large beads. The child uses pincer grasp to pick up small objects. The child can build a tower of several cubes. The child can scribble to and fro on paper.
2 years (24 months)	The child is very mobile and can run safely. The child can climb up onto furniture. The child can walk up and down stairs, usually two feet to a step. The child tries to kick a ball with some success but cannot catch yet.	The child can draw circles, lines and dots, using preferred hand. She can pick up tiny objects using a fine pincer grasp. She can build tower of six or more blocks (bricks) with longer concentration span. She enjoys picture books and turns pages singly.
3 years	The child can jump from a low step. She can walk backwards and sideways. The child can stand and walk on tiptoe and stand on one foot. She has good spatial awareness. The child rides tricycle using pedals. She can climb stairs with one foot on each step – downwards with two feet per step.	The child can build tall towers of bricks or blocks. She can control a pencil using thumb and first two fingers – a dynamic tripod. The child enjoys painting with large brush. She can use scissors to cut paper. She can copy shapes, such as a circle.
4 years	A sense of balance is developing – the child may be able to walk along a line. The child can catch, kick, throw and bounce a ball. She can bend at the waist to pick up objects from the floor. She enjoys climbing trees and frames. She can run up and down stairs, one foot per step.	The child can build a tower of bricks and other constructions too. She can draw a recognisable person on request, showing head, legs and trunk. She can thread small beads on a lace.
5 years	The child can use a variety of play equipment – slides, swings, climbing frames. She can play ball games. She can hop and run lightly on toes and can move rhythmically to music. The sense of balance is well developed. She can skip.	The child may be able to thread a large-eyed needle and sew large stitches. She can draw a person with head, trunk, legs, nose, mouth and eyes. She has good control over pencils and paintbrushes. She copies shapes, such as a square.
6 and 7 years	The child has increased agility, muscle co-ordination and balance. The child develops competence in	The child can build a tall, straight tower with blocks and other constructions too.

riding a two-wheeled bicycle.
She hops easily, with good balance.
The child can jump off apparatus.
at school.

The child can draw a person with detail, e.g. clothes and eyebrows.
She can write letters of alphabet with similar writing grip to an adult.
She can catch a ball thrown from one metre with one hand.

Table 5.2 Normative language development, 0–8 years.

Age	Language development
0–3 months	Babies need to share language experiences and cooperate with others from birth onwards. From the start babies need other people.
From birth to 4 weeks	The baby responds to sounds, especially familiar voices. She quietens when picked up. She makes eye contact. The baby cries to indicate need. The baby may move her eyes towards the direction of sound.
4–8 weeks	The baby recognises the carer and familiar objects. She makes non-crying noises such as cooing and gurgling. Her cries become more expressive. She looks for sounds.
8–12 weeks	The baby is still distressed by sudden loud noises. She often sucks or licks lips when she hears sound of food preparation. She shows excitement at sound of approaching footsteps or voices.
During the first three months	Babies listen to people's voices. Babies 'call out' for company. When adults close to them talk in motherese or fatherese (a high-pitched tone referring to what is around and going on) babies dance, listen, reply in babble and coo. Babies cry with anger to show they are tired, hungry, and to say they need to be changed. A hearing-impaired baby babbles and cries too. Babies are comforted by the voices of those who are close to them and they will turn especially to the voices of their family.
3–6 months	Babies become more aware of others so they communicate more and more. As they listen, they imitate sounds they can hear, and they react to the tone of someone's voice. For example, they might become upset by an angry tone, or cheered by a happy tone. Babies begin to use vowels, consonants and syllable sounds, e.g. 'ah', 'ee aw'. Babies begin to laugh and squeal with pleasure. Babies continue to do everything they did in the first three months. Look back to remind yourself about what babies do throughout 0–6 months.
6–9 months	Babble becomes tuneful like the lilt of the language the baby can hear (except in hearing-impaired babies). Babies begin to understand words like 'up' and 'down', raising their arms to be lifted up, using appropriate gestures. The baby repeats sounds. Babies continue to do everything they did in the first six months. Look back to remind yourself about this.
9–12 months	Cooperation develops further from the early protoconversations of early fatherese and motherese. For example, when adults wave bye-bye, or say, 'Show me your shoes' the babies enjoy waving and pointing. Babies can follow simple instructions, e.g. 'Kiss teddy.' Word approximations appear, e.g. hee haw = donkey or more typically mumma, dadda and bye-bye in English-speaking contexts. The tuneful babble develops into 'jargon' and babies make their voices go up and down just as people do when they talk to each other. 'Really? Do you? No!' The babble is very expressive. Neuroscientists are finding that babies' brains develop to think better if they are

spoken to in a warm tone of voice, rather than in a sharp, shouting one. Intonation is important.

Children are already experienced and capable communicators by this time.

They are using emergent language or protolanguage.

It is nothing short of amazing that all this happens within 1 year. They know about: facial expressions, combined sounds (hee haw), gestures, shared meanings, persuading, negotiating, cooperating, turn-taking, interest in others, their ideas, their feelings, what they do.

They know that words stand for people, objects, what they do and what happens. They are taking part in the language of their culture.

1–2 years	Children begin to talk with words or sign language. They add more and more layers to everything they know about language and communication in the first year. Look back and remind yourself of what children can manage at this stage.
By 18 months	They enjoy trying to sing as well as to listen to songs and rhymes. Action songs (for example pat-a-cake) are much-loved. Books with pictures are of great interest. They point at and often name parts of their body, objects, people and pictures in books. They echo the last part of what others say (echolalia). One word or sign can have several meanings (holophrases). For example, C-A-T = all animals, not just cats. This is sometimes called 'extension'. They begin waving their arms up and down which might mean start again, or I like it, or more. Gestures develop alongside words. Gesture is used in some cultures more than in others.
By 2 years	Researchers used to say that children are using a vocabulary of 50 or so words but they understand more. Modern researchers do not use vocabulary counts so much and they simply stress that children are rapidly becoming competent speakers of the languages they experience. They over-extend the use of a word, e.g. all animals are called 'doggie'. They talk about an absent object when reminded of it, e.g. seeing an empty plate, they say 'biscuit'. They use phrases, (telegraphese) 'Doggie-gone,' and they call themselves by their name. They spend a great deal of energy naming things and what they do. For example, chair, and as they go up a step they might say 'up'. They can follow a simple instruction or request; for example, 'Could you bring me the spoon?' They are wanting to share songs, dance, conversations, finger rhymes, etc. more and more. They also name movements, e.g. 'up' and 'gone'.
2–3 years	During this period, language and the ability to communicate develop so rapidly that they almost seem to explode. Children begin to use plurals, pronouns, adjectives, possessives, time words, tenses and sentences. They make what are called virtuous errors in the way that they pronounce (articulate) things. It is also true of the way they use grammar (syntax). They might say 'two times' instead of 'twice'. They might say 'I goed there' instead of 'I went there.' They love to chat and ask questions (what, where and who). They enjoy much more complicated stories and ask for their favourite ones over again. It is not unusual for children to stutter because they are trying so hard to tell adults things. Their thinking goes faster than the pace at which they can say what they want to. They can quickly become frustrated.
3–4 years	During this time children ask why, when and how questions as they become more and more fascinated with the reasons for things and how things work (cause and effect). They wonder what will happen 'if' (problem solving and hypothesis making). They can think back and they can think forward much more easily than before. They can also think about things from somebody else's point of view, but only fleetingly. Past, present and future tenses are used more often.

They can be taught to say their name, address and age.

As they become more accurate in the way they pronounce words, and begin to use grammar, they delight in nonsense words which they make up, and jokes using words. This is called metalinguistics.

They swear if they hear swearing (see page 153).

4–8 years	They try to understand the meaning of words. They use adverbs and prepositions. They talk confidently, and with more and more fluency.
	As they become part of their culture they become aware of the roles of the language(s) they speak. They use language creatively.
	They add vocabulary all the time.
	Their articulation becomes conventional.
	They are explorers and communicators – they begin to be able to define objects by their function, e.g. 'What is a ball?' 'You bounce it.'
	Young children do not learn well in isolation from other children and adults. They begin to share as they learn. Sharing sharpens and broadens their thinking. This helps them to learn better, e.g. they begin to understand book language, and that stories have characters and a plot (the narrative). They begin to realise that different situations require different ways of talking. They establish a sense of audience (whom they are talking to).

Table 5.3 Normative intellectual/cognitive and symbolic development.

Age	Development
0–4 weeks	Concepts (ideas) are already beginning to develop. Concepts are based in the senses and in what is perceived (i.e. the baby is aware of sensations). Babies explore through their senses and through their own activity and movement.

❑ **Touch and movement (kinaesthetic development)**
From the beginning babies feel pain.
Their faces, abdomens, hands and the soles of their feet are also very sensitive to touch. They perceive the movements that they themselves make, and the way that other people move them about.
For example, they give a 'startle' response if they are moved suddenly. This is called the 'Moro' response.

❑ **Sound**
Even a newborn baby will turn to a sound. Babies might become still and listen to a low sound, or quicken their movements when they hear a high sound. A baby often stops crying and listens to a human voice by two weeks of age.

❑ **Taste**
Babies like sweet tastes, for example breast milk.

❑ **Smell**
Babies turn to the smell of the breast.

❑ **Sight**
Babies can focus on objects 20 cm (a few inches) away.
Babies are sensitive to light.
Babies like to look at human faces – making eye contact.
They can track the movements of people and objects.
They will scan the edges of objects.
They will imitate facial expressions (for example, they will put out their tongue if you do). If you know any newborn or very young babies, try it and see!
Psychologists think that babies may not see in colour during the early stages of development.

4–16 weeks	They recognise (or have a concept of) differing speech sounds. By three months they can even imitate low- or high-pitched sounds. By four months they link objects they know with the sound, for example mother's voice and her face. They know the smell of their mother from that of other mothers.
4–5 months	By 4 months babies reach for objects, which suggests they recognise and judge the distance in relation to the size of the object. This is called **depth perception**. It also suggests that the baby is linking the immediate perception with previous ones and predicting the future, which is an early concept of dimensional objects.
5–6 months	Babies prefer complicated things to look at from 5 to 6 months. They enjoy bright colours. They know that they have one mother. Babies are disturbed if they are shown several images of their mother at the same time. They realise that people are permanent before they realise that objects are too. Babies can coordinate more, e.g. they can see a rattle, grasp the rattle, put the rattle in their mouths (they coordinate tracking, reaching, grasping and sucking). They can develop favourite tastes in food and recognise differences by 5 months.
6–9 months	The baby understands **signs**, e.g. the bib means that food is coming. Soon this understanding of signs will lead into symbolic behaviour. From 8 to 9 months babies show they know objects exist when they have gone out of sight, even under test conditions. This is called the concept of object constancy, or the **object permanence test** (as described by **Piaget**). They are also fascinated by the way objects move. They understand that two objects can occupy space. One toy can be covered by a cloth. See also page 269.
9 months–1 year	Babies are beginning to develop images. Memory develops. They can remember the past. They can anticipate the future. This gives them some understanding of routine daily sequences, e.g. after a feed, being changed, and having a sleep with teddy. This thinking is linked to people and objects. They imitate actions, sounds, gestures and moods after an event is finished, e.g. they may imitate a temper tantrum they saw a friend have the previous day, wave bye-bye, remembering Grandma has gone to the shops. They catch the moods and feeling of other people, e.g. sadness or joy. This **emotional contagion** is the beginning of sympathy for others.
1–4 years	Children develop **symbolic behaviour**. This means that they: ❑ talk ❑ **pretend play** – often talking to themselves as they do so ❑ take part in simple non-competitive games ❑ represent events in drawings, models, etc. Personal images dominate, rather than the conventions used in the culture, e.g. writing is 'pretend' writing: ~ + o + + + Children tend to focus on one aspect of a situation. It is difficult for them to see things from different points of view. The way people react to what they do helps them to work out what hurts and what helps other people. They begin to understand, typically from 18 months, that other people might think differently from them, e.g. they might like biscuits and dislike broccoli. This is called developing **Theory of Mind** (understanding how others may feel). It leads to having empathy for others. Being able to sympathise and empathise makes this an important time for **moral development**. They often enjoy music and playing sturdy instruments, and like to join groups to sing and dance.

4–8 years	Children begin to move into deeper and deeper layers of symbolic behaviour.
	Communication through body language, facial gestures and language is well established, and opens the way into literacy (talking, listening, writing and reading).
	Personal symbols still dominate until 6 or 7 years of age.
	Cultural conventions in writing and drawing begin to influence children increasingly. Where there is a balance in the way children use personal and conventional symbols, children are described as creative. Lack of creativity is linked with a lack of personal symbols. Colouring-in templates and tracing discourage children from developing personal symbols.
	Thinking becomes increasingly coordinated as children are able to hold in mind more than one point of view at a time. **Concepts** – of matter, length, measurement, distance, area, time, volume, capacity and weight – develop steadily.
	They enjoy chanting and counting (beginning to understand number). They can use their voice in different ways to play different characters in their pretend play. They develop play narratives (stories) which they return to over time. They help younger children into the play.
	They are interested in their own development – from being babies to the present.
	They are beginning to establish differences between what is real and unreal or fantasy. This understanding is not always stable, and so they can easily be frightened by supernatural characters.
	They begin to try to work out right and wrong – e.g. hurting people physically or their own feelings – as language develops and deeper discussion of issues becomes more possible. But remember that even adults have difficulty knowing what is right in some situations.

Table 5.4 Normative emotional and social development.

Age	Development
Birth to 4 weeks	Baby's first smile in definite response to carer is usually around 5–6 weeks. The baby often imitates certain facial expressions. She uses total body movements to express pleasure at bathtime or when being fed. The baby enjoys feeding and cuddling. In the first month babies are learning where they begin and end, e.g. a hand is part of them but mother's hand is not.
4–8 weeks	Baby will smile in response to adult. The baby enjoys sucking. She turns to regard a nearby speaker's face. The baby turns to a preferred person's voice. She recognises the face and hands of a preferred adult. The baby may stop crying when she hears, sees or feels her carer.
8–12 weeks	The baby shows enjoyment at caring routines such as bathtime. She responds with obvious pleasure to loving attention and cuddles. She fixes the eyes unblinkingly on carer's face when feeding. The baby stays awake for longer periods of time.
4–5 months (16–20 weeks)	The baby enjoys attention and being with others. She shows trust and security. She has recognisable sleep patterns. By 5 months babies have learnt that they only have one mother. They are disturbed when shown several images of their mother at the same time.
6–9 months	The baby can manage to feed herself with fingers. She is now more wary of strangers, sometimes showing **stranger fear**. She might offer toys to others. She might show distress when her mother leaves. Babies typically begin to crawl and this means they can do more for themselves, reach for objects and get to places and people.

Babies are now more aware of other people's feelings. They cry if their brother cries, for example. They love an audience to laugh with them. They cry and laugh with others. This is called recognition of an emotion. It does not mean they are really laughing or crying, though.

9–12 months	The baby enjoys songs and action rhymes. She still likes to be near to a familiar adult. She can drink from a cup with help. She will play alone for long periods. She has and shows definite likes and dislikes at meal- and bedtimes. She thoroughly enjoys peek-a-boo games. She likes to look at herself in a mirror (use a plastic safety mirror). She imitates other people, e.g. clapping hands, waving bye-bye, but there is often a time lapse so that she waves after the person has gone. She cooperates when being dressed.
1–2 years	The child begins to have a longer memory. ✳ She develops a **sense of identity** (I am me). She expresses her needs in words and gestures. She enjoys being able to walk, and is eager to try to get dressed, saying, 'Me do it!' Toddlers are aware when others are fearful or anxious for them as they climb on and off chairs, for example.
2–3 years	**Pretend play** develops rapidly when adults foster it. ✳ The child begins to be able to say how she is feeling. She can dress herself and go to the lavatory independently, but needs sensitive support in order to feel success rather than frustration.
3–4 years	Pretend play helps children to **decentre** and develop Theory of Mind. They are beginning to develop a gender role as they become aware of being male or male. They make friends and are interested in having friends. They learn to negotiate, give and take, experiment with feeling powerful, having a sense of control, and they quarrel with other children. Children are easily afraid, for example, of the dark. As they become capable of pretending, they imagine all sorts of things.
4–8 years	Children have developed a stable self-concept. They have internalised the rules of their culture. They can hide their feelings once they can begin to control their emotions. They can think of the feelings of others. They can take responsibility, e.g. in helping younger children.

Table 5.5 Spiritual aspects of a child's development.

Age	Development
0–1 year	Even a tiny baby experiences a sense of self, and of awe and wonder, and values people who are loved by them. Worship is about a sense of worth. People, loved teddy bears, a daisy on the grass grasped and looked at (put in the mouth!) are all building the child's spiritual experiences. This has nothing to do with worship of a god or gods. Spirituality is about the developing sense of relationship with self, relating to others ethically, morally and humanely and a relationship with the universe.
1–3 years	Judy Dunn's work suggests that during this period children already have a strongly developed moral sense. They know what hurts and upsets their family (adults and children). They know what delights them and brings about pleased responses. Through their pretend play, and the conversations in the family about how people behave, hurt and help each other, they learn how other people feel. They learn to think beyond themselves.

3–8 years	With the help and support of their family, early years workers and the wider community, children develop further concepts like being helpful and forgiving, and having a sense of fairness.
9 years onwards	These concepts become more abstract – such as justice, right, wrong, good versus evil, beauty and nature, the arts and scientific achievements.

Assessing the development of children with disabilities

Lilli Nielsen, a Danish specialist working with children who have multiple disabilities (complex needs), stressed the importance of carefully assessing the development of the whole child. For example, she observed a child with cerebral palsy (see page 33 for information about cerebral palsy). He was lying on his stomach on a mat, with toys around him. He looked at a toy, but each time he reached for it, his shoulder jerked involuntarily and he pushed the toy away. She gently weighted down his shoulder. He reached for the toy and was able to grab it. He smiled and made a contented sound.

It would have been easy to check his physical development, and say '**cannot reach and grasp**'. Instead, we have a picture of a boy who:

* **had an idea** (to reach for the toy);
* **knew what to do** (but his body could not manage it);
* **was given the right help**, based on Nielsen's careful observation;
* **experienced success and pleasure**;
* **developed the motivation to have another go**.

Intellectual, physical, emotional and social aspects all merge together.

CRITICAL PERIODS, OR OPTIMAL, SENSITIVE AND BEST TIMES FOR DEVELOPMENT

Are there critical times for development?

Until recently it was thought that there were **critical times** when children learned to talk and walk, for example. If a child missed out on bonding with people by being able to crawl – perhaps through having an operation on the feet – or being kept confined in a cot without objects for play, it was believed that the damage was irreparable.

However, recent research suggests that it is **not always too late to catch up**. This is a much more positive way of thinking about a child's development. As neuroscience develops we are seeing that catching up is only possible if the physical mechanisms are present. They may have become latent, buried or weakened through being restrained.

A visually-impaired woman, who had been blind throughout her life, had an operation on her eyes. She was delighted to find that every oak tree looked completely different. She had learnt that there were things called oak trees, but had not realised how completely different every oak tree's shape is. She was able to catch up once her sight had been restored. In the same way, a child who learns to walk after an operation at 3 years of age can catch up on learning about walking and what it involves.

Optimal, sensitive and best times

Rather than critical periods, it seems much more likely that there are **optimal** times, **best** times or **sensitive** times in the child's development for learning to talk, walk, ride a bike, draw, sort out right from wrong, and so on.

Children who for any reason are held back from development during these sensitive or best times for learning have more difficulty becoming skilled in these areas later on. However, this does not always mean that they cannot catch up after the best time has passed.

These optimal times usually last for a number of months, except in the case of the critical time for the baby's development in utero (in the womb). Once born, it is as if nature has designed children so that there is plenty of time to learn things at every stage of their development. This is why it is so important not to rush children in their learning.

While it is never too late to catch up, bear in mind that it does seem to get harder and harder once the sensitive period is missed. It is easier for babies to learn about holding rattles and toys in their hands than it is for a child of 3 or 4 years. You should understand that it will take more time to introduce such skills to the older child.

Early is not always best

The existence of optimum periods does not mean that early is best for young children. In fact, neuroscientists think that a window of opportunity for a particular area of development is also a period of great *vulnerability* for the child's development in

that area. Those working with children need to develop the skill of observing children in enough detail to support them at the optimal or best moment for development, whenever this should come. This means not pushing children to do things too early, and it also means not waiting for maximum signs of 'readiness' until it is rather late for children to attempt things – the window may have passed.

* Children who are pushed on in advance of optimal times of development usually survive, but can also 'burn out' by 8 or 9 years of age. When children are being pushed to do academic work (reading, writing and number work) too early and too fast, they can be put off school. This pushing of children is sometimes called **intellectual abuse** (see Chapter 15).

* Children who are held back during optimal times of development through lack of stimulation also usually survive, but often suffer low self-esteem because they cannot do things. They lack the competence and skill which they know they need. In an extreme form, this lack of stimulation is sometimes called **intellectual neglect** (see Chapter 15).

* Children who are helped appropriately, at their optimal or best times of development, in a stimulating environment by people who are sensitive and observant of what an individual child can manage (regardless of norms and average ages for doing things) usually do better than survive. They flourish in their own unique way. Malaguzzi, the Italian who pioneered the **Reggio Emilia approach**, calls these 'rich' children.

Adults working with young children need to know about child development so that they are informed enough to use their observations of children to encourage them into appropriate activity at the appropriate point of development: not too early, not too late, but just right. Because development is uneven and each child is a unique person – different from everyone else in the world – each child will need what is just right *for them*. What helps a certain child will not necessarily help another. Different children need different sorts of help in learning.

Case Study

Tom and Hannah

Tom and Hannah, both from the same family, needed completely different help. At 6 years of age, Tom, the second child in the family, liked his parents and older sister to read stories to him at bedtime. He enjoyed quite different stories from his sister, especially *The Tales of Narnia* by C.S. Lewis. He showed no interest in looking at the book. He preferred to lie down and listen before he settled down to sleep. Tom did enjoy looking at non-fiction books about beetles and bugs. He would willingly look up pictures of spiders, ladybirds and ants to identify the creatures he found in the garden. He would read the short sentences describing them – this was his way into reading, rather than being read to.

Hannah, when she was 6 years of age, liked to find books that she could read easily. She would read these aloud to her parents at bedtime. She also liked to read them to her younger brother Tom, who was then 4 years old. She read books like *Spot*. Then she wanted her parents to take a turn at reading, asking them to read books that were too difficult for her to read on her own. She liked to sit and follow the text as a parent read to her. In this way, Hannah began to fill in bits of reading and even to take over from the adult when she could manage it. She felt in control when tackling more difficult texts and did not lose the flow of the story because the adult took over as soon as she stopped reading.

Guidelines for thinking about child development

1 Children are whole people. It can be useful to focus on one area of development (e.g. communication and language), but it is not useful to isolate thinking about one aspect from thinking about the whole child's development.

2 Children seem to go through the same sequences of development but will vary in the exact way that they do so.

3 Milestones can be very misleading (for the reason outlined in point 2 above). Children with disabilities or exceptionally gifted children (children with a great talent or intellectual gift, for example in dance, music or mathematics) may not be 'normal' in the way they go through a sequence.

4   Cultural differences mean that norms vary across the world in terms of what young children are expected to do at different points. For example, in some cultures children are expected to speak only one language, while in others they are expected to speak several languages from the moment they can form words.

5   Normative development tends to make us compare children with each other. It is also important to compare the child with his or her own previous development. We must not forget to ask, 'Is this good progress for this particular child?'

THE DIFFERENCE BETWEEN DEVELOPMENT AND LEARNING

It is important to be clear about the difference between development and learning.

Development is about the general way in which a child *functions*.

Example: Matthew (2 years old) can run and jump. He cannot hop or skip yet. He runs across spaces. He jumps to music. Matthew's development is spontaneous and depends on his physical progress, his ability to think about a concept of 'hop' or 'skip', his mood, and whether he has seen someone else hop or skip.

Learning is *provoked*. Learning occurs in a specific situation, at a specific moment, or when a specific problem needs to be tackled. People help children to learn, by creating environments and atmospheres which promote learning.

Example: Matthew is taken to the fair, where he learns to jump in a new way – on an inflatable castle. Most of the learning children do happens while they are developing. We do not even notice that they are learning. It is one of nature's safety mechanisms. It is actually difficult to stop children learning as long as they are with people who encourage their general development (e.g. if the adult

knows and understands that 2-year-olds need to run and jump).

Children are held back in their learning if they are not allowed to develop. There have been tragic instances of this in the orphanages of Romania, where children who have been left sitting in a cot all day have been held back intellectually because their general development has not been allowed to move forward. This example shows that an environment that is not stimulating can hold back development.

It is important to take care that children with disabilities are not held back in their learning just because their general development is constrained in some way. For example, the child with a hearing impairment needs to communicate; otherwise learning about relating to other people will be held back. Use of facial expression, gestures, sign language and finger spelling, as well as a hearing aid and help with lip-reading, will all help the child's general development. The child can then communicate, and learn to think and socialise in particular situations.

WHAT IS A THEORY OF CHILD DEVELOPMENT?

A theory of child development is someone's idea about how a child might develop. Theories help people to predict, for example, that before children talk, they usually babble. Theories about how children develop are products of research and so are influenced by the culture in which they are thought out. Research by human beings provides all the evidence for and against various theories of child development. It is very important to remember this, because humans are not objective – they agree and disagree. You must realise that there is no such thing as 'the truth' about child development. We always need to stop and ask: who is doing the research? Who is formulating the theory?

Two examples illustrate this point:

1   The child psychologist Lev **Vygotsky** (1896–1935) grew up in the Soviet Union, where Marxist and Communist ideas dominated. He came from a large family. Is it coincidence that his theory emphasises social relationships and the community?

2   The psychologist Jean **Piaget** (1896–1980) grew up in Europe. He was an only child. Is it coincidence that his theory emphasises the child as an individual and as an active learner trying to experiment and solve problems?

Using theories in your work

You need to have an open mind and to look at various different theories, bringing together those ideas that are useful from each so that you can use them in your work. Some theories will help you to make predictions about a child's learning. You need to see where theories like those of Vygotsky and Piaget are the same and where they are different.

Sometimes the differences between theories are so big that it is not possible to use them together. But, as with Piaget's and Vygotsky's work, they are often very similar. This means they can be blended into a useful template for our work with children. Both theories help us to look at how children learn.

THEORIES OF CHILD DEVELOPMENT AND LEARNING

Historically, theories of child development have tended to fall into one of two groups. Some theories take the view that learning is closely linked with development. Examples of this type of theory are '**leave it to nature**' theories and **social constructivist** theories. The other group of theories dismisses the importance of a child's development as the basis of learning. These theories follow the transmission model, which says that children learn what they are shown by adults. When describing how children learn, therefore, it is important to say which theory is being used. In the following section, we will look first at transmission theories, and then at 'leave it to nature' and social constructivist theories.

Transmission models of learning

In the seventeenth century the British philosopher John Locke thought that children were like lumps of clay, which adults could mould into the shape they wanted. At the beginning of the twentieth century in the USA a psychologist John Watson, and the Russian psychologist Ivan Petrovich **Pavlov**, were developing similar theories about how people learn. In the past, these theories have had a strong influence on thinking about development.

CLASSICAL CONDITIONING
Ivan Petrovich Pavlov (1849–1936) experimented with conditioned responses in

dogs. He liked to be described as a physiologist, rather than as a psychologist, because he believed that psychological states (such as conditioning) are identical to physiological states and processes in the brain. He thought this approach was useful and scientific. In his experiments, there was a neutral conditioned stimulus, which was a church bell ringing. This was paired with food, which was an unconditioned stimulus. The dogs were fed when the church bells rang. This produced an unconditioned response, which was saliva flowing in the dog's mouth when the food appeared.

Gradually, the sound of any bell would produce a conditioned response in the dogs, which would produce saliva ready for the food that usually accompanied the ringing of the bell.

Classical conditioning is the way in which responses come under the control of a new stimulus. In this case, food normally produces salivation. Classical conditioning changes the stimulus, so that the sound of a bell produces salivation. Pavlov would have fed the dogs whether or not they salivated at the sound of the bell.

Table 5.6 The advantages and disadvantages of the transmission model of learning.

Advantages	Disadvantages
❖ Adults feel secure. They feel that they know what to teach children about different subjects, behaviour, etc.	❖ Adults think they know what they have taught children. In fact the child might have learned something quite different. Example: the child might stop hitting a younger child in front of the adult; but they may have learned that they can still hit the younger child – but not when an adult can see them doing it.
❖ They can make up ways of testing children in order to check what they have learned.	❖ This approach encourages children to be passive receivers of the learning that adults think is important for them; but they are not likely to want to attempt something new and also less likely to take risks in case they make mistakes.
❖ They can see if children are doing things properly (i.e. are doing what adults think children should do).	❖ Children will only want to do things if they think they can do it successfully and get it right.
❖ This approach produces quick success, which makes adults feel they are good teachers.	❖ The child's learning is controlled by the adult. This quickly leads to a narrow approach to the curriculum.
❖ It makes children who succeed in performing adults' tasks feel that they are good learners, who can perform as adults require them to do.	❖ Children are likely to be labelled as poor learners, or even as failures, if they do not complete adult tasks and tests in the way the adult wants.
	❖ The approach undermines creativity and imagination.

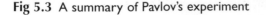

CS	+	UCS	→	UCR
bell		food		salivation

gradually turned into

CS	→	CR
bell		salivation

Fig 5.3 A summary of Pavlov's experiment

Case Study

An example of learning through classical conditioning

Year-2 children (aged 6 and 7 years) in a primary school were working in groups. One group was painting, one group was writing, another group was involved in a maths game and a fourth group was cooking. The school bell rang. Immediately the children stopped what they were doing and started to tidy up quickly and go out to play. The children were conditioned to expect playtime when the bell sounded, so they tidied up in readiness. They would have tidied up even if they had not been allowed to go out to play subsequently.

bell (conditioned stimulus) + playtime (unconditioned stimulus) = tidy up (unconditioned response)

bell (conditioned stimulus) = tidy up (conditioned response)

Fig 5.4 Pavlov's dog: an illustrated summary of the experiment

OPERANT CONDITIONING

Burrhus Frederic **Skinner** (1905–1990) was a behavioural psychologist who worked in the USA. He did not believe it was useful to theorise about mental states that could not be observed. He thought this was unscientific.

Whereas Pavlov fed his dogs when the bell rang whether or not they salivated, Skinner only fed his rats or pigeons if they did as he required. For example, he gave rats a reward of food if they pressed a lever. This was positive reinforcement: the desired behaviour was rewarded. Conversely, undesired behaviour could be negatively reinforced. For example, the rats might receive an electric shock each time they went near one area of a maze. They would then begin to avoid that area. The undesired behaviour was extinguished and the desired behaviour was encouraged.

Chris Rice is a lecturer in early childhood courses at Clydebank College in Scotland. This is how she explains positive and negative reinforcement.

If behaving in a certain way leads to a pleasing outcome, then the behaviour will be repeated. For example, a baby points to a toy monkey and looks at the adult. The adult hands her the toy, making appropriate monkey noises, which they both find funny. The baby then repeats the behaviour with

elements of both into something that is helpful to those working with children.

Piaget, Vygotsky and Bruner all used a social constructivist/interactionist approach and their work is discussed below.

JEAN PIAGET (1896–1980)

The important elements of Piaget's theory of how children learn are that they:

* go through stages and sequences in their learning;

* are active learners;

* use first-hand experiences and prior experiences in order to learn;

* imitate and transform what they learn into symbolic behaviour.

Piaget did not explicitly emphasise the importance of social and emotional aspects of learning and he did not dwell on social relationships as much as the other social constructivists. This means he took social and emotional development for granted and he did not write about it in detail. Instead, his writing emphasises intellectual/cognitive development and learning. Piaget's theory is called **constructivist** (rather than social constructivist) for this reason.

LEV VYGOTSKY (1896–1934)

Vygotsky stressed the importance for development of someone who knows more than the child and who can help the child to learn something that would be too difficult for the child to do on his or her own. Vygotsky described:

* the **zone of potential development**, sometimes called the zone of proximal development. It means that the child can do with help now what it will be possible for him or her to do alone with no help later in life.

* the **importance of play** for children under 7 years. Play allows children to do things beyond what they can manage in actual life (such as pretend to drive a car). It is another way through which children reach their zone of potential development.

* the **zone of actual development**. This is what the child can manage without help from anyone.

Vygotsky believed **social relationships** are at the heart of a child's learning, So his theory is called a social constructivist theory. Barbara Rogoff (1997) has extended Vygotsky's work and writes about the way adults and toddlers co-construct their learning, learning from each other.

Case Study

An example of a social constructivist/interactionist view of development and learning
Using a team approach to record keeping in an early years setting, staff had built up observations of children. They noted that Damian (5 years) kept punching; he punched other children, furniture and other objects. It seemed to be his main way of exploring.

The staff decided to introduce activities which allowed punching:

* They put huge lumps of clay on the table.

* They made bread and encouraged energetic kneading.

* They sang songs like 'Clap your hands and stamp your feet' and 'Hands, knees and bumps-a-daisy'.

Case Study continued

- ❖ They encouraged vigorous hand-printing and finger-painting.
- ❖ They helped children to choreograph dance fights when acting out a story.
- ❖ Damian told the group about 'baddies' from another planet.
- ❖ He helped to 'beat' the carpet with a beater as part of spring cleaning.
- ❖ He spent a long time at the woodwork bench, hammering nails into his model.

Damian soon stopped hitting other children and began to talk about what he was doing in the activities with adults and other children. Observation enabled adults to support Damian's learning in educationally worthwhile ways. Adults were also able to extend his learning so that hitting people stopped and became learning to hit in a rich variety of ways that did not hurt anyone.

JEROME BRUNER (B. 1915)

The essence of Bruner's theory is that children learn through:

- ❖ **doing** (the **enactive** mode of learning);
- ❖ **imaging** things that they have done (the **iconic** mode of learning);
- ❖ making what they know into **symbolic codes**, for example talking, writing or drawing (the **symbolic** mode of learning).

Adults can tutor children and help them to learn. They do this by 'scaffolding' what the child is learning in order to make it manageable for the child. This means that children can learn any subject at any age. They simply need to be given the right kind of help. For example, when a baby drops a biscuit over the side of the high chair, the baby can learn about gravity if the adult scaffolds the experience by saying something like: 'It dropped straight down on to the floor, didn't it? Let's both drop a biscuit and see if they get to the floor together.' Bruner's theory is also called a social constructivist theory, as social relationships are central to scaffolding.

Fig 5.5 Using dough to express feelings

THE NATURE–NURTURE DEBATE

The nature–nurture debate is concerned with the extent to which development and learning are primarily to do with the child's natural maturing processes, and the extent to which development and learning progress as a result of experience.

The debate has been very fierce, and it is not over yet. Modern psychologists, such as Sir Michael Rutter, believe that the child's learning is probably about 60 per cent nature and 40 per cent nurture. Neuroscientists, such as Colin Blakemore, stress the importance of relationships (nurture) and how these actually cause the brain to change and be altered physically. What do you think?

We can think about the developmental theories in terms of nature and nurture:

❖ The transmission approach stresses experience and nurture.

❖ The 'leave it to nature' approach stresses maturation and nature.

❖ The social constructivist approach to learning stresses both nature and nurture.

A modern way of describing this is to say that both the biological and sociocultural paths of development are important for learning.

(The nature–nurture debate is discussed in more detail in Chapters 6 and 10.)

ADULTS' LEARNING

Remember, theories about learning are not just about how children learn; they are about how adults learn too. Adults who enjoy learning and being with children are much more likely to provide a high-quality early childhood setting for children and their families. When a setting is described as demonstrating good practice, or high-quality practice, it is usually seen that adults and children are *both* active in their learning.

Table 5.9 Advantages and disadvantages of the social constructive/interactionist view of learning.

Advantages	Disadvantages
❖ This approach is very rewarding and satisfying because adults and children can enjoy working together, struggling at times, concentrating hard, stretching their thinking and ideas, celebrating their learning, and sharing the learning together. ❖ Trusting each other to help when necessary creates a positive relationship between children, parents and staff. It means taking pride in the way that indoor and outdoor areas of the room are set up, organised, maintained and cared for. ❖ It means teamwork by the adults, which is the way to bring out everyone's strengths in a multiprofessional group of teachers and early years workers. ❖ It means sharing with parents and children all the learning that is going on. ❖ It means adults need to go on learning about children's development. When adults continue to develop as people and professionals, learning alongside children, they have more to offer the children. ❖ Adults and children respect and value each other's needs and rights, and help each other to learn. ❖ Although it takes time, training and experience for adults to build up skills for working in this way, it is very effective in helping children to learn during their early years.	❖ It is very hard work compared with the other two approaches to learning that we have looked at in this chapter. This is because there is much more for adults to know about, more to think about, more to organise and do. ❖ It is much more difficult for those who are not trained to understand how to work in this way. ❖ In Sweden there are now local plazzas where early years workers explain the way they work to parents, those working with older children, governing bodies and politicians.

Guidelines for using the different approaches to development and learning

1   Figure 5.6 shows that in a 'leave it to nature' approach to learning, children make a very high contribution to the learning they do, but adults hold back and take a very small part.

2   This is very different from the transmission model. In this approach the adult has a very high input into the child's learning, taking control over the child's learning. The child's contribution is quite low.

3   The by-the-book approach to learning is not valuable and has not been covered in this chapter. Here, both the adults and the children have a very low level of participation. It is not really an approach to learning; it is just a way of keeping children occupied. Worksheets, colouring–in, tracing, templates, filling in gaps and joining the dots all fall under this heading.

4   In the social constructivist (sometimes called interactionist) approach to learning both the adult and the child put an enormous amount of energy into active learning.

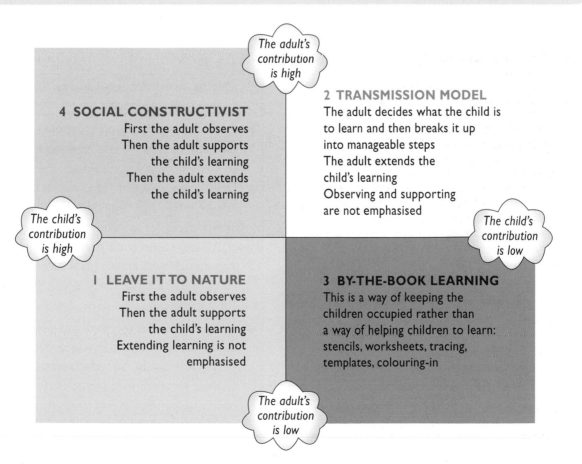

Fig 5.6 The four approaches to development and learning

PIONEERS IN QUALITY, INTEGRATED, EARLY YEARS PROVISION

Throughout history there have been people who have been prepared to stand up and fight for what young children need. They are the pioneers who help everyone working with young children, past and present, to move forward. Not all of us have the kind of personality which makes a pioneer, but we can all do our bit for the children in our care.

The pioneers in this chapter are often called educational pioneers, but each one of them cared for children as much as they educated them. Each one of them believed in integrated early years provision. This has a long and respected heritage, and the greatest influence in the UK in the last century has been that of Friedrich Froebel. Other pioneers include Maria Montessori, Rudolf Steiner, Margaret McMillan and Susan Isaacs.

Friedrich Froebel (1782–1852)

Froebel, who founded the first kindergarten in 1840, studied for a time with Pestalozzi in his school in Switzerland. Through his observations of children, Froebel learned how important it was for children to have real experiences which involved them in being physically active. Froebel's ideas are now very much part of everyday thinking about the integration of early years services. But most people have never heard of the man himself – only his ideas remain.

Froebel believed that everything links and connects with everything else: he called this the **Principle of Unity**. But he also believed in what he called the **Principle of Opposition**. For example, the first Gift is a soft ball, but the second Gift is a hard wooden ball (see the summary below for more on Gifts). He thought that these kinds of contrasts were important in helping children to think.

A summary of Froebel's ideas

❖ Froebel thought schools should be communities in which the parents are welcome to join their children.

❖ He believed that parents were the first educators of their child.

❖ Froebel thought that children learned outdoors in the garden, as well as indoors. He encouraged movement, games and the study of natural science in the garden.

❖ He invented finger play, songs and rhymes.

❖ He encouraged the arts and crafts and a love of literature, as well as mathematical understanding.

❖ He thought that children should have freedom of movement, clothes that were easy to move about in, and sensible food that was not too rich.

❖ Froebel deeply valued symbolic behaviour, and he encouraged this even in very young children. He realised how important it is for children to understand that they can make one thing stand for another; for example, a daisy can stand for a fried egg, a twig can stand for a knife, a leaf can stand for a plate, a written word can stand for a name.

❖ He thought that the best way for children to try out symbolic behaviour was in their play. He thought that children show their highest levels of learning as they pretend and imagine things. He thought that children's best thinking is done when they are playing.

- He also designed various items and activities to help symbolic behaviour. He encouraged children to draw, make collages and model with clay.
- He encouraged play with special shaped wooden blocks, which he called the Gifts.
- He made up songs, movements and dancing, and the crafts, which he called his Occupations.
- He allowed children to use the Gifts and Occupations as they wished, without having to do set tasks of the kind that adults usually asked of them. Thus he introduced what is now called free-flow play.
- He emphasised the expressive arts, mathematics, literature, the natural sciences, creativity and aesthetic (beautiful) things. He believed that each brought important but different kinds of knowledge and understanding.
- He also placed great emphasis on ideas, feelings and relationships. Relationships with other children, he believed, were as important as relationships with adults.

Maria Montessori (1870–1952)

Maria Montessori began her work as a doctor in the poorest areas of Rome at the beginning of the 1900s. She worked with children with learning difficulties. She spent many hours **observing** children and this is one of the great strengths of her work. She came to the conclusion, now supported by modern research, that children pass through sensitive periods of development when they are particularly receptive to particular areas of learning. Like Piaget (and others), she saw children as active learners.

A summary of Montessori's ideas

- Montessori devised a structured teaching programme which she based on her observations of children who were mentally challenged, and she believed she was making Froebel's work more scientifically rigorous in doing so.
- She also used the work of an educator called Seguin, who had given manual dexterity exercises to children who were handicapped. He did this because he believed that if they could learn to use their hands, they would be able to find work later.
- Montessori designed a set of what she called **didactic materials**, which encouraged children to use their hands. Her approach moved children through simple to complex exercises.
- Whereas Froebel stressed the importance of relationships, feelings and being part of a community, Montessori stressed that children should work alone. She thought this helped children to become **independent learners**.
- For her, the highest moment in a child's learning was what she called **the polarisation of the attention**. This means that the child is completely silent and absorbed in what they are doing.
- Unlike Froebel, Montessori did not see the point in play. She did not encourage children to have their own ideas until they had worked through all her graded learning sequences: she did not believe that they were able to do free drawing or creative work of any kind until they had done this. Montessori has had less influence on the maintained sector of education than she has had on private schools.

Rudolf Steiner (1861–1925)

Steiner believed in three phases of childhood. These involved:

1   The **will**, 0–7 years: he believed the spirit fuses with the body at this stage.

2   The **heart**, 7–14 years: he believed that the rhythmic system of the beating heart, the chest and the respiratory system meant that feelings were especially important during this time.

3   The **head**, 14 years onwards: this is the period of thinking.

There are a few schools in the UK which use Steiner's methods. These **Waldorf Schools** are all in the private sector. Like Montessori, Steiner has had less influence on the statutory public sector than on the private sector.

A summary of Steiner's ideas

❖ Steiner believed in reincarnation. To him, this meant that, during the first 7 years of life, the child is like a newcomer finding their way, and the child's reincarnated soul needs protection.

❖ The child needs a carefully planned environment to develop in a rounded way.

❖ What the child eats is very important (Steiner was a vegetarian). The child also needs proper rest (rest and activity need to be balanced).

❖ The child's temperament is also considered to be very important. A child might be calm (**sanguine**), easily angered (**choleric**), sluggish (**phlegmatic**), or peevish (**melancholic**). Often children are a combination of types.

❖ The golden rule for the adult is never to go against the temperament of the child, but always to go with it.

❖ Steiner was like Froebel in that he believed in the importance of the community. He believed that maintaining relationships with other people is very important, and for this reason children would keep the same teacher for a number of years.

❖ When children are about to sing and act out a circle game, everyone waits for the last child to join the group. The song is sung many times so that quicker children learn to help and support slower children.

❖ Steiner's curriculum is very powerful for children with special educational needs, who can integrate because other children are actively helped to care about them.

❖ Steiner thought the **symbolic behaviour** of the child was important, but in a different way from Froebel. In the first 7 years of life, he told special Steinerian fairy tales. He believed children 'drink' these in and absorb them. He gave them dolls without faces, wooden blocks with irregular shapes, silk scarves as dressing-up clothes and particular colour schemes in rooms (pink at first). Baking, gardening, modelling, painting and singing would all take place in a carefully designed community.

Margaret McMillan (1860–1931)

Margaret McMillan, like Montessori, began her work using the influence of Seguin. This meant that she emphasised manual dexterity exercises long before Montessori's ideas reached the UK. However, as time went on, she used Froebel's ideas more and more (she became a member of the Froebel Society in 1903).

A summary of McMillan's ideas

❖ McMillan believed **first-hand experience** and **active learning** to be important.

❖ She emphasised relationships, feelings and ideas, as much as the physical aspects of moving and learning.

❖ She believed that children become whole people through play. She thought play helps them to apply what they know and understand.

❖ McMillan pioneered nursery schools, which she saw as an extension of, not a substitute for, home.

❖ She believed in very close **partnership with parents**, encouraging parents to develop alongside their children, with adult classes in hobbies and languages made available to them.

❖ The British nursery school, as envisaged by McMillan, has been admired and emulated across the world. Nursery schools have gardens and are communities which welcome both parents and children. Such nursery schools stood out as beacons of light in the poverty-stricken areas of inner cities like Deptford and Bradford in the 1920s.

❖ McMillan said that in a nursery school families could experience 'fresh air, trees, rock gardens, herbs, vegetables, fruit trees, bushes, opportunities to climb on walls, sandpits, lawns, flowers and flower beds and wildernesses'. In her book, *The Nursery School*, she wrote, 'most of the best opportunities for achievement lie in the domain of free play, with access to various materials'. This was published in 1930.

❖ Perhaps her most important achievement of all is to have been described as the 'godmother' of school meals and the school medical services. She believed that children cannot learn if they are undernourished, poorly clothed, sick or ill, with poor teeth, poor eyesight, ear infections, rickets, and so on. Recent reports emphasise that poor health and poverty are challenges still facing those who work with families in the UK today.

❖ McMillan placed enormous importance on the training of adults working with children, and on the need for them to be inventive and imaginative in their work.

Susan Isaacs (1885–1948)

Susan Isaacs, like Margaret McMillan, was influenced by Froebel. She was also influenced by the theories of Melanie Klein, the psychoanalyst (see page 240). Isaacs made detailed observations of children in her Malting House School in Cambridge during the 1930s.

A summary of Isaacs's ideas

❖ Isaacs valued play because she believed that it gave children freedom to think and feel, and relate to others.

❖ She looked at children's fears, their aggression and their anger. She believed that, through their play, children can move in and out of reality. This enables them to balance their ideas, feelings and relationships.

❖ She said of classrooms where young children have to sit at tables and write that they cannot learn in such places because they need to move just as they need to eat and sleep.

❖ Isaacs valued parents as the most important educators in a child's life. She spoke to them on the radio, and she wrote for parents in magazines. In her book, *The Nursery Years*, she wrote:

If the child had ample opportunity for free play and bodily exercise, if this love of making and doing with his hands is met, if his interest in the world around him is encouraged by sympathy and understanding, if he is left free to make-believe or think as his impulses take him, then his advances in skill and interest are but the welcome signs of mental health and vigour.

❖ Isaacs encouraged people to look at the inner feelings of children. She encouraged children to express their feelings. She

thought it would be very damaging to bottle up feelings inside.

❖ She supported both Froebel's and McMillan's view that nurseries are an extension of the home and not a substitute for it, and she believed that children should remain in nursery-type education until the age of 7 years.

❖ She kept careful records of children, both for the period they spent in her nursery and for the period after they had left. She found that many of them regressed when they left her nursery and went on to formal infant schools. Modern researchers have found the same.

ACTIVITY: ASPECTS OF DEVELOPMENT

When you have looked at these milestones of normative development, turn to Figure 5.2.

1 Draw seven circles with the same diameter.

2 Cut them out.

3 Write in the aspects of development.

4 Thread the circles on a string.

5 Bunch them together to remind yourself these are seven parts of a whole.

6 Spread them out to focus on a single aspect of the child, but return them to the whole at the end.

ACTIVITY: REMEMBERING OUR LEARNING

Think back to your own schooldays. Were any of the lessons based on a transmission model of learning? Evaluate your learning experience.

ACTIVITY: A SCALE OF NORMATIVE DEVELOPMENT

Make your own scale of normative development, trying to make it as holistic as possible. Apply it in each of the following four ways. In each case, ask yourself this question: 'Do I know this child better than I did before, and in what ways?'

1   Observe a baby girl and then, in a different family, a baby boy. Both children should be 6–9 months in age. Use the circles activity above and the holistic child development chart (Figure 5.2) in this chapter to find out everything you can about the children under those headings.

2   Observe a boy toddler of 15–20 months in age. Again, use the circles activity and the holistic child development chart.

3   Observe two children aged 3–4 years and repeat exercise 1. Choose children from different cultural backgrounds, with different language backgrounds, or observe a child with a disability and another without. Remember, it is not useful to do this just to see if children are behind or ahead of 'norms'. Instead, you are using guidelines to help you to build up a complete picture of each child. Then you can see where help is needed, and how to facilitate and extend each child's development and learning.

4   Observe two children aged 5–7 years in the same spirit.

ACTIVITY: MODELS OF LEARNING

Make a chart with the following three headings:

❖   Transmission model of learning;

❖   Laissez-faire or 'leave it to nature' model of learning;

❖   Social constructivist or interactionist model of learning.

Which sentences go under which heading?

1   Adults should mould children's learning. After all, adults know more than children.

2   Children know what they need in order to learn.

3   Do you want to have a story first or tidy up first?

4   We need to tidy up; we'll have the story after.

5   Children are full of ideas if they are encouraged to have them.

6   Do it because I say so.

7   That child has been off-task all morning.

8   Children are born with everything they need in order to learn.

9   Children enjoy conversations with adults.

10 Children must be free to try things out.

11 Children will learn when they are ready and not before.

12 That child performed the task successfully today.

13 Nature knows best.

14 Adults know best.

15 Children must be free to try things out and to learn from the mistakes they make.

Compare your answers with a working partner. Discuss your answers together.

ACTIVITY: INVESTIGATING FROEBEL'S WORK

1 Research a set of wooden hollow blocks and wooden unit blocks (examples of these are made by Community Playthings). Can you find any mathematical relationships between the different blocks? Plan how you could help children to learn about shape using wooden blocks. Implement your plan and evaluate your observations with children aged 3–7 years.

2 Try to find 12 examples of finger rhymes. These are songs or rhymes using the fingers for actions. Make a book of them for children to enjoy. Make sure you include a multicultural range of action songs and also think about children with disabilities. Share the book with a child of 2–7 years. Evaluate your observations.

3 Research what children did in kindergartens in the last century. For example, each child had their own little garden.

   ❖ Plan how you will organise a garden activity. What equipment will you need? Where will you do this? How will you clear up?

   ❖ Plant some flowers or vegetables with children and watch them grow.

   ❖ Observe a child of 2–7 years and evaluate your garden activity in relation to that particular child's cognitive and language development.

4 Imagine that you are Friedrich Froebel today. What do you think he might like or dislike about your early years setting?

ACTIVITY: INVESTIGATING MARGARET MCMILLAN'S WORK

Plan an outdoor area for an early years setting. Emphasise the child's need for movement and curiosity about nature, and provide an area for digging and playing in mud. Evaluate your plan.

ACTIVITY: INVESTIGATING EDUCATION AND CARE

1 Research the age at which children start compulsory schooling in six countries, including one country each in Africa, Asia, Europe and Australia/New Zealand. You can use the Internet or telephone the relevant embassies, who will help you track down this information.

2 Research the different ways in which Froebel, Montessori and Steiner would (a) introduce children to a set of wooden blocks and (b) help children to use the blocks. Implement each approach with a group of children in three separate sessions. Evaluate your observations, noting the way your role as an early years worker changed according to which approach you used. Note the differences in the way the children responded, especially in relation to creativity (see Chapter 6), language and communication (see Chapter 7) and play (see Chapter 12). Which approaches encouraged the child to be a symbol user? Evaluate your observations.

which does not change throughout their lives, was not seriously challenged until the 1960s.

Intelligence can grow

During the 1960s, Piaget's work made researchers think again about what intelligence is. His theory suggested that intelligence is not fixed and unchangeable – it is not something people are born with or without. His theory suggested that intelligence is plastic. This means it can stretch, grow and increase. The idea that intelligence is plastic has been supported by recent studies in neuroscience. We now think that children can increase their intelligence if they:

❖ mix with adults and other children who help them to develop their intelligence;

❖ experience a stimulating environment which encourages thinking and ideas, and emotional intelligence.

IQ TESTS AND COMPENSATORY EDUCATION

Children were often tested in the past to find their IQ (intelligence quotient) using scales such as the Standford-Binet or Merrill-Palmer intelligence tests. Because these tests were developed by white, male psychologists with middle-class ways of looking at life, they favoured white, middle-class, male children, who thus scored higher than other groups of children. It became obvious after the 1944 Education Act that mainly white, middle-class children went to grammar schools, and there were more places in grammar schools for boys than for girls. Children from other groups went to secondary modern schools and technical schools. This began to worry some researchers, who found that IQ tests:

❖ favour children from the culture from which the tests emerged – this means

the tests are not as objective as they were first thought to be;

❖ measure particular kinds of intelligence, such as memory span and ability with numbers – this means that they only look at intelligence in a narrow way; they do not help us to look at outstanding ability in dancing, music or interpersonal sensitivity, for example.

Multiple intelligence

The psychologist Howard Gardner says that there are seven kinds of intelligence. He calls this multiple intelligence. The different domains of intelligence proposed by Gardner are:

1 linguistic intelligence;

2 logico-mathematical intelligence;

3 bodily kinaesthetic intelligence;

4 social intelligence;

5 musical intelligence;

6 spatial intelligence;

7 personal intelligence (access to personal feelings and relationships with others).

Howard Gardner believes these seven aspects of intelligence are partly genetic, but are also open to cultural influences, and so can be helped through education. According to Gardner, IQ tests:

❖ only measure a small part of intelligence;

❖ often give children labels which are likely to stick, such as 'bright or 'average ability' or 'low ability';

❖ do not encourage teachers to have high enough expectations of children – a teacher might say, 'After all, she's only got an IQ of 80.'

Intelligence tests can be useful as part of a whole barrage of different ways of making an assessment of a child's needs (especially for children with special educational needs). They are not useful, however, when used in isolation from other forms of assessment.

A child's motivation (will) to learn is very important. Two children might have the same IQ, but the one with the greater will to learn might do better simply because of this disposition.

Case Study

Fountain Hospital and the Brook Experiment

A group of children with severe learning difficulties were taken from the wards of the Fountain Hospital during the 1960s. They were placed in a stimulating environment of people and first-hand interesting experiences. Their intelligence was found to develop rapidly. This research project was called the Brook Experiment. Research like this led, in 1971, to children with special needs in hospitals and day centres being given, by law, education as well as hospital-type care. Until then, such children, and young people with IQs below 50 on the IQ scale, had been considered ineducable.

Compensatory education

During the 1960s and 1970s, programmes of compensatory education developed in the USA and the UK. In the USA, these were called the Head Start Programmes, and in the UK a series of research projects was set up under the direction of Albert Halsey, a sociologist. Researchers were beginning to realise that intelligence can grow, and so children who were thought to be growing up in non-stimulating environments were placed on these education programmes. The idea was that a good education would compensate for the poverty and social disadvantage of their lives. However, this view rejected and ignored some important influences on a child's developing intelligence, thinking and understanding:

* It did not put enough emphasis on the language and cultural background of children.
* It did not emphasise the importance of the child's parents and family life.

By contrast, the Froebel Nursery Research Project, directed by Chris Athey in 1972–77, worked in close partnership with parents. The home language of children was respected and valued, and they were offered interesting, real experiences through a quality curriculum. This included:

* cooking;
* play;
* stories and books;
* outdoor play;
* a home area;
* a workshop area with clay, paint, junk modelling and woodwork;
* a graphics area.

The IQs of the children rose, especially the IQs of the younger children who joined the project when they were babies. This project had a long-lasting effect on children's development because it:

* worked in close partnership with parents;
* offered children a stimulating, well-planned environment (i.e. a quality curriculum);
* valued the children's language and culture.

IMAGINATION AND DEVELOPMENT

Intelligence tests favour people who are convergent thinkers – these are people who can give 'correct' answers and who are able to solve questions that are set by the testers. However, intellectual development is also about having imaginative and creative ideas.

What is the imagination?

Having imagination is about being able to rearrange your past experiences and to put them together to make new ideas. Imaginative people have all sorts of ideas in art (drawing, painting, sculpture), architecture, music, dance, drama, scientific research and mathematics. These people are divergent or creative thinkers. This means they can gather together many different ideas and organise them into a single interesting idea. Imagination is about having new and fascinating ideas.

What is creativity?

Creative people – children or adults – take an imaginative idea they have had (which is a rearrangement of past experience in new and fascinating ways) and turn it into an act of creation (which is made up of the process of gathering an idea unconsciously, incubating it, becoming aware that something is developing and hatching it into a creation). They might make a dance, devise a recipe for a cake, compose a poem or develop a new scientific theory. (For more detail of what is involved in creativity, see *Cultivating Creativity: Babies, Toddlers and Young Children*, Bruce 2004.) Marian Whitehead, an expert on the teaching of reading and writing, believes that creativity and the imagination are basic in learning to read and write. Imaginative children read and write with more pleasure and interest. They have imaginative ideas and make (create) stories. (See also Chapter 12.)

BARRIERS TO CREATIVITY

Activities which discourage imagination and creativity use:

- ❖ templates;
- ❖ colouring-in;
- ❖ tracing;
- ❖ the screwed-up-tissue-paper syndrome of filling in a pre-cut outline, colouring in or using stencils.

These activities are all pre-structured by adults and allow almost no opportunity for the children's own ideas and thinking to develop. Such activities are sometimes referred to as 'busy work', but they are low-level ways of keeping children occupied. Children might enjoy doing them, but then they enjoy all sorts of things which are not good for them, such as eating sweets.

Templates are not helpful to a child who is becoming creative by developing their own thinking and ideas. In the long term, they can even undermine a child's self-esteem by making them believe that they cannot draw or make things without a template or an outline. Children can become very preoccupied with the 'right' or 'correct' ways of doing things, and they often end up by learning other people's formulas for drawing. This destroys creativity. Children should be encouraged to develop their own style in their drawings and paintings, models, dances and stories. A child who has learnt to become creative might be rather frustrated and even miserable if their creativity is undermined by pre-structured activities.

Guidelines for encouraging imagination and creativity

Young children need support and help if their creativity is to develop well. Imagination and creativity do not arise naturally, although it is true that some children learn about being creative much more easily than others.

❖ Children need a wide range of material provisions and to be encouraged to use them in lots of different ways (see Chapter 12).

❖ Children need plenty of opportunities to represent their ideas (see Chapter 12). Having an idea of your own and making it come alive is creative.

❖ Children need plenty of time for their play. They must not be over-organised by adult-led tasks (see Chapter 12). Play helps them to have imaginative ideas and to turn these into creative pretend play.

❖ Children learn about becoming creative thinkers through the people they meet and the materials they are encouraged to use.

BEING CREATIVE MEANS TAKING RISKS

A child who has never 'had a go', taken risks or experimented with different ways of doing things will not become a confident active thinker. Instead, such children only know how to carry out adult instructions or ideas. They do not become imaginative or creative.

THE IMPORTANCE OF PLAY

The strength of play lies in the way it helps children to be agents of their own learning. Children who play are good at choosing and selecting, concentrating with deep focus on what they choose; they are flexible thinkers, who are highly motivated to learn (see Chapter 12).

Case Study

The importance of play for thinking actively

Dale, 2 years, saw a fireman's hat in the dressing-up clothes. He carried it upside down like a shopping bag, and put his pretend shopping in it. He had never seen a fireman in his uniform, but he knows about shopping. He used the hat to fit the play scenario he had selected to use. He concentrated deeply as he did his 'shopping' and he made flexible (imaginative) use of the helmet, using it as a pretend bag instead of a hat. Play is good for active thinking.

PROBLEM SOLVING – MAKING HYPOTHESES AND PREDICTIONS

There is a saying, 'Happiness is not the absence of problems. It is being able to solve them.' Children are natural problem solvers from the moment they are born. It used to be thought that there is a rigid developmental sequence by which children learn to solve problems. It was thought that, at first, children tried to solve problems through trial and error, and that only later could they develop a theory or hypothesis. However, more recently researchers have found that even newborn babies can make a hypothesis.

Making a hypothesis means having a theory which can be tested to see if it is right. It is amazing to think that babies can do this. But researchers have found that they do not behave in a trial-and-error way. They do not try random solutions until, by luck, they solve the problem.

Case Study

Jo

Jo was given a card with the outline of a butterfly on it. She was asked to fill in the outline with pieces of screwed-up coloured tissue paper. She cried. She found a piece of paper and made her own picture. She made a path through a wood. This was an imaginative idea and a creative piece of work. The butterfly would only have been a low-level piece of 'busy work'.

The butterfly cards were going to be given to mothers as Mother's Day cards. The family worker explained to Jo's mother why Jo's card was different. Mum was pleased that her daughter had been so creative and did not mind the fact that Jo's card did not look so good. The imaginative thinking that went into the card and the creative result were far more important than how it looked.

Case Study

Baby makes a hypothesis

Every time a newborn baby heard a buzzer and turned towards it, the baby would find a honeyed dummy to suck on. Every time a bell rang, the baby would turn towards it, but would not find a honeyed dummy (this experiment took place in the 1970s; as evidence now shows that honey is dangerous to babies under one year old, it would need consideration if undertaken now). Soon the baby only turned for the buzzer. Once the baby had made the hypothesis that the buzzer signified honey and the bell did not, the baby felt the problem had been solved. The hypothesis the baby had made was correct. Soon it became boring to keep solving the same old problem repeatedly, and so the baby would not do it over and over again. The baby's interest was to solve the problem rather than to get the honey. Once the hypothesis was found to be correct and the problem was solved, there was no reason to carry on with this activity.

Newborn babies can hypothesise and make theories to solve such problems even when they are only a few hours old.

Making a false hypothesis

Children aged 2 years and onwards will often make a 'false' or incorrect hypothesis. They can be very obstinate about an idea they have! Experts think that finding out that a hypothesis is wrong is a very important part of learning to solve problems. In order to learn about problem solving, children need to test out their false or wrong hypotheses, as well as correct and true ones.

Case Study

Segun's hypothesis

Segun (4 years) saw some paint which glowed in the dark. His mother told him (wrongly) that it was called fluorescent paint. He asked his mother for some fluorescent paint. Having painted the stone owl from the garden, Segun put it in his bed so that it would glow in the dark. It did not glow in the dark! He then painted all sorts of stones from the garden. He put these in his bed each night. They did not glow in the dark either! Next he painted sticks from the garden and put them on his bed each night. They did not glow in the dark!

Segun's uncle visited him and told him that what he needed was iridescent paint. Segun, however, carried on with his idea of making objects glow in the dark using fluorescent paint. Then he saw a pot that glowed in the dark. He asked the owner what sort of paint they had used. The answer was, 'Iridescent'. Segun finally agreed to try the new sort of paint. His owl glowed in the dark. So did his stones. So did his sticks.

Segun had worked out, by thoroughly exploring his mistaken hypothesis, that fluorescent paint does not make things glow in the dark. Segun will now know this for the rest of his life. And he also knows that iridescent paint does make things glow in the dark. This is real learning which no one can take away from him. It shows he is making predictions and a hypothesis, concentrating and problem solving actively.

Guidelines for encouraging children with problem solving

❖ Encourage children to make a hypothesis by asking, 'What do you think is going to happen?'

❖ Help children to use their prior experience – what they already know. You could ask, 'What happened when you did…?'

❖ Let children try out their ideas. If something does not work, do not argue or dismiss it as wrong. Just point out the bits that did not work as if you are interested in 'why', and leave it at that.

❖ Try to set up situations which help children to go on testing their hypothesis and talking about it. Ask, 'Does that give you any ideas for trying again?'

MEMORY

Imitation and memory are closely linked. If you poke out your tongue at a newborn baby, the baby will imitate you, after a time. You can see the baby concentrating hard and then managing to imitate the adult. Gradually, as babies become toddlers, they begin to remember things and to imitate them after a time delay. One famous example is Piaget's daughter Jacqueline. She saw a friend have a temper tantrum when she was about 18 months old. She was very impressed by this dramatic event! The next day she tried it out herself – she imitated the temper tantrum.

The influence of having a longer memory

Between 2 and 3 years, children are able to remember more. This means that, when they are in unfamiliar situations, they tend to be able to plan things. They do not immediately rush to try new things. Instead they pause until they have an idea about what they would like to do. In this way, they organise their thinking. They remember what they have done before with similar or different objects and people, and they use this memory to help them plan ideas for this new situation. This is called 'inhibition to the unfamiliar', and it means the children can 'think before they do'.

Different kinds of memory

Neuroscientists now think that our feelings, sensory perceptions and memories are bound together as a seamless whole. In other words, the feelings children have are of central importance in the way their thinking develops, and the way they remember what they learn and feel as they learn. There are different kinds of memory:

* **Procedural memory:** for example, how to ride a bike. Remembering how to do this is a deeply ingrained habit.
* **Fear memory:** for example, flashbacks and phobias.
* **Semantic memory:** facts we remember.
* **Episodic memory:** such memories are clothed in personal experiences which are emotional, such as the day you dropped your ice cream and a dog rushed over and ate it, and you cried! This kind of memory develops rapidly as children begin to walk, talk and pretend.

BECOMING AWARE: FROM SENSATION TO PERCEPTION

When we say someone is a very perceptive person, we mean that they are very aware of things. Children and adults perceive and understand the world through their senses. The senses and what they tell us about the movements of our body give us immediate feedback about how we are moving and what is happening to us.

If you sit awkwardly and your leg goes to sleep, it is very difficult to walk. There is not enough sensory feedback from your leg to enable you to walk! You cannot perceive your leg!

Perceiving something means constructing an idea of that thing which is based on information you have received through your senses. The senses make it possible for us to perceive and experience life. For some children with severe learning difficulties it can be difficult to be sure whether they have awareness. Are they receiving messages through their senses which tell them they are having an experience? Observing children is always important, but it is particularly important in this situation. For most babies, the senses help them to perceive experiences, even in the first months of their life. Remember, all the senses are important – touch, smell, taste, hearing and sight, along with movement or kinaesthesia (see Chapter 8 for how the senses develop in babies). Most people are very aware that babies need love and care, and need to feel secure. However, it is also very important to give interesting and new experiences to newborn babies:

* We need to choose the right moment to introduce a baby to a new experience.

* The feedback from their senses (perceptions) helps babies to develop ideas (concepts). Researchers are beginning to realise that concepts develop much earlier than had been thought previously.

* Research is also showing that proprioception, being aware of how different bits of your body work together, through a sense of embodiment (feeling comfortable inside your own body), helps children to develop a sense of self.

Embodiment and a sense of self

Knowing yourself is important for learning. Can you climb that high? Will you trip on the rug? Can you reach that far without toppling over? All this is important as children begin to know themselves and develop a sense of self and identity. Our feelings, thoughts and physical selves all work together as we learn.

EARLY CONCEPTS

Researchers have shown that concepts develop early in babies, as follows:

* Very early on babies think beyond their immediate perceptions (that is, they have an awareness beyond their immediate sensory feedback about things). They begin to link present feedback with their past perceptions.

* Then babies use these links to predict the future – what will happen next.

* When babies think back to prior experience and forward to the future, they begin to develop early concepts, which become stable thoughts in their mind.

So, early concepts link past, present and future around a particular idea. This means that children can predict and plan ahead. They get better at this as their memory develops. These factors are important for thinking, and for creativity to develop. Concepts enable children to:

* organise their thinking;

* organise previous experience and perception – Piaget calls this assimilation;

* predict things about the future;

* have ideas;

* take in new knowledge and understand it – Piaget calls this **accommodation**.

Case Study

Bill

Bill is 10 months old. He stands at a coffee table and bangs a biscuit on it. His mother comes in. He perceives his mother by using his sense of sight (i.e. he is aware that she has come into the room). Bill then links the prior experience he has of his mother with this present one. He has a concept that she will come and talk to him – she has always done this in the past.

Case Study

Concepts of food
A baby of 5 months is beginning to take solids on a spoon and is often offered mashed banana. This is a taste that is known. It fits the baby's previous experience (assimilation). If the baby is given apple purée, which is a new taste, this will mean taking in a new experience (accommodation). The baby might spit the apple out.

Balancing assimilation and accommodation

Piaget would say that we are never quite balanced, but that we are always trying to keep balanced! This is what Piaget calls the process of equilibration. The balancing act between: assimilation (taking in what is known) and accommodation (adjusting to what is new) helps children and adults to organise past experiences into concepts (ideas). This is an active process, so Piaget refers to **active learners**.

Stranger fear and children's concepts

The phenomenon of stranger fear is very interesting in relation to children's concepts. The child (usually at about 6–9 months) is exploring and getting to know about faces. A face that looks different is frightening because it does not fit with what they know. Babies might cry with fear when they see someone with glasses, a bald head, a different skin colour or a beard if they have not seen this before. A reassuring adult helps babies to broaden their experience and make the unfamiliar more familiar. The case study of Hannah (below) also shows how closely linked the child's ideas are with their feelings and their relationships with people. Cognitive, emotional, physical and

social development are all combined in this story.

Case Study

Hannah
One baby, Hannah, cried when her Uncle Dan, who was bald, came to the house. She had never seen a bald person before. She cried. This happened every time Hannah saw her Uncle Dan for a month or so.

Hannah had to accommodate her new knowledge that some people do not have hair on the tops of their heads. At first Uncle Dan was very upset, but he was reassured when this was explained.

Schemas

Even babies as young as 1 month are organising their perceptions and linking them with previous experiences of people and events. They are using these concepts to work out what will happen next. Piaget calls these ready concepts **schemas**. Recent researchers have developed this part of his work. Schemas are patterns of linked behaviours which the child can generalise and use in a whole variety of different situations. For example, children are often fascinated by things that rotate. We see this in toddlers particularly, but in older children too. For example, a 4-year-old might:

❖ be fascinated by the way the water rotates as it swirls down the plughole;

❖ try to touch the steering wheel in the car (a dangerous interest);

❖ want to watch an adult mixing food round and round in a bowl;

❖ be interested in the wheels going round on a toy car;

❧ do a roly-poly down a grass slope;

❧ join in with a movement song such as 'Round and round the garden, like a teddy bear'.

Every time the child meets a situation which involves rotation, either the situation will fit the experience of what is already known and the child will assimilate it, or the child will have to change their concept to accommodate the situation. Rotating as in the song 'Round and round the garden' means taking turns and not rotating all the time. And it means standing up straight as you rotate. This is very different from the kind of rotation involved in doing a roly-poly down a grass slope, which means rotating on your side.

THE DIFFERENT LEVELS OF SCHEMA

'Up' and 'down' are important schemas that children often explore at the same time. Their exploration will be at a different level, depending on their stage of development and on their existing concepts of up and down.

1   **Senses and actions level of schemas.** At first, schemas occur when babies and toddlers use their senses and movements to link past and present perceptions. For example, a baby might move their arms up and down when shaking a rattle. The baby already knew how to move her arms in this way and applied it to a new situation.

2   **Symbolic level of schemas.** Typically during the second year, the child begins to use schemas in a new way. As well as using feedback from actions and senses, the child begins to experiment with symbolic behaviour. For example, a 2-year-old child might be painting at the table, making a line that goes up and down on the paper. The child might then say 'Daddy'. The line on paper stands for Daddy, and the drawing of the line is, therefore, an example of symbolic behaviour.

3   **Cause and effect level of schemas.** A 3-year-old child makes a thin line go up and down on the paper with the paintbrush. Then with a different paintbrush makes a wide line, saying, 'Big one, little one.' The child is interested in the causes and effects of using different paintbrushes.

The 'up' and 'down' schemas have thus been used in three different ways:

❧ The **sensori-motor** level was used by the child with the rattle.

❧ The **symbolic behaviour** level was used by the child who painted Daddy.

❧ The **cause and effect** level was used by the child who was interested in the thick and thin painted lines.

Operational concepts

Between the ages of 2 and 7 years, children become able to combine early concepts or schemas in a logical way. They start to link the different aspects of their experiences, developing what Piaget calls operational thinking. Most children become proficient in operational thinking from middle childhood onwards (from 7 years), but during early childhood (2–7 years) they are already moving towards this, although they still find it difficult to think about more than one aspect at a time. Young children cannot easily go forwards and backwards through their ideas in quick succession, because every event is a bit like a separate photograph. They need to focus on one thing at a time. Piaget calls this **centration**: they centre on something. It is a very good way of making sense of things. This period when children 'centrate' is often called the start of pre-operations. However, most early years workers do not like the idea that children are 'pre' anything, because it undervalues what children can do. Indeed, it concentrates too much on what children cannot do, conveying a negative image of the young child. It is much more useful to think in terms of developing operations, of the development into operational thinking or of the move from early childhood to middle childhood. As children start to develop operational concepts during early childhood, they begin to use the following ways of thinking.

* **Sequencing:** a sequence has a beginning, a middle and an end. Understanding how sequences work helps children to learn about cause and effect. For example, if I roll the clay, it will change its shape from a lump to a sausage.

* **Seriating:** this is seeing the differences between things. Think of a xylophone. It has many keys that are lines, but they are all of different lengths.

* **Classifying:** this is seeing the similarities between things. For example, pigs, dogs, cats and cows are all animals.

* **Transformation:** children begin to ask if a process can be reversed. For example, water freezes into ice, but you can melt it back to water again. However, if you break an egg you cannot put it back together again; if you burn the wood from a tree, you cannot get the wood back again; after cooking a cake, you cannot get the original ingredients back. Reversibility is an important concept.

CLASS INCLUSION

As children develop they gradually begin to link their previous experiences together much more easily: the experiences become more like a video film than a sequence of still photographs. As well as the operational concepts outlined above, children also form concepts about the shapes, sizes, colours and classes of objects and animals. The class of animals might be divided into pets and farm animals, while the class of cutlery might be divided into knives, forks and spoons. This is called class inclusion.

CONCRETE OPERATIONS AND CONSERVATION

As concept formation elaborates, children begin to understand that things are not always as they seem to be. This typically occurs as children (aged 7–12 years) begin to go to junior school, according to Piaget. Children can now hold in mind several things at once when they are thinking and they can run backwards and forwards through their thoughts. Piaget says the child's thinking gradually becomes more mobile. Children's concepts develop to include concrete operation, such as the conservation of mass and number.

Conservation of mass

Give children two balls of clay, play dough or plasticine. Check that the child agrees that there is the same amount in each ball. Roll one into a sausage shape while the child is watching. Then ask if there is the same amount of clay in both pieces as before. Children under 7 years usually do not conserve mass in a formal test situation like this. This means that they all think that either the sausage shape or the ball shape has more clay in it. This is because these children cannot hold in mind several ideas at once (the balls were the same), but can only concentrate on one aspect (the sausage versus the ball).

Table 6.1 Schema focus sheet

Name of schema	Description
Transporting	A child may move objects or collections of objects from one place to another, perhaps using a bag, pram or truck.
Positioning	A child may be interested in placing objects in particular positions, for example on top of something, around the edge, behind. Paintings and drawings also often show evidence of this.
Orientation	This schema is shown by interest in a different viewpoint, as when a child hangs upside down or turns objects upside down.
Dab	A graphic schema used in paintings, randomly or systematically, to form patterns or to represent, for example, eyes, flowers or buttons.
Dynamic vertical (and horizontal)	A child may show evidence of particular interest by actions such as climbing, stepping-up and down, or lying flat. These schemas may also be seen in constructions, collages or graphically. After schemas of horizontality and verticality have been explored separately, the two are often used in conjunction to form crosses or grids. These are very often systematically explored on paper and interest is shown in everyday objects such as a cake-cooling tray, grills or nets.
The family of trajectories	(a) VERTICAL (up) and HORIZONTAL (down) A fascination with things moving or flying through the air – balls, aeroplanes, rockets, catapults, frisbees – and indeed, anything that can be thrown. When expressed through child's own body movements, this often becomes large arm and leg movements, kicking, or punching, for example. (b) DIAGONALITY Usually explored later than the previous schemas, this one emerges via the construction of ramps, slides and sloping walls. Drawings begin to contain diagonal lines forming roofs, hands, triangles, zig-zags.
Containment	Putting things inside and outside containers, baskets, buckets, bags, carts, boxes, etc.
Enclosure	A child may build enclosures with blocks, Lego or large crates, perhaps naming them as boats, ponds, beds. The enclosure is sometimes left empty, sometimes carefully filled in. An enclosing line often surrounds paintings and drawings while a child is exploring this schema. The child might draw circles, squares and triangles, heads, bodies, eyes, wheels, flowers, etc.
Enveloping	This is often an extension of enclosure. Objects, space or the child herself are completely covered. She may wrap things in paper, enclose them in pots or boxes with covers or lids, wrap herself in a blanket or creep under a rug. Paintings are sometimes covered over with a wash of colour or scrap collages glued over with layers of paper or fabric.

Table 6.1 (continued)

Name of schema	Description
Circles and lines radiating from the circle	(a) SEMI-CIRCULARITY Semi-circles are used graphically as features, parts of bodies and other objects. Smiles, eyebrows, ears, rainbows and umbrellas are a few of the representational uses for this schema, as well as parts of letters of the alphabet. (b) CORE and RADIALS Again common in paintings, drawings and models. Spiders, suns, fingers, eyelashes, hair and hedgehogs often appear as a series of radials.
Rotation	A child may become absorbed by things which turn – taps, wheels, cogs and keys. She may roll cylinders along, or roll herself. She may rotate her arms, or construct objects with rotating parts in wood or scrap materials.
Connection	Scrap materials may be glued, sewn and fastened into lines; pieces of wood are nailed into long connecting constructions. Strings, rope or wool are used to tie the objects together, often in complex ways. Drawings and paintings sometimes show a series of linked parts. The opposite of this schema may be seen in separation, where interest is shown in disconnecting assembled or attached parts.
Ordering	A child may produce paintings and drawings with ordered lines or dabs; collages or constructions with items of scrap carefully glued in sequence. She may place blocks, vehicles or animals in lines and begin to show interest in 'largest' and 'smallest'.

It is important to remember that the sensori-motor stage of the schema is at an earlier level, and that the cause and effect, together with the symbolic levels, both emerge out of this.

Conservation of number

Show the child two rows of similar buttons. Check that the child agrees that the rows have the same number. Spread one row out to make it longer. Ask the child which row has the most buttons. Children under 7 usually do not conserve number in a formal test situation like this. This means they are likely to think that the spread-out row has more buttons. Again, young children usually cannot yet hold in mind more than one thing at a time.

JEAN PIAGET

Piaget is often talked of as the elder statesman of child development study. He has left us a very rich description of how children develop in their thinking, and he has given us detailed observations which are very sensitively made. He deserves great respect for this. His contribution has also helped others to extend, modify and add to his findings. His work has helped people who study child development to move forward in their understanding of how young children think. The following section – which brings together many of the elements discussed above –outlines the four stages that occur in a child's thinking and ideas, according to Piaget. The exact ages vary, but the sequences are still thought to be useful.

Piaget's stages of cognitive development

1 Sensori-motor stage (0–18 months);

2 Developing operations (18 months–7 years);

3 Concrete operations (7–12 years);

4 Formal operations (12 years–adulthood).

Recent research actually questions whether all children go through these stages in the same way. It also questions whether all adults reach the stage of formal operations. Piaget did not believe it possible to 'teach' conservation, and researchers disagreeing with his point of view have not managed to prove conclusively that it is possible.

THE SENSORI-MOTOR STAGE, 0 TO 18 MONTHS

❖ Babies explore and recognise people and objects through their senses and through their own activity and movements.

❖ Schemas are patterns of action which the baby can generalise, and which become increasingly coordinated. For example, at 4½ months the baby can see a rattle, reach out for the rattle, grasp the rattle and put the rattle in their mouth – tracking, reaching, grasping and sucking schemas.

❖ Toddlers still see things mainly from their own point of view, and cannot **decentre** to look at things from somebody else's point of view. Furthermore, they tend, at any one time, to focus on only one aspect of an event (centration). Piaget says they are **intellectually egocentric**.

❖ By the end of their first year, most children have understood that people and objects are permanent and constant, that is, they go on existing even when they cannot be seen, for example if they are under a cloth or in another room.

PRE-OPERATIONAL PERIOD, 18 MONTHS TO 7 YEARS

❖ Action schemas – for example, rotation or trajectory (up and down) – now become **representational**. This means that children begin to use symbolic behaviour, which includes language, representational drawings and pretend play. Action schemas are internalised by the child, and they become **thinking**. Thinking backwards and forwards with ideas (concepts) is still heavily linked, however, with perception of immediate experiences (i.e. the perception of objects, people and events).

❖ The development of memory – recalling past perceptions and prior experiences – is now important. In their minds, children will form images of a smell, of something they have seen, of something they have heard, of something that moved, of something they tasted or something they touched. They also now anticipate the future.

❖ They imitate things they remember from past experiences.

❖ Using past and future, as well as immediate, experiences, children now begin to develop ideas (concepts). This frees them to think more about time and space.

❖ Children begin to refer to things and people who are not present.

❖ They begin to try to share what they know, feel and think with other people.

❖ Because children still only look at one aspect of a situation, it influences the way that they classify or seriate things.

❖ At this stage, children also tend to assume that objects have consciousness (**animism**), for example they get cross with a door for slamming shut. Furthermore, they form an idea of what is right or wrong in what actually happens (moral realism).

CONCRETE OPERATIONS, 7 TO 12 YEARS
❖ Children now begin to understand **class inclusion**.

> **Moral realism**
> If a cup breaks, children think the person who broke it has been naughty. They are not, at this stage, interested in how the event came about (i.e. the motive). They are likely to think that a child who breaks a cup helping to wash up is naughtier than the child who takes a valuable cup from the dresser when they had been told not to, even if they did not break it.

❖ They begin to understand about the **conservation of mass**, **number**, area, quantity, volume, weight.

❖ They realise that things are not always as they look.

❖ However, they still need real situations to help them to think **conceptually**, and they have great difficulty thinking in the abstract. For example, they need practical work in understanding number or time concepts in mathematics.

❖ Although the children can now see things from somebody else's point of view (this means they have established **Theory of Mind**), they still tend to try to make ideas fit other ways of thinking.

❖ They will use symbols in writing, reading, notation in music, drawing, maths and dance if they are introduced to these.

❖ Children at this stage of development can also take into account several features of an object at the same time when they are classifying and seriating. This means that they no longer centrate, that is, they no longer concentrate on just one thing at a time. They realise that there might be several correct solutions to a problem or several outcomes of an event or action.

- Children also now enjoy games and understand about rules.

FORMAL OPERATIONS, 12 YEARS TO ADULTHOOD

- Children can now understand abstract concepts, such as fairness, justice or peace.

- They also understand that it is possible to create laws and rules which help them to test things out, to have a hypothesis and to solve problems.

- They think about time, space and reasons through **formal operations**, and this means they can speak in an abstract way about subjects – they do not need to do things practically to work them through.

- Some adults never reach this stage and continue to rely on concrete situations rather than being able to think in the abstract. Most adults remain concrete-operational for large parts of their lives. For example, a car mechanic might use high levels of formal thought to find out what is wrong with a car, but not do so when organising a weekly shop for the family. In fact, it is possible to live a fulfilled adult life without using formal thinking at all.

Guidelines for promoting cognitive development

Throughout cognitive intellectual development it is important to:

- see the child as an active learner;
- offer a wide range of experiences (look at Chapter 12);
- use skilled observations to inform planning of the next step in the child's learning.

FURTHER DEVELOPMENTS IN PIAGET'S WORK

Piaget concentrated on children's thinking, intellectual development and ideas. This does not mean that he did not think that social, emotional and physical development were also important – he did. It is just that he did not make these the main area of study in his theory. Some people have argued that Piaget ignored social relationships and the cultural aspects of the child's life. In fact, Piaget thought they were so important that he took these for granted.

- Social and cultural relationships with other people are now thought to be just as central to a child's development as the other kinds of experience which Piaget emphasised more, such as the way children build up an understanding of objects.

- People, first-hand experiences of materials and all sorts of provision in indoor and outdoor areas are all of great importance because they help children in the development of their ideas. Neuroscience supports this approach.

- Piaget – as already pointed out – tended to start with what children cannot do, rather than what they can do. However, we now realise that even very young children, including babies, can decentre and see things from somebody else's point of view, providing they are in a situation that holds personal meaning for them.

* Children are not isolated from other people when they learn. Piaget did not emphasise this fact, although he did know it. Recent research stresses the importance of interdependent relationships with others in order for children to learn effectively.

* Children know that people and objects are permanent much earlier than Piaget realised. His test of object permanency (see page 273) proved difficult for babies at 5 months who did not realise two objects – a cloth over a cup, for example – could occupy the same space. By the age of 9 months they have worked this out and they remove the cloth to get the object underneath. However, the multiple-mother image test demonstrates that at 5 months, babies know they only have one mother.

When children are in a situation which makes what researchers call 'human sense', they can conserve and they can understand reversibility. It is just that children find formal test situations rather difficult. This is because it is very hard for a child to understand what it is the questioner is asking.

Instead of Piaget's rather linear stages of development, researchers now tend to look at **networks** of sequences of development. These give us the basic order, rules and strategies that children develop and learn through.

Piaget worked with a Western, middle-class, white, industrialised model of society – after all, that is what he knew about – so his stages of development are culturally biased towards this kind of society. In cultures where there is a different lifestyle, children

might appear to be 'backward' according to Piaget's theory. For example, the Swiss children he studied had a much better-developed understanding of the different points of view you would get from different mountaintops than, for example, a child living on the flat Norfolk Broads would have had. It is very important to remember this point when studying Piaget's work. These biases are called contextual sensitivities, and they result in variations in the way children think, depending on the different places and cultures in which they live (Moss, Pence and Dahlberg 1999).

Recent researchers are beginning to look more at the importance of context:

* Piaget's work was used to focus on intellectual processes in the child until the 1970s.

* By the 1970s and 1980s **social cognition** was emphasised. **Vygotsky's** work was influential. The context, and the people especially, moderated the way a child's thinking developed.

* In the 1980s researchers were beginning to think that both the **social** and **physical contexts**, including the physical and biological development of the child, are crucial to the development of thinking. It is important to look at the situation in which a child thinks and learns. This approach is called **situational cognition**.

Piaget has been criticised mostly for what he did not say, and he left lots of gaps which more recent researchers have been trying to fill in. It is a bit like putting more pieces into the jigsaw puzzle. Although Piaget started our thinking in this area of symbolic behaviour, other people have then developed his work.

Was Piaget right or are the modern researchers who criticise him right? They are both right! This often happens when we look at Piaget's work. Piaget is not wrong, but in one lifetime he did not have time to discover all the pieces of the jigsaw puzzle. Modern researchers are helping us to put more pieces into the puzzle so that we can have a fuller picture than the one he gave us.

Permanence of the object

Piaget used a test called 'the permanence of the object'. He would cover an object, and the baby had to sit and watch this. By 9 months of age, the baby would reach for the object by uncovering it and picking it up; younger babies did not do this. It is now thought that babies have to realise that two objects (the object and the cover) can be in one place in order to complete the test.

Later researchers gave babies of 5 months of age an object which might be put in either their right hand or their left hand. When the light went out they found that the babies reached for the object as soon as it was dark. The object could not be seen, but the babies still reached out and almost always they reached out in the right direction. The babies seemed to know that the object was still there, even though they could not see it in the dark. They also know that they only have one mother and so become disturbed if they are shown multiple images of her as early as 5 months old.

LEV VYGOTSKY

Vygotsky believed that:

* Play helps children to make sense of what they learn. During play they are free from all the practical constraints of a real-life situation.

* Children can have better ideas and do better thinking when an adult or child who knows more is helping them. For example, an adult can help a child to experience a story like *Spot the Dog* by reading the book for the child. Later on the child will be able to read the story for themselves. Vygotsky called the things that children can only do with help the **zone of potential development**.

* The zone of potential development is as important as the zone of actual development (what the child can do alone, without any help from anyone else). He said that the zone of actual development shows the results, the fruits of learning, while the zone of potential learning shows the buds, the future of learning.

JEROME BRUNER

Bruner believed that:

* Children need to move about and be active, having real, first-hand, direct experiences. This helps their ideas to develop, and it helps them to think. He agrees with Piaget in this, and he calls the thinking involved here **enactive thinking**.

* 'Codes' are important. Languages are very important kinds of code. Codes also include drawing, painting, dancing, making stories, play, music and maths. He calls the thinking involved here **symbolic thinking**.

* That children need books and interest tables with objects displayed on them to remind them of prior experiences. He calls the thinking involved here **iconic thinking**.

* That adults can be a great help to children in their thinking, because adults can be like a piece of scaffolding on a building.

Adults scaffolding children's thinking

At first, the building needs a great deal of scaffolding (adult support of the child's learning), but gradually, as the children extend their competence and control of the situation, the scaffolding is removed until it is not needed any more. When scaffolding, the adult arranges the experience, rather than transmitting what is to be learnt. For example, a child learning to weave among the Zinacantecon in Southern Mexico goes through six steps of learning, each scaffolded by the adult. First, the child learns to set up the loom and to finish off the piece of weaving. The first time the child weaves, the child is helped most of the time.

LEARNING STYLES OR A MULTI-SENSORY ENVIRONMENT

Some researchers think that different people have different dominant learning styles (visual, tactile, auditory and kinaesthetic). Others stress the importance of offering children a multi-sensory environment with opportunities for freedom of movement, which is language-rich, so that all kinds of learning styles are encouraged.

YOUR ROLE IN PROMOTING COGNITIVE DEVELOPMENT

Guidelines for promoting cognitive development

Your role is to:

❖ observe children carefully and to record your observations;

❖ act on those observations as various points in the sequence are recognised;

❖ make sure that you do not underestimate children, just as it is very important not to overestimate them;

❖ encourage children to try new things and to express their own ideas and creativity;

❖ ensure that children are neither rushed along in their learning by adults, nor held back while adults wait for the correct age or stage of development to occur;

❖ offer appropriate activities and experiences; these should be planned to suit individual interests and the needs of each individual;

❖ to ensure a wide range of materials is available;

❖ to intervene when appropriate, with sensitivity;

❖ to adapt activities and experience to suit children with special educational needs and sensory impairments.

CHILDREN WHO EXPERIENCE SENSORY IMPAIRMENT

A child with one or more sensory impairments is challenged in learning, but there are famous role models who have shown that cognitive development can be very deep. Helen Keller is a famous example. She was both blind and deaf. Now she would probably be described as having both a visual and hearing impairment.

Given that learning through the senses and movement feedback is central to the learning of young children, it is important to offer children with sensory impairments the kind of support which allows them to do this as much as possible.

Hearing impairment

For the child with a hearing impairment it is important to get the most out of a hearing aid(s). This means having expert help in finding the optimal settings for the child. This will vary with each child. For a partial loss of hearing, a loop system might help the child to pick up normal conversational voice levels while cutting out the background noise. For a child with a profound hearing loss there may be benefits in using British Sign Language (BSL) as well as organising expert help for the child to learn to lip-read. Although hearing aids can be a huge help to children with partial hearing loss, and may give considerable help to a child with a profound loss through vibrations and rhythms of language patterns, which help them to decipher what is being said, it is important to remember that a hearing aid never gives a child normal hearing. Communication and language are of great importance in learning, so great effort needs to be made to help children with a hearing loss in this respect. Hearing loss can also bring loneliness when communication is very difficult. Children appreciate people explaining things to them one-to-one when they miss what is said in a group. They are helped if they can face the adult directly at group times, and if the sun falls on the group leader's face. They are not helped if people keep holding their face and turning it to look at them, because this is invasive.

Visual impairment

Just as a hearing aid does not give a child normal hearing, so a pair of glasses will not bring normal eyesight. The child who is partial-sighted is not just a child who is, for example, short-sighted, and so wears glasses. There will be a considerable loss of sight for a child to be identified as partial-sighted. Children with a sight-challenge lose things easily. They try to stay in touch with people by chatting to them, so that they feel very connected and can work out where they are in space; or they 'still', so that they can listen carefully and work it out that way. It is helpful if things are put on trays, so that they do not fall off the edge of the table. If adults explain where things are it helps too. 'Your lunch is straight in front of you on the table. The peas are on the side of the plate nearest to you.' It does not help if people grab a child suddenly. In fact it can frighten them if they are picked up without warning or taken by the hand, and it is difficult if they are left suddenly, because they cannot see that you have gone!

ACTIVITY: CHILDREN AT PLAY

1 Set up an area using found materials (see Chapter 12 for ideas to help you in this). Observe what children do in general. Describe how a child aged 3–7 years uses the area.

❖ Did you see any imaginative ideas developing?

❖ Did any of the children make anything creative?

❖ Are the children used to being creative, or are they already dependent on adults giving them outlines or templates?

❖ How can you help them to have more confidence in their own ideas?

2 Evaluate your observations, relating them to your target child's development.

ACTIVITY: CHILDREN PROBLEM SOLVING

1 Plan an area with a water tray or sand tray. Observe children (try to have as wide a range of ages as possible) to see if they demonstrate any examples of problem solving. Evaluate your observations. What role did you take in helping the child? If possible, repeat the observation of water play, observing a child at bath-time, in a paddling pool or in a swimming pool. How do children solve problems in these settings?

2 Try to observe children in a sandpit in a park, or using sand on the beach. Focus on the children's problem solving and how you supported them. Evaluate your observations, in whatever settings you made them.

ACTIVITY: ENCOURAGING CREATIVITY AND CONCENTRATION

1 Plan some ways to encourage creativity in the development of young children. Set up an area of the room for this purpose, making sure materials are appropriate and accessible, and that children can use them freely. Evaluate the help you have given in the way you communicated with the children and through the materials you offered.

2 Plan ways of encouraging a child's concentration and involvement. See how successful you have been by finding out about and using the Leuven Involvement Scale to observe a child in your setting who you have noticed lacks concentration (use time-sampling or event-sampling observation techniques – see Chapter 2). When does the child concentrate most? Evaluate your observations.

ACTIVITY: INTERESTS AND SCHEMAS OF THE YOUNG CHILD

1   Plan ways of finding out about what fascinates a child aged 2–5 years. Observe and note what the child does on a particular day. If possible, observe the child continuously for an hour. Write down a description of what the child does and says. You might use video and photographs to enhance your observations. Use Table 6.1 on schemas (page 000) to help you identify and name the areas of interest the child has. Remember, children are interested in a variety of things, but might particularly enjoy one activity. Use your observations to add to the available materials. For example, if the child is particularly interested in rotation, add whisks and spinners or cogs. If the child is interested in covering things over, you could provide finger-painting activities, dressing-up clothes such as cloaks, or sand for burying things.

2   Evaluate your observations.

3   Look at the basic equipment in the room. How does it support the children's schemas? Either look at a book on the subject or visit a museum of childhood. Look at the toys children had, for example, in the last century. How do traditional toys encourage children to develop their schemas?

ACTIVITY: NEUROSCIENCE AND CHILDREN

1   Neuroscience is showing us that young children need to learn through movement, rhythm, sounds and their senses. Plan a learning experience for a child aged 0–3 years or 3–5 years. Use songs with actions. Evaluate your observations.

2   Play short extracts of different kinds of music to a group of children, again aged 0–3 or 3–5 years. How do they react? What movement or sounds do they make? Evaluate your observations.

ACTIVITY: TESTING PIAGET'S WORK

1   Plan and carry out Piaget's conservation of mass test (see page 266) with children aged 3, 5 and 7 years. Can the children conserve? Evaluate the activity.

2   Then try the conservation of number test devised by Piaget (see page 269). You can use buttons or other objects, as long as they are all the same. Do children aged 3, 5 and 7 years conserve? Evaluate your findings.

3   Carry out an experiment with a child, based on the work of Martin Hughes in the 1980s. You will need two small dolls, the size of doll's house dolls. One will be the 'parent', the other the 'child'. Keep the mother fixed to one point. Ask your target child to move the child doll around, so that sometimes the mother can see the child and sometimes not. Does the target child know when the mother doll will be able to see the child doll and when she will not? Margaret Donaldson found that when a situation made 'human sense', children were able to decentre and see things from other people's points of view (or from the doll's point of view). However, if the task was very formal, removed from real-life experience, the children could not manage it.

4   Try also the object permanency test (see page 273). Evaluate your observations of a baby of 6 months and one of 10–18 months. Refer to the cognitive development of the baby.

5   Plan how you can promote a child's cognitive development in ways which also value the social relationships and feelings of children. Plan experiences with number, seriation and classification. You might decide to help children to choose a recipe, go with them to shop for ingredients, and then help them to cook the recipe. Evaluate your activity, commenting on the cognitive, social and emotional aspects of the child's development, as well as on the way you provided the experiences.

7

Communication, including language development

Contents

COMMUNICATION AND LANGUAGE

When we communicate, we connect with other people, but we also connect with ourselves. Some forms of communication are spoken/signed, but about 85 per cent of communication is non-verbal.

From the beginning, babies seem to want to communicate with other people. Remember that babies with a disability may have difficulty in this, or their carers may find it hard to 'read' the baby's communication signals. Babies love to share experiences with people, and communication is a huge part of the way in which people relate to each other. Communication in babies involves:

❖ **facial expressions** (a smile, frown, raised eyebrows) and eye contact;

❖ **gesture and body language** (hugs, beckoning, clapping hands and applause, a shrug, jumping with surprise, being stiff and ill at ease) – body language varies according to the culture;

❖ **verbal** or **sign language** – this can be a very limited kind of communication, through a personal language that is only understood by those who are very close to the baby; for example, 'bubba' might stand for all children and young animals;

❖ **intonation** (how the baby's voice sounds – angry, gentle, playful, sharp, cooing, pausing, encouraging);

❖ **pauses** – these are very important; often we do not give babies, toddlers or young children enough time to respond;

❖ moving in tune (in **synchrony**) with someone when they 'talk' together – a proto-conversation. It is like a conversation without words, and it lays the foundations for later conversations with words. Moving in tune with each other has several aspects. It can mean doing the same movement together at the same time – mirroring – or imitating;

❖ **'Oogly Boogly'** is for young children aged 12–18 months on the edge of spoken/signed language, who attend, eight at a time, with their parent/carer. A group of professional actors/dancers, trained in improvisation, mirror what the toddlers do and the sounds they make. The children seem to understand quickly that they can lead the adults in a kind of dance that unfolds. Some children stay close to their important adult and watch the others, although they seem to appreciate the actors mirroring their smallest movements too. Many children have now experienced 'Oogly Boogly', and at the end of the session, which typically lasts for about 45 minutes, they and their parents/carers report that the children and they feel calm and have a sense of deep wellbeing. Perhaps this is because the children, their important adults and the actors/dancers have all connected in deep forms of non-verbal communication. (It seems to be a powerful experience for children with autism on the edge of language.)

Using language usually means talking aloud and listening to the spoken word. However, talking and listening can also be done through signs (e.g. British Sign Language, which is now an officially recognised language). Babies, toddlers and some children with special educational needs – for example, children with complex needs – will use personal communication systems which are known and understood by those who live with and care for them. Two examples are **Objects of Reference** and **Makaton**.

Both spoken and sign languages use agreed codes which develop according to the cultures in which they arise. They suit that culture, and they are an expression of its important ideas and values. The rhythms, tone and melody of language (its musical aspects) are each of great importance as children's language develops. So are the gestures and movements, especially of the face and hands, as recent studies in neuroscience show. The brain actually develops abilities in music, movement and language at the same time. If spoken language is not possible (perhaps the child is deaf) the brain develops the movement aspects more extensively (sign language).

Fig 7.1 Elementary cross-cultural marks made by children

Fig 7.2 Coordinated marks

China

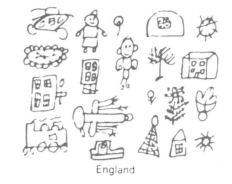

England

Egypt

Spain

Germany

Vietnam

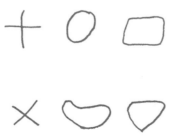

Fig 7.3 Although children's marks are personal and idiosyncratic, there are common basic features

Language:

❀ helps people to communicate internally: children (and adults!) often talk out loud to themselves; they begin to internalise speech more and more until they can think of the words rather than saying them out loud;

❀ can be spoken, signed or thought;

❀ helps people to move from here and now into the past or the future;

❀ helps people to use symbolic behaviour;

❀ helps people to put ideas (concepts) into words and to express imaginative thoughts;

❀ helps abstract thinking;

❀ helps people to express feelings and to think about emotions.

In order to use language effectively, we need to master its two modes:

1 listening or watching, and understanding (reception of language);

2 communicating, which involves facial expressions, gestures and verbal or sign speech (expression of language).

LANGUAGE DEVELOPMENT AS SYMBOLIC BEHAVIOUR

It is not possible to study language development without looking at the rich variety of symbols that human beings use. Before studying the development of language in young children it is important to know a little bit about symbolic behaviour.

What are symbols?

Symbols are a way of making one thing stand for another. For example, a drawing of mum and saying the word 'Mum' are both symbols for mother. She does not have to be there. These symbols, the drawing and the word stand for her when she is not there.

IS IT ONLY HUMANS WHO ARE SYMBOL USERS? Whether animals use symbols has been debated for centuries. Until recently it was argued that humans were superior to other animals. Nowadays there are many people who prefer to look at similarities and differences between humans and other animals. One similarity, for example, is that animals such as chimpanzees, gorillas and orang-utans also seem to use symbolic systems. This means that all these animals can make one thing stand for another. Children make connections like Washoe the chimpanzee did as they learn to share the language of their culture. Washoe was a symbol user just like a human child (see below). However, it does seem that humans can go further and deeper in their ability to make one thing stand for something else. For a start, humans have a larynx, so they can talk. In addition, humans can:

❀ draw and paint;

❀ make dances;

❀ make sculptures;

❀ write;

❀ make music;

❀ think scientifically;

❀ use mathematical notations, such as those for numbers, geometry and algebra.

Layers of symbols

There is a huge variety in the kinds of symbol that human children begin to use, even very early in their development. And the symbolic layers keep on accumulating throughout life as the culture is taken in and used by the child as he or she grows up. Indeed, we never stop adding to our symbolic layers as long as we live. Since

Case Study

Washoe the chimpanzee

There was a famous example of an animal using symbols in Washoe the chimpanzee in the 1960s. She was taught American Sign Language by her researchers, the Gardners, and she knew the signs for both water and bird. One day, she saw a duck fly over a pond. She did not know the sign for a duck, but without any prompting, she signed 'water bird'.

Piaget began his pioneering work in the 1930s, researchers have been finding deeper and deeper layers in the symbolic behaviour of people. More is now known about how children start to become symbol users. The psychologist Howard Gardner (see Chapter 6) believes that we have multiple intelligences which help us to use a wide range of different kinds of symbols. Neuroscientists like Trevarthen, however, do not see the brain as having separate domains in this way. Instead they show that the brain forms connected networks which feed off and into each other, so that sound, gesture and movement are linked, but can be used for music, language, dance or other things. There

is now a training project led by Penny Lancaster (Coram Family) called 'Listening to Children'. We already know that symbolic behaviour is about making one thing stand for another. It also involves thinking about the **past**, the **present** and the **future**.

Fig 7.4b Drawing

Fig 7.4a Drawing

Fig 7.4c Science

Fig 7.5 Sharing a home-made book together

Symbols help people to think at an abstract level. This means they can go beyond the here and now in their imagination, ideas, feelings and relationships.

THE GRAMMAR OF A LANGUAGE

Every language has its own kind of grammar. In some languages, such as Latin and British Sign Language, the verb is not placed the same way as it is in English. This can make languages seem ungrammatical. The grammar of a language is the rules that make it work. To set out the rules of grammar is not to specify how people ought to speak. It is simply a way of describing how a language works. For example, the grammar of the English language includes:

- ❖ **verbs** (doing words) – 'I am *going* home';
- ❖ **nouns**, which might involve either a **subject** – 'The *cat* is asleep in the chair' – or an **object** – 'The cat is asleep in the *chair*';
- ❖ **adjectives** (words which describe nouns) – 'The baby likes the *red* rattle best';
- ❖ **adverbs** (words which describe verbs) – 'The baby *quickly* grabs the red rattle';
- ❖ **pronouns**, such as 'they', 'you', 'he' or 'she', as well as the personal pronouns, 'I' and 'me';
- ❖ **apostrophes** (which indicate possession) – 'The *child's* rattle' (the rattle that belongs to the child).

COMMUNICATION DIFFICULTIES

It can be very difficult for some children – those who may have a hearing impairment, severe learning difficulties, moderate learning difficulties or physical challenges such as cerebral palsy – to talk or listen. Not

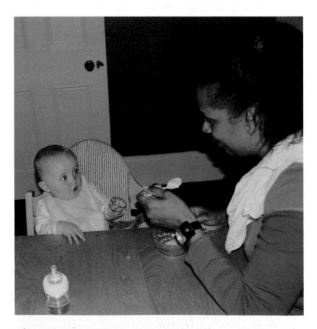

Fig 7.6 Children's language develops as they are talked to during a meal

being able to talk or listen with ease can bring frustration, loneliness and a feeling of powerlessness. It is very important, therefore, that every child be encouraged to find ways of communicating with other people. Research on the brain now suggests that when people learn to speak they do not use rules of grammar at all. When a sound is heard, it fires certain neurons and impedes the firing of others. Gradually, as the sound is heard over and over again, a neural pathway is forged and a language pattern forms. This fire dance, as it is called by neuroscientists, is part of the connectionist theory of how language develops. The language involved here does not have to be a verbal language, and a considerable minority of children are now taught to use sign languages or personal references.

These can be based on:

❖ gestures or touch;

❖ agreed shared signs;

❖ finger spelling, computers and keyboards.

A small number of children will not use shared signs which are understood by others. They will continue to use personal communication signs, which only those close to them will understand. Most children, but not all, will move gradually into the world of shared language, and may learn to speak in a verbal language. It is important to remember that all children – and adults too – find it difficult to express their feelings and thoughts when they are:

❖ put under pressure to speak;

❖ under stress for any reason (such as a child who has been hit by another child).

No child should be put in a position where they feel uncomfortable about talking – for example in a large group – or where they are rushed by adults who do not take the time to listen to what they are trying to say. All children need adults to take time to listen to them.

REPRESENTATION

Representation means keeping hold of an experience by bringing it back to the mind and making it into some kind of product.

(**Time to choose:** if you do not want to study the different kinds of early representation in the next section, it is not necessary for you to do so. Studying is a kind of travelling: some people like to go directly to their destination; other people like to go down country lanes, stopping off along the way to explore things. This takes longer, but they enjoy the journey. What about you? If you want to go direct, turn to page 288. If you want to explore and find out more about representation in young children, read this next section.)

Keeping hold of experiences – procedural representations

Researchers believe that babies (typically at 5 months) can:

❖ remember;

❖ anticipate;

❖ make images;

❖ conceptualise people and objects that are not present.

Babies are starting to 'keep hold' of experiences, which is what representation is about. The next step is for babies to begin to share their highly personal ways of doing this.

Case Study

Sharon

Sharon, 4 years, ate an ice cream on a hot day. It melted and dripped down her hand. Later she did a painting. She chose white paint and made it run all over the paper. She then said, 'It's my ice cream.' Sharon was keeping hold of her experience of a dripping ice cream by representing it in a painting.

Declaring is sharing – declarative representations

Babies (typically at around 9 months) begin to be able to share their representations of things with other people. In fact, they want to share very much. They seem to have a deep need to do things with other people. Sharing symbols is only possible with those who are close to the child because the symbols are unique to each particular child.

Gesturing, **naming** and **pointing** begin around this time. Naming is likely to be very idiosyncratic – the child might say 'hee haw' when they see a horse. A baby of 9 months will often wave 'bye-bye' *after* a person has gone. When babies do this it is cause to celebrate and, perhaps, to say to the baby, 'Yes, you are right, Jill has gone, hasn't she, and we said bye-bye to her.'

Gradually, other kinds of representation become possible. A child begins to be able to draw or paint a person waving bye-bye. A child might make a model of someone waving bye-bye or do a dance about waving bye-bye. A child might make music, singing 'bye-bye', or write about saying bye-bye to Jill. There are many ways in which children begin to keep hold of their experiences and to represent them.

From 1 to 8 years of age, there is amazing development in the way that children begin to represent their experiences and share symbolic behaviour with other people. They now begin adding cultural layers to what they know about symbols.

Experience and representation

The most important thing to remember about representing experiences is that children cannot represent an experience they have not had! Some other important things to bear in mind are that children need:

❖ real first-hand experiences;

❖ to experience things, actively;

❖ to feel ownership of the experiences they have – it is difficult for them to think deeply if their ideas are controlled by other people all the time;

❖ to be encouraged to think back and to think forward about experiences they have had or are looking forward to.

Case Study

Experience and representation

A teacher of a class of 5-year-olds asked the children to paint pictures of people skiing. There was a problem: none of the children in the class had been skiing! This meant that they had no experience of skiing and so could neither think back to when they had skied nor think forward to when they would ski again. Skiing was not included in their own experience of life.

Representation and the ability to decentre

Very young children simply have not had enough experiences of their own to be able to:

❖ think what it is like to experience something as if they were someone else;

❖ understand an experience from someone else's point of view, unless it is very like their own experience.

As we have seen, the ability to understand what it is like to be someone else is called being able to decentre, or to have **Theory of Mind**.

Case Study

Helping children to remember a first-hand expedience

Consider a walk to the shops. There is lots of chatting and you all make stops to look at things. The children might see a dog, or they might help to buy things, give the money to the shopkeeper, or carry the bags. Then they might go back to the setting and help to do cooking. Later you might set up an interest table to remind the children about the shopping and cooking they have done. Books and cooking utensils might be put on the table.

You could display packaging. Children might want to do cooking again the following day.

The children might want to represent some of their experiences. They might want to make a model of the dog. They might want to make a model of the food they cooked. They might want to act out the way somebody walked down the street. There are many different ways the children might represent the walk to the shops. There are many different aspects of the experience that they might have enjoyed and will choose to represent.

Fig 7.7 An interested adult takes time to listen and support a child's thinking

Before children can learn to decentre they need help in finding ways of keeping hold of their own experiences, not those of other people. This means that tracing someone else's outline, colouring-in someone else's outline with tissue paper or coloured pencils, or drawing round a template, are low-level activities because they do not allow children to represent their *own* experience in their *own* way.

GRAPHIC REPRESENTATION

Watch out for the first marks that young children make: they are cross-cultural. Children use them quite naturally and without needing to be taught, although they do need to see other people drawing and mark-making. Initially children use these marks separately (as shown in Figure 7.1). Later on they will begin to use them in combination; that is, they can coordinate them (see Figure 7.2). Remember, if you ask children to copy these shapes, they will not 'own' them. They will be doing it for you as an adult-led task – this will not be their own representation of their own experience which they have chosen to do. It is easy to make children copy; it is not so easy to help children express their own ideas, feelings and relationships with others on paper. As they grow up, many children leave behind these early and personal ways of representing their experiences of life. As they grow older, they only use the conventional symbols and ways of representing which are specific to their culture. When this happens, the creative side of the child disappears and learned formulas take its place. This is why it is very important to keep representation alive, at the same time as introducing children to the shared and agreed conventions of writing and other ways of representing. Creative,

imaginative children *keep* their personal representations and symbols, but can also use the conventional symbols of their culture.

LANGUAGE AND LITERACY

Researchers believe that people are capable of using many complex symbolic layers in what they do. Language is only one kind of symbolic behaviour, and it accumulates more symbolic layers when it moves into writing and reading (see also Chapter 12). Developing writing and reading is called literacy.

Writing

Writing means that the person has to put language into a **code** (encoding).

Reading

Reading means that the person has to decode what is written. Young children use pictures in books as an extra help when they try to decode what is written. Reading and writing move along together with the development of spoken language. Some psychologists think that children are rather like scientists trying to discover things: they seem to try to find out how language systems work in the culture in which they are growing up. Not being able to read or write (illiteracy) is a serious disadvantage in many cultures. However, not all cultures use the written word. Although there is a written form, the Celtic language has an oral culture. This is why Celtic stories and songs have lasted so well: they are handed down orally and use dance and song to great effect. The Maori culture in New Zealand also has an oral tradition.

THEORIES OF LANGUAGE DEVELOPMENT

Some terminology

In order to take part in discussions about language theory, you need to know the meanings of some words:

- **Phonology:** the sounds of the language (or the visual aspects of a sign language).

- **Grammar**, sometimes called **syntax:** the word order, and the rules which describe how a language works (but not how we ought to speak).

- **Arbitrary symbols:** these refer to the past, help speakers to learn from the past, imagine the future, make jokes, tell lies and have fantasies.

- **Articulation:** how words are spoken in order to be understood.

- **Intonation:** the mood of the language and the way sounds go up and down.

- **Vocabulary** or **lexicon:** the words.

- **Semantics:** meanings of the language.

- **Communication:** shared meaning with self and others.

- **Conversations:** these require a sense of audience (meaning a sense of who you are talking to and listening to).

There are four approaches to studying language:

1 The **normative approach,** devised by Gesell in the 1930s–1960s.

2 The **behaviourist** theory (or the **nurture** approach), put forward by Skinner in the 1920s–1960s.

3 The **nature** theory that language development is innate and genetically predetermined, proposed by Chomsky in the 1960s.

4 The **social constructivist** theory of Piaget, Vygotsky and Bruner (see Chapter 6).

Literacy around the world

In the USA, the UK and Holland about 15 per cent of adults are illiterate. In some parts of the USA, the UK and Holland, children are expected to start using shared, conventional ways of writing and to read from 4 years of age. This is exceptionally early compared with most countries in the world.

In Finland, children are read to by adults, but they do not begin the formal learning of reading and writing until they are 7 years old. Statistically, they are the best readers and writers in the world.

What do you think about this? Is earlier best? Are long-term results more important than short-term successes?

Normative accounts of language development

Until the 1960s, experts like Gessell studied the development of language in young children mainly by using vocabulary counts. They counted the number and types of words that children used. They looked at whether children used single words, phrases and different types of sentence. This approach tended to stress what children could do at particular ages, and it could be very misleading. For example, recent research suggests that babies say words like 'up' and 'gone', but this is not recognised by adults. Adults do seize on babble like 'Mum', which adults want babies to say. Research shows that in fact the first word children in different parts of the world say is usually a comment on how people or objects have 'gone'. In Korea, adults say, 'It's moving in' when they give babies a drink. In Western cultures adults are more likely to say, 'Here's your cup.' Korean babies say 'moving in' before they say 'cup'. Western babies say 'cup' before they say 'moving in'. Although it is not always useful to take a normative approach, it is important that those working with young children know about the general way in which all languages develop. (The terminology explored above, on page 289, is useful in this respect.) It will help you to remember that there is more to language development than vocabulary building.

The language development revolution of the 1960s

From the 1920s a group of theorists called the **behaviourists** thought that language had to be 'put into' children, who started out as empty vessels. An exciting revolution occurred when the behaviourist view – that children learn language entirely by imitating – was challenged in 1968. Chomsky showed that children can invent new sentences that they definitely had not heard before. He believed children are born ready to learn whatever languages they hear around them. He proposed that they did this through what he called a **language acquisition device (LAD)**. Chomsky said that:

❖ babies are born with a predisposition to learn, talk and listen;

❖ children learn to talk because they are genetically equipped to do so; they learn partly through the people they meet, communicate and socialise with.

Researchers studied the mistakes or errors that children make when they talk. They found that these gave important clues about the innate language rules that children all over the world seem to be born with. This was also true for children using sign languages rather than spoken languages.

THE SOCIAL CONTEXT OF LANGUAGE DEVELOPMENT

It became apparent in the 1960s and 1970s that some children were not as developed in language as others. At that time it was thought that children from working-class homes were disadvantaged because they used what the researcher Bernstein called a restricted language code. Their language seemed to have limited vocabulary and used less complex forms. He believed that this held them back in school. This code contrasted with children from middle-class backgrounds, who Bernstein said used an elaborated language code. He thought that this was why they achieved more in school. As a result, in both the UK and the USA, compensatory education programmes were launched which tried to enrich the school language environment of the so-called disadvantaged children.

In fact, it is much more likely that, because staff in schools often come from different cultures and backgrounds from the children they work with, they do not always understand the richness of the child's own particular language and culture. Recent research shows that children growing up in Japan who are described as lower class do badly in school compared with the children described as upper class, but if their family moved to the USA, they were simply thought of as Japanese. Whether they were lower-class or upper-class Japanese, they did well in the USA, perhaps because there is a perception among American people that Japanese children study well at school.

Early years workers can promote children's language development if they:

❖ value and respect the child's language and culture, and try to learn about it;

❖ have real everyday conversations with children, using gestures, eye contact, props and spoken language;

❖ encourage children to listen to and enjoy stories, including those from their own culture;

❖ introduce children to what is sometimes called 'storytelling language' or 'book language', for example, 'Once upon a time, far, far away. . .'.

These measures help children to take a full part in school life, in ways which build on their language or culture.

The theories of Piaget, Vygotsky and Bruner help practitioners to look at the social aspects of language development. This is the sociocultural approach. It is now thought that positive relationships and communications between people who respect each other are the most important factors in language development and in the development of the child's thinking. To be part of a culture is a need human beings are born with. There is a wide variation in the way that children begin to:

❖ understand;

❖ communicate;

❖ represent and express things through new language.

This variation depends on the culture in which the child grows up, as much as on the child's genetic and biological development.

SUPPORTING LANGUAGE DEVELOPMENT

All children need a supportive language environment. The DfES/SureStart have initiated an accredited training course for practitioners at level 2 and above, 'Communicating Matters' (from Autumn 2005), which will be taught through the local authorities. This will look at how to support language development in all children. It gives guidance on working with children using English as an additional language, who may benefit from gestures and actions when learning (action songs for example). Chapter 1 gives details about ways of supporting and extending the language development of bilingual and multilingual children.

It is essential for anyone working with young children to understand the importance of the child's first or home language. If you have not read Chapter 1 yet, you should do so now before continuing with this chapter.

Appreciating language and bilingualism

Children are more likely to feel that they belong if their first language or home language is understood and encouraged in the early years setting, as well as in their family. It is also important to value dialect or regional accents.

❖ **Dialect** is a variant form of a language. In the Caribbean, for example, Patois is spoken. It might seem to a standard English speaker that a Patois speaker is speaking ungrammatical and poor English. However, Patois is actually a combination of French language with the local (mainly English) language, as used on the different islands. In Trinidad, it will be a combination of French and the particular way English is used on that island. The word, phrases and speed of speaking will sound a bit like English, but Patois is not English.

❖ **Accent** is mostly to do with the way the words are pronounced. Some accents, such as Geordie or Glaswegian, can be difficult to understand for those who are not used to hearing them spoken.

Being bilingual should never be considered a disadvantage. In fact, the opposite is true. Learning how to communicate in more than one language helps children to learn in a much broader way. Recent studies in neuroscience give evidence to support this. So, it is very important that you value a child's first language. It has been known for children to be labelled as having 'no language' when in fact they simply speak a different language from English.

❖ **Balanced bilingualism** – this is when children speak more than one language, each with equal fluency. In fact, a child's home language is usually more fluent than English. Very few children are completely balanced across two languages. Most children are unbalanced with one language more developed than the other.

❖ **Transitional bilingualism** – in some early childhood settings the first language has been valued only as a bridge for learning English. This is transitional bilingualism. It is assumed that the child will no longer need to speak the first language once English begins to take over. For example, a child who speaks Punjabi at home might be expected to speak English at school and gradually to speak English rather than Punjabi at home. In fact children need to continue to use their first language to help them transfer later on to reading and writing in the second language, which is usually English. If the child's first language is not valued as well as the new language that is being learnt, the opportunities for bilingualism and the advantages that bilingualism brings will be wasted.

Helping children towards balanced bilingualism

In order for balanced bilingualism to occur, rather than just transitional bilingualism, children need to be given appropriate help. You can help in the following ways.

Guidelines for promoting balanced bilingualism

Providing comprehensible input

This phrase, used by Stephen Krashen, means enabling the child to make sense of what is being said. If an adult picks up a cup, points at the jug of orange juice and asks: 'Would you like a drink of orange juice?' the meaning is clear. If the adult just says the words without the actions and props, the meaning is not at all clear to the child. The adult could be saying anything.

Allowing for a period of silence

At first there is often a period of silence on the part of the child, while he or she listens to all the sounds of the new language, and becomes familiar with them. The adult should understand this and be patient.

Providing 'opportunities' for listening

Children need plenty of opportunity to listen to what is being said and to make sense of it before they begin to speak in the new language. The process of learning occurs in three phases:

1   First there is understanding (**comprehension**).
2   Then the child speaks (**production**).
3   Eventually they become fluent (**performance**).

Exposure to fluent speakers

When children first being to speak a new language they will not be fluent. They will make approximate sounds and communicate by **intonation** (tone of voice), rather than use words. They are greatly helped if they can talk with people who are completely fluent and comfortable with the new language. This is why children are no longer separated and taken out of classrooms to be 'taught' English. They learn much more effectively in a real-life setting, which is relaxed and not formal, and with other children and adults who can already speak the language.

Above all, children need to feel that becoming bilingual is a benefit and not a disadvantage. This is a message that we can help to support.

Some children are fortunate enough to grow up learning more than one language. This helps them to learn in a broader way. When children learn more than one language they are, at the same time, being introduced to more than one culture in a deeply meaningful way. By doing several things at once, the brain learns to think more flexibly.

❧   They are learning two languages.

❧   They are learning the culture that is linked with each language. In Gujarati, the words 'thank you' are used in special situations. In English they are used often, but usually just as a way of being polite rather than as an expression of deep gratitude. And while in English there are two separate words for 'teaching' and 'learning', in Swedish there is only one, which is translated as 'helping children to learn'.

❧   They can think in different ways about the same thing. For example the Inuit language has seven words for snow. This makes it possible to think about snow in much greater detail.

❧   They grow up understanding different ways of thinking, and different cultural layers. This helps them to respect and value differences between people.

❧   They understand more easily that names are arbitrarily assigned to objects and that names for things can be changed. This helps them with concept formation.

❧   They find it easier to separate meanings and sounds.

❧   They are more sensitive to the emotional aspects of language, such as intonation, and they can interpret situations more easily.

❦ They can think more broadly. This is often called divergent thinking.

Practitioners need to support the language development of children who have special educational needs and disabilities. It is important to remember that some children do not use verbal ways of communicating. They will need to be introduced to British Sign Language (BSL), Makaton or Objects of Reference.

LANGUAGE DELAY

A child who has a hearing or visual impairment, Asperger syndrome or is **autistic** may be constrained in understanding and using language (i.e. in their *reception* and *expression* of language). (A definition of the term 'autistic' can be found on page 39.) Speech therapists, specialist teachers and other professionals may be needed to support the language development of these children. All children need to mix with other children and adults who speak *fluently* so that they can hear the patterns of the language they are trying to learn.

However, if they are always in the company of other people who are also learning a new language, they will not hear the correct patterns of the language in question and may learn incorrect grammar patterns. They may have to unlearn some of the things they have picked up. Hearing other people speak fluently means experiencing what is called comprehensible output (see page 295).

Children who do not speak

❦ It does not help development if children are made to speak. But it does help if they are invited to speak, as long as they can turn down the invitation without

being made to feel bad or a failure.

❦ It is very important to check that a silent child can still see and hear.

❦ It is crucial to be sure that the child understands what is being said.

❦ It is important to monitor children who do not speak through your **observations**. Share your observations with your line manager and the rest of the team.

❦ Bear in mind that children under emotional stress sometimes become withdrawn.

❦ Other children can sometimes be a great help in explaining things meaningfully to a child.

❦ Stories and rhymes can be made clearer by using props and pictures (see again Chapter 1).

TALKING TO BABIES – LANGUAGE AND ACTION

When adults talk to babies, they tend to talk about things that are happening all around. They speak slowly, in a high-pitched voice, and use a lot of repetition. This is called 'Motherese' or 'Fatherese'. Adults will pause, waiting for the baby to 'reply', using babble. However, in some cultures adults do not speak in Motherese or Fatherese to babies, but instead the babies watch their mothers working and talking with other adults.

Language needs to accompany action. For instance, the adult lifts the baby and says, 'Up we go. Let's put you in the pram now.' It is important that adults *continue* to describe what is happening when babies become young children – 'You've got to the top of the slide, haven't you? Are you going to come down now?' Actions help children to

Fig 7.8 Discussion that is two-way is important in developing language

understand what is being said to them. Actions give children clues about meaning. This is comprehensible input (see page 294).

LANGUAGE AND THOUGHT/COGNITION

Remember that all areas of a child's development are interrelated. Language and thought (or cognition) are often considered to be particularly closely linked. Can we think without words? Some psychologists have suggested that thinking is not possible without language. Language is especially

important for abstract thinking. This means that it would be difficult to understand the idea, for example, of what is fair or honest unless a child has enough language. Piaget, however, emphasised that children learn to think using a variety of different ways to represent their experiences, ideas, feelings and relationships symbolically. Indeed, he thought that language is only one kind of symbolic mode that people use to do this. Piaget's work has been very positive in helping those working with children with language delay or impairment, and with all children who do not begin to use coded or shared language systems. This is because he stressed the personal and individual ways through which children can communicate, as well as their later use of the arbitrary symbols of their culture. Personal communication can include:

❖ gestures;

❖ props – the handbag represents mother when she goes for coffee, and the child knows she is coming back because her handbag is there;

❖ evidence – the footprint in the sand tells the child someone was there;

❖ links – the child has a teddy bear while the mother is away; this gives the child a link with the absent mother; the communication is personal between this particular child and this particular mother.

Thinking about thinking, and thinking about language

❖ **Cognition** means thinking and having ideas (concepts).

❖ **Metacognition** means that children begin to think about their own thinking. They reflect on their own ideas, such as, 'That was a good idea', 'That was a bad idea.'

❖ **Metalinguistics** means children beginning to think about what they say. By 4 years, children usually make jokes and 'play' with words, devising nonsense words for fun.

LANGUAGE AND FEELINGS

Children experience problems when they are not able to put their feelings into words or to express themselves in any way. This has a damaging impact on the development of their self-esteem. If children are full of anger, anxiety, frustration or fear, they need to

express this. Talking about feelings is just as important as talking about ideas. Children who cannot explain or put into words how they feel often have temper tantrums or show other kinds of challenging behaviour. In fact, it is often easier to help children to put their ideas into words than it is to help them to express their feelings or emotions in words. The next section contains some suggestions for promoting talk, including talk about feelings.

LANGUAGE AND CONVERSATION

Talking to oneself

Children talk to themselves when they:

❖ need to think through different ideas;

❖ are feeling frustrated;

❖ need to talk about their feelings;

❖ need to organise their thinking;

❖ want to regulate what they do (i.e. tell themselves what to do).

Textbooks often say that this egocentric speech fades when children begin to internalise their thinking more easily. In this context, egocentric does not mean selfish, it just means thinking from their own point of view. Young children can put themselves in someone else's shoes if that person's experience is linked with their own (see Chapter 6).

Conversations with another person

'Conversations' begin when tiny babies are spoken to by adults close to them in Motherese or Fatherese. Visually impaired babies respond by becoming still and listening intently. Sighted babies 'dance' in response to speech. 'Conversations' continue as toddlers babble in response to adult talking. It is quite possible to have a conversation with sounds but no words. Researchers have noticed that although toddlers often turn their backs during a conversation and say 'No!' to their mother's suggestions, they do in fact take up and imitate the ideas that are offered to them. It is as if toddlers need to have conversations with other people, even when they can still only say a few words, even if the words do not fit the situation.

Small-group discussions

Children also need help when taking part in group discussions. Stories, songs and dances are useful catalysts. These are best used with children aged 3–8 years, in small groups. Having to wait for a turn frustrates children. It will not help them to discuss and enjoy things. In fact, it could put them off stories, songs and dancing. Even children aged 5–8 years cannot wait too long before being allowed to have their say in a discussion or a conversation. Chapter 1 gives examples of strategies for storytelling with small groups.

Encouraging conversations and group discussions

Conversations need to:

❖ be two-way;
❖ involve sharing ideas and feelings;
❖ involve thinking of each other;
❖ be a real exchange of ideas and feelings between adults and children;
❖ include taking turns;
❖ involve thinking about things of interest to each other, as well as about things of interest to oneself.

LANGUAGE AND CONTEXT

Different situations bring about different sorts of language. A **formal situation** – being introduced to the mayor or buying a bus ticket – is different from an **informal** one, for example chatting with friends over a cup of coffee or playing in the park. It takes years for children to learn the different ways of talking which are appropriate to formal and informal situations. Understanding the difference in context is important in most cultures.

Guidelines for promoting language skills

❖ Children need to be spoken to as individuals.

❖ Be patient: young children find it hard to put their thoughts and feelings into words, so listening takes patience. It is very tempting to prompt children and say things for them. Instead, try nodding or saying, 'Hmm.' This gives children time to say what they want to.

❖ It does help children when adults elaborate on what they have just said and give the correct pattern. For example, Shanaz, at 2 years, says, 'I falled down.' The adult replies, 'Yes, you did, didn't you? You fell down. Never mind, I will help you up.'

❖ However, research indicates that children are not helped when adults make them pronounce things properly or repeat things to get the grammar 'right'. Remember, grammar is not about how children 'ought' to speak, but about showing adults that children understand things about the language they speak.

❖ It is important that all children experience unrushed, one-to-one conversations with both adults and other children, for example when sharing a drink together at the snack table, or chatting while using the clay.

Being with familiar adults

Children need to be with the same adults each day, so that they learn the subtle signals about how people talk to each other in different situations. In different situations people comment, describe, give opinions, predict, give commands, use formal phrases, reminisce, and so on. Meaning changes according to context. For example, 'Go into the hall!' when said at home might be a reference to the small area near the front door. In another setting, it might be a reference to a huge room, full of chairs, with a platform at one end.

Children can tell the difference between someone who sincerely wants to talk with them and someone who is being patronising and puts on a 'talking to children' voice. They appreciate adults who take their ideas and feelings seriously and respect and value them.

Fig 7.9 Children learn through talking together as they engage in solving a problem

Fig 7.10 A relaxed atmosphere and a shared focus of attention between adults and children help conversations to develop

Guidelines for encouraging conversations

- ❧ It is important to remember that anybody in a group can start or end a conversation.
- ❧ Two speakers can talk together, even using different languages.
- ❧ In good conversation, there must be comprehensible input. This means using actions and props which show *meaning*, as well as gestures and facial expressions. The lack of comprehensible input is probably one reason why many people dislike talking on the telephone, which only gives intonation (mood and sounds) clues. Communication is 85 per cent non-verbal.
- ❧ Children must not be rushed to speak, and they must feel relaxed.
- ❧ It is better to elaborate on what children say, rather than to correct their errors. This respects children's feelings and promotes their wellbeing. It gives them confidence in themselves as learners.

LANGUAGE DEVELOPMENT 0–8: A SUMMARY

From birth to 1 year: emerging language

The first year of a baby's life is sometimes called 'pre-linguistic'. This is an inaccurate, negative and misleading term. It gives us a much more helpful and positive image of a baby if we think of this stage as one of early communication before words or signs are used. Thus it is sometimes called the stage of emerging language.

From 1 to 4 years: symbolic development

This is sometimes called the period of language explosion. Every aspect of language seems to move forward rapidly at this time. language development is part of symbolic behaviour, so this is often called the period of symbolic development. It is the best time to learn other languages, or to become bilingual or multilingual.

From 4 to 8 years: consolidating learning

This is the time when what has been learnt and understood about language is consolidated, so further developments are

---

A summary of representation, communication and language development

1 Language development is deeply linked with the processes of **representation and play**, and **communication**.

2 Language makes it easier for us to represent (to keep hold of experiences), to communicate (to share these experiences with the self and other people) and to think in abstract ways beyond the here and now (as in play).

3 Once children can listen and talk, they are well on the way to adding more layers of symbolic behaviour. The **symbolic layers** in language acquisition are:

❖ non-verbal communication (gesture, etc.);
♣ listening;
❖ talking;
❖ writing;
❖ reading.

---

enhancements rather than being brand new. For example, children now become better at articulation, conventional grammar patterns, thinking about whom they are talking to, the context and situation, and putting ideas and feelings into words. (Chapter 5 helps you to link language development with the holistic development of the child.)

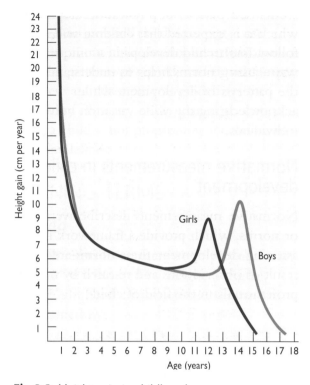

Fig 8.2 Height gain in childhood

development (see Chapter 5). They are useful in helping parents and carers to know what to expect at a certain age, especially when planning a safe, stimulating environment. However, their use can lead people to label children as 'slow' or 'bad' if they fall behind the norm. Using norms in this way is not helpful and will not enable you to promote development. Although professionals caring for children need to have a framework of the patterns of expected development to help them promote children's health and to stimulate the children's all-round development, they should be aware of the pitfalls of using norms.

The development of gross motor skills

These are sometimes called skills of **movement**. Gross motor skills use the large muscles in the body and include walking, running, climbing, and so on.

The development of fine motor skills

These use the smaller muscles and include:

❖ **gross manipulative skills**, which involve single-limb movements, usually the arm, for example throwing, catching and sweeping arm movements;

❖ **fine manipulative skills**, which involve precise use of the hands and fingers for drawing, using a knife and fork, writing, doing up shoelaces and buttons.

The skills of locomotion and balance

❖ **Locomotion** is the ability to move around on one's own. It is central to the pattern of development changes which occur at the end of the baby's first year, and begins with crawling or bottom-shuffling.

❖ **Balance** is the first of all the senses to develop. It is crucial to posture, movement and **proprioception** (see page 307).

The 8-month-old child who rolls backwards and forwards across the floor with no particular goal in sight is preparing her balance for:

❖ sitting;

❖ standing;

❖ walking.

Eye–hand coordination

The ability to reach and grasp objects in a coordinated way requires months of practice and close attention:

❖ In the first months after birth eye–hand coordination takes effort.

❖ By around 9 months, a baby can usually manage to guide their movements with a single glance to check for accuracy, for example when feeding themselves with a spoon.

WHAT IS PHYSICAL DEVELOPMENT?

Physical development is the way in which the body gains skills and becomes more complex in its performance. Physical development is the most visible of all the abilities shown in childhood and includes the less observable development of all the senses: hearing, vision, touch, taste and smell.

Sensory development

Sensation is the process by which we receive information through the senses. These include:

❖ vision;

❖ hearing;

❖ smell;

❖ touch;

❖ taste;

❖ proprioception.

Perception is making sense of what we see, hear, touch, smell and taste. Our perception is affected by previous experience and knowledge, and by our emotional state at the time. There are therefore wide variations in the way different individuals perceive the same object, situation or experience.

Visual development

A newborn baby's eyes are barely half the size of an adult's and, although they are structurally similar, they differ in two ways:

1 A baby's focus is fixed at about 20 cm, which is the distance from the baby to her mother's face when breastfeeding. Anything nearer or further away appears blurred. She will remain short-sighted for about 4 months.

2 The response to visual stimuli is slower in babies because the information received by the eye takes longer to reach the brain via the nervous pathway. A newborn baby is able only poorly to fix her eyes upon objects and follow their movement. Head and eye movement is also poorly coordinated; in the first week

Table 8.1 A summary of activities related to physical skills development.

Gross motor skills (locomotion or movement)	Fine motor skills (manipulation)	Balance and stabilisation
walking	throwing	bending
running	catching	stretching
skipping	picking up	twisting
jumping	kicking	turning
hopping	rolling	balancing
chasing	volleying	squatting
dodging	striking	transferring
climbing	squeezing	landing
crawling	kneading	hanging

Fig 8.3 (a) and (b) Gross motor skills (locomotion)

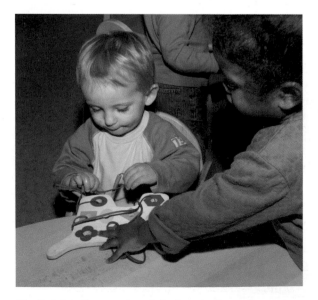

Fig 8.3 (c) Fine motor skills (manipulation)

or two, the eyes lag behind when the baby's head is turned to one side, a feature known by paediatricians as the 'doll's eye phenomenon'.

Research has shown that babies prefer looking at:

❖ patterned areas rather than plain ones, especially stripes;

❖ edges of objects in 3D;

❖ anything which resembles a human face – babies will actually search out and stare at human faces during their first 2 months of life;

❖ brightly coloured objects.

By around 4 months a baby can focus on both near and distant objects and her ability to recognise different objects is improving steadily. By 6 months the baby will respond visually to movements across the room and will move her head to see what is happening. By 1 year her eye movements are smoother and she can follow rapidly moving objects with the eyes (a skill known as **tracking**). A squint is normal at this point.

The development of hearing

Newborn babies are able to hear almost as well as adults.

- Certain rhythmic sounds – often called 'white noise' – seem to have a special soothing effect on babies. The drone of a vacuum cleaner or hairdryer is calming!

- The sound of a human voice evokes the greatest response and the rhythms of lullabyes have been used for centuries in all cultures to help babies to sleep or to comfort them.

- Babies can recognise their own mother's voice from the first week and can distinguish its tone and pitch from those of other people.

- Sudden changes in noise levels tend to disturb very young babies and make them jump.

- From about 6 months a baby learns to recognise and distinguish between different sounds; for example the sound of a spoon in a dish means that food is on its way.

- Babies can also discriminate between cheerful and angry voices, and will respond in kind.

The development of smell, taste and touch

The senses of smell and taste are closely linked. If our sense of smell is defective, for example because of a cold, then our sense of taste is also reduced. Babies as young as 1 week old who are breastfed are able to tell the difference between their own mother's smell and other women's smells. From birth babies are also able to distinguish the four basic tastes – sweet, sour, bitter and salty.

The sense of touch is also well-developed in infancy, as can be demonstrated by the primitive reflexes (see page 000). Babies seem to be particularly sensitive to touches on the mouth, the face, the hands, the soles of the feet and the abdomen. Research has shown that babies would rather be stroked than fed.

Proprioception is the sense that tells the baby the location of the mobile parts of his body (e.g. his legs) in relation to the rest of him – in other words, where his own body begins and ends.

Sensory deprivation

A congenitally blind baby (i.e. a baby who is born blind) will develop a more sophisticated sense of touch than a sighted baby, although they both start life with the same touch potential. As the sense of touch develops, so the area of the brain normally assigned to touch increases in size for the blind baby, and the area of the brain normally assigned to sight decreases.

Similarly, in a congenitally deaf baby, the part of the brain that normally receives auditory stimuli is taken over by the visual and movement input from sign language.

FACTORS AFFECTING PHYSICAL DEVELOPMENT

Children's physical development is influenced by their:

* growing confidence and sense of identity;
* enjoyment of physical play;
* increasing ability to control their own bodies through movement;
* physical wellbeing and strength.

As children develop, they become faster, stronger, more mobile and more certain of their balance, and they start to use these skills in a wider range of physical activities. There are many other factors that affect children's physical development:

1 **Genetic factors:** the genes children inherit from their parents affect both growth and development.

2 **Nutrition:** family income, lifestyle and culture all affect the diet a child receives. Children who are on poor diets are more susceptible to infection as their immunity is affected by the lack of adequate minerals and vitamins.

3 **Environmental factors:** these include:
   * overcrowded housing;
   * air pollution (e.g. lead poisoning from traffic exhausts and adults smoking in the home);
   * lack of access to a play area or garden.

4 **Social factors:** such as:
   * love and affection;
   * stimulation;
   * opportunities to play.

Healthy growth and development can be affected when a child receives too little (or too much) stimulation.

NORMATIVE PHYSICAL DEVELOPMENT, BIRTH TO 7 YEARS AND 11 MONTHS

From 0 to 4 weeks

GROSS MOTOR SKILLS

* Baby lies supine (on her back) with head to one side.
* When placed on her front (the prone position), she lies with head turned to one side and by 1 month can lift her head.
* If pulled to sitting position, her head will lag, her back curves over and her head falls forward.

FINE MOTOR SKILLS

* She will turn her head towards the light and stare at bright, shiny objects.
* She is fascinated by human faces and gazes attentively at her carer's face when fed or held.
* Her hands are usually tightly closed.
* She reacts to loud sounds, but by 1 month may be soothed by particular music.

From 4 to 8 weeks

GROSS MOTOR SKILLS

* Baby can now turn from her side to her back.
* She can lift her head briefly from the prone position.
* Her arm and leg movements are jerky and uncontrolled.
* There is head lag if she is pulled to a sitting position.

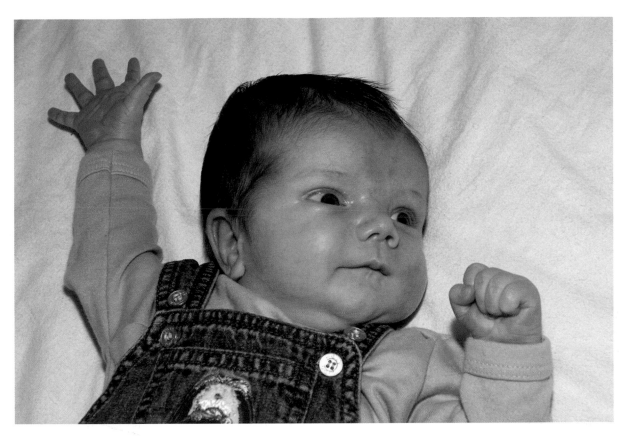

Fig 8.4 0–4 weeks

Guidelines for promoting development: birth to 4 weeks

- ❖ Encourage the baby to lie on the floor to kick and experiment safely with movement.
- ❖ Provide an opportunity for her to feel the freedom of moving without a nappy or clothes on.
- ❖ Always support the baby's head when playing with her as her neck muscles are not strong enough to control movement.
- ❖ Use bright colours in furnishings.
- ❖ Provide a mobile over the cot and/or the nappy-changing area.
- ❖ Feed on demand, and talk and sing to her.
- ❖ Provide plenty of physical contact and maintain eye contact.
- ❖ Talk lovingly to her and give her the opportunity to respond.
- ❖ Introduce her to different household noises. Provide contact with other adults and children.
- ❖ Encourage bonding with main carer by enjoying the relationship.
- ❖ Expect no set routine in the first few weeks. Pick her up and talk to her face-to-face.

Guidelines for stimulating development: 4 to 8 weeks

❖ Use a special supporting infant chair so the baby can see adult activity.

❖ Let her kick freely, without nappies.

❖ Massage her body and limbs during or after bathing.

❖ Use brightly coloured mobiles and wind chimes over her cot and/or changing mat.

❖ Let her explore different textures.

❖ Light rattles and toys strung over her pram or cot will encourage focusing and coordination.

❖ Talk to and smile with the baby.

❖ Sing while feeding or bathing her – allow her time to respond.

❖ Learn to distinguish her cries and to respond to them differently.

❖ Tickling and teasing her may induce laughter.

❖ Talk to her and hold her close.

Fig 8.5 4–8 weeks: baby looking at mobile

FINE MOTOR SKILLS

❖ Baby turns her head towards the light and stares at bright shiny objects.

❖ She will show interest and excitement by facial expression and will gaze attentively at her carer's face while being fed.

❖ She will open her hand to grasp your finger.

From 8 to 12 weeks

GROSS MOTOR SKILLS

❖ When lying supine, baby's head is in a central position.

❖ She can now lift her head and chest off the bed in a prone position, supported on forearms.

❖ There is almost no head lag in the sitting position.

❖ Her legs can kick vigorously, both separately and together.

❖ She can wave her arms and brings her hands together over her body.

FINE MOTOR SKILLS

❖ Baby moves her head to follow adult movements.

❖ She watches her hands and plays with her fingers.

❖ She holds a rattle for a brief time before dropping it.

Guidelines for stimulating development: 8 to 12 weeks

* Place the baby in a supporting infant chair so that she can watch adult activity.
* Encourage her to kick without nappies.
* Massage and stroke her limbs when bathing or if using massage oil.
* Use brightly coloured mobiles and wind chimes to encourage focusing at 20 cm.
* Place a rattle in her hand and attach objects which make a noise when struck above the cot.
* Read her nursery rhymes.
* Talk sensibly to her and imitate her sounds to encourage her to repeat them.
* Holding her close and talking lovingly will strengthen the bonding process.
* Encourage contact with other adults and children.
* Respond to her needs and show enjoyment in caring for her.

From 4 to 5 months

GROSS MOTOR SKILLS

* Baby has good head control.
* She is beginning to sit with support and can roll over from her back to her side.
* She is beginning to reach for objects.
* When supine, she plays with her own feet.
* She holds her head up when pulled to a sitting position.

Guidelines for stimulating development: 4 to 5 months

* Practise sitting, with the baby on the carer's knee.
* Play rough-and-tumble games on the bed.
* Play bouncing games on the carer's knee to songs.
* Offer rattles and soft, squashy toys to give a variety of textures.
* Offer home-made toys (e.g. transparent plastic containers with dried peas inside or empty cotton reels tied together). **NB** Check lids are secure and always supervise play.
* Continue talking to the baby, particularly in response to her own sounds.
* Provide different toys with a range of textures and sounds.
* Sing nursery rhymes combined with finger play ('This little piggy. . .').
* Give her the opportunity to find out things for herself and begin to choose play activities.
* Encourage playing alone and in the company of other children.
* Waterproof books in the bath give a lot of pleasure.

FINE MOTOR SKILLS

* She is beginning to use palmar grasp.
* She can transfer objects from hand to hand.
* She is very interested in all activity.
* Everything is taken to her mouth.
* She moves her head around to follow people and objects.

From 6 to 9 months

GROSS MOTOR SKILLS

* The baby can roll from front to back.
* She may attempt to crawl, but will often end up sliding backwards.
* She may grasp her feet and place them in her mouth.
* She can sit without support for longer periods of time.
* She may 'cruise' around furniture and may even stand or walk alone.

FINE MOTOR SKILLS

* The baby is alert to people and objects.
* She is beginning to use pincer grasp with thumb and index finger.
* She transfers toys from one hand to the other.
* She looks for fallen objects.
* Everything is explored by putting it in her mouth.

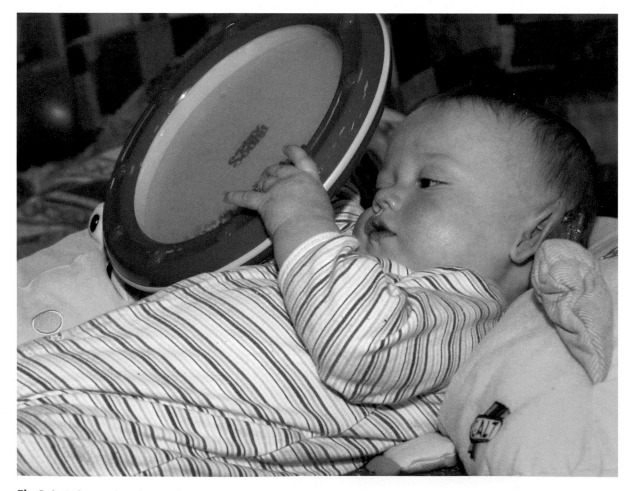

Fig 8.6 6–9 months: playing alone

Guidelines for stimulating development: 6 to 9 months

✤ Encourage confidence and balance by placing toys around the sitting baby. Make sure furniture is stable and has no sharp corners when baby is using it to pull herself up.

✤ Encourage mobility by placing toys just out of baby's reach.

✤ Encourage visual awareness by providing varied experiences.

✤ Small objects, which must be safe if chewed by the baby, will encourage the pincer grasp (small pieces of biscuit are ideal, but always supervise).

✤ Build a tower of bricks with her and watch her delight when they all fall down.

✤ Look at picture books together and encourage her to point at objects by naming them.

✤ Talk to her about everyday things.

✤ Widen her experiences by going on outings which include animals.

✤ Imitate animal sounds and encourage her to copy you.

✤ Allow plenty of time for play.

✤ Provide simple musical instruments (xylophone or wooden spoon and saucepan).

✤ Use a safety mirror for the baby to recognise herself.

From 9 to 12 months

GROSS MOTOR SKILLS

✤ The baby will now be mobile; she may be crawling, bear-walking, bottom-shuffling or even walking.

✤ She can sit up on her own and lean forwards to pick things up.

✤ She may crawl upstairs and onto low items of furniture.

✤ She may bounce in rhythm to music.

FINE MOTOR SKILLS

✤ Her pincer grasp is now well-developed and she can pick things up and pull them towards her.

✤ She can poke with one finger and will point to desired objects.

✤ She can clap her hands and imitate adult actions.

✤ She throws toys deliberately.

✤ She manages spoons and finger foods well.

Guidelines for stimulating development: 9 to 12 months

✤ Provide large-wheeled toys to push around – brick trucks serve the dual purpose of walking and stacking games.

✤ Ensure furniture is safe and stable for climbers.

✤ Go swimming, or walking in the park.

- Provide small climbing frames – closely supervised – to increase her balance and coordination.

- Offer stacking and nesting toys.

- Roll balls for her to bring back to you.

- Encourage sand and water play – always supervised.

- Offer cardboard boxes and saucepans to put things into and take things out of.

- Partake in plenty of talking to the baby which requires a response that will develop language ability.

- Encourage self-feeding – tolerate messes.

- Talk constantly to her and use rhymes and action songs.

- Offer lots of play opportunities with adult interaction – sharing, taking turns, and so on.

- Encourage her to join in and help with regular chores.

- Foster a feeling of self-worth by providing her with her own equipment and utensils (e.g. she will need her own flannel, toothbrush, cup and spoon).

Fig 8.7 9–12 months: baby crawling or bottom-shuffling

At 15 months

GROSS MOTOR SKILLS

❖ The baby probably walks alone, with feet wide apart and arms raised to maintain balance.

❖ She is likely to fall over and land suddenly on her bottom.

❖ She can probably manage stairs and steps, but will need supervision.

Figure 8.8 15 months: child looking at a book

❖ She can stand without help from furniture or people.

❖ She kneels without support.

FINE MOTOR SKILLS

❖ The baby can build with a few bricks and arrange toys on the floor.

❖ She holds crayons in palmar grasp.

❖ She turns several pages of a book at once.

❖ She can point to desired objects.

❖ She shows a preference for one hand, but uses either.

At 18 months

GROSS MOTOR SKILLS

❖ The baby walks confidently and is able to stop without falling.

❖ She can kneel, squat, climb and carry things around with her.

❖ She can climb forwards onto an adult chair and then turn round to sit.

❖ She comes downstairs, usually by creeping backwards on her tummy.

FINE MOTOR SKILLS

❖ The baby can thread large beads.

❖ She uses a pincer grasp to pick up small objects.

Guidelines for stimulating development: at 15 months

❖ Provide stacking toys and bricks.

❖ Provide push-and-pull toys for children who are walking.

❖ Read picture books with simple rhymes.

❖ Offer big empty cardboard boxes for play (very popular).

❖ Provide thick crayons or thick paintbrushes.

❖ Arrange a corner of the kitchen or garden for messy play involving the use of water or paint.

NB This is a high-risk age for accidents – be vigilant at all times.

Guidelines for stimulating development: at 18 months

❖ Push-and-pull toys are still popular.

❖ Teach the baby how to manage stairs safely.

❖ Provide threading toys, and hammer and peg toys.

❖ Encourage and praise early attempts at drawing.

Fig 8.9 18 months: child bending down to pick up an object

❖ She builds a tower of three or more cubes.

❖ She scribbles to and fro on paper.

At 2 years

GROSS MOTOR SKILLS

❖ The child is very mobile and can run safely.

❖ She can climb up onto the furniture.

❖ She walks up and down stairs, usually two feet to a step.

❖ She tries to kick a ball with some success, but cannot yet catch a ball.

FINE MOTOR SKILLS

❖ The child can draw circles, lines and dots, using preferred hand.

❖ She can pick up tiny objects using a fine pincer grasp.

❖ She can build a tower of six or seven bricks, with a longer concentration span.

❖ She enjoys picture books and turns pages individually.

Guidelines for stimulating development: at 2 years

❖ Provide toys to ride and climb on, and space to run and play.

❖ Allow trips to parks and opportunities for messy play with water and paints.

❖ Encourage use of safe climbing frames and sandpits, always supervised.

❖ Provide simple models to build (e.g. Duplo), as well as jigsaw puzzles, crayons and paper, picture books and glove puppets.

Fig 8.10 2 years: trying to kick a large ball

Fig 8.11 3 years: standing on one leg

At 3 years

GROSS MOTOR SKILLS

❖ The child can jump from a low step.

❖ She walks backwards and sideways.

❖ She can stand and walk on tiptoe and stand on one foot.

❖ She has good spatial awareness.

❖ She rides a tricycle using pedals.

❖ She can climb stairs with one foot on each step – downwards with two feet per step.

FINE MANIPULATIVE SKILLS

❖ The child can build a tower of nine or ten bricks.

❖ She can control a pencil using her thumb and first two fingers – the dynamic tripod grasp.

❖ She enjoys painting with a large brush.

❖ She can copy a circle.

Guidelines for stimulating development: at 3 years

❖ Provide a wide variety of playthings – dough for modelling, sand and safe household utensils.

❖ Encourage play with other children. Allow swimming, trips to the park, maybe even enjoy long walks.

- ❖ Read to the child and discuss everyday events.
- ❖ Encourage art and craft activities.
- ❖ Promote independence by teaching her how to look after and put away her own clothes and toys.
- ❖ Encourage visits to the library and story-times.

At 4 years

GROSS MOTOR SKILLS

- ♣ Sense of balance is developing; she may be able to walk along a line.
- ♣ She can catch, kick, throw and bounce a ball.
- ♣ She can bend at the waist to pick up objects from the floor.
- ♣ She enjoys climbing trees and on climbing frames.
- ♣ She can run up and down stairs, one foot per step.

FINE MANIPULATIVE SKILLS

- ♣ The child can build a tower of ten or more bricks.
- ♣ She can draw a recognisable person on request, showing head, legs and trunk.
- ♣ She can thread small beads on a lace.

Fig 8.12 4 years: building a tower of ten bricks

Guidelines for stimulating development: at 4 years

- ❖ Provide plenty of opportunity for exercise.
- ❖ Play party games – musical statues, and so on.
- ❖ Use rope swings and climbing frames.
- ❖ Obtain access to a bike with stabilisers.
- ❖ Provide small-piece construction toys, jigsaws and board games.
- ❖ Encourage gluing and sticking activities, as well as paint, sand, water and play dough.
- ❖ Prepare child for school by teaching her how to dress and undress for games, and to manage going to the toilet by herself.

At 5 years

GROSS MOTOR SKILLS

- The child can use a variety of play equipment – slides, swings, climbing frames.
- She can play ball games.
- She can hop and run lightly on toes, and move rhythmically to music.
- Her sense of balance is well-developed.

FNE MOTOR SKILLS

- The child may be able to thread a large-eyed needle and sew large stitches.
- She can draw a person with head, trunk, legs, nose, mouth and eyes.
- She has good control over pencils and paintbrushes.
- She can copy a square and a triangle.

From 6 years to 7 years and 11 months

GROSS MOTOR SKILLS

- The child has increased agility, muscle coordination and balance.
- She develops competence in riding a two-wheeled bicycle.

Fig 8.13 5 years: drawing a person

Guidelines for stimulating development: at 5 years

✤ Provide plenty of outdoor activities.

✤ Encourage non-stereotypical activities (e.g. boys using skipping ropes, girls playing football).

✤ Team sports may be provided at clubs such as Beavers, Rainbows and Woodcraft Folk.

✤ Encourage the use of models, jigsaws, sewing kits and craft activities, as well as drawing and painting.

✤ Introduce tracing and image patterns.

✤ She hops easily, with good balance.

✤ She can jump off apparatus at school.

FINE MOTOR SKILLS

✤ The child can build a tall, straight tower with bricks.

✤ She can draw a person with detail (e.g. clothes and eyebrows).

✤ She writes letters of the alphabet with a similar writing hold to an adult.

✤ She can catch a ball thrown from a metre away with one hand.

Fig 8.14 6/7 years: doing cartwheels

Guidelines for stimulating development: from 6 years to 7 years and 11 months

✤ Provide opportunity for vigorous exercise.

✤ Team sports, riding a bike and swimming can all be encouraged; give plenty of praise for new skills learnt and never force a child to participate.

✤ Provide books and drawing materials, board games and computer games.

✤ Encourage writing skills.

✤ Display the child's work prominently to increase self-esteem.

PHYSICAL DEVELOPMENT IN RELATION TO OTHER AREAS

Physical development is linked to other areas of development, such as emotional and social development, and cognitive and language development. Each affects and is affected by the other areas. For example:

* Once babies have mastered crawling, they are free to explore the world on their own. They become more independent and confident when away from their familiar adults.

* The ability to reach and grasp objects (usually achieved at around 6 months) develops their understanding of the nature of objects. This often results in a surprise, for example when they try to pick up a soap bubble or a shaft of sunlight. Babies are interested in edges (e.g. of a book on a floor). Where does one object end and the next object begin?

PHYSICAL ACTIVITY AND EXERCISE

Exercise is essential for children's growth and development, because it:

* reduces their risk of developing heart disease in later life;

* strengthens muscles;

* helps strengthen joints and promotes good posture;

* improves balance, coordination and flexibility;

* increases bone density, so bones are less likely to fracture.

Apart from these obvious physical benefits, regular exercise develops a child's **self-esteem** by creating a strong sense of purpose and self-fulfilment; children learn how to interact and cooperate with other children by taking part in team sports and other activities.

Promoting exercise in children

Children need to learn that exercise is fun; the best way to convince them is to show by example. Bear in mind that some team games do not provide all children with the same opportunity for exercise, as they often involve several children standing around for long periods. Some children dislike being competitive and prefer to dance, for example. Early years workers and parents should try to find an activity that the individual child will enjoy, such as swimming or roller-skating. Older children could be encouraged to join a local sports or gym club; some areas provide 'gym and movement' or yoga classes for toddlers. It is often easier to persuade a child to take up a new activity if she knows she will meet new friends. Family outings could be arranged to include physical activity, such as swimming, walking or boating.

THE IMPORTANCE OF PHYSICAL PLAY

Through opportunities for physical play, children steadily become better at those skills requiring coordination of different parts of the body; for example:

* hands and eyes for throwing and catching;

* legs and arms for skipping with a rope.

Physical play helps children to:

* **express ideas and feelings:** children become aware that they can use their bodies to express themselves by moving in different ways as they respond to their moods and feelings, to music or to imaginative ideas.

* **explore what their bodies can do:** children become aware of their increasing

abilities, agility and skill; their awareness of the space around them and what their bodies are capable of can be extended by climbing and balancing on large-scale apparatus, such as a climbing frame, wooden logs and a balancing bar, and by using small tricycles, bicycles and carts.

❖ **cooperate with others:** children become aware of physical play both as an individual and a social activity, in playing alone or alongside others, in playing throwing and catching with a partner, in using a see-saw or pushcart, or in joining a game with a larger group.

❖ **develop increasing control of fine motor skills:** for example, playing musical instruments and making sounds with the body, such as clapping or tapping, help develop fine movements of their hands and fingers, while also reinforcing the link between sound and physical movement; helping with household tasks (washing up, pouring drinks, carrying bags) also develops fine motor skills.

❖ **develop balance and coordination:** energetic play, which involves running, jumping and skipping, helps children to develop these skills, which also encourage an appreciation of distance and speed.

❖ **develop spatial awareness:** for example, dancing and moving around to music develop a spatial awareness while also practising coordination and muscle control.

Providing opportunities for physical play

Opportunities for physical activity should be provided both inside and out. Regular sessions of indoor physical play or visits to local sports and leisure centres are particularly important when the weather limits opportunities for outdoor play. The outdoors can provide a scale and freedom for a type of play which is difficult to replicate indoors. For example, outdoors there are opportunities for children to:

❖ dig a garden;

❖ explore woodland;

❖ run on the grass and roll down a grassy slope;

❖ pedal a toy car across a hard surface.

Visits to swimming pools, where these can be arranged, can help children to enjoy and gain confidence in the water at an early stage.

Case Study

Petra

Petra walks towards a ball. She wants to pick it up. She leans over to touch the ball, but instead her foot hits it and the ball slides across the floor. She walks towards it again, and this time she tries to kick the ball on purpose. She misses the ball; her foot goes past the left side of the ball. Petra tries again, and again. She kicks it and she begins to run after the ball, tries to stop in front of it, and falls forward. She stands up and kicks it to a new location and she laughs.

ACTIVITY: A LEARNING EXPERIENCE

1 How old do you think Petra is?

2 What has Petra learnt during this activity? Try to list at least six

things and then compare them with the list at the end of this chapter (see page 326).

Problem solving, physical development and play

Any conscious movement involves making judgements or assessments. Assessment of the situation and of your ability (speed, power, etc.) will help you to make the appropriate movement. For example, a child might make an assessment of:

❖ how hard to throw;

❖ how fast to run;

❖ how much effort to use to jump so high;

❖ when to start to stop.

These are all examples of decision making needed in school and social life.

PROMOTING PHYSICAL DEVELOPMENT

Physical development is the easiest aspect of development to observe and measure. Parents are usually proud of their child's physical achievements, but children are often unfavourably compared with their peers and may also be judged by others. We should always stop and consider how both parents and their child may feel when the child is not able to perform certain physical tasks. Rather than feeling sorry for the child who has a physical disability or illness, we should aim to maximise their individual potential for development.

Children do not need lots of expensive toys and play equipment in order to grow and develop physically. The most important factors for healthy development are that you should:

1 recognise the skills a child has developed and provide plenty of opportunities for him or her to practise them;

2 ensure that children have the freedom to explore their environment in safety;

3 be there for the child, to offer reassurance, encouragement and praise;

Guidelines for promoting physical development

❖ Always focus on all aspects of development; the child's self-esteem and wellbeing are paramount.

❖ Help children to see physical activities as fun rather than as tests of competency.

❖ Help children to compete with themselves – can I do this better than I managed last time? – rather than comparing themselves with others.

❖ Provide a balance of activities, exposing children to as many experiences as possible.

❖ Be sensitive to insecurities; be aware of why a child might be hesitant.

❖ Always acknowledge effort, rather than results.

❖ Never ridicule a child for being 'clumsy'.

❖ Use technology where possible to help in the development of skills.

❖ Help children to develop the ability to praise others' achievements without feeling degraded.

❖ Be fair to all children; encourage patience, understanding and teamwork.

❖ Recognise and allow differences between siblings and friends – try not to compare.

> ## ACTIVITY: PROMOTING PHYSICAL DEVELOPMENT IN A CHILD WITH SPECIAL NEEDS
>
> Either visit a school for children with special needs, or invite an early years worker with experience of working with children with special needs into college. Prepare the questions you need to ask to find out:
>
> ❖ how a child with difficulties in coordination can be helped to develop these skills;
>
> ❖ what activities may be used to promote physical development in a child who is a wheelchair-user;
>
> ❖ what the role of the early years worker is in promoting physical development in children with special needs.

4 provide access to a range of facilities and equipment (this need not be expensive – for example, a visit to the local park or toddler's playgroup will provide facilities not available in a small flat).

Promoting the development of fine motor skills

Children should be provided with a rich variety of opportunities to develop their skills in using different materials and a range of tools. They also need to develop the skills required to take care of their own bodies, for example in washing and dressing themselves, cleaning their teeth and becoming more independent at mealtimes.

To strengthen the hands and promote the development of **fine motor skills**, you should provide:

1 **play dough** or clay for squeezing, rolling, squashing, making holes with fingers and tools;

2 **newspaper** for scrunching up, using one hand at a time, or tearing into strips and crumpling them into balls;

3 **scissors** – when safety scissors are held correctly, and when they fit a child's hand well, simple cutting activities will exercise the same muscles that are needed to manipulate a pencil in a mature **tripod grasp**. The correct scissor position is with the thumb and middle finger in the handles of the scissors, the index finger on the outside of the handle to stabilise, with fingers 4 and 5 curled into the palm. For cutting, provide:

❖ junk mail or similar thick paper;

❖ straws;

❖ play dough;

4 **mark-making** opportunities with chunky pens, pencils and paintbrushes for drawing, writing, painting, tracing, and so on;

5 a **peg game** to promote the development of the **pincer grasp** – give each child a cardboard plate and provide lots of brightly coloured plastic pegs; using a sand-timer or clock-timer, see how many pegs the children can arrange around their plate

(this activity is also good for learning their colours);

6   a **finger gym** to promote the development of fine manipulative skills, such as pinching, screwing, threading, winding, and so on. Provide a basket or box in which you have collected items that need small fingers to work, but that are also attractive and appealing to children, for example:

- old clocks and radios;
- spinning tops;
- squeezy toys;
- eye droppers to 'pick up' coloured water for colour mixing or to make patterns on paper;
- buttons and fasteners;
- dried pasta shapes and chopsticks for picking them up;
- wind-up toys;
- jar tops for opening and closing, or other twisting toys;
- cotton reels, chunky beads (and smaller ones as the children get older) for threading;
- shape sorters and 'posting' toys;
- pegs of various sizes with boards.

Promoting hand–eye coordination

This involves accuracy in placement, direction and spatial awareness:

- Throw beanbags or soft 'koosh' balls into a hoop placed flat on the floor. Gradually increase the distance.
- Play throwing and catching with a ball; start with a large ball and then work towards using a smaller ball.
- Practise hitting skittles with a ball (improvise by using weighted plastic bottles).

Promoting physical development in children with special needs

Although the sequence of physical development may remain the same for a child with a special need, the rate at which a 'stage' is achieved may be slower. The attitudes and actions of parents and early years workers will have a great influence on the child's behaviour and self-esteem.

- All children should be appreciated and encouraged for any personal progress made, however small, and should not be compared to the normative measurements. This is because children with special needs often seem to 'dance

ACTIVITY: TOYS FOR BABIES

1   Visit a toy shop and look at the range of toys for babies under 1 year. List the toys and activities under two headings:

- Toys that strengthen muscles and improve coordination.
- Toys which particularly stimulate the sense of touch and sight.

What **safety symbols** are shown on the toys?

2   If you are asked to suggest toys and activities for a baby with a visual impairment, what specific things could you suggest?

the developmental ladder' – they move through developmental stages in unusual and very uneven ways; for example; they might sit or walk at the usual time, but not talk.

❧ Adults should recognise and understand that a child who is having difficulty in acquiring a skill may become frustrated and may need more individual attention or specialist help; also that the child may not yet be ready to acquire the particular skill.

❧ Every child must be seen as an individual first; activities and equipment should be tailored to the specific needs of that child.

❧ Plan activities to encourage exercise and movement of all body parts.

ANSWERS TO ACTIVITY: A LEARNING EXPERIENCE (PAGE 322)

1 Petra has just had her second birthday.

2 These are some of the things you may have listed (you may have found more) that Petra has learned:

❧ That you need to watch your feet as well as your hands.

❧ If you hit something with your foot it moves.

❧ You have to aim at the ball, not just swing your leg.

❧ Do not give up even when it is difficult.

❧ Do not run too fast when you go after a ball.

❧ Slow down before trying to stop.

❧ Start stopping at a certain distance ahead, depending on the speed you are moving.

❧ How to assess speed, distance and force.

❧ The connections between cause and effect.

❧ Keep trying because you can succeed.

❧ Learning is fun.

9

Emotional and social development

Contents

THE STAGES/SEQUENCES OF EMOTIONAL AND SOCIAL DEVELOPMENT: BIRTH TO 7 YEARS AND 11 MONTHS

From birth to 3 months

Researchers do not think that babies, in their first month, know that they are separate from other people. Babies are only beginning to learn where they begin and end: a toe is part of them; a bed cover is not, neither is the mother's hand. Up to 3 months babies start to:

❖ recognise people they know well – feelings and relationships develop;

❖ smile;

❖ turn to familiar person's voice, especially their mother;

❖ know their own face and hands;

❖ react when they hear, see or feel their carer (they may stop crying, for example).

Babies who are visually impaired often become very still, as if listening and waiting for more information. Researchers believe that it is almost as if babies are born in order to relate to people.

From 3 to 6 months

From the beginning, babies find faces interesting to look at. They turn to their mother's voice, in particular, and they like to be held in the arms of someone they love and know. Even very young babies prefer being held by those they are emotionally close to.

By 5 months babies have learnt that they have only one mother. They are very disturbed if several images of their mother are shown to them. They might cry or look away because they are worried.

From 6 to 12 months

Babies begin moving about. As they crawl and begin to walk they develop more of a self-image and are able to do more things for themselves. They become more aware of other people's feelings. They realise that people and objects are separate from them.

* They love to play peek-a-boo.

* They like to look at themselves in the mirror.

* They know their name and respond to it.

* They love to have an audience. They use social referencing, looking to see how other people react to what they do.

* They imitate other people, for example clapping hands or copying sounds.

* They are very affectionate when they are shown love.

* They often show fear of strangers.

* They recognise how other people feel. They become anxious if someone they love begins to cry. They express their own feelings too. The way they are influenced by the feelings of other people is called being **affectively tuned**.

* They understand the word 'no'.

* They can become full of rage.

* They cooperate when they are being dressed.

From 1 to 2 years

* Babies start to show that they have a mind of their own.

* They are developing a sense of identity.

* They are developing a longer memory span.

* They are beginning to express their needs using words and gestures.

* They love to do things for themselves – this is called **autonomy**. They enjoy their developing physical skills, such as walking.

* However, when they try things which are new, they quickly sense when others fear for them, for example when they try to climb onto or off a chair at the meal table (this awareness is called **social referencing**).

* They love their efforts to be appreciated.

* It is still easy to distract children and take their attention from one thing to another.

From 2 to 3 years

* Children imitate what other people do and begin to become engrossed in symbolic **play**. This means they pretend to be someone else, for example someone pouring out the tea or the person who delivers the post. This is called **role play** because children rehearse adult roles.

* They begin to explain how they are feeling.

* They are very anxious to try things for themselves.

* They quickly become frustrated, for example when something does not go well. They need a great deal of support from adults as they learn to go to the toilet, put their clothes on and feed themselves.

From 3 to 4 years

* Children begin to develop a more complex **Theory of Mind** as they try out what it is like to be someone else in their imaginative role play.

* During this time, children are becoming more influenced by each other. They

begin to be interested in having friends. They love to use 'silly talk' and to laugh together.

✤ They often have one special friend. They value companionship, but they also value being alone. This means that they need:

1 solitary times;

2 times to do things in parallel;

3 times to be cooperative.

✤ Sometimes they follow the lead of another child; sometimes they show leadership. Children of this age love to feel power and to have control: over things and people. Sometimes they negotiate at their own level.

✤ Children are easily afraid at this time. For example, they might be afraid of the dark and so need a night light in their bedroom.

✤ During this time children are beginning to think about things that are right and things that are wrong. They are developing moral values. They often argue with adults in a dogmatic way, and will not shift their position.

From 4 years to 7 years and 11 months

✤ During this period, the child is establishing a stable self-concept.

✤ They take in and internalise the social rules of their culture. They have begun to work out the difference between:

1 **social rules:** which vary from culture to culture (e.g. the way to greet somebody);

2 **display rules:** which govern when we hide our feelings (e.g. disappointment that a present is not what we hoped for);

3 **moral values:** which are to do with respect for other people (e.g. not hitting people).

✤ Children respond very positively to being given explanations and reasons.

✤ They are able to follow a series of events from beginning to end, and to be sensitive to the needs of other people as they do so.

✤ They are also able to take considerable responsibility, and enjoy helping other younger children. There is a terrific desire to be accepted by other children and adults. It is also important to encourage children to be people in their own right and not simply to conform to what others want. Children with a strong sense of identity learn to be strong people. They learn to be assertive without being aggressive.

INFLUENCES ON EMOTIONAL AND SOCIAL DEVELOPMENT

Environmental influences

There are many reasons why children may experience a lack of emotional and social wellbeing. In the government initiative, Every Child Matters, the importance of being healthy, staying safe, achieving and enjoying, making a positive contribution and experiencing economic wellbeing are emphasised. A child who has poor physical and mental health will be challenged in this respect. When children experience physical, emotional or sexual abuse, or neglect over time, this has a detrimental impact on their emotional lives and their social relationships. When children do not have any sense of personal achievement, their self-esteem is low. When children do not feel any sense of belonging to a family, a community or an early childhood group, they do not have the enriching experience of feeling that they are contributing. Poverty has a damaging effect on emotional and social relationships, especially when it is of the grinding and long-term kind.

Fig 9.1 Sensitive, consistent, loving care from familiar adults gives children high wellbeing

Personality and temperament

Every person has a different **personality**. Recently researchers have begun to realise that a child's temperament in early childhood is the beginning of their later personality. It used to be thought that personality was fixed at birth (just as it used to be thought that intelligence was fixed at birth and unchangeable thereafter). As in other areas of development, it seems that a child's temperament is partly biological, but is also influenced by other factors:

❖ the experiences of life;

❖ physical challenges;

❖ the people children meet.

Temperament is the style of behaviour that is natural to the child. So the child's temperament influences the personality that emerges later on, during late childhood and early adolescence. For example, some babies seem almost 'prickly' when you hold them, while others are full of smiles. Some children are always crying and may seem unattractive to adults. Some children are accident-prone because their temperament is to be very impulsive and active. They move into less safe situations more readily than a child with a more cautious temperament.

It is very important that adults working with young children do not favour smiling children. And it is critical that they do not take against children with more difficult temperaments. Working professionally with children means being determined to uphold principles of equality of opportunity and inclusivity (see Chapter 1). The way adults help children willingly and with pleasure has a deep influence on how they develop and learn. People's reactions to a child's temperament can influence that child's self-esteem. Different temperaments can lead children to behave in different ways:

1 Emotionality and feeling.

❖ Some children have more happy moods.

❖ Others are sad or distressed.

❖ Some children are more at ease than others in unfamiliar situations.

❖ Some children can manage better than others when they are bored.

❖ Some children can wait longer than others to eat when they are hungry.

❖ Some children are more serious temperamentally, while others love to have a go at things.

2   Activity.

  ❖ Some children are very vigorous and active, and always on the go.

  ❖ Some children are able to change and modify what they do more easily.

  ❖ Some children are very flexible.

  ❖ Some children are impulsive, while others hold back.

3   Sociability.

  ❖ Some children are easily comforted when they are upset and distressed, while others are not.

  ❖ Some children positively enjoy meeting new people and going to new places, while others do not.

4   Variation in concentration.

  ❖ Some children are easily distracted, while others are not.

The child's temperamental features will be stable across different times of the day and night, and in different places and with different people. This means that they will have their own style of doing things and of relating to people. Shy, timid children will be more cautious than communicative, sociable children.

TEMPERAMENT AND PERSONALITY CLASHES

Sometimes people clash: adults clash with other adults; children clash with other children. Sometimes an adult can have a personality clash with a child. This is why it is so helpful to work in a team with other members of staff (see page 580). It is very important that every early years worker tries their best to get on with every child, even though it is easier to do this with some children than with others. It is only natural, according to researchers, that there is sometimes a better 'goodness of fit' between some people than others, but this does not give us an excuse to show favouritism.

The interdependency between physical, emotional, intellectual and social development

It is important to remember that it is not possible to isolate emotional and social development from any other areas of development. Piaget thought that it was unfortunate that there are two separate words for thinking and feeling. He thought the two were completely inseparable: he said that it was impossible to think without feeling, or to feel without thinking. In the same way, relationships with other people (emotional and social development) cannot be separated from intellectual (cognitive) aspects of development.

Is love a feeling? The development of thoughtful feelings

We have seen that it is not possible to separate feelings (emotions) from social relationships (which involve thoughts about the people we love). Love is a feeling in yourself and it is also a social relationship with another person. People who love each other care about each other's feelings as much as they care about their own feelings. As people share their feelings they use words or a cuddle, for example. The words contain ideas and cuddles are physical demonstrations. There may be a spiritual experience too. Knowing how the person who is loved thinks about things is an important part of loving someone. For example, to organise a surprise birthday party for someone who would hate it would not be loving. Making breakfast in bed for them, when they love to get up slowly as a treat, would be a loving thing to do.

Cultural influences

Different families and different cultures show or do not show their feelings in different ways. The neuroscientist Damasio says that feelings are 'preludes to emotion'. They can stay hidden, but we cannot hide our emotions so easily, because these are physical reactions. Helping children to manage their emotions so that they learn to understand their feelings and how they lead to emotional reactions is very important.

For cultural or personality reasons, some people are very private about their feelings, but it is important for mental health that they learn to understand how they feel, and to feel that they have some control over this emotionally. Bottling up feelings by trying to suppress emotion is damaging long-term, and so is expressing feelings in emotional outbursts which are socially unacceptable.

The sociocultural aspect of development and the influence of social exchanges with other people, especially those who are close to and love the child, are crucial. Babies have feelings and emotions from the moment they are born. As children become increasingly aware of themselves, they can be helped to become more aware of how other people feel. Children who feel loved and receive plenty of warm affection and cuddles will find it easier both to give love to other people and to like themselves. Neuroscientists call the first years of life the period when children develop an understanding of 'personhood'.

THE IMPORTANCE OF PLAY IN SOCIAL AND EMOTIONAL DEVELOPMENT

In the 1930s, Mildred Parten identified the following different kinds of play:

1 **Solitary play:** children sometimes want to have personal space and do things alone.

2 **Spectator play:** a child may choose to watch what others do, and not want to join in.

3 **Parallel play:** there are times when children want companionship but not much interaction; for example, two children may sit side by side and draw together, but not look at each other or talk very much about what they are doing.

4 **Associative play:** two children might both choose to be the chef in a cafe, each oblivious to what the other is doing. They are each busy with their own play agenda. If their agendas do conflict, then there will be a problem! When each child has a separate idea that is not shared by the other, there will be frequent conflicts. This is partly why young children need help and support in their social play or when sharing materials together. It is often not appropriate, however, to force sharing. Instead adults might need to bring in another saucepan for the extra chef. Separate ideas are separate, and if children are not able to share ideas, they cannot share materials! Helping children at moments like this is an important role for the early years worker

5 **Cooperative play:** this develops as the children grow older, especially when they experience help and positive treatment from adults. The peek-a-boo game enjoyed by babies as young as 6 months of age is an early kind of cooperative behaviour. Gradually children begin to share; for example, a set of wooden building blocks. They decide, together, to make a road. They negotiate and exchange ideas. If the sharing breaks down, adults can help

by stating each child's ideas. For example, 'Sean, you want to build a bridge. Meg, you want to build a row of shops. You both want to use the same blocks. What can we do about this?' Children often find solutions and then return to work together again.

In Chapters 3 and 12 play is discussed in more detail. Play helps children to understand their feelings and to experiment with showing emotions. They become the cross mum, the grumpy shopkeeper, the kind aunty when a child falls over, or the angry bus driver. It also helps them to experience what someone else might feel when someone is cross, grumpy, kind or angry towards them. It is important to know the features of play (Bruce) and what play gives to children who are developing emotionally and socially.

THE ROLE OF THE ADULT IN PROMOTING EMOTIONAL AND SOCIAL DEVELOPMENT

Babies

Encourage babies to bond with their main carer by allowing time for them to enjoy the relationship. Once weaned, encourage babies to feed themselves and be tolerant of any messes. Tune in to the baby. When a baby is upset, help the baby to return to what Sue Gerhardt calls their **comfort zone**. Babies and very young children experience constantly changing emotional states. They need a huge amount of support and help in moving back to their comfort zone once it has been wobbled or disturbed. Try to enter the baby's state of emotion by mirroring the sound he or she is making, and gradually leading the way into a calmer sound by

toning your voice down and taking the baby into a calmer state. Babies usually like to be held gently while you do this; some like to be rocked in time to your heart beating. Try it. It is one of the most satisfying things you will ever experience when you tune in to a baby and calm them.

Children aged 2–3 years

It is very important, during this time, that adults help children to experience success as they try to become more autonomous. This helps children to deal positively with problems. They need clothes which are easy to put on and take off, and easy to do up and undo – straps, laces and small buttons are not helpful, whereas elasticated waistbands and Velcro on shoes are great for children who want to dress themselves.

General advice

✤ It is very important that children be encouraged to learn about being cooperative, positive and caring towards each other. During the last 20 years, the work of Judy Dunn has shown how children learn through quarrels with others. They need a great deal of support from adults when learning in this way; they need to be helped to turn difficult situations into positive ones.

✤ They are helped if principles of inclusion and equality of opportunity are explained, so that they do not stereotype people and see them narrowly.

✤ It is important that children are prepared to have a go at things, to take risks and not be anxious about making errors.

✤ If children are smacked or hit by adults, they learn that it is acceptable behaviour for bigger people to hit smaller, less powerful people. It is illegal for early years workers in institutions to hit or smack children.

RELATING TO OTHERS

❧ From the start, it seems as if babies are born to relate to other people. This is called pro-social behaviour. It is important to encourage sociability by providing opportunities for babies and young children to meet other children and adults. As early as 6 months of age, babies enjoy each other's company. When they sit together, they touch each other's faces. They look at each other and smile at each other. They enjoy peek-a-boo games with adults and older children. This is cooperative social behaviour. It involves turn-taking. Babies delight in having a shared idea, and they really laugh with delight.

❧ Toddlers' behaviour also shows how very young children cooperate socially. One might pick up a toy, and the other will copy. They laugh together. There is plenty of eye contact. One drops the toy intentionally, and the other copies. They laugh with glee. They have a shared idea which they can enjoy together.

❧ By the age 2 or 3 years, the widening social circle becomes important. Children need varying amounts of help and support as they have new social experiences. This might include joining an early childhood group of some kind. Settling children into a group is probably one of the most important aspects of the role of the early years worker (see later sections of this chapter).

When beginning to explore social relationships it is important that children are not frightened by aggressive and demanding behaviour from their peers. Different kinds of social behaviour can show themselves at different times of the day, in different situations and according to the child's mood,

personality, physical comfort (tired, hungry or needing a nappy change/lavatory) and previous experiences of relating to people.

Getting on with other children

A young child, seeing a friend distressed, may make a gesture spontaneously – such as giving them a treasured teddy bear – to ease the pain and provide comfort. This means that young children are, in their own way, very *giving*. They are also very *forgiving*. Being able to give means that a young child has managed to think of someone else's need and to control their behaviour accordingly. It takes enormous effort for young children to do this. It is an ability that will come and go depending upon the situation, the people involved and how tired the children are. Children who become skilled in this way are often popular leaders, and other children want to be with them. Children tend to behave according to the way they experience life. If they are ridiculed or smacked, they are likely to laugh at and hit others, especially children younger or smaller than themselves. This is because children use adults as a model of how to behave. As already mentioned, this is called **social referencing**. Some children need a great deal of support to play well and get on with other children. Children who know how to join in get on better with other children. They have good 'access strategies':

1 First a child will tend to circle around the edge of an activity, perhaps on a tricycle, trying to work out what is happening, or will watch what is happening from the safe viewpoint of being at the sand tray or water tray.

2 Then they will imitate what the other children are doing, for example pouring sand in and out of pots and laughing as

each pot is upturned. We call this using a **side-by-side** strategy. Doing the same helps the child to join in with other children.

You might say to the child, 'Do you want to join in? Let's look at what they are doing, shall we? Don't ask if you can do the same as them, just do the same as them.' This advice is given because if children ask if they can join in, they are usually rejected. If, on the other hand, children simply do what the other children are doing, they are very likely to be accepted into the group. This is an important access strategy which adults can help children to develop. It is also a useful strategy for adults to use if they are joining a group of children.

Friendships

Early friendships are important and may last throughout life, or they may be more fleeting. As a child's interests change and they go off in a different direction, the old friendship may fade. Early friendships are like adult ones; they are based, at least in part, on people sharing the same interests. As children become more able to play imaginatively together, the possibilities grow for sharing and enjoying each other's company. This is because, in play, children can rearrange the real world to suit themselves: you can pretend anything when you play!

Sharing

Young children can only manage to socialise cooperatively for a small part of their day: it is too much to expect them to cooperate with others for large parts of the day. Indeed, children who are just settling in might not manage to share at all: instead all their energy is going into adjusting to the new social setting.

How adults can help children to relate positively to others

No one gets on with everyone all the time. Children are just like adults in this way. All children need:

* the **personal space** to do things on their own, without interruptions or pressure from anyone else;
* to feel **nurtured and loved** as a person in their own right;
* **to be able to choose** whom to be with and what to do for most of the day (always having to do adult-led tasks is a great pressure for young children);
* their **difficulties to be addressed with sensitivity and care** by adults;
* **individual attention** so that they feel they have enough time to talk and share without the pressure of being in a group (e.g. a child might appreciate a one-to-one story); individual attention is especially important for younger children.

Guidelines for helping children with social difficulties

❖ Give children the words they need: teach them to say, 'I need some help.'

❖ Help children to understand social rules: 'If you stamp your feet and cry, I can't help you. I need to know the problem. Can you show me the problem?' 'Can you see my face? It is easier for us to listen to each other if I look at your face. You look unhappy. How can I help?'

❖ Help children to make sense of what you want them to do.

❖ Try to ensure that children see you as someone who wants to help, who does not nag, who is warm and encouraging, and who does not stop what the children are doing by saying 'no' all the time. Be positive.

❖ Look at what the children are doing and find things in the room and outdoors that you think make a good fit with their interests and moods. Children who are constantly frustrated in what they do become angry children. Angry children are very challenging to work with.

EVERY CHILD NEEDS THE ONE-TO-ONE ATTENTION OF AN ADULT

If children do not receive individual attention they may begin to demand it. It is important to have a policy that every child and every parent should be greeted on arrival, and that goodbyes should also be said at the end of the day. This gives an important message that 'you matter to me'. In some families, bedtime stories or going to the shops give these experiences to the child. If children have access to the full attention of an adult they do not need to use attention-seeking behaviour. Every child matters, and every child needs to feel that they matter to people they love and who are important to them because they spend time with them.

Helping children to manage their feelings in their social relationships

LEARNING TO BE ASSERTIVE

Children who bully have low self-esteem. Name-calling and shouting insults are one kind of bullying. Children pick on weaker children or children who are different. For example, they tease or make racial, gender or disability insults. Physical hitting or menacing is another kind of bullying. Teaching children to be assertive helps to prevent bullying and the creation of victims.

How you can help to develop assertiveness

❖ Try not to use the words 'bully' or 'disruptive'. Instead, talk to children about learning to be assertive by being less timid or less aggressive. This creates a positive image of all children.

❖ Swearing can create similar problems to name-calling. Often it is simply the case that swearing is an everyday part of the child's language experience. However, it is quite a different thing when children swear in order to shock. Any child who swears needs help in:

1 learning which are the words they cannot use in the early years setting;

2 finding new words to replace the swear words (they still have to be able to express their thoughts and feelings);

3 building up their vocabulary so that they have wider choice of words.

Formal social relationships and role behaviour

As children experience and understand the culture and society in which they are growing up, they gradually learn how to relate to people in ways which are not about friendship, companionship, family or carers in the early years setting. These formal relationships occur, for example, when you buy something in a shop, go to the post office or thank someone for giving directions in the street. Such relationships do not develop and they do not last. They demand certain kinds of behaviour. It is not until adulthood that formal behaviour becomes totally stable (if then). Each society has rules which shape formal relationships and create role behaviour. For example, MPs in Parliament have to ask questions and speak in formal ways; they take on the role of an MP. Children learn how to answer the telephone and take messages; they are assuming the role of 'message taker'. When parents ask, 'Have they been good?', they are expressing a hope that their children are beginning to learn about formal social relationships. As children become more able to do this, they are described as socially skilled.

CHILDREN'S FEELINGS

Children live life to the full. This means that they have powerful feelings. They need adult help to learn to deal with the strength of their feelings. Feelings are hard to manage – even adults do not always succeed in dealing with how they feel. These strong feelings can quickly overwhelm the child. This can lead to:

❖ sobbing and sadness;

❖ temper tantrums that are full of anger and rage;

❖ jealousy that makes a child want to hit out;

❖ joy that makes a child literally jump and leap with a wildness that is unnerving to many adults.

The fears children develop

The fears children have are very real to them. Some (especially babies and toddlers) are afraid that their parent or carer might leave them. Some are afraid of loud noises like thunder, of heights (perhaps they do not like to come down from the climbing frame) or of sudden movements, such as a dog leaping up at them. Going to a strange place, like the clinic, might bring on feelings of fear, and many children are afraid of the dark.

Children's body language

Children need to express their feelings. They do so through:

❖ **physical actions:** like stamping with rage, screaming with terror, hitting out, jumping with joy or seeking a cuddle;

❖ **facial expression:** a pout tells the adult the child is not happy, compared with eyes that are shining with joy;

❖ **the position of the body:** playing alone with the doll's house or hovering on the edge of a cooking session might indicate that the child wants to join in but does not know how; playing boats right in the centre of a group of children tells an adult something quite different;

❖ **body movements:** children who keep twisting their fingers together are not at ease, compared with children who sit in a relaxed way.

Guidelines for dealing with children's fears

❖ Talking about fearful feelings and showing the child that you understand is important.

❖ Later on children can use imaginative play – for example in the home area, doll's house or toy garage – to face and deal with their fears and worries.

❖ Feeling jealous and anxious about the arrival of a new baby at home can be helped by allowing children to take out their aggressive feelings on a soft toy. This channels the aggression, giving the child permission to express their feelings.

❖ The traditional provision of the early childhood curriculum provides well for children's feelings to be expressed: for example, boisterous outdoor play, bashing lumps of clay, knocking down wooden blocks or working at the woodwork bench all allow children to channel their energies.

Putting feelings into words

It helps children to manage their feelings if they can put them into words. The child who can say, 'Stop hitting me! That hurts! I don't like it!' has found an appropriate way to deal with an unpleasant situation.

❖ The cries that babies make are early attempts to 'tell' others how they feel.

❖ Early on, children may shout a term of abuse in a difficult situation rather than using appropriate words. Adults need to decide whether this is a step forward along the way from physical hitting (via use of unacceptable language) to an appropriate expression of feelings in words.

❖ It takes time, experience and adult support for young children to learn how to express their feelings in words and to negotiate in dialogue with others. It can help to give them examples of rather staccato-sounding words, such as

'Stoppit!' so that they can take control of situations. Children learn the language of feelings through real situations that hold great meaning and that engage their whole attention.

Helping children under emotional stress

When children do not experience warm, loving relationships, they react differently according to their personality. They may:

❖ become aggressive;

❖ be very quiet, watchful and tense;

❖ begin bedwetting or soil themselves;

❖ find it difficult to eat;

❖ return to babyish ways – they may want a bottle again or a comforter; they might want to be held and cuddled, or carried about; they could want help with eating and dressing.

When children are under emotional stress, their behaviour can change quite quickly. It is important, therefore, that early years workers be alert to the changes listed above and that they respond sensitively, with understanding. If you suspect a problem of this kind it is important to talk with your line manager about your observations. The discussion will probably open up to the staff team and the parents. You will all look at the child's progress and agree what steps should be taken, depending on whether the situation is a temporary one for the child or one that is more likely to be long-term.

Guidelines for developing the social behaviour of children by helping them to understand their feelings and manage their emotions positively

❖ Children need to understand, express and deal with their feelings.

❖ They need to develop positive relationships with people.

❖ Children feel things deeply and they need a great deal of help in coming to terms with their emotions. Feelings are hard to deal with. It is important to remember that even adults do not succeed all the time in coping with how they feel.

❖ Helping children to express and deal with their feelings constructively and positively is probably one of the most important things an adult can do if children are to feel they matter, and are valued and respected.

❖ Remember to work as a team to decide together on what is unacceptable behaviour and how to deal with it. Many early years settings now have behaviour policies. These should always use positive images of the child as the starting point. Negative images, for example that of a bully, can be made positive through visualisation techniques: the bully becomes a child who needs help to become assertive without being aggressive. They need to emphasize the development of self-discipline by the child, rather than adults managing the behaviour for the child.

❖ It is important that adults working with young children be guided by each child's personality. What helps one child might not help another. Every child is different.

❖ Remember that all children need:

1 personal space;

2 one-to-one attention;

3 friends;

4 to feel part of the group;

5 to feel secure.

CHILDREN WHO EXPRESS THEMSELVES OR RELATE TO OTHERS IN PARTICULAR OR CHALLENGING WAYS

The shy or withdrawn child

Although it is important for every child to have their own personal space and to be allowed opportunities to do things alone, some children have difficulty socialising with other children or with adults. These children have too much personal space. There are a number of things that you can do to help a child overcome their shyness:

* **Making introductions:** when the adults are new to the child, you can introduce them. 'Michael, this is Jane. Jane wants to do a painting. Can you help her to get started? Can you tell her how to find the colours she wants?'

* **Being welcoming:** if a child is shy with adults it can be helpful to join the child with a warm smile, but to say nothing. You might find that a welcoming gesture, such as handing the child a lump of clay if they join the clay table, reassures them.

* **Observing children:** keeping good observations of children's social relationships is important. If a child who is normally outgoing and has the full range of social behaviour suddenly becomes quiet, withdrawn and solitary, this should be discussed with the team and parents should be included in the discussion. Outside, multi-professional help may be required if the problem cannot be solved within the team.

The over-demanding child

Having too much individual adult attention can lead to children being labelled as 'spoilt' or 'over-demanding'. This negative image of the child is not helpful. Some children, for example only children, are the main focus of their family and are given one-to-one attention by adults most of the time. They have not experienced waiting for things or taking turns. Is it the child's fault if he or she seems demanding of adult attention, insecure or ill at ease with other children? This child needs sensitive help to become involved in parallel, associative and cooperative social behaviour with other children. Some children gain attention by being dominant and demanding. These are the so-called bossy children. But this is another negative and unhelpful image. Such children need help in turn-taking and learning to give and take. They are usually afraid of losing control of situations; for example, in the play and home area, they may control the other children by saying what the storyline is going to be and by making the other children do as they say. These children need an adult to help them

---

Moving into free-flow play

Adults can help bossy children into the give and take of play, as the following example shows.

Adult: Did you say you had a dog in your story?

Child: Yes. I call it to come here.

Adult: But Jack says it is a horse. You could call the horse over. See what happens.

Child: Horsey, come here!

Adult: Ah, here comes the horse. Shall we stroke it?

to see that the 'story' will be better if other children's ideas are allowed in. It takes a bit of courage for the child to dare to let the play 'free-flow', because no one knows quite how the story will turn out. Once children experience this kind of free-flow play, however, they usually want more of it!

Sibling jealousy

When a new baby is born, it can be hard-going for a child who is used to having a lot of attention. Sibling jealousy often results in very demanding behaviour, which may last for some time, until the family adjusts to its new social relationships. Recent research shows that the older child needs to feel that they are being treated in exactly the same way as the new baby.

Children who own status possessions

Children in capitalist societies often have difficulties with possessions. From 2 years of age they may become eager to own objects. Owning possessions helps them to gain attention and enables them to control things. Children who have not experienced secure social relationships are often especially anxious to possess fashionable objects which carry high status, for example a special toy or particular clothes and shoes. The status accorded to these usually comes through advertising. Adults can help children to see that these objects are not vital for having friends and being part of the group. Children need to learn that friends like you because of who you are, and not because you own a fashionable hat. Sometimes children are so desperate to 'have' that they will steal. If such children cannot return an object on their own because this is too difficult for

them emotionally, they need to be helped to do so. Many children steal, but when a child does so regularly it is usually a sign that he or she is under stress. The child needs individual warmth, love and attention from an adult. Sometimes such children need the help of a specialist such as an educational psychologist.

Angry children

Hitting, kicking, spitting, biting, swearing and disrupting other children's activities are behaviours that children use to demand attention. But these behaviours all lead to negative images of a naughty or disruptive child. In order to help such children, adults need to clear their heads of negative images. This can be done by using a visualisation technique:

❖   Try to think of the child positively.

❖   Try to see *why* the child might be angry.

❖   Try to create a better atmosphere for all the children in the group.

Bored and frustrated children

The way the indoor and outdoor areas are set up may be causing boredom and frustration in the children, leading to challenging behaviour. Thus it is important to bear in mind that children need:

❖   a good choice of activities, and interesting people to be with;

❖   interesting and exciting things to do;

❖   new and challenging activities;

❖   comfortable and familiar things to do.

Dealing with temper tantrums

Temper tantrums can be:

❖ **noisy** – the child might hurl themselves about, perhaps hurting themselves, usually in rather a public way;

❖ **quiet** – the child holds their breath, and might even turn blue.

Positive images of children are vital

Children need positive images of themselves. Such positive messages come, in part, from the social behaviour of the staff in the early years setting. Discriminatory practice, by children or adults, that applies negative labels to children – even if these are not conveyed directly to the child – damages social and emotional development, and can result in difficult behaviour and poor development of social skills. There may be certain experiences in the child's life which are causing the anger and distress. Bad behaviour needs to be monitored carefully, reported to your supervisor and acted on by the team. Again, it may be necessary to involve outside help such as a social worker, educational psychologist, health visitor or GP.

SELF-IMAGE, SELF-ESTEEM AND WELLBEING

Children develop a sense of self (self-conceptual sense of identity) during the first year of life, and this becomes more stable as they develop socially. The way we feel about ourselves is called our self-image, and this is deeply influenced by how we think that others see us. If we feel loved, valued, appreciated and that we matter to people who matter to us, then our sense of well-being is high. Developing a positive self-image is about:

❖ realising you exist;

❖ developing self-esteem and good well-being;

❖ learning to like and respect yourself;

❖ knowing who you are;

❖ knowing and understanding yourself;

❖ developing skills of caring for and looking after yourself;

❖ feeling you are making a caring contribution to others.

Having strong attachments to people and learning about feelings helps babies to develop socially. Being loved and shown warm affection also helps babies to learn

Fig 9.2 Attachment is an important part of making positive relationships with people

socially. It is now thought that emotions cause chemical reactions which influence the development of the brain. Upset and fear bring corrosive cortisol, while wellbeing opens up the brain to learning and positive relationships, with feel-good chemicals. Neuroscientists are suggesting, for example, that a baby who is shouted at will not develop intellectually as much as a baby who is spoken to gently and lovingly.

It used to be thought that once children turned into mature adults this was the end point of social development. This is not true: we go on developing socially throughout our lives, from birth to death. The psychologist Erikson helped us to begin thinking about this with his 8 stages of social and emotional development, which go from birth to old age (see page 360). It is important for each of us to know ourselves, and to be able to respect and value ourselves. People who value and respect themselves have:

❖ a positive sense of self (self-concept)

❖ a positive self-image (feel valued and that they matter to others)

❖ good wellbeing (self-esteem).

From an early age children are aware of differences between them and others. This can be a positive or negative aspect of their lives. Many things influence our self-image, including:

❖ ethnicity;

❖ gender;

❖ language;

❖ particular and special needs;

❖ abuse;

❖ economic circumstances.

Every child needs to know that they matter. From a loving beginning, a child can face and cope with the emotions of life.

Name-calling and harassment can damage a child's self-image. It is important to help children to be self-aware in ways which bring positive comments about difference. Because young children are very interested in differences in physical appearance, they are also very aware of differences in skin colour or clothing. For example, Sam says to Susu, a refugee from Somalia, 'Why do you wear that hat?' The practitioner joins and says, 'Susu has come from Somalia with her family, and so her clothes are different. If you went to another country, your clothes would look different.' Sam replies, 'If I went to Somalia, what would I wear?' This positive conversation is helping Sam and Susu to gain knowledge of each other's cultural backgrounds, so that each develops positive images of different cultures and people. This makes a child feel they matter, that they belong and that they are valued.

When English is an additional language, it is important that the child's first language and home languages are valued (see Chapter 7 on languages).

The child who has special needs can also quickly lose a good self-image. Children who use a wheelchair, wear glasses, use a hearing aid, walk differently or think differently, such as a child with a learning difficulty, would all need to be supported so that they develop a good self-image. Other children also need support to understand how and why children are different, and what this involves. They need to understand that when everyone makes it a priority to learn how to help each other and be well-informed, the whole community gains and everyone in it can then make a strong and positive contribution.

Because of the embarrassment and ignorance of many people, children with a disability have to come to terms not only with their disability, but also with the way people react to it. It is very important that children meet a wide range of people so that this kind of 'stranger fear' gradually disappears from society. This will make it easier for every child to develop a positive self-image with good wellbeing. Wellbeing does not mean being in a constant state of happiness. It brings a state of mind which is positive and forward-looking.

Every Child Matters emphasises the importance of economic background. Of course, making poverty history is a huge challenge for governments and needs large-scale action, but the small-scale aspects matter too. It is important not to charge for extra visits, outings and resources, and to be sensitive to the fact that families may not be able to afford to contribute.

Children who experience different kinds of abuse are very vulnerable in relation to the development of self-image. Poor self-image is associated with emotional, intellectual, physical and sexual abuse. It is especially important to show a child they are valued and appreciated as a unique person.

Boys and girls are different, and research is beginning to help our understanding of the gender aspects of brain development. Boys often prefer non-fiction books (about fish, trains or dinosaurs, for example) to fiction. They often develop spatial concepts earlier than girls. Girls tend to start enjoying reading at an earlier age than boys, which is why attention is now being paid to helping boys enjoy reading. If boys are always expected to read from storybooks and never encouraged to share books about nature or other facts with others, they lose confidence and interest in books.

Principles of equality and inclusivity help early years workers to encourage a good self-concept in young children. The same is true of very young babies and children. Very young babies, when they begin to move about, will keep looking at the adult who is caring for them. Babies need to see adults' reactions and to seek their approval. This is called **social referencing**.

Babies have individual personalities and need to settle into their particular family and its way of life. In the same way, the family learns about this new person who has come to live with them. There will be huge adjustments on all sides.

The way children feel about themselves and their bodies (how comfortable you feel in your body is part of your sense of self, and is called **embodiment**) is also linked to self-image. This develops in children as they feel unconditionally valued, respected and that they are of worth.

The role of adults in promoting a positive self-image and sense of wellbeing in children

❖ Value children for *who they are*, not what they do or how they look.

❖ A child needs love, security and a feeling of trust. There is no one way to give these feelings to children. It will depend on where children live, their family and culture. There is no standard family. There is no standard institution. There is no one best way to love children and give them self-esteem.

❖ People who give children positive images about themselves (in terms of skin colour, language, gender, disability, features, culture and economic background) help children to develop good self-esteem. Look at the book area and the displays on the walls in your setting. Are you giving positive messages?

❖ Visitors to the nursery can provide positive images. The people children meet occasionally or on a daily basis will all have a strong influence on them. If children almost never see men working in early years settings or women mending pieces of equipment, they form very narrow ideas about who they might become. Books, pictures, outings and visitors can all offer positive images which extend children's ideas of who they might be.

❖ Adults who are positive role models help a child's self-esteem. However, adults need to have a positive self-concept; a depressed, self-doubting adult will not be a really good role model for a child.

❖ Children need to feel some success in what they set out to do. This means that adults must avoid having unrealistic expectations of what children can manage, for example dressing, eating or going to the lavatory. It is important to

appreciate the efforts that children make. They do not have to produce perfect results. The effort is more important than the result.

❖ Adults help children's self-esteem if they are encouraging. When children make mistakes, do not tell them they are silly or stupid. Instead say something like, 'Never mind, let's pick up the pieces and sweep them into the bin. Next time, if you hold it with two hands it will be easier to work with.'

❖ Children need to feel they have some choices in their lives. Obviously, safety and consideration for others are important, but it is usually possible to allow children to make some decisions.

❖ Children need clear, consistent boundaries or they become confused. When they are confused they begin to test out the boundaries to see what is consistent about them.

❖ Children need consistent care from people they know. Many early years settings have now introduced a key worker or family worker system, which provides continuity.

❖ Children need to have a feeling of trust that their basic needs for food, rest and shelter will be met. Rigid rituals are not helpful, but days do need a shape or routine. This will give children a predictable environment. They will have the know-how to help in setting the table, for example, or washing their hands after going to the lavatory.

❖ Children and their families need first to be given respect in order that they can then develop self-respect. So children, parents and staff need to speak politely and respectfully to each other.

❖ Children have strong and deep feelings. They need help, support and care from adults.

THE EFFECTS ON CHILDREN OF ATTACHMENT, SEPARATION AND LOSS

Separation of children from primary carers

D.W. Winnicott (1896–1971) was involved with children at the Tavistock Clinic. His work has helped early years workers to be sensitive to how children feel when they separate from those they live with and love. Winnicott taught us to see the importance of the teddy bears and other comforters that children seem to need to carry about with them. He called these transitional objects. He believed that children need such objects to help them through the times when they begin to realise that they are a separate person. The teddy might stand for the mother when she leaves the baby in the cot; it is a symbol of the mother who will return. It helps children through being alone or feeling sad. Naturally, the child might enjoy the teddy's company more when the mother is there. This reinforces the value of the teddy as a transitional object when the mother is absent.

Many adults still use transitional objects when they first leave home or when their partner goes away. It is not only children who have to deal with feelings of being separated from someone they love. Until recently children were not allowed to take teddy bears into hospital in case they carried germs. In some early years settings, transitional toys are still taken away from children when they arrive, in case they get lost. Adults working in early years settings need to discuss this as a team and plan a policy which takes care of the deep feelings that children have about their transitional objects. Some children have imaginary friends. These are another kind of transitional object, but they are imaginary rather than real. Children may use other early comfort behaviour, such as sucking, stroking or smelling. These do not have an imaginative dimension as in the case of a transitional object or an imaginary friend, but they are important ways in which children cope with transitions and separation. Children usually grow out of this behaviour quite naturally, and it is best to let this happen in its own time.

Case Study

Tracey's imaginary dog
Tracey, 4 years, pretended that she had a dog. On holiday in the summer, she led the dog about wherever she went, feeding and stroking it. The dog helped her to get ready in her mind for starting at school after the holiday. It helped her to think about separating from her parents for a whole day, instead of just the half-day she spent at her nursery.

Bowlby's theory of attachment, separation, loss and grief

John Bowlby (1907–1990) looked at:

- how babies become attached to the mother figure (**attachment**);
- what happens when babies are separated from the mother figure (**separation**);
- what happens when babies experience **loss** and grief when separated from the people they feel close to.

Babies and the people who care for them usually form close bonds. As the baby is fed, held and enjoyed, these emotional, loving relationships develop and deepen. Babies who find that adults respond quickly to their cries become trusting of life and are well-attached in stable, warm relationships. They know that they will be fed, changed when soiled, comforted when teething, and so on.

Babies and parents who, for one reason or another, do not make close emotional bonds experience general difficulty in forming stable, warm and loving relationships.

Mary Ainsworth, who worked with Bowlby, found that if adults responded quickly to a baby's cries, the child, by 3 years of age, was less demanding than those babies who had generally been left to cry. The individual temperament of a baby becomes obvious very early on and has an effect on the carers. For instance, some babies become hysterical very quickly when hungry, while others have a calmer nature. Bonding is partly about adults and babies adjusting to each other and understanding each other – learning how to read each other's signals. Bowlby thought that early attachment was very important – that the relationship between the mother figure and the baby was the most important. This was because mothers tended to be at home with their babies. He did not believe that the most important attachment figure should be the natural mother, but he did say that babies need one central person, or a mother figure. It is now realised that babies can have deep relationships with several people – mother, father, brothers, sisters, carers and grandparents. Indeed, babies develop in an emotionally and socially healthy way only if they bond with several different people. In many parts of the world, and in many cultures, this is usual.

Babies might enjoy playing with one person and having meals with another. It is the quality of the time the child spends with people which determines whether or not the child becomes attached to them. Attachment can be difficult at first, especially in cases

where it is hard for the adult and child to communicate. For example, if:

❖ the birth has caused mother and baby to be separated and the mother is depressed;

❖ the child is visually impaired and eye contact is absent;

❖ the child is hearing-impaired and does not turn to the parent's voice; eye contact is also harder to establish here because the child does not turn to the parent's face when he or she speaks;

❖ the child has severe learning difficulties and needs many experiences of a person before bonding can become stable.

Bowlby's work was important because it led to the introduction of key worker systems in institutions. (This will be looked at in more detail later in the chapter, page 351.) Children no longer had a series of different nurses looking after them as each work shift changed. They were placed in smaller 'family' groups and were consistently looked after by the same team of staff. Furthermore, increasing numbers of children began to be fostered in family homes rather than placed in large institutions. This helped children to form good attachments with a limited number of people who cared for them. Children could develop warm, physical, loving relationships, and found it easier to communicate with their carers. By 5 or 6 months, many babies are so closely attached to the people they know and love that they show separation anxiety when they are taken away from these attachment figures. When a baby is handed from the parent figure to a new carer, it is best if the new carer:

❖ approaches slowly;

❖ talks gently before taking the baby from the parent;

holds the baby so that he or she can look at the parent during the handover.

Researchers have found that toddlers will happily explore toys and play with them if an attachment figure (usually their parent) is present. If the parent goes out of the room, however, young children quickly become anxious, and stop exploring and playing. They need the reassurance of someone they know to be able to explore, play and learn. Children who have had many separations from those with whom they have tried to bond find it very difficult to understand social situations and relationships. The extract below, 'A truly unethical experiment', was reported in *Dagens Nyheter*, a Stockholm newspaper, in 1990. These babies may have died because they were not able to learn the important signals that people give to each other when they are together. When young children's social signals for help and attention are ignored they:

* become frustrated;
* do not learn how to ask for help or attention or indeed how to give help in the usual ways;
* do not understand the social conventions that adults and children expect to use when they get together in a group.

Bear in mind that it is not helpful to concentrate on what children in this kind of difficulty *cannot* do. It is helpful to begin with what they can do. There is a famous series of films by James and Joyce Robertson which show Bowlby's theory of loss and grief in action. Children who were hospitalised and separated from their families went through various stages in their loss and grief:

1 **They protested:** they were angry, cried out and tried to resist the change.

2 **They despaired:** they acted as if they were numb to any feelings or interest in life.

3 **They became detached:** they related poorly to people, although they began to join in with their new situation.

We now know that children (and adults) move in and out of these stages, and that the stages do not occur in any strict order. Bowlby's findings have led to important work on how best to deal with the hospitalisation of children. His work has also helped early years workers to settle children into nurseries using positive strategies, and has led to the establishment of an organisation to help parents understand why their children become detached in their relationships after being sent to boarding preparatory schools at 6 or 7 years.

A truly unethical experiment

The thirteenth-century historian, Sallimbeni of Parma, Italy, reports that Emperor Fredrik II of the Holy Roman Empire conducted an experiment to find out man's original language. He gathered a number of babies and employed wet nurses to care physically for the children, but they were strictly forbidden to talk, cuddle or sing to the babies.

By not having any human contact, these children were supposed to develop as naturally as possible. The Emperor never found out about man's original language – the children died one after another without any apparent reason.

Examples of separation

Sometimes separations are temporary, but sometimes they are permanent:

* A mother goes to hospital to have a new baby and the child stays with people he does not know well.

* A child is taken into care and experiences a series of caregivers.

* A family is split up in a war zone and perhaps never find each other again.

* A family become refugees and they are split up.

* One parent no longer sees the child, perhaps as a result of divorce.

* A parent is in hospital and is unable to see the child, for example after a serious accident or through clinical depression.

* A loved one is sent to prison.

* A loved one goes abroad.

* A loved one dies.

The separation process involves working through feelings of:

* disbelief and numbness;

* shock and panic;

* despair and yearning for the lost person;

* anger;

* interest in life – it takes time to reach this stage.

There are several far-reaching consequences of Bowlby's work:

* These days babies and mothers usually stay together on maternity wards.

* Often parents can stay in hospital with their children: there may be a bed for a parent next to the child's bed.

* Social workers are more careful about separating children and parents when families experience difficulties.

* There is more awareness of the seriousness of the situation of many asylum seekers and refugees, and understanding of the need for more positive action to be taken.

* Most early years settings now have policies on how to settle children so as to make it a positive experience.

TRANSITION FROM THE HOME ENVIRONMENT TO OTHER SETTINGS

It is important that times of transition are as positive as possible for both the individual child and the family as a whole. Transitions can be painful, and some of the separations in the list of examples could never be happy experiences for children or those who love them and whom they love. However, it is always possible to ease the impact of difficult separations through thoughtful, sensitive support. But this needs to be well-thought-out and organised.

The first meeting with the family

This might be when the family visits the early childhood setting or it might be through a home visit. It is important that parents do not feel forced into accepting a home visit from staff. Often home visits are welcomed by families as an opportunity to get to know the early years worker. A home visit, or a visit to the setting before the child starts there, gives staff the chance to find out what the parents are expecting from the setting. See Chapter 16 for more details about working in a close partnership with parents or carers.

All this helps parents and children to make the transition from being at home to starting in a group setting. Childminders and nannies often make photograph albums with short captions in the same spirit.

Parents and children often appreciate having a booklet of their own to keep, and this can build into a record of the child's time with the setting, childminder or nanny, and often helps a child to make future transitions.

When settling a child and family, transitions are made easier if there is sensitivity about the way you use gesture and body language, such as eye contact. The photographs in the brochure can be invaluable when staff and family do not share the same language.

Settling children into the setting

Probably the most important thing an early years worker does is to settle a child into an early years group, in partnership with the parent(s). Many settings have a very clear policy on admissions and settling–in. This is discussed in greater detail in Chapter 16, Working with Parents.

Supporting times of transition

* Remember that if the parent is anxious about leaving their child, the child will be anxious about being separated from the parent. Make sure that each adult and child is welcomed. Put notices in the languages of the community as well as in English.
* A noticeboard with photographs of staff and their role helps people to feel part of things.
* An attractive display of some of the recent experiences children have gained helps people to tune in to the setting's way of working.
* A notice with the menu for the week gives valuable information to parents/carers.
* Something for children to do is vital; watching fish in a fish tank or having a turn on a rocking-horse are popular examples.

Typical points of transition for children are:

* The first time parents leave their baby with a relative or friend after birth.
* If the baby/toddler/young child starts attending a group setting regularly.
* When the child begins school (in England this is at the end of the Foundation Stage; in Scotland it is when entering Primary 1, and so on).
* When leaving infant school years (England – Key Stage 1) to enter the junior school years.

What went before?

Whenever there is a transitional point for a child and family, it is important to look at what went before. This is so that we can learn about and tune in to the child, and support them and make as seamless a transition as possible. There should be continuity, not discontinuity of experience for the child and family.

This means that every practitioner working with children in the birth-to-7-years range should know what comes before and what comes after the time the child will spend with them.

For example, an English practitioner will need to know about:

* Early Years Foundation Stage;
* *Birth to Three Matters*;
* *Curriculum Guidance for the Foundation Stage*;
* Key Stage 1.

The DfES has developed a mainstream training package for the transition between the Foundation Stage and Key Stage 1, called *Continuing the Learning Journey*.

Always focus on the child's wellbeing.

STRATEGIES TO ENABLE CHILDREN AND FAMILIES TO COPE WITH CHANGE AND SEPARATION

Being separated from our loved ones is difficult at any age, and a kind of bereavement is experienced, similar in some ways to that when someone loved dies. In situations when children are repeatedly separated from their families, through home circumstances or war and conflict, it helps when those the child is left with understand the elements discussed in this chapter, so that vulnerable children feel a sense of belonging and wellbeing, and feelings of being valued, loved and respected.

It is also important to remember that Anna Freud, working with children who had experienced the Holocaust, found that their friendships with each other were very important, and so was having a normal childhood with opportunities for sensitively supported play. Play seemed to have a self-healing power.

The key person

In many settings there is a system of a key person for the child. The important thing is that there are opportunities for warm, intimate relationships between practitioners and babies and young children spending time together. For this to be possible, children need constant and stable people, and to be in very small groups. Then there are opportunities to listen to children and tune in to them. Whether or not there is an allocated key person, it is this approach of respecting the child as unique, with emotional need for warm, affectionate relationships and feeling valued, which forms the crucial elements.

Some families will have a lead professional working with them to ensure that there is more joined-up thinking and that different professionals link with each other. This has developed through the Children Act 2004 and the embedding of the *Every Child Matters* agenda. It will also be an important way of reducing inequality, which becomes a local authority duty under the Childcare Act 2006.

Supporting parents

Parents who have experienced war and conflict are often anxious about leaving their children with those outside the family. They appreciate:

* having their youngest children in the next room while they learn English and learn about life in England;
* their older children being near them in school in the same building;
* all their children joining them at the end of the session, to try out a story they have learnt, using props (e.g. Goldilocks and the Three Bears);
* meeting other parents who have experienced war, conflict and trauma;
* meeting practitioners who help them and their children to develop and learn and who care for their emotional wellbeing.

ACTIVITY: INVESTIGATING EMOTIONAL AND SOCIAL ASPECTS OF DEVELOPMENT

1 Think about getting up in the morning. Choose a cultural tool – an alarm clock, telephone or a spoon – and discuss with a friend how you think it has influenced your behaviour in your culture, and how you in turn have influenced the culture you live in by using that cultural tool.

2 Plan ways to find out about the friendships young children develop. Observe a group of children aged 3–4 years playing together. Who is friends with whom? Look again a few weeks later at the same children. Are they still friends? Evaluate your observations.

3 Research the role of a key worker or family worker. Make a list of pros and cons of using a key worker or family worker. Discuss this with the group.

4 What are three important things about theories which support: (a) nurture, (b) nature, (c) nature and nurture?

10
Understanding the behaviour of children

Contents

MANAGING BEHAVIOUR (OR DEVELOPING SELF-DISCIPLINE)

There are two ways of looking at the behaviour of children:

❖ When we try to manage the child's behaviour, we work from the outside in. We try to control how the child behaves, using a variety of techniques. But what will happen when we are not there?

❖ When we give children strategies to develop their own self-discipline, we work from the inside out. We try to help the child to manage their own behaviour; this is called self-discipline. But what will happen when we are not there?

Research shows that self-discipline is the only kind of discipline worth having if we want behaviour to be lastingly good for the child, and for us as a society. When Judge Tumin, who died recently, was the Chief Inspector of Prisons, he found that the predominantly male prisoners (18–25 years)

had low self-esteem and no self-discipline. They were dependent on others to manage their behaviour.

OFFERING ALTERNATIVE DISTRACTIONS TO CHILDREN

Sometimes an adult can see trouble looming and can avoid a confrontation by offering an alternative. Alternatives are better than confrontations, which often result in temper tantrums and more challenging behaviour.

BEING A ROLE MODEL

Remember that children notice and learn from your feelings, actions and reactions. You are a powerful source of learning for the child. So you should:

❖ give children a predictable environment (but not necessarily a rigid routine);

❖ try to avoid confrontations or humiliation by respecting a child's personality and mood, and knowing what the child can manage without too much struggle;

❖ explain that there is a real boundary if a confrontation becomes unavoidable – a boundary that a child cannot cross.

BEHAVIOUR MANAGEMENT STRATEGIES WHICH ENCOURAGE SELF-DISCIPLINE

Young children often do not realise that they are doing something unacceptable. They need help to begin to understand when something is inappropriate.

Froebel believed that every bad act has a good intention. He thought that adults should try to find out what this intention was, and help the child by acknowledging it. Then, he believed, it is easier to put right the 'bad' that the child has done. When children do things that we do not want them to do, it is easy to feel annoyed and impatient. However, thinking positively and keeping a sense of humour enable us to remain professional with children who challenge our patience and stamina. There are four main approaches to the management of behaviour (the fourth type is most appropriate to your work and you should always use it in preference to the other strategies):

1   Using punishment as revenge;

2   Behaviour modification;

3   Time out;

4   Focusing on reform.

Using punishment as revenge

This *unacceptable* and *unethical* approach can be summed up in the statement, 'An eye for an eye, a tooth for a tooth.' This means that what you do to me, I will do to you; if you hit me, I will hit you. In many countries, such as Sweden, it is now illegal to smack, beat or 'strap' a child. In the UK it is illegal in early years settings. Children who are smacked often hit other children, usually younger and smaller children. They are imitating the fact that big adults smack small children. Children do not understand punishment as revenge – as well as being a cruel strategy, it simply does not work.

Behaviour modification

This strategy takes two forms,

❖ **negative reinforcement** (see Chapter 9);

❖ **positive reinforcement**.

Adults can also encourage children to do what they want them to do by giving them rewards. However, the strategy only works in the short term, and the effect wears off quite quickly. The problem is that rewards do not make children think about why they want to do things. Any motivation is short-lived.

Case Study

Using rewards may not be effective
Marion Dowling gives this example:

. . . in one study in a nursery school, a group of children were provided with drawing materials and told that they would receive a prize for drawing which, in due course, they did. Another group were given the same materials but with no mention of prizes. Some time after, drawing was provided as one of a range of optional activities . . . significantly, the children who chose to spend the least time on drawing were those who had been previously rewarded.

Time out

The adult might say to the child, 'If you scribble on the books again, you will have to sit on the time-out chair for a few minutes.' This might put the child off scribbling in books, but in a different situation, for instance when staying at grandma's, it will not prevent the child scribbling on the wall of the bedroom. Children can only make the obvious connection and may not be able to extend what they have learned to a different context. Vivian Gussin-Paley has written a book about the limitations of the time-out chair; the book is *Wally's Stones*. In a similar way, it is not helpful to punish children some time after the event. They do not connect what they did earlier with what is being done to them now.

Always remember, it is a mistake to make children do a drawing or look at a book as a punishment because this will give the message that these are unpleasant activities.

Focusing on reform

Research shows that from about 3 years children begin to feel guilt and shame about the things they do. However, they cannot learn about social behaviour if they cannot make sense of what is done to them. That is why a focus on reform rather than on revenge or deterrent is effective in the long term. In the section below strategies are given which encourage reform and the development of self-discipline.

CONTAINMENT AND HOLDING

It is important not to leave a child in the middle of a tantrum. Quietly holding them and being there for them provides support through this time until they begin to feel calm. Psychologists refer to this as **containment**. Containing a child's feelings with gentle and calm physical support helps the child to feel cared for. It also reassures the child that they will not be left alone to lose control. It is important that children have a good relationship with adults who hold their feelings of anger for them in this way. The adult acts as a 'container' which holds the child's anger in a safe way so that the child does not feel out of control. This helps the child to regain a sense of calm. It is no good trying to discuss what has happened with a child who is in the middle of a temper tantrum or who is being aggressive. The child needs to become calm before talking.

PREVENTING AGGRESSIVE BEHAVIOUR

Aggressive behaviour (hitting, shouting or spoiling another child's painting, for example) can sometimes be prevented if adults put on their running shoes! The adult must get there before the behaviour happens, gently saying 'no' and removing the child. This can be a very useful strategy, particularly with children under 3 years.

DISCUSSING THE SITUATION

Eye contact is very important in your dealings with children. So are your body language and the gestures you use. These can be more important than what you say. Communication is 85 per cent non-verbal.

CHALLENGING BEHAVIOUR IN A GROUP SITUATION

Disruptive behaviour in a group is best dealt with by not giving the challenging child attention: concentrate instead on all the other children who are not being disruptive. You might say: 'I can see most of you are ready for the story. You have all found your cushions and are sitting there looking really interested. I am so looking forward to reading this story because it is one of my favourites.'

Being ignored is not what an attention seeker hopes for. Children are helped if they realise that they gain positive and warm attention from you if they are cooperative.

SETTING CLEAR BOUNDARIES

Children need clear, consistent boundaries in order to manage their own behaviour. They will test out boundaries that are not clear or consistent: they will check to see if a boundary is still there; to see if it can be moved; whether all the adults will uphold a particular boundary. This can become very tedious from the adult's point of view! It is best to have just a few boundaries, agreed to by everyone in the team – and agreed by the children, if at all possible. It helps children to feel secure when a boundary is strong, clear and comforting – 4-year-olds often say with great satisfaction, 'You're not allowed!' When a child oversteps a boundary, it is important that they are not made to feel worthless or disliked for what they have done. This can be avoided if the child's actions are criticised, rather the child themselves. For example say, 'Kicking hurts. Jo is very upset because it hurt,' rather than, 'Don't do that. You are very naughty, and I am cross with you.' The message needs to be: I am not rejecting you; I am rejecting what you did.

OPPORTUNITIES FOR MOVEMENT

Often children simply need opportunities for play involving extensive physical movement. This is becoming increasingly important now that more children spend time in extended provision. Children who do not spend time on the floor, spinning and tilting, and climbing and jumping often develop behaviour problems, and even a mild form of ADHD, which has been socially induced because they are required to sit and be still too much.

THEORIES OF EMOTIONAL AND SOCIAL DEVELOPMENT

The nature–nurture controversy

NATURE AND INHERITANCE

In the past it was thought that personalities are fixed from the moment we are born (this is the nature argument). It is probably too extreme a view, just as the view that intelligence is fixed at birth is extreme. Children who have grown up without other people do not seem to show the kind of social behaviour we think of as human; they do not make human sounds, smile, use eye contact or walk like humans. This suggests that their social behaviour is not simply fixed in their genes and inherited. Such children include:

❖ feral children, sometimes known as 'wolf children';

❖ children who are kept isolated from other people.

The nature approach includes the psychodynamic theories of Freud, Erikson, Winnicott and Bowlby, which concentrate on the feelings we have inside us, and on how other people can help us to **express and deal with** these. These theorists believe that our early feelings and experiences never leave us. They are always deep inside us and they affect us throughout our lives.

SOCIAL BEHAVIOUR AS A RESULT OF NURTURE

Nurture theories include:

❖ Skinner's behaviourist theory;

❖ socialisation theory;

❖ Bandura's social learning theory.

These theories, which state that social behaviour is learned, have been challenged since the 1980s.

Case Study

Jody hits Amandip

The adult says, 'Amandip is crying because that hurt. He is very upset. What happened? He took your toy? Did you take Jody's toy, Amandip?' [Amandip nods]
'Next time, Jody, try saying "It's mine." Then he will know how you feel about it.'

This approach signals to Amandip that he must not snatch Jody's toy, but it also allows him to find a way out with dignity.

Furthermore, it gives Jody the words that she needs to use instead of hitting. It rejects what both children did, but it does not reject either child. It helps both children to have some ideas of how they might tackle the situation next time. This is punishment as reform, and it will help the children to think about moral matters and to develop self-discipline. It helps children to examine the results of what they do.

Fig 10.1 When children are bored they behave badly. Here the adult is providing interesting experiences and supporting the baby in the choice she has made so that she does not become frustrated

Guidelines for managing children's behaviour

❖ Can you distract the child? If a child keeps grabbing the paint pot from another child, ask the first child to help you mix more pots of paint. This distracts the child and takes you both out of a negative situation.

❖ Does the child need personal space? Sometimes children cannot share or be with other children for too long. They need to do their own thing. Respect this and help the child to move into a solitary activity.

❖ Does the child need help to express and talk about how they feel? Opportunities for role play or to bash and bang a lump of clay can be very helpful in this situation.

❖ Does the child need help with a side-by-side strategy?

❖ Should two children be left together? They may have been together too long, or perhaps their personalities are clashing and they find it hard to spend time together. When this happens it is usually best to find a way of separating the children.

❖ Can you help children to negotiate? (Remember, they may be too angry or upset to do this.)

❖ Sometimes children's feelings just erupt. They can be a danger to themselves or to other children. It is always best if children can be helped before this point is reached, but sometimes the eruption of feelings is unavoidable. Children can be very frightened by the power of their feelings and may be overwhelmed if they lose control. They need you to contain their anger and feelings for them.

❖ Are the children bored? Are the room and outdoor area interesting enough places? Are the children free to choose activities for themselves?

❖ Is the child hungry? Hunger can make us all crabby.

❖ Is there any physical reason for the behaviour? Does the child lack pain sensation in some aspects, and is the child clumsy?

❖ Is the child tired or uncomfortable? If so, try to find out why. (Maybe they have wet themselves.)

❖ Do they need rough-and-tumble play? Children need safe movement spaces where they can be noisy and move about freely, both indoors and outdoors.

❖ Do they need to slow down? Children need calmer periods where they have personal space, perhaps making a little den for themselves, reading alone in the book area or having a story read by an adult.

❖ Can you redirect the situation? Sometimes you will see something building up and may be able to prevent the situation arising by moving in before it happens.

❖ Do you value children's efforts and express your feelings? Children are able to tidy up with adult help, but they need their efforts to be recognised and warmly appreciated.

❖ Do the children have enough opportunities to play? Indoors and outdoors?

❖ Do you know about the child's background? It is important to remember that what is positive behaviour in one culture might be interpreted differently in another. For example, owning possessions and learning to respect other people's possessions might be valued in one family culture or society more than in another.

❖ Are you taking a flexible view? Showing initiative and negotiating might be valued in some situations, but conformity might be more important in others, such as crossing the road.

❖ Remember that behaviour which is valued universally in the world has to do with helping others, having feelings for others, sharing and taking turns, and understanding somebody else's feelings and ideas.

Fig 10.2 Listening to children and respecting their ideas and feelings are important

Nature and nurture theories

Theories which involve both nature and nurture include:

❖ The social **constructivist theories** of Trevarthen, Dunn and Vygotsky. According to this approach, children and adults are constantly adjusting to each other and learning from each other.

❖ Dawkins's **social evolution theory**, which concentrates on the whole

human race and does not look at individuals at all.

❖ **Brain studies**. Colin Blakemore, a neuroscientist at Oxford University, says that nurture shapes nature. The experiences we have with people and objects quite literally change the physical chemistry of our brains. For example, children who are exposed to music from an early age develop more auditory cortex than most people.

Psychodynamic theories

SIGMUND FREUD (1856–1939)

Freud is the founder of psychoanalytic theory. He believed that:

❖ our unconscious feelings direct the way we behave; we are not aware of these feelings, and this means that we often do not know why we behave as we do in a particular situation;

❖ our earliest childhood experiences deeply influence what we believe and how we feel as adults;

❖ people go through psychosexual stages of development which he called oral, anal, phallic, latency and genital stages;

❖ he could help the people he psychoanalysed to understand their behaviour and feelings, and even to change.

Freud thought that people have:

- an **id:** which makes 'want' demands;
- an **ego:** which tries to resolve conflicts between the id and the superego;
- a **superego:** which conveys the demands made by parents or society about how to behave.

ERIK H. ERIKSON (1902–1994)

Erikson took Sigmund Freud's work as the rock on which he based his own personality theory. He was also a pupil of Anna Freud, Sigmund's daughter. Erikson concentrated on the superego and on the influence of society on a child's development. He showed how, when we meet a personal crisis or have to deal with a crisis in the world (for example, living through a war), we are naturally equipped to face the difficulties and to deal with them. Erikson thought that there were eight developmental phases during a person's life (five during childhood and three during adulthood). He said that during each phase we have to face and sort out the particular kinds of problem that occur during that phase.

In the days before equal opportunities, Erikson called his developmental stages the eight phases of Man. It is important to bear in mind that theories evolving from Freud's ideas are based on white, middle-class patients in Western Europe. The theories need to be used carefully for that reason. However, they still seem to be useful in many of Erikson's eight developmental phases.

- **Phase 1: babyhood.** We have to sort out whether we feel a basic sense of trust or mistrust in life. This phase is about being a hopeful person or not.
- **Phase 2: the toddler and nursery years.** We develop either a basic sense of being able to do things ourselves (autonomy) or a basic sense of doubt in ourselves, leading to shame. This phase is about our self-identity.

- **Phase 3: the infant school years.** We either take the initiative and go for it or we feel guilty and hold back in case we upset people. This phase is about leading an active life with a sense of purpose, or not.
- **Phase 4: the junior years.** We either begin to be determined to master things or we do not try hard in case we cannot manage something. This phase is about becoming skilled.
- **Phase 5: adolescence.** We either begin to be at one with ourselves or we feel uncertain and unsure. We learn to have faith in ourselves, or not.
- **Phase 6: young adults.** We begin to have a sense of taking part in our society and of taking responsibility in it as a shared venture, or we think only of ourselves and become isolated.
- **Phase 7: middle age.** We begin to be caring of the next generation and the future of our society, or we reject the challenge.
- **Phase 8: old age.** We return to our roots and overcome feelings of despair, disgust about new lifestyles or fear of death, or not. This is Erikson's phase of wisdom.

THE CHILD'S CONCEPT OF DEATH

People say different things when someone dies. For example, they may tell children that the person has:

- gone to heaven;
- gone to sleep;

❖ gone away;

❖ turned into earth.

Children can become very confused. They get frightened that they will be taken away to this place called heaven, or that if they go to sleep they might not wake up. Children need honest and straightforward explanations of death which make it clear that the person will not come back, and that it is not their fault that the person died.

Guidelines for helping children to grieve

❖ Explain things. Say that someone is terminally ill, that parents are divorcing or that a person is going to prison. Children need to be told of the reality of the situation.

❖ Make sure the child does not feel responsible for what has happened.

❖ Do not exclude the child – let them be part of the family. If someone has died, let the child go to the funeral or visit the grave and share the sadness.

❖ Be especially warm and loving; cuddle the child, be calm and quietly be there for them.

❖ Give the child reassurance that it is okay to feel grief; help the child to know that, although these feelings will last for a long time, they are normal. Tell them that the pain will ease over time.

❖ Find photographs and evoke memories.

❖ Some children are helped by play therapy, but ordinary childhood play heals most children.

Be prepared for the child to regress; do not demand too much of the child. When the child begins to show an interest in things once more, gently encourage them.

Children need to grieve, just as adults do. If they are not helped to grieve, they may experience mental ill health later on in adult life. If they are helped, however, they will experience positive relationships with other people and come to terms with their loss in a positive way.

BEHAVIOURIST THEORY

Until the mid-1980s this theory had a great influence. It suggested that adults regulated children's behaviour. Skinner thought that adults shape children's behaviour, so that children conform to the expectations and conventions of the culture in which they grow up. Skinner believed that children could be positively or negatively reinforced so as to behave in the ways adults wanted (see examples of positive and negative reinforcement on page 000). Adults often give children rewards (sweets, badges, stars, smiley faces, verbal praise) for good behaviour. 'Good' behaviour in this context means behaviour that adults want to see. 'Good' behaviour in one culture might be bad behaviour in another. For example, in some cultures it is considered rude for a child to look an adult in the eye when being reprimanded, but it is very rude not to do so in other cultures. It is important for adults working with young children to decide whether or not they believe in extrinsic rewards – for example, stars for good behaviour. Research suggests that this approach can quickly bring successful results, but that these are short-lived. It is probably more successful in the long term if children do something because they realise its benefits, for example sitting quietly ready for a story because they know they will enjoy listening to it. This is called intrinsic motivation, and it helps children to become self-disciplined.

SOCIALISATION THEORY

Socialisation is the process by which children learn the expected behaviour for their culture and society. The theory of socialisation, which developed out of behaviourist theory, found favour between the 1960s and 1980s. According to this theory, children learn the rules of the society they live in, which vary from society to society and from culture to culture. Being socialised in certain cultures can mean that children learn about things that we should consider unacceptable, for example the denying of human rights to blacks in South Africa under the regime of apartheid. There are two levels associated with this theory:

Primary socialisation theory: this is about the way the family and those close to the child help the child's social development. The child learns to behave as part of the family, adapting to its social ways.

Secondary socialisation theory: the child's social circle begins to widen to include neighbours, perhaps an early childhood group and society at large. The influences on social development thus become broader.

SOCIAL LEARNING THEORY

This emphasises that young children learn about social behaviour by:

* watching other people;
* imitating other people.

Albert Bandura found that children tend to imitate people in their lives who they believe hold status, especially if those people are warm or powerful personalities. This research study did not replicate a natural situation for the children, but it does suggest that adults can be very influential on a child's behaviour. This should lead us to think about our own behaviour and the effect we have on children:

* If children are smacked by adults, they are likely to hit other children.
* If children are shouted at by adults, they are likely to shout at others.
* If children are given explanations, they will try to explain things too.
* If children are comforted when they fall, they will learn to do the same to others.

People who work with young children are very important status figures in the child's social learning.

Case Study

Bandura's work
Bandura showed three groups of children a film in which an adult was hitting a Bobo doll and shouting at it. The film had a different ending for each of the three groups:

First ending: the adult was given a reward for hitting the doll.

Second ending: the adult was punished for hitting the doll.

Third ending: nothing was done to the adult for hitting the doll.

Then the children were given a Bobo doll like the one in the film. The children who saw the adult rewarded for hitting the doll tended to do the same.

Case Study

Joe, 4 years
Joe pretended to be an early years worker. He told a story to a group of dolls and imitated the way in which the worker talked gently to the children, smiled and held the book.

Role play as social learning

Children copy directly what adults do, but they also pretend to be adults (they role-play being adults) when they begin to play imaginatively. The home area is an important area for this, and so is the outdoor area, which can become all sorts of places (shops, markets, streets and building sites, for example). The problem with this approach is that it does not see role play as children experimenting with different ways of doing things: it suggests that children merely copy what they see. We now know that role play is a more complex activity than the social learning theory would suggest.

SOCIOBIOLOGICAL THEORY

Modern research has revealed that how adults and children relate to each other is a two-way process. From a very early age, babies and children:

* actively choose whom they want to be with;

* have an influence on the way their family, carers and friends behave towards them;

* are influenced by those they care about;

* develop social and emotional relationships through this two-way process.

This means that children are not passively 'shaped' or 'regulated' to do what adults want. Some adults find it hard to understand and accept that even a young baby can have preferences for particular people, and that they can 'call' adults to them and get them to do the things that they want. In fact, from the start of their lives, young children give and take, contributing to relationships just as adults do.

* Sometimes they need other adults or children.

* Sometimes they follow what other people do.

* Sometimes they negotiate with other people.

JUDY DUNN

Judy Dunn has studied family social life in the Cambridge area of the UK for a number of years. She believes that the social and moral development of children is closely linked with their family relationships. In the first year of life, babies begin to notice and be sensitive to the actions of people in their family. She calls this affective tuning; it is sometimes also called social referencing. From 1 to 3 years children show self-concern. They need to:

* get the attention of others;

* understand what other people feel and say;

* comfort someone in distress.

If they do these things they can get what they want and need for themselves. Children also begin to work out what is allowed. They begin to understand what behaviours will meet with disapproval from other people, and how other people will respond to the way they express their feelings. Young children are curious about other people, and they experiment to discover what happens when they try to:

✤ hurt other people;

✤ help other people;

✤ show care for other people.

The concern that children have for themselves leads them to consider the needs of other people. In order to feel that they are getting fair treatment, children have to find out if they are being treated in the same way as other children. Children learn about these things through their family relationships. Before they can talk and discuss these events, they also learn through situations. Children learn about situations which make them angry, for example. Being angry makes people react to the child; and children also learn what makes other people angry!

Through their relationships with people in their families, they also learn how to care and to be considerate, kind and helpful. These are the basic experiences needed for moral development. In contrast to the behaviourist, social learning and socialisation approaches, the sociobiological approach supposes that children learn more through experimenting in social situations than just by copying what other people do. Children experiment in social situations:

✤ when they do things that other people do not allow or do not approve of;

✤ when people share fun together;

✤ through having conversations and discussing things;

✤ when people confront or tease each other;

✤ when playing with other children.

Every culture in every early years setting is based on a different set of relationships. Learning how to ask for things means that children learn how things get done in their particular family, in their particular early years setting and in their particular culture. Sociobiological theory says it is the way that people interact together which is important for social development. These are important aspects of the theory:

✤ Social development is a two-way process.

✤ Children learn as much from confrontation and angry exchanges as they do from having fun with other people.

✤ Adults such as early years workers are very important influences in the social constructivist approach.

✤ The way that children are helped to believe in themselves enables them, in turn, to develop positive relationships with other people.

It is important that adults help children to negotiate with other people, rather than to manipulate them. If adults manipulate children using bribes – 'If you do the clearing up quickly, you can have the first go on the swings when we get to the park' – they damage the child's developing self-discipline and moral development. When adults negotiate with children it shows that they respect each other. Adults and children should try to find the best solution together, in a spirit of being partners.

When children are helped to negotiate, this enhances both their social and their emotional development, and this in turn affects their moral development.

Behaviourist, socialisation and social learning theory: a summary

The following points are true according to these theories:

1 Children are born with reflexes. They do not inherit social behaviour; it is thought to be learned.

2 Children copy what adults do and thus learn accepted behaviour in their culture. They will experience:

❖ **role transition** (e.g. when they go from nursery to school);

❖ **role loss** (e.g. when an only child has a baby brother or sister born into the family);

❖ **role conflict** (e.g. when other children want the child to do something that he or she knows adults will disapprove of);

❖ the learning of a **gender role** (e.g. what it means to be a boy/male or a girl/female).

3 Children are influenced by other children: they want to be like their friends, perhaps wearing the same shoes. This can mean that some children are easily led because they copy others, or that they are easily bullied because they fear losing the approval of other children.

4 Children rehearse adult life through role play. For example, they learn the correct adult roles for a mother, doctor or receptionist, and these are rehearsed in their play. Children imitate the roles of people who have high status for them.

5 Children experience positive reinforcement. They are praised and extrinsically rewarded for their good behaviour (behaviour that is wanted by adults).

6 Children may experience negative reinforcement. They will avoid an unpleasant situation (which involves behaviour not wanted by adults). Instead, they do something adults approve of.

7 Children begin to sort out how adults expect them to behave, and also how they can expect adults to behave. Children thus begin to realise that different people have different roles, and that people behave according to their own particular role.

SOCIAL EVOLUTION THEORY

The development of social behaviour in different cultures

Throughout this book, we stress that modern researchers think about development in terms of two linked strands:

❖ the biological path;

❖ the sociocultural path.

Social evolution theory focuses on the interplay between the two strands over thousands of years, and we consider social development in this light. The brain, especially in the first 5 years of life, is constantly modified by experience, for example by the food eaten or by emotional and social encounters. Human beings are social animals. This means that when they work together adults can solve jointly all sorts of problems which would be much too hard for one person to manage alone. The same is true of children. For example, moving a truck that is stuck in the mud in the garden is difficult for a 4–year-old on his own, but a group of children working together may well solve the problem. Working together can be hard for children:

❖ They need to hold in mind others' ideas as well as their own.

❖ They have to be able to think in quite abstract ways to manage their own and others' ideas.

❖ All this takes a lot of brain power. It means thinking deeply.

❖ Each child has to control their feelings if the group is to work well together.

❖ They will work better together if they can use words or signs to communicate. New knowledge can then be handed on to other people: 'I know a good way to move a truck,' shouts Lee to Jo.

Once humans began to walk about on two legs instead of four, their hands became free. They began to make and use tools. They worked together when foraging and hunting for food, and when defending themselves as a group from enemies. Social cooperation has evolved because it makes people successful in managing new and difficult situations. Over time humans developed larger brains so that social and cultural learning could be handed down to other people. This transfer of social and cultural knowledge is still important today. It helps people to deal with things that are uncertain in life and to cope with lives which are full of changes.

Negotiating with children

The adult might say to the child, 'I know that you want to go to the shops, but we haven't cleared the toy cars away yet. It will leave a mess behind that won't be very nice for the other children and some of the toys might get broken. I think we need to clear up before we go. Do you want to do that while I get the coats ready, or shall we clear up together and get the coats afterwards?' Given a choice which is simple and clear, the child usually negotiates a solution that is positive.

Cultural tools and social evolution

Ever since Neanderthal men and women devised practical tools, social development has involved the development of cultural tools which help shared group thinking. These tools are not necessarily physical instruments. They help the exchange of ideas and information between people and include:

* a shared number system and languages;
* the sharing of plans and ideas;
* social rules, for example about sitting down for a meal together;

* practical tools which are used in technology and science.

Richard Dawkins, the biologist, believes that social learning is a shared process, based around cultural tools. He calls this the **social evolution** approach.

The social evolution approach in practice

At first a baby uses a spoon (which is a cultural tool) in their own way. Once the baby has got used to the spoon, the adult might help by putting some food on it. The baby then tries to do this. The baby's behaviour is influenced by being given the spoon in the first place, by watching what the adult does and by experimenting in their own way.

The baby might use the spoon in a new and interesting way. For example, they might balance a pea on the upturned spoon and take it into their mouth that way. The baby is developing an idea about how to use a spoon, as well as taking ideas from the way the adult uses the spoon.

OPEN SOCIETIES AND CLOSED SOCIETIES

In some cultures new ideas are very acceptable. These societies are called open societies, rather than closed societies where new ideas are less welcome. Every culture develops particular ways of doing things. These become customs and rituals which are handed down and give a sense of continuity with the past. The laws of the society and the rules of its different institutions give an indication of the society's values and show how they are put into practice. Cultures which are rich in the expressive arts – exciting dance groups, music events, drama performances – and the sciences – with original research and novel ideas in abundance – usually value these activities and provide the cultural tools which are needed to help these things blossom. It is only humans, with their cultural tools, who have achieved such activities. People are very influenced by the culture in which they grow up and each person can also influence that culture. In the same way, each child is influenced by the people and cultural tools in the early years setting; but just as surely each child also influences the people and cultural tools that they find.

ACTIVITY: COPING WITH CHANGE

Make a book which helps a child to develop a concept of death, or which looks at the birth of a sibling. Evaluate your book.

ACTIVITY: READING

Choose one of the books from the list below. Read to a child aged 3–5 years. Observe the child, concentrating on their feelings. Evaluate your observations and the book you chose.

* Ruth Brown, *Copycat*, Andersen Press.
* Marilyn Talbot, *Shy Roland*, Andersen Press.
* Selina Young, *Whistling in the Woods*, Heinemann.
* Catherine and Laurence Anholt, *What Makes Me Happy*, Walker Books.
* Anni Axworthy, *Along Came Toto*, Walker Books.

* Sue Lewis, *Come Back Grandma*, Red Fox.
* Susan Varley, *Badger's Parting Gifts*, Collins Picture Lions.
* Catherine Robinson, *Leaving Mrs Ellis*, Bodley Head.
* Sue Cowlishaw, *When My Little Sister Died*, Merlin Books.
* Bryan Mellonie and Robert Ingpen, *Lifetimes*, Hill of Content (Australia).
* John Burningham, *Granpa*, Jonathan Cape.

11

Health and community care

Contents

Section 1: The promotion and maintenance of health

WHAT IS HEALTH?

The World Health Organization (WHO) defines health as 'a state of complete physical, mental and social wellbeing and not merely the absence of disease or infirmity'. Health and social wellbeing can best be viewed as a holistic concept, encompassing the different aspects of a person's health needs (see Figure 11.1 and box below).

Aspects of health

❖ **Physical health:** this is the easiest aspect of health to measure, and is concerned with the physical functioning of the body.

❖ **Emotional health:** how we express emotions such as joy, grief, frustration and fear; this includes coping strategies for anxiety and stress.

❖ **Mental health:** this relates to our ability to organise our thoughts coherently, and is closely linked to emotional and social health.

❖ **Social health:** how we relate to others and form relationships.

❖ **Spiritual health:** this includes religious beliefs and practices, as well as personal codes of conduct and the quest for inner peace.

* **Environmental health:** an individual's health depends also on the health of the society in which they live; for example, in famine areas health is denied to the inhabitants, and unemployed people cannot be healthy in a society which only values those who work.

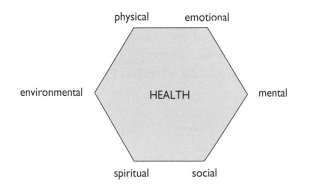

Fig 11.1 The six aspects of health

Maintenance of health and social wellbeing

It is now recognised that people's lifestyles and behaviour contribute to their health and wellbeing. Important factors are:

* diet;
* stress;
* smoking;
* sexual behaviour;
* exercise and maintaining mobility;
* recreation and leisure activities;
* alcohol and substance abuse;
* housing and sanitation.

FACTORS AFFECTING HEALTH IN INFANCY AND CHILDHOOD

There are very many factors that affect the healthy growth and development of children.

These factors work in combination, so it is often difficult to estimate the impact of any single factor on child health. They are:

* nutrition;
* infection;
* poverty and social disadvantage;
* housing;
* accidents;
* environmental factors;
* lifestyle factors;
* emotional and social factors.

Many of the factors that adversely affect child health are closely interrelated, and make up a **cycle of deprivation**. For example, poorer families tend to live in poorer housing conditions and may also have an inadequate diet. Lack of adequate minerals and vitamins as a result of poor diet leads to an increased susceptibility to infectious diseases, and so on.

Nutrition

Milk, whether human or formula, is the fuel that makes babies grow more rapidly during the first year than at any other time. Both human and formula milk provide the right nutrients for the first months of life, with just the right balance of carbohydrates, proteins, fats, vitamins and minerals (see Chapter 4).

Eating habits that are developed in childhood are likely to be continued in adult life. This means that children who eat mainly processed, convenience foods will tend to rely on these when they leave home. There are various conditions that may occur in childhood that are directly related to poor or unbalanced nutrition:

* **failure to thrive (or faltering growth):** poor growth and physical development;

- **dental caries or tooth decay:** associated with a high consumption of sugar in snacks and fizzy drinks;
- **obesity:** children who are overweight are more likely to become obese adults;
- **nutritional anaemia:** due to an insufficient intake of iron, folic acid and vitamin B12;
- **increased susceptibility to infections:** particularly upper respiratory infections, such as colds and bronchitis.

Infection

During childhood there are many infectious illnesses that can affect children's health and development. Some of these infections can be controlled by childhood immunisations; these are diphtheria, tetanus, polio, whooping cough, measles, meningitis, mumps and rubella. Other infections can have long-lasting effects on children's health.

Poverty and social disadvantage

There is now an official definition of poverty in the UK; poverty is defined as:

- absolute low income;
- relative low income;
- material deprivation and low income combined.

The government has pledged to eradicate child poverty by 2020, with immediate targets to halve it by 2010.

It is estimated that about 2.7 million children live in poverty in Great Britain today. Poverty is linked with the health of children for the following reasons:

- **Healthy eating costs more:** it costs more to provide a nutritionally balanced diet than one that is based on foods that tend to be high in sugar and fats.

- **Poor housing conditions:** low-income families tend to live in poorer housing, which may also be overcrowded, compared with those who are better off.
- **Unemployment:** parents who are unemployed have a higher incidence of mental health problems, long-term physical illness, disability and also higher mortality rates.

All these factors can have a lasting impact on the physical, emotional and social wellbeing of the child and family. Poverty is closely linked with **social disadvantage**; this means that families who have low incomes are likely to have fewer physical and personal resources to cope with illness. They will be at a disadvantage socially. They are also less likely to attend health clinics and, therefore, to receive adequate medical care, both preventive and in response to illness.

The inverse care law

The inverse care law is a term used to describe the fact that the amount of health care available to the individual is in an **inverse** proportion to the level of need. In other words, the people who have most need of health care are the very people who are least likely to receive it. There are various reasons why this happens:

- The National Health Service is not geared to meet these individuals' needs.
- There may be a lack of awareness about the health services available; for example, children from poor families are less likely to attend for routine screening services.
- Parents who have not experienced positive health care themselves are often unaware of its importance for their children.

* People who have had previous bad experiences of professional services may be suspicious of health professionals who are seen as interfering and authoritarian.

* Those whose first language is not English may find accessing health services difficult.

* Those from cultural backgrounds other than the white middle classes often find that the services offered do not meet their needs; for example, screening for conditions such as sickle-cell disorder, which affects African-Caribbean people, is not routine in these communities.

Housing

Poor housing is another factor that puts people at a social disadvantage. Low-income families are more likely to live in:

* homes which are damp and/or unheated – this increases the risk of infection, particularly respiratory illnesses;

* neighbourhoods that are unattractive and densely populated, with few communal areas and amenities – children without access to a safe garden or play area may suffer emotional and social problems;

* overcrowded conditions – homeless families who are housed in 'hotels' or bed-and-breakfast accommodation often have poor access to cooking facilities and have to share bathrooms with several other families (often children's education is badly disrupted when families are moved from one place to another).

Homelessness

It is estimated that about 180,000 children become homeless in England each year. Most of them will be living in temporary hostel accommodation or bed-and-breakfast housing. The vast majority of these children are in single-parent families, with very little financial or extended family support. Most of these families become homeless to escape from violence from a male partner or ex-partner, or from neighbours. The experience of homelessness causes many health problems for the children of such families:

* mental health problems, including delays in social or language development;

* behavioural problems;

* disruption of social relationships and difficulty in forming new friendships;

* experience of marital conflict and domestic violence.

Accidents

Some childhood accidents have lasting effects on a child's healthy growth and development, and many are preventable (see Chapter 4).

Emotional and social factors

A child who is miserable and unhappy is not healthy, although he or she may appear physically healthy. Children need to feel secure and to receive unconditional love from their primary carers. Child abuse, although not common, is bound to affect a child's health and wellbeing, and can have long-lasting health implications. (See Chapter 15 for information about child abuse.)

Environmental factors

Pollution of the environment can have a marked effect on children's health and development. The three main threats to health are water pollution, air pollution and noise pollution.

Water pollution

We all need clean, non-polluted water to prevent the spread of infectious diseases and poisoning. Many harmful germs are carried in water, including cholera, typhoid and the polio virus. In developing countries, over 4 million children die each year from drinking unclean water, mainly because it is contaminated with harmful organisms. Toxic chemicals in industrial, agricultural and domestic waste are common pollutants of water. In the UK water is purified before we use it. Although water treatment can remove bacterial contamination, it does not remove heavy chemical pollution. Examples of chemical pollutants in water that can affect children include:

- **Lead:** this can enter our bodies via air, food and water. It concentrates in the liver, kidney and bones and can cause mental retardation.
- **Nitrates:** these enter water from fertilisers that leach out of the soil; too much nitrate in drinking water has been found to cause a serious blood disorder in babies under 3 months, called blue-baby syndrome.

Air pollution

Children are particularly vulnerable to air pollution. This is partly because they have a large lung surface area in relation to their small body size; this means that they absorb toxic substances quicker than adults and are slower to get rid of them. The effects of air pollution from factory chimneys, the use of chemical insecticides and car exhausts include:

- **Lead poisoning:** children are particularly susceptible to lead poisoning, mostly caused by vehicle exhaust fumes.

Even very low levels of lead in the blood can affect children's ability to learn. Higher levels are associated with damage to the kidneys, liver and reproductive system.

- **Asthma:** air pollution can act as a trigger for asthma and can make an existing condition worse. The incidence of asthma is much higher in traffic-polluted areas.
- **Cancer:** the use of insecticides and fertilisers by farmers has been linked with various childhood cancers. Radioactivity from nuclear power stations has also been found to cause cancer.

Noise pollution

Noise pollution can also be a hazard to child health. There is evidence to suggest that high levels of noise, mostly caused by heavy traffic, are responsible for medical and social problems. For example, it has been found that children living on noisy main roads had far fewer friends than those in quiet suburbs, and that traffic noise adversely affects children's progress at school.

Lifestyle factors

SMOKING

Children who live in a smoky atmosphere are more likely to develop:

- coughs and colds;
- asthma;
- chest infections (temperature with a bad cough);
- ear infections and glue ear.

Every year 17,000 children are admitted to hospital with respiratory infections; research has found that many of these children are exposed daily to cigarette smoke. There is also an increased risk of children taking up the smoking habit themselves if one or both of their parents smoke.

EXERCISE

Some children take no regular physical exercise, apart from at school, and this is often because of the family's attitude and habits. Taking regular exercise allows children to develop their motor skills and to run off any pent-up feelings of frustration and aggression.

❖ Coronary heart disease is the greatest single risk to health in the UK.

❖ Adults who are physically inactive have about double the chance of suffering from coronary heart disease.

❖ Children who do not take much exercise tend to become inactive adults.

❖ Obesity is more common in children who take little exercise.

WHAT IS HEALTH EDUCATION?

Health education is a method of self-empowerment; it enables people to take more control over their own health and that of their children. Health education can be divided into primary, secondary and tertiary categories.

1   **Primary health education** is directed at healthy people. It is a prophylactic (or preventive) measure that aims to prevent ill health arising in the first instance.

2   **Secondary health education** is directed at people with a health problem or a reversible condition. It emphasises the importance of the early detection of defects and ways in which people can make lifestyle changes to improve their condition.

❖ **Screening:** by routinely examining apparently healthy people, screening aims to detect those who are likely to develop a particular disease and those in whom the disease is already present but has not yet produced symptoms. Screening may detect a problem with hearing, sight, or physical, emotional or behavioural development.

❖ **Reducing behaviours likely to damage health:** overweight people can be encouraged to change their dietary habits, or a smoker to quit smoking.

3   **Tertiary health education** is directed at those whose ill health has not been, or could not be, prevented and who cannot be completely cured. However, the quality of their lives can still be influenced:

❖ Children with brain damage can achieve their own potential with good support in communication and structured play.

❖ Patients dying of cancer can do so with dignity if their pain is kept under control.

Rehabilitation programmes are chiefly concerned with tertiary health education.

The aims of health education

❖ To provide information and to raise awareness.

❖ To change people's behaviour and attitudes.

❖ To meet national and local health targets, for example promoting self-examination of the breasts to aid in the early detection of breast cancer.

The areas of health education relevant to children are:

- good nutrition;
- prevention of tooth decay;
- immunisation;
- prevention of childhood accidents, including road safety and sunburn;
- prevention of emotional and behavioural problems;
- basic hygiene.

Five approaches to health education

1   **The medical approach:** this promotes medical intervention to prevent or improve ill health; it uses a persuasive and authoritarian method – for example, persuading parents to bring their children for immunisation.

2   **The behaviour-change approach:** this aims to change people's attitudes and behaviour so that they adopt a healthy lifestyle – for example, teaching people how to give up smoking.

3   **The educational approach;** this aims to give information and to ensure understanding of health issues. Information is presented in as value-free a way as possible, so that the people targeted feel free to make their own decisions; for example, clients are given information about the effects of smoking and can then make a choice to stop smoking if they want to.

4   **The client-directed approach:** this aims to work with clients so that they can identify what they want to know about, and make their own decisions and choices; for example, the antismoking issue is only considered if the clients identify it as a concern.

5   **The social change approach:** this aims to change the environment to facilitate the choice of healthier lifestyles; for example, the change taking place in school dinners (see page 202) and the no-smoking policy being implemented in restaurants, bars and workplaces.

Advertisers often use scare tactics to get the message across; this has been called the **fear creation approach**. A recent example is the Barnardos campaign, which aims to raise public awareness about the issues of:

- abuse through prostitution;
- domestic violence;
- parental neglect;
- drug and alcohol misuse.

Health education campaigns

Recent health education campaigns of particular relevance to children include:

- **The Water is Cool in School Campaign:** aims to improve the quality of provision and access to fresh drinking water for children in UK primary and secondary schools.

- **The School Fruit and Vegetable Scheme (SFV):** part of the **five-a-day** programme to increase fruit and vegetable consumption. Under the SFV Scheme, all children aged 4–6 years in LEA-maintained infant, primary and special schools are entitled to a free piece of fruit or portion of vegetables each school day.

- **'Sleep safe, sleep sound, share a room with me':** the latest campaign from the Foundation for the Study of Infant Deaths; leaflets and posters have been sent to all midwives and health visitors.

- **Birth to Five:** a comprehensive guide to parenthood and the first 5 years of a child's life. It covers child health, nutrition and safety and is given free to all first-time mothers in England.

Health education by private companies

Manufacturers of 'healthy' products, such as wholemeal bread or high-protein balanced foods for babies, often promote their products both by advertising and by using educational leaflets. Such leaflets are offered free in health clinics, postnatal wards and supermarkets. Examples of this type of health promotion are:

* booklets on feeding your baby, published by formula milk manufacturers;
* leaflets on child safety on the roads, produced by manufacturers of child car seats and harnesses;
* the promotion of herbal remedies to encourage a stress-free lifestyle.

There are strict controls over the claims that manufacturers can make about the health-giving properties of their product.

Health education by the voluntary sector

Voluntary organisations are in a strong position to enhance the health of the population. They use a variety of methods:

* **Self-help:** some organisations bring people together to share common problems and to help them to gain more confidence and control over their own health.
* **Direct service provision:** the British Red Cross has a network of shops for the rental of equipment in the home (including walking frames, commodes and chairs).
* **Community health:** voluntary organisations work with local people to

identify and solve problems affecting their health. GASP – Group Against Smoking in Public – is a Bristol-based group that campaigns for an increase in the provision of no-smoking areas in bars and restaurants.

* **Health education and promotion:** some organisations undertake fundraising to provide support for research. The Wellcome Trust is a medical research charity that provides funding for research in the biomedical sciences.

Charities with health promotion agendas also employ advertising methods to get across their message; they often work in conjunction with the Health Development Agency or with private companies, or both. For example, the Child Accident Prevention Trust, with financial support from Start-rite and Volvo, produced a safety leaflet for parents entitled 'First ride, safe ride'. This was aimed at keeping a baby safe in the car.

Fig 11.2 Barnardo's campaign poster

Fig 11.3 Sleep safe poster

Health education leading to preventive action

All **immunisation** programmes are an attempt to prevent disease and, therefore, to promote health – both in the individual and in the general population. The campaign to prevent sudden infant death syndrome is another example of an important health message reaching those who need it.

YOUR ROLE IN CHILD HEALTH EDUCATION

There are many ways in which you can contribute to health education programmes in early years settings. The most important part of your role is to be a **good role model** for children. Opportunities for

teaching children about health and safety are covered in the box below.

CHILD HEALTH PROMOTION

Child health promotion is a programme of care managed by professionals – family doctors, nurses, health visitors and other members of the primary health care team. It has four main aims:

1   to promote good health and development;

2   to prevent illness, accidents and child abuse;

3   to recognise and, where possible, eradicate potential problems affecting development, behaviour and education;

4   to detect abnormality, in order to offer investigation and treatment.

Safety in other people's homes

However careful parents are in making their own home a safe place for children, other people's homes may not be so safe. For example, the commonest cause of death in children in the USA and Australia is from children falling into friends' or neighbours' swimming pools. Always be alert to the possible hazards in any environment and keep children safe.

Safety when travelling in cars

Children travelling in a car who are not strapped in with a seat belt or not placed in a child seat are at risk of serious injury or death in the event of a car accident. The relatively large weight of a child's head makes them particularly vulnerable if they are thrown forward. Recommended safety measures for babies in cars are as follows:

❖   If using a child car seat in the front passenger seat, the front seat must be moved as far back as possible. A distance of at least 20 cm must be left between the dashboard and the child seat, in order to reduce the risk of injury to the child in the event of a head-on collision.

❖ The advice from the Child Accident Prevention Trust (CAPT) and paediatricians is that babies should travel rearward-facing in a special child safety seat, at least until they are able to sit on the floor unaided for at least half an hour.

❖ If there are front passenger airbags fitted to the car, make sure the baby always travels in a special baby seat fitted on the back seat.

Recommended safety measures for children aged 3–6 years are as follows:

❖ Children in this age group (weighing 15 to 25 kg) should be carried in the back seat in approved child seats, which must be fastened with the car's three-point seat belt.

❖ Bigger children should use a booster cushion with an adult safety belt.

❖ Make sure you always get children out of the car on the pavement side.

Strangers and child safety

Many parents worry that their child might be abducted or murdered by a stranger. In fact this is rare compared with the risk of a traffic accident, for example. However, it makes sense to teach children the following rules:

❖ Never go with anyone (even someone they know well) without telling the grown-up who is looking after them.

❖ If someone they do not know tries to take them away, it is okay to scream and kick.

❖ Always to tell you if they have been approached by someone they do not know.

❖ What to do if they become separated from you or are lost.

Guidelines for teaching children about health and safety

❖ Provide healthy meals and snacks.

❖ Practise good hygiene routines, such as hand washing and teeth brushing.

❖ Choose books and displays which reinforce healthy lifestyles.

❖ Use drama and music sessions to encourage children to express their feelings in a safe environment.

❖ Create interesting board games with a healthy theme (e.g. how to avoid accidents when playing outside).

❖ Welcome visitors to talk about their work in health care (e.g. invite a health visitor or dentist to explain the importance of good hygiene routines).

❖ Demonstrate safety and hygiene routines (e.g. a road safety officer or police officer could visit the setting to teach children how to cross the road safely).

❖ Make the home area into a hospital ward and encourage role play as patients, nurses and doctors.

* If they are in a crowded place, they should stand still and wait to be found.
* They can tell a police officer that they are lost.
* They can go into a shop and tell someone behind the counter.
* They could tell someone who has other children with them.
* As soon as they are old enough, teach a child his or her address and phone number, or the phone number of another responsible person.

Road safety

Road traffic accidents (RTAs) account for 50 per cent of all accidental deaths. Every year more than 400 children under the age of 15 years are killed, and many more are seriously injured, on the roads of the UK. In the 1970s Denmark had the highest rate of child deaths from traffic accidents in western Europe. The Danish government took action by creating a network of traffic-free foot and cycle paths, cutting accidents in those areas by 85 per cent. There are signs that the UK may follow this example. Educating children about safety on the roads should begin at a very early age, the best method being by example.

The Child Accident Prevention Trust

The Child Accident Prevention Trust is a voluntary organisation that works closely with health and education professionals to increase public awareness of safety issues. Recently it launched the Seven Steps for Safety initiative:

1 Plan and practise a safer route to school.

2 Use a car seat that fits your child and your car.

3 Fit and check a smoke alarm.

4 Use a harness and reins when out and about with your toddler.

5 Keep household products and medicines locked up or high out of reach.

6 Plan your next safety move – keep one step ahead as your baby grows.

7 Check your safety equipment – does it fit and does it work?

PREVENTING ILL HEALTH THROUGH IMMUNISATION

The immune system in children

Babies are born with some **natural immunity** as they are able to make their own infection-fighting cells. They may be further protected by antibodies and other substances found in breast milk. A child's own experiences of infection boost his or her immunity. For some infections immunity is life-long, while for others it is short-lived. Some illnesses, such as the common cold, are caused by one of several strains of virus, which is why having one cold does not automatically prevent another one later. Sometimes the immune system does not work properly, as in the case of AIDS infection and some other rare conditions. Sometimes it *overworks* and causes allergy. It can also be affected by emotional distress and physical exhaustion.

There are two types of immunity: **active immunity** and **passive immunity**. As discussed above, immunity can be induced by contact with an infection. It can also be induced by **immunisation** against certain infective agents. This is covered in more detail below.

Guidelines for teaching children about road safety

- Children need to learn about road safety in the same way as they learn any new skill: the message needs to be repeated over and over again until the child really has learned it.

- The Green Cross Code is a very good method of teaching road safety (see Figure 11.4).

- Every local authority employs a road safety officer, and the Royal Society for the Prevention of Accidents (ROSPA) runs the Tufty Club for children aged 3 years or over. Invite someone to talk to the children about road safety.

- Children should wear light-coloured clothes or luminous armbands – or both – when out at dusk or when walking on country roads without pavements.

- Children should have lights on their bikes if they cycle in the dark.

ACTIVE IMMUNITY

Active immunity is when a vaccine triggers the **immune system** to produce antibodies against the disease as though the body had been infected with it. This also teaches the body's immune system how to produce the appropriate antibodies quickly. If the immunised person then comes into contact with the disease itself, their immune system will recognise it and immediately produce the antibodies needed to fight it.

PASSIVE IMMUNITY

Passive immunity is provided when the body is given antibodies rather than producing them itself. A newborn baby has passive immunity to several diseases, such as measles, mumps and rubella, from antibodies passed from its mother via the placenta. Passive immunity only lasts for a few weeks or months. In the case of measles, mumps and rubella it may last up to 1 year in infants – this is why MMR is given just after a child's first birthday.

HERD IMMUNITY

If enough people in a community are immunised against certain diseases, then it is more difficult for that disease to get passed between those who are not immunised – this

is known as herd immunity. Herd immunity does not apply to all diseases because they are not all passed on from person to person. For example, tetanus can only be caught from spores in the ground.

What is immunisation?

Immunisation is a way of protecting ourselves against serious disease. Once we have been immunised against a certain disease, our bodies can fight that disease if we come into contact with it. An immunisation programme protects people against specific diseases by reducing the number of people getting the disease and preventing it being passed on.

With some diseases – like **smallpox** or **polio** – it is possible to eliminate them completely.

In the past 15 years there has been a dramatic reduction in the incidence of common childhood illnesses, due to:

- greater public awareness of the availability of immunisation;

- the introduction of two major new vaccines: MMR and Hib;

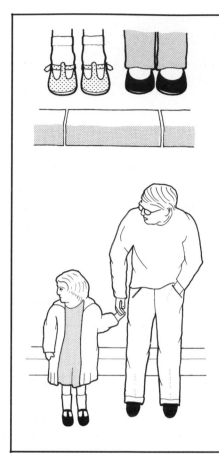

The Green Cross Code

1. **Find a safe place to cross, then stop. Safe places include zebra and pelican crossings.**

2. **Stand on the pavement near the kerb.**

3. **Look all round for traffic and listen.**

4. **If traffic is coming, let it pass. Look all round again.**

5. **When there is no traffic near, walk straight across the road. Never run.**

6. **Keep looking and listening for traffic while you cross. Repeat and use the code every time.**

Fig 11.4 The Green Cross Code

❖ a government policy which has led to national strategies on immunisation and better uptake.

Immunisations are usually carried out in child health clinics. The doctor will discuss any fears the parents may have about particular vaccines. No vaccine is completely risk-free, and parents are asked to sign a consent form prior to immunisations being given. Immunisations are only given if the child is well, and may be postponed if the child has had a reaction to any previous immunisation or if the child is taking any medication that might interfere with their ability to fight infection. The effects of the disease are usually far worse than any side effects of a vaccine.

The **advantages of immunisation** include the following:

❖ Avoiding catching diseases and having complications (children who are not immunised remain at risk).

❖ Immunisation is the safest way to protect children from particular diseases which may have long-lasting effects.

❖ Having children immunised at an early age means they are well-protected by the time they start playgroup or school, where they are in contact with lots of children.

❖ Immunisation also protects those children who are unable to receive immunisation, by providing herd immunity (see above, page 379).

Table 11.1 Recommended Immunisation Schedule

Routine childhood immunisation programme

When to immunise	What vaccine is given	How it is given
Two, three and four months old	Diphtheria, tetanus, pertussis (whooping cough), polio and Hib (DTaP/IPV/Hib)	One injection
	MenC	One injection
Around 13 months	Measles, mumps and rubella (MMR)	One injection
Three years four months to five years old	Diphtheria, tetanus, pertussis and polio (dTaP/IPV or DTaP/IPV)	One injection
	Measles, mumps and rubella (MMR)	One injection
Ten to 14 years old (and sometimes shortly after birth)	BCG (against tuberculosis)	Skin test then, if needed, one injection
Thirteen to 18 years old	Tetanus, diphtheria and polio (Td/IPV)	One injection

The **disadvantages of immunisation** include the possibility of side effects.

Diseases, immunisation and side effects

THE NEW **5-IN-1 VACCINE** (DTaP/IPV/Hib) GIVES PROTECTION AGAINST DIPHTHERIA, TETANUS, PERTUSSIS, POLIO AND HAEMOPHILUS INFLUENZAE TYPE B (Hib).

❖ **Diphtheria:** this disease begins with a sore throat and can progress rapidly to cause problems with breathing. It can damage the heart and the nervous system, and in severe cases it can kill. Diphtheria has almost been wiped out in the UK, but it still exists in other parts of the world and it is on the increase in parts of eastern Europe.

❖ **Tetanus:** tetanus germs are found in soil. They enter the body through a cut or burn. Tetanus is a painful disease that affects the muscles and can cause breathing problems. If it is not treated it can kill.

❖ **Pertussis (whooping cough):** this can be very distressing. In young children it can last for several weeks. Children become exhausted by long bouts of coughing that often cause vomiting and choking. In severe cases pertussis can kill.

❖ **Polio:** this is a virus that attacks the nervous system and can cause permanent muscle paralysis. If it affects the chest muscles it can kill. The virus is passed in the faeces of infected people or those who have just been immunised against polio. Routine immunisation has meant that the natural virus no longer causes cases of polio in the UK, but polio is still around in other parts of the world, especially in India.

❖ **Hib:** this is an infection that can cause a number of serious illnesses, including blood poisoning, pneumonia and meningitis. All these diseases can be dangerous if not treated quickly. Children under 4 years are most at risk, with the peak incidence of Hib infection being among babies of 10–11 months. The Hib vaccine protects children against this specific type of meningitis. The Hib vaccine does not protect against any other type of meningitis.

Side effects: any side effects of the new 5-in-1 vaccine are usually mild. They can include:

* irritability;
* a slightly high temperature;
* redness or a small lump at the injection site;
* sickness or diarrhoea.

Fewer than 1 in 1000 children has a more severe reaction to the vaccine 1 or 2 days after the injection. If any of the following symptoms develop, call your GP immediately:

* a fit called a **febrile convulsion** (babies usually recovery quickly from this);
* the baby seems less responsive than usual and floppy;
* a very high temperature;
* an unusual, high-pitched cry.

It is also possible, though rare, for babies to have a severe reaction immediately after the vaccine is given. Any parent who is concerned about their child's reaction to the vaccine should talk to a GP, nurse or health visitor.

NB Take care when changing the child's nappy after the immunisation. The **polio vaccine** is passed into a child's nappies for up to 6 weeks after the vaccine is given. If someone who has not been immunised against polio changes the child's nappy, it is possible for them to be affected by the virus.

THE **MMR VACCINE** PROTECTS CHILDREN AGAINST MEASLES, MUMPS AND RUBELLA (GERMAN MEASLES).

* **Measles:** this virus is very infectious. It causes a high fever and a rash. About 1 in 15 children with measles is at risk of complications that may include chest infections, fits and brain damage. In severe cases measles can kill.
* **Mumps:** this virus causes swollen glands in the face. Before immunisation was introduced, mumps was the commonest cause of viral meningitis in children under 15. It can also cause deafness, and swelling of the testicles in boys and ovaries in girls.
* **Rubella:** this is usually very mild and is not likely to cause your child any problems. However, if a pregnant woman catches it in her early pregnancy it can harm the unborn baby.

Before the vaccine was introduced, about 90 children a year in the UK died from measles.

Information from the Department of Health:

Side effects: it is not possible to say that MMR, or any vaccine, is absolutely safe. Some children do get side effects to the MMR vaccine, especially after the first injection. Side effects of the vaccine are usually mild and, crucially, they are milder than the potentially serious effects of having measles, mumps or rubella. MMR contains three separate vaccines in one injection. Each vaccine has different side effects at different times:

* About 1 week to 10 days after the MMR immunisation some children become feverish and they may develop a measles-like rash and go off their food. This is because the measles part of the vaccine is starting to work.

❖ About 3–4 weeks after the injection a child might occasionally get a mild form of mumps as the mumps part of MMR kicks in.

❖ In the 6 weeks after MMR a child may, very rarely, get a rash of small bruise-like spots which may be caused by the measles or rubella parts of the immunisation. This usually gets better on its own.

❖ Very rarely, children can have severe allergic reactions straight after any immunisation (about 1 in 100,000 immunisations for MMR). If the child is treated quickly, he or she will recover fully. People giving immunisations are trained to deal with allergic reactions.

❖ Rarely, children may get mumps-like symptoms (fever and swollen glands) about 3 weeks after their immunisation. The child will not be infectious at this time, so they can mix with other people as normal.

❖ Fewer than 1 child in 1 million develops encephalitis (infection of the brain) after the MMR vaccine – although there is very little evidence that it is the vaccine that causes it. If a child catches measles, however, the chance of developing encephalitis is between 1 in 200 and 1 in 5000.

❖ About 1 child in 1000 will have a fit (or convulsion), but a child who actually has measles is 10 times more likely to have a fit as a result of the illness.

AUTISM AND BOWEL DISEASE

The speculation over a link between the MMR vaccine and autism started in 1998 when a paper was published in a medical journal about 12 autistic children who also had bowel problems. Although the research stated that it did not prove a link between autism and the MMR vaccine, the resulting publicity gave the impression that there was a link. If a child has autism, parents typically start to notice the signs when their child is 1–2 years. As the MMR injection is given at around 13 months of age, it is easy to understand why some people think they may be linked. Although the number of cases of autism appears to have risen significantly in the last 20 years, this is probably due to better diagnosis of the condition, and a change in the way that doctors classify disorders so that autism is used more frequently than terms such as developmental delay.

In October 2005, an international team of researchers reported that the MMR vaccine has been cleared of causing long-term developmental problems, such as autism; the report was claimed to be the most systematic review of evidence concerning the effectiveness and safety of the MMR vaccine.

The **Meningitis C vaccine** protects against group C meningitis and septicaemia. It does not protect against other causes of meningitis and septicaemia (see page 398 for information on meningitis).

Side effects: these may include the following in children of different ages:

❖ Babies: some swelling and redness where the injection is given.

❖ Toddlers over 12 months: some swelling and redness where the injection is given. About 1 in 4 toddlers may have disturbed sleep. About 1 in 20 toddlers may have a mild fever.

❖ Nursery-age children: about 1 in 20 may have some swelling at the injection site. About 1 in 50 may have a mild fever within a few days of the vaccination.

❖ Children and young people: about 1 in 4 may have some swelling and redness at the injection site. About 1 in 50 may have a mild fever. About 1 in 100 may have a very sore arm from the injection, which may last a day or so.

❖ On very rare occasions, vaccinations may cause serious complications.

Care of children after immunisations

Children should be observed closely after any immunisation. Look out for any of the signs and symptoms given above:

❖ If fever occurs, keep the child cool, offer plenty to drink and give children's paracetamol.

❖ If the temperature remains high or if there are any other symptoms, such as convulsions, call a doctor immediately.

Alternatives to immunisation

There is no proven, effective alternative to conventional immunisation. Homeopathic medicine has been tried as an alternative to the whooping cough vaccine, but it was not found to be effective. The Council of the Faculty of Homeopathy (the registered organisation for doctors qualified in homeopathy) advises parents to have their children immunised with conventional vaccines.

CHILD HEALTH SURVEILLANCE

Surveillance is defined as close supervision or observation, and its primary purpose is to detect any abnormality in development so that the child can be offered treatment. For example, early detection of a hearing impairment gives the young child a better chance of receiving appropriate treatment and/or specialist education.

The inverse care law (again)

The families who are most in need of child health surveillance are often those who are least likely to make use of the services provided. Although children in the UK today enjoy better health than at any other time, the provisions of a National Health Service have not led to equality of health experience. The following box outlines people who might be seen as priority groups by health visitors and the primary health care team when organising caseloads and targeting resources. The health care of such priority groups is difficult and often involves a working partnership with other community services, such as social service departments or housing departments.

Priority groups for health surveillance

❖ Very young or unsupported parents, particularly those with their first baby.

❖ Parents thought to be at particular risk of abusing their children.

❖ Parents who are socially isolated, due to mental health problems or linguistic or cultural barriers.

❖ Families living in poor housing, including bed-and-breakfast accommodation or housing where there is overcrowding.

❖ Parents with low self-esteem or a lack of confidence.

❖ Parents with unrealistic expectations about the child or with a poor understanding of the child's needs.

❖ Parents and/or children suffering significant bereavement (or separation as a result of a recent divorce).

❖ Parents who have experienced previous SIDS (sudden infant death syndrome) in the family.

6-8 WEEK REVIEW

This review is done by your health visitor or a doctor. Below are some things you may want to talk about when you see them. However, if you are worried about your child's health, growth or development you can contact your health visitor or doctor at any time.

	yes	no	not sure
Do you feel well yourself?	☐	☐	☐
Do you have any worries about feeding your baby?	☐	☐	☐
Do you have any concerns about your baby's weight gain?	☐	☐	☐
Does your baby watch your face and follow with his/her eyes?	☐	☐	☐
Does your baby turn towards the light?	☐	☐	☐
Does your baby smile at you?	☐	☐	☐
Do you think your baby can hear you?	☐	☐	☐
Is your baby startled by loud noises?	☐	☐	☐
Are there any problems in looking after your baby?	☐	☐	☐
Do you have any worries about your baby?	☐	☐	☐

Any other issues you would like to discuss? ....

....

....

Results of newborn bloodspot screening

Condition	Results received? yes / no / not done	Follow up required? no / yes & reason	If follow up, outcome of follow up
PKU			
Hypothyroidism			
Sickle Cell			
Cystic Fibrosis			
Other			

Fig 11.5 Sample page from a personal child health record

Personal child health record

All parents are issued with a personal child health record that enables them to keep a record of their child's development (see Figure 11.5). This form is completed by doctors, health visitors and parents, and is a useful source of information if the child is admitted to hospital or is taken ill when the family is away from home.

Screening as part of surveillance

The aim of a screening programme is to examine all children at risk from a certain condition; the term 'screening' refers to the examination of apparently healthy children to distinguish those who probably have a condition from those who probably do not. Hearing defects are often detected in this way at one of the routine checks carried out at the child surveillance clinic (see below).

SCREENING FOR HEARING IMPAIRMENT

1   **Otoacoustic Emissions Test (OAE):** newborn babies are usually screened using the otoacoustic emissions (OAE) test. A tiny earpiece is placed in the baby's outer ear and quiet clicking sounds are played through it. This should produce reaction sounds in a part of the ear called the cochlea, and the computer can record and analyse these. It is painless and can be done while the baby

is asleep. Sometimes clear results are not obtained from the OAE test. A different method can then be used, such as automated auditory brainstem response.

2 **Automated auditory brainstem response (AABR):** small sensors are placed on the baby's head and neck, and soft headphones are placed over the ears. Quiet clicking sounds are played through the earphones and a computer analyses the response in the brain, using information from the sensors.

3 **Distraction test:** this is likely to be phased out in areas phasing in the neonatal screening tests (the OAE and the AABR). The reasons for this include the following:

*   studies have shown that the distraction test is not very reliable;

*   even when hearing loss is found, it does not identify children with permanent sensori-neural deafness until they are over 6 months, which is not satisfactory; also, many children who 'fail' the test have temporary **glue ear** that needs no treatment;

*   neonatal screening will identify most cases of congenital hearing loss, so there is little justification for a second screening test in older babies.

4 **Hearing 'sweep' test:** at school age (4–5 years) all children should have the hearing 'sweep' test. This is an audiogram test across the main speech frequencies (high and low pitches), using sounds of different volumes (loudness), which are played through earphones. The child has to indicate whether they have heard them, or perform various actions depending on the type of noise.

SCREENING FOR VISUAL DISORDERS

Screening tests for visual problems are carried out on all children at the following points:

*   newborn examination;

*   6–8 week review;

*   preschool (or school entry) vision check.

THE NEWBORN EXAMINATION AND 6–8 WEEK REVIEW

The eyes of newborn babies are examined for any obvious physical defects, including cross-eyes, cloudiness (a sign of cataracts) and redness. This examination includes:

1 **The red reflex:** this uses an **ophthalmoscope**. Light is directed into the baby's eyes and a red reflection should be seen as the light is reflected back. If the reflection is white instead, the child will be referred to a specialist immediately, as it can be a sign of a cataract or other eye condition.

2 **The pupil reflex:** this is checked by shining a light into each eye from a distance of 10 cm. The pupils should automatically shrink in response to brightness.

3 **General inspection of the eyes:** this may suggest other conditions. For example, one eye larger than the other may indicate glaucoma.

4 **A specialist examination** is indicated in babies who:

*   have an abnormality detected in the above routine examinations;

*   have a known higher risk of visual disorders. For example, low birth-weight babies at risk of **retinopathy of prematurity**; babies who have a close relative with an inheritable eye

disorder; and babies with a known hearing impairment.

PRESCHOOL VISION SCREENING

The school entry vision check which was carried out by school nurses is being replaced by a vision check carried out by an **orthoptist**. The main aim is to detect **amblyopia**. Amblyopia is reduced visual acuity, not correctable with glasses, in an otherwise 'healthy' eye. The brain has suppressed, or failed to develop, the ability to see properly with the affected eye. The commonest cause is a manifest **squint** (strabismus) where there are two competing images, so one is suppressed.

DEVELOPMENTAL REVIEWS

Parents will want to know if their child has problems as soon as possible: it is easier to come to terms with a serious problem in a young baby than in an older child. Health professionals should always take the parent's worries seriously and never assume that parents are fussy, neurotic or overanxious. Early childhood practitioners are usually very astute in recognising abnormalities in development because of their experience with a wide variety of children.

Developmental reviews give parents an opportunity to say what they have noticed about their child. They can also discuss anything that concerns them about their child's health and behaviour. Child development is reviewed by doctors and health visitors, either in the child's home or in health clinics. The areas that are looked at are:

* **gross motor skills:** sitting, standing, walking, running;
* **fine motor skills:** handling toys, stacking bricks, doing up buttons and

tying shoelaces (gross and fine manipulative skills);

* **speech and language:** including hearing;
* **vision:** including squint;
* **social behaviour:** how the child interacts with others (e.g. family and friends).

Early detection is important as:

* early treatment may reduce or even avoid permanent damage in some conditions;
* an early diagnosis (of an inherited condition) may allow **genetic counselling** and so avoid the birth of another child with a disabling condition.

When do developmental reviews take place?

Parents are usually invited to developmental reviews when their child is:

* 6–8 weeks;
* 6–9 months;
* 18–24 months;
* 3–3½ years;
* 4½–5½ years (before or just after the child starts school).

In some parts of the UK the age that children are reviewed may vary slightly from those given above, especially after the age of 3 years. During a developmental review some health visitors may ask parents or carers questions about their baby; others may ask the child to do simple tasks such as building with blocks or identifying pictures; others may simply watch the child playing or drawing, getting an idea from this observation and from the adult's comments of how the child is doing. If the child's first language is not English, parents may need to ask if development reviews can be carried out with the help of someone who can speak the child's language.

After the child has started school, the **school health service** takes over these reviews.

Neonatal examination

All babies are examined as soon as possible after birth.

The 6–8-week check

PARENTAL CONCERNS

This check usually takes place in the child health clinic. The doctor will enquire about any parental concerns over:

❖ feeding;

❖ bowel actions;

❖ sleeping;

❖ micturition (the act of passing urine).

OBSERVATION

While the parent is undressing the baby for examination, the doctor will look out for:

❖ the responsiveness of the baby – smiles, eye contact, attentiveness to parent's voice, and so on;

❖ any difficulties the parent has holding the baby – a depressed mother will not give much visual attention and may not use a good supporting hold;

❖ jaundice and anaemia.

MEASUREMENT

❖ The baby is weighed naked and the weight plotted on the growth chart.

❖ The head circumference is measured and plotted on the growth chart.

EXAMINATION

This examination follows the same lines as the examination at birth:

❖ The general appearance of the baby will give an indication of whether the child is well-nourished.

❖ The eyes are inspected using a light – the baby will turn their head and follow a small light beam; an ophthalmoscope is used to check for a cataract.

❖ The heart is auscultated, that is, listened to with a stethoscope, to exclude any congenital defect.

❖ The hips are manipulated, again to exclude the presence of congenital dislocation of the hips.

❖ The baby is placed prone and will turn her head to one side; hands are held with the thumbs inwards and the fingers wrapped around them.

❖ The posterior fontanelle is usually closed by now; the anterior fontanelle does not close until around 18 months.

HEARING

Most babies will have been screened soon after birth (see above). There is no specific test at this age; the parent is asked if they think the child can hear. A baby may startle to a sudden noise or freeze for some sounds.

Health education points at 0–8 weeks

❖ Nutrition: breastfeeding, preparation of formula feeds, specific feeding difficulties.

❖ Immunisation: discuss any concerns and initiate a programme of vaccinations.

❖ Passive smoking: babies here are at risk of respiratory infections and middle ear disease.

❖ Illness in babies: how to recognise symptoms.

❖ Crying: coping with frustration and tiredness.

❖ Reducing the risk of cot death: SIDS (sudden infant death syndrome).

The doctor will discuss health topics, give the first immunisation and, finally, complete the personal child health record.

The 6–9-month check

PARENTAL CONCERNS

The doctor or health visitor will enquire again about any parental concerns.

OBSERVATION

The doctor will look out for:

* socialisation and attachment behaviour;
* visual behaviour;
* communication – sounds, expressions and gestures;
* motor development – sitting, balance, use of hands, any abnormal movement patterns.

MEASUREMENT

Head circumference and weight are plotted on the growth chart.

EXAMINATION

* Manipulation of the hips is carried out.
* The heart is listened to with a stethoscope.
* The testes are checked in boys.
* The eyes are checked for a squint – if this is present, the child is referred to an ophthalmologist (eye specialist); visual behaviour is checked.
* Hearing is *sometimes tested* by the distraction test (see page 386).

Health education points

* Nutrition: weaning; control of sugar intake.
* Immunisations: check they are up-to-date.
* Teeth: regular brushing once teeth appear; information on fluoride; visit the dentist.
* The need for play and language stimulation.
* Accident prevention.

The 2-year check

This check is similar to the previous tests. It is often easier for the health visitor to carry out the check on a home visit. The parent is asked about any concerns. A physical examination is not normally carried out at this age.

* The height is measured if the child is cooperative.
* Weight is only checked if there is reason for concern.
* The parent is asked if there are any concerns about vision and hearing, and the child is referred to a specialist if necessary.
* A check is made that the child is walking and that the gait (manner of walking) is normal.
* Behaviour and any associated problems are discussed, for example tantrums, sleep disturbance, poor appetite or food fads.
* The possibility of iron deficiency is considered. It is common at this age and may be a cause of irritability, and developmental and behavioural problems, as well as of anaemia.

The 'school readiness' check at 4–5 years

This check is usually carried out by the GP and the health visitor. The parent is asked if

---

Health education points

* Nutrition and dental care: the child will be referred to the dentist if teeth are obviously decayed.
* Immunisations: check they are up-to-date.
* Common behavioural difficulties: such as temper tantrums, sleep disturbance, toilet training.
* Social behaviour: learning to play with other children and to share possessions.
* Accident prevention.

---

there are any general concerns about the child's progress and development, or any behavioural or emotional problems.

OBSERVATIONS

* Motor skills: can the child walk, run and climb stairs? Does the child tire more quickly than other children?

* Fine manipulative skills: can the child control pencils and paintbrushes?

* Behaviour: parents are asked about the child's ability to concentrate, to play with others and to separate from them without distress.

* Vision, language and hearing: observation and discussion with the parent will determine any problems which may need specialist assessment.

MEASUREMENT

Height and weight are measured and plotted on the growth chart.

EXAMINATION

* The heart is listened to for any abnormal sounds.

* The lungs are listened to for wheezing.

* In a boy, the testes will be checked again; if still not descended, he will be referred to a surgeon.

* The spine is inspected for signs of curvature or spina bifida occulta.

Health education points

* Immunisation: preschool booster.
* Dental care: diet – danger of sweets and snacks; brushing teeth; dental decay; visits to the dentist.
* The child's needs for play, conversation and social learning.
* The recognition and management of minor ailments.
* Accident prevention.

---

* Blood pressure is usually only measured if the child has a history of renal disease or growth problems.

The 8-year check

This is carried out by the school nurse, and parents are encouraged to attend the sessions at school. It involves the following:

* A general review of progress and development; the parent may voice concerns, such as bedwetting (enuresis) or food fads.

* Height and weight are measured.

* Vision is tested, and if a problem is found the child is referred to an ophthalmologist or optician.

Health education points

* Accident prevention: particularly safety on the roads and awareness of 'stranger danger'.
* Diet.
* Exercise.
* Dental health.

Parents who are concerned that their child is not hearing properly should have access to hearing testing. This is particularly important if the child has had:

* meningitis;
* measles or mumps;
* recurrent ear infections or glue ear.

Speech discrimination test

Any child who is suspected of having a hearing loss, or whose language development is delayed, may have the speech discrimination test. This involves using a set of toys, each with a single-syllable name – for example, dog, horse, key, tree, spoon, house, cup – which will test the child's ability to hear different consonants like 'd', 'g', 'p', 'm', 's', 'f' and 'b'. The child is gently encouraged to cooperate with the tester and together they name the toys using a normal voice. The child is then asked to find the toys with decreasing voice intensity, for example 'Show me the house', 'Put the duck in the box'. Each ear is tested through the complete range of sounds.

THE PRIMARY HEALTH CARE TEAM AND HEALTH SERVICES

The primary health care team (PHCT) is made up of a team of professionals which generally includes one or more of the following:

- **General practitioner (GP) or family doctor:** cares for all members of the family and can refer for specialist services.
- **Health visitor:** carries out developmental checks and gives advice on all aspects of child care.
- **Practice nurse:** works with particular GP; provides services such as immunisation and asthma and diabetes clinics.
- **Community midwife:** delivers antenatal care and cares for the mother and baby until 10–28 days after delivery.
- **District nurse:** cares for clients in their own homes.

Some health authorities also employ a **community paediatric nurse** – a district nurse with special training in paediatrics to care for sick children at home.

Services offered by the primary health care team

Services will include some or all of the following:

- child health clinics (see below);

- antenatal clinics;
- immunisation clinics;
- specialist clinics (e.g. for asthma or diabetes);
- family planning clinics;
- speech and language therapy;
- community dietician;
- community physiotherapists;
- community occupational therapists;
- community paediatrician;
- clinical medical officer (CMO);
- community dental service.

Child health clinics

Child health clinics are often held at the health centre or in a purpose-built centre. In rural areas the clinic may take turns with other community groups in village halls or community centres. Depending on the population served, clinics may be weekly or fortnightly and are run by health visitors, health care assistants and nursery nurses. A doctor or community paediatrician is usually present at specified times. Services provided at a child health clinic include:

- routine developmental surveillance (or reviews);
- medical examinations;
- immunisations;
- health promotion advice;
- antenatal and parent craft classes.

The School Health Service

The school health service is part of the community child health service and has direct links with those who carry out health checks on children before they start school. The aims of the school health service are to:

- ensure that children are physically and emotionally fit so that they can benefit fully from their education and achieve their potential;

❖ prepare them for adult life and help them to achieve the best possible health during the school years and beyond.

SERVICES PROVIDED BY THE SCHOOL HEALTH SERVICE

1 **Routine testing for vision, hearing or speech** to discover which children may need further tests or treatment. If treatment is thought to be required, the child's parents will be informed and consent requested.

2 The school nurse may work with one or more schools, and provides an important link between the school and health services. School nurses provide the following services:

  ❖ **growth measurements** – height and weight;

  ❖ advice on management of **health conditions**; for example, if a child has a long-term illness or special need the nurse will discuss possible strategies with the child's teacher;

  ❖ **enuresis** (bedwetting) support and advice, including providing an enuresis alarm;

  ❖ **immunisation**;

  ❖ advice on **health and hygiene**, sometimes running workshops or similar sessions;

  ❖ advice for parents on **specific health issues**, such as treating head lice or coping with asthma;

  ❖ **eyesight tests** from time to time;

  ❖ liaison with the **school doctor**.

3 The attention of the school doctor is drawn to any possible problems, and parents and the GP or family doctor are informed if any further action is considered necessary. The school doctor visits the school regularly and meets with the school nurse (or health visitor) and with teachers to find out whether any pupils need medical attention. In addition, the doctor reviews the medical notes of all children in Year 1 and of all new pupils transferring to the school.

4 Parents are usually requested to complete a **health questionnaire** about their child at certain stages, and are asked if they would like their child to have a full medical examination. In addition, the school doctor may ask for parental consent to examine a child if his or her medical records are incomplete or if the doctor particularly wishes to check on the child's progress. Parents are invited to be present at any medical examination and kept informed if the school doctor wishes to see their child again or thinks that they should be seen by the family doctor or a specialist.

5 The **audiometry team** checks children's hearing on a number of occasions before the age of 13 or 14 years. The school doctor will be told if a child seems to have a hearing problem. The doctor will then examine the child and let the family doctor know the result.

6 The **speech and language therapist** can provide assessment and treatment if the parent, a teacher or the school doctor feels that a child may have a speech or language problem.

Your role in child health screening and surveillance

Many methods have been devised to record growth and development in a systematic manner; none of them alone provides a diagnosis. Their aim is to assist in the detection of those children who need further examination. Early childhood practitioners are in an ideal position to be able to notice if a child is not making progress in any area of development. Continuous, structured **observation** is the most effective tool for assessing development, and any cause for concern should be noted and referred to the health visitor or paediatrician.

Throughout your training you will have learnt about child development and the importance of knowing what to expect from children at each developmental stage. When working with children you can use this knowledge and your powers of **skilled observation** to detect any developmental or health problems. Increasingly, trained early childhood practitioners are being employed in child health clinics to assist doctors and health visitors in carrying out routine screening tests and to offer parents advice on all aspects of child health and development.

Section 2: The effects of ill health on children and families

INFECTION

Infectious diseases are extremely common in childhood. An infection starts when certain microorganisms enter the body and start to multiply. The body, in turn, reacts to this infection and uses various methods to try to destroy the microorganisms. The illness that results is due partly to the effects of the multiplying microorganisms and partly to the body's subsequent reactions. Infections may be localised to one part of the body (e.g. **conjunctivitis** is limited to the eye) or they may be more widespread, affecting many of the body systems (e.g. **measles**). Not all microorganisms are **pathogenic** (disease-causing in humans). Pathogenic

microorganisms are also called **germs** and can only be seen with the aid of a powerful microscope. Germs may be subdivided into these categories:

❖ bacteria;

❖ viruses;

❖ protozoa;

❖ fungi;

❖ animal parasites.

Bacteria

Bacteria are abundant almost everywhere – in the air, soil and water – and most are harmless to humans. Indeed some bacteria are beneficial, such as those that live in the intestines and help to break down food for digestion. Bacteria need warmth, moisture and food to survive

Examples of diseases caused by bacteria include:

❖ food poisoning, or salmonella;

❖ cholera;

❖ typhoid;

❖ whooping cough (pertussis);

❖ tuberculosis;

❖ tetanus;

❖ gonorrhoea (a sexually transmitted disease);

❖ tonsillitis.

Viruses

Viruses are the smallest known type of pathogenic microorganism and cannot be seen under an ordinary microscope. They can only replicate *inside* host cells, which makes them difficult to treat because killing the virus also puts the host cell at risk. The best defence against viruses, therefore, is to stop them getting into the cells in the first place.

Examples of diseases caused by viruses include:

❖ flu;

❖ cold;

❖ measles;

❖ mumps;

❖ rubella;

❖ chicken pox;

❖ shingles (herpes zoster);

❖ tetanus;

❖ HIV/AIDS;

❖ rabies.

Protozoa

All types of protozoa are simple, one-celled animals and are of microscopic size. About 30 different types of protozoa are troublesome parasites of humans.

Examples of diseases caused by protozoa include:

❖ diarrhoeal infections;

❖ trichomoniasis (a sexually transmitted infection);

❖ malaria;

❖ toxoplasmosis (a disease acquired from cats).

Fungi

Fungi are simple, parasitic life forms, including moulds, mildews, mushrooms and yeasts. Some fungi are harmlessly present all the time in areas of the body such as the mouth, skin, intestines and vagina, but are prevented from multiplying through competition from bacteria. Other fungi are dealt with by the body's immune system.

Examples of fungal infection include:

❖ thrush (candidiasis);

❖ athlete's foot;

❖ ringworm.

Animal parasites

Parasites are organisms which live *in* or *on* any other living creature. They obtain their food from the host's blood or tissues and are thus able to reproduce. Parasites may remain permanently with their host or may spend only part of their life cycle in association.

Examples of infection by parasites include:

❖ head lice;

❖ scabies mites;

❖ fleas;

❖ threadworms.

The chain of infection

Infective microorganisms cannot survive without their essential needs being met; these needs are:

❖ warmth;

❖ moisture;

❖ food;

❖ time.

Some also require oxygen, but others do not.

The source or reservoir

All infection starts with either a source or a reservoir.

The **source** may be:

❖ a person who is already infected with the disease;

❖ someone who is unaware that they have the disease but is **incubating** it;

❖ a carrier of the disease, that is, someone who has either had the disease and is convalescent or who carries the causative organism with no obvious effects;

❖ a household pet – cats and dogs may be sources of streptococcal infections, as well as sources of infestation by fleas and roundworms.

A **reservoir** of infection may exist which allows organisms to survive and multiply. Examples include:

❖ dust;

❖ organic matter (e.g. food);

❖ secretions (e.g. saliva, sputum and mucus);

❖ excretions (e.g. urine and faeces);

❖ discharges (e.g. pus from a wound or a boil);

❖ sinks, taps, waste pipes and drains.

The route of spread

Organisms may spread from the reservoir or source by *direct* or *indirect* means (see Figure 11.7).

DIRECT INFECTION

❖ **Touch:** skin which is unbroken (i.e. with no cuts or grazes) provides an effective barrier to most organisms, although diseases such as **impetigo** can be transferred onto skin already infected by eczema. Scabies is also spread by skin contact.

❖ **Droplet or airborne infection:** if a person coughs or sneezes without covering their nose and mouth, the droplets may be carried several metres. Droplets are inhaled by people in the room; similarly, infection may be spread in this way by talking closely with others.

❖ **Kissing:** organisms are transferred directly from mouth to mouth; glandular fever (mononucleosis) is often referred to as the 'kissing disease'.

❖ **Injection:** the sharing of needles and syringes by drug addicts may cause infection to be transmitted by the blood. HIV infection and hepatitis B may both be transmitted in this way.

❖ **Sexual contact:** the transmission of diseases such as syphilis, gonorrhoea, HIV and non-specific genital infection (NSGI) is via sexual intercourse.

INDIRECT INFECTION

❖ **Water:** the contamination of water used for drinking is a major cause of the spread of diseases (e.g. typhoid fever, cholera, viral hepatitis A). Swimming in polluted water may cause ear infections. Schistosomiasis is a parasitic disease which afflicts over 200 million people worldwide; it is acquired by bathing in lakes and rivers infested by the schistosome fluke, which enters the human skin. Eating shellfish that live in

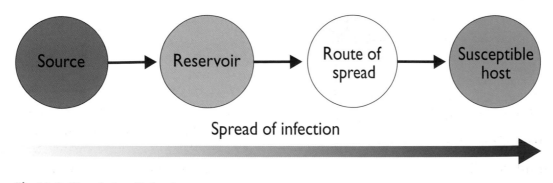

Fig 11.6 The chain of infection

polluted water may cause food poisoning or tapeworm infestations. Legionnaire's disease is a form of bacterial pneumonia caused by the inhalation of water droplets from contaminated air-conditioning tanks.

❖ **Food:** animals that are kept or caught for food may harbour disease organisms in their tissues. If meat or milk from such an animal is taken without being thoroughly cooked or pasteurised, the organisms may cause illness in the human host (e.g. food poisoning).

❖ **Insects:** many types of fly may settle first on human or animal excrement and then on our food, to lay eggs or to feed. Typhoid fever and food poisoning are diseases spread in this way. Biting insects can spread serious infections through their bites. Examples include the mosquito (malaria and filariasis), the tsetse fly (African trypanosomiasis), the rat flea (plague) and the sand fly (leishmaniasis).

❖ **Rats:** rats may harbour the leptospirosis bacterium, which is excreted in their urine and may be transmitted to humans. (Leptospirosis is also known as Weil's disease.)

Some common terms

INCUBATION PERIOD

This is the time gap between the entry of the microorganism into the body and the first appearance of symptoms. This period varies considerably with each infection. During the incubation period the infected child is likely to pass on the microorganism to others.

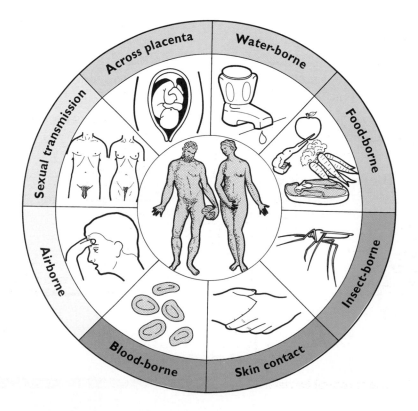

Fig 11.7 The spread of infection

Quarantine period

This refers to the amount of time for which children who have been in contact with the disease are advised to remain at home or otherwise isolated. As some diseases are highly infective even before symptoms appear (e.g. chickenpox), the quarantine period may have little relevance.

Fomites

Fomites are inanimate articles – such as clothing, books, toys, towels or a telephone receiver – which are not harmful in themselves, but which may harbour an infection that can then be passed to another person. They are responsible particularly for the spread of respiratory infections and gastroenteritis.

Immunity

Immunity is the ability of the body to resist infection. When the body is attacked by bacteria there may be a localised reaction in the form of inflammation and a general response, including fever. There is also a specific immune response when the body recognises the bacteria as foreign and produces antibodies (proteins with a protective role) which resist the particular bacteria.

RECOGNISING GENERAL SIGNS OF ILLNESS IN BABIES AND CHILDREN

Small children are not always able to explain their symptoms and may display non-specific complaints such as headache, sleeplessness,

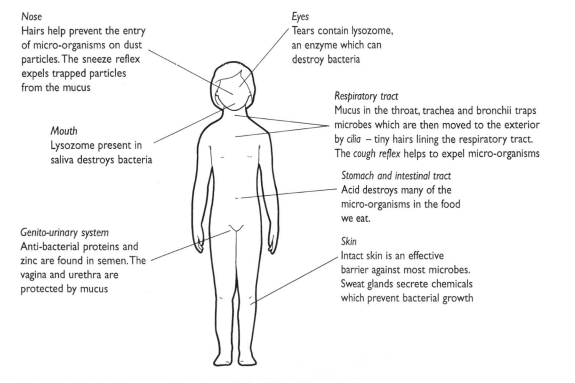

Nose
Hairs help prevent the entry of micro-organisms on dust particles. The sneeze reflex expels trapped particles from the mucus

Mouth
Lysozome present in saliva destroys bacteria

Genito-urinary system
Anti-bacterial proteins and zinc are found in semen. The vagina and urethra are protected by mucus

Eyes
Tears contain lysozome, an enzyme which can destroy bacteria

Respiratory tract
Mucus in the throat, trachea and bronchii traps microbes which are then moved to the exterior by *cilia* – tiny hairs lining the respiratory tract. The *cough reflex* helps to expel micro-organisms

Stomach and intestinal tract
Acid destroys many of the micro-organisms in the food we eat.

Skin
Intact skin is an effective barrier against most microbes. Sweat glands secrete chemicals which prevent bacterial growth

Fig 11.8 The body's natural barriers to infection

vomiting or an inability to stand up. Babies have even less certain means of communication, and may simply cry in a different way, refuse feeds or become listless and lethargic. In most infectious illnesses, there will be **fever**.

Signs of illness are those that can be **observed** directly, for example a change in skin colour, a rash or a swelling. **Symptoms** of illness are those **experienced** by the child, for example pain, discomfort or generally feeling unwell. Detection of symptoms relies on the child being able to describe how they are feeling.

Identifying signs of illness in children with different skin tones

Both within and between different ethnic groups there is a wide variety of skin tones and colours affecting the way skin looks during illness. When dark-skinned children are ill they may show the following signs:

- Skin appearance: normal skin tone and sheen may be lost; the skin may appear dull and paler or greyer than usual. You must pay attention to those parts of the body with less pigmentation – the palms, the tongue, the nail beds and the conjunctiva – the insides of the bottom eyelids – all of these will be paler than usual.

- Rashes: in children with very dark skin raised rashes are more obvious than flat rashes.

- Bruising: the discoloration that is obvious in pale skin may not be easily observed in darker-skinned children. When bruised the skin may appear darker or more purple when compared with surrounding skin.

- Jaundice: in a fair-skinned child, you would gently press your finger to his forehead, nose or chest, and look for a yellow tinge to the skin as the pressure is released. In a darker-skinned child, you should check for yellowness in his gums or the whites of his eyes.

Recognising illness in babies

The responsibility of caring for a baby who becomes ill is enormous; it is vital that carers know the signs and symptoms of illness and when to seek medical aid. (See Chapter 13, page 555, for general signs of illness in babies.)

WHAT YOU SHOULD DO

- **Observe the baby carefully** and note any changes; record his or her temperature and take steps to reduce a high temperature (see page 400).

- **Give extra fluids** if possible and carry out routine skin care. The baby may want extra physical attention or prefer to rest in his cot.

MENINGITIS IN BABIES

Meningitis is an inflammation of the lining of the brain. It is a very serious illness, but if it is detected and treated early, most children make a full recovery. The early symptoms of meningitis – such as fever, irritability, restlessness, vomiting and refusing feeds – are also common with colds and flu. However, a baby with meningitis can become seriously ill within hours, so it is important to act quickly if meningitis is suspected.

SYMPTOMS OF MENINGITIS

In babies under 12 months, these include:

- Tense or bulging fontanelles.
- High temperature.
- A stiffening body with involuntary movements, or a floppy body.
- May be difficult to wake.
- Blotchy or pale skin.
- May refuse to feed.
- A high-pitched, moaning cry.
- Red or purple spots (anywhere on the body) that do not fade under pressure. Do the 'glass test' (see below).

In older children, these include:

❖ Headache.

❖ Neck stiffness and joint pains; the child may arch the neck backwards because of the rigidity of the neck muscles.

❖ An inability to tolerate light.

❖ Fever.

The glass test

Press the side or bottom of a glass firmly against the rash – you will be able to see if the rash fades and loses colour under the pressure. If it does not change colour summon medical aid immediately. If spots are appearing on the child's body this could be septicaemia, a very serious bacterial infection described as the 'meningitis rash'.

General signs and symptoms of illness

When children feel generally unwell you should ask them if they have any pain or discomfort and treat it appropriately. Take their temperature and look for other signs of illness, such as a rash or swollen glands. Often, feeling generally unwell is the first sign that the child is developing an **infectious disease**. Some children can also show general signs of illness if they are anxious or worried about something, either at home or at school.

EMOTIONAL AND BEHAVIOURAL CHANGES

Children react in certain characteristic ways when they are unwell. Some of the more common emotional and behavioural changes include:

❖ being quieter than usual;

❖ becoming more clingy to their parents or primary carer;

❖ attention-seeking behaviour;

❖ changed sleeping patterns – some children sleep more than usual, others less;

❖ lack of energy;

❖ crying – babies cry for a variety of reasons (see Chapter 13); older children who cry more than usual may be physically unwell or you may need to explore the reasons for their unhappiness;

❖ regression – children who are unwell often regress in their development and behaviour; they may:

1 want to be carried everywhere instead of walking independently;

2 go back to nappies after being toilet-trained;

3 start to wet the bed;

4 play with familiar, previously outgrown toys.

Common signs and symptoms of illness in children

❖ **Loss of appetite:** the child may not want to eat or drink; this could be because of a sore, painful throat or a sign of a developing infection.

❖ **Lacking interest in play:** he may not want to join in play, without being able to explain why.

❖ **Abdominal pain:** the child may rub his or her tummy and say that it hurts – this could be a sign of gastroenteritis.

❖ **Raised temperature (fever):** a fever (a temperature above 38°C) is usually an indication of viral or bacterial infection, but can also result from overheating.

❖ **Diarrhoea and vomiting:** attacks of diarrhoea and/or vomiting are usually a sign of gastroenteritis.

❖ **Lethargy or listlessness:** the child may be drowsy and prefer to sit quietly with a favourite toy or comfort blanket.

> ❖ **Irritability and fretfulness:** the child may have a change in behaviour, being easily upset and tearful.
>
> ❖ **Pallor:** the child will look paler than usual and may have dark shadows under the eyes; a black child may have a paler area around the lips and the conjunctiva may be pale pink instead of the normal dark pink.
>
> ❖ **Rash:** any rash appearing on the child's body should be investigated – it is usually a sign of an infectious disease.

HIGH TEMPERATURE (FEVER)

The normal body temperature is between 36 and 37°C. A temperature of above 37.5°C means that the child has a fever. Common sense, and using the back of your hand to feel the forehead of an ill child, is almost as reliable in detecting a fever as using a thermometer.

A child with a fever may:

❖ look hot and flushed; complain of feeling cold, and shiver (this is a natural reflex due to the increased heat loss and a temporary disabling of the usual internal temperature control of the brain);

❖ be either irritable or subdued;

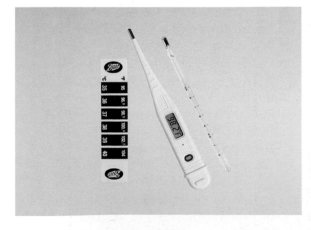

Fig 11.9 Different thermometers: strip, digital and clinical

❖ be unusually sleepy;

❖ go off his or her food;

❖ complain of thirst.

Children can develop high temperatures very quickly. You need to know how to bring their temperature down to avoid complications, such as dehydration and febrile convulsions.

All family first-aid kits should contain a thermometer. There are three types: clinical thermometer, digital thermometer and temperature strips.

A **clinical thermometer** is a glass tube with a bulb at one end containing mercury. This tube is marked with gradations of temperature in degrees Centigrade and/or Fahrenheit. When the bulb end is placed under the child's armpit, the mercury will expand, moving up the tube until the temperature of the child's body is reached.

A **digital thermometer** is battery-operated and consists of a narrow probe with a tip sensitive to temperature. It is easy to read via a display panel and is unbreakable.

A **plastic fever strip** is a rectangular strip of thin plastic which contains temperature-sensitive crystals that change colour according to the temperature measured. It is not as accurate as the other thermometers, but is a useful check.

Whatever the cause of a high temperature, it is important to try to reduce it (see box below). There is always the risk that a fever could lead to convulsions or fits.

Using a clinical thermometer

1   Explain to the child what you are going to do.

2   Collect the thermometer; check that the silvery column of mercury is shaken down to 35°C.

Table 11.2 Illness in babies.

Condition (and cause)	Signs and symptoms	Role of the carer
Colic	This occurs in the first 12 weeks. It causes sharp, spasmodic pain in the stomach, and is often at its worst in the late evening. Symptoms include inconsolable high-pitched crying, drawing her legs up to her chest, and growing red in the face.	Try to stay calm! Gently massage her abdomen in a clockwise direction, using the tips of your middle fingers. Sucrose solution (3.35 ml teaspoons of sugar in a cup of boiling water and left to cool) is said to have a mild pain-killing effect on small babies. Dribble 2 ml of this solution into the corner of the baby's mouth twice a day. If the problem persists, contact the doctor.
Diarrhoea	Frequent loose or watery stools. Can be very serious in young babies, especially when combined with vomiting, as it can lead to severe dehydration.	Give frequent small drinks of cooled, boiled water containing glucose and salt or a made-up sachet of rehydration fluid. If the baby is unable to take the fluid orally, she must be taken to hospital urgently and fed intravenously, by a 'drip'. If anal area becomes sore, treat with a barrier cream.
Gastroenteritis (virus or bacteria)	The baby may vomit and usually has diarrhoea as well; often has a raised temperature and loss of appetite. May show signs of abdominal pain, i.e. drawing up of legs to chest and crying.	Reassure baby. Observe strict hygiene rules. Watch out for signs of dehydration. Offer frequent small amounts of fluid, and possibly rehydration salts.
Neonatal cold injury – or hypothermia	The baby is cold to the touch. Face may be pale or flushed. Lethargic, with runny nose, swollen hands and feet. Pre-term infants and babies under 4 months are at particular risk.	Prevention. Warm *slowly* by covering with several light layers of blankets and by cuddling. No direct heat. Offer feeds high in sugar and seek medical help urgently.
Reflux	Also known as gastro-intestinal reflux (GIR) or gastro-oesophageal reflux (GOR). The opening to the stomach is not yet efficient enough to allow a large liquid feed through. Symptoms include grizzly crying and excessive **possetting** after feeds.	Try feeding the baby in a more upright position and bring up wind by gently rubbing her back. After feeding leave the baby in a semi-sitting position. Some doctors prescribe a paediatric reflux suppressant or antacid mixture to be given before the feed.
Tonsillitis (virus or bacteria)	Very sore throat, which looks bright red. There is usually fever and the baby will show signs of distress from pain on swallowing and general aches and pains. May vomit.	Encourage plenty of fluids – older babies may have ice lollies to suck. Give pain relief, e.g. paracetamol. Seek medical aid if no improvement and if fever persists.
Cough (usually virus)	Often follows on from a cold; may be a symptom of other illness, e.g. measles.	Keep air moist. Check the baby has not inhaled an object. Give medicine if prescribed.

Table 11.2 (continued)

Condition (and cause)	Signs and symptoms	Role of the carer
Croup (virus)	Croup is an infection of the voice box or larynx, which becomes narrowed and inflamed. Barking cough (like sea lions), noisy breathing, distressed; usually occurs at night.	If severe, seek medical help. Reassure her and sit her up. Keep calm and reassure the baby. Inhaling steam may also benefit some babies. You can produce steam by boiling a kettle, running the hot taps in the bathroom, using a room humidifier or putting wet towels over the radiator. If using steam, take care to avoid scalding.
Bronchiolitis (virus)	A harsh dry cough which later becomes wet and chesty; runny nose, raised temperature, wheeze, breathing problems, poor feeding or vomiting. May develop a blue tinge around the lips and on the fingernails (known as cyanosis).	Observe closely. Seek medical help if condition worsens. Increase fluids. Give small regular feeds. Give prescribed medicine. Comfort and reassure.
Febrile convulsions (high temperature)	Convulsions caused by a high temperature (over 39° Centigrade, 102° Fahrenheit) or fever are called febrile convulsions. Baby will become rigid, then the body may twitch and jerk for one or two minutes.	Try not to panic. Move potentially harmful objects out of the way and place the baby in the recovery position. Loosen clothing. Call doctor. Give tepid sponging. Comfort and reassure.
Otitis media (virus or bacteria)	Will appear unwell; may have raised temperature. May vomit, may cry with pain. May have discharge from ear.	Take to doctor, give antibiotics and analgesics (or painkillers). Increase fluids; comfort and reassure.
Conjunctivitis (virus or bacteria)	Inflammation of the thin, delicate membrane that covers the eyeball and forms the lining of the eyelids. Symptoms include a painful red eye, with watering and sometimes sticky pus.	Take to doctor who may prescribe antibiotic eye drops or ointment. Bathe a sticky eye gently with cool boiled water and clean cotton wool swabs. Always bathe the eye from the inside corner to the outside to avoid spreading infection.
Common cold (coryza) (virus)	Runny nose, sneeze; tiny babies may have breathing problem.	Keep nose clear. Give small frequent feeds. Nasal drops if prescribed.
Meningitis (virus or bacteria)	Raised temperature, may have a blotchy rash. May refuse feeds, have a stiff neck, have a seizure. Bulging fontanelles; may have a shrill, high-pitched cry.	Seek medical help urgently. Reduce temperature. Reassure.

3   Sit the child on your knee and take their top layer of clothing off.

4   Place the bulb end of the thermometer in the child's armpit, holding her arm close to her side for at least 2 minutes.

5   Remove the thermometer and, holding it horizontally and in a good light, read off the temperature measured by the level of the mercury. Record the time and the temperature reading.

6   After use, wash the thermometer in tepid water, and shake the column of mercury down again to 35°C. Dry carefully and replace in case.

7   Decide whether to contact the parents – you may need to obtain their consent to give paracetamol.

A clinical thermometer should never be placed in a child's mouth, because of the danger of biting and breaking the glass.

USING A DIGITAL THERMOMETER

1   Place the narrow tip of the thermometer under the child's arm, as described above.

2   Read the temperature when it stops rising (some models beep when this point is reached).

USING A FEVER STRIP

1   Hold the plastic strip firmly against the child's forehead for about 30 seconds.

2   Record the temperature revealed by the colour change.

Guidelines for bringing down a high temperature

✤   **Offer cool drinks:** encourage the child to take small, frequent sips of anything he will drink (though preferably clear fluids like water or squash, rather than milky drinks). Do this even if the child is vomiting as some water will still be absorbed.

✤   **Remove clothes:** keep the child as undressed as possible to allow heat to be lost.

✤   **Reduce bedclothes:** use a cotton sheet if the child is in bed.

✤   **Sponge the child down:** use tepid water (see below).

✤   **Give the correct dose of children's paracetamol:** make sure you have written consent from the parents to use it in case of emergency. If not, contact the parents and try to obtain consent.

✤   **Cool the air in the child's room:** use an electric fan or open the window.

✤   **Reassure the child:** they may be very frightened. Remain calm yourself and try to stop a baby from crying as this will tend to push the temperature higher still.

✤   **If the temperature will not come down, call the doctor:** always consult a doctor if a high fever is accompanied by symptoms such as severe headache with stiff neck, abdominal pain or pain when passing urine.

Early childhood practitioners are advised that medicines should not be given unless the written permission of the parent or next of kin is obtained.

Guidelines for tepid sponging to reduce a temperature

1   Make sure the air in the room is comfortably warm – not hot, cold or draughty.

2   Lay the child on a towel on your knee or on the bed and gently remove their clothes; reassure them by talking gently.

3   Sponge the child's body, limbs and face with tepid or lukewarm water – not cold. As the water evaporates from the skin, it absorbs heat from the blood and so cools the system.

4   As the child cools down, pat the skin dry with a soft towel and dress only in a nappy or pants; cover them with a light cotton sheet.

5   Keep checking the child's condition to make sure that he does not become cold or shivery; put more light covers over the child if he is shivering or obviously chilled.

6   If the temperature rises again, repeat sponging every 10 minutes.

COMMON INFECTIOUS DISEASES IN CHILDHOOD

Everyone concerned with the care of babies and young children should be aware of the signs and symptoms of common infectious diseases, and should know when to summon medical aid.

When to call a doctor or call for an ambulance

If you think the child's life is in danger, dial 999 if you are in the UK, ask for an ambulance urgently and explain the situation. Contact the family doctor (GP) if the child has any of the following symptoms (if the doctor cannot reach you quickly, take the child to the accident and emergency department of the nearest hospital):

❖   Has a temperature of 38.6°C (101.4°F) that is not lowered by measures to reduce **fever**, or a temperature over 37.8°C (100°F) for more than one day.

❖   Has **convulsions**, or is limp and floppy.

❖   Has severe or persistent **vomiting** and/or **diarrhoea**, seems **dehydrated** or has projectile vomiting.

❖   **Cannot be woken**, is unusually drowsy or may be losing consciousness.

❖   Has symptoms of **meningitis**.

❖   Has symptoms of **croup**.

❖   Is pale, listless and **does not respond** to usual stimulation.

❖   **Cries or screams** inconsolably and may have severe pain.

❖   Has bulging **fontanelle** (soft spot on top of head) when not crying.

❖   Appears to have severe abdominal pain, with symptoms of **shock**.

❖   **Refuses** two successive feeds.

❖   Develops **purple–red** rash anywhere on body.

❖   Passes bowel motions (stools) containing **blood**.

❖   Has **jaundice**.

❖   Has a suspected **ear infection**.

Table 11.3 Common infectious illnesses.

disease and cause	spread	incu-bation	signs and symptoms	rash or specific sign	treatment	complications
COMMON COLD (coryza) Virus	Airborne/droplet, hand-to-hand contact	1–3 days	Sneeze, sore throat, running nose, headache, slight fever, irritable, partial deafness		Treat symptoms*. Vaseline to nostrils	Bronchitis, sinusitis, laryngitis
CHICKENPOX (varicella) Virus	Airborne/droplet, direct contact	10–14 days	Slight fever, itchy rash, mild onset, child feels ill, often with severe headache	Red spots with white centre on trunk and limbs at first; blisters and pustules	Rest, fluids, calamine to rash, cut child's nails to prevent secondary infection	Impetigo, scarring, secondary infection from scratching
DYSENTERY Bacillus or amoeba	Indirect: flies, infected food; poor hygiene	1–7 days	Vomiting, diarrhoea, blood and mucus in stool, abdominal pain, fever, headache		Replace fluids, rest, medical aid, strict hygiene measures	Dehydration from loss of body salts, shock; can be fatal
FOOD POISONING Bacteria or virus	Indirect: infected food or drink	½ hour to 36 hours	Vomiting, diarrhoea, abdominal pain		Fluids only for 24 hours; medical aid if no better	Dehydration – can be fatal
GASTROENTERITIS Bacteria or virus	Direct contact. Indirect: infected food/drink	Bacterial: 7–14 days Viral: 1 hour to 36 hours	Vomiting, diarrhoea, signs of dehydration		Replace fluids – water or Dioralyte; medical aid urgently	Dehydration, weight loss – death
MEASLES (morbilli) Virus	Airborne/droplet	7–15 days	High fever, fretful, heavy cold – running nose and discharge from eyes; later cough	Day 1: Koplik's spots, white inside mouth. Day 4: blotchy rash starts on face and spreads down to body	Rest, fluids, tepid sponging. Shade room if photophobic (disliking bright light)	Otitis media, eye infection, pneumonia, encephalitis (rare)

Table 11.3 (continued).

disease and cause	spread	incu-bation	signs and symptoms	rash or specific sign	treatment	complications
MENINGITIS (inflammation of meninges which cover the brain) Bacteria or virus	Airborne/droplet	Variable – usually 2–10 days	Fever, headache, drowsiness, confusion, photophobia arching of neck	Can have small red spots or bruises	Take to hospital; antibiotics and observation	Deafness, brain damage, death
MUMPS (epidemic parotitis) Virus	Airborne/droplet	14–21 days	Pain, swelling of jaw in front of ears, fever, eating and drinking painful	Swollen face	Fluids: give via straw, hot compresses, oral hygiene	Meningitis (1 in 400), orchitis (infection of testes) in young men
PERTUSSIS (Whooping cough) Bacteria	Airborne/droplet; direct contact	7–21 days	Starts with a snuffly cold, slight cough, mild fever	Spasmodic cough with whoop sound, vomiting	Rest and assurance; feed after coughing attack; support during attack; inhalations	Convulsions, pneumonia, brain damage, hernia, debility
RUBELLA (German measles) Virus	Airborne/droplet; direct contact	14–21 days	Slight cold, sore throat, mild fever, swollen glands behind ears, pain in small joints	Slight pink rash starts behind ears and on forehead. Not itchy	Rest if necessary. Treat symptoms	Only if contracted by woman in first 3 months of pregnancy – can cause serious defects in unborn baby
SCARLET FEVER (or Scarlatina) Bacteria	Droplet	2–4 days	Sudden fever, loss of appetite, sore throat, pallor around mouth, 'strawberry' tongue	Bright red pinpoint rash over face and body – may peel	Rest, fluids, observe for complications, antibiotics	Kidney infection, otitis media, rheumatic fever (rare)
TONSILLITIS Bacteria or virus	Direct infection, droplet		Very sore throat, fever, headache, pain on swallowing, aches and pains in back and limbs		Rest, fluids, medical aid – antibiotics, iced drinks relieve pain	Quinsy (abscess on tonsils), otitis media, kidney infection, temporary deafness

Table 11.4 When to call a doctor

If you think the child's life is in danger, dial 999 if you are in the UK, ask for an ambulance urgently and explain the situation.

Contact the family doctor (GP) if the child has any of the following symptoms. If the doctor cannot reach you quickly, take the child to accident and emergency department of the nearest hospital:

❖ Has a temperature of 38.6°C (101.4°F) which is not lowered by measures to reduce **fever**, or a temperature over 37.8°C (100°F) for more than one day.	❖ Has **convulsions**, or is limp and floppy.
❖ Has severe or persistent **vomiting** and/or **diarrhoea**, seems dehydrated or has projectile vomiting.	❖ **Cannon be woken**, is unusually drowsy or may be losing consciousness.
❖ Has symptoms of **meningitis**.	❖ Has **croup** symptoms.
❖ Is pale, listless, and **does not respond** to usual stimulation.	❖ **Cries or screams** inconsolably and may have severe pain.
❖ Has bulging **fontanelle** (soft spot on top of head) when not crying.	❖ Appears to have severe abdominal pain, with symptoms of **shock**.
❖ **Refuses** two successive feeds.	❖ Develops **purple-red rash** anywhere on body.
❖ Passes bowel motions (stools) containing blood.	❖ Has **jaundice**.
❖ Has a suspected **ear infection**.	❖ Has been **injured**, e.g. by a burn which blisters and covers more than 10% of the body surface.
❖ Has inhaled something, such as a peanut, into the air passages and may be **choking**.	❖ Has swallowed a **poisonous** substance, or an object, e.g. a safety pin or button.
❖ Has bright pink cheeks and swollen hands and feet (could be due to **hypothermia**).	❖ Has difficulty in **breathing**.

❖ Has been injured (e.g. by **a burn which blisters and covers** more than 10 per cent of the body surface).

❖ Has inhaled something, such as a peanut, into the air passages and may be **choking**.

❖ Has swallowed a **poisonous** substance, or an object (e.g. a safety pin or button).

❖ Has bright pink cheeks and swollen hands and feet (could be due to **hypothermia**).

❖ Has difficulty **breathing**.

DISORDERS OF THE DIGESTIVE TRACT

One of the most common signs that something is wrong with the digestive system is diarrhoea, when the bowel movements are abnormally runny and frequent. Other symptoms of infection or illness are vomiting and abdominal pain. Although these symptoms are often distressing – both to the child and his carer – they are rarely a serious threat to health.

Vomiting

Vomiting is the violent expulsion of the contents of the stomach through the mouth. A single episode of vomiting without other symptoms happens frequently in childhood. It could be a result of overeating or too much excitement. Vomiting has many causes, but in most cases there is little warning, and after a single bout the child recovers and quickly gets back to normal. The chart below details possible causes of vomiting in children over 1 year, and what to do about it.

Possible causes of vomiting with accompanying symptoms	What to do
Gastroenteritis The child also has diarrhoea.	See the doctor within 24 hours. **Prevent dehydration** (see page 409).
Intestinal obstruction The child's vomit is greenish-yellow.	**Call an ambulance.** Do not give the child anything to eat or drink.
Meningitis The child has a fever, a stiff neck or flat, purplish spots that do not disappear when pressed.	**Call an ambulance.**
Head injury The child has recently suffered a blow to the head.	**Call an ambulance.** Do not give the child anything to eat or drink.
Appendicitis The child has continuous abdominal pain around the navel and to the right side of the abdomen.	**Call an ambulance.** Do not give the child anything to eat or drink.
Infection The child seems unwell, looks flushed and feels hot.	**Reduce the fever.** See the doctor within 24 hours.
Hepatitis The child has pale faeces and dark urine.	See the doctor within 24 hours.
Travel sickness When travelling, the child seems pale and quiet and complains of nausea.	Give the child a travel sickness remedy before starting journey. Take plenty of drinks to prevent dehydration.
Migraine The child complains of a severe headache on one side of the forehead.	See the doctor if accompanied by severe abdominal pain (it could be appendicitis).
Whooping cough (pertussis) The child vomits after a bout of coughing.	See the doctor within 24 hours.

Helping a child who is vomiting

❖ Reassure the child, who may be very frightened.

❖ Stay with the child and support their head by putting your hand on their forehead.

❖ Keep the child cool by wiping the face with a cool, damp cloth.

❖ Offer mouthwash or sips of water after vomiting.

❖ Give frequent small drinks of cold water, with a pinch of salt and a teaspoon of glucose added – or you can buy special rehydrating powders.

❖ Encourage the child to rest, lying down with a bowl by their side. Do not leave them until they have fallen asleep – and stay within call in case they vomit again.

Diarrhoea

Most children have diarrhoea at some time, usually after an infection involving the digestive tract, for example **gastroenteritis**. If the fluid lost through passing frequent, loose, watery stools is not replaced, there is a danger the child will become **dehydrated**. Babies become dehydrated very quickly and can become seriously ill as the result of diarrhoea. Diarrhoea can also be caused by:

❖ emotional factors – overtiredness, excitement and anxiety;

❖ allergy;

❖ reaction to certain drugs and medicines.

Toddler's diarrhoea

Toddler's diarrhoea occurs when an otherwise healthy child (aged 1–3 years) passes loose, watery faeces. The cause is uncertain, but it is thought to be the result of poor chewing of food.

Care of a child with diarrhoea

❖ Reassure the child, who may be very distressed.

❖ Prevent dehydration by giving regular drinks of water.

❖ Keep a potty nearby.

❖ Be sympathetic when changing soiled underwear; soak any soiled clothing in a nappy sterilising solution before washing.

❖ Maintain a high standard of hygiene; hand washing by both you and the child is vital in preventing the spread of infection.

❖ Unless it is toddler diarrhoea, keep child away from other children; early years settings will have an exclusion policy in the case of infectious illness, such as gastroenteritis.

SIGNS AND SYMPTOMS

❖ Loose, watery faeces often containing recognisable pieces of food (e.g. raisins, corn, carrots and peas).

❖ Nappy rash if the child is in nappies.

WHAT TO DO

❖ Consult a doctor to exclude other causes of diarrhoea, such as an infection.

❖ Encourage the child to chew foods thoroughly.

❖ Mash or liquidise foods which are difficult to chew and digest.

Children generally grow out of toddler's diarrhoea by 3 years. As it is not an infectious condition there is no need for the child to be kept away from friends or from nursery.

Dehydration

Children can lose large amounts of body water through fever, diarrhoea, vomiting or exercise; this is called **dehydration**. In severe cases they may not be able to replace this water simply by drinking and eating as usual. This is especially true if an illness stops them taking fluids by mouth or if they have a high fever.

SIGNS OF DEHYDRATION IN BABIES

❖ **Sunken fontanelles** – these are the areas where the bones of the skull have not yet fused together; they are covered by a tough membrane and a pulse may usually be seen beating under the **anterior fontanelle** in a baby without much hair.

❖ **Fretfulness**.

❖ **Refusing feeds**.

❖ **Dry nappies** – because the amount of urine being produced is very small.

SIGNS OF DEHYDRATION IN CHILDREN

Mild to moderate dehydration:

❖ Dry mouth.

❖ No tears when crying.

+ Refusing drinks.

+ At first thirsty, then irritable, then becomes still and quiet.

+ Inactive and lethargic.

+ Increased heart rate.

+ Restlessness.

Severe dehydration:

+ Very dry mouth.

+ Sunken eyes and dry, wrinkled skin.

+ No urination for several hours.

+ Sleepy and disorientated.

+ Deep, rapid breathing.

+ Fast, weak pulse.

+ Cool and blotchy hands and feet.

WHAT TO DO

If you think a baby or child might have dehydration, do not try to treat them at home or in the setting. Call the doctor immediately or take the child to the nearest accident and emergency department. The doctor will prescribe oral rehydrating fluid to restore the body salts lost.

Infestations of the digestive tract

THREADWORMS

Threadworms are small, white worms that infest the bowel (see Figures 11.10(a) and (b)). People of any age can get threadworms, but they are most common in children aged 5–12 years. They *cannot* be caught from animals.

+ They are highly contagious, and pass easily from one person to another.

+ The eggs are usually picked up by the hands and then transferred to the mouth.

+ The eggs hatch in the small intestine, and the worms migrate downwards to the rectum where they emerge at night.

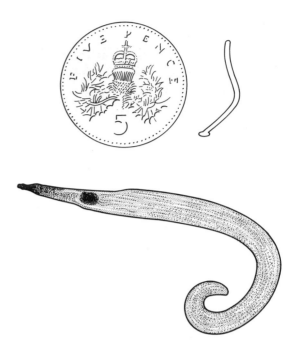

Fig 11.10 (a) The size of a threadworm in relation to a 5p coin; (b) Threadworm

+ They cause intense itching: the child will then scratch, eggs will be caught under the nails and the cycle may repeat itself.

+ Treatment will be prescribed by the doctor, and it is important that the whole family be treated at the same time.

+ Strict hygiene measures – scrubbing the nails after a bowel movement, the use of separate flannels and towels, and daily baths – help to prevent infestation.

TOXOCARIASIS

This is an infection of the roundworms that usually live in the gut of dogs and cats. The eggs of the worm are excreted in the faeces of the animal, and young children may pick them up and transfer them to their mouths. Infection can, occasionally, be serious, leading to epilepsy or blindness. Prevention is through public awareness: all dog and cat owners must regularly worm their pets, and dogs should not be allowed in areas where young children play.

SKIN DISORDERS

Up to 3 million microorganisms exist on each square centimetre of skin. Most of these are **commensals** (literally 'table companions' from the Latin) and are harmless to their host. These commensals have become adapted through evolution to live off human skin scales and the slightly acid secretions produced by the skin. Babies are born with no resident microbial flora. Pathogens (the organisms which cause disease) are discouraged by the presence of commensals.

Some important points to note regarding skin conditions are:

❖ **Newborn babies** are particularly prone to skin infection.

❖ **Microorganisms thrive in moist conditions** (e.g. at the axillae – the armpits – and the groin).

❖ **Washing and bathing** increases the number of bacteria released from the skin for up to 10 hours.

❖ **The skin can never be sterilised**. Iodine preparations used to prepare skin for surgical operations kill a large percentage of organisms but cannot remove the bacteria that colonise the hair follicles.

❖ To provide a **defence against infection**, the skin must be **intact** (i.e. unbroken).

There are two main reasons why the skin should be kept clean:

1   **To prevent infection** by microorganisms via the sweat pores.

2   **To prevent the accumulation of oil, sweat and microorganisms**, which will encourage insect parasites.

Parasitic skin infections

The three most common causes of parasitic skin infection in the Western world are:

❖ the head louse (pediculus capitis);

❖ the clothing or body louse (pediculus humanus);

❖ the scabies mite.

HEAD LICE

Head lice are a common affliction. Anybody can get them, but they are particularly prevalent among children. Head lice:

❖ are tiny insects with six legs;

❖ only live on human beings – they cannot be caught from animals;

❖ have mouths like small needles which they stick into the scalp and use to drink the blood;

❖ are unable to fly, hop or jump;

❖ are not the same as nits, which are the egg cases laid by lice (nits may be found 'glued' on to the hair shafts; they are smaller than a pinhead and are pearly white);

❖ are between 1 and 4 mm in size – slightly larger than a pinhead (see Figure 11.11);

❖ live on, or very close to, the scalp, and they do not wander down the hair shafts for very long;

❖ are caught just by coming into contact with someone who is infested – when heads touch, the lice simply walk from one head to the other;

❖ do not discriminate between clean and dirty hair, but tend to live more on smooth, straight hair.

If you catch one or two lice, they may breed and increase slowly in number. At this stage, most people have no symptoms. Many people only realise that they have head lice when the itching starts, usually after 2–3 months. The itching is due to an allergy, not to the bites themselves. Sometimes a rash may be seen on the scalp or lice droppings (a black powder, like fine pepper) may be seen on pillowcases.

THE LIFE CYCLE OF THE HEAD LOUSE

The female head louse lays 6–8 eggs a day; these eggs are dull, well-camouflaged and glued to the base of hair shafts. Hatching increases in warm, moist atmospheres. Once the eggs have hatched, the empty egg cases (called **nits**) remain glued to the hair and grow out with it at a rate of 1 cm per month, so distracting attention from the live eggs and lice. The nits are white and shiny and may be found further down the scalp, particularly behind the ears. They may be mistaken for dandruff, but unlike dandruff, they are firmly glued to the hair and cannot be shaken off.

PREVENTION

The best way to stop infection is for families to learn how to check their own heads. This way, parents can find any lice before they have a chance to breed. Families can then treat the lice and stop them being passed round. If a living, moving louse is found on one of the family's heads, the others should be checked carefully. Then any of them who have living lice should be treated at the same time.

HOW TO DETECT HEAD LICE

You will need a plastic detection comb (from the chemist), good lighting and an ordinary comb. Lice are most easily detected by fine tooth-combing wet hair. Some parents find that using a hair conditioner helps to lubricate the hair and ease the combing process; others report that such lubricants make it more difficult to see the eggs.

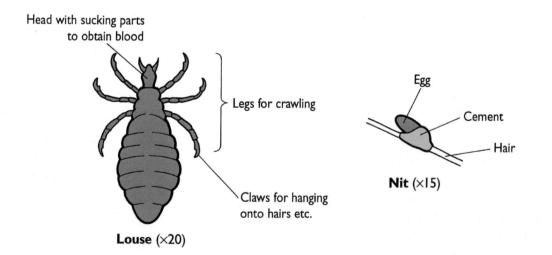

Head with sucking parts to obtain blood

Legs for crawling

Claws for hanging onto hairs etc.

Louse (×20)

Egg

Cement

Hair

Nit (×15)

Fig 11.11 A head louse and egg case (or nit)

Guidelines for detecting head lice

- ❧ Brush and comb the child's hair daily, preferably at night and in the morning until the child is old enough to do it alone.

- ❧ Comb thoroughly. Contrary to popular belief, head lice are not easily damaged by ordinary combing. However, regular combing may help to detect lice early and so help to control them.

- ❧ Inspect the child's hair prior to washing it; pay special attention to the areas behind the ears, the top of the head and the neckline.

- ❧ Examine the child's hair closely if he or she complains of an itchy scalp or if there is a reported outbreak of head lice at school or nursery.

TREATMENT

Treatment should only be used if you are sure that you have found a living, moving louse. Special head louse lotions should never be used 'just in case' or as a preventive measure, since the lotions may be harmful to young children when used repeatedly. So, check the heads of all the people living in your home, but only treat those who have *living, moving* lice. Treat them all at the same time, using a special lotion or aromatherapy mixture, not a shampoo. There are two main methods of treatment for head lice:

1   **Insecticide lotions:** lotions and rinses that are specifically formulated to kill lice and their eggs are available from pharmacists and from some child health clinics. Your school nurse, health visitor or pharmacist will advise you on which lotion to use. The lotion is changed frequently, as the lice become resistant to it and it no longer works. If you cannot afford the lotion, you can ask your GP for a prescription. Follow the instructions on the product carefully.

2   **Aromatherapy lotions:** these have been found to be very effective by parents in treating head lice. They are based on essential oils (containing extracts from plants such as rosemary, lavender, eucalyptus, geranium, tea tree, etc.). They can be applied to the hair in the evening – massaging the whole scalp with the oil to ensure the hair is completely covered in it – left overnight and then rinsed out in the morning. Alternatively, they are thoroughly massaged into the hair at bath time, left for half an hour and then rinsed out. Check with the supplier for their advice on the method to use.

The **Community Hygiene Concern** charity has developed the **bug buster** kit; this contains specially designed combs, which can rid a child of head lice without having to subject them to chemical treatments. This method has been approved by the Department of Health.

THE CLOTHING OR BODY LOUSE

Another name for this louse is the bedbug. It is similar to the head louse and is distinguished mainly by its different habitat: these lice hide during the day in cracks and crevices, and are often attached to clothing or blankets. They usually feed on people while they sleep at night, visiting their host to suck blood four or five times a night.

Transmission is mostly by contact, but may also occur through shared bedding and clothing.

TREATMENT

Treatment should be carried out with tact and sympathy in order to preserve self-respect:

* The floors and walls of the bedroom should be sprayed with liquid insecticide.
* Bedding should be treated with insecticide powder.
* Affected clothes should be treated by fumigation, washing in very hot water or dry-cleaning.

TREATMENT

For adults: insecticide is applied. Shaving is not necessary. Crab lice cause much distress to the sufferer and tend to discourage attendance at GUM (genito-urinary medicine) clinics.

THE SCABIES MITE

Scabies is largely a disease of families and young children. The scabies mite differs from the louse in that it does not have a recognisable head, thorax and abdomen.

* It has a tortoise-like body, with four pairs of legs.
* It is about 0.3 mm in size.
* It lives in burrows in the outer skin. These can be mistaken for the tracks made by a hypodermic needle.
* It is usually found in the finger webs, wrists, palms and soles.
* Transmission is mainly by body contact, which must last for at least 20 minutes.
* Cleanliness does not prevent infestation.
* A widespread itchy rash appears, which is most irritating at night.

* If untreated, secondary sepsis may occur, with boils and impetigo.

TREATMENT

Insecticide lotion is applied to the whole body below the neck; treatment is usually repeated after 24 hours. Calamine lotion may be used to soothe the itch that often lasts after treatment.

Allergic skin conditions

ECZEMA

Eczema (from the Greek 'to boil over') is an itchy and often unsightly skin condition that affects millions of people to some degree. The most common type which affects children is **atopic eczema**. About 1 in 8 children will show symptoms at some time, ranging from a mild rash lasting a few months, to severe symptoms that persist over years.

* Eczema is *not* infectious.
* It often starts as an irritating red patch in the creases of the elbows or knees, or on the face.
* It can spread quickly to surrounding skin, which becomes cracked, moist and red.
* In severe cases it can blister and weep clear fluid if scratched.
* Later, the skin becomes thickened and scaly.
* Skin damaged by eczema is more likely to become infected, particularly by a bacterium called **staphylococcus aureus** that produces yellow crusts or pus-filled spots.

CAUSES

There is no single known cause, but certain factors predispose a child to suffer from eczema:

* an allergy to certain foods (e.g. cow's milk);

❧ an allergy to airborne substances like pollen, house dust, scales from animal hair or feathers, or fungus spores;

❧ environmental factors (e.g. humidity or cold weather);

❧ a family history of allergy;

❧ emotional or physical stress.

Guidelines for managing eczema

In mild cases where the child's life is not disrupted, the following measures are usually advised:

❧ **Do not let the child's skin get dry**. Apply a moisturising cream or emollient to the skin several times a day. **Aqueous cream** is a good moisturiser and can also be used for washing instead of soap. **Apply the cream** with *downward* strokes – do not rub it up and down. (Try to put some cream on when you feed the baby or change a nappy.)

❧ **Identify triggers**. Identify and avoid anything that irritates the skin or makes the problem worse (e.g. soap powder, pets and other animals, chemical sprays, cigarette smoke or some clothing).

❧ **Avoid irritants**. These are substances that dry or irritate the baby's skin, such as soap, baby bath, bubble bath or detergents, and bathe the child in lukewarm water with a suitable skin oil added. Avoid wool and synthetics – cotton clothing is best.

❧ **Prevent scratching** – use cotton mittens for small children at night; keep the child's nails short.

❧ **Avoid certain foods**. Do not cut out important foods, such as milk, dairy products, wheat or eggs, without consulting the GP or health visitor. Citrus fruits, tomatoes and juice can be avoided if they cause a reaction.

❧ **House dust mite**. The faeces of the house dust mite can sometimes make eczema worse. If the child has fluffy or furry toys in the bedroom, the house dust mite collects on them. Limit these toys to one or two favourites, and either wash them weekly at 60°C or put them in a plastic bag in the freezer for 24 hours to kill the house dust mite.

❧ **Apply steroid creams** as prescribed by the GP; these must be used sparingly as overuse can harm the skin.

In severe cases, the GP will refer the child to a skin specialist (dermatologist).

CARING FOR A CHILD WITH ECZEMA IN THE EARLY YEARS SETTING

❧ **Food allergies** can create problems with school lunches and the cook having to monitor carefully what the child eats.

❧ **Clothing**. Wearing woolly jumpers, school uniform (especially if it is not cotton) and football kits can all make the eczema worse.

❧ **A special cleaner** may be needed rather than the school soap; the child may also need to use cotton towels as paper towels can cause a problem.

❖ **Extra time and privacy** may be needed for applying creams at school; children may need to wear bandages or cotton gloves to protect their skin.

❖ **Changes in temperature** can exacerbate the condition – getting too hot (sitting by a sunny window) or too cold (during PE in the playground).

❖ **Difficulty holding a pen**. If the eczema cracks they may not be able to hold a pen.

❖ **Pain and tiredness**. Eczema may become so bad that the child is in pain or needs to miss school, due to lack of sleep, pain or hospital visits.

❖ **Irritability and lack of concentration** can result from tiredness – sleep problems are very common as a nice warm cosy bed can lead to itching and therefore lack of sleep.

❖ **Using play dough, clay and sand**. Some children with eczema may have flare-ups when handling these materials.

❖ **Early childhood practitioners** should find out from the child's parents or specialist nurse which activities are suitable and which should be avoided; you should also provide **alternatives** so that the child is not excluded from the normal daily activities in the setting.

Other common skin disorders

❖ **Impetigo:** this is a highly contagious bacterial infection of the skin; the rash commonly appears on the face but can affect the rest of the body. The rash consists of yellowish crusts on top of a reddened area of skin. The child should not mix with others until the condition is treated. Impetigo is easily spread by contact with infected flannels and towels, so scrupulous attention to hygiene is necessary. Treatment is with antibiotic medicines and creams.

❖ **Warts:** these are the most common viral infection of the skin. They appear as raised lumps on the skin and are quite harmless. Most warts occur in children aged 6–12 years and disappear without treatment. If they become painful the local hospital's outpatient department will arrange for their removal, usually by freezing with liquid nitrogen (a form of cryosurgery).

❖ **Verrucae:** also known as plantar warts, these are warts on the sole of the foot, and may hurt because of pressure. They are picked up easily in the warm, moist atmosphere of swimming baths. Treatment is by the application of lotions or by freezing. Tincture of thuja is an effective homeopathic remedy.

❖ **Molluscum contagiosum:** this is a viral infection which consists of clusters of small, whitish-yellow, pearl-like spots on any part of the body. No treatment is necessary as the spots disappear within a few weeks or months.

❖ **Pytiriasis rosea:** this is an unidentified viral infection that affects mainly school-age children. The rash is scaly, consisting of beige-coloured oval patches that appear on the chest, back and limbs. Sometimes the rash will cause irritation and can be controlled by use of a mild steroid cream.

❖ **Ringworm:** this is not due to a worm at all; it is a fungal infection, often acquired from an animal. On the body it forms a reddish patch with a ring of small pimples at the edge. Usually it affects the scalp, causing the hair to break and sore, bald patches to appear. Treatment is by medicine (griseofulvin), and the hair does grow again.

* **Athlete's foot:** this is the name for ringworm that grows on the skin of the feet. It appears as a pink, flaky rash, particularly between the toes, and is intensely irritating. Treatment is by powder or cream; and the child should not walk barefoot around the house as the condition can easily spread to others.

* **Cold sores:** these are small, painful blisters that develop on or around the lips. They are caused by the herpes simplex virus and are caught by close contact with an infected person; they can be triggered by illness, cold winds, bright sunlight and emotional upset. Treatment is by an antiviral cream.

RESPIRATORY DISORDERS

Asthma

Asthma is a condition that affects the airways – the small tubes that carry air in and out of the lungs. If you have asthma, your airways are almost always sensitive and inflamed. When you come into contact with something you are allergic to, or something that irritates your airways (a trigger), your airways will become narrower, making it harder to breathe. The muscles around the walls of your airways tighten. The lining of the airways becomes inflamed and starts to swell; often sticky mucus or phlegm is produced.

ASTHMA IN CHILDREN

About 1 in 10 children will have an asthma attack (or episode) at some time. There are 1.2 million children in Britain who are currently receiving treatment for asthma. In general, children who have mild asthma are more likely to be free of symptoms once they grow up, but this is not guaranteed. Some people find that their asthma goes away when they are teenagers, but comes back again when they are adults.

Although there is no guarantee that symptoms will go away, they can usually be controlled with **medication**. Asthma should never be left untreated in the hope that a child may grow out of it.

CAUSES OF ASTHMA

There is no single cause of asthma. Most children who develop asthma have several **triggers**, or predisposing factors, and these vary from one child to another. Triggers include the following:

* **colds** and **viruses**;
* **pollen** – from grass;
* **pet hairs** and **feathers**;
* **tobacco smoke**;
* **stress** and excitement;
* **weather changes**;
* **exercise**;
* **mould**;
* **dust** and house dust mites;
* certain types of **medication**;
* **chemicals** and fumes (e.g. from car exhausts, paints and cleaning fluids);
* **certain foods** (e.g. peanuts, eggs).

It is important to try to identify possible triggers so they can be avoided. Generally, the more triggers present, the worse the attack. Typically, a child's first attack will follow 1 or 2 days after the onset of a respiratory illness, such as a cold.

SYMPTOMS OF ASTHMA

* **wheezing** (although some children with asthma do not experience wheezing);

- **elevated breathing rate** (the normal rate is under 25 breaths per minute; over 40 is cause for calling the doctor);
- **coughing**, especially in the early morning;
- **longer expiration** (breathing out) than inspiration (breathing in);
- **sweating**;
- the child may appear **very frightened**;
- the child **becomes pale**; a darker-skinned child may also appear drained of colour, particularly around the mouth.

Attacks may build over days or occur within seconds. There are two types of asthma:

1 **Acute asthma** (or an asthma attack or episode) – this may require medical stabilisation within a hospital setting.

2 **Chronic asthma** – this produces symptoms on a continual basis, and is characterised by persistent, often severe symptoms, requiring regular oral steroid medication.

WHAT TO DO IN THE EVENT OF AN ACUTE ASTHMATIC ATTACK

Not all asthma attacks can be prevented. When the child is having an acute attack of wheezing – the difficulty is in breathing *out* rather than catching one's breath – he needs a reliever drug (a bronchodilator, usually in a blue inhaler case). Most children will have been shown how to deliver the drug by an aerosol inhaler, a spinhaler or a nebuliser.

PREVENTION OF ASTHMA

- Where possible, avoid likely triggers of asthma (see above, page 417).
- **Preventer inhalers** are usually brown and contain corticosteroids. These have to be taken regularly every day, even when the child is feeling well; they act by reducing the inflammation and

swelling in the airways. Corticosteroid drugs should not be confused with the anabolic steroids taken by athletes to improve their performance.

Guidelines for helping a child who is having an asthmatic attack

- If the attack is the child's *first*, **call a doctor** and the parents.
- Stay calm and **reassure the child**, who may be very frightened.
- **Encourage the child to sit up** to increase lung capacity.
- If the child has a **reliever inhaler** or nebuliser, then supervise him while using it.
- **Never leave the child alone** during an attack.
- Try not to let other children crowd round.
- If these measures do not stop the wheezing and the child is exhausted by the attack, call a doctor. He or she will either give an injection of a bronchodilator drug or arrange admission to hospital.

Croup

This is a condition usually caused by a cold virus. It causes the child's windpipe (or trachea) to swell, and results in a characteristic barking cough – it sounds like crowing or sea lions barking. The child will feel panic and may wheeze.

Provide a steamy atmosphere by:

- running a hot bath and directing the steam at the child;
- using a vaporiser with special vaporising fluid – available from any chemist.

If the breathing becomes rapidly worse, take the child to hospital for emergency treatment.

ACUTE ILLNESS

An acute illness is one that occurs suddenly, and often without warning. It is usually of short duration. Examples are:

❖ gastroenteritis;

❖ otitis media – inflammation of the middle ear (see page 402);

❖ appendicitis;

❖ tonsillitis;

❖ an acute asthmatic attack.

Symptoms of acute illness

Signs of such illness in a child include:

❖ anorexia or **loss of appetite**;

❖ a lack of interest in **play**;

❖ unusual **crying** or screaming bouts;

❖ **diarrhoea** and **vomiting**;

❖ **abdominal pain** – babies with colic or abdominal pains will draw their knees up to their chest in an instinctive effort to relieve the pain;

❖ **lethargy** or listlessness;

❖ **pyrexia** (fever);

❖ **irritability** and fretfulness;

❖ **pallor** – a black child may have a paler area around the lips, and the conjunctiva may be pale pink instead of red;

❖ **dehydration** – any illness involving fever or loss of fluid through vomiting or diarrhoea may result in dehydration; the mouth and tongue become dry and parched, and cracks may appear on the lips. The first sign in a baby is a sunken anterior fontanelle (see page 409).

THE NEEDS OF SICK CHILDREN

Children who are sick have:

❖ **physical needs:** food and drink, rest and sleep, temperature control, exercise and fresh air, safety, hygiene and medical care;

❖ **intellectual and language needs:** stimulation, appropriate activities;

❖ **emotional and social needs:** love, security, play and contact with others.

The most important part of caring for sick children is to show that you care for them and to respond to all their needs. If a child is going to be nursed for some weeks, it is often useful to draw up a plan of care, just as nurses do in hospital. This has the following benefits:

❖ It helps you to keep a record of any changes in the child's condition and to ask for outside help if necessary.

❖ It reassures you that you are providing for all the child's needs.

❖ It enables you to plan a simple programme of activities to keep the child entertained and occupied.

❖ It enables another family member or colleague to assist in the general care, allowing you a break.

Meeting physical needs

BED REST

Children usually dislike being confined to bed and will only stay there if feeling very unwell. There's no need to keep a child with a fever in bed; take your lead from the child. Making a bed on a settee in the main living room will save carers the expense of extra heating and of tiring trips up and down stairs. The child will also feel more included in family life and less isolated. The room does not have to be particularly hot – just a comfortable temperature for you. If the child *does* stay in bed in his own room, remember to visit him often so that he does not feel neglected.

HYGIENE

All children benefit from having a routine to meet their hygiene needs, and this need not be altered drastically during illness.

TEMPERATURE CONTROL

If the child has a fever you will need to take their temperature regularly and use tepid sponging to reduce it (see page 400).

FEEDING A SICK CHILD AND PROVIDING DRINKS

* Children who are ill often have poor appetites – a few days without food will not harm the child, but fluid intake should be increased as a general rule.

* Drinks should be offered at frequent intervals to prevent dehydration – the child will not necessarily request drinks.

SAFETY WHEN CARING FOR A CHILD AT HOME

* Keep all medicines safely locked away in a secure cupboard.

* Supervise the child at all times; watch out for any sudden changes in their condition.

* Be aware of any potential complications of the child's condition and watch for warning signs.

Guidelines for caring for a child in bed

* Use cotton sheets – they are more comfortable for a child with a temperature.

* Change the sheets daily if possible – clean sheets feel better.

* Leave a box of tissues on a table next to the bed.

* If the child has bouts of vomiting, pillows should be protected and a container should be kept close to the bed. This should be emptied and rinsed with an antiseptic or disinfectant, such as Savlon, after use.

* Wet or soiled bed linen should be changed to prevent discomfort. Paper tissues that can be disposed of either by burning or by sealing in disposal bags are useful for minor accidents.

* A plastic mattress cover is useful as a sick child's behaviour may change and cause him or her to wet the bed.

Guidelines for a hygiene routine for a sick child

* The child's room should be well-ventilated and uncluttered. Open a window to prevent stuffiness, but protect the child from draughts.

* Provide a potty to avoid trips to the lavatory.

* Protect the mattress with a rubber or plastic sheet.

* A daily bath or shower is important. During an acute phase of illness, this can be done in the form of a bed bath – an all-over wash in bed (see below).

❖ Brush hair daily.

❖ Clean teeth after meals and apply Vaseline to sore, cracked lips.

❖ Keep the child's nails short and clean, and prevent scratching of any spots.

❖ Dress the child in cool, cotton clothing; put a jumper and socks or slippers over pyjamas if the child does not want to stay in bed the whole time.

Guidelines for giving a bed bath

❖ Make sure that the room is warm enough; close the windows to avoid draughts.

❖ Collect the things you will need and place on a table next to the bed: a bowl with warm water, soap, flannel or sponge, and towels.

❖ Remove the child's nightie or pyjamas.

❖ Cover the child with a sheet and remove the top bedding.

❖ Place a towel under each part of the body as it is washed.

❖ Start by washing the face and upper body.

❖ Use a separate flannel to wash the bottom and genital area.

Guidelines for encouraging sick children to drink

❖ Provide a covered jug of fruit juice or water; any fluid is acceptable according to the child's tastes (e.g. milk, meaty drinks or soups).

❖ If the child has mumps, do not give fruit drinks because the acid causes pain to the tender parotid glands.

❖ A sick toddler who has recently given up his bottle may regress. Allow him to drink from a bottle until he is feeling better.

❖ Try using an interesting curly straw.

❖ Give the child an 'adult' glass to make them feel special.

❖ Try offering drinks in a tiny glass or egg cup, which makes the quantities look smaller.

❖ Offer fresh fruit juices, such as pear, apple or mango; dilute them with fizzy water to make them more interesting, but avoid giving more than one fizzy drink a day; vary the drinks as much as possible.

❖ If the child does not like milk, add a milkshake mix or ice cream.

Guidelines for encouraging a sick child to eat

❖ Most children with a fever do not want to eat, so while you should offer food, you should never force a child to eat.

❖ Allow the child to choose their favourite foods.

❖ Give the child smaller meals, but more often than you would normally.

❖ If the child has a sore throat, give ice cream or an ice lolly made with fruit juice or yoghurt.

❖ If the child is feeling slightly sick, offer mashed potato.

❖ Offer snacks regularly and always keep the child company while they eat.

❖ Most children who are sick do not find ordinary food very appetising, but may be tempted to eat with 'soldiers' of fresh bread and butter, slices of fruit or their favourite yoghurt.

❖ Try to make food as attractive as possible; do not put too much on the plate at once and remember that sick children often cope better with foods that do not require too much chewing (e.g. egg custard, milk pudding, thick soups, chicken and ice cream).

GIVING MEDICINES

The medicine cabinet

Every home should have a properly stocked medicine cabinet, preferably locked, but always out of reach of children. The cabinet should contain:

❖ **children's paracetamol** – paracetamol elixir and junior paracetamol tablets (the doses for children of different ages should be on the bottles);

❖ **zinc and castor oil cream** for nappy rashes;

❖ mercury **thermometer** or digital thermometer and a fever strip;

❖ a **measuring spoon**, dropper or small cup for liquid medicines;

❖ a pack of assorted fabric **plasters** and one of hypoallergenic plasters;

❖ blunt-edge **tweezers**, safety pins and scissors;

❖ a small bottle of liquid **antiseptic** or mild antiseptic cream;

❖ a **hot-water bottle** – when wrapped in a towel it can relieve the pain of an aching abdomen;

❖ **calamine lotion** for soothing itchy spots and rashes;

❖ **wound dressings** (e.g. cotton wool and gauze pad already attached to a bandage);

❖ a small packet of **cotton wool**;

❖ packet of **skin closures**;

❖ **crêpe bandages**, open-weave bandage and triangular bandage;

❖ **surgical tape**.

Discard all the half-empty or improperly labelled bottles and any medicines that are over 6 months old.
Keep down costs by buying non-branded products.

Using prescribed medicines

Here is a list of essential points to bear in mind when medicines are prescribed for a child:

❖ Store all medicines out of reach of children and in childproof containers.

❖ Ask the doctor for as much information as possible about the medicines (e.g. if there are likely to be side effects or if certain foods should be avoided).

❖ Measure doses of medicine accurately, using a marked medicine spoon for liquid (teaspoons are not equivalent to a 5 ml spoon).

❖ Always follow instructions carefully.

❖ Most medicines for young children are made up in a sweetened syrup to make them more palatable.

❖ Remember that your attitude is important – if you show anxiety when giving medicine to a child, they will be anxious too.

❖ Store medicines at the correct temperature (i.e. in the fridge or away from direct heat if that is the direction on the bottle).

❖ Make sure you understand the instructions for giving the medicine before leaving the chemist (e.g. how much, how often and when; check whether it should be given before or after meals).

❖ Make sure that all the medicine is swallowed – this can be difficult with babies (see tips below).

❖ Throw away any leftover prescribed medicines on completion of treatment.

❖ If a child needs to take medicine contained in syrup regularly, remember to brush her teeth afterwards to prevent tooth decay.

❖ Never put medicines into a child's drink or food as the child may not take it all. If necessary, tablets can be crushed and added to a teaspoon of jam or honey. Follow this with a drink.

❖ *Do not* give aspirin to any child under the age of 10 years, because of the risk of **Reye's syndrome.**

❖ Always obtain **written consent** from the child's parents before giving any medicines.

Oral medicines

Most medicines for children are given as sweetened syrups or elixirs. They can be given with a spoon, tube or dropper.

Guidelines for giving oral medicines

1 Wash your hands before giving any medicine.

2 Always check the label on the bottle, and the instructions. If the medicine has been prescribed by the doctor, check that it is for your child and follow the instructions exactly; for example, some medicines have to be taken with or after food. Generally, oral medicines are best given before meals as they enter the bloodstream quickly.

3 Shake the bottle before measuring the dose. Always pour any medicine bottle with the label uppermost so that the instructions remain legible if the medicine runs down the side of the bottle.

4 Some medicines do not taste good (e.g. iron preparations). Always be truthful when the child asks, 'Does it taste bad?' Answer, 'The medicine doesn't taste good, but I'll give you some juice as soon as you've swallowed it.'

5 If the child is reluctant, you should adopt a no-nonsense approach and be prepared to resort to bribery if necessary (e.g. a favourite story or a chocolate). Never punish or threaten a child who refuses to take medicine.

Giving medicines to a baby or young child

❖ If possible, get someone to help you in case the baby wriggles.

❖ Cradle the baby comfortably on your lap, in the crook of your arm, so that he is slightly raised, with the head tilted back. (Never lay a baby down flat while giving medicine, because of the risk of inhalation.)

❖ Put a bib on the baby and have some baby wipes or a flannel close at hand to wipe him clean.

❖ If you are on your own, wrap a blanket around the baby's arms so that you can stop him wriggling.

❖ Only put a little of the medicine in his mouth at a time.

You can use a spoon, a dropper, a tube or a syringe to give medicine to a baby.

1 Using a spoon

❖ If the baby is very young, sterilise the spoon by boiling it or placing in sterilising solution. Gently pull down the baby's chin if he will not open his mouth – or get someone else to do this.

❖ Place the spoon on his lower lip, raise the angle of the spoon and let the liquid run into his mouth.

2 Using a dropper

❖ Take up the required amount of medicine into the dropper.

❖ Place the dropper in the corner of the baby's mouth and release the medicine gently.

3 Using a tube

❖ Pour the required dose into the tube.

❖ Place the mouthpiece on the baby's lower lip and let the medicine run gently into the mouth.

4 Using a syringe

❖ Fix the special adapter to the bottle and withdraw the required dose.

❖ Place the end of the syringe in the child's mouth, pointing towards the cheek, and slowly squeeze in the dose.

Giving medicines and tablets to older children

Older children do not seem to mind taking medicine and often want to pour it out for themselves. Always supervise children and make sure that they take the medicine

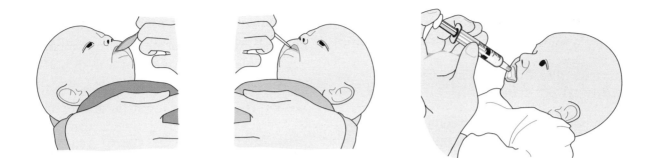

Fig 11.12 Giving medicines to a baby (a) by spoon; (b) by dropper; (c) by syringe

exactly as prescribed. After giving any medicine to a child, write down the time and the dosage.

How to give ear drops

❖ The child should lie down on one side – on a bed or on your lap – with the affected ear uppermost. Place a pillow under the child's head to keep it steady and comfortable.

❖ Pull the pinna (the top of the outer ear) gently backwards, towards the back of the head – this straightens out the ear canal.

❖ Hold the filled dropper just above the canal entrance. (Many ear drops are supplied in plastic bottles with pointed nozzles. If so, invert the bottle and squeeze gently.)

❖ Release the required number of ear drops into the ear.

❖ Gently massage the base of the ear to help disperse the liquid.

❖ Encourage the child to remain lying down in the same position for a few minutes.

❖ Put a piece of cotton wool loosely in the outer ear to prevent any leakage; do not pack it in too tightly as it may cause harm and be difficult to remove.

How to give nose drops

To a baby:

❖ Put the baby on a flat surface before you begin and get someone to help you if possible.

❖ Tilt the baby's head backwards slightly and gently drop liquid into each nostril.

❖ Count the number of drops as you put them in; two or three drops are normally sufficient – any more will run down the throat and cause the baby to cough and splutter.

❖ Keep the baby lying flat for 1 or 2 minutes.

To an older child:

❖ Ask the child to blow their nose and to lie down on a comfortable surface, with their head tilted slightly backwards.

❖ Gently release the prescribed number of drops into each nostril. Encourage the child to stay lying down for 1 or 2 minutes.

❖ Both ear drops and nose drops can be warmed slightly to make them more comfortable; stand the bottle in warm, not hot, water for a few minutes.

❖ Do not let the dropper touch the child's nose, or you will transfer the germs back to the bottle. If the dropper does touch the child, wash it thoroughly before replacing it in the bottle.

How to give eye drops or eye ointment

An important part of the healing process after an eye operation or an injury to the eye is the instillation of the prescribed eye drops and/or ointment. This is often a new experience for most children and their parents or carers, and the following guidelines may be useful.

PREPARATION

* A simple and honest explanation of what you are about to do, and perhaps a demonstration on the child's favourite doll or teddy, will help.

* It may be easier for you if the child lies flat, on a bed or a settee, with the head tilted back.

* Babies and young children may wriggle and put their hands up to their face – try wrapping them in a blanket so that they feel secure and their arms are tucked out of the way.

* Try to distract the child afterwards. This will reinforce the idea that having eye drops is quick and easy, and there is nothing for them to be afraid of.

GENERAL DIRECTIONS

* Read the label on the bottle or tube for directions.

* Wash your hands.

* Position the child.

* Gently pull down the lower lid with one finger and squeeze one drop into the eye. If using ointment, squeeze about 1 cm of ointment into the lower surface of the inside of the lower eyelid.

* Try not to allow the bottle or tube end to touch the child's eye.

* Replace the top of the bottle or tube immediately after use.

* Discard the medicine once treatment is completed; otherwise use a fresh bottle or tube every 4 weeks.

* Do not save it or use it for anyone else.

FIRST AID FOR BABIES AND CHILDREN

First aid is an important skill. By performing simple procedures and following certain guidelines, it may be possible to **save lives** by giving basic treatment until professional medical help arrives. Practice of first-aid skills is vital; in an emergency there is no time to read instructions. If you have memorised some of the most basic procedures, it will help you to react quickly and efficiently.

All those who work with children should take a recognised first-aid course, such as those run by the St John's Ambulance Association or the British Red Cross Society. You should also take refresher courses periodically, so that you feel competent to deal with any medical emergency.

The following pages explain the major first-aid techniques for babies and children. They should not be used as a substitute for attending a first-aid course with a trained instructor.

An ABC of resuscitation, 0–1 years

If a baby appears unconscious and gives no response:

A: Airway – open the airway.

* Place the baby on a firm surface.

* Remove any obstruction from the mouth.

* Put one hand on the forehead and one finger under the chin, and gently

tilt the head backwards **very slightly** (if you tilt the head too far back, it will close the airway again).

B: Breathing – check for breathing.

❖ Put your ear close to the baby's mouth.

❖ Look to see if the chest is rising or falling.

❖ Listen and feel for the baby's breath on your cheek.

❖ Do this for 5 seconds.

If the baby is not breathing:

1   Start **mouth-to-mouth-and-nose resuscitation**:

❖ Seal your lips around the baby's mouth and nose.

❖ Blow **gently** into the lungs until the chest rises.

❖ Remove your mouth and allow the chest to fall.

2   Repeat 5 times at the rate of 1 breath every 3 seconds.

3   Check the pulse.

C: Circulation – check the pulse.

Lightly press your fingers towards the bone on the inside of the upper arm and hold them there for 5 seconds.

If there is no pulse, or the pulse is slower than 60 per minute, and the baby is not breathing, start **chest compressions**:

1   Find a position a finger's width below the line joining the baby's nipples, in the centre of the breastbone.

2   Place the tips of two fingers on this point and press to a depth of about 2 cm (3/4 inch) at a rate of 100 times per minute.

3   After 5 compressions, blow gently into the lungs once.

4   Continue the cycle for 1 minute.

5   Carry the baby to a phone and dial 999 for an ambulance.

6   Continue resuscitation, checking the pulse every minute until help arrives.

If the baby is not breathing, but does have a pulse:

1   Start **mouth-to-mouth-and-nose resuscitation**, at the rate of 1 breath every 3 seconds.

2   Continue for 1 minute, then carry the baby to a phone and dial 999 for an ambulance.

If the baby does have a pulse and is breathing:

1   Lay the baby on its side, supported by a cushion, pillow, rolled-up blanket or something similar.

2   Dial 999 for an ambulance.

3   Check breathing and pulse every minute, and be prepared to carry out resuscitation.

An ABC of resuscitation, 1–10 years

A: Airway – open the airway.

❖ Lay the child flat on their back.

❖ Remove clothing from around the neck.

❖ Remove any obstruction from the mouth.

❖ Lift the chin and tilt the head back slightly to open the airway.

B: Breathing – check for breathing.

❖ Keep the airway open and place your cheek close to the child's mouth.

❖ Look to see if their chest is rising and falling.

❧ Listen and feel for their breath against your cheek.

❧ Do this for 5 seconds.

❧ If the child is not breathing, give 5 breaths, then check the pulse.

C: Circulation – check the pulse.

❧ Find the carotid pulse by placing your fingers in the groove between the Adam's apple and the large muscle running down the side of the neck.

❧ Do this for 5 seconds.

If the child is not breathing and does not have a pulse:

1 Begin a cycle of 5 chest compressions and 1 breath. Continue for 1 minute.

2 Dial 999 for an ambulance.

3 Continue at the rate of 1 breath to 5 compressions until help arrives.

If the child is not breathing but does have a pulse:

1 Give 20 breaths in 1 minute.

2 Dial 999 for an ambulance.

3 Continue mouth-to-mouth resuscitation, rechecking the pulse and breathing after each set of 20 breaths, until help arrives or until the child starts breathing again. When breathing returns, place the child in the recovery position.

Choking

Check inside the baby's mouth. If the obstruction is visible, try to hook it out with your finger, but do not risk pushing it further down. If this does not work, proceed as follows:

Mouth-to-mouth resuscitation

1 Open the airway by lifting the chin and tilting back the head. Check the mouth is clear of obstructions.

2 Close the child's nose by pinching the nostrils.

3 Take a deep breath and seal your mouth over the child's.

4 Blow firmly into the mouth for about 2 seconds, watching the chest rise.

5 Remove your mouth and allow the child's chest to fall.

6 Repeat until help arrives.

Chest compression

1 Make sure the child is lying on their back on a firm surface (preferably the ground).

2 Find the spot where the bottom of the ribcage joins on to the end of the breastbone, and measure a finger's width up from this point.

3 Using one hand only, press down sharply at a rate of 100 times a minute, to a depth of about 3 cm (1¼ inches). Counting aloud will help you keep at the right speed.

4 Continue until help arrives

❧ Lay the baby face down along your forearm, with your hand supporting her head and neck, and her head lower than her bottom (an older baby or toddler may be placed face down across your knee, with head and arms hanging down).

❧ Give 5 brisk slaps between the shoulder blades.

❧ Turn the baby over, check the mouth and remove any obstruction.

❧ Check for breathing.

❧ If the baby is not breathing, give 5 breaths (see **mouth-to-mouth-and-nose resuscitation**, page 427).

❧ If the airway is still obstructed, give 5 chest compressions (see **chest compressions**, page 428).

❧ If the baby is still not breathing, repeat the cycle of back slaps, mouth-to-mouth-and-nose breathing and chest compressions.

❧ After 2 cycles, if the baby is not breathing, dial 999 for an ambulance.

NB Never hold a baby or young child upside down by the ankles and slap their back – you could break their neck.

Head injuries

Babies and young children are particularly prone to injury from falls. Any injury to the head must be investigated carefully. A head injury can damage the scalp, skull or brain.

SYMPTOMS AND SIGNS

If the head injury is mild, the only symptom may be a slight headache and this will probably result in a crying baby. More seriously, the baby may:

❧ lose consciousness, even if only for a few minutes;

❧ vomit;

❧ seem exceptionally drowsy;

❧ complain of an ache or pain in the head;

❧ lose blood from her nose, mouth or ears;

❧ lose any watery fluid from her nose or ears;

❧ have an injury to the scalp which might suggest a fracture to the skull bones.

TREATMENT

If the baby or young child has any of the above symptoms, dial 999 for an ambulance or go straight to the accident and emergency department at the nearest hospital. Meanwhile:

❧ if the child is unconscious, follow the ABC routine described on page 427;

❧ stop any bleeding by applying direct pressure, but take care that you are not pressing a broken bone into the delicate tissue underneath; if in doubt, apply pressure around the edge of the wound, using dressings;

❧ if there is discharge from the ear, position the child so that the affected ear is lower, and cover with a clean pad; do not plug the ear.

Burns and scalds

Burns are injuries to body tissue caused by heat, chemicals or radiations. Scalds are caused by wet heat, such as steam or hot liquids.

Superficial burns involve only the outer layers of the skin, cause redness, swelling, tenderness and usually heal well. Intermediate burns form blisters, can become infected and need medical aid. Deep burns involve all layers of the skin, which may be pale and charred, may be pain-free if the nerves are damaged, and will **always** require medical attention.

TREATMENT FOR SEVERE BURNS AND SCALDS

❧ Lay the child down and protect burnt area from ground contact.

❧ Check ABC of resuscitation and be ready to resuscitate if necessary.

❖ Gently remove any constricting clothing from the injured area before it begins to swell.

❖ Cover the injured area loosely with a sterile, unmedicated dressing or use a clean, non-fluffy tea towel or pillowcase.

DO NOT remove anything that is sticking to the burn.

DO NOT apply lotions, creams or fat to the injury.

DO NOT break blisters.

DO NOT use plasters.

❖ If the child is unconscious, lay the child on her side, supported by a cushion, pillow, rolled-up blanket or something similar.

❖ Send for medical attention.

TREATMENT FOR MINOR BURNS AND SCALDS

❖ Place the injured part under slowly running water, or soak in cold water for 10 minutes.

❖ Gently remove any constricting articles from the injured area before it begins to swell.

❖ Dress with clean, sterile, non-fluffy material.

DO NOT use adhesive dressings

DO NOT apply lotions, ointments or fat to burn or scald

DO NOT break blisters or otherwise interfere

If in doubt, seek medical aid.

TREATMENT FOR SUNBURN

❖ Remove the child to the shade and cool the skin by gently sponging the skin with tepid (lukewarm) water.

❖ Give sips of cold water at frequent intervals.

❖ If the burns are mild, gently apply an after-sun cream.

❖ For extensive blistering, seek medical help.

Drowning

If a baby or small child is discovered under water, either in the bath or a pool, follow these guidelines:

❖ Call for emergency medical attention. Dial 999.

❖ Keep the child's neck immobilised as you remove him/her from the water.

❖ Restore breathing and circulation first.

❖ If child is unconscious or you suspect neck injuries, do not bend or turn neck while restoring breathing.

❖ Give rescue breathing if the child is not breathing but has a pulse. Breathe forcefully enough to blow air through water in the airway. Do not try to empty water from child's lungs.

❖ Do not give up. Give CPR (cardiopulmonary resuscitation) if the child does not have a pulse. Continue until child is revived, until medical help arrives or until exhaustion stops you.

SIGNS AND SYMPTOMS

Look for one or more of the following:

❖ unconsciousness;

❖ no pulse;

❖ no visible or audible breath;

❖ bluish-coloured skin;

❖ pale lips, tongue and/or nail bed.

IMMEDIATE TREATMENT

1   Lay child on flat surface or begin first aid in the water.

2   Check ABC (Airway, Breathing, Circulation).

3 If child is not breathing, open airway and start rescue breathing.

4 Check pulse and continue CPR if necessary to restore circulation.

5 When breathing and pulse have been restored, treat for shock.

6 Have child lie down on his/her side to allow water to drain from the mouth.

7 Restore child's body heat by removing wet clothing and covering child with warm blankets.

8 Do not give up if breathing and pulse are not restored. Continue CPR until help arrives.

Cuts and bleeding

Young children often sustain minor cuts and grazes. Most of these occur as a result of falls and only result in a very small amount of bleeding.

NB Always wear disposable gloves in an early years setting to prevent cross-infection.

FOR MINOR CUTS AND GRAZES

❖ Sit or lay the child down and reassure them.

❖ Clean the injured area with cold water, using cotton wool or gauze.

❖ Apply a dressing if necessary.

❖ Do not attempt to pick out pieces of gravel or grit from a graze; just clean gently and cover with a light dressing.

Record the injury and treatment in the accident report book and make sure the parents/carers of the child are informed.

FOR SEVERE BLEEDING

1 Summon medical help – dial 999 or call a doctor.

2 Try to stop the bleeding:

    ❖ Apply direct pressure to the wound.

❖ Wear gloves and use a dressing or a non-fluffy material, such as a clean tea towel.

❖ Elevate the affected part if possible.

3 Apply a dressing. If the blood soaks through, **DO NOT** remove the dressing; apply another one on top, and so on.

    ❖ Keep the child warm and reassure them.

    ❖ **DO NOT** give anything to eat or drink.

    ❖ Contact the child's parents or carers.

    ❖ If the child loses consciousness, follow the ABC procedure for resuscitation.

NB Always record the incident and the treatment given in the accident report book.

How to get emergency help

1 Assess the situation: stay calm and do not panic.

2 Minimise any danger to yourself and to others (e.g. make sure someone takes charge of other children at the scene).

3 Send for help. Notify a doctor, hospital and parents, and so on, as appropriate. If in any doubt, call an ambulance: dial 999.

CALLING AN AMBULANCE

Be ready to assist the emergency services by answering some simple questions:

❖ Give your name and the telephone number you are calling from.

❖ Tell the operator the location of the accident. Try to give as much information as possible (e.g. familiar landmarks, such as churches or pubs nearby).

❖ Explain briefly what has happened: this helps the paramedics to act speedily when they arrive.

❖ Tell the operator what you have done so far to treat the casualty.

REPORTING AND RECORDING ACCIDENTS IN AN EARLY YEARS SETTING

Any accident, injury or illness that happens to a child in a group setting must be reported to the child's parents or primary carers. If the injury is minor, such as a graze or a bruise, the nursery or school staff will inform parents when the child is collected at the end of the session. If someone other than the child's parent collects the child, a notification slip should be sent home. Parents are notified about:

❖ the nature of the injury or illness;

❖ any treatment or action taken;

❖ the name of the person who carried out the treatment.

In the case of a major accident or illness, the child's parents must be notified as quickly as possible.

Accident report book

Every early years setting is required by law to have an **accident report book** and to maintain a record of accidents. Record the injury and treatment in the accident report book and make sure the parents/carers of the child are informed. Information may be recorded in the format shown below.

Name of person injured:	Callum Rogers
Date and time of injury:	Tuesday 9 May 2006, 10.43 a.m.
Where the accident happened:	In the outdoor play area
What exactly happened:	Callum fell in the outdoor play area and grazed his right knee
What injuries occurred:	A graze
What treatment was given:	Graze was bathed and an adhesive dressing applied
Name and signature of person dealing with the accident:	LUCY COWELL *Lucy Cowell*
Signature of witness to the report:	*Paul Hammond*
Signature of parent or guardian:	*Maria Rogers*

MEETING CHILDREN'S INTELLECTUAL, EMOTIONAL AND SOCIAL NEEDS

Play and the sick child

Play is an important part of recovery for a sick or convalescent child. Children who are ill often regress and may want to play with toys that they have long since outgrown.

While they are ill, children have a short attention span and tire quickly, so toys and materials should be changed frequently. You will need to be understanding and tolerant of these changes in behaviour. Never put pressure on a child to take part in an activity they do not want to do. If a child is ill for some time, you can achieve variation in toys and games by borrowing them from a local toy library.

If the child wishes to draw or paint, or do some other messy activity, use protective sheets to protect the bed covers. Many activities are easier to manage if you supply a steady surface such as a tray with legs or a special beanbag tray.

ACTIVITIES WHICH SICK CHILDREN MIGHT ENJOY

❖ Jigsaw puzzles: the child could start with simple puzzles and progress to more challenging ones, perhaps with family help.

❖ Board games: such as Lotto, Ludo and Halma.

❖ Card games: such as Uno, Snap and Happy Families.

❖ Making a scrapbook: provide magazines, photos, flowers, scissors and glue to make a personal record.

❖ Drawing and painting: provide poster paints, lining paper and a protective plastic apron; children also love to paint with water in 'magic' painting books.

❖ Play dough: either bought or home-made; playing with dough is creative and provides an outlet for feelings of frustration.

❖ Making models with Duplo or Lego. Playing with small-world objects, such as toy farms, zoos and Playmobil.

❖ French knitting or sewing cards can be used with older children.

❖ Crayons, felt-tip pens and a pad of paper.

❖ Books to be read alone or with an adult.

❖ Audiotapes of songs, rhymes and favourite stories.

❖ Videos, cartoons and computer games.

❖ Encourage other children and adults to visit once the child is over the infectious stage.

CARING FOR SICK CHILDREN AT HOME

Wherever possible, children should stay at home when ill, within the secure environment of their family and usual surroundings. The child will want their primary carer available at all times. The parents may need advice on how to care for their child, and this is provided by the family GP and primary health care team – some health authorities also have **specialist paediatric nursing** visiting services.

Limiting infection

If the illness is infectious, advice may be needed on how it spreads; visits from friends and relatives may have to be reduced. The most infectious time is during the incubation period, but the dangers of infecting others remain until the main signs and symptoms (e.g. a rash) have disappeared. A child attending nursery or school will usually be kept at home until the GP says he is clear of infection.

CARING FOR SICK CHILDREN IN EARLY YEARS SETTINGS

Children who are sick should not be at school or nursery; playgroups and schools are not appropriate places in which to care for sick children. However, it is often at a day-care setting that the child first shows signs and symptoms of an illness. Childminders and nannies working in the family home also need to know how to act to safeguard children's health.

❖ Nannies and childminders should always contact the child's parents directly in case of accident or illness.

❖ In schools or nurseries you should notify a senior member of staff if you notice that a child is unwell; that person will then decide if and when to contact the child's parents.

Keeping records and recording illness

Every child's record should contain the following information:

❖ child's full name;

❖ address and telephone number of child's home;

❖ address and telephone number of child's GP and health visitor;

❖ date of birth;

❖ address and telephone number of parent or carer's place(s) of work;

❖ names and addresses of child's primary carers;

❖ additional emergency contact telephone number, possibly a relative.

Records of a child's illness should be kept so that the child's parents and doctor can be informed; as with the accident report book, these records should include:

❖ when the child first showed signs of illness;

❖ the signs and symptoms;

❖ any action taken (e.g. taking the temperature);

❖ progress of the illness since first noticing it (e.g. any further symptoms).

Helping a child who becomes unwell

Staff in schools and nurseries should offer support and reassurance to a child who may have to wait a while to be taken home. Any incident of vomiting or diarrhoea should be dealt with swiftly and sympathetically to minimise the child's distress and to preserve their dignity.

A member of staff should remain with the child at all times and keep them as comfortable as possible.

Illness policies

All early years settings should have a written policy on when to exclude children for childhood infections.

Giving medicines in an early years setting

Children may have a condition that requires medication, yet still be well enough to attend nursery or school; examples include asthma, eczema and glue ear. Prescribed medicines and paracetamol may be given to these children only after the parent or carer's written consent is obtained. The consent should be on a form that includes the following details:

❖ the child's name;

❖ the name of the medicine to be given;

❖ the precise dose to be given;

❖ the timing of each dose or, if given irregularly, parents must detail the precise circumstances or symptoms that would mean the medicine should be given;

Table 11.5 Guidelines for exclusion periods relating to childhood illnesses

Ilness	Incubation period	Periods when infectious	Minimum period of exclusion
Chickenpox	11–21 days	1 day before to 6 days after appearance of rash	6 days from onset of rash
Rubella (German measles)	14–21 days	few days before to 4 days after onset of rash	4 days from onset of rash (avoid contact or warn women who are under 14 weeks pregnant)
Measles	10–15 days	few days before to susidence of rash	7 days from onset of rash
Mumps	12–26 days (commonly 18)	few days before to 5 days after onset of swelling	until swelling has gone
Whooping cough	About 7 days	from 7 days after exposure to 21 days after onset of the bouts of bouts of coughing	21 days from onset of the bouts of coughing

❖ how it should be given (e.g. oral medicine, eye drops, inhaler);

❖ parent's name and signature.

Keeping medicines in an early years setting

❖ Keep medicines in a locked cupboard, except for inhalers, which must be easily available at all times.

❖ Make sure that each medicine is labelled for a particular child; always check the label for the child's name before giving it.

❖ Keep a written record of medicines given, including the child's name, date, time, the medicine and dose, and any problems with giving it.

PREPARING FOR HOSPITALISATION

Every year 1 in 4 children under 5 years goes into hospital and over 2 million children are seen in accident and emergency units. How a child reacts to a hospital visit depends on:

❖ their age;

❖ the reason for hospitalisation;

❖ the tests and treatment needed;

❖ the ambience of the ward;

❖ their personality;

❖ their previous experience of hospitals;

❖ the attitude and manner of the doctors, nurses and other staff;

❖ the carer's own anxieties and perceived ability to cope with what is often a very stressful situation.

When a child has to be admitted to hospital, either for medical treatment or for a surgical operation, it is best to prepare them in advance, if possible. Often the experience is stressful for parents, particularly if they have their own negative childhood memories of hospitalisation. In the event, the majority of children do enjoy their hospital stay, but adverse reactions can be avoided in younger children by careful preparation and complete honesty in all information given.

Isolation

Some conditions (e.g. **leukaemia**) result in damage to the child's immune system, and hospital care in such cases may involve **reverse barrier nursing**. This technique provides the child with protection from infection that could be introduced by those people who have regular contact:

❧ A separate cubicle is used.

❧ Gowns and masks must be worn by any person who is in contact with the child.

❧ Gloves and theatre caps may be worn during certain procedures.

❧ Items such as toys and clothes cannot be freely taken in or out.

Children in isolation need a parent or carer to stay with them to an even greater extent than do those on an open ward, because of the strain of loneliness or boredom. Parents, in turn, need support from friends and relatives as they are having to cope with many stressful events: the anxiety over their child's illness and treatment; the unnaturalness of being confined with their child; the lack of privacy because of the need for continuous observation by nursing staff. Some hospitals provide a parents' room where they can go to have a cup of tea and share problems with others in similar situations.

Guidelines for preparing children for hospitalisation

❧ If possible, arrange to visit the ward a few days before admission – most wards welcome such visits and are happy to talk with carers. (This helps to overcome fear of the unknown.)

❧ Encourage children to talk about their feelings so that you know how to help them.

❧ Always be honest – never say that something will not hurt if it might, and only tell them that you will be there all the time if that is your plan.

❧ Keep explanations simple – reading a book about a child going to hospital may help allay fears.

❧ If the child is going to have an operation, explain that they will have a 'special hospital sleep' which will stop them from feeling any pain.

❧ Do not let the child see your own worry, as this will make him feel frightened.

❧ Play hospital games, using toys to help the child act out any fears.

❧ Try to be involved in the child's care as fully as possible.

❧ Take the child's favourite toy or 'comforter' as a link with home – the child could even help to pack their case.

❧ Tell the ward staff about the child's eating and sleeping patterns, and about particular preferences or special words that may be used for the toilet, and so on.

❧ If the child is of school age, the hospital school will provide educational activities. Play specialists, nursery nurses or teachers will provide play activities for younger children.

CHRONIC ILLNESS

Strauss (1984) states that chronic illness has the following characteristics:

* It is permanent.
* It leaves residual disability.
* It is non-reversible.
* It requires special training of the patient for rehabilitation.
* It is likely to require a long period of supervision, observation and care.

Chronic disorders are usually contrasted with acute ones (i.e. those of sudden onset and of short duration). A child with a chronic illness shows little change in symptoms from day to day and may still be able – though possibly with some difficulty – to carry out normal daily activities. The disease process is continuous, with progressive deterioration, sometimes in spite of treatment. The child may experience an acute exacerbation (flare-up) of symptoms from time to time.

Some examples of chronic illness in children are:

* juvenile rheumatoid arthritis;
* psoriasis – a skin disorder;
* diabetes mellitus (Type 1);
* thalassaemia major – an inherited blood disorder;
* chronic renal failure;
* atopic eczema;
* sickle-cell disorders (sickle-cell anaemia).

Hugh Jolly defined the needs of children with chronic illness as:

* **medical:** diagnostic tests, the use of drugs, and so on;
* **involving nursing:** having their physical and emotional needs looked after;
* **emotional:** love, security, belongingness;
* **surgical:** treatment by direct physical intervention, organ transplant, and so on;
* **social:** interacting with others;
* **intellectual:** stimulation, play, education.

Long-term illness may mean that the child's ability to exercise freedom of choice in daily activities is curtailed. Frequent periods of hospitalisation disrupt family and social life, and impose strain on all members of the family; siblings often resent the extra attention given to the sick child, and the parents themselves may also need financial support. Social workers based at hospitals will give advice on any benefits and can provide a counselling service. They may also be able to put parents in touch with a voluntary organisation for the parents of children with similar conditions. Most children's units in hospitals have a separate playroom, with trained staff who provide the sick child with an opportunity for a choice of play activities.

Cystic fibrosis (CF)

Cystic fibrosis is caused by a faulty recessive gene that *must* be inherited from both parents – the parents are **carriers** if they do not display any symptoms. In people with CF the abnormal gene causes unusually sticky secretions of mucus that clog the airways, leading to **chest infections**. The gene also affects **food digestion**, leading to an inability to absorb nutrients from the intestines. Although cystic fibrosis is present from birth, the condition may not become apparent for many months or years. By the time it is detected, damage to the lungs may have begun already. Among west Europeans and white Americans, 1 child in 2000 is born with CF and 1 person in 25 is a carrier of the faulty gene.

FEATURES OF CYSTIC FIBROSIS

❧ Failure to grow normally, due to **malabsorption** of nutrients (failure to thrive).

❧ A cough that gradually gets worse.

❧ Recurrent chest infections.

❧ Severe diarrhoea, with pale, foul-smelling faeces.

Children with cystic fibrosis have a higher concentration of salt in their sweat; a sample of the child's sweat can be taken and analysed for diagnosis. Genetic tests will also be carried out. Recent research has succeeded in locating the gene that causes cystic fibrosis. This means that it is now possible to detect the carrier state, and also to test for cystic fibrosis before birth. Once cystic fibrosis is suspected in the young baby, simple laboratory tests will confirm or refute the diagnosis. Early treatment can limit lung damage and can help to ensure that failure to thrive is averted.

TREATMENT AND CARE

❧ **Vitamin supplements** and pancreatin (a replacement enzyme) will be prescribed for the child to take with meals; this helps in the proper digestion of food.

❧ **A high-energy diet** (a diet high in calories) will be recommended.

❧ Parents and carers will be shown how to give **physiotherapy** (postural drainage) to clear mucus or phlegm from the lungs.

❧ Children with this condition are susceptible to lung infections, and **antibiotic treatment** is very important in protecting the lungs.

There is no cure for cystic fibrosis, but due to earlier diagnosis and new methods of treatment most people survive into adulthood.

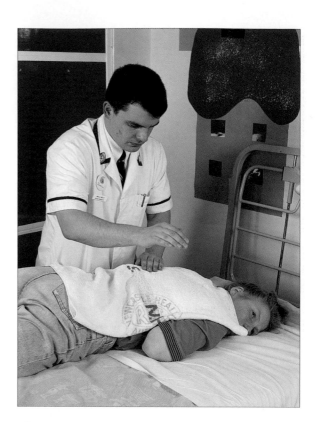

Fig 11.13 Postural drainage and chest physiotherapy

Case Study

Lisa

Lisa is the second child of healthy parents. She appeared to be a healthy baby until she was 5 months, when she caught a cold from her brother, Matthew, who is 3 years older. Her cough rapidly worsened. After bouts of high fever and vomiting at every feed, pneumonia (inflammation of the lungs) was diagnosed. Lisa was rushed into hospital. She responded well to antibiotic treatment and intravenous feeding, but X-ray pictures revealed an abnormality of the bronchial tubes. Pancreatic enzyme tests confirmed the diagnosis as cystic fibrosis.

Lisa's parents began the daily routine, so familiar to anyone coping with cystic fibrosis, of physiotherapy (postural

Case Study

drainage and coughing to clear the lungs), antibiotic medicine, vitamin supplements and vital pancreatic enzymes. Lisa received some of these drugs via a nebuliser, worked by a compressor; this delivers mist containing tiny droplets of the drugs which can get right down into the lungs where they are needed. (Some asthmatic patients also take their drugs via a **nebuliser**.)

Lisa progressed normally until she was in her first year at infant school; she began to complain of 'colicky' pain and had bouts of vomiting and constipation – this was diagnosed as meconium ileus equivalent, which is a type of intestinal obstruction caused by CF. Lisa was admitted to hospital for intravenous fluids, pain-relieving medicine and special enemas given under X-ray control. Lisa has also been a hospital inpatient during two severe bouts of pneumonia. She attends regular outpatient appointments to see her specialist.

Lisa is now a happy, optimistic 7-year-old, who enjoys PE and games. Although small for her age group, she can keep up with her peers, apart from a tendency to wheeze with any strenuous exertion. Lisa's parents share her care and try to ensure that family life is not centred around their daughter's condition.

Guidelines for working with children who have cystic fibrosis

❧ Children with CF can join in with whatever the other children are doing, but they have to remember to carry out their physiotherapy, enzymes and exercise programmes.

❧ The lungs of a child with CF must be kept clear to prevent infection. If appropriate, learn how to perform the necessary postural drainage and physiotherapy techniques (see Figure 11.13). Always obtain permission from the child's parents or guardians before performing any of these techniques.

❧ Children with CF can eat a normal diet, but also need to take enzyme and vitamin supplements; and they may also need salt tablets if they are undertaking strenuous exercise in hot weather.

❧ A child with CF may tire easily, but should be encouraged to take lots of exercise to keep healthy. Good exercises are running, swimming, cycling and skipping.

Sickle-cell disorders (SCD)

Sickle-cell disorder is an inherited blood condition caused by abnormal haemoglobin. Under certain conditions the red blood cells that contain the haemoglobin and are normally round become sickle- or crescent-shaped. They clump together and lodge in the smaller blood vessels, preventing normal blood flow and resulting in **anaemia** (a lack of haemoglobin).

In the UK the disorder is most common in people of African or Caribbean descent, but may also occur in people from India, Pakistan, the Middle East and the East Mediterranean. It affects about 1 in 2500 babies born each year

FEATURES OF SICKLE-CELL DISORDERS

Children with a sickle-cell disorder can almost always attend a mainstream school, but are subject to *crises* that may involve the following:

* **pain:** often severe, occurring in the arms, legs, back and stomach, and due to the blockage of normal blood flow;

* **infection:** these children are more susceptible to coughs, colds, sore throats, fever and other infectious diseases;

* **anaemia:** most sufferers are anaemic; only if the anaemia is severe, however, will they also feel lethargic and ill;

* **jaundice:** this may show as a yellow staining of the whites of the eyes.

TREATMENT AND CARE

Blood transfusions may be necessary. Infections should be treated promptly, and immunisation against all the normal childhood diseases is recommended.

Diabetes mellitus

Diabetes mellitus is a condition in which the amount of glucose (sugar) in the blood is too high because the body is not able to use it properly. Normally the amount of glucose in our blood is carefully controlled by the hormone **insulin**, which helps the glucose to enter the cells where it is used as fuel by the body. Most children will have **Type 1 diabetes**, meaning they can no longer produce insulin because the cells in the pancreas that produce it have been destroyed – and without insulin, the body cannot use glucose.

SIGNS AND SYMPTOMS

* **Increased thirst**.

* **Breath smells** of pear drops (acetone).

Guidelines for working with children who have a sickle-cell disorder

* Know how to recognise a crisis. If the child suddenly becomes unwell or complains of severe abdominal or chest pain, headache, neck stiffness or drowsiness, contact the parents without delay: the child needs urgent hospital treatment.

* Make sure the child is always warm and dry. Never let a child get chilled after PE or swimming.

* Make sure the child does not become dehydrated. Allow them to drink more often and much more than normal.

* Advise parents that the child should be fully immunised against infectious illnesses and ensure that any prescribed medicines (e.g. vitamins and antibiotics) are given.

* Give support. The child may find it difficult to come to terms with their condition; make allowances when necessary.

* Talk to the parents to find out how the illness is affecting the child.

* Help with schoolwork. If badly anaemic, the child may find it difficult to concentrate, and regular visits to the GP or hospital may entail many days off school.

- **Frequent passing of urine** – especially at night. (Children who have previously been dry at night might start to wet the bed: **enuresis**; this is caused by the body trying to rid itself of excess glucose.)
- **Genital itching** – sometimes leading to thrush (a yeast infection).
- **Extreme tiredness** and lack of energy.
- **Loss of appetite**.
- **Blurred vision**.
- **Loss of weight**. The amount of weight lost can be quite dramatic – up to 10 per cent of the child's total body weight can be lost in as little as 2 months – caused by the body breaking down protein and fat stores as an alternative source of energy.

TREATMENT AND CARE

Diabetes cannot be cured, but it can be treated effectively. The aim of the treatment is to keep the **blood glucose** level close to the normal range, so it is neither too high (**hyperglycaemia**) nor too low (**hypoglycaemia**, also known as a **hypo**). Most children with diabetes will be treated by a combination of **insulin** and a **balanced diet**, with the recommendation of regular physical activity.

Insulin has to be injected – it is a protein that would be broken down in the stomach if it were swallowed like a medicine. The majority of children will take **two injections** of insulin a day, one before breakfast and one before the evening meal. They are unlikely to need to inject insulin at school, unless on a school trip. In most cases the equipment will be an insulin **pen** rather than a syringe. The child's parents or carers, or a diabetes specialist nurse, can demonstrate the device used and discuss where the pen

and insulin should be kept while the child is in school.

HYPOGLYCAEMIA (HYPO)

Hypoglycaemia is the most common complication in diabetes where there is not enough sugar in the blood – usually because of too much insulin. It must be treated promptly to avoid possible brain damage from prolonged low blood sugar levels. **Hypoglycaemic attacks** – or hypos – are especially likely to happen **before meals**. They can also happen as a result of:

- too much **insulin**;
- not enough food to fuel an **activity**;
- **too little food** at any stage of the day;
- a **missed meal** or delayed meal or snack;
- **cold weather**;
- **vomiting**.

RECOGNISING A HYPO

Hypos happen quickly, but most children will have **warning signs** that will alert them, or people around them, to a hypo. Signs include:

- weakness or hunger;
- confused or aggressive behaviour;
- loss of concentration or coordination;
- rapid, shallow breathing;
- sweating;
- dizziness;
- glazed eyes and pallor;
- headache;
- trembling or shakiness.

HOW TO MANAGE A HYPO

- Stay with the child – never leave them alone or expect them to go and get their own food or drink.

❖ Sit the child down and reassure him or her.

❖ Give the child a sugary drink (e.g. fizzy non-diet drink) or sweet food.

❖ If the child recovers quickly after a sweet drink or food, give some more and allow the child to rest.

❖ If the child does not recover quickly or becomes unconscious, call an ambulance immediately and place the child in the recovery position. Always inform the parents of any hypoglycaemic attack so that adjustments can be made to the treatment.

Epilepsy

Epilepsy is a condition of the nervous system affecting 150,000 children in the UK. It is not a mental illness and cannot be transmitted to others. A person with epilepsy

Guidelines for meeting the needs of a child with diabetes in an early years setting

❖ Children with diabetes should be treated as any other child. Diabetes is *not* an illness and children should be encouraged to take part in all the activities and daily routine.

❖ Make sure that all contact details are up-to-date – home contact numbers, GP, diabetic specialist nurse, and so on.

❖ Always contact parents immediately if the child becomes unwell, and keep them informed of the child's progress.

❖ Ensure there is always a supply of glucose tablets or sweet drinks in the setting.

❖ When on outings, take a supply of sweet drinks or glucose tablets with you.

❖ Allow the child to take glucose tablets or snacks when required – most children with diabetes carry glucose tablets with them.

❖ Make sure you and all other members of staff know how to recognise and deal promptly with a child who has a hypoglycaemic attack.

❖ Always stay with the child if he or she feels unwell, and allow privacy if blood glucose testing is necessary during the day.

❖ Observe the child carefully during any vigorous exercise, such as swimming or climbing.

❖ Be understanding if the child shows emotional or behaviour problems caused by the necessary restrictions to their routine.

❖ Inform the child's parents if you are planning an activity which might involve extra strains and excitement.

❖ Make sure that the child eats regularly and that cooks are consulted about the child's dietary needs.

experiences seizures or fits. A **seizure** is caused by a sudden burst of excess electrical activity in the brain, causing a temporary disruption in the normal message passing between brain cells. This results in the brain's messages becoming temporarily halted or mixed up. Seizures can happen at any time and they generally only last a matter of seconds or minutes, after which the brain usually returns to normal.

The **type of seizure** a child has depends on which area of the brain is affected. Some seizures involve **convulsions**, or strange and confused behaviour, but others, such as **absences**, may be harder to recognise. Some may be unnoticeable to everyone except the child experiencing the seizure (see Table 11.6).

NB Some very young children have convulsions when there is a sudden rise in their body temperature; this is called a febrile convulsion. This is *not* classified as epilepsy.

CAUSES

In most cases of epilepsy there is no known cause, but sometimes a structural abnormality of the brain is found. In some children individual attacks may be brought on by a trigger, for example a flashing light; in others the attacks have no trigger.

TREATMENT

The aim of medical treatment is to control the child's tendency to have seizures, so that they can get on with life with as little disruption from epilepsy as possible. Avoiding the things which may trigger seizures and taking **anti-epileptic drugs** are the main treatment methods. Different anti-epileptic drugs are best for different seizures, so each drug is selected according to the type of seizures that the child is experiencing. Although each drug has a slightly different way of acting, they all act on the brain to suppress seizures. They do not treat the underlying cause and do not 'cure' epilepsy.

Guidelines for meeting the needs of a child with epilepsy in an early years setting

❖ Children with epilepsy should be treated as any other child. Epilepsy is *not* an illness and children should be encouraged to take part in all the activities and daily routine, unless otherwise advised by the child's parents or doctor.

❖ Teachers and nursery managers should be aware of the child's **individual needs** and what is best for them should they have a seizure (e.g. What kind of seizure does the child have? Are there any known triggers? How long does the seizure usually last? Does the child need to sleep after a seizure? Do they need to go home? Are they usually confused afterwards? Does the setting have a medical room where the child can recover before going back to class? Is there a school nurse to advise or help if needed?).

❖ Make sure that all contact details are up-to-date – home contact numbers, GP, and so on.

❖ Record exactly what happened during a seizure; this will help in an initial diagnosis and also to build up a picture of the child's condition.

❖ Always contact parents immediately if the child has a seizure, and keep them informed of the child's progress.

❖ Record any seizure in the appropriate record book.

❖ Make sure you and all other members of staff know what to do when a child has a seizure.

❖ Try to minimise embarrassment for the child; if the child has been incontinent during the seizure, deal with it discreetly.

❖ Always stay with the child during a seizure and until they have recovered completely.

❖ Supervise activities such as swimming and climbing.

❖ Try to deal with seizures matter-of-factly. Your attitude will influence the attitude of other children towards the child with epilepsy.

Table 11.6 Types of epileptic seizures and first aid

Type of seizure and what might happen	First aid
Generalised tonic-clonic (used to be called grand mal) The child: ❖ suddenly falls unconscious, often with a cry (caused by a tightening of the voice muscles); ❖ goes rigid, arching the back (**tonic phase**); ❖ may stop breathing and the lips go blue; ❖ begins convulsive movements (**clonic phase**); ❖ the limbs make rhythmic jerks, the jaw may be clenched and the breathing noisy; ❖ shows saliva at the mouth; ❖ loses bladder or bowel control. Then the muscles relax and breathing becomes normal. Usually in just a few minutes the child regains consciousness and may fall into a deep sleep or appear dazed. The child will not remember anything about the seizure when they come round and will need time to recover. Recovery time varies from minutes for some children to hours for others.	*Do:* ❖ Protect the child from injury by moving any furniture or other solid objects out of the way during a seizure. ❖ Make space around the child and keep other children away. ❖ Loosen the clothing around the child's neck and chest and cushion their head. ❖ Stay with the child until recovery is complete. ❖ Be calmly reassuring. *Do not:* ❖ Restrain the child in any way. ❖ Try to put anything in their mouth. ❖ Try to move them unless they are in danger. ❖ Give the child anything to eat or drink until they are fully recovered. ❖ Attempt to bring them round. Call an ambulance *only if:* ❖ It is the child's first seizure and you do not know why it happened. ❖ It follows a blow to the head. ❖ The child is injured during the seizure. ❖ The seizure is continuous and show no sign of stopping – a rare condition called status epilepticus.
Absence (used to be called petit mal) The child: ❖ may appear to be daydreaming, in a trance or 'switched off';	*Do:* ❖ Sit the child down in a quiet place. ❖ Stay with the child until the symptoms go away. ❖ Talk calmly and reassuringly to the child.

❖ have slight twitching movements of the lips, eyelids or head;
❖ make strange 'automatic' movements, such as chewing, fiddling with their clothes or making odd noises.

Simple partial
Epileptic activity occurs in just part of the brain; the symptoms depend on the area of the brain affected and the child remains fully conscious.

The child may experience:
❖ twitching, dizziness and numbness;
❖ sweating;
❖ nausea;
❖ 'feeling strange'.

Complex partial
Epileptic activity occurs in just part of the brain; the symptoms depend on the area of the brain affected. The child might appear to be fully aware of what they are doing – but this is not actually the case.
The child may experience:
❖ an 'aura' or warning – such as a funny taste in the mouth, flashing lights or a peculiar sound;
❖ plucking at the clothes;
❖ smacking of the lips;
❖ swallowing repeatedly;
❖ wandering around.

❖ Tell the child what happened while their seizure was happening.

Do not:
❖ Try to restrain the child.
❖ Try to shake them out of the seizure.

Do:
❖ Stay with the child until the symptoms go away.
❖ Talk calmly and reassuringly to the child.

Do not:
❖ Try to restrain the child.

Do:
❖ Guide the child from danger.
❖ Stay with the child until the symptoms go away.
❖ Talk calmly and reassuringly to the child.
❖ Explain anything they might have missed.

Do not:
❖ Try to restrain the child.
❖ Assume the child is aware of what is happening or has happened.
❖ Attempt to bring them round.
❖ Give the child anything to eat or drink until they are fully recovered.

Call an ambulance *only if*:
❖ It is the child's first seizure and you do not know why it happened.
❖ The seizure lasts longer than 5 minutes.

LIFE-THREATENING AND TERMINAL ILLNESS

Life-threatening conditions are those for which there is not always a cure, such as cancer, irreversible kidney failure or AIDS. The course of a life-threatening condition can be unpredictable. Not all children die of these conditions – some are cured. Many degenerative or severe neurological conditions could also be described as life-threatening – when the effects of the condition cause weakness and vulnerability to serious health complications.

Kawasaki disease

This inflammatory disease affects up to 2000 children a year, mainly in those aged under 5 years, but it is not very well known. Its cause is unknown, but it is thought that a **virus** or **bacterial infection** may be responsible; this means that it is not possible to prevent the illness, which is **fatal** in about 1 in 50 children. It is important to be able to recognise the disease because of the risk of serious complications – which include **coronary artery disease**. Although it can affect any children, it appears to be more common in children of Asian and African-Caribbean origin. The affected child usually starts with all the symptoms of a heavy cold or flu and then develops the following symptoms:

1   a **high fever** lasting more than 5 days without any obvious cause;

2   **within 3 days** of the sudden onset of fever, the following symptoms occur:

*   **conjunctivitis** (bloodshot, infected eyes with no discharge);

*   a **red, blotchy rash** over the whole body;

*   **dry, red, cracked lips**;

*   swollen, red and cracked tongue – commonly known as a **strawberry tongue**;

*   redness and/or swelling of the **hands and feet**;

*   **swollen glands** in the neck, usually just on one side.

3   During the second week of the illness, the skin will flake and peel from the hands and feet.

4   Children are usually acutely ill for about 10 days. Most recover completely within 5–6 weeks, and the disease is unlikely to affect the same child twice.

TREATMENT AND CARE

Treatment is usually with intravenous gamma globulin (purified antibodies). High-dose aspirin is also given to reduce the risk of coronary artery disease.

NB Never give aspirin to a child because of the risk of Reye's syndrome. Kawasaki disease is the only childhood condition for which aspirin is the recommended treatment, but it must be given by a doctor.

Cancer

Children with cancer – the most common life-threatening disease – number 1 in 600. **Chemotherapy** (treatment by drugs) and **radiotherapy** (treatment by deep X-rays) may alter the course of the disease and can sometimes effect a complete cure.

WHAT IS CANCER?

Children's cancers are rare. Only 1 in every 600 children under 15 years develops a cancer, and these are quite different from cancers affecting adults. They tend to occur in different parts of the body; they look different under the microscope; and they respond differently to treatment. In general, cancer occurs when cells in the body become out of control and multiply. They stop working properly and, as their numbers increase, they form a lump or **tumour**. When cancer cells break away and spread to other parts of the body they may produce secondary tumours known as **metastases**.

Nobody knows the cause of cancer, although there are many theories. A great deal of research is currently under way to study a number of possible causes. Sometimes two or three children develop cancer in the same school or village, causing local concern. These cases are carefully investigated, but at present they do seem to arise by chance. Some current but unproven theories are that childhood cancer may be caused by:

*   exposure to **radiation:** both the radiation that occurs naturally in the environment and through the use of X-rays;

*   exposure to **chemicals:** some chemicals are known to be associated with specific cancers in adult life;

*   exposure to **infection:** for example, by viruses which cause cells to behave in an unusual way;

* exposure to **electromagnetic fields:** for example, where the child is living close to power lines or electricity substations.

The signs and symptoms of cancer in children vary according to which part of the body is affected. Warning signs include:

* a marked change in bladder or bowel habits;

* excessive tiredness and lethargy;

* weight loss;

* generally appearing unwell and lacking energy, in spite of a good diet and plenty of sleep;

* an unexplained swelling or lump anywhere on the body;

* nausea and vomiting with no apparent cause;

* unexplained pain or persistent crying in a baby or child;

* anaemia and easily bruised skin.

Leukaemia

The most common form of childhood cancer is leukaemia. In leukaemia, abnormally growing white blood cells are scattered throughout the bone marrow, rather than being grouped into a single tumour. The age of onset is most likely around 5 years. Symptoms include:

* bleeding from the gums – this is due to an insufficient production of platelet cells needed to stop bleeding;

* headache – due to anaemia;

* epistaxis (nosebleeds);

* enlarged lymph nodes – in the neck, armpits and groin;

* anaemia – causing tiredness, breathlessness on exertion, and pallor;

* bone and joint pain – due to abnormality of the bone marrow;

* frequent bruising – due to reduced platelet production;

* infections – the immature white cells are unable to resist infections (e.g. chest or throat infections, herpes zoster or skin infections).

The diagnosis of acute leukaemia is based on a bone marrow biopsy that confirms an abnormal number of immature white blood cells (blasts).

Treatment is by:

* blood and platelet transfusions;

* anti-cancer drugs;

* radiotherapy;

* bone marrow transplantation;

* protective isolation nursing (reverse barrier nursing).

Of those children with the commonest form of leukaemia, 75 per cent are well again 5 years after diagnosis.

Some anti-cancer treatments have distressing side effects:

* **Sudden hair loss:** wigs are provided for children who lose their hair during treatment, but they should not be forced to wear them if it makes them feel uncomfortable.

* **Nausea and vomiting:** the child will need much support to cope with these acute symptoms during treatment.

* **A change in body shape:** some corticosteroid drugs cause the young patient to develop a characteristic 'moon face' and there is a build-up of fatty tissue.

It is often difficult for parents to appreciate the benefits of a treatment which causes such distressing side effects, especially when they are trying to adjust to the diagnosis of the illness – the treatment can seem more unpleasant than the effects of the illness it is trying to fight.

SUPPORT FOR THE CHILD AND FAMILY, IN HOSPITAL AND IN THE COMMUNITY

Any illness as serious as cancer is bound to have an effect on the whole family. Family members will be worried and under considerable stress. While a child is being treated for cancer, it is best for everyone if life continues as normally as possible. Parents are often tempted to spoil their child and relax the usual rules, but this can cause more problems in the long run. The child will feel more secure if discipline is as usual.

In hospital, the child and family are helped and supported by a team of professionals:

* **paediatric nurses;**
* **doctors;**
* **social workers;**
* **play therapists** and **hospital play specialists** (they may hold the Diploma in Child Care and Education, the Hospital Play Specialist Board Certificate, a psychotherapy qualification or other child care qualification);
* **counsellors;**
* representatives of different **religious faiths**.

In the community support is offered by:

* the **primary health care team** – the GP, district nurse, health visitor and practice nurse;
* **Macmillan nurses** – trained district nurses who specialise in caring for people with life-threatening conditions.

Guidelines for supporting a child with cancer and their family

* The child should be able to continue with most of his usual activities if he feels able to, so long as parents and carers are aware of some basic precautions. Hospital staff will give guidance on issues connected with the child's treatment and everyday care.

* It is important for the child to continue normal schooling and, for much of the time, there will be no limitation on his activities. The child's head teacher should be kept informed of the child's illness and any side effects of treatment.

* There is still a great fear of death when cancer is mentioned and most parents react to the diagnosis of their child's cancer in similar ways. First of all they have feelings of shock, fear, numbness and disbelief. They may deny diagnosis and consult one doctor after another. As well as shock and disbelief, parents may feel guilty. Most parents ask themselves if they could have prevented the cancer from happening. Reassure parents that there is no evidence to suggest this is the case.

* Many centres treating children have parents' groups where parents can meet others in the same situation. They may be able to offer support and encouragement. There are also other kinds of support groups, such as for siblings, in some hospitals.

Guidelines for playing with sick children in hospital

❖ The sick child usually regresses and may prefer to play with toys intended for a younger child.

❖ The child will tire quickly, so provide a range of activities within the child's capacity.

❖ Allow the child to exercise choice.

❖ Children who are immobile (e.g. in orthopaedic traction) also need to play, but require practical support to do so; parents usually welcome ideas on ways of amusing their child.

❖ Toys and activities should be changed frequently.

❖ Big and complicated toys tire a child more quickly than small and simple toys which can be changed easily.

❖ Supply a good steady surface, such as a tray, for a child who is confined to bed or cot.

❖ The value of any toys is quickly lost if they are left lying around, neglected or broken. Always tidy away toys, and maintain them regularly.

❖ A variety of craft and play materials, including real and miniature medical equipment, should be available.

VOLUNTARY SUPPORT AGENCIES

1 **Action for Sick Children** offers:

   ❖ **family support:** through a national parent advice service and family information booklets;

   ❖ **information and research:** by publishing and disseminating standard-setting reviews on child health issues, such as mental health care, adolescents and the needs of black and minority ethnic children;

   ❖ **campaigns:** by working at national and local levels to influence policy to improve the standards of health care for all children.

2 **Dial-a-Dream** was set up to allow children with life-threatening and debilitating illnesses to fulfil their aspirations by making a dream come true. Attaining a dream can help children to regain the will to say, 'Let me live another day' – the charity's motto – giving them the strength to face further treatment or hospitalisation. Dial-a-Dream has organised all sorts of dreams, from meeting the child's favourite celebrity to trips abroad.

3 **The Compassionate Friends** is a nationwide organisation of bereaved parents who have experienced heartbreak, loneliness and isolation, and who seek to help other bereaved parents.

4 **Cruse** is a national charity that exists to help all who are bereaved. It offers counselling, advice and information on practical matters, and opportunities for contact with others. Cruse has local branches throughout the UK.

5 **The Child Bereavement Trust** promotes support and counselling for bereaved families. It focuses particularly on providing training for health care professionals in order that bereaved families can obtain the best possible help from their carers.

6 **Children's hospices:** the **Association of Children's Hospices** (ACH) is the national voice for children's hospice services, and through them the children and families who use them. ACH works together with other organisations to support the development of best practice and provision of children's hospice services across the UK.

ACTIVITY: HEALTH PRODUCT ADVERTISING

1 Collect advertisements from magazines and newspapers for any product that claims to promote better health. Discuss their aims and objectives:

❖ Which groups are they targeting?

❖ Do they give any useful information on healthy living, in addition to information on using their product?

2 Find out about the advertising standards which apply to health product advertising.

3 Which television advertising campaigns for such products are memorable? Why?

ACTIVITY: HEALTH PROMOTION ON TV AND RADIO

In small groups, discuss a serial on TV or radio. List all the health promotion messages you can remember that have been contained within the storylines:

1 Do you think that TV or radio programmes are a good way of getting a health message across?

2 Does the inclusion of a telephone helpline number detract from or enhance the impact of a health problem in a storyline?

3 Does the programme mirror real life or is it viewed as escapism?

ACTIVITY: FIRST-AID BOXES AND SAFETY INFORMATION

The contents of a first-aid box in the workplace are determined by the Health and Safety at Work Act.

1   Find out and list the items that should be in the workplace first-aid box.

2   Make a list of all the items that you feel should be in a home first-aid box.

3   As a group, compare your lists and discuss the following points:

   ❧ the cost of all the items;

   ❧ possible reasons why the contents of the workplace first-aid box are fairly limited;

   ❧ the contents of the first-aid box in your own workplace;

   ❧ how accessible the first-aid box is;

   ❧ how many members of staff are designated first-aiders, and how they are trained.

4   Design a poster to illustrate the Seven Steps to Safety (see page 378).

5   Where would be the best places to display the poster, and why?

ACTIVITY: AWARENESS OF HEAD LICE

Prepare a pamphlet for parents whose 5-year-old child has head lice. Include the following information in an easy-to-read format:

   ❧ what head lice are;

   ❧ where to go for treatment;

   ❧ how to prevent a recurrence;

   ❧ how to treat the condition.

ACTIVITY: PROMOTING AWARENESS ABOUT ASTHMA

Design a poster, for use in a nursery or primary school, which presents the following information in a lively style:

   ❧ the main factors known to trigger an asthma attack;

   ❧ what to do when a child has an asthma attack;

   ❧ how preventers and relievers – via inhalers – work.

ACTIVITY: LEARNING ABOUT HOSPITAL PLAY

Invite a play specialist or nursery nurse working in hospital to come and talk about their job. Prepare a list of questions beforehand and collect as much information as you can about the needs of children in hospital.

ACTIVITY: INFORMATION ON IMMUNISATION

1 Read through the section on common childhood diseases and the information on immunisation (see page 378).

2 Prepare a booklet for parents on those childhood diseases for which there is immunisation. Include the following information:

   * the causes, signs and symptoms of the diseases;

   * possible complications and treatment;

   * the immunisation schedule;

   * contraindications to immunisation;

   * where to go for further advice and help on immunisation.

   * Make the booklet as eye-catching as possible, using illustrations.

ACTIVITY: INVESTIGATING CHILD HEALTH SURVEILLANCE

Arrange to visit a child health clinic and find out the following information:

   * What surveillance programmes are routinely carried out, and by whom?

   * If further tests are necessary, to whom is the child referred?

   * What records do health visitors maintain?

   * How do health personnel try to ensure equality of access to health surveillance?

12

Play, curriculum and early learning

Contents

CREATING A RICH LEARNING ENVIRONMENT

In Chapter 3 you will find many examples of what makes a rich learning environment, so that you select equipment and materials which provide a non-biased and positive world view. You will find that there are many links between Chapter 3, which looks at working with children, and this chapter, which focuses on how adults can plan for rich play, learning environments indoors and outdoors, and developing learning.

How to provide an environment that supports and encourages learning

Children gain access to a quality curriculum through **people** and **provision**.

Every child needs full access to the curriculum regardless of their ethnic background, culture, language, gender, special educational needs or disability, or economic background. No child should be held back in their learning because of restricted access to the curriculum.

The role of the adult in supporting children's development and learning through developmentally appropriate materials, equipment and resources is of huge importance.

EFFECTIVE COMMUNICATION WITH BABIES AND YOUNG CHILDREN

Adults who tune in to children are affectionate and sensitive to non-verbal ways in which babies, toddlers and young children communicate. Research shows that personal rhythms and patterns as children move and learn to speak make a contribution to their later language and reading development. Children with poor timing and rhythm do less well. The rhythm, tone and way babies and toddlers are talked to help them to develop verbal/signed language with confidence and understanding. Throughout our lives, 85 per cent of communication is non-verbal.

The Basic Skills Agency has reported a decline in basic language development in young children in recent years. This fits with a survey of findings by the National Association of Head Teachers, who also found children less developed in basic language skills. Children need direct eye contact with adults in order to develop shared sustained conversations and communications. The National Literacy Trust is responding to the findings of health visitors through the 'Talk to your Baby Campaign' (managed by Liz Attenborough). The Trust found that only two types of less expensive buggy have reversible seats. In 2006 there should be more on the market, according to companies who manufacture buggies.

It is important to remember that babies do not communicate verbally or use signs. The communications we have with them are non-verbal. Their skin is very sensitive to touch. They turn their head if we stroke their cheek. They love to be cuddled and held and spoken to gently. They enjoy eye contact and looking at faces, and if you give them time to reply when you gently say 'Coo' to them at about 3 months, they might reply, after a pause. The tone of voice you use is important as babies quickly become startled and frightened by sudden shouting or sudden movements.

It is fascinating to observe a sleeping baby too. Their facial expression constantly changes from smile, to pout, to frown, to relaxed.

Babies are helped by those who:

* observe the baby's unique way of telling us they are distressed;

* learn the signals that indicate a baby is about to become very upset, such as squirming, arching the back, yawning and turning away, possetting that is not linked to feeding;

* act on the signals the baby is giving before becoming very distressed;

* avoid undressing a baby who finds this difficult, by wrapping their upper body, including their arms, in a towel during changing. This stops the arms shooting out and causing 'startle' movements which further upset the baby;

* cradle a baby in their arms and rock them gently, with the baby's head on their shoulder and gently stroking the baby's back;

* respond to a baby becoming tired during a proto-conversation (conversation with no words), when the baby signals this by yawning or turning away; the adult responds and stops the 'conversation' and simply cuddles the baby to allow them to relax and rest after such an exhausting 'chat';

* know that being in a quiet, dimly lit place can help babies to sleep when they need to;

* share a book with a baby, which can calm them (they love to look at patterns of grids and circles);

* help babies to find what self-calms them, such as sucking a fist, and place the baby so that they easily find their fist to suck;

* know how important pushchair design is for communication and language; chairs which face the adult encourage

communication and shared experience, while those which face the child forward do not; given that many children spend long periods in pushchairs (which is constraining development and learning), both language development and learning to 'read' centrally important non-verbal signals, such as eye contact, pointing/looking at a shared focus, reading facial expression, are at risk of underdevelopment.

CREATING A GOOD LEARNING ENVIRONMENT FOR BABIES AND YOUNG CHILDREN

A good learning atmosphere (**ethos**) is one in which the adults support and extend the development and learning of the children.

Guidelines for effective communication with babies and young children

❖ Sing to, talk to and hold the baby. Carry the baby and show him things as they happen, objects and people.

❖ **Play games** with babies – stick your tongue out, and after a delay the baby does the same; peek-a-boo games are greatly enjoyed by older babies.

❖ Allow the child **personal space** – let the baby quietly lie or sit and watch a mobile. Babies like to lie under a tree, watching the leaves rustling. Babies need to listen to sounds around them, for example the sound of someone opening a door or dropping something in the next room. Having a radio on all the time stops them from doing this.

❖ Babies need places where they can be propped up safely (e.g. with cushions on a mat on the floor so they can watch people).

❖ Babies like to explore **objects** – find out about Elinor Goldschmied's **treasure baskets**, which are suitable for sitting babies. A video is available from the National Children's Bureau.

❖ Make available a bag with various low-cost odds and ends in it, such as a bath sponge and a cotton reel. Choose objects that can be changed or thrown away regularly, and check them for safety.

❖ Use home-made or commercial toys, such as a baby safety mirror (really worth buying), a pop-up toy, a wobbling toy, bath toys that float and sink, a teddy bear or soft doll, rattles (which are good for hands to hold and make interesting sounds) and baby books which can be chewed and sucked.

❖ Provide comfortable flooring to crawl over, a mixture of carpets and other surfaces to explore, and grass to crawl on. Soft surfaces are great for beginner-walkers, who fall over a lot!

❖ Provide stable furniture for babies to pull themselves up on and to cruise between.

❖ The book *Play It My Way* by the RNIB has a wealth of activities suitable for children from birth to 3 years and children with complex needs.

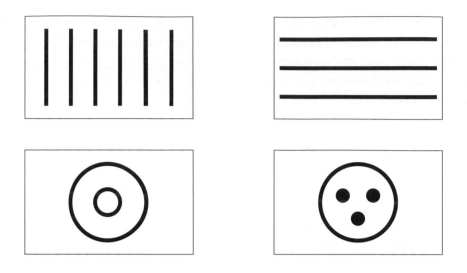

Fig 12.1 Babies love books (based on *The Social Baby,* Murray and Andrews 2003)

The adults create a warm, affectionate atmosphere, have high aspirations, observe and tune in to the child's learning, and make individual plans to help the child to learn with a high sense of wellbeing in ways which are appropriate for them. In a quality learning environment, adults value the uniqueness of each child. It is essential to create a learning environment in which children feel appreciated, valued and where those close to them (usually their families) are also valued.

It is through other people that children learn to feel valued, or not. When children feel their *efforts* are appreciated and celebrated, they develop a positive self-image with high wellbeing. This helps learning more than almost anything else.

On the other hand, if children spend time with adults who only praise and recognise results, most are bound to fail. We learn from our mistakes and errors and things that do not go as planned only if we feel that our efforts have been valued. This keeps children (and adults) highly motivated and interested in learning more.

It is important that early childhood practitioners work in a close partnership with parents/carers, in a spirit of trust, with a genuine exchange of information and knowledge. When this happens, everyone gains, especially the child.

Children need adults who provide a safe learning environment indoors and outdoors, which is predictable. This means that staff work together as a team to create consistent boundaries and ways of doing things, so that children feel secure and safe. This enables children to become explorers and problem solvers, and encourages reasoning and enquiring minds.

Some babies are more sensitive to others in dealing with transitions:

❖ from day to night sleep cycle;

❖ the stress of being undressed for a nappy change;

❖ sudden noises;

❖ being handed over to someone new to hold them.

If during the first months babies are not helped to return to their comfort zone at these times, they might become increasingly unsettled or very passive. This will constrain their development and learning.

For children who are mobile – crawlers and toddlers who are beginner-walkers

1   Make room for vigorous movement and provide places to run and jump. Offer a soft ball or a larger bouncy ball to kick and throw outside.

2   Wooden and natural material objects to feel, mouth and hold, and make simple towers to knock down.

3   Finger painting.

4   Non-toxic crayons and paper.

5   Wet and dry silver sand (not builder's sand).

6   Find some good recipes for play dough. Some involve cooking, which makes the dough last longer. Check the dough is safe to put in the mouth and even to eat, as some children might do so.

7   Provide opportunities for water play, carefully supervised, at bath-time, in paddling pools or with bowls of water. Remember, children can drown in very shallow water, so always supervise this.

8   Babies who sit enjoy treasure baskets, developed by Elinor Goldschmied; and toddlers enjoy heuristic play, which she also devised.

9   A tea set, toy cars and other play props will encourage pretend symbolic play with an interdependent adult to connect with.

10   The learning environment indoors and outdoors should facilitate schemas and their development, as part of brain development. For example:

❖ small trucks on wheels to transport objects about;

❖ soft toys to throw (trajectories);

❖ boxes, baskets and bags to put things in (inside and outside);

❖ blankets to cover teddies, dolls, and so on (enveloping).

11   Picture books and simple texts, such as *Spot the Dog*.

12   Dressing-up clothes – hats, shoes and belts are best for toddlers.

13   Flowers are for picking, as far as toddlers are concerned. Encourage children to pick daisies and dandelions rather than flowers from the flowerbed. They enjoy putting flowers in a vase of water to place on the meal table.

14   Sing action songs and rhymes.

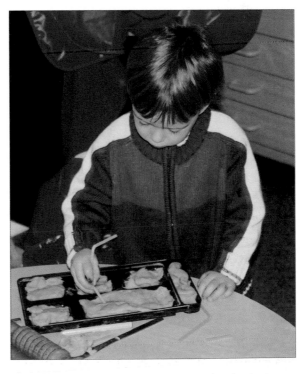

Fig 12.2 Supporting and extending a grid schema using open-ended materials (dough)

OUTDOORS

A variety of resources is needed:

❧ bats, balls, hoops, beanbags (called small apparatus);

❧ climbing frame (large apparatus);

❧ wheeled trucks, pushchairs for dolls and teddies;

❧ plants and growing area, with a wild area to encourage butterflies; perhaps a pond with a safety fence;

❧ grassy area and other soft surfaces;

❧ hard surface to make contrasting surfaces;

❧ well-drained sandpit.

Case study

Using everyday events for learning 1

When Joey (10 months) is changed he dislikes the plastic changing mat. He tries to move off it. His key worker respects his feelings and puts a towel on the mat. She talks about what she is doing and why, and she sings 'Ten little toes' to help him relax. He giggles in anticipation of each toe being gently touched.

This everyday event has helped Joey learn about:

❧ himself and where he ends;

❧ affectionate and sensitive communication between people;

❧ making sense of what someone says;

❧ music, with its melody (tune) and pitch (loudness);

❧ eye contact when people talk to each other, and facial expressions;

❧ having fun together.

Babies and toddlers learn better if they are not anxious. Laughing releases chemicals into the brain which open it up to learning. Anxiety closes the brain off to the possibility of learning.

Case study

Using everyday events for learning 2

At lunchtime, a group of sitting babies and toddlers were encouraged to choose their pudding. A plate of freshly prepared fruit was placed on the table. A tiny portion was given to the babies to try out. Several showed they wanted more through their movements. The key worker passed the plate to the babies, who were allowed to take more for themselves.

This encouraged:

❧ learning that one portion of fruit is the same as the next;

❧ physical coordination;

❧ a feeling of control over what happens;

❧ decision making.

Case study

Playing with an adult – interdependent relationships

The key worker sat on the floor facing Rebecca and sang 'Row, row, row the boat' with her. She sang the song and did the actions twice through, and then stopped. Rebecca touched her on the thigh and the key worker responded, 'Again? You want to sing again?' The singing and moving were repeated, and Rebecca smiled with pleasure.

In this play:

❧ Rebecca is helped to be imaginative;

❧ her idea to repeat the song is taken up;

❧ she is encouraged to use initiative and not be passive;

❧ she is learning the basis of drama, music and dance.

Children aged 3–6 years: indoors and outdoors

❖ Children should be offered a full range of provision whether they choose to be indoors or outdoors.

❖ There should be pictures with word labels on shelves and boxes.

❖ There should be progression in what is offered; for example, the water tray would have elaborate waterfall, pipes and guttering, canals, and challenges and problem-solving opportunities, in an atmosphere where children's reasoning is valued.

❖ Small-world equipment should be separated into clearly labelled boxes with pictures, with zoo, prehistoric and farm animals separated, and transport separate from space travel, hospital, domestic play, and so on.

❖ There should be a warm, light and cosy book corner, with cushions and chairs, and a book den outdoors, preferably under a shady tree.

❖ Children need opportunities for weighing balances, and calibrated equipment such as measuring jugs, sieves, colanders and egg whisks to encourage scientific and mathematical exploration, such as reasoning, problem solving and hypothesising – developing a theory, such as when the water gets to the top of this jug, it spills over all the outside edges; if I do this, then that happens every time. *If* and *then* are important aspects of making a hypothesis.

❖ There should be a mark-making area, with a variety of paper and different kinds of pencils and pens. This is usually placed next to the workshop area, which will contain materials and glue, scissors, masking tape, and so on. The workshop will offer paint and clay every day. One of the reasons why clay is not always provided is that practitioners do not know how to care for it. It is a valuable natural material, which children use with pleasure and great skill if they have access to it daily.

It is best kept in a thick polythene bag, placed in a covered plastic bucket. It can be cut into manageable chunks with a wire cheese cutter. A hole can be made using the thumb, and a tiny amount of water can be poured into the hole. This is then covered with a clay lid, smoothed over it. If the clay seems rather sticky when taken from the bucket, it can be thrown on to a porous surface to dry it out. Children love to help with this.

They quickly learn how to make thumb pots and coil pots, especially if shown examples on a display table. Showing children how people made pots in the past is a good way of introducing history in a meaningful way.

❖ A well-planned home corner is essential, and basic. Shops, cafes, garages, and so on, can be offered as well, but never instead of a home corner for this age group. Many children need this play for their wellbeing. Dressing-up clothes need to be offered alongside this.

❖ There will need to be a construction area (e.g. Duplo or Brio). It is best not to have a huge number of different kinds of construction kit, as each one will be expensive and there will not be enough of any set for children to use them with satisfaction. It is worth spending time deciding which to buy in bulk, with perhaps two types which offer children a rich range of experiences and endless possibilities. There will need to be simple ways of using the kit, but ways of using it with greater sophistication and elaboration too.

❖ There should be an area for wooden blocks which are free-standing and mathematically related shapes and sizes. Community Playthings unit blocks are basic. Hollow blocks are additional. Again, so that the mathematical relationships can be developed fully, it is best to add more of the same brand, rather than having a huge number of incompatible sets of blocks.

❖ There will be a cookery area with baking materials and equipment. This requires a shelf with easy-to-handle containers of basic ingredients, aprons, wooden spoons and easy-to-hold pans to cook in, and metal spoons to measure ingredients. A child-friendly cookery book is essential, so that children learn the sequences and how to find their way through a recipe.

❖ There should be growing things, such as mustard and cress, hyacinths, a fish aquarium or a wormery. Having magnifying lenses, and pots to put objects and creatures in for nature study without damaging them is important. Teaching children to return live spiders and other mini-beasts to their natural habitat safely and gently is essential.

❖ There needs to be an interactive interest table and display at child height, with fascinating objects to handle, beautifully and accessibly presented. More is written abut display elsewhere in this book (see pages 163 and 164).

❖ There should be an area for movement. This should have sufficient clean floor space on which children can roll and crawl. Having a floor mat can help, although it does indicate that the learning environment is not of a high standard of cleanliness.

❖ There should be a computer, and ideally a word processor, as well as digital cameras for children to use.

❖ The outdoor area needs to be available for most of the day. In some settings children remain indoors until it is safe to let them in the garden, as it is difficult to supervise families arriving and leaving, and a child could slip out of the building

---

Learning through Landscapes (LTL)

This is the national school grounds charity, campaigning for positive outdoor learning and play experiences for all children in education and child care.

Since 1990, LTL has been undertaking research and evaluation, developing innovative projects and programmes, and providing training and support to raise awareness of the importance and special nature of the outdoors. Today, both school and early years communities, and those working on their behalf, turn to LTL for guidance in developing and implementing improvements to their outdoor environment for the benefit of children.

LTL has been involved in the production of more than 100 high-quality publications, including books, videos and teaching resources. All are designed to help schools and early years settings realise the full potential of the outdoors – for all aspects of play and learning.

For further details on the work of Learning through Landscapes and information about the early years and primary membership schemes, **Early Years Outdoors** and **Schoolgrounds UK**, you can visit the website at www.ltl.org.uk or write to: Learning through Landscapes, Third Floor, Southside Offices, The Law Courts, Winchester SO23 9DL.

unnoticed. Ideally the garden is separate from the main entrance to the setting.

✤ The outdoor area should complement the indoor area, so that, for example, there are opportunities for mark making, but indoors there may be pencils and felt-tip pens, while outdoors there may be buckets of water and paint brushes to make water markings on the ground.

There is no one way to set out the areas indoors and outdoors, but the layout should not be constantly changed. When you go to the supermarket and find the layout changed, how do you feel? Is it difficult to find things?

✤ The layout of the room should reflect the multicultural society of the UK.

✤ There should be appropriate attention to the layout for children with SEN and disabilities.

✤ The environment should be safe and easy to explore, with easy access to the materials, encouraging autonomy.

Children aged 5–8 years

The provision should be the same, but there will be elaboration of the writing and reading areas; and the nature of the decision making, child choices and freedom of movement will need to show progression.

Fig 12.3 Outdoor space is an important part of the provision

Guidelines for timetabling the curriculum

❧ Children learn best when they are in a **predictable environment**. This means that although their activities should not be controlled by adults all the time, there *should* be a shape to the day. Children feel safe if they have some sense of what is coming next, for example if there are regular mealtimes.

❧ The way that the day is organised should fit with children's natural rhythms. Adults need to keep in mind that it is important not to work to a tight, inflexible routine for their convenience. There are times when children go at a fast pace, and times when they tire, times when they want to be alone or to have a quiet cuddle, and times when they enjoy working with other children or adults.

Children benefit from having their own dictionary, in which they are helped to put words that are important for them. They find word banks helpful, for example words about shopping in a box placed near the 'shop', or words about plants and flowers in a box next to the nature table. Doing words (verbs) such as 'go' and 'jump', are well-situated near the movement area. There will need to be reference books carefully placed to help children find out more.

Children with disabilities

There should be a tray on the table to stop objects falling off the edge for children with disabilities such as visual impairment or movement restriction, and ramps for children who are wheelchair users.

It is important to avoid clutter, so that everything provided is there for a reason. Clutter is confusing and distracting. If children know where to put things they use the learning environment more effectively, and they develop awareness of participating positively in the community.

It is important not to underestimate what any child can do, while offering the support and encouragement they need. This is

especially important if a child has special educational needs or disabilities.

Learning with and through other children

Children learn with and through other children as well as with and through adults they trust and like. They identify children they wish to be friends with. However, this is only possible if they are free to choose what they do for large parts of the day. Even babies who crawl and sit, who are not yet walking, like to choose their friends.

Learning with and through adults

Children need adults to provide a safe and predictable environment, and a warm, affectionate atmosphere. They learn only if adults are sensitive to their needs and interests, providing stimulating things to experience, and encouraging them to have a go at things, explore and be autonomous.

Adults need to be consistent, so that different messages are not given by different people. For example, if one adult allows children to sit on tables and another does not, children will push the boundaries until they find out whether or not this is allowed!

Adults need to be sensitive to when children need help so that children receive:

❧ the right help;

❧ at the right time;

❧ in the right way.

Adults need to observe children carefully to see if the child:

❧ is struggling;

❧ is avoiding doing something;

❧ is interested but does not know what to do.

Direct teaching can help to avoid temper tantrums, frustration, anxiety and sadness.

A child may pick up a cloak in the dressing-up area, but find he cannot tie a bow. He puts it down and instead chooses a jacket which fastens with Velcro. But really he wanted the cloak, and if an adult had helped him to tie the strings, he would have carried out his plan.

Children usually need direct teaching when they try to cut with scissors.

The **Effective Early Learning** project at CREC in Birmingham emphasises the need for the adult to:

❧ show sensitivity to children;

❧ encourage the child's autonomy;

❧ offer stimulating experiences which are challenging and interesting.

SELF-RELIANCE, SELF-CONFIDENCE, INDEPENDENCE AND AUTONOMY – WHAT IS THE DIFFERENCE?

It is important to know the difference between a child being self-reliant, self-confident, independent and autonomous.

❧ **Self-reliant** children do not expect help from others. This is not always a good thing, as they can be left to themselves, but may actually appreciate an offer of help. It can mean that they only attempt to do what they know they can manage unaided, and are not very adventurous about trying new things.

❧ **Self-confident** children will have a go at things and ask for help when they need it. They trust their ability to learn.

❧ **Independent** children can carry out certain tasks of life without help, such as getting dressed or managing a Sellotape dispenser. They are confident that they can manage themselves and have developed the dispositions which will help them to learn, such as problem solving, knowing the sequence for toileting and washing, or finding what they need to model with clay.

❧ **Autonomous** children can be independent, but they also enjoy the company of those who know more than they do, and from whom they can learn and find out more. For example, they might not be able to read stories of Beatrix Potter when they are 4 years old, because they are not yet fluent readers (and nor should they be), but they do enjoy being read to and sharing the pictures in the book. They enjoy acting out the story of Miss Moppet, the cat trying to catch the mouse, while the adult reads the story out loud. According to Vygotsky, what we can do with help today, we can do alone tomorrow.

Fig 12.4 Children read books to enjoy from babyhood. This is the beginning of learning to read.

Fig 12.5 Children benefit when adults enjoy sharing stories with them in a relaxed unhurried way.

WHY SHOULD CHILDREN PLAY?

Play is one of the most difficult aspects of a child's development to understand and support. It is also one of the most important for development and learning. Play lays down neural patterns in the brain which are important foundations for future learning, such as being a flexible, imaginative thinker, understanding other points of view, and appreciating the feelings and lives of others.

Childhood memories of play

Before you read this section, think back to your own childhood. Talk about your childhood memories of play with your friends. It is one of the best ways to find out what is important to children as they grow up.

❖ Did you make dens in the garden, under a table or with your bedclothes?

❖ Did you pretend you were in outer space, on a boat, on a desert island, going shopping or keeping house?

❖ Did you feel you had hours and hours to play?

❖ Did you enjoy using inexpensive play props, or were your favourite toys expensive, commercially produced toys?

Children who do not play

It is a myth to say that all children play – they do not. In different parts of the world and according to the culture in which children grow up, play may or may not be encouraged. It is often seen as something children grow out of, possibly the quicker the better, rather than part of deep learning.

There are various reasons why children might not play:

* A sick, unhappy or over-occupied child will not play.

* Children who are abused verbally, sexually or physically, or who have experienced upheaval in their close relationships with people, may have difficulty playing.

* The culture or family does not encourage play.

Children are biologically driven to play, but they need people to develop their play fully. Play takes great energy and commitment on the part of the child.

PLAY THERAPY

In some cases, children who do not play can be helped by play therapy. Play therapists undertake specialist training, and help children who are emotionally vulnerable to heal. They are often based in hospitals and special schools. Most children will begin to play if given sensitive adult help in any early years setting or at home. Once children know how to play, there is usually no stopping them. Most children therefore do not need the specialist help of a play therapist. Their natural childhood play helps them to self-heal.

Play in children with special educational needs

Children with special educational needs have often been underestimated in their ability to play. Even children with severe learning difficulties can play – if play is seen as a combination of being allowed to wallow deeply in feelings, ideas and relationships and exploring the physical self, together with the application of skills and competencies. This gives us a very positive view of play and makes it a possibility for most children.

Case Study

Jo

Jo, who is 4 years old, has autism, and is fascinated by strips of material, which he loves to wave in front of his face and brush across his nose. The practitioner does not label this an obsession, but instead builds on his interest. She provides a variety of ribbon-like strips, and over several weeks he begins to experiment with a wider range. After a few months he is interested in eye contact with her, provided the ribbons are swaying in front of his face. One day, he parts the ribbons and looks her directly in the eye. He says, 'Boo.'

Children with special educational needs and disabilities often dance the developmental ladder. They may do some things at the same time as most children their age, or they may have a different timescale for different aspects of their development. One of the helpful things about having the *Birth to Three Matters* framework is that it supports practitioners in developing the learning (including play) of a diverse range of children, in ways which are inclusive.

Too busy to play

Some children lead over-occupied lives, which leave them little time, energy or personal space for play. They are mainly involved in adult-dictated activities, being encouraged to read and write early, do number work, perhaps learn a musical instrument, ballet dancing, take part in drama sessions, join woodwork and PE clubs and play computer games, so that they almost never have any time for themselves. Researchers suggest it is likely that many children in the UK could be described as experiencing over-occupied childhoods. These children often became very dependent

Case study

Children with English as a second language

Noor (3 years) is a new arrival in England. She has been separated from most of her family, but her mother is reunited with three of her children after fleeing from a war zone. She is in the home corner. She finds a sheet from the doll's bed and wraps it round her. She puts the doll into the sling she has made. She finds the broom and sweeps the floor. She finds the saucepan and puts it on the stove, pretending to prepare a meal. The practitioner smiles when she catches her eye, and sits near her, but does not invade her focused play.

It is difficult to do two new things at once. Adjusting to a new country is dealt with by playing out familiar everyday things, such as caring for the baby and meal preparation. It would be very difficult to talk in a new language too. This will come later. Now she needs the sensitive encouragement of the practitioner.

on adults. They will say things like, 'I don't know what to do,' or, 'I need you to help me.' Such children are very easily bored. This is because they are not developing their inner resources and do not know how to harness the energy that is needed in order to play.

Recent research suggests that children, especially boys, who do not play are more likely to bring personal and social tragedy on themselves and their communities, for example by becoming persistently drunken drivers. Lack of early childhood play is also becoming linked by some researchers with attention deficit hyperactivity disorder (ADHD). Some researchers believe that play and laughter actually 'fertilise' the brain.

Second-hand experiences in play

The themes of television programmes and computer games are very often taken up by children in their play. When children pretend to be fantasy characters – such as those appearing in cartoon programmes and computer games – whose activities they have not experienced in their own lives, their play is usually at a very low level. Only when children can link their own real experiences with the second-hand experiences they see on television can their play be rich. It is therefore best to limit the time that children spend on second-hand experiences, unless these link directly to first-hand experiences that the child has had.

Case study

Work and play

In Sweden, researchers found that 6-year-olds, when asked the difference between work and play, explained that work needs adults to help, but that children cannot do this for very long. Play is much more difficult because children have to have their own ideas. One girl said that in order to play she needed acres of time.

THE CHILD'S RIGHT TO PLAY

The Charter of Children's Rights (1989) states that every child in the world should have the right to play. Play is not the same as recreation or relaxation. Play is about high levels of learning, while recreation is about relaxing and not thinking very hard.

So why should children have the right to play? Play is central to a child's learning. It makes a very big contribution to development and to learning about:

- ideas and imagination;
- feelings;
- relationships;
- flexible and abstract ways of thinking;
- the moral and spiritual self;
- the physical self.

Sometimes people say that play is the only way a child learns. In fact, it is not. However, play is a major part in a network of learning, and it is important because it enables the child to bring together, coordinate and make whole everything they learn.

WHAT IS PLAY?

Through play, children bring together and organise their ideas, feelings, relationships and their physical life. It helps them to use what they know and to make sense of the world and people they meet. When they play, children can:

Fig 12.7 Through play, children try out their skills and competencies

- rearrange their lives;
- rehearse the future;
- reflect on the past;
- be creative and imaginative;
- organise their learning for themselves;
- get their thoughts, feelings, relationships and physical bodies under their own control.

The act of playing gives children a sense of mastery and competence that helps them to face the world and cope with it. This is crucial for the development of good self-esteem and for becoming a rounded personality.

Learning to play

Some people believe that children are born knowing how to play naturally. In fact, children learn to play, although they are also

Fig 12.6 A child will sometimes enjoy playing alone

predisposed towards it. So it is both nature and nurture. Often it is older children who teach younger children how to play. In situations where children play in mixed age groups, younger children easily learn about quality play from those who are experienced and good at it. For example, Maori children traditionally learn in this way.

However, in modern life, in places where parents often feel that it is dangerous to play out in the streets, where families are smaller, and where children are at school in classes of children of the same age, there are not many opportunities for younger children (2–5 years) to learn about play from older children (5–8 years or older). This means that many modern children increasingly depend on adults to help them into quality play. The prior (childhood) experience of adults who play with children is therefore very important. Research suggests that it is especially important that adults working professionally with young children know and understand what play is. They need to be trained to understand its central contribution to the learning that children experience. Adults need to support and extend children's play with sensitivity and skill.

Defining play

Play is one of the most complicated concepts to study and understand, and there is a mass of literature written about it. People are often afraid of things they do not know much about and do not understand. In addition, play has become a political issue. There are those who think it has no place in a child's education and there are those who believe it must have a central place. This debate has gone on for 200 years. On the whole, it is those who work with children

on a daily basis, and experts in child development who have contact with young children all over the world, who argue that play is central to a child's learning.

Play from the inside out

Play comes from within children. Bruce argues that the way children develop in their play should not be seen as progress through a prescribed sequence or hierarchy. This is because any child can be helped to play – babies, toddlers, children and children who have disabilities. Early years workers will form a positive view of play if they approach its development as a learning web that the child weaves (see Figure 12.8).

Bruce has elaborated and enhanced this definition with her 12 features of play (see page 469).

Assessing quality play

Bruce's 12 features are often used to assess and evaluate the quality of play. If most of these 12 features are present (7 or more) when children are observed in their play, then probably they are involved in quality play. If only a few features are present, it does not necessarily mean that the child is not doing anything of quality. It may mean that the child is doing something other than play – the child might be representing things, be involved in a game with rules or be enjoying a first-hand experience. It is very useful for staff working with young children in a whole variety of early years settings to become skilled at knowing what is play and what is not, even though this is not always easy. It is certainly not helpful to call everything that children do 'play'.

There is a biological reason for children's play – it stops the brain from getting too set

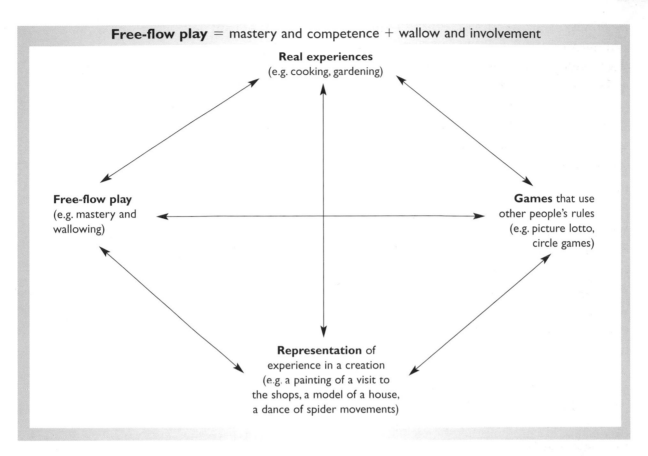

Free-flow play = mastery and competence + wallow and involvement

Real experiences
(e.g. cooking, gardening)

Free-flow play
(e.g. mastery and
wallowing)

Games that use
other people's rules
(e.g. picture lotto,
circle games)

Representation of
experience in a creation
(e.g. a painting of a visit to
the shops, a model of a house,
a dance of spider movements)

Fig 12.8 Bruce's definition of play

The 12 features of play – to recognise, monitor and cultivate free-flow play

1 Using first-hand experiences.

2 Making up rules.

3 Making props.

4 Choosing to play.

5 Rehearsing the future.

6 Pretending.

7 Playing alone.

8 Playing together.

9 Having a personal agenda.

10 Being deeply involved.

11 Trying out recent learning.

12 Coordinating ideas, feelings and relationships for free-flow play.

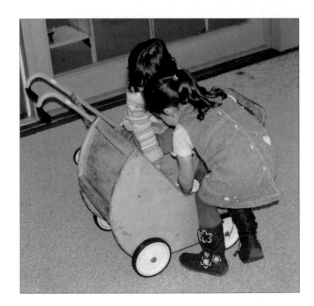

Fig 12.9 Free-flow play

in its ways. It allows ideas, feelings and relationships to flow and it opens up a child's thinking. It helps reasoning, problem solving and creativity.

The development of free-flow play

EARLY STAGES

Babies and toddlers are beginning to find out through their senses, movements and relationships with other people what play is, for example by playing with their own hands.

EMERGENT PRETEND PLAY

Children begin to pretend and develop spontaneous, creative and imaginative play, known as free-flow play. This means they are beginning to use symbolic behaviour. This is one of the most important stages of development for human beings.

MORE ELABORATE PLAY

Play elaborates pretend themes, includes more people, involves props and ideas, sustained characters and stories or narratives, leads to expression of feeling and requires more skill. Creative free-flow play is often left out of the school curriculum at this stage in the UK, but in countries like Denmark, Germany and Japan, children still play in school at this age. Unfortunately for us in the UK, this means that just at the stage when play is beginning to flow well, it is often cut off in its prime. Without safe streets to play in or friends to play with at home, children cannot compensate for the play they miss out on at school. Free-flow play is very important for a child's development and learning at this stage.

Childhood play turns to creative pursuits

Play consolidates and becomes very sophisticated (if it survives). At this stage, play

> ### Creative, imaginative adults
> Play continues to be important for adults who are creative and imaginative, and innovative thinkers (*Cultivating Creativity*, Bruce 2004). There is also participation in leisure pursuits, as in the previous stage of development. People who play are less likely to become stressed, depressed, bored or narrow. They are more interested in life, more interesting to be with and tend to be more sensitive to other people (Bruce 1991).

divides into hobbies, games and leisure pursuits, and into creative pursuits, for example drama, sculpture, making computer programmes, dancing, singing and playing music.

The play spiral, devised by Janet Moyles, suggests that children first play freely with materials, such as play dough, and are then directed through play tutoring, for example to play shops, being shown how to make the dough into play props for the shop. They are then encouraged to engage in free play about shops.

Piaget and Vygotsky both thought that play led to the enjoyment of games. They proposed that play turns into games in middle childhood (from about 8 years), unlike Erikson, Winnicott or Bruce, who see play as turning into adult creativity.

Time to play

Children need a free choice of activity in order to play. They also need *time* to play. A rigid timetable makes it very difficult for them to develop quality, free-flowing play. Play cannot flow under these circumstances, and so learning will be held back. If adults truly believe that play is central to learning, play – including free-flow play – needs to be encouraged by flexible timetabling of the day.

Table 12.1 Moyles's forms of play

Basic form	Detailed form	Type of play	Examples
1 Physical Play	Gross Motor	Construction	Building blocks
		Deconstruction	Clay, sand and wood
	Fine motor	Manipulation	Interlocking blocks
		Coordination	Musical instruments
	Psychomotor	Adventurous play	Climbing apparatus
		Creative movement	Dance
		Sensory exploration	Junk modelling
		Object play	Finding-out table
2 Intellectual play	Linguistic	Communication and explanation	Hearing and telling stories
		Acquisition	
	Scientific	Exploration	Water play
		Investigation	
		Problem solving	
	Symbolic and mathematical	Representation and pretend mini-worlds	Doll's house
			Homes and drama
			Number games
3 Social and emotional play	Therapeutic	Aggression and regression	Wood, clay and music
		Relaxation/solitude/ parallel Play	
	Linguistic	Communication, interaction and cooperation	Puppets and telephone
	Repetitious	Mastery and control	Anything
	Empathetic	Sympathy and sensitivity	Pets and other children
		Emulation of roles	Home corner and
		Morality	shop
			Discussion
	Gaming	Competition and rules	Word and number games

Piaget's stages of play

* **Babyhood (0–18 months):** play involves sensori-motor behaviour (the senses and movement).
* **The early years of symbolic play (18 months–5 years):** play involves making something stand for (represent) something else.
* **The school years (5–8 years):** children move from play to taking part in games. Children are able to play more cooperatively. The rules of games are quite different from the rules of play. In games the rules are given; in play children make up the rules as they go along.

THE DEVELOPMENTAL ASPECTS OF PLAY

Babies

Natural materials give a wider range of possibilities for learning through the senses and movement.

* Lying under a tree and watching the leaves through dappled sunlight.
* Crawling on grass in the garden.
* Sitting and manipulating fir cones in a heap on the floor.

These encourage creative, imaginative, manipulative and physical play.

Toddlers

✤ Sliding down a small slide on the tummy, feet first.

✤ Rolling down a grassy slope.

✤ Pushing a cart along with a doll in it.

These encourage creative, imaginative, manipulative and physical play.

Young children

✤ Making a den and gathering play props (child-initiated).

✤ Picking daisies, dandelions, twigs and pebbles to make a play scenario, with a house, garden and shops.

✤ Making a cake with a face decorated on it from raisins and cherries.

These encourage creative, imaginative, manipulative and physical play.

MAKING PROVISION FOR PLAY

Space for play – indoors and outdoors

Play does not happen to adult order. Both the indoor and outdoor areas need to be made into spaces which encourage children to develop their *own* play. For example, both the environment and the equipment must be safely maintained. There should be appropriate materials to encourage play, such as dressing-up clothes, den-making materials and small-world objects. There must be space to run and jump and corners to hide away in.

Material provision

Children need things to play with – play props. Sometimes children will make their own props, or they may select play clothes and objects from the material that you provide. Staff will be continually making plans for new activities based on their observations of how children play. As part of these plans they will provide play props which encourage the children to play more deeply.

Choosing play materials

Children do not need expensive equipment in order to play. For example, they may find and play with twigs and pebbles. In the park they will be running and using the space. In the garden they might climb or dig. On the seashore they will collect pebbles, seaweed and shells. They might splash in rock pools and build castles out of sand. In a setting they will use the material provisions that adults put there. So it is very important that adults choose materials carefully and plan the physical environment to support play. Then children can get the most out of opportunities for free-flow play. Children can use scissors, for example, to develop fine motor skills, and they can learn to put straws in cartons of fruit juice, rather than doing fine motor exercises that are not connected to real life. Performing exercises which do not relate to the day-to-day context of a child's life can actually stop them from learning well. When life becomes a drudge, full of boring, repetitive tasks, children quickly lose the excitement of learning. So it is better to avoid pre-structured toys and to provide open-ended and more traditional toys, such as dolls, cars, wooden blocks and play dough.

Adult support for play

There may to be a visit to a real shop before a play shop scenario can develop. Children need interdependent relationships with other children and often an adult in order to develop their play agenda. When adults 'teach' play this can constrain children. When children are left without support, the play is

Guidelines for selecting play materials

1 **Pre-structured materials**, such as a miniature post box, more often hold back rather than encourage free-flow play. If there is only one way of doing things, children cannot develop in their imaginative play and they will probably carry out a very narrow range of physical actions. So-called educational toys, made by commercial manufacturers and usually very expensive, are often pre-structured in this way.

2 **Open-ended materials** encourage children to think, feel, imagine, socialise and concentrate deeply. They will tend to use a range of fine and gross motor skills. Examples of open-ended materials are:

   ❖ **found materials**, such as those used in junk modelling;

   ❖ **transforming raw materials**, like clay and dough;

   ❖ **self-service areas** in the provision;

   ❖ **wooden blocks**;

   ❖ dressing-up clothes and cookery items in the **home area**.

low-level. Interdependent relationships mean adults take up and help children to develop their ideas, supported as they do so, so that the 12 features of play emerge.

Children really appreciate adults who help them to keep their play flowing, provided the adult is sensitive to their play ideas.

PLANNING FOR PLAY

Remember that you are planning for play, and not planning the play. The difference is

Guidelines for encouraging free-flow play

❖ Use adult-led sessions to introduce children to the materials first through **real experience** (part of the learning web, see page 469). For example, do some cooking and then use the experience in a play scenario in the home area. Children will still see how to use their experiences in their own free-flow play, both safely and creatively.

❖ Do not make children complete adult-led tasks, that is, 'work', *before* being allowed to play, as this undermines play. But play is also undervalued when adults leave children without *any* help when they play. In these situations the play quickly becomes repetitive and superficial. If adults are only found in those areas where children are doing 'work', while children are being sent off to 'play' without any help, children will receive unfortunate messages about how adults value their play.

❖ Free-flow play literally occurs when the play begins to flow with quality according to the 12 features described earlier in this chapter (see page 469). Free-flow play can fade and vanish in a moment, but adults can be a great help to children in keeping going.

that planning for play means you plan the environment so that children can initiate their own spontaneous play, whereas planning the play means that you direct the children in what to do in their play.

Well-planned play

Some of the children have visited the market and shown great interest. You set up a market in the garden, with stalls and play props. Children begin to play markets, and you support them, sensitively tuning in to their play ideas.

The same approach is important when working with babies and toddlers.

Planning for play – the baby likes to sit and reach for objects and put them in her mouth. The practitioner makes a selection of objects, some easy to put in the mouth, some less so, and presents these on the floor. The baby spends nearly half an hour trying these out.

This is very different from a situation where the practitioner decides to introduce sphere-shaped objects to all the babies. She holds a ball and presents it to the baby, who takes it and tries to put it in her mouth. The baby drops the ball. The practitioner tries a different ball and the same thing happens again. The baby loses interest when a third ball is presented. This would not be well-planned play.

TYPES OF PLAY

Different types of play have been linked to particular kinds of material provision and to different aspects of a child's development:

* **Particular kinds of material provision:** the home area, construction kits, the outdoor area, natural materials, a messy area, a computer, wooden blocks, climbing frames, bats and balls, hoops, clay, paint.

* **Different aspects of a child's development:** manipulative play, practice play and repetitive play, symbolic play, superhero play, exploratory play, discovery play, investigative play, pretend play, ludic play, heuristic play, role play, therapeutic play, solitary play, parallel play, cooperative play, epistemic play, imaginative play, physical play, manipulative play, creative play, rough-and-tumble play, boisterous play, fantasy play, phantasy play and socio-dramatic play. (Some of these forms are defined below.)

Considering play in terms of the different definitions has become increasingly unwieldy, with more and more categories being added all the time. It is probably better to focus on:

* Setting up the basic areas of provision to give quality play opportunities.

* How adults can help children to play both alone and together, through interdependent relationships.

All the types of play listed in the box below can be catered for if the setting is arranged with great care. This is why it is very important for staff to plan the curriculum that they intend to provide for young children.

THEORIES ABOUT PLAY

Some of the early theories about play suggested it was just recreation after work, or a way of burning off excess energy. We now know that play is far more important than these theories would suggest.

Types of play

❖ **Symbolic play:** usually occurs from 1 year and includes pretend play, role play, socio-dramatic play and imaginative play. A symbol is when one thing stands for another.

❖ **Creative play:** this label is often given to describe play with natural materials, such as sand, water, clay, dough, musical instruments and sensory materials. It is also used to describe the creation (making) of an idea that the child has, and may not need any play props. The child might 'create' the idea of being a dog or an engine. The links between the processes of creativity, the imagination and play are strong. (You can read more about cultivating scientific, artistic and humanitarian creativity in Bruce 1991.)

❖ **Pretend play or ludic play:** when an action or object is given a symbolic meaning which is different from real life – a clothes peg becomes a door key.

❖ **Role play:** this occurs when pretend symbols are used together – the child pretends to drive to the shops and unlocks the car door with a pretend clothes-peg key, sits on a box (a car seat) and turns the steering wheel (a dinner plate).

❖ **Socio-dramatic play:** when children role-play and pretend-play together.

❖ **Imaginative play or creative play:** children use their own real-life experiences and rearrange them – they might make a pretend swimming pool out of wooden blocks. One of them pretends to be a lifeguard and rescues someone who cannot swim. The children already know about learning to swim and rescue. Imaginative play links with creative play, role play, domestic play, fantasy play, phantasy play and play with dolls and small world.

❖ **Fantasy play:** here children role-play situations they do not know about, but which might happen to them one day – the experience of getting married, going to the moon in a space rocket or going to hospital.

❖ **Phantasy play:** here children role-play unreal events, using characters from cartoons on TV – Power Rangers, Superman. The theme of war tends to dominate this kind of play. Because it is not rooted in real experience, it is difficult to help children to use this kind of play for their benefit.

❖ **Manipulative play:** this occurs when children use and celebrate physical prowess – playing on a skateboard with great competence or riding a two-wheeled bicycle. It is about what they can do, not about what they are struggling to do (which would not be play). This kind of play helps children to develop their motor skills. It links with physical play with large equipment indoor and outdoors.

❖ **Physical play:** this also helps children to develop their gross and fine motor skills.

❖ **Play using props:** sometimes children make their own props and use them to pretend-play – they might make a telephone out of boxes and then pretend to book a doctor's appointment. This is sometimes called constructive play, but it is really a representation.

❖ **Rough-and-tumble play:** this often involves chasing, catching, pretend fights and pillow fights. Unless children are sufficiently coordinated to manage their play safely, it often ends in tears; it requires great sensitivity to other people in order not to hurt them physically. This form of play often occurs before going to sleep and it bonds those playing emotionally and socially. It is difficult to cater for in the early years setting, as it tends to frighten those not taking part.

❖ **Therapeutic play:** this kind of play helps children who are in emotional pain to find out more about how they feel, to face their feelings and to deal with them, so that they gain some control over their lives. Helping children through play therapy requires professional training, but every child can improve their mental health through the feeling of control that play gives. Some children need more help than early years workers can give, and specialists may be called in.

Helping babies, toddlers and young children to play – a summary

❖ Think back to your own childhood memories of play. What did you enjoy doing? Remembering will help you to help children to play.

❖ Take time to observe babies, toddlers and young children as they play. This will help you tune in to children's play agendas and help you play along.

❖ Think about equality of opportunity (see Chapter 1). Some children might be left out of the play when they want to join in. Use what you know about access strategies.

❖ Both boys and girls need to experience a broad range of play. Pay attention to gender issues.

❖ Babies and children with special educational needs might require extra help to develop their play; all children can play at some level.

❖ When babies, toddlers and young children play, they learn at a very high level.

❖ You cannot *make* children play, because play only happens when conditions are right. Work at getting conditions right for play in your setting.

❖ People matter. Adults who help babies, toddlers and children to play are adults who help children to learn.

❖ Give play a high priority – it is a central form of learning.

❖ The provision of play props is important. These should be open-ended and flexible. Do not pre-structure props and equipment so that there is only one way to use them.

❖ Children need places for play, indoors and outdoors.

❖ Babies and children need uninterrupted time for play.

❖ Allow children freedom of movement indoors and outdoors.

❖ Give children freedom of choice for activities. Some children like doll play, while others prefer to play on climbing frames.

❖ Mixed age groups encourage play because older children will help toddlers and younger children and teach them how to play.

❖ Adults can help play by play tutoring. This is not actually play: it is a way that adults can help children take a step towards their own play.

❖ Adults can also help children by entering into the spirit of play. You can play with children as long as you do not try to take over their play and control it.

❖ Know about and provide for each aspect in the network of learning (see page 469).

❖ Encourage quality first-hand experiences through carefully chosen provision both indoors and outdoors.

❖ Help children to represent and keep hold of their experience by using a range of materials and activities.

❖ Organise games.

❖ Observe children at play, and add provision to support and extend their play. For example, add shoes to the dressing-up box if children are playing 'shoe shops'.

❖ Do not invade, dominate or change the direction of the children's play. Join the free-flow play and try to catch what it is about so that you can help it along.

❖ Make a safe and healthy environment.

❖ Maintain the environment. For example, if the block area has become very messy ask a group of children to help you tidy it. No one can play well in a chaotic area.

❖ Watch out for the 12 features of play (see page 469) so that you know what a child is doing. Then you can help out if necessary by joining in or by extending the provision.

❖ Help the children to stay in character when they are making a play story. Help children to keep in mind the storyline of their play scenario.

❖ Remember, babies, toddlers and young children use what they already know to learn more, and they need other people to help them.

(Gopnik, Melzoff and Kuhl 1999).

ACTIVITY: MAKING TIME FOR PLAY

1 Plan ways of giving children sufficient *time* to develop rich, free-flow play. Include a flexible routine for children, with a balance between leaving children to get on with it (a leave-it-to-nature approach) and adult-led activities (a transmission model). Implement your plan and observe a child of 3–4 years. Evaluate your observations.

2 Research how the day is timetabled for children in a reception class compared to children in Key Stage 1, Years 1 and 2. Observe a child of 4–7 years for a day: remember to include the mid-morning, afternoon and lunchtime play periods.

3 Plan an outdoor area suitable for children aged 3–7 years. Remember, it should be possible for a child to do everything that is on offer indoors in the outdoor play area also. How will you organise outdoor experiences of paint, water, sand, drawing, home area, clay? In one school there was a clay table indoors and a mud patch to dig in outdoors. In this way, the outdoor provision complemented the indoor provision. Observe a child aged 3–7 years in the outdoor area. Evaluate their experiences and compare these with your plan of an outdoor area.

ACTIVITY: INVESTIGATING PLAY

1 Plan how you could assess what kind of learning a child is involved in – is it play or is the child benefiting from a quality first-hand experience, for example cooking?

2 Observe children aged 1 year (if possible), 2–3 years, 3–5 years and 5–7 years. Use the 12 features of play (see page 469) as observation tools. Evaluate your findings.

3 Observe children aged 1–3 years, 3–5 years and 5–7 years playing in the home area or the small-world area (doll's house, farm, road). Again, use the 12 features to understand (assess) the learning. Plan how you could add to the provision in the light of your observations. Evaluate your activity.

4 Observe a child with special educational needs. Is the child playing according to the 12 features of free-flow play? Evaluate your observations.

5 Observe a child who is sick but able to play – at home in bed or in a hospital. Identify which of the 12 features of free-flow play the child exhibits. Plan how to help the child. Implement your plan and evaluate the activity.

6 Describe how you could encourage play opportunities through the structured telling of a story.

7   Make a miniature garden using twigs and shells, and so on, and make a little pond. Tell a story to a small group, for example *Rosie's Walk* by Pat Hutchins. When you have finished telling the story, leave the garden out on a table with some story props. If a child begins to play

spontaneously with the garden, observe the play. Write down what the child says and does. Evaluate your activity.

8   Make a den. Who lives in it? Imagine the characters and make up a story. You might act it out for a group of children at story-time.

Fig 12.11 Sharing a story in a group

With the emergence of psychology as a discipline of study in the 1920s, theories suggested that play helps children:

❖   rehearse adult roles and prepare for their future lives (Groos, 1920s);

❖   sharpen their wits, keep their bodies functioning well through movement play, and engage in flexible and adaptable thinking (play helps adults to do these things too) (Huizinga, 1940s);

❖   experience a natural childhood, which helps them, supported by sensitive adults, to self-heal after emotional trauma (Anna Freud, 1940s and 1950s);

❖   find out what is important to them and resolve dilemmas – childhood play reveals the fears and fascinations of children (Erikson, 1950s);

❖   develop transitional objects and imaginary friends, which are used by the child deal with separations from those they love (e.g. sleeping with teddy or needing teddy when parting from mother), and develop imaginative play, so that teddy becomes a character with a full life; they try things out as they are, as they were, as they might be and as they want them to be; they gain control of their lives (Winnicott, 1960s);

❖   make the most of learning through the senses and movement, and using first-hand experiences, such as going shopping when learning about pretending (playing shops), gradually developing games with rules, such as snakes and ladders, snooker or football (Piaget, 1930s to 1980s);

❖   operate on a higher, more abstract plane than they can manage in ordinary life – Vygotsky emphasised that other people, especially adults, are important to children as they play; he believed that play helps children to do things in advance of what they can manage in real life, such as drive a car or pour the tea from a teapot (Vygotsky's influence reached the West in the 1980s).

THE CURRICULUM

Different educational and philosophical approaches to the curriculum for babies and young people

Every culture decides what the children should learn, and there are variations across the world. In India spirituality is emphasised, while in Laos and Hong Kong literacy and numeracy are the focus.

The approach in **Reggio Emilia** in Northern Italy emerged after World War II, and by 1976 governed the schools in that region for young children (from birth to 6 years). It took away the monopoly the Roman Catholic Church held over education, despite a campaign suggesting that this model of education was corrupting for children. Loris Malaguzzi, the pioneer, realised that **pedagogy** (understanding the relationship between developing, learning and teaching) must not be 'the prisoner of certainty'. He thought Piaget was right in warning us that we need a balance by informing our practice through theory and research. In the 1840s the educational pioneer Friedrich Froebel had similarly experienced the resistance of the German churches to his kindergartens, and placed emphasis on linking theory with practice. This is a recurring theme in the history of education that is centred on the child's development and learning rather than on the transmission of knowledge

identified as important by those who hold power.

Malaguzzi coined the phrase **the hundred languages of the child** to refer to all the different ways in which children express themselves, through talking, singing, dancing, painting, making models, role play, and so on. He considered each of these to be a language.

In New Zealand the Maori people and the Pakeha (white people) have worked together to make a major contribution to the early childhood curriculum (birth to 6 years) in the **Te Whariki** curriculum framework, which is based on four principles:

- empowerment – Whakamana;
- holistic development – Kotahitanga;
- family and community – Whanau Tangata;
- relationships – Nga Hononga.

There are five strands, each with goals:

1   Wellbeing – Mana Atua

    Goals: health is promoted; emotional wellbeing is nurtured; kept from harm.

2   Belonging – Mana Whenua

    Goals: connecting links with the family and wider world are affirmed and extended; children know they have a place; they feel comfortable with the routines, customs and regular events; they know the limits and boundaries of acceptable behaviour.

3   Contribution – Mana Tangat

    Goals: there are equitable opportunities for learning, irrespective of gender, ability, age, ethnicity or background; children are affirmed as individuals; they are encouraged to learn with and alongside others.

4   Communication – Mana Reo

Goals: children develop non-verbal communication skills for a range of purposes; they develop verbal communication skills for a range of purposes; they experience the stories and symbols of their own and other cultures; they discover and develop different ways to be creative and expressive.

5   Exploration – Mana Aoturoa

Goals: children's play is valued as meaningful learning and the importance of spontaneous play is recognised; children gain confidence in and control of their bodies; they learn strategies for active exploration, thinking and reasoning; they develop working theories for making sense of the natural, social, physical and material worlds.

The Centres of Innovation (COIs), a ministerial initiative led by Anne Meade, are further building on the good practice emerging from Te Whariki:

* through encouraging action research in settings which are innovating practice;

* supporting them in sharing their practice, knowledge and understanding.

Wherever children grow up they need to experience a curriculum framework which is broad, deep, balanced and meaningful to them. The following are considered important across the UK, although the different curriculum frameworks will present them differently (see Chapter 3).

THE EARLY CHILDHOOD CURRICULUM IN UK COUNTRIES

England

Birth to Three Matters: A framework to support children in their earliest years and *Curriculum Guidance for the Foundation Stage* inform the Early Years Foundation Stage.

BIRTH TO THREE MATTERS
The emphasis in **planning is on observation**.

'When we plan for children we base our ideas for activities and experiences on our knowledge of the children in our care. We notice one child's interest in water, another's curiosity about snails or the pleasure at listening to a story. This is where our planning begins.' (*Birth to Three Matters*, 2002)

This is also built around a set of principles to form a framework. It is important to understand that a framework is not seen as something like a curriculum syllabus, which is a very prescribed and rigid approach. Rather, this emphasises:

* the central importance of parents to the wellbeing of the child;

* relationships with adults and other children and the key staff at home and in the setting;

* recognising that babies and young children are social beings, and competent learners from birth.

The principles are as follows:

* Learning is a shared process, most effective when children are actively involved and interested, and with a trusted adult.

❧ Caring adults are more important than resources and equipment.

❧ Schedules and routines should flow with the child's needs.

❧ Children are learning when they are given appropriate responsibility, allowed to make errors, decisions and choices, and respected as autonomous and competent learners.

❧ Children learn by doing rather than being told.

❧ Young children are vulnerable. They learn to be independent and autonomous when they can depend on someone and trust them.

❧ Parents/carers are seen as central in the child's life.

There are four 'Aspects':

1   A Strong Child

Components:

❧ Me, myself and I;

❧ Being acknowledged and affirmed;

❧ Developing self-assurance;

❧ A sense of belonging.

2   A Skilful Communicator

Components:

❧ Being together;

❧ Finding a voice;

❧ Listening and responding;

❧ Making meaning.

3   A Competent Child

Components:

❧ Making connections;

❧ Being imaginative;

❧ Being creative;

❧ Representing.

4   A Healthy Child

Components:

❧ Emotional wellbeing;

❧ Growing and developing;

❧ Keeping safe;

❧ Healthy choices.

CURRICULUM GUIDANCE FOR THE FOUNDATION STAGE

This document is also based on a set of principles. It emphasises the importance of:

❧ meeting the diverse needs of children;

❧ children with special educational needs and disabilities;

❧ children with English as an additional language;

❧ learning and teaching;

❧ working with parents;

❧ play.

This is the most important part of the document, and it is not possible to embed the six areas of learning which follow without embedding the sections in the first part of the document. The six areas of learning (2006) are:

1   Personal, social and emotional development;

2   Communication, language and literacy;

3   Mathematical development;

4   Knowledge and understanding of the world;

5   Physical development;

6   Creative development.

Stepping stones help practitioners and parents to see the significant markers in a child's highly individual learning journey towards the early learning goals, which are aspirations (not expectations).

Scotland

The key documents are *Birth to Three: Supporting Relationships, Responsive Care and Respect* and *A Curriculum Framework for Children 3 to 5*.

In Scotland there is a move towards a generic framework for the curriculum, known as the '3–18 framework'.

BIRTH TO THREE

The document is based on principles summarised as:

* the best interests of children;
* the central importance of relationships;
* the need for all children to feel included;
* an understanding of the ways in which children learn.

The document shares the belief (stated in the *National Care Standards: Early Education and Care up to the Age of 16*) that children have a right to:

* dignity;
* privacy;
* choice;
* safety;
* realising potential;
* equality and diversity.

There is a strong emphasis on recognising and valuing the important role of parents. (This is so in all four countries of the UK.) Parents constantly ask for more information about their child's development and learning. Talking together with other parents and practitioners, including health visitors, empowers parents, along with television programmes and magazines aimed at supporting parents positively. This helps to ease anxieties parents experience, for example about their child's behaviour, or eating and sleeping patterns.

A CURRICULUM FRAMEWORK FOR CHILDREN 3 TO 5

This is also a document based on principles. There are five key aspects of children's development and learning:

1 Emotional, personal and social development;

2 Communication and language;

3 Knowledge and understanding of the world;

4 Expressive and aesthetic development;

5 Physical development and movement.

The framework:

* **promotes effective learning:** looking at the roles and responsibilities of adults in organising for children's learning; looking at the assessment and planning process; valuing observations that inform these; recording, reporting and evaluating;

* **sees each child as a unique individual:** working together with homes and families, children with special educational needs, fostering equal opportunities, collaborating with other agencies and supporting transitions.

Wales

THE FOUNDATION PHASE (3–7)

Between 2004 and 2008, 41 settings in Wales (The Learning Country) are being trialled as part of a pilot project integrating:

* desirable outcomes for children's learning before compulsory school age;

* the programmes of study and focus statements in the current Key Stage 1 national curriculum in Wales.

This is described as the draft **Framework for Children's Learning**.

There are seven areas of learning in the Foundation Phase, with an emphasis on experiential learning, learning by doing and by solving real-life problems both inside and outdoors:

1 Personal and social development and wellbeing;

2 Language, literacy and communication skills;

3 Mathematical development;

4 Bilingualism and multicultural understanding;

5 Knowledge and understanding of the world;

6 Physical development;

7 Creative development.

Northern Ireland

CURRICULAR GUIDANCE FOR PRESCHOOL EDUCATION

The document emphasises the importance of valuing the diverse experiences children bring to preschool, and building on this through providing a rich play environment. Children need to learn without experiencing a sense of failure. This requires:

❖ a stimulating environment, with adequate supervision, in which children are safe, secure and healthy;

❖ an environment inside and outside the playroom with opportunities to investigate, satisfy curiosity, explore and extend their sense of wonder, experience success and develop a positive attitude towards learning;

❖ appropriate periods of time for learning through sustained involvement in play;

❖ adults who are sensitive and encouraging, with whom children feel secure in their relationships, knowing that adults are there to support them;

❖ adults who treat children as individuals and participate in their play sensitively.

The curriculum framework needs to include opportunities, through play and other experiences, to develop the learning associated with:

1 Personal, social and emotional development;

2 Physical development;

3 Creative/aesthetic development;

4 Language development;

5 Early mathematical experiences;

6 Early experiences in science and technology;

7 Knowledge and appreciation of the environment.

PERSONAL, SOCIAL AND EMOTIONAL DEVELOPMENT

In every country in the UK there is great emphasis in the curriculum frameworks from birth to 6 years on the emotional wellbeing of the child.

These are basic emotions: anger, pride, shame, humiliation, disgust, surprise, love, enjoyment, fear, sadness.

Emotional development requires:

❖ emotional self-awareness;

❖ self-managing your emotions;

❖ empathy with how others feel and think;

❖ handling relationships.

Adults can help children to develop emotionally (and become **emotionally literate**) if they encourage children to:

❖ stop and calm down before they act;

❖ say, or show the adult, what the problem is;

❖ be clear what it is they want or hope for;

❖ think of different ways to solve the problem;

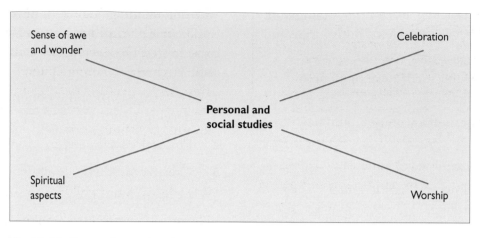

Fig 12.12 Personal, social and emotional development

* work out the consequences;
* try out what seems to be the best plan.

Adults also help children to develop emotionally if they encourage participation in nature (awe and wonder and spirituality) and in the arts (dance, music, visual arts, drama, pottery, and so on).

Sue Gerhardt, in her book *Why Love Matters*, stresses the importance of children developing warm, affectionate relationships with those who care for them, to whom they become attached. Early friendships are also important. (Look again at Chapter 9 to remind yourself about this.)

Celebration

It is important to realise that celebrations such as Diwali, Ramadan and Christmas can only be celebrated by Hindus, Muslims or Christians. It is therefore easy to introduce these to children in ways which are tokenist and superficial. We can learn about the celebrations of others, but we cannot actually celebrate with them unless we are of that faith. This may be why events such as New Year's Eve and New Year's Day are gaining in popularity. They are ways in which everyone can celebrate together in the UK, because they are not faith-based.

COMMUNICATION, LANGUAGE AND LITERACY

Again and again in this book (and particularly in Chapter 7), the importance of tuning in to the body language and early efforts to talk of babies and young children

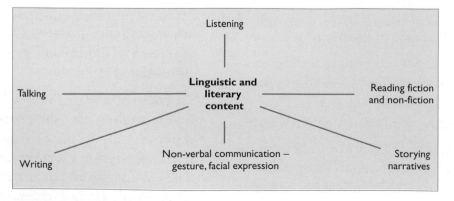

Fig 12.13 Elements of communication, language and literacy

> **Non-verbal communication**
> Facial expression, gesture, body movement/language, hand movements, pauses, rhythms of speech, eye contact, moving in synchrony with someone speaking to you, blushing, intonation of the voice, narrowed or wide-open eyes.

has been emphasised. Parent/carer-facing prams and buggies are important, and getting down to the child's level is too. Talking with babies and children at their height, face-to-face, helps language to develop.

Conversations develop with quality when adults and children are:

* talking about the same things;

* looking at things together (shared focus);

* sharing an experience they both find interesting.

Having a conversation is different from making children reply to questions that have definite answers (**closed questions**). In a real conversation people take it in turns to say things that they are thinking or feeling. One speaker does not decide what the other speaker has to reply.

When questions are asked they should be **open-ended, and asked for a real reason**. Children quickly realise when adults are asking questions just for the sake of it.

Turn-taking

Young children find it difficult to wait for their turn.

Singing songs or saying rhymes *together* means that no one has to wait and everyone can join in. This is very important at large-group time.

Research suggests that knowing about rhyme and rhythm helps children to learn to *read and write*. For this reason it is very important to encourage children to play with words.

Communicating Matters (DfES 2005) is a multi-professional initiative which helps practitioners to develop the communication and language of young children, including those with special educational needs and disabilities. This is part of every local authority's training now.

Reading

Why do we want children to read?

The aim is to produce children who are bookworms, who want to read for pleasure and understanding, information and knowledge, and not children who only look at books when directed to do so, who are just dutiful readers.

Reading, across the world, begins by listening to stories and rhymes.

MUSICAL DEVELOPMENT AND LEARNING TO READ AND WRITE

The areas of the brain which are for movement, gestures, sound and language are close to each other and form interactive networks. Ring games and traditional songs and dances help the brain along in a natural way, and this helps children learn to read – and later to write.

If you sing, 'Dinner-time, it's dinner-time' to children, especially children with special needs, complex needs, or who are learning English as an additional language, you will probably find they understand more easily what you are saying. It helps children to segment the sounds, and to identify and pronounce them.

Of course, the sound of words is important in learning to read, but we have to remember that saying or singing 'duck' in the north of England is different from the south. The context is very important too, especially when words are spelt differently, such as,

'When you have **read** this book, you might like to **read** another one.'

Singing helps children because many of the words rhyme, and this makes the text predictable; it is also more manageable because the poetry is in a verse or small chunk.

Clapping the rhythm or dancing to the song while singing also helps the brain to sort things out.

LISTENING TO STORIES

It is important to remember that stories are not always in written form:

❖ stories can be told (the Gaelic, Celtic and Maori traditions use storytelling powerfully);

❖ stories can be told in pictures, which are subtle.

Stories have a special way of using language called **book language**, such as, 'Once upon a time. . .'. Children need a wealth of experience of book language before they can read well and become enthusiastic readers.

Children need many different forms (genres) of stories they need core texts, favourite stories and new stories.

Criteria for selecting appropriate books

❖ **Everyday events:** these help children to recognise common events and feelings. They help children to heighten their awareness of words which describe everyday situations.

❖ **Poems:** these help rhyming and rhythm, and the chorus often gives a predictable element; the repetition helps children. This is also true of many stories, but poems are an enjoyable experience for young children, who may not be able to concentrate on a whole story in the early stages.

❖ **Folk stories:** these introduce children to different cultures. However, avoid stories in which animals behave as if they were humans or in which animals behave in a way which is out of character (e.g. a spider who saves the life of a fly in an act of bravery). These are called anthropomorphic stories. They can confuse young children who are trying to sort out what is and is not true.

❖ **True stories:** these lead to an understanding of non-fiction books, which are full of information on different topics and subjects.

❖ **Make-believe stories:** these lead to an understanding of fiction. Avoid stories of witches and fairies for very young children (under 4 years); children need to be clear about the distinction between reality and imagination, otherwise they may be fearful and have nightmares. Bear in mind that it is one thing for a 4-year-old to make up their own stories about monsters, witches or ghosts (the child has control), but if an adult introduces these characters the child may be scared.

❖ **Action rhymes and finger rhymes:** these help children to predict what is in a text. Predicting is a very large part of learning to read; knowing what comes next is important.

❖ **Repeating stories:** knowing a story well helps children begin to read. Sometimes adults say, 'Oh, but he is not reading, he just knows it off by heart.' Knowing what comes next is probably one of the most important parts of learning to read.

❖ Think about issues of gender, ethnicity, culture and disability, and be sure that all children see positive images of themselves in the stories you tell and in the books that you offer.

CHILDREN NEED ADULTS TO TELL AND READ THEM STORIES

❖ Children need one-to-one stories. These are called bedtime-type stories. The child can interact with the reader and get

and action songs with very large groups (eight or more children). This gives children the rhythm, intonation and pace and small manageable chunks of text in a song. This makes for a good community experience of reading together.

Poetry cards are of great benefit. They can be made out of cardboard boxes, and can be large and rather like theatre props. Children enjoy playing with them afterwards if they are left near the book corner. Children are often to be seen pointing at the print, in word approximation, landing at the end, and starting at the beginning. They are often joined by a friend. Encouraging children to share stories together, whether or not they can read fluently, is very helpful. This encourages emergent readers to **approximate-read**, and to pick out the words they know with confidence. Being able to have a go and to do so with confidence and pleasure are crucial.

HELPING CHILDREN TO READ

You can help children to read by enjoying a book or poetry card together, without any pressure. Children can see how a book is used, where to begin, how to turn a page and the direction of print, using pictures as clues, finding familiar words and guessing. Being able to guess and predict what the print says is important. Children are usually fascinated by guesses that go wrong, realising this as they learn to link what they read with meaning, and to work out the words using their increasing ability to segment and blend the graphemes and phonemes. It is important to say, 'What do you think he says next?' Show the child any patterns, for example a phrase that is repeated, and talk about the letters, words and sentences as you go. Picture cues are very important when learning to read, so talk about these and the clues they give.

Fig 12.14 One-to-one stories are like bedtime stories and they are an important part of learning to read

deeply involved. The adult and child can pause, chat, go back and revisit, and read at their own pace.

❖ Small-group stories, with two to four children, are more difficult for children because the adult needs to keep the story going, and so cannot allow constant interruptions. Skilled adults are able to welcome many of the children's contributions, but the larger the group, the more important it becomes for children to be able to listen. Large groups, with four to eight children, are less sensitive to the individual needs of children, so these need to be more of a theatre show or performance by the adult in order to keep the attention of the children. They cannot be so interactive. It is better to use poetry cards

Fig 12.15 Photographs and names: picture cues help children to read

Alphabet books and friezes are important as they help children to segment words, and to focus on the initial grapheme and phoneme in a word, while offering a meaningful picture to help the child along. Regularly singing the alphabet is helpful too. Pointing out children with the same letter at the beginning of their name helps, and there can be fascinating discussions about why George is pronounced with a 'J' sound, while Gary is with a 'G'

sound. English speakers need to learn early to spot exceptions with detective joy!

Children often know favourite stories by heart. This gives children a sense of control and ability to feel they can predict what the text says. It gives them a can-do feeling, crucial in learning. Decide as a team which books you will introduce as core texts, to help children become familiar with them. Note which books are favourites of particular children, and use these with the child in the same way.

Above all, remember that learning to read should be fun, and it should hold meaning for the child.

Aspects of print which are important when learning to read

* The meaning of the words (**semantic** aspect).
* The flow of the words (the **syntax** or grammar).
* The look and sound of the print (**grapho-phonic** aspects).
* Discriminating between a sentence, a word and the smallest aspects (**graphemes** and phonemes).
* Segmenting words into **phonemes** (**decoding**) and blending phonemes into words (**encoding**), using onset and rime to help this along in rhymes and songs, poetry cards, dance and actions.
* Book language (**vocabulary**).

ACTIVITY: STAGES OF READING

Observe children aged 3–7 years. Identify which children are emergent, beginner or fluent readers. What are the factors that you use to decide? Evaluate the advantages and disadvantages of shared stories.

Remember that the child's own name is the best starting point for learning letters, because children are emotionally attached to their name.

ONSET AND RIME — A TYPE OF PHONICS PARTICULARLY USEFUL FOR ENGLISH SPEAKERS

Because English is an irregular language, it is particularly hard to learn to read and write using it. Some argue that we should get children off to an early start for just this reason. Most early childhood experts take the view that the human brain needs to be sufficiently matured to tackle the fine detail of discriminating the sounds and look of English print. Even in countries where the language is very regular, such as Finland and Sweden, this is the approach. However, the brain does function easily and without stress in relation to learning about communication (both non-verbal and spoken/signed language) and music, gesture and movement. This means that singing and dancing, and talking with and listening to children, all have a huge contribution to make in helping children towards reading and writing by 6 or 7 years of age. This age is generally regarded, throughout the world, as the best time to learn to read and write, because the structures dealing with this level of symbolic functioning are there.

These words are nearly the same: 'pot', 'dot', 'got'; 'mess', 'cress', 'dress'; 'mum', 'chum', 'drum'.

The last chunk rhymes, but the first chunk is different in each case. This is a type of **analytic phonics** called **onset and rime**. Many early childhood reading and writing experts consider that learning about onset and rime through poems, songs and action rhymes, poetry cards and books are more powerful ways of helping young children to read in English than teaching isolated sounds

using flashcards (**synthetic phonics**) as the main strategy. A fierce debate about this seems to arise roughly every 10 years. Most experts argue that the more strategies we have to offer children as they learn to read, the more we can find the ones that suit them best. One size does not fit all children.

The Rose Review on Reading (2006), commissioned by the Secretary of State for Education, emphasises the importance of a rich language environment, encouraging children to enjoy being read to from fiction and non-fiction books from babyhood; it sees reading and writing as inextricably intertwined and emphasises the importance of a broad range of experiences, as advocated by *Birth to Three Matters* and *Curriculum Guidance for the Foundation Stage*. It focuses on the importance of song, rhythm and rhyme for young children in encouraging them to make the important connections needed between the letter and sound relationships.

There is great opposition by early childhood experts to the suggestion that young children should be directly taught synthetic phonics through daily drill in large groups. However, daily group time (remember, large groups are four to eight children), with song, dance and rhyme, and encouragement to make children phonologically aware and able to discriminate sounds with more and more ease, and to link these with the print in the rhymes using poetry cards, would be welcomed. Practitioners doing this need to be aware that onset and rime is a type of phonics which also encourages synthetic phonics in a meaningful context.

Children need to learn to **segment** (break down) sounds and print. They also need to learn to **blend** (join) sounds and print. The smallest sounds are phonemes and the smallest print is a grapheme. Children need to make **grapho-phonic** relationships. They need to begin to see that what they have segmented can be blended back into a word. The ideal age to do this, experts in most countries say, is between 6 and 7 years of age.

Songs like 'Humpty Dumpty' are simple examples of this:

Humpty Dumpty sat on a wall,

Humpty Dumpty had a great fall.

Children quickly begin to see the last chunk is the same (-umpty), while the beginnings are different ('H' and 'D').

Studies of the brain suggest that the brain loves complexity, and that singing, dancing, moving, doing action songs and seeing print in meaningful patterns is part of the interconnectedness of different parts of the brain.

The brain develops important interconnecting networks, which include those in the chart below. Movement, communication, play, symbol use, problem solving and understanding why things happen (cause and effect), become more complex, coordinated and sophisticated as the networks for learning in the brain develop.

Many experts believe that removing the meaningful context and teaching letter–sound relationships in isolation and separately, although systematic to those adult readers devising the system, actually make reading and writing more difficult for many children. This is particularly so for children who have low-incidence disabilities, such as visual or hearing impairments, or children with English as an additional language.

Pioneers of education such as Froebel and Steiner used song and dance with action songs to great effect in helping children

towards reading and writing. In most countries of the world this is the approach, particularly in countries like Finland and Sweden, where children start to learn to read late (6–7 years), yet within weeks become the best readers in the world. These languages are regular compared with the many exceptions in English. This is another reason why using a single strategy of synthetic phonics is not likely to be as effective in English literacy development as a broader approach, which includes both synthetic and analytic phonics (especially onset and rime). The brain works in an interconnected way to make sense of the sounds and relationships with print. This is the opposite of the accretion model, which builds from the simple to the more complex, using isolation and removing context as part of the simplification. This approach was widely used at the beginning of the 1900s.

The big debate is really about whether, as with other aspects of development, children begin with the whole, gross aspects of movement, sound and visual discriminations before picking out the fine detail, or whether they begin with the detail and piece together the whole out of all the parts. For children with little language experience, or with English as an additional language, this is a challenge, many experts believe. Most adults report that when learning a new language they understand the finer parts of the sounds and look of the words more easily if they learn songs and rhythms. This is because it is easier to pick out the detail of the patterns. Adam Ockelford is a musician who is also an educator (RNIB). He has pointed out that when children with complex needs are sung to, for example, 'Dinner is ready', they react when they might not do so if the words are simply said.

Fig 12.16 Children's writing

Writing

Writing has two aspects:

❖ what it says – the construction of meaning;

❖ the look of it – the handwriting and letter shapes (transcription).

When children begin to write, they are constructing a **code**. Most languages have a written code. Writing develops when children begin to use symbols. Often they begin by putting letter-type shapes into their drawings. These gradually get pushed out to the edges of the drawing, to look more like words and sentences. Practitioners need to observe the shapes, sizes and numbers children experiment with. Children need to be free to experiment without criticism or

pressure. Left-handed children must never be encouraged to write with the right hand.

Young children find capital letters, which are more linear, easier to write than lower-case letters, which have more curves, and so they tend to experiment with capitals first. It is when children begin to experiment with curves that they are indicating they have more pencil control, and so can begin to form letters more easily.

Children need:

❖ to manipulate and try out different ways of 'writing' using their own personal code – tracing or copying letters undermines this because their own movement patterns and laying down of neural pathways are an important part of the process;

❖ to explore what writing is;

❖ adults who point out print in books and in the environment, on notices and street signs, for example.

It is important to value writing from different cultures, for example Urdu, Arabic (which is read from right to left) and Chinese (which is read up and down on the page).

The pace and sequence of events which leads to writing and the age at which it occurs will vary greatly from child to child, depending on the child's interest, mood and personality, aptitude and, very importantly, prior experience and understanding of what writing is about. Compared with other countries, children in England are expected to begin formal writing and reading exceptionally young. There is a high illiteracy rate in England, and many experts are concerned that this is because, by starting too soon, many children lose heart and are put off by the end of their primary school years. Young children are more likely to enjoy and see the point of reading and writing for the rest of their lives if they are introduced to reading and writing carefully and without feeling pressured. The first words that children write are full of their own feelings. These words need to be valued and respected. A child's own name is important

Guidelines for encouraging later creative writing

❖ Learning about different roles, characters and themes is essential if children are going to learn to write stories.

❖ Having dressing-up clothes to act out stories helps children to create narratives, a skill needed for later writing.

❖ Ask children to act out a story you have told.

❖ Encourage children to act out stories that *they* have made up, and which you have written down for them. Vivian Gussin-Paley, in her school in Chicago, did this as a daily part of the curriculum.

❖ Act out stories in an atmosphere of *sharing*. This should *not* involve a *performance* of the story. The idea is to help children to understand *how* stories are made. This will help them later when they want to write their own stories.

❖ Young children should not be expected to perform stories in school assemblies, or in situations with audiences full of strangers (e.g. for the summer or Christmas show). It is not good practice to encourage children to perform before they have gone through the sequence: make – share – show. They need to be able to make their own stories, and to share these with friends and adults whom they know well before they perform.

❖ To perform becomes appropriate only in junior school. Any earlier, and some children begin over-acting and playing to the audience rather than becoming involved in the story; other children are put off forever because of the stress of being made to perform. Waving at people in the audience during a performance may be very sweet for adults to see, but it is a clear sign that the child is not involved in what they are doing and so is not ready to perform. The exercise is a failure in terms of involving a child in a story.

❖ Research suggests that, if children are encouraged to play in the early years, they will be better at creative writing at 7 years of age.

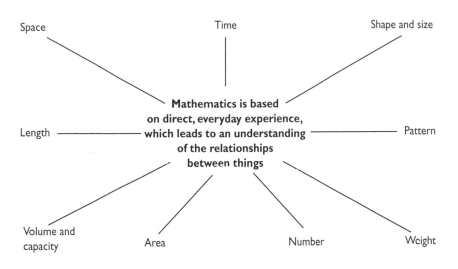

Fig 12.17 Elements of mathematics

to them, and they often write the names of people they love, plus the words 'love from'.

It is important to talk with children about environmental print, and to pick out their favourite letters (often those in their name).

MATHEMATICAL DEVELOPMENT

Mathematics involves problem solving and reasoning in particular ways. Of course, these aspects of thinking are part of every area of learning, creative and physical development, emotional, social and personal development, learning to use language, to communicate with or without words or signs, and to read and write, as well as in developing scientific thinking and other aspects of knowledge and understanding of the world.

In mathematics, finding an elegant, logical and beautiful answer to a problem is deeply satisfying to a child, providing the problem is one generated by the child. Then it will have meaning.

Children learn about **topological** space (on/off, over/under, in/out, surrounding,

across, near/far) before they learn about **Euclidian** space (circles, squares, etc.). Learning the words for these in everyday situations helps children to develop reasoning and the ability to solve problems. 'Put the chair under the table' uses a topological term. These topological words link with **schemas**, which are patterns in the brain that help learning. They also feature in the 250 most used words in the English language. They are, researchers at Warwick University have

Fig 12.18 Talking together about reflections in the mirror

shown, very important in learning to read because they are used so frequently. Children quickly recognise them, and so do not need to segment and blend as they read them. Instead they just recognise them from sight.

Number

Number has several different aspects:

❖ **Matching:** this looks like this – two identical cups in the home corner.

❖ **Sorting:** this looks different from this – the cup and the saucer.

❖ **One-to-one correspondence:** one biscuit for you, one biscuit for me.

❖ **Cardinal numbers:** the two cups remain two cups however they are arranged (this means that the child understands the number, e.g. two).

❖ **Ordinal numbers:** this is first, second, third (e.g. the sequence in cooking: first I wash my hands, second I put on my apron. . .).

Children learn about number in these ways:

❖ reciting – number songs;

❖ nominal understanding – they pick out numbers on house doors, buses, in shops, on shoe sizes;

❖ subitising – remembering number patterns to recognise how many, for example, four dots, one on each corner of a square, or on a domino (chimpanzees can do this with numbers up to seven);

❖ counting backwards – 5, 4, 3, 2, 1, lift-off!

There are three counting principles:

1 A number word is needed for every object that is counted. This is the one-to-one correspondence principle.

2 The numbers always have the same order, 1, 2, 3 (not 1, 3, 2). This is called the stable order principle.

3 When children count, they have grasped the cardinal number principle if they understand both points 1 and 2, because they know that a number is an outcome. This means that when you count, 1, 2, 3, the answer is 3.

Time

Time has two aspects:

1 Personal time: it feels a long time before a car journey ends – it might be an hour, but it feels like a day.

2 Universal time, including:

❖ succession: Monday, Tuesday, Wednesday. . .

❖ duration: day, night, an hour, a minute. . .

Guidelines for learning number

❖ Do not do exercises or tasks with young children which are isolated from their experience.

❖ Remember that children learn mathematics through cooking, tidy-up time, playing in the home area, painting and being in the garden. Mathematics is everywhere.

❖ Numbers are found on rulers, calibrated cooking jugs, the doors of houses, and so on.

❖ Counting is only one part of exploring numbers. It is one thing for children to be curious about numbers on calibrated jugs, weights and measures, but they need to be free to experiment and explore. This is very different from formally teaching them numbers through adult-led tasks, unrelated to real life.

Do not be too specific with young children. Begin by teaching the time with '1 o'clock', 'half past ten', and so on. Introduce more exact time-telling later. When children look at the watch and enjoy finding the numbers they are learning in an informal way.

Shape and size

Use general terms to help children learn about these aspects of mathematics. Talk about shape and size when you do things together. Children need experience of action and language. This means plenty of talking while they do things. Children need adults to describe things that are 'bigger than' and 'smaller than' to learn that these things are **relative**, not **absolute** sizes. Something is 'big' only in relation to something else. Always use relative terms with children.

Children are very three-dimensional in their perception, so introduce words like cube and cylinder before oblong and circle. Use everyday things, like tins of food or a football to explain that this is a cylinder and a sphere.

Length

Again, it is helpful to children if relative words are used, such as 'longer than' or 'shorter than'. Young children do not yet understand the absolute nature of 1 metre, although it is helpful to show them that there is a metre behind the car in the parking space. Children need to be surrounded by rulers and tapes so that they become aware that things can be measured. Which is the tallest plant? Who has the longest foot? Gradually they develop an understanding of the exactness of absolute measurements.

Volume and capacity

'This glass is full.' 'This bucket is nearly empty.' Listen to yourself speak and you will be surprised at how often you use mathematical language in everyday situations. This informal approach encourages children's dispositions towards learning in an enjoyable and relaxed way.

Area

Area is about ideas such as the blanket that covers the *area* of the mattress on the bed. Another example would be a pancake covered with lemon and sugar – the lemon and sugar cover the area of the pancake. Children often explore area in their block play.

Weight

Again, it is best to introduce the concept of weight using relative ideas. 'This tin of soup is heavier than that apple.' Rather than using a weighing machine, use a balance, so that children see this. Remember that young children need to experience weight physically. They love to carry heavy things. They love to lift each other up, and often carry bags around.

Case Study

Exploring weight

Kit, 3 years, carried a huge piece of ice about one freezing winter. He enjoyed throwing it and watching it skim across an icy stream. He kept saying, 'This is heavy.' His parents helped him to make comparisons: 'Is it heavier than this stone?' 'Is it heavier than this twig?'

Computers

There is an urgent need for better computer programmes to be developed for the use of young children. Many current examples are nothing more than technological forms of template-type activities. This does not encourage children to think at a deep level.

It might be fun, but it is certainly not educational. The most appropriate computer programmes invite children to be interactive.

Children benefit from using a word processor and printer, as well as using digital cameras. They enjoy picking out letters and punctuation marks, and through this kind of play they learn about important aspects of reading, writing and numbers, which will be used in a more elaborate way later.

CREATIVE DEVELOPMENT

Creative development is often seen as linked only with the arts. In fact, it is a very important part of human development which applies to the:

❖ arts (dance, music, drama, the visual arts, including sculpture, ceramics and pottery, painting and drawing, collage);

❖ sciences (biology, chemistry, physics, applied engineering, environmental studies, industry);

❖ humanities (history, geography, cultural aspects).

You can read more about creative development in *Cultivating Creativity: Babies, Toddlers and Young Children* (Bruce 2004).

Creativity in the arts and crafts

Children need experiences which are real, direct and first-hand, such as using clay and paint regularly. Some children choose solid media, such as dough, clay and wood. Others choose to draw and paint on paper. Representing a dog is quite different when using clay, wood at the woodwork bench, paint or pretending to be a dog in the home corner. It is important that adults directly

Guidelines for promoting children's creativity

Remember, the idea is for the child to become involved in these activities. Adults often use children's art lessons as a chance to do art for themselves! Resist the temptation.

❖ *Do not* draw for children.

❖ *Do not* use templates.

❖ *Do not* ask children to trace.

❖ *Do not* ask children to colour in.

❖ *Do not* ask children to copy your model step by step.

❖ *Do* give children real, first-hand experiences, such as looking at plants or mini-beasts in the pond.

❖ *Do* give children opportunities to represent things, and to keep hold of their experiences (e.g. by making a model of the plant out of clay).

❖ *Do* encourage lots of different ideas. It is best when every child in a group has made a different model. This means that children are doing their own thinking and are not dependent on adults for ideas.

❖ *Do* remember that children are creative in lots of different ways. Arts and crafts are only one area in which children are creative. Children can be creative scientists, creative mathematicians, creative writers, and so on.

teach children skills with the woodwork bench, or in using clay or scissors, as and when the need arises. Teaching skills in context is important. Often when children stand and watch other children use scissors, they are indicating that they are interested to learn. Adults need to be good observers and tune in to these situations.

SCULPTURE AND POTTERY

Children need to have opportunities to make three-dimensional models, with clay, wet sand, wax, soap carving, wood, dough, junk and recycled materials. This will involve them in using Sellotape, scissors, rolling pins, string, wire and other materials. Most of the time these materials can be offered as general areas of provision, available all the time. Clearly, the woodwork can only be used when an adult joins the children, in order to maintain a safe environment. However, sometimes, each of these areas can become a focused group, where an adult is anchored to teach directly. For example, a group of children might be taught how to make coil pots with clay in the clay area. If a child has been enjoying making paper spirals, the adult would make a point of inviting them to do this. Children should be able to decline such an invitation, however.

DRAWING AND PAINTING

For drawing it is best to use plain white paper of varied sizes, plus pencils, wax crayons, felt-tip pens, chalks and slates, and charcoal.

For painting there should be powder paints and different thicknesses of brushes. Materials should be stored carefully so that children can take and access what they need when they need it. Children should be offered pots of basic coloured paints, but they should also be able to mix paints, provided they are taught to do so. They simply need the basic colours – red, yellow, blue, and white and black for light and dark shades of colour.

BOOK MAKING

Children love to make books, but need help to do so initially. If they see that you have made recipe books, books of stories and poems, and books for display with information, they will want to do the same. They need to learn how to fold and cut the paper. An adult may need to be with them so that they do not give up.

COLLAGE AND WORKSHOP AREA

This requires glue, found materials, junk and recycled materials and scissors. Materials can be set out in attractive baskets or boxes

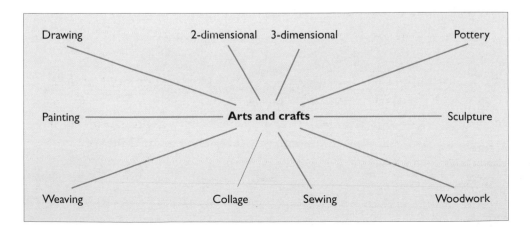

Fig 12.19 Elements of arts and crafts

covered in wallpaper. Glue should always be non-toxic.

Creativity in dance, music and drama

DANCE

Use what children do naturally – spinning, running, jumping, stamping, to make into a dance. A 'Singing in the Rain' dance was made by a group of 5-year-olds in Year 1 Key Stage 1, helped by their teacher, Dee De Wet. The children watched a video extract from the film, 'Singing in the Rain', and then they experimented with moving about:

❖ with fancy feet;

❖ by jumping in puddles;

❖ by swishing through puddles;

❖ by dashing about under an umbrella.

They made a dance sequence. Each child had an umbrella and raincoat, and used the above sequences in line with the traditional music from the film. Every child made their own dance, and yet they all danced at the same time, and were sensitive to each other's movement and ideas.

Guidelines for helping children to make dances

❖ Use an action phrase, for example 'shiver and freeze'. Ask the children to move like the words in the phrase.

❖ Show different objects, perhaps something spiky. Ask the children to move in a spiky way and make a dance.

❖ Take an idea from nature or everyday life: rush and roar like the wind; be a machine or a clock; dance like shadows moving or fish in the aquarium.

❖ For inspiration only use experiences which the children have had very recently.

The book by Mollie Davies, *Movement and Dance in Early Childhood* (2003), gives more ideas on how to help young children dance, both boys and girls.

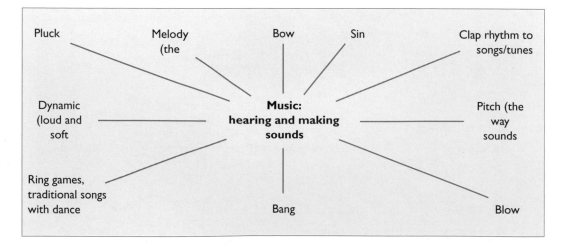

Fig 12.20 Music; hearing and making sounds

MUSIC

Recent studies in neuroscience show that music is important in helping language and memory to develop. Adults naturally sing, 'Up we go' when they lift a baby or toddler out of a pram. Music helps children to remember words. But music is important in its own right. Everyday sounds have rhythm, such as the tick-tock of an alarm clock. Tearing paper, shaking the salt box, jangling a bunch of keys, fire engines. . . Children love to go on listening walks, and to make the sounds they have heard using home-made musical instruments you help them to make. The importance of singing and listening to a wide range of music from different cultures cannot be overemphasised.

DRAMA

Some people argue that drama began in ancient times when people tried to explore the forces of good versus evil. In their play, children experiment with goodies and baddies, friendship and foes, kindness and unkindness. Penny Holland's work shows how adults can help children to explore these major themes of what it is to be human. Telling children stories and sharing poetry cards with them also helps. Retelling stories with props is beneficial. The adult might help children to act out the story of Pegasus using 'My Little Pony', with paper wings attached with sticky tape. Children might wear dressing-up clothes to retell the story of *The Wild Things* by Maurice Sendak, including the rumpus dance.

Creativity in the sciences and technologies

Creative scientists and technicians see new connections and new ways of doing things. They look at the same old things in a new way, which changes things for ever. Seeing the barbs on a teasel when walking the dog by the river led one scientist to invent Velcro.

Creativity in the humanities

Thinking in new ways about what has gone before can have a huge impact on history, geography and culture. Nelson Mandela changed the world when, instead of following tradition and having trials to condemn the atrocities which had taken place during apartheid in South Africa, he developed a council of truth and reconciliation, so that people admitted and faced publicly the full horror of their actions, but without fear of reprisal in doing so. He was given the Nobel Prize for Peace.

SCIENTIFIC KNOWLEDGE AND UNDERSTANDING

Just as mathematics is everywhere, so science is everywhere. Einstein, the famous scientist, said that science is really just the refinement of everyday life.

Use all the provision, indoors and outdoors, sand, water, wood, clay, paint. Use the nature around you. Look at animals, insects, birds, amphibians. Do not just look at these in books. Find ways to show children real-life examples. Use books only to follow up and remember real experiences.

THE PHYSICAL SCIENCES

❖ **Electricity:** electrical circuits are easy to make with children and can be used to make a light for the doll's house or the train tracks.

❖ **Heat:** remember, heat is not just about temperature. Heat is energy. Temperature is a measure of how much

Guidelines for looking at animals

- ❖ **Where do animals live?** You can find ants, spiders and birds and look at their habitats. Remember, never kill animals, and always return them to their habitat; make a point of explaining this to the children. There are now pots with magnifying glasses in them, which make it easier to look at these creatures without squashing them accidentally.

- ❖ **What do animals eat?** Study cats, birds, fish and talk about their diets.

- ❖ **How do animals eat?** Talk about claws, type of feet, mouths, beaks, types of teeth, jaws which chew (cows), jaws which gnash. Study dogs, cats, humans. A bird that eats nuts needs a beak that is a good nutcracker! A bird that catches fish needs a long beak.

- ❖ **How do animals protect themselves?** Look at camouflage, claws, tusks, fur for warmth, oil on ducks' feathers to make them waterproof.

There are reasons why animals, birds and insects have developed as they have done. The points above will give children an introduction to the evolution of the animal world in ways they can understand.

Guidelines for looking at plants

- ❖ Why do plants have leaves? Do all plants have leaves?

- ❖ Why is a tree trunk like it is? Do all trees have exactly the same sort of trunk? Make some bark rubbings. Hug trees to see if you can reach all the way round them with your arms.

- ❖ Why do flowers have colours? Insects are important for plant life.

- ❖ Why do some flowers have scent and nectar? Again, plants might need to attract insects and birds to visit them.

energy. Cookery is the best way to help children understand about temperature. Making a jelly or ice cream is a good way of looking at coldness. Making something which needs to be cooked in the oven shows children about high temperatures. Look at a central-heating system and the radiators. Think about the sun and how it makes the tarmac on the playground feel warm on a sunny day in the summer. Look at the fridge. Play with ice cubes in the water tray.

Again, talk about relative heat. Is this hotter than that? Describe what is happening, think about the cause and effect, why things happen as they do. Metal feels colder than wood, but why? They are both at room temperature. Does the metal conduct the heat out of your hand?

- ❖ **Sound:** listen to the sounds around you. Help children to be aware of them. Children love to tape-record sounds and find ways to imitate sounds they hear.

Some sounds are quieter and some are noisier than others. Children are not very concerned about how many decibels a sound is, but they are interested that a shout is louder than an whisper.

- **Light:** use torches and lanterns. Make rainbows with prisms. Put on puppet shows and have lighting effects. Use cellophane to make different colours of light. Children in Key Stage 1 enthusiastically make light effects for stories they have made up or enjoyed from books. Experiment with shadows and shadow puppets.

- **Gravity:** use parachutes, or drop objects from heights.

- **Floating and sinking:** this is a difficult concept. Young children benefit from a waterwheel and different experiments with boats, but true understanding takes time.

THE NATURAL SCIENCES

Use **mixtures** to demonstrate how materials can be changed and recovered (salt and water, sugar and water, earth and water, flour and water, mud pies, and mud and straw to make bricks.) All these mixtures have properties which children can explore:

- Salt dissolves in water. So does sugar. When the water evaporates the salt or sugar can be seen again.

- Flour and mud do not dissolve. They become suspended in water.

- You can look at transformations using water, ice and steam. You can reverse these, and turn steam into water again.

- Study what happens when you cook an egg. You cannot reverse this transformation.

Early technology can be explored by looking at activities such as weaving. If you have a frame with string going up and down and from side to side, near the entrance, then children and families will enjoy the in- and out-movement of threading pieces of material, wool, ribbon, and so on. These weavings often become attractive wall hangings in the office or entrance hall of the setting.

It is important to use technology which is easy for children to understand. Examples would be a tin opener, an egg whisk or scissors. Encourage children to use wooden blocks and construction kits.

Look at both types of technology:

- low technology, such as an egg whisk, waterwheels;

- high technology, such as digital cameras, tape recorders for music and stories, computers, word processors and printers, telephones for conversations.

GEOGRAPHY, HISTORY AND CULTURE

Young children are interested in people, families and homes. They like to learn about what people in the community do. They show this in their role play. Through role play and visits to offices, shops, clinics, the vet, the station, they learn about different communities. They develop a sense of geography.

They are also interested in old objects, in what things were like when they were babies or when their parents were babies, and what sort of childhood their grandparents had. Collecting artefacts of bygone days and inviting older people to share and talk about their lives, often with the help of photographs, help children to develop a sense of history. Having a timeline helps too, again using photos to show the order and sequence of events.

PHYSICAL DEVELOPMENT

Remember:

❖ Children need to move as much as they need to eat and sleep.

❖ They learn through action and language that gives it meaning.

❖ They need to be skilled in a range of movements, using both fine and gross motor skills.

❖ They need repetition to consolidate.

❖ Movement needs to be appropriate – stroke a dog gently, but throw hard to make a splash with a pebble in a puddle.

Large apparatus

This can include:

❖ climbing frame;

❖ ropes to swing on;

❖ planks to walk on with ladders;

❖ things to jump off.

Children need to be encouraged to become generally skilled in movement.

Small apparatus

This includes bats, balls, hoops, beanbags and ropes. It is very important to encourage turn-taking and cooperation.

Floor work

This enables children to explore:

❖ weight transfer from one part of the body to another;

❖ travel from one spot to another;

❖ flight: jumps – the five basic jumps are: on two legs, from one leg to the other, on the left leg, on the right leg, from two legs to one leg.

Give children a general theme to investigate through floor work, for example starting low and getting higher. Do not make children do just one thing, such as a handstand. There are lots of ways of changing your balance – a handstand is only one. To help children enjoy creating and solving problems about weight transfer, you can say, 'Can you start on your feet and stop with another bit of you touching the floor?' In this way you are helping children with **reasoning** and **problem solving** as they think about their own movements. Being aware of your own body and comfortable in it is called embodiment. This increases **wellbeing** and self-confidence.

KEYSTAGE 1 IN ENGLAND – CONTINUING THE LEARNING JOURNEY

This is a DfES teaching package designed to help schools give children a positive

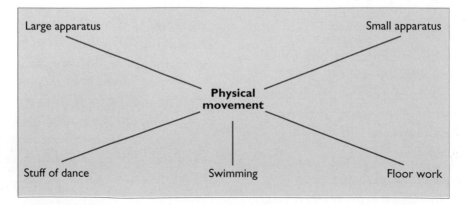

Fig 12.21 Elements of movement

experience as they move into Key Stage 1 in England, so that there is an effective building upon the Foundation Stage.

The principles of the Foundation Stage should be used to promote continuity in learning, so that teachers are aware of children's achievements and can implement the next steps in their learning. Information from the Foundaion Stage Profile supports this process. The curriculum in year 1 of the primary school should be responsive to children's needs.

If this is effectively achieved, a features transition is brought about, and children undertake the programme of Key Stage 1 positively building on the 6 areas of the Foundation Stage.

THE ENGLISH NATIONAL CURRICULUM

The English National Curriculum was established by the **Education Reform Act 1988 (ERA)**. It provides a *minimum requirement* for a curriculum and it has recently been reviewed. It states that the curriculum of each school should be 'balanced and broadly based' to promote the 'spiritual, moral, cultural, mental and physical development of pupils … and of society' and to prepare pupils for 'the opportunities, responsibilities and experiences of adult life'.

In England, there are **programmes of study** for each subject, plus **attainment targets** in each subject, through which teachers can make rounded assessments of children using **levels of description**. Teachers are encouraged to make plans of work and to keep observation-based records. Checklists for record-keeping are not encouraged.

The subjects in the English National Curriculum are:

* Three core subjects – English, maths and science (soon to be four, including citizenship)

* foundation subjects – design and technology, information technology, history, geography, art, music, physical education and a modern language (from 11 years old).

There is a trend towards allowing schools to use the National Curriculum more flexibly provided that they receive a good Inspection Report. Most schools have decided against a rigid application of the **National Literacy Hour** or daily mathematics lesson. The teaching of religious education must be provided under the heading cultural, moral and spiritual and sex education.

There are four **key stages** in the English National Curriculum:

* **Foundation Stage** (from 3 years to the end of the Reception Year)
* **Key Stage 1** (Years 1 and 2: 5–7 years)
* **Key Stage 2** (7–11 years)
* **Key Stage 3** (11–14 years)
* **Key Stage 4** (14–16 years).

Children are assessed through **Standard Assessment Tasks** (SATs) at the end of each Key Stage, with a Foundation Profile at the end of the Foundation Stage (from 2002). Staff in early years settings will be able to use the end of the Foundation Stage Profile assessment to:

* support and encourage a multi-lingual classroom

* identify children with special educational needs

* encourage a dialogue between home and school, perhaps building on a home visit which is made just before the child starts school.

However, research shows that summer-born children, especially if they are boys, have lower SAT scores than older children. Many early years experts interpret this as evidence suggesting an early start to formal education carries long-term disadvantages for a large proportion of children.

THE WELSH NATIONAL CURRICULUM

There are three or four core subjects depending on whether Welsh is the first language of the child and on whether the child is being educated in a Welsh-medium school: English, maths, science and Welsh. Welsh is tested at the end of each Key Stage if it is a core subject, as are the other core subjects. Welsh is studied by all children up to Key Stage 3, but tests are optional if it is the child's second language. The other subjects are the same as for the English National Curriculum, except:

❖ at Key Stage 4, when modern language and technology are optional;

❖ in art and music, where there is still a requirement to make and perform dances, music and art.

There will no longer be SATs at the end of Key Stage 1 and children will follow an extension of the curriculum for 3–5 year-olds.

THE SCOTTISH CURRICULUM

The Scottish Curriculum is for 5–14 years. It has been designed largely by practising teachers. Teachers decide when a child is ready to move to the next level. A sample of teacher assessments are monitored as a moderation exercise. This checks that all teachers are using the same criteria correctly. The results of the teacher assessments are share with parents. 79% of parents voted against SATs being introduced into the Scottish system. The subject areas are also organised differently, with six different areas of learning. There are:

❖ English

❖ mathematics

❖ science

❖ design and technology

❖ creative and expressive studies

❖ language studies.

THE NORTHERN IRELAND CURRICULUM

In some ways, the Northern Ireland Curriculum is more likely the Scottish Curriculum, with similar areas of study, though religious education lies outside these. In other ways, it is like the English National Curriculum in that it follows similar testing procedures: children are tested at the end of each Key Stage.

The areas of study are:

❖ English – at Key Stage 1 – this includes drama and media studies; mathematics; science

❖ design and technology – which may soon be combined with science

❖ environment and society – which includes geography and history, and may soon include home economics

❖ creative and expressive studies – which includes PE and dance; art and design; music

❖ language studies – only at secondary level. When the Irish language is offered, another modern language must also be offered by the school.

Caring for babies in the first year of life

Contents

PRE-CONCEPTUAL CARE

Life does not begin at birth; an individual is already 9 months old when born. In China a person's age is determined, not by his birth date, but by the date of his conception.
A couple who are planning to start a family will certainly hope for a healthy baby; pre-conceptual care means both partners reduce known risks before trying to conceive in order to create the best conditions for an embryo to grow and develop into a healthy baby. The first 12 weeks of life in the womb (or uterus) are the most crucial, as this is the period during which all the essential organs are formed.

CONCEPTION AND DEVELOPMENT OF THE UNBORN BABY

Conception occurs in the fallopian tube when a male sperm meets the female egg (the ovum) and fertilises it. The fertilised ovum now contains genetic material from both mother and father – a total of 46 chromosomes (23 pairs) – and a new life begins.

Early days of life

Within about 30 hours of fertilisation, the egg divides into 2 cells, then 4, and so on (see Figure 13.1); after 5 days it has reached the 16-cell stage and has arrived in the uterus (womb). Sometimes a mistake happens and the ovum implants in the wrong place, such as in the fallopian tube; this is called an **ectopic pregnancy** and it is not sustainable. By about the tenth day, the **blastocyst** has embedded itself entirely in the lining of the uterus and the complex process of development and growth begins. The outer cells of the blastocyst go on to form:

❖ The **placenta** (called chorionic villi during early development). The placenta (afterbirth) provides the foetus with

Table 13.1 Guidelines for preconceptual care.

Use barrier methods of contraception	Stop smoking
Use a condom or a diaphragm for three months before trying to conceive. It is advisable to discontinue the Pill so that the woman's natural hormonal pattern can be re-established.	Smoking cuts the amount of oxygen supplied to the baby through the placenta and can result in miscarriage or low birth weight. Some men who smoke are less fertile because they produce less sperm.

Eat well
A balanced diet allows a woman to build up reserves of the nutrients vital to the unborn baby in the first three months: <ul><li>**eat something from the four main food groups** every day (potato and cereals, fruit and vegetables, milk and milk products and high protein foods);</li><li>**cut down on sugary foods** and eat fresh foods where possible;</li><li>**avoid prepacked foods** and any foods which carry the risk of salmonella or listeria;</li><li>**do not go on a slimming diet**; follow your appetite and do not eat more than you need;</li><li>**vegetarian diets** which include milk, fish, cheese and eggs provide the vital protein the baby needs;</li><li>**vegans** should eat soya products and nuts and pulses to supply protein and vitamin B12 may need to be taken as a supplement.</li><li>**folic acid tablets and a diet rich in folic acid** taken preconceptually and in pregnancy help the development of the brain and spinal cord.</li></ul>

Genetic counselling	Avoid hazards at work
If there is a fairly high risk that a child may carry a genetic fault, such as cystic fibrosis or sickle cell disease, genetic counselling is offered. Tests may be done to try to diagnose any problem prenatally but all carry some element of risk in themselves.	Some chemicals and gases may increase the risk of miscarriage or birth defects. Women should be aware of the risks and take precautions after discussion with the environmental health officer.

Substance misuse and abuse	X-rays
Do not take any drugs unless prescribed by a doctor. Existing conditions such as epilepsy or diabetes will need to be controlled before and during pregnancy. Many addictive drugs cross the placental barrier and can damage the unborn baby.	X-rays are best avoided in the first three months of pregnancy although the risks to the foetus are thought to be very small.

Sexually transmitted diseases (STDs)	Cut down on alcohol
STDs should be treated – if either partner thinks there is any risk of syphilis, gonorrhoea, genital herpes or HIV infection, then both partners should attend a 'special clinic' for advice and tests. STDs can cause miscarriage, stillbirth or birth defects.	The best advice is to cut out alcohol completely; moderate drinking (1–2 glasses of wine or beer a day) increases the risk of miscarriage and babies are born smaller and more vulnerable. Heavy drinking, especially in the first few weeks of pregnancy, can cause **foetal alcohol syndrome** in which the baby is seriously damaged.

oxygen and nourishment from the mother via the umbilical cord and removes the foetal waste products. The placenta also acts as a barrier to certain microorganisms, but some may cross this barrier and cause damage to the embryo or foetus.

❖ The **membranes** or **amniotic sac**. This sac is filled with amniotic fluid and provides a cushion for the foetus as it grows and becomes more mobile.

The inner cell mass goes on to form the embryo proper. Until 8 weeks after conception the developing baby is called an embryo; from 8 weeks until birth the developing baby is called a **foetus**. The embryonic cells are divided into three layers:

1 The **ectoderm** forms the outer layer of the baby: the skin, nails and hair; it also folds inwards to form the nervous system (brain, spinal cord and nerves).

2 The **endoderm** forms all the organs inside the baby.

3 The **mesoderm** develops into the heart, muscles, blood and bones.

Development of the embryo

❖ **At 4–5 weeks** the embryo is the size of a pea (5 mm) and yet the rudimentary heart has begun to beat, and the arms and legs appear as buds growing out of the sides of the body (see Figure 13.2).

❖ **At 6–7 weeks** the embryo is 8 mm long and the limb buds are beginning to look like real arms and legs; the heart can be seen beating on an ultrasound scan (see Figure 13.3).

❖ **At 8–9 weeks** the unborn baby is called a foetus and measures about 2 cm. Toes and fingers are starting to form, and the major internal organs (brain, lungs, kidneys, liver and intestines) are all developing rapidly (see Figure 13.4).

❖ **At 10–14 weeks** the foetus measures about 7 cm and all the organs are complete. By 12 weeks the unborn baby is fully formed and just needs to grow and develop. The top of the mother's uterus (the fundus) can usually be felt above the pelvic bones (see Figure 13.5).

❖ **At 15–22 weeks** the foetus is large enough for the mother to feel its movements. A mother who has had a child before may feel fluttering sensations earlier as she is able to identify them. At 22 weeks the greasy, white protective film called **vernix caseosa** has begun to form and the foetus is covered with a fine, downy hair called **lanugo** (see Figure 13.6).

❖ **At 23–30 weeks** the foetus is covered in vernix and the lanugo has usually disappeared. From 28 weeks the foetus is said to be viable, that is, if born now, he has a good chance of surviving, although babies have survived from as early as 23 weeks. The mother may be aware of his response to sudden or loud noises and he will be used to the pitch and rhythm of his mother's voice. At 30 weeks the foetus measures 42 cm (see Figure 13.7).

❖ **At 31–40 weeks** the foetus begins to fill out and become plumper; the vernix and lanugo disappear and the foetus usually settles into the head-down position, ready to be born. If his head moves down into the pelvis it is said to be 'engaged', but this may not happen until the onset of labour (see Figure 13.8).

PREGNANCY

The signs and symptoms of pregnancy occur after the fertilised ovum has implanted in the lining of the uterus. The pregnancy is usually confirmed by a simple urine test – the **HCG** test, which detects the presence of **human chorionic gonadotrophin** in the urine.

The significance of the rhesus factor in pregnancy

As well as belonging to one of four different blood groups (A, B, AB and O), your blood can be rhesus (Rh) positive or rhesus negative. Most people are rhesus positive. Problems may result if the mother is Rh negative and the baby inherits the father's

Rh positive gene. If the baby's blood enters the mother's bloodstream during delivery, the mother's body reacts to these foreign blood cells by producing antibodies to fight them. These antibody molecules are able to cross the placenta and go back into the baby, resulting in anaemia or, more seriously, haemolytic disease of the newborn, which may require several blood transfusions in pregnancy and sometimes also after birth. Usually the level of antibodies is not high enough to do serious damage in a first pregnancy, but the antibodies remain in the mother's blood and may cause serious problems in subsequent pregnancies. Prevention of this situation is by regular tests to assess the antibodies in the maternal blood and by giving an injection of anti-D globulin (anti-rhesus factor) within 72 hours of the first delivery to prevent further formation of antibodies.

Fertilisation: only one sperm can fertilise the egg   Two-cell stage   Four-cell stage   Blastocyst

Fig 13.1 The early days of life

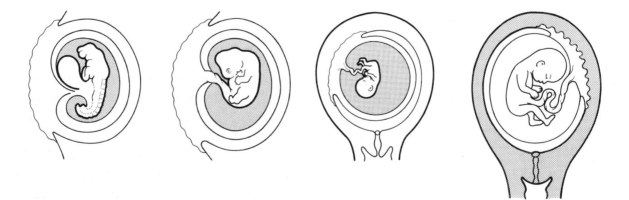

Fig 13.2 Embryo 4–5 weeks; **13.3** Embryo 6–7 weeks; **13.4** Foetus 8–9 weeks; **13.5** Foetus 10–14 weeks

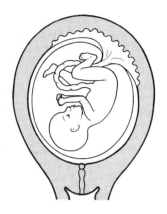
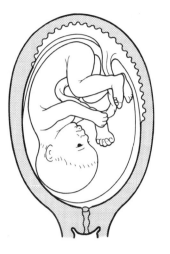
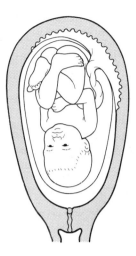

Fug 13.6 Foetus 15–22 weeks; 13.7 Foetus 23–30 weeks; 13.8 Foetus 31–40 weeks

Signs and symptoms of pregnancy

MISSED PERIOD (AMENORRHOEA)

Missing a period is a very reliable symptom of pregnancy if the woman has no other reason to experience a change to her menstrual cycle; occasionally periods may be missed because of illness, severe weight loss or emotional upset.

BREAST CHANGES

Sometimes the breasts will tingle and feel heavier or fuller immediately; surface veins become visible and the primary **areola**, the ring around the nipple, will become darker. This is more noticeable on fair-skinned women. As pregnancy continues (at about 16 weeks) colostrum can be expressed from the nipple.

PASSING URINE FREQUENTLY

The effect of hormones and the enlarging uterus result in women having to pass urine more often than usual.

TIREDNESS

This can be noticeable in the first 3 months of pregnancy, but usually lifts as the pregnancy progresses.

SICKNESS

Nausea (feeling sick) or vomiting can occur at any time of the day or night, but is usually referred to as 'morning sickness'. Some unlucky women experience nausea throughout pregnancy.

Nutrition during pregnancy

Every pregnant woman hears about 'eating for two', but the best information available today suggests that this is not good advice. Research shows that the quality (not quantity) of a baby's nutrition before birth lays the foundation for good health in later life. Therefore, during pregnancy women should eat a well-balanced diet (see the guidelines in the box below).

Guidelines for a healthy diet in pregnancy

❖ Lean meat, fish, eggs, cheese, beans and lentils are all good sources of nutrients. Eat some every day.

❖ Starchy foods like bread, potatoes, rice, pasta and breakfast cereals should – with vegetables – form the main part of any meal.

❖ Dairy products, like milk, cheese and yoghurt, are important as they contain **calcium** and other nutrients needed for the baby's development.

NB Pregnant women should avoid eating all types of pâté and mould-ripened cheese, like Brie, Camembert and similar blue-veined cheeses, because of the risk of the bacterial infection, **listeria** (this is a rare cause of serious problems in a newborn baby and can also cause stillbirth).

❖ Citrus fruit, tomatoes, broccoli, blackcurrants and potatoes are good sources of **vitamin C**, which is needed to help the absorption of iron from non-meat sources.

❖ Cut down on sugar and sugary foods like sweets, biscuits and cakes, and sugary drinks like cola.

❖ Eat plenty of fruit and vegetables that provide **vitamins**, **minerals** and **fibre**. Eat them lightly cooked or raw.

❖ Green, leafy vegetables, lean meat, dried fruit and nuts contain iron, which is important for preventing anaemia.

❖ Dairy products, fish with edible bones like sardines, bread, nuts and green vegetables are rich in calcium, which is vital for making bones and teeth.

❖ Margarine or oily fish (e.g. tinned sardines) contain **vitamin D** to keep bones healthy.

❖ Include plenty of **fibre** in the daily diet; this will prevent constipation and help to keep calorie intake down.

❖ Cut down on fat and fatty foods. Reducing fat has the effect of reducing energy intake; it is important that these calories are replaced in the form of carbohydrate. Fat should not be avoided completely, however, as certain types are essential for body functioning, as well as containing **fat-soluble vitamins**.

❖ **Folic acid** is a B vitamin, which is very important throughout pregnancy, but especially in the first 12 weeks when the baby's systems are being formed. (Most doctors recommend that pregnant women take a folic acid supplement every day, as more folic acid is required than is available from a normal diet.)

❖ Department of Health advice is to eat according to appetite, with only a small increase in energy intake for the last 3 months of the pregnancy (200 kcal a day).

Some women are at risk from poor nutrition during pregnancy. Any woman who restricts her diet for personal, religious or cultural reasons may have to take care, although well-balanced vegetarian and vegan diets should be safe. The following groups of women are potentially at risk:

- adolescents who have an increased nutritional requirement for their own growth, as well as providing for the foetus;
- women with closely spaced pregnancies;
- recent immigrants;
- women on low incomes;
- women who are very underweight or overweight;
- women with restricted and poorly balanced diets;
- women with pre-existing medical conditions, such as diabetes mellitus and food allergies;
- women who have had a previous low birth-weight baby.

ANTENATAL CARE

The main aim of antenatal (or prenatal) care is to help the mother deliver a live, healthy infant. Women are encouraged to see their family doctor (GP) as soon as they think they may be pregnant. The team of professionals – midwife, doctor, health visitor and obstetrician – will discuss the options for antenatal care, delivery and post-natal care with the mother. Antenatal care has the following principles or aims:

- A safe pregnancy and delivery, resulting in a healthy mother and baby.
- The identification and management of any deviation from normal.

- Preparation of both parents for labour and parenthood.
- An emotionally satisfying experience.
- Promotion of a healthy lifestyle and breastfeeding.

The management of antenatal care

STATUTORY SERVICES RELATING TO ANTENATAL CARE

The first decision to be made by the prospective parents is where the birth will take place. Facilities and policies vary a great deal around the UK and some people have more choices than others. The options are:

- **Home:** some doctors do not agree with home births in any circumstances as they are concerned about the lack of hospital facilities if anything should go wrong during labour; the woman is entitled to register with another doctor if she wishes to have a home birth. Antenatal care is shared between the community midwife, who visits the woman in her own home or at a health centre, and the GP.
- **Hospital:** a full stay in hospital is usually 7 or 8 days, but there are often options to stay only 48 hours or even 6 hours. Antenatal care is shared between the hospital, the GP and the community midwife.
- **GP units:** these are run by GPs and community midwives, often using beds within a district hospital or in a separate building near the hospital.
- **Midwife unit:** this type of unit is run entirely by midwives, who undertake all the antenatal care, delivery and post-natal care. The mother and baby usually stay in the unit from 6 hours to 3 days after birth. Midwife units are not widely available.

❖ **Domino schemes:** Domino is an abbreviation of Domiciliary-in-out. Care is shared between the community midwife and the GP. When labour starts, the midwife comes into the hospital or GP unit to deliver the baby. Back-up care can be from the woman's GP or from a hospital doctor. If both mother and baby are well, they can often go home within hours of the birth and the midwife continues to look after them at home.

The booking clinic

Wherever the woman decides to give birth, early in her pregnancy she will attend a lengthy interview with the midwife, and the medical team will perform various tests. If necessary, a bed is booked for a hospital delivery for around the time the baby is due. Recognition of cultural differences and personal preferences, such as a woman's wish to be seen by a female doctor, is important and most antenatal clinics try to meet such needs. Relatives are encouraged to act as interpreters for women who understand or speak little English, and leaflets explaining common antenatal procedures are usually available in different languages.

Professionals involved in antenatal care and childbirth

❖ **Midwife:** a registered nurse who has had further training in the care of women during pregnancy and labour. They can work in hospitals, clinics or in the community. Most routine antenatal care is carried out by midwives, and a midwife delivers most babies born in the UK. In the community, midwives have a statutory responsibility to care for both mother and baby for 10 days after delivery.

❖ **Obstetrician:** a doctor who has specialised in the care of pregnant women and childbirth. Most of their work is carried out in hospital maternity units and they care for women who have complications in pregnancy or who need a Caesarean section or forceps delivery.

❖ **General practitioner (GP) or family doctor:** a doctor who has taken further training in general practice. Many GP group practices also have a doctor who has taken further training in obstetrics.

❖ **Gynaecologist:** a doctor who has specialised in the female reproductive system.

❖ **Paediatrician:** a doctor who has specialised in the care of children up to the age of 16. Paediatricians attend all difficult births in case the baby needs resuscitation.

❖ **Health visitor:** a qualified nurse who has taken further training for the care of people in the community, including midwifery experience. They work exclusively in the community and can be approached either directly or via the family doctor. They work primarily with mothers, and children up to the age of 5 years. Their main role is health education and preventive care.

Private services relating to antenatal care

There are many options available to the woman who can afford to pay for private antenatal and post-natal care. She may choose a home birth with a private or independent midwife. The midwife will undertake all antenatal and post-natal care and also deliver the baby. Another option is to have the baby in a private hospital or maternity unit, attended by an obstetrician.

Table 13.2   The Booking Clinic, early pregnancy.

Taking a medical and obstetric history	Medical examination
This is usually carried out by the midwife and covers the following areas:	A doctor will need to carry out the following physical examinations:
❖ details of the **menstrual cycle** and the date of the last period; the expected delivery date (EDD) is then calculated;	❖ **listening to the heart and lungs;**
❖ details of any **previous pregnancies,** miscarriages, or births;	❖ **examining breasts** for any lumps or for inverted nipples which might cause difficulties with breast feeding;
❖ **medical history** – diabetes, high blood pressure or heart disease can all influence the pregnancy;	❖ noting the presence of **varicose veins** in the legs and any swelling of legs or fingers;
❖ **family history** – any serious illness, inherited disorders or history of twins;	❖ **internal examination** to assess the timing of the pregnancy – a cervical smear may be offered.
❖ **social history** – the need for support at home and the quality of housing will be assessed, especially if the woman has requested a home or Domino delivery.	

Clinical tests

❖ **Height** – this can give a guide to the ideal weight; small women (under 1.5m) will be more carefully monitored in case the pelvis is too narrow for the baby to be delivered vaginally.

❖ **Weight** – this will be recorded at every antenatal appointment; weight gain should be steady (the average gain during pregnancy is 12–15kg).

❖ **Blood pressure** – readings are recorded at every antenatal appointment, as **hypertension** or high blood pressure in pregnancy can interfere with the blood supply to the placenta.

❖ **Urine tests** – urine is tested at every antenatal appointment for:
- **sugar:** occasionally present in the urine during pregnancy, but if it persists may be an early sign of **diabetes;**
- **protein:** traces may indicate an infection or be an early sign of **pre-eclampsia** – a special condition only associated with pregnancy where one of the main signs is high blood pressure;
- **ketones:** these are produced when fats are broken down; the case may be constant vomiting or dieting or there may be some kidney damage.

❖ **Blood tests** – a blood sample will be taken and screenef for:
- **blood group:** in case transfusion is necessary; everyone belongs to one of four groups: A, AB, B or O;
- **Rhesus factor:** positive or negative (see page 507);
- **syphilis:** can damage the baby if left untreated;
- **rubella immunity:** if not immune, the mother should avoid contact with the virus and be offered the vaccination after birth to safeguard future pregnancies;
- **sickle cell disease** – a form of inherited anaemia which affects people of African, West Indian and Asian descent;
- **thalassaemia** – a similar condition which mostly affects people from Mediterranean countries;
- **haemoglobin** levels – the iron content of the blood is checked regularly to exclude **anaemia.**

Many district hospitals also offer private facilities for paying patients.

Antenatal care during the middle months

Visits to the antenatal clinic, GP or community midwife will be monthly during this stage of pregnancy, or more often if problems are detected. On each occasion the following checks are made and recorded on the cooperation card, which is given to every woman to enable appropriate care to be given wherever she happens to be:

❖ weight;

❖ blood pressure;

❖ foetal heart (heard through a portable ear trumpet or using electronic equipment);

❖ urine (checked for sugar and protein);

❖ fundal height (the size of the uterus);

❖ any **oedema**, or swelling, of ankles and/or fingers.

By 28 weeks the hospital will expect to have the mother booked in for a hospital delivery and visits to the antenatal clinic, GP or midwife are weekly in the final month of pregnancy.

A summary of the tests carried out during pregnancy is shown in Table 13.3.

Health education

The midwife, doctor and health visitor are available throughout pregnancy to give advice on diet, rest, exercise or any issue causing concern; they can also offer advice on the current maternity benefits and how to apply for them.

The inverse care law operates in this area of health (see also page 370). The women most at risk of developing complications during pregnancy are those in poor housing, on a poor diet or whose attendance at antenatal clinics is infrequent or non-existent. The midwife and health visitor will be aware of the risks such factors pose for both mother and baby, and will target such individuals to ensure that preventive health care, such as surveillance and immunisation, reaches them.

Parent craft classes

Childbirth preparation classes are offered, usually in later pregnancy, and are held in hospitals, health centres, community halls and private homes. They usually welcome couples to attend and aim to cover:

❖ **all aspects of pregnancy:** diet and exercise; sexual activity; how to cope with problems such as nausea, tiredness and heartburn;

❖ **labour:** what to expect; pain control methods; breathing and relaxation exercises;

❖ **birth:** what happens at each stage and the different methods of delivery;

❖ **the new baby:** what to expect and how to care for a newborn; common problems, including post-natal depression.

The classes usually include a tour of the maternity unit at the hospital.

They are also valuable meeting places for discussion with other parents-to-be about all the emotional changes involved in becoming a parent. Separate classes may also be held for women with **special needs** – expectant mothers who are schoolgirls, or in one-parent families, or whose first language is not English. Some areas provide classes earlier in pregnancy (8–20 weeks) or aqua-natal classes where women can practise special exercises standing in shoulder-high water.

Table 13.3 Screening tests in pregnancy.

Name	Procedure	When	Procedure performed to assess	Comments
Chorionic villus sampling (CVS)	A small piece of the placenta is removed via the cervix (neck of the womb) and the cells examined	At about 8–11 weeks	❖ the risk of Down's syndrome, haemophilia, cystic fibrosis, thalassaemia, sickle-cell disease or other inherited disorders	
Amniocentesis	After an ultrasound scan a hollow needle is inserted through the abdomen to draw off a sample of amniotic fluid from inside the uterus; the foetal cells are examined under a microscope to detect chromosomal abnormality	At about 16–18 weeks	❖ the presence of an extra chromosome, i.e. Down's syndrome ❖ any missing or damaged chromosomes	May be offered to any woman with a history of chromosomal abnormalities or sex-linked disorders, or who is over 35 years old
Triple test	A blood test which measures levels of the hormones, HCG (Human Chorionic Gonadotrophin) and oestriol and a protein, AFP – alpha-fetoprotein; the levels of the three substances are used in conjunction with the woman's age	At about 16 weeks	❖ the risk of the baby having Down's syndrome ❖ the risk of the baby having spina bifida	The triple test does not make a diagnosis of these conditions but indicates if further tests such as amniocentesis are necessary
Ultrasound scan	Ultrasound (sound at higher frequency than can be heard by the human ear) is used to produce pictures of the foetus in the uterus	At any stage, but usually 16–20 weeks	❖ the size, age and position of the foetus ❖ the position of the placenta ❖ if there is more than one baby ❖ if the foetus is developing normally ❖ if there are fibroids in the womb ❖ if the pregnancy is in the right place or ectopic	

Some organisations, such as the National Childbirth Trust (NCT), also offer parent education classes; these are usually held in small groups in the tutor's home. Fees vary according to circumstances.

Maternity rights and benefits

All pregnant women are entitled to the following rights and benefits:

* free NHS maternity care;
* if employed, paid time off for antenatal care; this care includes not only medical examinations but also parent craft classes;
* protection against detrimental treatment and unfair dismissal because of pregnancy;
* 14 weeks' maternity leave, regardless of service;
* free prescriptions until the baby is 1 year old;
* free dental care until the baby is 1 year old;
* the right to return to work up to 29 weeks after the baby is born.

Other maternity benefits are paid only to those who meet certain qualifying conditions or who are on a **low income**. The **Sure Start Maternity Grant** is a one-off payment for pregnant women on a low income – currently £500 – to help towards the costs of a new baby. The grant comes from the Social Fund and does not have to be repaid. Free milk and vitamin tokens are also available to expectant mothers and to children under 5 years, in families receiving income support.

FACTORS AFFECTING PHYSICAL DEVELOPMENT OF THE FOETUS

Various factors affect growth and development of the foetus (see Figure 13.9).

The mother's age

The best age to have a baby from a purely *physical* point of view is probably between 18 and 30 years. Complications of pregnancy and labour are slightly more likely above and below these ages.

* **Younger mothers**: under the age of 16 years there is a higher risk of having a small or premature baby, of becoming anaemic and suffering from high blood pressure. In addition, emotionally and socially, very young teenagers are likely to find pregnancy and motherhood hard to cope with and they will need a great deal of support.

* **Older first-time mothers:** first-time mothers over the age of 35 run an increased risk of having a baby with a chromosomal abnormality. The most common abnormality associated with age is Down's syndrome. A woman in her twenties has a chance of only 1 in several thousand of having an affected baby, but by 40 years the risk is about 1 in every 110 births, and at 45 the risk is about 1 in every 30. Amniocentesis can detect the extra chromosome which results in Down's syndrome; it is usually offered routinely to women who are 37 or over.

Number of pregnancies

Some problems occur more frequently in the first pregnancy than in later ones, for example, breech presentation, pre-eclampsia (see page 518), low birth weight and neural tube defects. First babies represent a slightly higher risk than second and third babies do. The risks begin to rise again with the fourth and successive pregnancies; this is partly because the uterine muscles are less efficient, but it also depends to a certain extent on age and on the social factors associated with larger families.

The use of drugs

Most drugs taken by the mother during pregnancy will cross the placenta and enter the foetal circulation. Some of these may cause harm, particularly during the first 3 months after conception. Drugs that adversely affect the development of the foetus are known as **teratogenic**.

* **Prescription drugs:** drugs are sometimes prescribed by the woman's doctor to safeguard her health during pregnancy, for example antibiotics or anti-epilepsy treatment; they have to be very carefully monitored to minimise any possible effects on the unborn child.

* **Non-prescription drugs:** drugs such as aspirin and other painkillers should be checked for safety during pregnancy.

* **Alcohol:** can harm the foetus if taken in excess. Babies born to mothers who drank large amounts of alcohol throughout the pregnancy may be born with **foetal alcohol syndrome**. These babies have characteristic facial deformities, stunted growth and mental retardation. More moderate drinking may increase the risk of miscarriage, but many women continue to drink small amounts of alcohol throughout their pregnancy with no ill effects.

* **Illegal drugs:** drugs such as cocaine, crack and heroin are teratogenic and may cause the foetus to grow more slowly. Babies born to heroin addicts are addicted themselves and suffer painful withdrawal symptoms. They are likely to be underweight and may even die.

* **Smoking:** during pregnancy smoking reduces placental blood flow and,

therefore, the amount of oxygen the foetus receives. Babies born to mothers who smoke are more likely to be born prematurely or to have a low birth weight.

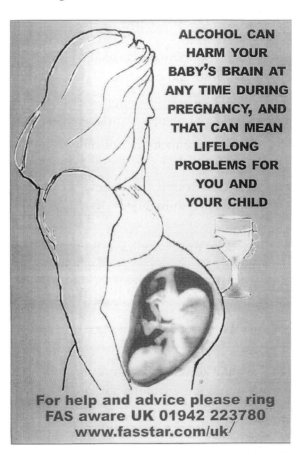

Fig 13.9 Foetal alcohol syndrome poster

Infection

Viruses and small bacteria can cross the placenta from the mother to the foetus and may interfere with normal growth and development. During the **first 3 months** (the first trimester) of a pregnancy, the foetus is particularly vulnerable. The most common problematic infections are:

1   **Rubella** (German measles) – this is a viral infection that is especially harmful to the developing foetus as it can cause congenital defects such as blindness,

deafness and mental retardation. All girls in the UK are now immunised against rubella before they reach childbearing age, and this measure has drastically reduced the incidence of rubella-damaged babies.

2 **Cytomegalovirus** (CMV) – this virus causes vague aches and pains, and sometimes a fever. It poses similar risks to the rubella virus, that is, blindness, deafness and mental retardation, but – as yet – there is no preventive vaccine. It is thought to infect as many as 1 per cent of unborn babies, and of those infected about 10 per cent may suffer permanent damage.

3 **Toxoplasmosis** – this is an infection caused by a tiny parasite. It may be caught from eating anything infected with the parasite, including:

❖ raw or undercooked meat, including raw cured meat such as Parma ham or salami;

❖ unwashed, uncooked fruit and vegetables;

❖ cat faeces and soil contaminated with cat faeces;

❖ unpasteurised goat's milk and dairy products made from it.

In about one-third of cases, toxoplasmosis is transmitted to the foetus and may cause blindness, hydrocephalus or mental retardation. Infection in late pregnancy usually has no ill effects.

4 **Syphilis** – this is a bacterial sexually transmitted disease (STD). It can only be transmitted across the placenta after the twentieth week of pregnancy. It causes the baby to develop congenital syphilis, and can even lead to the death of the foetus. If the woman is diagnosed as

having the disease at the beginning of pregnancy (see page 506), it can be treated satisfactorily before the twentieth week.

Pre-eclampsia

Pre-eclampsia is a complication of later pregnancy that can have serious implications for the wellbeing of both mother and baby. The oxygen supply to the baby may be reduced and early delivery may be necessary. It is characterised by:

❖ a rise in blood pressure;

❖ **oedema** (swelling) of hands, feet, body or face, due to fluid accumulating in the tissues;

❖ protein in the urine.

In severe cases, pre-eclampsia may lead to **eclampsia**, in which convulsions (seizures) can occur. This can occasionally threaten the life of both mother and baby. If pre-eclampsia is diagnosed, the woman is admitted to hospital for rest and further tests.

Premature birth

Babies who are born before the thirty-seventh week of pregnancy are now called pre-term babies. Around 4 per cent of babies are born pre-term and most of them weigh less than 2.5 kg. Therefore, they are also described as **low birth-weight** babies. The main problems for pre-term infants are:

❖ **Temperature control:** heat production is low and heat loss is high, because the surface area is large in proportion to the baby's weight and there is little insulation from subcutaneous fat.

❖ **Breathing:** the respiratory system is immature and the baby may have difficulty breathing by himself – a condition called **respiratory distress** syndrome (RDS). This is caused by a deficiency in **surfactant**, a fatty substance which coats the baby's lungs and is only produced from about 22 weeks of pregnancy.

❖ **Infection:** resistance to infection is poor because the baby has not had enough time in the uterus to acquire antibodies from the mother to protect against infection.

❖ **Jaundice:** due to immaturity of the liver function.

THE BIRTH PROCESS

Stage 1: the neck of the uterus opens

Towards the end of pregnancy, the baby moves down in the uterus and usually lies

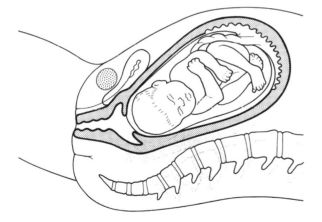

Fig 13.10 The first stage of labour

head downwards. A woman will recognise the onset of labour (the three-stage process of birth) by the following signs:

❖ **a 'show'** – a discharge of blood-stained mucus from the vagina;

❖ **the breaking of the waters,** or rupture of membranes, when some amniotic fluid escapes via the vagina;

❖ **regular muscular contractions,** which may start slowly and irregularly, but become stronger and more frequent as labour progresses. They open up the cervix at the neck of the womb.

Stage 1 may last for up to 24 hours and is usually longer for the first-time mother. Once the membranes have ruptured, which may not occur until late in stage 1, the woman should contact the midwife or hospital, as there is a risk of infection entering the uterus if labour is prolonged.

Stage 2: the birth of the baby

This begins when the cervix is fully **dilated** (open) and the baby starts to move down the birth canal; it ends when the baby is born. The contractions are very strong and the midwife encourages the mother to push with each contraction until the baby's head is ready to be born. When the baby's head stays at the entrance to the vagina, it is said to be

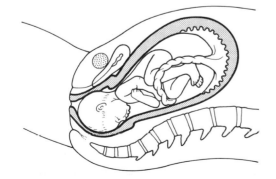
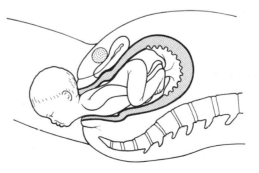

Fig 13.11 The second stage of labour

crowning and the mother is asked to pant as the head is born. The baby will then rotate so that the shoulders are turned sideways and the rest of the body is born.

Many mothers prefer to have their baby placed on their abdomen immediately after birth, to feel the closeness and warmth. This is also thought to benefit the baby. The midwife will clamp and cut the umbilical cord and the baby is labelled with the mother's name on wrist and ankle bands.

Stage 3: the delivery of the placenta and membranes

Normally the placenta separates from the lining of the uterus within 20 minutes of the birth and is pushed out through the vagina. The process is often speeded up by medical intervention.

Pain relief during labour

Labour is usually painful, but a thorough understanding of what is happening throughout the birth process can help to reduce the fear of the unknown. It is fear that makes the body tense up and fight the contractions, instead of relaxing and working with them. There are various different methods of pain relief:

* **Relaxation and breathing** exercises – these are taught at parent craft classes, and the support of a sympathetic partner or friend is invaluable.

* **Gas and air (Entanox)** – this is a mixture of oxygen and nitrous oxide (laughing gas); it is often offered to the mother towards the end of the first stage of labour, via a rubber mask or plastic mouthpiece attached to the gas cylinder; it does not affect the baby and the mother is able to control her own intake.

* **Pethidine** – this is a strong pain-killing drug given by injection; it relaxes the muscles and makes the mother very drowsy.

* **Epidural anaesthetic** – this is injected into the space around the mother's spinal cord; it usually gives total pain relief and leaves the mother fully conscious.

* **Transcutaneous nerve stimulation (TENS)** – this is delivery of electric pulses via wires from a small control box, called a pulsar, to rubber pads on either side of the spine; the mother controls the delivery of the pulses, which block the sensations of pain before they reach the brain; the technique has no side effects.

Acupuncture and hypnosis are also used by some women to relieve the pain of labour, but these are not routinely offered within NHS units.

Medical interventions in the birth process

INDUCTION

This means starting labour artificially; it involves rupturing the membranes and/or giving artificial hormones, either via a vaginal pessary or by an intravenous infusion or drip. It is necessary if:

* the baby is very overdue;
* the placenta is no longer working properly;
* the mother is ill, for example with heart disease, diabetes or pre-eclampsia.

EPISIOTOMY

An episiotomy is a small cut made in the **perineum** (the area between the vagina and the rectum) and is used during the second stage of labour to:

* deliver the baby more quickly if there are signs of **foetal distress**;

* prevent a large, ragged, perineal tear, which would be difficult to repair;
* assist with a forceps delivery.

FORCEPS

Forceps are like tongs which fit around the baby's head to form a protective 'cage', and are used during the second stage of labour to help deliver the head. They may be used:

* to protect the head during a breech delivery, that is, when the baby presents bottom-first;
* if the mother has a condition such as heart disease or high blood pressure, and must not overexert herself;
* if the labour is very prolonged and there are signs of foetal distress;
* if the baby is very small or pre-term (premature).

VACUUM DELIVERY (VENTOUSE)

This is an alternative to forceps, but can be used before the cervix is fully dilated; gentle suction is applied via a rubber cup placed on the baby's head.

CAESAREAN SECTION

A Caesarean section is a surgical operation done under either a general or an epidural anaesthetic; the baby is delivered through a cut in the abdominal wall. The need for a Caesarean section may be identified during pregnancy – an '**elective**' or planned operation – or as an emergency:

* when induction of labour has failed;
* when there is severe bleeding;
* when the baby is too large or in a position which makes vaginal delivery difficult;
* in placenta praevia – when the placenta is covering the cervix;

* in cases of severe foetal distress;
* if the mother is too ill to withstand labour.

Post-natal care

The post-natal period lasts for 6 weeks from the time of birth. For the first 10 days the mother will receive help and advice from a midwife, either in hospital or at home. From 10 days onwards the health visitor visits mother and baby at home. The purpose of these visits is to:

* offer advice on health and safety issues;
* check that the baby is making expected progress;
* offer support and advice on any emotional problems, including referral to a specialist if necessary;
* advise the parents to attend a baby clinic;
* discuss a timetable for immunisations;
* put the parents in touch with other parents locally.

Giving birth is a momentous event; everyone reacts differently and while many mothers feel an immediate rush of love and excitement, others can feel quite detached, needing time to adjust. Early contact with their newborn baby is equally important for fathers as for mothers, and learning how to care for a newborn baby can make couples feel closer. Many mothers experience the 'baby blues' – a feeling of mild depression caused by hormonal changes, tiredness and reaction to the excitement of the birth. If these feelings persist for longer than a few days, the mother may develop a more serious condition, **post-natal depression**, and she will need medical help.

THE NEWBORN BABY OR NEONATE

Neonatal tests

The first question usually asked by parents is, 'Is the baby okay?' The doctor and midwife will observe the newborn baby closely and perform several routine tests which will show whether the baby has any obvious physical problem (see Figures 13.12 and 13.13).

THE APGAR SCORE

This is a standard method of evaluating the condition of a newborn baby by checking five vital signs (see Table 13.4). The **Apgar score** is assessed at 1 minute and 5 minutes after birth; it may be repeated at 5-minute intervals if there is cause for concern.

Most healthy babies have an Apgar score of 9, losing 1 point for having blue extremities; this often persists for a few hours after birth. A low score at 5 minutes is more serious than a low score at 1 minute. In hospital the paediatrician will be notified if the score is 6 or under at 5 minutes. Dark-skinned babies are assessed for oxygenation by checking for redness of the conjunctiva and inside the mouth.

The face is examined for cleft palate – a gap in the roof of the mouth, and facial paralysis – temporary paralysis after compression of the facial nerve, usually after forceps delivery

Eyes are checked for cataract (a cloudiness of the lens)

Hands are checked for webbing (fingers are joined together at the base) and creases – a single unbroken crease from one side of the palm to the other is a feature of Down's syndrome

The head is checked for size and shape: any marks from forceps delivery are noted

The heart and lungs are checked using a stethoscope; any abnormal findings will be investigated

The neck is examined for any obvious injury to the neck muscles after a difficult delivery

Feet are checked for webbing and talipes (club foot), which needs early treatment

Genitalia and anus are checked for any malformation

Skin – vernix and lanugo may still be present, milia may show on the baby's nose; black babies appear lighter in the first week of life as the pigment, melanin, is not yet at full concentration

The spine is checked for any evidence of spina bifida

Hips are tested for cogenital dislocation using Barlow's test

The abdomen is checked for any abnormality, e.g. pyloric stenosis, where there may be obstruction of the passage of food from the stomach; the umbilical cord is checked for infection

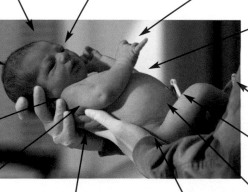

Fig 13.12 Examination of the newborn baby

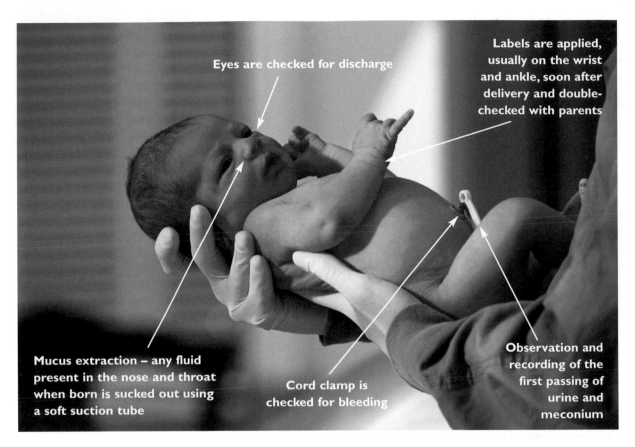

Eyes are checked for discharge

Labels are applied, usually on the wrist and ankle, soon after delivery and double-checked with parents

Mucus extraction – any fluid present in the nose and throat when born is sucked out using a soft suction tube

Cord clamp is checked for bleeding

Observation and recording of the first passing of urine and meconium

Fig 13.13 Examination of the newborn baby

Table 13.4 Assessing the condition of the newborn baby: the Apgar score.

Signs	0	1	2
Heartbeat	absent	slow – below 100	fast – over 100
Breathing	absent	slow – irregular	good; crying
Muscle tone	limp	some limb movement	active movement
Reflex response (to stimulation of foot or nostril)	absent	grimace	cry, cough, sneeze
Colour		body oxygenated, hands and feet blue	well oxygenated

Interpreting the Apgar Score

- ❖ 10: The baby is in the best possible condition.
- ❖ 8–9: The baby is in good condition.
- ❖ 5–7: The baby has mild asphyxia (lack of oxygen in the blood) and may need treatment.
- ❖ 3–4: The baby has moderate asphyxia and will need treatment.
- ❖ 0–2: The baby has severe asphyxia and needs urgent resuscitation.

Other screening tests are carried out on the newborn baby to check for specific disorders that can be treated successfully if detected early enough:

- ❖ **Barlow's test** is a test for congenital dislocation of the hip and is carried out soon after birth, at 6 weeks and at all routine developmental testing opportunities until the baby is walking. There are varying degrees of severity of this disorder; treatment involves the use of splints to keep the baby's legs in a frog-like position.

- ❖ **The newborn bloodspot test** screens all babies for **phenylketonuria** and **congenital hypothyroidism**; in some areas babies are also screened for **cystic fibrosis**, **sickle-cell disorders** and some other conditions. A small blood sample is taken from the baby's heel and sent for analysis. Phenylketonuria is very rare, affecting 1 in 10,000 babies; it is a metabolic disorder which leads to brain damage and learning delay. Early diagnosis is vital since treatment is very effective. This involves a special formula protein diet, which has to be followed throughout the person's life. Congenital hypothyroidism (CHT) affects 1 in 4000

babies in the UK. Babies born with this condition do not have enough **thyroxin**; untreated babies develop serious, permanent, physical and mental disability. Early treatment with thyroxin tablets prevents disability and should start by the time the baby is 21 days of age.

Features of the newborn baby

SIZE

All newborn babies are weighed and their head circumference is measured soon after birth; these measurements provide vital information for professionals when charting any abnormality in development.

1 **Length**: it is difficult to measure accurately the length of a neonate and many hospitals have abandoned this as a routine; the average length of a full-term baby is 50 cm.

2 **Weight**: the birth weight of full-term babies varies considerably because:

- ❖ first babies tend to weigh less than brothers and sisters born later;
- ❖ boys are usually larger than girls;
- ❖ large parents usually have larger babies, and small parents usually have smaller babies.

3 **Head circumference:** the average head circumference of a full-term baby is about 35 cm.

APPEARANCE

The baby will be wet from the amniotic fluid and she may also have some blood streaks on her head or body, picked up from a tear or an episiotomy.

1 The head is large in proportion to the body, and may be oddly shaped at first, because of:

- ❖ **moulding:** the head may be long and pointed as the skull bones overlap slightly to allow passage through the birth canal;

- ❖ **caput succedaneum:** a swelling on the head, caused by pressure as the head presses on the cervix before birth – it is not dangerous and usually disappears within a few days;

- ❖ **cephalhaematoma:** a localised blood-filled swelling or bruise caused by the rupture of small blood vessels during labour – it is not dangerous but may take several weeks to subside.

2 **Vernix** (literally, varnish) – or protective grease – may be present, especially in the skin folds; it should be left to come off without any harsh rubbing of the skin.

3 **Lanugo** – or fine downy hair – may be seen all over the body, especially on dark-skinned babies and those who are born pre-term.

4 **Head hair:** the baby may be born with a lot of hair or be quite bald; often the hair present at birth falls out within weeks and is replaced by hair of a different colour.

5 **Skin colour:** this varies and depends on the ethnic origin of the baby; at least half of all babies develop jaundice on the second or third day after birth; this gives the skin a yellow tinge – usually no treatment is necessary.

6 **Mongolian spot:** this is a smooth, bluish-black area of discoloration commonly found at the base of the spine on babies of African or Asian origin; it is caused by an excess of **melanocytes**, the brown pigment cells, and is quite harmless.

7 **Milia:** sometimes called milk spots, these are small, whitish-yellow spots which

may be present on the face; they are caused by blocked oil ducts and disappear quite quickly.

8 **Birthmarks:** the most common birthmark is a pinkish mark over the eyelids, often referred to as stork marks; they usually disappear within a few months. Other birthmarks, such as strawberry naevus, persist for some years.

Movements of the newborn baby

Babies display a number of automatic movements (known as **primitive reflexes**), which are reflex responses to specific stimuli (see Figure 13.14). These movements are inborn and are replaced by voluntary responses as the brain takes control of behaviour; for example, the grasp reflex has to fade before the baby learns to hold objects which are placed in her hand. The reflexes are important indicators of the health of the nervous system of the baby; if they persist beyond an expected time it may indicate a delay in development.

- ❖ **The swallowing and sucking reflexes:** when something is put in the mouth, the baby at once sucks and swallows; some babies make their fingers sore by sucking them while still in the womb.

- ❖ **The rooting reflex:** if one side of the baby's cheek or mouth is gently touched, the baby's head turns towards the touch and the mouth purses as if in search of the nipple (see Figure 13.14a).

- ❖ **The grasp reflex:** when an object or finger touches the palm of the baby's hand, it is automatically grasped (see Figure 13.14b).

- ❖ **The stepping or walking reflex:** when held upright and tilting slightly forward, with feet placed on a firm surface, the baby will make forward-stepping movements (see Figure 13.14c).

❧ **The startle reflex:** when the baby is startled by a sudden noise or bright light, she will move her arms outwards, with elbows and hands clenched (see Figure 13.14d).

❧ **The asymmetric tonic neck reflex:** if the baby's head is turned to one side, she will straighten the arm and leg on that side and bend the arm and leg on the opposite side (see Figure 13.14e).

❧ **The falling reflex (Moro reflex):** any sudden movement which affects the neck gives the baby the feeling that she may be dropped; she will fling out her arms and open her hands before bringing them back over the chest as if to catch hold of something.

BABIES NEEDING SPECIAL CARE

Low birth-weight babies

Any baby weighing up to 2.5 kg at birth, regardless of the period of gestation, is said to be of low birth weight. Low birth-weight babies can be divided into two categories:

1 **Pre-term:** babies born before 37 weeks of pregnancy.

2 **Light-for-dates:** babies who are below the expected weight for their gestational stage (length of pregnancy).

Some babies are both pre-term and light-for-dates.

Low birth-weight babies are at higher risk of death during the first year of life, but if they survive most catch up with their full-size peers by school age. Those with birth weights below 1.5 kg, or who are very light-for-dates, are more likely to have lasting

problems, but the frequency of such problems has declined as neonatal care has improved.

CAUSES

The reasons for low birth weight are often unknown, but common factors are:

❧ multiple births;

❧ toxaemia of pregnancy;

❧ a medical disorder in the mother (e.g. diabetes, heart disease, kidney infection);

❧ drug abuse by the mother (e.g. smoking, drinking or narcotic abuse).

CARE OF THE LOW BIRTH-WEIGHT BABY

Most low birth-weight babies are nursed in an **incubator**, which is an enclosed cot with controlled temperature and humidity; the baby is usually nursed naked, sometimes lying on a sheepskin for comfort. Feeding is often via a tube or a dropper until the baby has the strength to suck; extra oxygen is supplied to assist breathing.

Such an environment can be very frightening for the parents, and special care baby units (SCBUs, see page 528) strive to keep any separation to a minimum. If the baby is too ill or frail to leave the incubator, the hospital will take a photograph of the baby which the parents can have immediately. Staff caring for neonates value the importance of early mother–baby bonding and encourage parents and close family to talk to and touch the baby, after observing the required hygiene precautions. Low birth-weight babies usually sleep more and may seem less alert than full-term babies, and parents will welcome reassurance from staff that this is normal behaviour.

Post-term babies

When pregnancy is prolonged beyond the expected date of delivery there may be

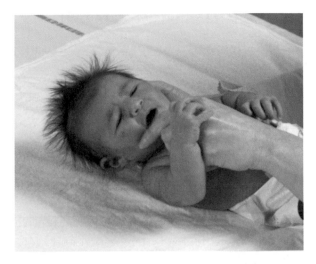

(a) Rooting reflex

(b) Grasp reflex

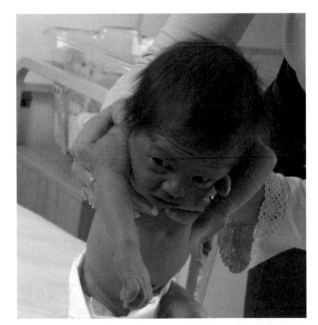

(c) Stepping reflex

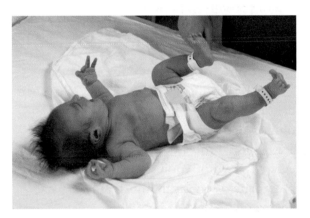

(d) Grasp reflex

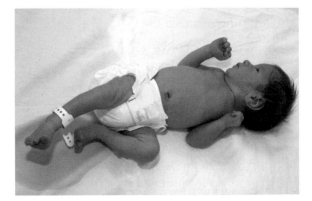

Fig 13.14 (a)–(e) Primitive reflexes in a newborn baby

(e) Assymetric tonic neck reflex

problems for the baby. These result from a decline in placenta function after the forty-second week of pregnancy (full term is 40 weeks). Where the expected delivery date is known accurately, induction of labour is usually undertaken before 42 weeks. The post-term baby has the following characteristics:

* being much thinner than normal;
* having parchment-like skin, which is often cracked and peeling;
* having a worried expression;
* being alert, restless and hungry for feeds.

Treatment is similar to that for light-for-dates infants, with hypoglycaemia (low blood sugar) presenting an additional problem.

Special care baby units (SCBUs)

Special care baby units are usually situated within the maternity departments of general district hospitals. They employ specially trained midwives and paediatric nurses and are designed to care for the 5 babies out of every 100 who require extra care that cannot be provided within the normal post-natal environment.

Each hospital has its own criteria for deciding which babies need special care. Usually these criteria are:

* babies born before 32 weeks;
* babies weighing less than 2 kg at birth;
* babies with breathing difficulties;
* babies with seizures or blood disorders.

The principles of care in a SCBU are to keep the newborn baby warm and free from infection. This is achieved by expert care of babies in incubators. Babies who are more seriously ill and who require more intensive care will be transferred to a neonatal intensive care unit.

The neonatal intensive care unit

Neonatal intensive care units are situated in large regional hospitals and care for the smallest and most ill babies, using the most sophisticated technology and specialist skills. SCBUs can ensure that the sick baby receives oxygen via a face mask within the incubator; the intensive care unit can provide a **ventilator** and staff who are trained to deliver such specialist care. Parents whose baby has had to be transferred to an intensive care unit often feel very frightened and helpless. The baby they had so eagerly anticipated now seems totally at the mercy of strangers and is surrounded by highly technical and noisy machinery. Often the parents feel that there is nothing they can do for their own child and the waiting is very hard to bear.

Multiple births

Multiple pregnancies – where there is more than one baby – always need special care and supervision. Twins are the most common multiple birth, occurring in about 1 in 87–100 pregnancies.

IDENTICAL (MONOZYGOTIC) TWINS
Identical twins develop after one sperm has fertilised one egg; the egg splits into two and each half becomes a separate baby. Identical twins are always the same sex and they share the same placenta (see Figure 13.15a).

NON-IDENTICAL (DIZYGOTIC) TWINS
Non-identical twins develop when two sperms fertilise two different eggs, the mother's ovaries having, for some reason, produced two eggs at ovulation. They grow together in the womb, with two separate placentas (see Figure 13.15b). Such twins are sometimes called fraternal

twins and can be the same sex or different sexes; they can be as alike or as unlike as any brothers and sisters.

The chances of a woman having non–identical twins increases if she herself is such a twin or if there is a history of twins in her family.

INFERTILITY TREATMENTS AND MULTIPLE PREGNANCIES

Fertility drugs work by stimulating follicle ripening and ovulation; sometimes they work too well and result in the ripening of more than one egg at a time. Women who are treated with fertility drugs are, therefore, more likely to conceive more than one child at a time.

DIAGNOSING MULTIPLE PREGNANCIES

A woman expecting more than one baby is likely to be larger than her dates would suggest and will put on more weight; routine ultrasound scanning can usually diagnose the presence of more than one baby, unless one baby is 'hiding' behind the other.

CARING FOR TWINS AND TRIPLETS

The main risk when there is more than one baby is that they will be born too early (be premature); this risk rises with the number of

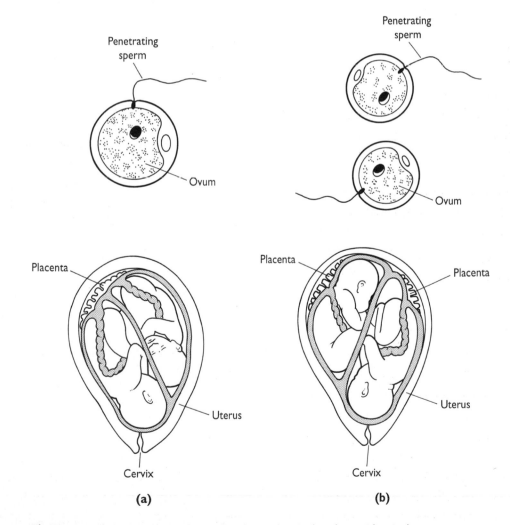

Fig 13.15 (a) and (b) Two types of twins – identical and non-identical

babies. Usually women expecting twins or more babies are admitted to hospital for the birth; twins may be delivered vaginally, provided both babies are in the head-down position, but triplets and quadruplets are usually born by Caesarean section.

FEEDING TWINS

There is no reason why mothers should not totally breastfeed twins and partly breastfeed any number of babies, but this requires great motivation, excellent health and a lot of extra help and support.

SUPPORT FOR PARENTS WITH TWINS AND MORE BABIES

The community midwife and health visitor will visit more frequently and will put the parents in touch with other parents in the same situation; extra help may be provided for a few weeks and arrangements are made for routine tests and immunisations to be done at home. The La Leche League and the Twins and Multiple Births Association (TAMBA) can offer practical advice and a list of local support groups (see addresses list at the end of this chapter).

If one of the babies dies, either before birth or afterwards, the parents will require specialist bereavement counselling; the Child Bereavement Trust can offer invaluable advice and support.

PRESERVING INDIVIDUALITY

Twins who survive together should each be recognised as an individual in their own right.

Guidelines for preserving the individual identity of twins

❖ Do not use terms such as 'the twins', but always use each child's own name.

❖ Take care if dressing twins and triplets alike, as this will draw attention to their sameness. Some twins insist on wearing identical outfits, but it is important to be aware of the disadvantages of this.

❖ Ensure that being 'a twin' is secondary to being 'an individual'. Sharing large equipment, such as a pram or buggy, in the early years is inevitable, but on birthdays, for example, two cakes could be made.

❖ Acknowledge that developmental milestones will be reached at different times by each child and that individual attention from parents is worthwhile, even though this may be difficult in practice.

COMMON NEONATAL PROBLEMS AND DISORDERS

Jaundice

Jaundice is a common condition in newborn infants that usually shows up shortly after birth. In most cases, it goes away on its own; if not, it can be treated easily. A baby gets jaundice when **bilirubin**, which is produced naturally by the body, builds up faster than the newborn's liver can break it down (usually it would be excreted in the baby's stool). Too much bilirubin makes a jaundiced baby's skin look yellow. This yellow colour will appear first on the face, then on the chest and stomach and, finally, on the legs. Older babies, children and adults get rid of this yellow blood product quickly, usually through bowel movements.

HOW IS JAUNDICE TREATED?

Mild to moderate levels of jaundice do not require any treatment. If high levels of jaundice do not clear up on their own, the baby may be treated with special light (**phototherapy**) or by another treatment. The special light helps to get rid of the bilirubin by altering it to make it easier for the baby's liver to excrete. Another treatment is to give more frequent feeds of breast milk or formula to help pass the bilirubin out in the stools. Increasing the amount of water given to a child is not sufficient to pass the bilirubin because it must be passed in the stools.

Common skin problems in babies

A newborn baby's skin has a unique tender quality, as it has not been exposed to the environment and to ultraviolet radiation. There are certain common disorders that may affect the newborn child.

DRY SKIN

Some babies have dry skin that is particularly noticeable in cold weather. It can be treated by using a water-soluble cream (e.g. Unguentum Merck) instead of soap for washing and by applying Vaseline to lips, cheeks or noses – the most commonly affected skin areas.

URTICARIA

Neonatal urticaria presents as red, blotchy spots, often around a small, white or yellow blister. They usually appear from around the second day after birth and disappear within a few days. They are harmless to the baby.

SWEAT RASH

A baby's sweat glands are immature and they do not allow heat to evaporate from the skin. This can lead to a rash of small red spots on the face, chest, groin and armpit. The baby should be kept cool and the skin kept dry; calamine lotion will soothe the itching.

MILIA

Milia – often called milk spots – occur in 50 per cent of all newborn babies. They are firm, pearly-white, pinhead-sized spots, which are really tiny sebaceous cysts. They are felt and seen mostly around the baby's nose, and will disappear without scarring in 3–4 weeks.

PEELING

Most newborn babies' skin peels a little in the first few days, especially on the soles of the feet and the palms. Post-mature babies may have extra-dry skin, which is particularly prone to peeling. Babies of Asian and Afro-Caribbean descent often have drier skin and hair than babies of European descent. No treatment is necessary.

CRADLE CAP

This is a type of seborrhoeic dermatitis of the scalp and is common in young babies. It is caused by the sebaceous glands on the scalp producing too much sebum, or oil. The scalp is covered with white or yellowish-brown, crusty scales which, although they look unsightly, rarely trouble the baby. It may spread as red, scaly patches over the face, neck, armpits and eyebrows. Sometimes it is caused by inefficient rinsing of shampoo. Treatment is by applying olive oil to the affected area overnight to soften the crusts, and by special shampoo.

INFANTILE ECZEMA

Infantile eczema (or atopic dermatitis) presents as an irritating, red and scaly rash, usually on the baby's cheeks and forehead, though it may spread to the rest of the body. It is thought to be caused by an allergy and appears at 2–3 months. It causes severe itching, made worse by scratching. It should be treated by rehydrating the skin with short, cool baths, using an unscented cleanser and applying special moisturisers frequently. If the eczema is severe the doctor may prescribe special cortisone creams. The baby's fingernails should be kept short and scratch mittens worn. Cotton clothing should be worn and antibiotics may be used to treat any infection. It is not contagious.

Maintaining body temperature

From birth, babies have a heat-regulating mechanism in the brain which enables them to generate body warmth when they get cold. However, they can rapidly become very cold for the following reasons:

❖ they are unable to conserve body warmth if the surrounding air is at a lower temperature than normal;

❖ they have a large surface area compared to body weight;

❖ they lack body fat, which is a good insulator.

Maternity units are always kept at a high temperature (usually about 29°C or 80°F) to allow for frequent undressing and bathing of newborn babies. At home, the room temperature should not fall below 20°C (or 68°C). A pre-term or light-for-dates baby is at an even greater risk of **hypothermia**.

THE PRINCIPLES OF PROMOTING DEVELOPMENT AND LEARNING

The normative development of babies is discussed in Chapter 5. You need to have a thorough knowledge of these norms of development in order to:

❖ be reassured that babies are developing normally;

❖ identify those babies and children who, for some reason, may not be following these normative stages;

❖ build up a picture of a child's progress over time;

❖ anticipate – and respond appropriately to – certain types of age-related behaviour;

❖ provide for the baby's developmental needs.

As well as knowing about babies' developmental milestones, you need to know how to promote a baby's development in a wider, holistic sense.

CARING FOR BABIES IN A SAFE, SECURE AND STIMULATING ENVIRONMENT

The importance of the quality of adult–baby interaction

The way in which babies are cared for has a huge impact on how they will respond to difficulties and relationships later in life. Babies are totally dependent on our ability to be responsive to their needs. If they learn to feel and enjoy their parents' love, care, comfort and protection, they will start to feel secure and understood. Being in warm, loving surroundings, with plenty of **physical contact**, is the single most important factor for improving a baby's physical and emotional wellbeing. Babies and toddlers are more likely to feel safe and loved when the same familiar people are looking after them each day. As early childhood practitioners, you need, above all, to have **empathy** – to be able to appreciate the world from a baby's point of view.

The importance of play

Play is important because it helps babies to:

❖ learn about and understand the world around them;

❖ socialise and form relationships with their primary carers.

From a very early age babies learn best by exploring the world through their senses – touch, sight, hearing, taste and smell – and through their movements. In other words, they learn by:

❖ doing;

❖ seeing;

❖ listening;

❖ tasting;

❖ smelling;

❖ touching.

During the first year of life, babies mostly play with objects, with someone they love or by themselves (**solitary play**). There are many ways in which you can play with a baby; babies do not need a room full of expensive toys in order to play. The most important part of a baby's development is to experience **continuous attention** and **affection** from their parents, caregivers, relations and other significant adults. Any toys and activities that you use with the babies in your care should be chosen carefully (see box below).

PROMOTING HOLISTIC DEVELOPMENT OF THE BABY

The information set out on the next pages provides guidance for promoting the overall development of the baby at each stage.

Guidelines for selecting toys for small babies

1 Is the toy or plaything clean and safe?

❖ no rough or broken edges;

❖ no small parts which could become loose and be swallowed (e.g. check the eyes on a soft toy);

❖ no strings to become tangled around a baby's neck;

❖ not so heavy that a young baby could be injured;

❖ no toxic paint;

❖ complies with safety standards.

2 Is the toy or activity appropriate for the child's developmental stage?

❖ if using household objects – wooden spoons, saucepans, keys or empty plastic containers – check that the baby is closely supervised;

❖ once the baby is able to walk, even if cruising by holding onto furniture, new safety checks will need to be made.

(See Chapter 4 for information on maintaining the safety of babies' toys and equipment.)

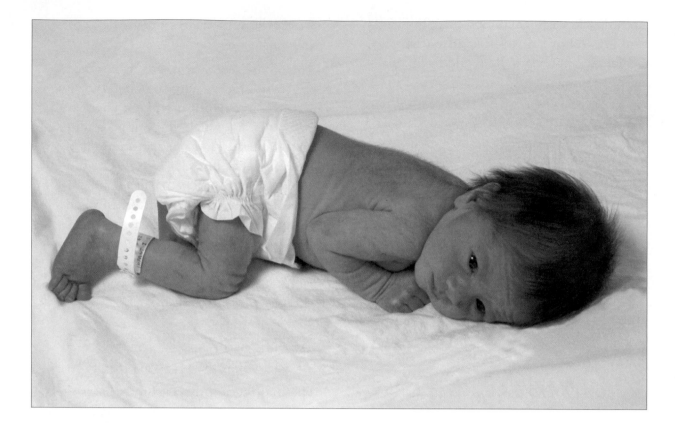

Newborn babies: birth to 4 weeks

GENERAL DEVELOPMENT

Babies:

* will turn their head towards the light and stare at bright shiny objects;

* are fascinated by human faces and gaze attentively at their carer's face when being fed or cuddled;

* enjoy feeding and cuddling;

* often imitate facial expressions;

* respond to things they see, hear and feel.

ROLE OF THE ADULT

* Meet the baby's primary needs for milk, warmth and hygiene.

* Provide plenty of physical contact and maintain eye contact.

* Talk lovingly to babies and give them the opportunity to respond.

* Feed on demand, and talk and sing to them.

EQUIPMENT, TOYS AND ACTIVITIES

* Pram or cot and bedclothes for sleeping.

* Nappy-changing mat and equipment.

* Bathing equipment.

* Clothes and laundry facilities.

* Light rattles and toys strung over the pram or cot to encourage focusing and coordination.

* Mobile hung over the nappy-changing area or cot.

* Use bright colours in furnishings.

* Try sticking out your tongue and opening your mouth wide; the baby may copy you.

* Try showing babies brightly coloured woolly pompoms, balloons, shiny objects and black and white patterns. Hold them

directly in front of the baby's face and give him time to focus before slowly moving them.

❋ Talk with babies; if you talk closely to a baby and leave time for a response, you will find that very young babies react with a concentrated expression, and later with smiles and excited leg kicking.

SAFETY POINTS

❋ When playing with a baby always support the head, as the neck muscles are not strong enough to control movement.

❋ Always place babies on their back to sleep.

❋ Keep the temperature in a baby's room at around 20°C (68°F).

Babies aged 4 to 8 weeks

GENERAL DEVELOPMENT

Babies:

❋ can turn from their side to their back;

❋ make jerky and uncontrolled arm and leg movements;

❋ are beginning to take their fist to their mouth;

❋ open their hands to grasp an adult's finger;

❋ show that they recognise their primary carers by responding to them with a combination of excited movements, coos and smiles;

❋ love to watch movement: trees in the wind, bright contrasting objects placed within their field of vision, and so on;

❋ enjoy listening to the sound of bells, music, voices and rhythmic sounds;

❋ love to look at shapes – particularly circles and stripes.

ROLE OF THE ADULT

❋ Meet the baby's primary needs for milk, warmth and hygiene.

❋ Massage the baby's body and limbs during or after bathing.

❋ Talk to and smile with the baby.

❋ Sing while feeding or bathing the baby – allowing time for the baby to respond.

❋ Learn to differentiate between the baby's cries and to respond to them appropriately.

❋ Encourage laughter by tickling the baby.

❋ Hold the baby close to promote a feeling of security.

EQUIPMENT, TOYS AND ACTIVITIES

❋ Pushchair or combination pram/ pushchair.

❋ Safety car seat.

❋ Use a special supporting infant chair so that babies can see adult activity.

❋ Light rattles and toys strung over their pram or cot will encourage focusing and coordination.

❋ Let them kick freely without a nappy on.

SAFETY POINTS

❋ Never leave rattles or similar toys in the baby's cot or pram as they can become wedged in the baby's mouth and cause suffocation.

❋ Do not leave a baby unattended on a table, work surface, bed or sofa; lie them on the floor instead.

Babies at around 3 months

GENERAL DEVELOPMENT

Babies:

❋ can now lift both head and chest off the bed in the prone position, supported on forearms;

❋ kick vigorously with legs, alternating or occasionally together;

❋ watch their hands and play with their fingers;

❖ can hold a rattle for a brief time before dropping it;

❖ are becoming conversational by cooing, gurgling and chuckling; they love to exchange coos with familiar person;

❖ enjoy exploring different textures, for example on an activity mat.

ROLE OF THE ADULT

❖ Meet the baby's primary needs for milk, warmth and hygiene.

❖ Provide brightly coloured mobiles and wind chimes to encourage focusing at 20 cm.

❖ Place some toys on a blanket or play mat on the floor so that the baby can lie on their tummy and play with them for short periods.

❖ Give babies a rattle to hold.

❖ Attach objects above the cot which make a noise when touched.

❖ Change the baby's position frequently so that they have different things to look at and experience.

EQUIPMENT, TOYS AND ACTIVITIES

❖ Rattles.

❖ Chiming balls.

❖ Cradle 'gym' to encourage focusing and reaching skills.

❖ Wind chimes.

❖ Imitate the sounds made by babies to encourage repetition.

❖ Sing nursery rhymes.

❖ Encourage contact with other adults and children.

❖ Try action rhymes with the baby on your lap (e.g. This little piggy went to market. . .).

❖ Respond to their needs and show enjoyment in caring for them.

SAFETY POINTS

❖ Always protect babies of all skin tones from exposure to sunlight. Use a special sun protection cream, a sun hat to protect face and neck, and a pram canopy.

❖ Never leave small objects within reach as everything finds its way to a baby's mouth.

❖ Always buy goods displaying an appropriate safety symbol.

Babies at around 6 months

GENERAL DEVELOPMENT

Babies:

❖ when lying on their backs, can roll over – moving from back to stomach;

❖ can sit with support; sometimes without support;

❖ bounce their feet up and down when held on the floor;

❖ move arms purposefully and hold them up to be lifted;

❖ reach and grab when a small toy is offered;

❖ explore objects by putting them in the mouth;

❖ enjoy playing with stacking beakers and bricks;

❖ play with a rolling ball when in sitting position;

❖ understand 'up' and 'down' and make appropriate gestures;

❖ show interest in the edges of mats on the floor.

ROLE OF THE ADULT

❖ Meet the baby's primary needs for milk, warmth and hygiene.

❖ Encourage confidence and balance by placing toys around the sitting baby.

❖ Provide rattles and toys which can be hung over the cot to encourage the baby to reach and grab.

❖ Encourage mobility by placing toys just out of the baby's reach.

❖ Provide safe toys for babies to transfer to their mouths.

❖ Look at picture books together and encourage the baby to point at objects with you.

EQUIPMENT, TOYS AND ACTIVITIES

❖ High chair with safety harness.

❖ Stacking beakers and nesting toys.

❖ Suction toys on tabletops.

❖ Provide cardboard boxes to put things into and take things out of.

❖ Build a tower of bricks with the baby and watch their delight when it topples over.

❖ Simple musical instruments (e.g. a xylophone or wooden spoon and saucepan).

❖ Safety mirror to develop the baby's recognition of self.

SAFETY POINTS

❖ Make sure that furniture is stable and has no sharp corners.

❖ Always supervise a baby when trying finger foods and at mealtimes.

❖ Always supervise water play.

Babies at around 9 months

GENERAL DEVELOPMENT

Babies:

❖ sit alone without support;

❖ stand, holding on to furniture;

❖ find ways of moving about the floor (e.g. by rolling, wriggling, or crawling on stomach);

❖ grasp objects between finger and thumb in a pincer grip;

❖ understand their daily routine and will follow simple instructions (e.g. 'kiss teddy');

❖ may drink from a cup with help;

❖ enjoy making noises by banging toys.

ROLE OF THE ADULT

❖ Meet the baby's primary needs for milk, warmth and hygiene.

❖ Allow plenty of time for play.

❖ Encourage mobility by placing toys just out of reach.

❖ Provide small objects for babies to pick up; choose objects that are safe when chewed, such as pieces of biscuit, but always supervise.

❖ Play peek-a-boo and hide-and-seek games.

❖ Roll balls for the baby to bring back to you.

EQUIPMENT, TOYS AND ACTIVITIES

❖ High chair with safety harness.

❖ Bath toys – beakers, sponges and funnels, and so on.

❖ Stacking and nesting toys.

❖ Picture books.

❖ Soft balls for rolling.

❖ Pop-up toys.

❖ Encourage self-feeding and tolerate messes.

❖ Talk constantly to babies and continue with rhymes and action songs.

SAFETY POINTS

❖ Always supervise eating and drinking. Never leave babies alone with finger foods such as bananas, carrots, cheese, and so on.

❖ Use childproof containers for tablets and vitamins, and ensure that they are closed properly.

❖ Use a locked cupboard for storing dangerous household chemicals, such as bleach, disinfectant and white spirit.

Babies at around 1 year

GENERAL DEVELOPMENT

Babies:

❖ crawl on hands and knees, bottom-shuffle or bear-walk rapidly about the floor;

❖ stand alone for a few moments;

❖ cruise along, using furniture as a support;

❖ point with index finger at objects of interest;

❖ understand simple instructions associated with a gesture (e.g. 'come to Daddy', 'clap hands' and 'wave bye-bye');

❖ help with daily routines, such as getting washed and dressed;

❖ enjoy playing with bricks and containers – for putting toys into and taking them out of;

❖ love to play with toys that they can move along with their feet;

❖ enjoy looking at picture books.

ROLE OF THE ADULT

❖ Meet the baby's primary needs for milk, warmth and hygiene.

❖ Read picture books with simple rhymes.

❖ Arrange a corner of the kitchen or garden for messy play, involving the use of water, play dough or paint.

❖ Talk to the baby about everyday activities, and always allow time for a response.

EQUIPMENT, TOYS AND ACTIVITIES

❖ Push-and-pull toys to promote confidence in walking.

❖ Stacking toys and bricks.

❖ Shape sorters.

❖ Baby swing.

❖ Cardboard boxes.

❖ Encourage creative skills by providing thick crayons and paintbrushes, and large sheets of paper (e.g. wall lining paper).

❖ Join in games of 'let's pretend' to encourage imaginative skills (e.g. pretending to be animals or to drive a bus).

❖ Think about attending a mother-and-toddler group.

SAFETY POINTS

❖ As babies become more mobile, you need to be vigilant at all times. This is a very high-risk age for accidents.

❖ Always supervise sand and water play.

❖ Use safety equipment, such as safety catches for cupboards and stair gates, ideally at the top and bottom of stairs.

Guidelines for promoting physical development

Babies master the physical skills of rolling over from front to back, crawling or bottom-shuffling, bear-walking and standing during their first year. Some babies walk unaided by the age of 1 year, and 70 per cent of babies walk by the age of 13 months. You can help babies in the following ways:

1   **Sitting:** by about 6 or 7 months, most babies can balance in a secure sitting position for a short while. You can help them by:

❖ providing a protective 'ring' so that any sudden overbalancing is safe and painless;

❖ placing the baby on the floor with legs wide apart for balance and then arranging cushions or rolled-up blankets all around her.

NB Never leave babies sitting alone on the floor, even for a few minutes, as they could fall and trap their arms awkwardly.

2   **Crawling:** by about 9 months babies are usually starting to crawl, even if they cannot always control their direction. You can help by:

❖ protecting their knees against friction on rough-textured carpets, and so on (e.g. by dressing them in light trousers or dungarees);

❖ foreseeing possible dangers, such as steps, splintery floors or unsuitable objects left lying around; follow the safety advice on page 189 onwards.

3   **Standing:** most babies can stand for a few moments at around 10 months, but are not able to balance and may suddenly sit down again. You can help them by ensuring that:

❖ furniture is stable (i.e. not likely to topple over when babies hold on to pull themselves up);

❖ there are no dangling cords, electrical flexes or tablecloths which the baby could pull on and cause themselves harm;

❖ they go barefoot as much as possible (it helps when babies can feel the floor and so can make sensitive adjustments with their toes to achieve balance).

4   **Walking:** towards the end of the first year, babies are usually standing alone and are able to cruise around the room, holding onto furniture. You can help them by:

❖ kneeling down one or two paces away from the baby and encouraging them to toddle into your arms;

❖ letting them walk in bare feet whenever possible; avoid slippery floors and use socks with non-slip soles, rather than shoes, until the baby is walking confidently;

❖ protecting them from falls and keeping older, more boisterous children out of their way when they are feeling unsteady and need to practise in a calm environment.

These milestones of physical development are all dependent on the individual baby's confidence and motivation, as well as on their muscles and coordination. You should never try to hurry a baby towards being able to stand or walk. You may hold their development back if, for example, they become afraid of falling over.

Guidelines for promoting language development

Talking to babies is easier for some people than for others; this applies to the baby's parents as well as to carers. Some people are naturally chatty; others are naturally quiet and may feel silly talking to a baby who cannot 'talk' back to them. While you cannot change your personality, there are a number of ways in which you can communicate effectively with babies:

❖ Always listen to babies; when they smile at you or make cooing sounds, try to answer in words. You do not have to keep up a running commentary – you just have to be responsive to the baby's efforts to communicate.

❖ Try to talk normally, without trying to simplify your language, so that it feels natural, like a real conversation with a friend.

❖ Tell babies what you are doing whenever you are handling them (e.g. if you are feeding a baby, talk about the food and about what the next course will be).

❖ Ask questions, such as 'Was that nice?' and 'Where's it gone?' The baby will answer with a gesture or a facial expression that speaks as clearly as any words.

❖ Bath-time is a good time to talk to babies; talk to them and tell them what you are doing: 'I'm just going to put some soap on your tummy now.'

❖ Read picture books to babies; point to the pictures and name them. Even though young babies cannot understand what is going on in the book, they will be very responsive and will enjoy taking part in the experience.

❖ Learn some simple nursery rhymes and action songs; babies love to hear the old favourites such as 'This little piggy went to market. . .' Try to find out some simple rhymes or songs from other cultures too.

POSITIVE OVERALL CARE AND SAFE PRACTICE

The needs of the young baby

All babies depend completely on an adult to meet all their needs, but how these needs are met will vary considerably according to family circumstances, culture and the personalities of the baby and the caring adult. To achieve and maintain healthy growth and all-round (holistic) development, certain basic needs must be fulfilled.

In Chapter 4, the factors that make up a safe, stimulating and caring environment for children over 1 year were described. The same principles apply when caring for babies in domestic and nursery settings. The **key worker system** is particularly important for providing continuity of care. Babies need to be cared for by just one person most of the time, so that they can form a close relationship. This also helps to minimise the difficulty of separation for babies from their parents or primary carers (see page 346).

The importance of routines

Routines – such as around mealtimes and bedtimes – can be very useful in helping

protection from infection and injury

food

cleanliness ·

sleep, rest and activity

responsibility

intellectual stimulation

praise and recognition

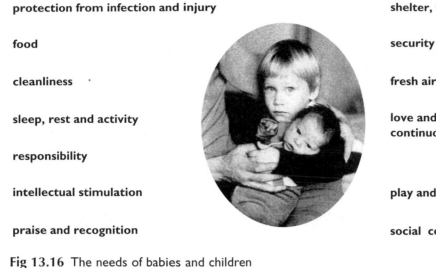

shelter, warmth, clothing

security

fresh air and sunlight

love and consistent and
continuous affection

play and new experiences

social contacts

Fig 13.16 The needs of babies and children

babies and toddlers to adapt both physically and emotionally to a **daily pattern**, which suits both them *and* those caring for them. This is especially helpful during times of **transition** and change in their lives, such as starting nursery or moving house. If certain parts of the day remain familiar, they can cope better with new experiences. Having routines for everyday activities also ensures that care is consistent and of a high quality. This does not mean that caring for babies is, or should be, in itself a routine activity. Anyone looking after babies should be able to adapt to their individual needs, which will change from day to day. Therefore, you need to be flexible in your approach and allow, whenever feasible, the individual baby to set the pattern for the day – as long as all the baby's needs are met.

Care for a baby's skin

A baby's skin is soft and delicate, yet forms a tough, pliant covering for the body. The skin has many important functions:

- **Protection:** it protects underlying organs and, when unbroken, prevents germs entering the body.

- **Sensation:** each square centimetre of skin contains up to 250 nerve endings called receptors; these detect different feelings, such as touch, cold, warmth, pressure, pain and hair movement.

- **Secretion of oil (sebum):** this lubricates the skin and gives hair its shine.

- **Manufacture of vitamin D:** vitamin D is made when the skin is exposed to sunlight and is essential for healthy bones and teeth; black skin protects against sunburn but is less efficient at making vitamin D, and black children may need a supplement of vitamin D in the winter.

- **Excretion:** the skin excretes waste products in sweat.

- **Temperature regulation:** the hypothalamus in the brain controls body temperature by causing the skin to release sweat, which evaporates from the skin's surface, cooling the body.

A young baby does not have to be bathed every day, because only her bottom, face, neck and skin creases get dirty and because her skin may tend to dryness. If a bath is not given daily, the baby should have the important body parts cleansed thoroughly – a process known as topping and tailing. This process limits the amount of undressing and helps to maintain good skin condition. Whatever routine is followed, the newborn baby needs to be handled gently but firmly, and with confidence. Most babies learn to enjoy the sensation of water and are greatly affected by your attitude. The more relaxed and unhurried you are, the more enjoyable the whole experience will be.

Topping and tailing

Babies do not like having their skin exposed to the air, so should be undressed for the shortest possible time. Always ensure the room is warm, no less than 20°C (68°F) and that there are no draughts. Warm a large, soft towel on a not-too-hot radiator and have it ready to wrap the baby in afterwards.

Collect all the equipment you will need before you start:

- ❧ changing mat;
- ❧ water that has been boiled and allowed to cool;
- ❧ cotton-wool swabs;
- ❧ lidded buckets for soiled nappies and used swabs, and clothes;
- ❧ bowl of warm water;
- ❧ protective cream (e.g. Vaseline);
- ❧ clean clothes and a nappy.

Guidelines for a topping and tailing routine

1 Wash your hands.

2 Remove the baby's outer clothes, leaving on her vest and nappy.

3 Wrap the baby in the towel, keeping her arms inside.

4 Using two separate pieces of cotton wool (one for each eye; this will prevent any infection passing from one eye to the other), squeezed in the boiled and cooled water, gently wipe the baby's eyes in one movement from the inner corner outwards.

5 Gently wipe all around the face and behind the ears. Lift the chin and wipe gently under the folds of skin. Dry each area thoroughly by patting with a soft towel or dry cotton wool.

6 Unwrap the towel and take off the baby's vest, raise each arm separately and wipe the armpit carefully as the folds of skin rub together here and can become quite sore; again, dry thoroughly and dust with baby powder if used.

7 Until the cord has dropped off, make sure that it is kept clean and dry using special antiseptic powder supplied by the midwife.

8 Wipe and dry the baby's hands.

9 Take the nappy off and place in lidded bucket.

10 Clean the baby's bottom with moist swabs, then wash with soap and water; rinse well with flannel or sponge, pat dry and apply protective cream.

11 Put on clean nappy and clothes.

Bathing the baby

When the bath is given will depend on family routines, but it is best not to bath the baby immediately after a feed, as she may be sick. Some babies love being bathed; others dislike even being undressed. Bath-time has several benefits for babies (see box below).

Benefits of bath-time
Bath-time provides:

* the opportunity to kick and exercise;
* the opportunity to clean and refresh the skin and hair;
* the opportunity for the carer to observe any skin problems, such as rashes or bruises;
* a valuable time for communication between the baby and the carer;
* a time for relaxation and enjoyment.

Before you start ensure the room is warm and draught-free, and collect all necessary equipment:

* small bowl of boiled and cooled water and cotton swabs (as for topping and tailing procedure);
* baby bath filled with warm water – test temperature with your elbow, not with hands, as these are insensitive to high temperatures; the water should feel warm, but not hot;
* changing mat;
* lidded buckets;
* two warmed towels;
* clean nappy and clothes;
* brush and comb;
* toiletries and nail scissors.

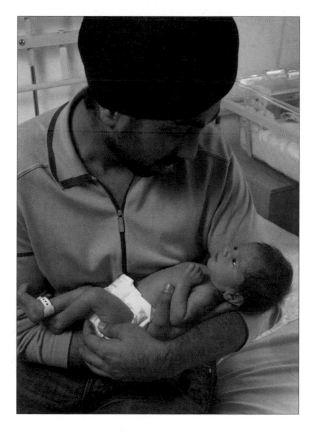

Fig 13.17 Father and son gazing at each other

Guidelines for a bathing routine

1 Undress the baby except for her nappy and wrap her in a towel while you clean her face, as for topping and tailing.

2 Wash her hair before putting her in the bath: support her head and neck with one hand, hold her over the bath and wash her head with baby shampoo or soap; rinse her head thoroughly and dry with second towel.

3 Unwrap the towel around her body, remove her nappy and place it in bucket.

4 Remove any soiling from the baby's bottom with cotton wool; remember to clean baby girls from front to back, to avoid germs from faeces entering the urethra or vagina.

5 Lay the baby in the crook of one arm and gently soap her body front and back with baby soap. (If preferred, use baby bath liquid added to the bath beforehand.)

6 Lift the baby off the towel and gently lower her into the water, holding her with one arm around the back of her neck and shoulders and holding the far arm to stop her slipping.

7 Talk to the baby and gently swish the water to rinse off the soap, paying particular attention to all skin creases – under arms, between legs and behind knees. Allow time for the baby to splash and kick, but avoid chilling.

8 Lift the baby out and wrap in a warm towel; dry her thoroughly by patting, not rubbing.

9 Baby oil or moisturiser may now be applied to the skin; do not use talcum powder with oils as it will form lumps and cause irritation.

10 Check if fingernails and toenails need cutting. Always use blunt-ended nail scissors and avoid cutting nails too short.

11 Dress the baby in clean nappy and clothes.

Additional advice: keeping babies clean

❖ Cultural preferences in skin care should be observed; cocoa butter or special moisturisers are usually applied to babies with black skin and their bodies may be massaged with oil after bathing.

❖ Always put cold water in the bath before adding hot – many babies have been severely scalded by contact with the hot surface of the bath.

❖ Do not wear dangling earrings or sharp brooches, and keep your own nails short and clean.

❖ Never leave a baby or child under 10 years alone in the bath, even for a few seconds.

❖ Do not top up with hot water while the baby is in the bath; make sure that taps are turned off tightly, as even small drops of hot water can cause scalds.

❖ From a few months old, babies may be bathed in the big bath, keeping the water shallow and following the same guidelines regarding temperature and safety. A non-slip mat placed in the bottom of the bath will prevent slipping.

❖ Avoid talcum powder because of the risk of inhalation or allergy; if it is used, place on your hands first and then gently smooth it on to completely dry skin.

❖ Do not use cotton-wool buds – they are not necessary and can be dangerous when poked inside a baby's ears or nose, which are self-cleansing anyway.

❖ Nail care should be included in the bathing routine. A young baby's nails should be cut when necessary. Do this after a bath when they are soft. Some parents use their own teeth to bite them off gently.

❖ Hair should be washed daily in the first few months, but shampoo is not necessary every day. A little bath lotion added to the bath water could be gradually worked into the baby's scalp until a lather forms and may then be rinsed off using a wrung-out flannel.

❖ If the baby dislikes having her hair washed, try to keep hair washing separate from bath-time so that they are not associated as unpleasant events.

Care for a baby's bottom

EXCRETION

The first stool a newborn baby passes is **meconium** – a greenish-black, treacle-like substance which is present in the baby's bowels before birth and is usually passed within 48 hours of birth. Once the baby starts to feed on milk, the stools change:

❖ A breastfed baby has fluid, mustard-coloured stools which do not smell unpleasant.

❖ A bottle-fed baby has more formed stools which may smell slightly.

Babies pass urine very frequently; bottle-fed babies tend to pass stools less often than breastfed babies. Constipation can occur in bottle-fed babies, but can be relieved by giving extra boiled and cooled water to drink.

NAPPIES

The choice of nappies will depend on several factors: convenience, cost, personal preference and concern for the environment.

There are two main types of nappy:

1 **Fabric nappies:** these are made from cotton terry towelling and come in different qualities and thickness. Two dozen are required for everyday use. Fabric nappies may be squares or shaped to fit. The latest style is similar in shape to the disposable nappy and has popper fastenings. If using fabric squares, you will also need special nappy safety pins and six pairs of plastic pants. Disposable one-way liners may be used with towelling nappies to keep wetness away from the baby's skin and to make solid matter easier to dispose of, by flushing down the toilet.

2 **Disposable nappies:** these are nappy, liner and plastic pants all in one and are available in a wide range of designs. Some have more padding at the front for boys and there are different absorbencies for day- and night-time use. Some makes have resealable tapes so that you can check if the nappy is clean.

CHANGING A NAPPY

Young babies will need several changes of nappy each day – whenever the nappy is wet or soiled. As with any regular routine, have everything ready before you begin:

- ❖ a plastic-covered, padded changing mat;
- ❖ a bowl of warm water (or baby wipes);
- ❖ baby lotion;
- ❖ barrier cream (e.g. zinc and castor oil cream);
- ❖ nappy sacks for dirty nappies;
- ❖ cotton wool;
- ❖ baby bath liquid;
- ❖ new, clean nappy.

If you are using a special changing table or bed, make sure the baby cannot fall off. Never leave the baby unattended on a high surface. As long as there are no draughts and the room is warm, the changing mat can be placed on the floor.

A nappy routine

Guidelines for cleaning a girl

1   First wash your hands and put the baby girl on the changing mat.

2   Undo her clothing and open out the nappy.

3   Clean off as much faeces as possible with the soiled nappy.

4   Use wet cotton wool or baby wipes to clean inside all the skin creases at the top of her legs. Wipe down towards her bottom.

5   Lift her legs using one hand (finger between her ankles) and clean her buttocks and thighs with fresh cotton wool, working inwards towards the anus. Keep clear of her vagina and never clean inside the lips of the vulva.

6   Dry the skin creases and the rest of the nappy area thoroughly. Let her kick freely and then apply barrier cream.

Guidelines for cleaning a boy

1   First wash your hands and place the baby boy on the changing mat. It is quite common for baby boys to urinate just as you remove the nappy, so pause for a few seconds with nappy held over the penis.

2   Moisten cotton wool with water or lotion and begin by wiping his tummy across, starting at his navel.

3   Using fresh cotton wool or a wet wipe, clean the creases at the top of his legs, working down towards his anus and back.

4   Wipe all over the testicles, holding his penis out of the way. Clean under the penis. Never try to pull back the foreskin.

5   Lift his legs using one hand (finger between his ankles) and wipe away from his anus, to buttocks and to back of thighs.

6   Dry the skin creases and the rest of the nappy area thoroughly. Let him kick freely and then apply barrier cream.

NAPPY RASH

Almost all babies have occasional bouts of redness and soreness in the nappy area. This may be caused by leaving wet and dirty nappies on too long, poor washing techniques, infections, skin disorders such as eczema or seborrhoeic dermatitis, or reaction to creams or detergents.

The most common types of nappy rash are:

1   **Candidiasis or thrush dermatitis:** this is caused by an organism called candida albicans, a yeast fungus which lives naturally in many parts of the body. The rash is pink and pimply and is seen in the folds of the groin, around the anus and in the genital area; it is sometimes caused in breastfed babies whose mothers have taken a course of antibiotics, or in bottle-fed babies where the teats have been inadequately cleaned and sterilised.

Treatment:

❖   Use a special antifungal cream at each nappy change. This is prescribed by the doctor.

❖   Do not use zinc and castor oil cream until the infection has cleared, as the thrush organism thrives on it.

❖   If oral thrush is also present a prescribed ointment may be used.

2   **Ammonia dermatitis:** this produces the most severe type of nappy rash. It is caused when the ammonia present in the baby's urine and stools reacts with the baby's skin; it is more common in bottle-fed babies because their stools are more alkaline, providing a better medium for the organisms to thrive. The rash is bright red, may be ulcerated and covers the genital area; the ammonia smells very strongly and causes the baby a lot of burning pain.

Treatment:

❖   Wash with mild soap and water, and dry gently.

❖   Expose the baby's bottom to fresh air as much as possible.

❖   Only use creams if advised and leave plastic pants off.

❖   If using towelling nappies, a solution of 30 ml vinegar to 2.5 l of warm water should be used as a final rinsing solution to neutralise the ammonia.

PROCEDURE FOR CHANGING NAPPIES IN A GROUP SETTING

Nappy changing is an important time and you should ensure that the baby feels secure and happy. Singing and simple playful games should be incorporated into the procedure to make it an enjoyable experience. Each setting will have its own procedure for changing nappies. The following is an example:

❖   Nappies should be checked and changed at regular periods throughout the day.

❖   A baby should never knowingly be left in a soiled nappy.

❧ Check nappy mats for any tears or breaks in the fabric and replace if necessary.

❧ **Never leave a baby or toddler unsupervised on the changing mat.**

1 Collect the nappy and the cream needed. Put on apron and gloves. Ensure you have warm water and wipes.

2 Carefully put the baby on the changing mat, talking to them and reassuring them.

3 Afterwards dispose of the nappy and discard the gloves.

4 Thoroughly clean the nappy mat and the apron with an antibacterial spray.

5 Wash your hands to avoid cross-contamination.

6 Record the nappy change on the baby's nappy chart, noting the time, whether it was wet or dry, and if there has been a bowel movement. Also note any change you have observed (e.g. in colour or consistency of the stools or if the baby had difficulty in passing the stool; also, if there is any skin irritation or rash present).

(For information on disposing of waste in the early years setting, see Chapter 4, page 142.)

Care of the feet

❧ Feet should always be washed and dried thoroughly, especially between the toes, and clean socks should be put on every day.

❧ All-in-one baby suits must be large enough not to cramp the baby's growing feet.

❧ Toenails should be cut straight across, not down into the corners.

Care for a baby's teeth

Although not yet visible, the teeth of a newborn baby are already developing inside the gums; a baby's first teeth are called deciduous teeth or milk teeth, and these start to appear at around 6 months (see page 169). Dental care should begin as soon as the first tooth appears, with visits to the dentist starting in the child's second year. Teeth need cleaning *as soon as they appear*, because **plaque** sticks to the teeth and will cause decay if not removed. Caring for the first teeth, even though they are temporary, is important because:

1 It develops a good hygiene habit which will continue throughout life.

2 Babies need their first teeth so that they can chew food properly.

3 First teeth guide the permanent teeth into position; if first teeth are missing the permanent teeth may end up crooked.

4 Painful teeth may prevent chewing and cause eating problems.

5 Clean, white, shining teeth look good.

CLEANING A BABY'S TEETH

Use a small amount – a smear – of baby toothpaste on a soft baby toothbrush or on a piece of fine cloth (e.g. muslin) to clean the plaque from the teeth. Gently smooth the paste on to the baby's teeth and rub lightly. Rinse the brush in clear water and clean her mouth. Brush twice a day – after breakfast and before bed. After the first birthday, children can be taught to brush their own teeth – but will need careful supervision. They should be shown when and how to brush, that is, up and down, away from the gum; they may need help to clean the back molars.

It is also important to keep sugary foods to feed-times.

TEETHING

Some babies cut their teeth with no ill effects; others may experience:

* general fretfulness (they may rub the mouth or ears);
* red or sore patches around the mouth;
* diarrhoea;
* a bright red flush on one or both cheeks, and on the chin;
* dribbling.

Teething should not be treated as an illness, but babies will need comforting if in pain. Teething rings and hard rusks usually provide relief. Teething powders and gels are not advised, as they are dangerous if given in large quantities. Infant paracetamol may be helpful in relieving pain, but is unsuitable for babies under 3 months unless advised by the doctor.

Fresh air and sunlight

Babies benefit from being outside in the fresh air for a while each day. When air is trapped in a house it becomes stale, the level of humidity rises and there is an increased risk of infections spreading. Carers working in nurseries should ensure that rooms are well-ventilated and that there are opportunities for babies to go outside. Sunlight is beneficial too, but care should be taken with babies and young children:

* Keep all children out of the sun when it is at its most dangerous, between 11 a.m. and 3 p.m.; carers of young children should plan outdoor activities to avoid this time unless children are well-protected by hats and sun protection cream. Permission must be obtained from the child's parent or guardian before applying sunscreen creams.

* Specialists advise keeping babies up to 9 months of age out of direct sunlight altogether to prevent the risk of developing skin cancer in later life.

* Use sun hats with a wide brim that will protect face, neck and shoulders on older babies.

* Use sun protection cream on all sun-exposed areas.

* Use sunshades or canopies on buggies and prams.

Sleep and rest

Everyone needs sleep, but the amount that babies sleep varies enormously, and will depend on the maturity of the brain (the pre-term baby may sleep for long periods) and the need for food. Sleep is divided into two distinct states:

1   **Rapid eye movement (REM)**, which is termed active sleep.

2   **Non-rapid eye movement (NREM)**, which is termed quiet sleep.

In REM sleep the mind is active and is processing daytime emotional experiences. In NREM sleep the body rests and restoration occurs. In babies under 1 year, more of the sleep is active (REM). It is important not to wake babies during deep sleep, as it plays a vital part in restoring energy levels.

Few aspects of parenthood are more stressful than months of broken nights. Carers could try the following strategies to encourage babies to adopt different sleep patterns for day and night.

Guidelines for encouraging a sleeping routine

❖ Allow the baby time to settle alone so that she begins to develop her own way of going to sleep. Some babies do cry for a short period as they settle; leave the baby but stay within hearing distance and check after 5 minutes to see if she is comfortable.

♣ Give the baby plenty of stimulation during the day by talking and playing with her when she is awake.

❖ Try to make night-time feeds as unstimulating as possible; feed, change and settle the baby in her cot.

❖ Make bedtime at night into a routine; by repeating the same process each night, the baby is made to feel secure and comfortable. These are both good aids to sleep.

Guidelines for establishing a bedtime routine

❖ Between 3 and 5 months, most babies are ready to settle into a bedtime routine.

❖ Give the baby a bath or wash and put on a clean nappy and nightwear.

❖ Take her to say goodnight to other members of the household.

❖ Carry her into her room, telling her in a gentle voice that it is time for bed.

❖ Give the last breast- or bottle-feed in the room where the baby sleeps.

❖ Sing a song or lullaby to help settle her, while gently rocking her in your arms.

❖ Wrap her securely and settle her into the cot or cradle, saying goodnight.

❖ If she likes it, gently 'pat' her to sleep.

❖ The routine can be adapted as the baby grows. Advice from FSID (The Foundation for the Study of Infant Deaths) is that the safest place for a baby to sleep is in a cot in the parents' room for the first six months. After 6 months, the baby can be left safely in her own room.

Exercise

Exercise strengthens and develops muscles. It also helps to promote sleep, as the body needs to relax after physical activity. Carers of young babies can provide opportunities for exercise in the following ways:

❖ Give plenty of opportunities for the baby to practise each new aspect of physical development as she becomes capable of it.

❖ Allow times for wriggling on the floor without being hindered by nappy or clothes.

❖ Allow freedom to look around, to reach and to grasp.

❖ Give opportunities to roll, crawl and eventually walk around the furniture safely.

❖ Provide objects and toys to exercise hand–eye coordination.

❖ After she has had her first 5-in-1 vaccination, the baby can be taken to special baby sessions at the local swimming pool.

Crying in young babies

Crying is a baby's way of expressing her needs. Finding out why a baby is crying is often a matter of elimination, so it is important that all carers should understand the physical and emotional needs of a baby at each stage of development (see Table 13.5).

PERSISTENT CRYING

Some babies do cry a great deal more than others, and are difficult to soothe and

Table 13.5 Causes of crying.

Hunger:	This is the most common cause of crying. It is quite likely unless the baby has just been fed. Breast-fed and bottle-fed babies should be fed on demand in the early weeks. By the age of four months, the baby will probably need solid foods.
Being undressed:	Most new babies hate being undressed and bathed, because they miss the contact between fabric and bare skin. One solution is to place a towel or shawl across the baby's chest and tummy when she is naked.
Discomfort:	Until they can turn themselves over, babies rely on an adult to change their position; babies show marked preferences for sleeping positions.
Nappy needs changing:	Some babies dislike being in a wet or dirty nappy and there may be nappy rash.
Twitches and jerks:	Most new babies make small twitching and jerking movements as they are dropping off to sleep. Some babies are startled awake and find it difficult to settle to sleep because of these twitches. Wrapping a baby up firmly – or swaddling – usually solves the problem.
Over-tired or over-stimulated:	Some babies can refuse to settle if there is too much bustle going on around them, e.g. loud noises, too much bouncing or bright lights in a shopping centre; take her somewhere quiet and try rhythmical rocking, patting, and generally soothing her.
Pain or illness:	A baby might have a cold or snuffles and be generally fretful or may have an itchy rash, such as eczema. (For signs and symptoms of illness in babies, see Chapter 14.)
Allergy:	An intolerance of cow's milk could cause crying; seek medical advice.
Thirst:	In particularly hot weather, babies may be thirsty and can be given cool boiled water. Breastfed babies may be offered an extra feed as breast milk is a good thirst-quencher.
Feeling too hot or too cold:	Temperature control is not well-developed in the young baby; if too hot, she will look red in the face, feel very warm and may be sweaty around the neck folds; loosen clothes and wrappings and remove some layers of bedding, but watch for signs of chilling. If too cold, she may also have a red face or may be pale; to check, feel the hands, feet, tummy and the back of the neck; cuddle the baby, wrap a blanket around her and try a warm feed.
Boredom/need for physical contact:	Babies find being cuddled or carried reassuring; talk to her and provide interesting objects for her to look at and a mobile; put pram under a tree or near a washing line so that she can see movements (NB: remember to fix a cat net to prevent insects and other unwanted visitors).
Colic:	If the baby cries after being fed or has long bouts of crying, especially in the evening, she may be suffering from colic.
Child abuse:	A baby who has been abused in any way may cry and the carer should seek help from appropriate professionals (see Chapter 16).

comfort. Parents and carers can feel quite desperate through lack of sleep and may develop personal problems; they may suffer guilt at not being able to make their baby happy, or lack confidence in caring for her. Such feelings of desperation and exhaustion can unfortunately result in physical violence to the baby – throwing her into the cot, shaking her or even hitting her. Parents experiencing such stress need a great deal of support.

Help and advice

Often just talking to others helps the carer to feel less isolated. Self-help groups such as Cry-sis or the National Childbirth Trust Post-natal Support System can help by offering support from someone who has been through the same problem. Talking to the health visitor or GP may help, and some areas run clinics with a programme to stop the spiral of helplessness.

Fig 13.18 Crying is a baby's way of expressing herself

Guidelines for helping a crying baby

❖ Make sure the baby is not hungry or thirsty.

❖ Check that the baby is not too hot or cold.

❖ Check that the baby is not physically ill (see page 555 for signs of illness in babies).

❖ Check if the baby's nappy needs changing.

❖ Treat colic or teething problems.

❖ Cuddle the baby and try rocking gently in your arms (the most effective rate of rocking is at least 60 rocks a minute; the easiest way to achieve this rapid and soothing rocking without getting exhausted is to walk while rocking her from side to side).

❖ Rock the baby in a cradle or pram.

❖ Talk and sing to the baby.

❖ Take the baby for a walk or a car ride.

❖ Leave the baby with someone else and take a break.

❖ Play soothing music or a womb-sounds recording.

❧ Talk to a health visitor, GP or a parents' helpline.

❧ Accept that some babies will cry whatever you do.

❧ Remember that this phase will soon pass.

If the crying ever feels too much to bear:

❧ Take a deep breath and let it out slowly. Put the baby down in a safe place, like a cot or a pram. Go into another room and sit quietly for a few minutes, perhaps with a cup of tea and the TV or radio on to help take your mind off the crying. When you feel calmer, go back to the baby.

❧ Ask a friend or relative to take over for a while.

❧ Try not to get angry with the baby. She will instinctively recognise your displeasure and will probably cry even more.

❧ Never let things get so bad that you feel desperate. There are lots of organisations at the end of a telephone line that can help.

Faltering growth

Faltering growth (formerly called failure to thrive) can be defined as a failure to gain weight at the expected rate. The first issue to be explored if a baby appears to be under-nourished is **feeding**; often a newly weaned baby will fail to gain weight due to intolerance of a newly introduced feed. Once the food is withdrawn from the diet, the baby will usually start to gain weight. There may be other problems associated with feeding a young baby, such as breathing difficulties or a poor sucking reflex in a premature baby. A baby who is **vomiting** frequently over a period of time is also likely to have faltering growth. Vomiting may be the result of pyloric stenosis, gastroenteritis or whooping cough (pertussis).

Sudden infant death syndrome (SIDS)

Sudden infant death syndrome is often called cot death. It is the term applied to the sudden, unexplained and unexpected death of an infant. The reasons for cot deaths are complicated and the cause is still unknown. Although cot death is the commonest cause of death in babies up to 1 year old, it is still very rare, occurring in approximately 2 out of every 1000 babies. Recent research has identified various risk factors and the Foundation for the Study of Infant Deaths has written the following guidelines.

Guidelines for parents from the Foundation for the Study of Infant Deaths

1 Cut smoking in pregnancy – fathers too!

2 Do not let anyone smoke in the same room as your baby.

3   Place your baby on their back to sleep.

4   Do not let your baby get too hot.

5   Keep baby's head uncovered – place your baby with their feet to the foot of the cot, to prevent wriggling down under the covers.

6   If your baby is unwell, seek medical advice promptly.

7   The safest place for your baby to sleep is in a cot in your room for the first 6 months.

8   It is dangerous to share a bed with your baby if you or your partner:

❖ are smokers (no matter where or when you smoke);

❖ have been drinking alcohol;

❖ take drugs or medication that makes you drowsy;

❖ feel very tired.

It is very dangerous to sleep together on a sofa, armchair or settee.

Guidelines for reducing the risk of cot death

❖ The room where an infant sleeps should be at a temperature which is comfortable for lightly clothed adults (16–20°C).

❖ If the baby is a natural tummy-sleeper, keep turning him over and tuck in securely with blankets (as long as the weather is not too hot); a musical mobile may help to keep him happy while lying on his back.

❖ Always invest in a brand-new mattress if the baby's cot is second-hand.

❖ A pillow should never be used for sleeping; if the baby is snuffly or has a blocked nose, place a small pillow *under* the mattress, but make sure he does not slide down to the end of his cot.

❖ Never allow the baby to come into contact with smoky rooms; ask visitors not to smoke in the house. The risk factor increases with the number of cigarettes smoked.

❖ Learn to recognise the signs and symptoms of illness and know how to respond.

❖ Use a room thermometer if necessary and check the baby's temperature by feeling his tummy, making sure your hands are warm beforehand.

❖ Babies over 1 month of age should never wear hats indoors, as small babies gain and lose heat very quickly through their heads.

❖ Learn and practise on a special baby resuscitation mannequin how to perform artificial ventilation and cardiac massage. This should always be practised under the supervision of a qualified first-aider.

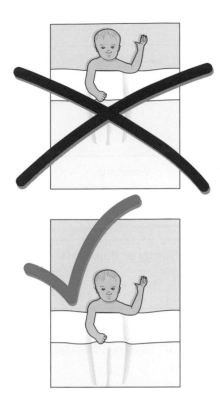

Fig 13.19 Preventing SIDS: the feet-to-foot position

GENERAL SIGNS OF ILLNESS IN BABIES

Babies are not able to explain how they are feeling to their carers, so it is important to recognise some of the general signs that accompany illness. Some babies may cry in a strange way – in a way that is different from their usual cry, indicating pain, hunger or thirst. They may refuse feeds or become unusually listless or lethargic. If the baby has an infection, there will be a raised temperature (or fever).

When to call the doctor

If you think the baby's life is in danger, dial 999 if you are in the UK. Ask for an ambulance urgently and explain the situation.

Contact the family doctor (GP) if the baby has any of the symptoms shown in Table 13.7. If the doctor cannot reach you quickly, take the baby to the accident and emergency (A&E) department of the nearest hospital.

Your role in reporting and recording illness in early years settings

* Nannies and childminders should always contact the baby's parents directly in the case of accident or illness.

* In schools and nurseries, you should notify a senior member of staff, who will then decide if and when to contact the baby's parents.

(Recording procedures in early years settings are discussed in Chapter 11.)

CLOTHING, FOOTWEAR AND EQUIPMENT

The layette

The layette is the baby's first set of clothes. Many shops specialising in baby goods supply complete layettes, and there is a vast range of clothing available. Baby clothes should be:

* **loose and comfortable** to allow for ease of movement; as babies grow rapidly, care should be taken that all-in-one stretch suits do not cramp tiny feet – there should always be growing space at the feet to avoid pressure on the soft bones;

* **easy to wash and dry**, as babies need changing often; natural fibres (e.g. cotton and wool mixtures) are more comfortable; any garment for babies up to 3 months old must carry a permanent label showing that it has passed the low flammability test for slow burning;

Table 13.6 Common signs of illness.

Raised temperature or fever	Refusing feeds or loss of appetite
The baby may look flushed or be pale, but will feel hot to the touch (black babies and those with dark skin tones may look paler than usual and the eyes may lose sparkle). Occasionally a high temperature may trigger a seizure (fit) or febrile convulsion.	A young baby may refuse milk feeds or take very little. An older baby may only want milk feeds and refuse all solids.
Diarrhoea	**Vomiting**
Persistent loose, watery or green stools can quickly dehydrate a baby. Dehydration means that the baby is losing important body salts.	This may be persistent or projectile (i.e. so forceful that it is projected several feet from the baby) – more violent than the usual **possetting**.
Excessive and persistent crying	**Lethargy or floppiness**
If the baby cannot be comforted in the usual way or if the cry is very different from usual cries.	The baby may appear to lack energy and does not exhibit the normal muscle tone.
Dry nappies	**Persistent coughing**
If the baby's nappies are much drier than usual because he or she has not passed urine, this can indicate **dehydration**.	Coughing in spasms lasting more than a few seconds. Long spasms often end with vomiting.
Difficulty with breathing	**Discharge from the ears**
If breathing becomes difficult or noisy with a cough, the baby may have bronchitis or croup.	Ear infections may not show as a discharge, but babies may pull at their ears and may have a high temperature.
Sunken anterior fontanelle	**Seizures (also called convulsions or fits)**
A serious sign of **dehydration**, possibly after diarrhoea and vomiting. The anterior fontanelle is a diamond-shaped 'soft spot' at the front of the head just above the brow. In dehydrated babies, this area is sunken and more visible.	During a seizure the baby either goes stiff or jerks their arms or legs for a period lasting up to several minutes. The eyes may roll upwards; the skin and lips become blue; the baby may dribble and will be unresponsive to you.

❖ **easy to put on and take off** – avoid ribbons, bows and lacy-knit fabrics, which can trap small fingers and toes;

❖ **non-irritant** – clothes should be lightweight, soft and warm; some synthetic fibres can be too cold in winter as they do not retain body heat, and too hot in the summer as they do not absorb sweat or allow the skin pores to breathe.

Note also that:

❖ several layers of clothing are warmer than one thick garment;

❖ clothing needs will vary according to the season, and the baby will need protective clothes such as a pram suit, bonnet or sun hat, mittens and booties.

Footwear for babies

Babies' feet are very soft and pliable. When choosing footwear bear in mind that:

❖ there must be room for the baby to wiggle his or her toes in a baby stretch suit or in socks or tights;

❖ socks should have a high cotton content so that moisture from the feet can

Table 13.7 When to call a doctor or take the baby to A&E.

❖ Has a temperature of 38.5°C which is not lowered by measures to reduce fever, or a temperature over 37.5°C for more than one day.	❖ Has convulsions, or is limp and floppy.
❖ Has severe or persistent vomiting and/or diarrhoea, or has projectile vomiting.	❖ Cannot be woken, is unusually drowsy or may be losing consciousness.
❖ Has symptoms of **meningitis**.	❖ Seems dehydrated – a sunken anterior fontanelle can indicate **dehydration**.
❖ Is pale*, listless, and does not respond to usual stimulation.	❖ Has **croup** symptoms.
❖ Has a bulging fontanelle (soft spot on top of head) when not crying.	❖ Cries or screams inconsolably and may have severe pain.
❖ Refuses two successive feeds.	❖ Appears to have severe abdominal pain, with symptoms of shock.
❖ Passes bowel motions (stools) containing blood.	❖ Develops a purple-red rash anywhere on body. Could be **meningitis**.
❖ Has a suspected ear infection.	❖ Has **jaundice**.
❖ Has inhaled something, such as a peanut, into the air passages and may be choking.	❖ Has been injured, e.g. by a burn which blisters and covers more than 10 per cent of the body surface.
❖ Has bright pink cheeks and swollen hands and feet (could be due to **hypothermia**).	❖ Has swallowed a poisonous substance or an object, e.g. a safety pin or button.
*Babies with black skins will show darker-coloured rashes than those on fairer-skinned babies.	❖ Has difficulty in breathing; rapid, difficult or noisy breathing.

escape; make sure that socks are not too loose as the friction can cause blisters;

❖ soft corduroy shoes called padders keep a baby's feet warm when crawling or walking, but should not be worn if the soles become slippery;

❖ outside shoes should not be worn until the baby has learnt to walk unaided, and then should be fitted properly by a trained shoe fitter.

Equipment for a young baby

Babies need somewhere to sleep, to be bathed, to feed, to sit, to play and to be transported.

FOR SLEEPING
Cradles and Moses baskets (wicker baskets with carrying handles) can be used

as beds for a young baby, but are unsuitable for transporting the baby outside or in a car.

Prams and carrycots come in a wide variety of designs; safety mattresses are available which are ventilated at the head section to prevent the risk of suffocation. Prams can be bought second-hand or hired for the first year of a baby's life; they must meet the following safety requirements:

❖ brakes should be efficient and tested regularly;

❖ a shopping basket should be positioned underneath to prevent shopping bags being hung on the handles and causing overbalancing;

❖ there must be anchor points for a safety harness;

the vehicle must be stable, easy to steer and the right height for the carer to be able to push easily without stooping;

the mattress must be firm enough to support the baby's back.

COTS

Often a baby will move into a cot for sleeping when he has outgrown his carrycot, but cots are also suitable for newborn babies. Cots usually have slatted sides – which allow the baby to see out – with one side able to be lowered and secured by safety catches. Safety requirements are:

bars must be no more than 7 cm apart;

safety catches must be childproof;

the mattress should fit snugly, with no gaps;

cot bumpers (foam-padded screens tied at the head end of the cot) are not recommended;

if the cot has been painted, check that lead-free paint has been used.

TRAVEL COT

This is a folding cot with fabric sides, suitable for temporary use only; it is especially useful if the family travels away from home a lot and it can double as a playpen when the mattress is removed.

BLANKETS AND SHEETS

These should be easy to wash and dry as they will need frequent laundering. The ideal fabric for sheets is brushed cotton; blankets are often made from cellular acrylic fabric, which is lightweight, warm and easily washable.

For bathing

Baby baths are easily-transportable (when empty) plastic basins which can be used with the fixed base bought for a carrycot, or within the adult bath. After a few months, the baby can be bathed in the adult bath; carers should guard against back strain, cover hot taps because of the risk of burns and always use a non-slip rubber mat in the base of the bath.

Never leave a baby alone in any bath, even for a few seconds.

For feeding

If the baby is being bottle-fed, eight to ten bottles and teats, sterilising equipment and formula milk will be required. If she is being breastfed, one bottle and teat are useful to provide extra water or fruit juice. A **high chair**, with fixed safety harness, is useful for the older baby.

For sitting

A bouncing cradle is a soft fabric seat which can be used from birth to about 6 months; it is generally appreciated by babies and their carers as it is easily transported from room to room, encouraging the baby's full involvement in everyday activities. It should always be placed on the floor, never on a worktop or bed, as even young babies can 'bounce' themselves off these surfaces and fall.

For playing

Babies like to be held where they can see faces clearly, especially the carer's face; they prefer toys which are brightly coloured and which make a noise. In the first 3 months, provide:

mobiles, musical toys and rattles;

soft balls and foam bricks;

toys to string over the cot or pram.

From about 3 months, provide:

cradle gym, bath toys and activity mat;

❖ chiming ball and stacking beakers;

❖ saucepans and spoons;

❖ building bricks;

❖ rag books.

(See also page 533 for ideas about providing play things and activities to promote holistic development.)

For transport

BABY SLINGS

Baby slings, used on the front of the carer's body, enable close physical contact between carer and baby, but can cause back strain if used with heavy babies; child 'back carriers', which fit on a frame like a rucksack, are suitable for larger babies.

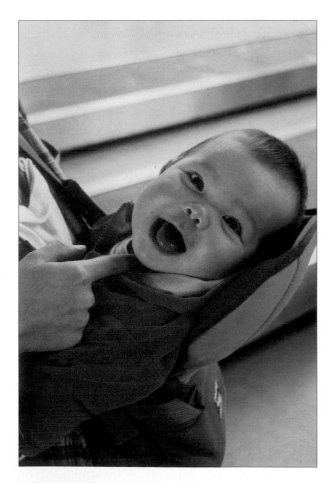

Fig 13.20 Baby in a front sling

PRAM OR BUGGY

A newborn baby can be transported in a special buggy with a tilting seat (the baby must be able to lie flat). This can then be used for as long as the baby needs a pushchair; the buggy has the advantage of being easier to handle, store at home and take on public transport than a pram. It is not possible to carry heavy loads of shopping on a buggy and lightweight buggies are not recommended for long periods of sleeping.

CAR SEATS

A baby should never be carried on an adult's lap on the front seat of a car. Small babies can be transported in a sturdy carrycot with fixed straps on the back seat or in a rearward-facing baby car seat – if the car has a passenger airbag, the baby seat should always be fitted in the back seat; for babies under 10 kg, these seats can also be used as a first seat in the home.

POSITIVE RELATIONSHIPS WITH PRIMARY CARERS

The diversity of child-rearing practices

Child-rearing practices vary across different cultures – they can also differ within cultural groups. Respecting cultural values and practices as they relate to the care of young children is not just a matter of having appropriate insight and a positive attitude towards diverse cultural practices. It may also demand a willingness to modify the routines in an early years setting in order to accommodate the needs of a particular child and their family.

Examples of different customs around the birth of a baby include:

❖ 'wetting the baby's head' (a euphemism for having an alcoholic drink to celebrate the birth);

- baby showers and the giving of gifts and cards;
- restricted visiting by male members of the family for up to 10 days following the birth;
- preparing special foods for the mother to eat;
- a Christian family may wish to have the baby christened;
- a Hindu family may wish to write the mantra 'Om' on the baby's tongue with honey;
- a Muslim family may wish that a male relative whisper the Islamic call to prayer into the baby's ear and perhaps attach an amulet around the baby's neck or wrist.

Weaning is also an important milestone in many cultures and the progression from milk feeds to solids may be marked by specific ceremonies:

- For Hindus, there is a rice-feeding ceremony at 6 months of age, when various members of the family, usually starting with the grandparents, feed the baby its first rice.
- Congee, a traditional Chinese weaning food of rice boiled in watery meat broth, is introduced at 6–10 months.

Avoiding stereotypical attitudes

It is important not to make assumptions about any individual, as this can lead to **stereotyping** (see Chapter 1). It is very important that you get to know the children in your care – and their parents – and that you consider each child as an individual with his or her own **unique needs**.

Families under pressure

Families come under a lot of pressure from friends, from advertising companies and from television programmes to provide the very best clothing and equipment for their new baby. The idealised picture of happy, smiling parents cuddling their precious bundle of joy is hard to resist; advertisers use these images to bombard the new parents with a dazzling array of objects that are deemed 'essential' to happy parenthood. You are in an important position to advise on the basic principles when choosing equipment. Parents should prioritise their needs by considering all factors relevant to their circumstances:

- **Cost:** how much can the parents afford to spend? What may be available on loan from friends who have children past the baby stage? Can some equipment (e.g. the pram) be bought second-hand or hired cheaply?
- **Lifestyle:** is the family living in a flat where the lifts are often out of action, in bed-and-breakfast accommodation or in a house with a large garden? These factors will affect such decisions as pram or buggy, and where the baby will sleep.
- **Single or multiple use:** will the equipment be used for a subsequent baby – in which case the priority may be to buy a large pram on which a toddler can also be seated? It may be worth buying new, high-quality products if they are to be used again.
- **Safety and maintenance:** does the item of equipment chosen meet all the British Safety Standards? What if it has been bought second-hand? How easy is it to replace worn-out parts?

FACTORS WHICH CAN CAUSE STRESS TO PARENTS

- **Financial:** if both parents have to go out to work, this can be stressful. One or both parents may need to reduce their hours of work or they may need to pay for child care.

* **Age of parents and support available:** very young parents or parents who are at the upper end of the childbearing age range may have less support from their peers and find the adjustment to parenthood more stressful. Some parents lack support from the **extended family**, who may live a long way away.

* **Tiredness:** having a young baby can disrupt parents' sleeping patterns; this is particularly stressful if both parents have to get up to go to work.

* **Responsibility:** some parents find the responsibility of looking after a young baby overwhelming; they may worry that they cannot cope or find that 'the baby' has completely taken over their life.

* **Conflict:** parents may have several other children to care for, all with their own needs. The needs of the new baby may conflict with the established routine within the family.

ACCESS TO HEALTH CARE AND SUPPORT

There are many voluntary organisations that can offer help and support to parents of young children. The **health visitor** will be able to advise parents about local groups, such as parent-and-toddler groups and **Home–Start**, which is a voluntary organisation that provides trained volunteers to work with families under stress.

Providing information for parents

When caring for babies – whether as a nanny in their home or in a nursery – you need to ensure that parents have information about their baby on a daily basis; most settings provide a **daily record chart**, which helps to make sure the parents are

involved in their child's care. Information includes:

* **Feeding:** what, when and how much their baby has consumed.

* **Excretion:** nappy changing information.

* **Health:** any concerns (e.g. nappy rash, unexplained rashes, teething symptoms).

* **Holistic development:** all aspects of development should be noted – physical, intellectual, language, emotional and social.

* **Behaviour:** what the baby has been doing during the session; how happy he has been; any problems that have arisen, and so on.

You need to be available to discuss any concerns a parent may have about their baby – ideally each key worker will hand over to 'their' baby's parent or carer at the end of each session.

Potential problems

Occasionally you might come across parents who have difficult or challenging attitudes towards the staff and the setting generally. You should always be patient, even when *you* are exhausted at the end of a busy day! There could be any number of reasons for a sudden, angry outburst, and you need to react in a professional and caring manner. Several factors – including competition, guilt and time constraints – may affect the relationship between a working parent and staff in an early years setting. For example:

* **Competition:** the parents may feel they are competing with you for the baby's affection, since both you and they have formed strong attachments to the baby.

* **Jealousy:** parents may feel jealousy if their baby takes her first steps in your presence – rather than at home.

- ❧ **Guilt:** parents often feel guilty; they may resent having to 'abandon' their children by leaving them while they work – this is even more difficult when separating from their baby causes *both* of them distress.

- ❧ **Time:** employed parents may feel that they have many roles and duties to perform, but not enough time to perform them; consequently, they often feel overwhelmed when they turn up to collect their children.

THE NUTRITIONAL NEEDS OF BABIES

The way babies and children are fed involves more than simply providing enough food to meet nutritional requirements; for the newborn baby, sucking milk is a great source of pleasure and is also rewarding and enjoyable for the mother. The ideal food for babies to start life with is breast milk and **breastfeeding** should always be encouraged as the first choice in infant feeding; however, mothers should not be made to feel guilty or inadequate if they choose not to breastfeed their babies.

Breastfeeding

The breast is made up of 15–20 segments or lobes, each of which contains alveoli or cells which produce milk (see Figure 13.21). Lactiferous ducts drain milk from the alveoli to reservoirs in the area of the areola (the pigmented ring around the nipple). Small glands in the areola, called Montgomery's tubercles, produce a fluid that keeps the skin of the nipples and the areola soft and supple. The nipple has several openings through which the baby can obtain milk.

During pregnancy the breasts produce colostrum, a creamy, yellowish fluid, low in fat and sugar, which is uniquely designed to feed the newborn baby. Colostrum also has higher levels of antibodies than mature milk and plays an important part in protecting the baby from infection. Mature milk is present in the breasts from around the third day after birth. Hormonal changes in the mother's bloodstream cause the milk to be produced and the sucking of the baby stimulates a steady supply. (Unfortunately, this mechanism also operates in the event of stillbirth or miscarriage and can cause the mother severe distress, especially if she has had no warning that this may happen.)

MANAGEMENT OF BREASTFEEDING

The most difficult part of breastfeeding is usually the beginning and it may take 2–3 weeks to establish a supply and to settle into some sort of pattern. Even if the mother does not intend to breastfeed her baby, she should be encouraged to try for the first few days so that the baby can benefit from the unique properties of colostrum. Many of the problems which cause women to give up breastfeeding can be overcome with the right advice and support.

Breast milk may be expressed by hand or by breast pump for use when the mother is unavailable; expressed breast milk (EBM) can be stored in a sterilised container in a freezer for up to 3 months.

The **UNICEF UK Baby Friendly Initiative** offers a range of assessment, training and information services to help the health services to **promote and support breastfeeding**. The initiative was started after research found that:

- ❧ Breastfed babies are less likely to suffer many serious illnesses: gastroenteritis, respiratory and ear infections are much less common in breastfed babies.

* They are less likely to suffer from eczema, wheezing and asthma as children, particularly if there is a family history of these conditions.
* Adults who were breastfed as babies are less likely to have risk factors for heart disease such as obesity, high blood pressure and high cholesterol levels.

Bottle-feeding

Commercially modified baby milks (formula milks) must be used for bottle-feeding. Soya-based milks can be used if the baby develops an intolerance to modified cow's milk. For the first 4–6 months the baby will be given infant formula milk as a substitute for breast milk; she may then progress to follow-on milk, which should be offered until the age of 12 months.

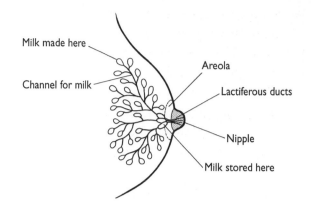

Fig 13.21 The lactating breast

PREPARATION OF FEEDS

A day's supply of bottles may be made and stored in the fridge for up to 24 hours. A rough guide to quantities is: 150 ml of milk per kilogram of body weight per day: thus a baby weighing 4 kg will require

Guidelines for the successful management of breastfeeding

* The mother should take a well-balanced diet; her diet will affect the composition of the breast milk and some foods may cause colic (vegetarian mothers who drink cow's milk, eat a varied vegetarian diet and take vitamin supplements produce breast milk that is similar in nutrient value to non-vegetarian mothers; vegan mothers may need to take calcium and vitamin B12 supplements while breastfeeding).
* Put the baby to the breast straight after the birth; this has been shown to be a key factor in successful breastfeeding.
* Feed on demand (i.e. when the baby is hungry), rather than routinely every 4 hours.
* Arrange extra help in the home if possible, at least until breastfeeding is established.
* Find the most comfortable position for feeding; if the mother has a sore perineum or Caesarean scar, the midwife or health advisor will be able to advise.
* Try not to give extra (complementary) milk feeds by bottle.
* Let the baby decide when she has had enough milk and allow her to finish sucking at one breast before offering the other.

Advantages of breastfeeding

* Human breast milk provides food constituents in the correct balance for human growth. There is no trial-and-error to find the right formula to suit the baby.

* The milk is sterile and at the correct temperature; there is no need for bottles and sterilising equipment.

* Breast milk initially provides the infant with maternal antibodies and helps protect the child from infection.

* The child is less likely to become overweight as overfeeding by concentrating the formula is not possible and the infant has more freedom of choice as to how much milk she will suckle.

* Generally, breast milk is considered cheaper, despite the extra calorific requirement of the mother.

* Sometimes it is easier to promote mother–infant bonding by breastfeeding, although this is certainly not always the case.

* Some babies have an intolerance to the protein in cow's milk (which is the basis of formula milk).

* The mother's uterus returns to its pre-pregnancy state more quickly, as a result of the action of oxytocin released when the baby suckles.

Advantages of bottle-feeding

* The mother knows exactly how much milk the baby has taken.

* The milk is in no way affected by the mother's state of health, whereas anxiety, tiredness, illness or menstruation may reduce the quantity of breast milk.

* The infant is unaffected by such factors as maternal medication. Laxatives, antibiotics, alcohol and drugs affecting the central nervous system can affect the quality of breast milk.

* Other members of the family can feed the infant. In this way the father can feel

equally involved with the child's care, and during the night could take over one of the feeds so that the mother can get more sleep.

* There is no fear of embarrassment while feeding.

* The mother is physically unaffected by feeding the infant, avoiding such problems as sore nipples.

approximately 600 ml in 24 hours. This could be given as 6 x 100 ml bottles.

The following equipment will be needed:

* a container for sterilising bottles, large enough to submerge everything completely; steam sterilisers are very effective, but costly;

* eight wide-necked feeding bottles and teats designed for newborn babies;

* a large plastic or Pyrex measuring jug and a plastic stirrer (or feeds can be made directly in bottles and shaken to mix);

* sterilising liquid or tablets – check the manufacturer's instructions for length of time and correct dilution.

The following steps should be followed:

1   Wash hands and nails thoroughly; boil some fresh water and allow it to cool; take bottles from the steriliser; shake but do not rinse because this would desterilise them.

2   Pour the correct amount of boiled and cooled water into each bottle (check quantity at eye level on a firm surface).

3   Measure the exact amount of formula milk powder using the scoop provided; level with a plastic knife but do not pack down; add powder to each bottle.

4   Take teats from steriliser, taking care to handle by the edges; and fit into the

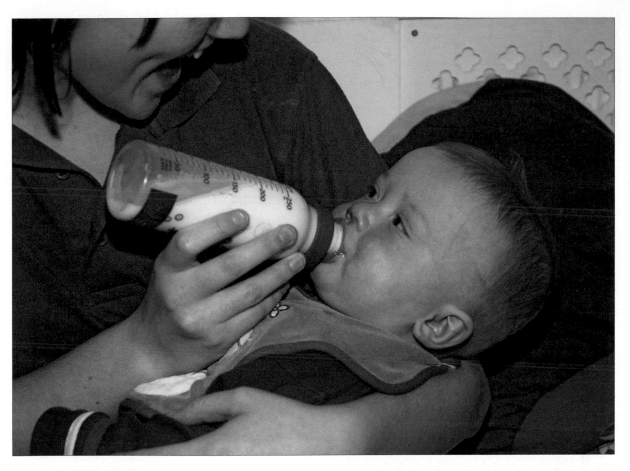

Fig 13.22 Bottle-feeding

bottles upside down; put caps, rings and tops on.

5 Shake each bottle vigorously until any lumps have dissolved.

6 If not using immediately, cool quickly and put bottles in the fridge; if using immediately, test temperature on the inside of your wrist.

STERILISING FEEDING EQUIPMENT
It is very important that all bottles and equipment are thoroughly sterilised.

❖ After use, scrub all the bottles, caps and covers, using hot soapy water and a special bottle brush. Rinse thoroughly in clean running water.

Guidelines for bottle-feeding

❖ Always wash hands thoroughly before preparing feeds for babies.

❖ Never add sugar or salt to the milk, and never make the feed stronger than the instructions state – this could result in too high a salt intake which can lead to severe illness.

❖ Always check the temperature of the milk before giving it to a baby.

❖ Do not use a microwave oven to warm the bottle as it may produce isolated hot spots.

❖ Always check that the teat has a hole of the right size and that it is not blocked.

❖ Never prop up a baby with a bottle – choking is a real danger.

❖ Always supervise siblings when feeding small babies.

❖ Teats may be cleaned using a special teat cleaner; turn teat inside out to ensure all milk deposits are removed and wash as the bottles.

❖ Submerge bottles, teats and all other equipment needed for bottle-feeding in the sterilising solution, checking that no bubbles are trapped inside bottles and that teats are completely immersed.

Feeding problems in babies

POSSETTING

The baby regularly vomits small amounts of her feed, but is generally healthy and has no signs of illness. The cause is a weakness of the muscle at the opening of the stomach and eventually the baby will grow out of it; although the condition is messy, there is no cause for alarm!

Guidelines for giving a bottle-feed

1 Collect all the necessary equipment before picking up the baby. The bottle may be warmed in a jug of hot water; have muslin square or bib and tissues to hand.

2 Check the temperature and flow of the milk by dripping it onto the inside of your wrist (it should feel warm, not hot or cold).

3 Make yourself comfortable with the baby. Do not rush the feed – babies always sense if you are not relaxed and it can make them edgy too.

4 Try to hold the baby in a similar position to that for breastfeeding and maintain eye contact; this is a time for cuddling and talking to the baby.

5 Stimulate the rooting reflex by placing the teat at the corner of the baby's mouth; then put the teat fully into her mouth and feed by tilting the bottle so that the hole in the teat is always covered with milk.

6 After about 10 minutes, the baby may need to be helped to bring up wind; this can be done by leaning her forwards on your lap and gently rubbing her back or by holding her against your shoulder. Unless the baby is showing discomfort, do not insist on trying to produce a burp – the baby may pass it out in the nappy.

A

B

C

D

E

F

Fig 13.23 Preparing a bottle-feed

The **National Children's Bureau** states that:

Babies who are bottle-fed should be held and have warm physical contact with an attentive adult while being fed. It is strongly recommended that a baby [in a child care setting] is fed by the same staff member at each feed. Babies should never be left propped up with bottles as it is dangerous and inappropriate to babies' emotional needs.

PYLORIC STENOSIS

This is a condition, more common in boys than girls, in which the muscle surrounding the channel at the end of the stomach (the pylorus) thickens, narrowing the outlet. Symptoms usually appear about 3 weeks after birth:

❖ The baby will vomit quite violently – projectile vomiting. The regurgitated food often shoots several feet away.

❖ The baby becomes constipated.

❖ Dehydration may occur and weight gain stops.

Medical advice should be sought; pyloric stenosis is easily diagnosed and is usually cured by a simple operation.

COLIC

Colic is an attack of abdominal pain caused by spasms in the intestines as food is being digested; sometimes called '3-month colic', as it usually disappears by the age of 3 months, the condition causes the baby to draw up her arms and legs and cry inconsolably. Attacks of colic can last anything from 15 minutes to several hours, and some babies only suffer in the evening. There is no known cause and really no effective cure. The obvious distress of the baby and the helplessness of the carer make caring for a colicky baby difficult; parents need a lot of support and reassurance that the baby will grow out of it and that there is no lasting damage.

CONSTIPATION

This occurs when stools are hard or infrequent; it can be caused by underfeeding and/or dehydration. The baby's fluid intake should be increased; if weaned, more fruit and vegetables should be included in the diet.

DIARRHOEA

Diarrhoea is caused by food passing through the intestines too quickly, not leaving enough time for it to be digested; the baby will pass frequent, loose, watery stools. It may be caused by poor food hygiene or by viral infection. It should always be taken seriously in a young baby, especially if accompanied by vomiting. Seek medical advice and give cooled, boiled water; bottle-feeding should be stopped completely, but breastfeeding may continue if the baby wants it.

FOOD INTOLERANCE

Only a small number of reactions to food are true allergic responses, in that they involve an immune reaction in the body. Some babies develop an intolerance to cow's milk protein; the most common symptoms are vomiting, diarrhoea and failure to thrive. After weaning, foods most likely to cause an adverse reaction in babies are:

❖ hen's eggs;

❖ fish;

❖ citrus fruits;

❖ wheat and other cereals;

❖ pork.

Allergies to food additives, such as the colouring agent tartrazine, have been blamed for many different problems, including eczema, asthma and hyperactivity (attention deficit disorder); however, there is no conclusive medical evidence to support this thesis. Sometimes an allergic reaction will be temporary, perhaps following an illness, but the offending food should always be removed from the baby's diet. Dietetic advice should be sought before any changes to a balanced diet are made. (Diets are discussed in more depth in Chapter 4.)

Weaning

Weaning is the gradual introduction of solid food to the baby's diet. The reasons for weaning are to:

❖ meet the baby's nutritional needs – from about 6 months of age, milk alone will not satisfy the baby's increased nutritional requirements, especially for iron;

❖ satisfy increasing appetite;

❖ develop new skills – use of feeding beaker, cup and cutlery, for example;

❖ develop the chewing mechanism; the muscular movement of the mouth and jaw also aids the development of speech;

❖ introduce new tastes and textures; this enables the baby to join in family meals, thus promoting cognitive and social development.

STAGES OF WEANING

Between 4 and 6 months is usually the right time to start feeding solids to a baby. Note that giving solids too early – often in the mistaken belief that the baby might sleep through the night – places a strain on the baby's immature digestive system; it may also make her fat and increases the likelihood of allergy.

❖ **Stage 1 (4–6 months):** give puréed vegetables, puréed fruit, baby rice, finely puréed dhal or lentils. Milk continues to be the most important food.

❖ **Stage 2 (about 6–8 months):** increase variety; introduce puréed or minced meat, chicken, liver, fish, lentils, beans. Raw eggs should not be used (see Table 13.8), but cooked egg yolk can be introduced from 6 months; wheat-based foods (e.g. mashed Weetabix, pieces of bread). Milk feeds decrease as more solids rich in protein are offered.

❖ **Stage 3 (about 9–12 months):** cow's milk can safely be used at about 12 months; lumpier foods such as pasta, pieces of cooked meat, soft cooked beans, pieces of cheese, a variety of breads; additional fluids, such as diluted, unsweetened fruit juice or water. Three regular meals should be taken as well as drinks.

METHODS OF WEANING

Some babies take very quickly to solid food; others appear not to be interested at all. The baby's demands are a good guide for weaning; mealtimes should never become a battleground. Even babies as young as 4 months have definite food preferences and should never be forced to eat a particular food, however much thought and effort have gone into the preparation. Table 13.8 gives guidelines on introducing new solids to babies. The best foods to start with are puréed cooked vegetables, fruit and ground cereals such as rice. Chewing usually starts at around the age of 6 months, whether the baby has teeth or not, and coarser textures can then be offered. The baby should be in a bouncing cradle or high chair – not in the usual feeding position in the carer's arms.

Food can be puréed by:

❖ rubbing through a sieve using a large spoon;

❖ mashing with a fork (for soft foods such as banana or cooked potato);

❖ using a Mouli-sieve or hand-blender;

❖ using an electric blender (useful for larger amounts).

Finger foods

Finger foods are any foods that can be given to a baby to manage by themselves. After weaning, encourage the baby to chew, even if there are no teeth, by giving finger foods, or foods which have a few lumps. Examples of finger foods include:

Guidelines for weaning

❖ Try to encourage a liking for savoury foods.

❖ Only introduce one new food at a time.

❖ Be patient if the baby does not take the food – feed at the baby's pace, not yours.

❖ Do not add salt or sugar to feeds.

❖ Make sure that food is the right temperature.

❖ Avoid giving sweet foods or drinks between meals.

❖ Never leave a baby alone when she is eating.

❖ Limit the use of commercially prepared foods – they are of poorer quality and will not allow the baby to become used to home cooking.

❖ Select foods approved by the baby's parents.

❖ wholemeal toast;

❖ pitta bread;

❖ banana or peeled apple slices;

❖ cubes of hard cheese (e.g. cheddar);

❖ chapatti;

❖ breadsticks;

❖ cooked carrot or green bean.

NB Always stay near to the baby during feeding to make sure they do not choke and to give encouragement.

THE PARTICULAR REQUIREMENTS OF YOUNG BABIES IN GROUP AND DOMESTIC CARE

The most important factor in any early years setting for babies is the people who are doing the caring – in other words, *you*. Obviously the physical environment should be attractive and planned to provide a safe and stimulating environment. Babies should be in rooms containing groups of no more than six children (and two adults). Staff

Table 13.8 Introducing new solids to babies.

	4–6 months	6–8 months	9–12 months
You can give or add	Puréed fruit Puréed vegetables Thin porridge made from oat or rice flakes or cornmeal Finely puréed dhal or lentils	A wider range of puréed fruits and vegetables Purées which include chicken, fish and liver Wheat-based foods, e.g. mashed Weetabix Egg yolk, well cooked Small-sized beans such as aduki beans, cooked soft Pieces of ripe banana Cooked rice Citrus fruits Soft summer fruits Pieces of bread	An increasingly wide range of foods with a variety of textures and flavours Cow's milk Pieces of cheese Fromage frais or yoghurt Pieces of fish Soft cooked beans Pasta A variety of breads Pieces of meat from a casserole Well-cooked egg white Almost anything that is wholesome and that the child can swallow
How	Offer the food on the tip of a clean finger or on the tip of a clean (plastic or horn) teaspoon	On a teaspoon	On a spoon or as finger food
When	A very tiny amount at first, during or after a milk feed	At the end of a milk feed	At established mealtimes
Why	The start of transition from milk to solids	To introduce other foods when the child is hungry	To encourage full independence
Not yet	Cow's milk – or any except breast or formula milk Citrus fruit Soft summer fruits Wheat (cereals, flour, bread, etc.) Spices Spinach, swede, turnip, beetroot Eggs Nuts Salt Sugar Fatty food	Cow's milk, except in small quantities mixed with other food Chillies or chilli powder Egg whites Nuts Salt Sugar Fatty food	Whole nuts Salt Sugar Fatty food

working with babies in group care or in a childminder's home should be adequately trained and supported in their work.

Babies need consistent, individual care

In nursery and crèche settings, each baby should be allocated to a **key worker**, who, ideally, is responsible for:

* the routine daily hands-on care (e.g. feeding, washing, changing);

* observing the baby's development;

* encouraging a wide range of play activities tailored to the baby's individual needs;

* recording and reporting any areas of concern;

* liaising with the baby's primary carers or parents and establishing a relationship which promotes mutual understanding.

Any setting which uses the key worker system should have a strategy for dealing with staff absence or holidays. (See also page 581 for information on the key worker role and the lead professional role.)

Respecting differences

All babies need respectful and individual care. Within the early years setting, physical care arrangements should allow for individual differences; for example:

* **food**: provide a variety of foods – do not expect each child to eat the same thing;

* **sleep:** allow babies to sleep when they need to, rather than having a set group time;

* **anti-discriminatory practice:** books, toys and ceremonies should reflect the cultural diversity of the nursery and

should be positively non-sexist and against violence (see Chapter 1);

* **stereotyping:** staff must avoid stereotyping language.

Attachment and separation

* **Primary attachments:** babies usually develop close attachments to those who care for them – at first with their parents or primary caregivers.

* **Multiple attachments:** babies can, and often do, make several attachments, often with other family members, close friends of the family and other carers.

* **Separation anxiety:** a baby may show signs of separation anxiety – typically at around 6 months; this may happen even when the primary carer, usually the mother, leaves the baby just for a few moments. The baby does not have certain feeling that the parent will return and can become very distressed in a short space of time. They might become tearful, uneasy or even filled with panic.

Your role in meeting the needs of babies in group and domestic care

Most parents are understandably anxious when they decide to leave their baby with a stranger. Unless their baby has had some experience of being left for long periods of time with anyone other than the primary carers, the parents will not be certain of their reaction. Some common worries include:

* What will happen if my baby will not stop crying?

* Will my baby settle to sleep immediately, but then be panic-stricken when she wakes up and finds that Mummy is not there?

* How will the nanny or key worker handle such a situation?

❖ Will the staff get annoyed with me if I want to know everything that has gone on in my baby's life since I left this morning?

It takes time for staff to get to know a parent, but you can help to alleviate some of their concerns, and to provide quality care and education for babies by:

❖ **Showing empathy:** try to put yourself in the parent's shoes and follow the guidelines on page 659 for settling-in new children.

❖ **Welcoming parents and making time for them:** make friendly contact with the child's parents; you need to be approachable; try not to appear rushed, even when you have a really busy nursery.

❖ **Helping parents to separate from their baby:** when a baby is handed from the parent to a new carer, it is best if:

1 you approach slowly;

2 you talk gently before picking up and taking the baby from the parent;

3 the baby is held looking at the parent during the handover.

❖ **Explaining how you will be caring for the baby:** for example, describing the daily routines and the layout of the setting.

❖ Being aware of your particular situation and your responsibilities: you need to maintain a **professional relationship** with parents (even if they also happen to be your friends) and work as a team member in an early years setting.

❖ Showing that you **enjoy** being with the baby: physical contact is important; encourage 'conversations' with babies; smile and talk to them.

❖ Always act in the **interests of the baby:** use your knowledge of holistic development and your powers of observation to enable you to tailor the care you give to the individual baby's needs.

❖ Keeping parents and other staff members **informed:** you need to know how and when to pass on information to parents about their baby's care; and to observe the rules of confidentiality.

ACTIVITY: ANTENATAL CARE

1 In groups, discuss the advantages and disadvantages of giving birth to a baby (a) in hospital and (b) at home.

2 (a) Research the effects that smoking when pregnant may have on the developing foetus. (b) Research the possible effects that alcohol consumption may have on the unborn baby.

3 Prepare a weekly menu plan for a pregnant woman: (a) who follows a vegan diet; (b) who follows a vegetarian diet; (c) who is on a limited income.

(You can also refer to the principles of nutrition in Chapter 4.)

ACTIVITY: THE SKILLS OF THE NEWBORN BABY

1 Make a list of all the things a newborn baby is able to do.

2 What is the name given to movements which are automatic and inborn?

Describe six such movements and explain their importance in the study of child development.

ACTIVITY: DESIGNING A MOBILE

1 Think of two or more designs for a mobile.

2 Compare your ideas, considering the following factors:

* availability of resources and materials;
* skills and time required;
* costs of materials;
* appropriateness of the design for its purpose;
* safety of the design.

3 Select one of the designs; if possible, use a computer graphics program to prepare patterns, and a word processor to write a set of instructions for making the mobile.

4 Follow your written instructions and make the mobile. Evaluate both the instructions (were they easy to follow or did you have to modify the plan?) and the mobile. If appropriate, offer the mobile as a gift to a baby known to you (perhaps in family placement) and conduct a detailed observation on the baby's reaction to the mobile and his or her associated behaviour.

ACTIVITY: BOTTLE-FEEDING

1 Find out the costs involved in bottle-feeding a baby:

   ❧ the initial costs of equipment – sterilising unit, bottles, teats, and so on;

   ❧ the costs of formula milk and sterilising tablets for 1 year.

2 Collect some advertisements for baby milk formulas and analyse their appeal:

   ❧ make a poster using a selection of advertisements, and discuss the similarities and differences between them;

   ❧ make a poster which 'sells' the idea of breast milk, using the same methods.

3 Discuss the statement on bottle-feeding by the National Children's Bureau, quoted in the text on page 568. Why is it important that babies are bottle-fed in the manner described?

4 Discuss the problems faced by developing countries when large companies promote bottle-feeding by mounting campaigns and distributing free infant milk samples.

ACTIVITY: WEANING

1 Prepare a booklet for parents on weaning. Include the following information:

   ❧ when to start weaning a baby;

   ❧ what foods to start with;

   ❧ when and how to offer feeds;

   ❧ a weekly menu plan which includes vegetarian options.

2 Visit a store which stocks a wide variety of commercial baby foods and note their nutritional content (e.g. protein, fat, energy, salt, sugar, gluten and additives). Make a chart which shows:

   ❧ the type of food (e.g. rusks and cereals, savoury packet food, jars of sweet and savoury food);

   ❧ the average cost of an item in each category;

   ❧ the packaging (note particularly if manufacturers use pictures of babies from different ethnic backgrounds).

3 Ask a parent who has recently used weaning foods what reasons they had for choosing one product over another.

ACTIVITY: WHAT SORT OF NAPPIES?

Research the advantages and disadvantages of terry-towelling and disposable nappies, including the following information:

* costs – initial outlay for purchase of nappies, liners and pants, and continuing costs of laundry;

* the effects of each method on the environment – chemicals used in laundering; disposal in landfill;

* convenience and suitability for the purpose.

ACTIVITY: CARING FOR A BABY'S TEETH

Prepare a leaflet for parents showing how teeth develop in a young baby and how to ensure their healthy development. Include tips for making caring for the teeth an enjoyable routine activity.

ACTIVITY: AN UNWELL BABY

1 Imagine you are a nanny looking after a 6-month-old baby in his home. When you pick him up from his morning nap, you notice that he is very hot and sweaty; he refuses his bottle-feed and cries fretfully. What would you do *first*?

2 Write an essay on the principles of caring for a sick baby.

ACTIVITY: SUDDEN INFANT DEATH SYNDROME (SIDS)

1 In groups, prepare a display which details the risk factors implicated in sudden infant death syndrome. Using the information provided, make a poster for each risk factor and state clearly the precautions that should be taken to prevent cot death.

2 In pairs, rehearse the procedure to follow if a young baby is found 'apparently lifeless' in his cot. Use a baby resuscitation mannequin to test each other's skills. **NB** Professional supervision will be required.

ACTIVITY: CLOTHING A NEW BABY

You have been asked to advise on the purchase of a layette for a newborn baby.

1 Make a list of the items you consider to be essential, excluding nappies and waterproof pants.

2 Visit several shops and find out the cost of all the items on your list.

3 Evaluate your selection, checking:

* the ease of washing and drying;

* the design and colours used (are you reinforcing the stereotypes of pink for girls or blue for boys?);

* the safety aspects (no fancy bows, ties, etc.);

* the suitability of the fabrics used;

* the quantity of clothes needed;

* the final cost of the layette.

14

Preparation for employment

Contents

● The role of the early childhood practitioner ● Understanding group dynamics and teamwork ●
Leadership and management ● Communication patterns within care organisations ● The
responsibilities of a professional early childhood practitioner ● Stress and conflict in the workplace
● Working in a team ● Staff appraisal and review ● Codes and policies in the workplace ●
Employment opportunities ● Conditions of employment ● Grievance and complaints procedures ●
Professional development

THE ROLE OF THE EARLY CHILDHOOD PRACTITIONER

Having satisfactorily completed a recognised course in Child Care and Education, a professional early childhood practitioner will be qualified to work in a variety of settings, including nursery, infant or primary schools or classes, family centres, hospitals and the private and voluntary sectors.

What qualities make a good early childhood practitioner?

Above all else, an early childhood practitioner needs to like children and enjoy being with them. Caring as a quality is largely invisible, difficult to quantify and more noticeable when absent than when present. The main individual characteristics required are shown in the box below.

Guidelines for important personal qualities in an early childhood practitioner

❖ **Listening:** attentive listening is a vital part of the caring relationship. Sometimes a child's real needs are communicated more by what is left unsaid than by what is actually spoken. Facial expressions, posture and other forms of body language all give clues to a child's feelings. A good carer will be aware of these forms of non-verbal communication.

❖ **Comforting:** this has a physical side and an emotional side. Physical comfort may be provided in the form of a cuddle at a time of anxiety, or by providing a reassuring, safe environment to a distressed child. Touching, listening and talking can all provide emotional comfort as well.

❖ **Empathy:** this should not be confused with sympathy. Some people find it easy to appreciate how someone else is feeling by imagining themselves in that person's position. A good way of imagining how a strange environment appears to a young child is to kneel on the floor and try to view it from the child's perspective (see Figure 14.1).

❖ **Sensitivity:** this is the ability to be aware of and responsive to the feelings and needs of another person. Being sensitive to others' needs requires the carer to anticipate their feelings (e.g. those of a child whose mother has been admitted to hospital, or whose pet dog has just died).

❖ **Patience:** this involves being patient and tolerant of other people's methods of dealing with problems, even when you feel that your own way is better.

❖ **Respect:** a carer should have an awareness of a child's personal rights, dignity and privacy, and must show this at all times. Every child is unique, and so your approach will need to be tailored to each individual's needs.

❖ **Interpersonal skills:** a caring relationship is a two-way process. You do not have to like the child you are caring for, but warmth and friendliness help to create a positive atmosphere and to break down barriers. Acceptance is important: you should always look beyond the disability or disruptive behaviour to recognise and accept the person.

❖ **Self-awareness:** a carer is more effective if they are able to perceive what effect their behaviour has on other people. Being part of a team enables us to discover how others perceive us and to modify our behaviour in the caring relationship accordingly.

❖ **Coping with stress:** caring for others effectively in a full-time capacity requires energy, and it is important to be aware of the possibility of professional burnout. In order to help others, we must first help ourselves: the carer who never relaxes or develops any outside interests is more likely to suffer burnout than the carer who finds his or her own time and space.

Values and principles

All early childhood practitioners should work within a framework that embodies sound values and principles. The **CACHE Statement of Values** is a useful tool for checking that you are upholding important child care values.

> **CACHE Statement of Values**
> You must ensure that you:
> 1 Put the child first by:
>   ❖ ensuring the child's welfare and safety;
>   ❖ showing compassion and sensitivity;
>   ❖ respecting the child as an individual;
>   ❖ upholding the child's rights and dignity;

* enabling the child to achieve their full learning potential.

2 Never use physical punishment.

3 Respect the parent as the primary carer and educator of the child.

4 Respect the contribution and expertise of staff in the child care and education field, and other professionals with whom they may be involved.

5 Respect the customs, values and spiritual beliefs of the child and their family.

6 Uphold the Council's Equality of Opportunity Policy.

7 Honour the confidentiality of information relating to the child and their family, unless its disclosure is required by law or is in the best interest of the child.

Fig 14.1 Empathising: the child's-eye view of the world

UNDERSTANDING GROUP DYNAMICS AND TEAMWORK

A group is a collection of two or more people who possess a common purpose.

1 **Formal groups** are deliberately created by their managers for particular planned purposes. It is the management who select group members, leaders and methods of doing work.

2 **Informal groups** are formed by people who feel they share a common interest. Members organise themselves and develop a sense of affinity both to each other and to a common cause.

Group norms

A group norm is a shared perception of how things should be done, or a common attitude, feeling or belief. Norms are closely linked to expectations: as the group norms emerge, individuals start to behave in ways in which they believe other group members expect them to behave.

Factors which create group cohesion

* **The frequency and closeness of interactions:** the more often people meet and the closer their contact, the more they will perceive themselves as belonging to a distinct group.

* **Exclusivity of membership:** if membership of the group is selective, members feel a sense of achievement in having been chosen.

* **The nature of the external environment:** the environment in which a group operates may offer protection from a hostile external environment (e.g. Neighbourhood Watch groups).

* **Good interpersonal communication:** if communication is easy, then a collective sense of purpose will readily emerge; and

the less contact with outsiders, the greater the internal cohesiveness.

* **The nature of the task:** if the individuals are all engaged in similar work, then they will more readily perceive themselves as a group.

* **Homogeneity of membership:** where members are alike in terms of background, education, age, social origin, and so on, they are likely to share some common attitudes.

* **Rewards and penalties:** a group that can offer rewards or bonuses, or even punish its own members, can exert great pressure on individuals to conform. In such cases, group cohesiveness tends to be very strong.

Group cohesion

Group cohesion is the extent to which group members are prepared to cooperate and to share common goals. Cohesion encourages compliance to group norms and causes groups to be more stable in their functioning.

Certain factors contribute to the creation of group cohesion. These are discussed in the box above.

The value of teamwork

In early years settings, a team is a group of people who work together to meet the aims of their establishment – for example, a day nursery with the aim of providing care for an early years group. Most early childhood practitioners are required to work alongside colleagues in a team; even someone employed as a nanny in a private home is operating in a team with the family. Furthermore, some people work in a multidisciplinary team – for example, a team consisting of a doctor, police officer, teacher, social worker and perhaps a parent may attend a case conference on a child at risk.

To function well as a team, the team members must be:

* motivated towards **common goals**;

* provided with the **support and encouragement** necessary to achieve these goals;

* able to **communicate** effectively.

LEADERSHIP AND MANAGEMENT

All organisations have to be managed, although the styles of management involved can vary considerably. The managerial team of most organisations must:

* plan;

* establish goals;

* control operations;

* appraise its employees.

A successful team needs good **leadership** or management. Leadership is the ability to influence the thoughts and behaviour of others. A leader's position may be formal, resulting from designated organisational authority (e.g. a nursery manager), or informal in nature (e.g. depending on the individual's personal ability to exercise power). There is a continuum of possible leadership styles, extending from complete autocracy at one extreme to total democracy at the other.

Autocratic leadership

CHARACTERISTICS OF THE AUTOCRATIC STYLE

* The leader tells the subordinates exactly what to do, without comment or discussion.

* There are rewards for good performance and penalties or threats of sanctions for underperformance.

❧ There is strict control and a highly formal network of interpersonal relations between the leader and team members.

ADVANTAGES OF THE AUTOCRATIC STYLE

❧ Everyone knows precisely what is expected of them: tasks, situations and relationships are clearly defined.

❧ Time management is usually good as the manager sets the standards and coordinates the work.

❧ Decisions are arrived at speedily as there is no consultation with others.

❧ Employees receive direct and immediate help towards achieving their goals.

DISADVANTAGES OF THE AUTOCRATIC STYLE

❧ It stifles the workers' own initiative.

❧ It does not make maximum use of the employees' knowledge, skills and experiences.

❧ Staff cannot reach their true potential.

❧ If the group leader is absent (e.g. ill or on holiday), important work may not be completed.

Autocratic styles of leadership are not often seen in early years settings.

Democratic styles

CHARACTERISTICS OF THE DEMOCRATIC STYLE

❧ At its extreme, this style uses the laissez-faire approach. A group may not even have a leader, but may have someone who acts as a facilitator.

❧ There is much communication and consultation between the leader/facilitator and the group. It is recognised that everyone has a contribution to make.

❧ Group members actively participate in the leader's/facilitator's decisions. If unanimity is impossible, then a vote is taken.

ADVANTAGES OF THE DEMOCRATIC STYLE

❧ The job satisfaction of group members is greater, through widening their responsibilities and making their work more interesting and varied.

❧ The morale of group members is improved as they have a key role in planning and decision making.

❧ Specialist knowledge and skills are recognised and used towards achieving goals.

❧ Targets are more likely to be achieved because they have been formulated by group consensus.

DISADVANTAGES OF THE DEMOCRATIC STYLE

❧ Some group members may not want to become involved in the decision-making process.

❧ Time management may be more problematic because of the extra time necessary for full consultation of the group.

❧ A lack of positive direction may prevent goals from being attained.

❧ Employees may feel resentful because they are only involved in minor day-to-day issues and do not have any real say in the major issues.

❧ Subordinates may require closer supervision.

COMMUNICATION PATTERNS WITHIN CARE ORGANISATIONS

Business structures

Most business organisations are **hierarchical** in structure. Those at the top of the hierarchy take the most important decisions, and are rewarded by the highest salaries. They communicate their decisions downwards through a chain of command.

The number of levels within the hierarchy can vary a great deal, but the fewer there are, generally the greater the efficiency.

Information can flow within the hierarchy in three directions:

1 downwards from top to bottom;

2 upwards from bottom to top;

3 sideways at various levels.

Whatever system of management is used, a large amount of information must flow down the hierarchy from top management to the shop floor (or domestic staff). Research has proved that downward communication can be very inefficient, with only 20 per cent of information reaching the bottom of the pyramid.

Communication from the bottom upwards has two important purposes:

* to feed back information on the action that has been taken in response to messages sent downwards;

* to alert the decision makers to the feelings and attitudes of those lower down the organisation.

Line managers

Many large organisations with grouped specialities use line authority. Line managers are directly responsible for achieving the organisation's objectives, and exert direct authority over their subordinates. In line authority:

* authority flows through the chain of command from the apex to the base;

* the chain of command is illustrated by means of an organisation chart;

* each position in the line system involves points of contact between manager and subordinates, and shows clearly both the authority of its occupant and to whom that person is responsible;

* vertical communications proceed only through the line system.

THE RESPONSIBILITIES OF A PROFESSIONAL EARLY CHILDHOOD PRACTITIONER

The skills required by the professional early childhood practitioner need to be practised with regard to certain responsibilities (see below).

Good practice as a team member will depend on liaising with others, and reporting on and reviewing your activities. Conflicts between team members often arise from poor communication: for example, an early childhood practitioner who fails to report, verbally or in writing, that a parent will be late that day to collect their child may cause conflict if a colleague challenges the parent's conduct.

Guidelines for your responsibilities as a professional early childhood practitioner

1 **Respect the principles of confidentiality.** Confidentiality is the preservation of secret (or privileged) information concerning children and their families which is disclosed in the professional relationship. It is a complex issue which has at its core the principle of trust. The giving or receiving of sensitive information should be subject to a careful consideration of the needs of the children and their families; for example, a child who is in need of protection has overriding needs which require that all relevant information be given to all the appropriate agencies, such as social workers or doctors. Within the child care and education setting, it might be appropriate to discuss sensitive issues, but such information must never be disclosed to anyone outside the setting.

2 **Commitment to meeting the needs of the children.** The needs and rights of all children should be paramount, and the early childhood practitioner must seek to meet these needs within the boundaries of the work role. Any personal preferences and prejudices must be put aside; all children should be treated with respect and dignity, irrespective of their ethnic origin, socioeconomic group, religion or disability. The equal opportunities code of practice involved will give detailed guidelines.

3 **Responsibility and accountability in the workplace.** The supervisor, line manager, teacher or parent will have certain expectations about your role, and your responsibilities should be detailed in the **job contract**. As a professional, you need to carry out all your duties willingly and to be answerable to others for your work. It is vital that all workers know the **lines of reporting** and how to obtain clarification of their own role and responsibility. If you do not feel confident in carrying out a particular task, either because you do not fully understand it or because you have not been adequately trained, then you have a responsibility to state your concerns and ask for guidance.

4 **Respect for parents and other adults.** The training you have received will have emphasised the richness and variety of child-rearing practices in the UK. It is an important part of your professional role that you respect the wishes and views of parents and other carers, even when you may disagree with them. You should also recognise that parents are usually the people who know their children best; and in all your dealings with parents and other adults, you must show that you respect their cultural values and religious beliefs.

5 **Communicate effectively with team members and other professionals.** The training you have received will have emphasised the importance of effective communication in the workplace. You will also be aware of the need to plan in advance for your work with young children: a knowledge of children's needs in all developmental areas will enable you to fulfil these within your own structured role.

STRESS AND CONFLICT IN THE WORKPLACE

There are a number of reasons why conflicts arise in the workplace. The nature of the caring relationship imposes particular stresses that can lead to conflict between team members. There may be:

✤ **low morale** – individuals may feel unsupported and undervalued in their role;

✤ confusions over **individual roles** in the hierarchy of the organisation;

✤ stresses associated with the responsibility and accountability for providing care for children who are ill or disadvantaged;

✤ a **lack of communication** with superiors and colleagues;

✤ ambiguity over which tasks should take **priority** during the working day;

✤ an **excessive workload** in both quantitative (i.e. having too much to do) and qualitative (i.e. finding work too difficult) terms;

✤ feelings of **personal inadequacy and insecurity**, often following destructive criticism of one's work.

Anxiety

Unresolved anxiety will lead to stress. The physical effects of anxiety developed originally as aids to survival and were triggered by dangerous situations (the fight-or-flight responses).

There are two types of anxiety:

1 **Objective anxiety:** caused by genuinely stressful events.

2 **Neurotic anxiety:** subjective, often unconscious, feelings which arise within the individual.

Although they have different sources, both types of anxiety are experienced as the same painful emotional state.

Objective anxiety can be addressed by changing the circumstances of the environment in which a person functions; for example, a social worker who is worried about their own ability to cope with a difficult client can enlist help from their colleagues, or even transfer their responsibilities if necessary.

Neurotic anxiety cannot be removed by controlling external events. Consequently, the ego develops additional ways to protect itself from internal threats. These are called the ego defences.

Case Study

The stressful situation

Marsha recently obtained a qualification in child care and has been employed as a nursery nurse at Meadlands Day Nursery for 2 weeks. She has just been called in to see her supervisor as her colleagues have reported that she is frequently tearful and unable to contribute to activities in the nursery. Carol, her supervisor, asks why she is unhappy, and Marsha says that she does not like the atmosphere in the nursery, that there is a lot of bickering between the staff, and she feels that one particular child is constantly being ridiculed by her colleagues. Carol asks her to give more information about the complaints, but Marsha bursts into tears and asks if she can go home as she cannot cope any more.

ACTIVITY: THE STRESSFUL SITUATION

1   Identify and write down the stressors (the factors producing stress) which Marsha mentions.

2   How should Carol deal with this situation?

3   Find out about the Type A and Type B personalities from psychology textbooks. Are some personalities more suited to working in early years settings?

Ego defences for 'coping' with stress

✤ **Repression:** unpleasant memories and thoughts are banished from the consciousness and forced into the unconscious mind; this process of repression requires much mental energy, and can quickly lead to abnormal behaviour.

✤ **Regression:** the individual behaves as they did in an earlier phase of their life; immature behaviour is thus characteristic of those experiencing regression.

✤ **Displacement:** displacement occurs when an individual diverts their energies away from the area of work which they are finding difficult and instead devotes themselves completely to other things; for example, a nursery manager whose record-keeping skills are inadequate might channel all their energies into staff training issues, thereby replacing the need to deal with essential administration with an unnecessary concern for other matters.

✤ **Projection:** simple projection occurs when a person unconsciously attributes to another person a characteristic that is, in fact, their own. Personal feelings of dislike, hatred or envy that one person feels towards another and which give rise to internal feelings of neurotic anxiety are projected onto that person. What was originally an internal threat is now experienced as an external threat. Instead of feeling, 'I hate you,' projection changes this to, 'You hate me.' The extreme case is that of the paranoid individual who feels continually threatened by everyone with whom they come into contact.

WORKING IN A TEAM

Attending team meetings

In most work settings being part of the staff team means participating in meetings, to discuss and make decisions about a wide range of issues. You are expected to attend and you must make your apologies (to the person holding the meeting) if, for a genuine reason, you are unable to attend.

At any formal meeting, there is usually a set format:

1   **An agenda (or programme):** this is a list of items which will be discussed – some items will appear at every meeting. Apologies for absence are usually received and recorded at the start of any meeting.

2   **A written record, called the minutes:** most meetings begin by looking at the minutes of the last one to

remind everyone what was decided and to find out what has happened since. Someone will be given responsibility for taking the minutes.

3 **Any other business:** most meetings allow time for issues not included in the formal agenda to be brought up and discussed; for example, a problem with discipline that has arisen or equipment that has been damaged since the meeting was arranged.

4 **Date for the next meeting:** this is set and agreed by those attending the meeting.

After the meeting, the person who has taken the minutes will type or write them out neatly and arrange for copies to be sent to all the people who attended or who were invited but were unable to attend.

Some meetings are informal – perhaps arranged to talk about planning next month's topic or theme, or to finalise arrangements for an outing. Others may be more formal, perhaps covering policy matters. There is one person who leads (or chairs) the meeting and makes sure the items on the agenda are being dealt with – it is very easy for people to begin their own conversations or stray from the subject in hand!

Remember that you are there to contribute your ideas and thoughts and to listen to those of others.

At a meeting try to:

❖ listen carefully to information being given;

❖ check that you know what is expected of you at the meeting and afterwards;

❖ make sure you bring pen and paper and any other things that will be needed (e.g. an observation of a child who is being discussed);

❖ understand that you may not share the views of others, or agree with all decisions made;

❖ contribute your ideas and opinions clearly and at the appropriate time – not when everyone has started talking about the next item;

❖ ask questions about anything you do not understand.

Contribution to team meetings

In most settings team meetings are held regularly and conducted according to an agreed agenda. Ideally the written agenda should be given to all team members and should include a space for anyone to add their own item for discussion.

Certain factors may detract from the value of team meetings:

❖ **Distractions:** constant interruptions, from either telephone calls or visitors, will prevent progress being made.

❖ **Irrelevant topics:** some meetings become a forum for gossip or other topics that are irrelevant to the task in hand.

❖ **A dominating member:** one person may be aggressive and outspoken, blocking other people's contributions.

Assertiveness

Assertiveness makes communication at team meetings more effective; this should not be confused with loudness or aggressive behaviour. Assertiveness may be defined, in this context, as standing up for your own basic rights and beliefs, without isolating those of others, and as making your behaviour 'match' your feelings.

Guidelines for being assertive

If you are assertive in your behaviour, you:

❖ can express your feelings, without being unpleasant;

❖ are able to state your views and wishes directly, spontaneously and honestly;

❖ respect the feelings and rights of other people;

❖ feel good about yourself and others too;

❖ can evaluate a situation, decide how to act and then act without reservation;

❖ are true to yourself;

❖ value self-expression and the freedom to choose;

❖ may not always achieve your goals, but feel that is not as important as the actual process of asserting yourself;

❖ are able to say what you have to say, whether it is positive or negative, while also leaving the other person's dignity intact.

NON-VERBAL FORMS OF ASSERTIVENESS

❖ good eye contact;

❖ a confident posture – standing or sitting comfortably;

❖ talking in a strong, steady voice;

❖ not clenching one's fist or pointing with a finger.

VERBAL FORMS OF ASSERTIVENESS

❖ avoiding qualifying words (e.g. 'maybe', 'only' or 'just');

❖ avoiding disqualifying phrases (e.g. 'I'm sure this isn't important, but . . .');

❖ avoiding attacking phrases (e.g. those that begin with 'You'); instead use assertive phrases, such as 'I feel'.

STAFF APPRAISAL AND REVIEW

In any employee, the employer is looking for a range of personal and professional qualities. A system of appraisal and review helps you and your manager or employer to assess how you are performing in your job and whether you are happy. Often goals may be set and your performance may be measured in relation to these targets.

Guidelines for staff appraisal and review

❖ An appraisal interview provides an opportunity for both you and your employer to identify any aspects of the job that you are doing really well and any that need to be improved.

❖ It is on these occasions that you can raise any problems you have – about dealing with particular situations, children, parents or staff.

Fig 14.2 Working together as a team

❖ When you are carrying out all your duties well you may be given more responsibility or you may be moved to work in a different area to develop your experience with other age ranges or activities.

❖ Appraisal should be viewed by staff as a positive action which helps to promote good practice within the setting. This holds true even when there are criticisms of performance.

❖ Most appraisals are carried out annually and by interview.

❖ Appraisals are also useful in identifying staff development needs; for example, an early childhood practitioner who is lacking in assertiveness may be sent on an assertiveness training course.

CODES AND POLICIES IN THE WORKPLACE

A code of practice is not a legal document, but it does give direction and cohesion to the organisation for which it has been designed. Codes of practice and policy documents cover areas of ethical concern and good practice, such as:

* equal opportunities;
* confidentiality;
* safety aspects;
* partnerships with parents;
* first-aid responsibilities;
* staff training;
* food service;
* record keeping;
* child protection;
* staff-to-children ratios.

All workplace policies and codes of practice must be drawn up within the framework of current legislation. The laws which are most relevant to child care and education services are:

* The Children Act (2004);
* The Education Reform Act (1988);
* The Race Relations Act (1976);
* The Sex Discrimination Act (1975).

Equal opportunities policy

An equal opportunities policy represents a commitment by an organisation to ensure that its activities do not lead to any individual receiving less favourable treatment on the grounds of:

* gender;
* race;
* ethnic or national origin;
* age;
* disability;
* marital status;
* religious belief;
* skin colour.

Having such a policy does not mean reverse discrimination in favour of minority groups, but equality for all. An effective policy will establish a fair system in relation to recruitment, training and promotion opportunities, as well as the staff's treatment of children, parents and one another.

THE POLICY STATEMENT

Each employing organisation should set out a clear policy statement that can be made available to employees and service users. The statement should include:

* a recognition of past discrimination;
* a commitment to redressing inequalities;
* a commitment to positive action.

Training should be provided to explain to all staff the implications and practical consequences of the policy. The organisation must also provide information about the law on direct and indirect discrimination.

Any policy which attempts to promote equality is only effective if the individuals working in the organisation incorporate its principles into their individual practice.

Guidelines for an equal opportunities policy

❖ Ethnic minority staff should be kept informed about, and encouraged to apply for, training programmes and promotion.

❖ Racial and ethnic variations should not be ignored, but rather recognised positively in the context of care.

❖ All staff should be aware that attitudes or actions based on racial prejudice are unprofessional and unacceptable in the workplace.

❖ Avoid the use of negative labels – even in private – such as 'bully', 'thick' or 'spoiled brat'.

❖ Ensure that all children have equal access to resources and equipment.

❖ Treat all parents and carers with respect and warmth.

❖ Promote a sense of fair play and respect for others within the setting.

❖ Investigate the interests of ethnic minority staff and find out whether facilities are required in respect of the canteen, social or cultural issues, religious holidays, and so on.

❖ Try to ensure a higher level of participation of ethnic minority staff in team meetings and case conferences (e.g. include on the agenda 'Multiracial and multicultural aspects of care'.

Health and safety policies

(See Chapter 4, page 180.)

Trade unions and professional organisations

Trade unions and professional organisations exist to represent and protect their own members' interests. Their main functions are to:

❖ negotiate for better pay and conditions of service;

❖ provide legal protection and support;

❖ represent members at grievance and disciplinary hearings.

Two such organisations which early childhood practitioners can join are:

❖ UNISON – a union for health workers;

❖ the Professional Association of Nursery Nurses (PANN).

In addition to representing their members' interests, most trade unions and professional organisations publish newsletters and hold regular local meetings to discuss workplace issues.

EMPLOYMENT OPPORTUNITIES

There are many opportunities for employment for people with child care qualifications to work with children, for example in:

❖ the family home, as a nanny;

❖ private nurseries;

❖ special schools or special units within mainstream schools;

❖ Sure Start Children's Centres (see Chapter 15);

❖ local authority day nurseries;

❖ workplace crèches;

❖ primary and preparatory schools;

❖ maternity units in hospitals;

❖ nursery schools;

❖ child-minding;

❖ babysitting;

❖ children's units in hospitals;

❖ jobs within the holiday and leisure industry (e.g. abroad as a ski or summer resort nanny, or as a nanny in a special children's hotel).

Preparing a CV

It is always useful to compile a **curriculum vitae** (CV) and to keep it up-to-date. The purposes of a CV are to:

❖ provide a brief outline of your life history;

❖ set out basic factual information in a concise manner;

❖ help in filling out application forms.

Many word-processing packages have a useful format for preparing a CV or résumé. The main headings to include are:

Table 14.1 Working in the public, voluntary and private sectors.

THE PUBLIC SECTOR

Local Education Authority	Local Government Services	Health Authority
Areas of work	**Areas of work**	**Areas of work**
Maintained Nursery schools	Family centres	Health Visiting in the community
Nursery classes	Children's centres	Hospital
Infant, lower and primary schools	Holiday Playschemes	Hospital crèches and nurseries
Schools for children with special needs		Adventure Centres and One o'Clock Clubs
Types of job	**Types of job**	**Types of job**
Nursery Assistant	Nursery Assistant in Family Centres and Children's Day Care Nurseries	Health Visitor Assistant in dincs clinics and in client's homes
Classroom Assistant	Playworker in Holiday Playschemes and Adventure Centres	Play Assistants in crèches and nurseries
Special Needs Classroom Assistant		
Teacher's Assistant		

THE VOLUNTARY SECTOR

Areas of work	Types of job
Pre-school Playgroups	Childminders – belonging to the Childminding Network in the Local Authoriy
After-school Clubs	Nursery Assistants
Holiday Playschemes	After-school Club Assistants
Nurseries	Holiday Playschemes Workers
	Playworkers

THE PRIVATE SECTOR

Areas of work	Types of job
Day nurseries	Childminders – not registered with the local Childminding Network
Nursery schools	Nursery Assistants
Crèches (in workplaces, shopping centres or sports and leisure centres)	Playworkers or ski nannies
	Mother's help (looking after children and housework)
Holiday companies, e.g. ski chalets, watersports, cruise ships, hotels	Au pair – usually unqualified in child care; often young people from abroad who live with a family and offer childcare services
Families	Nanny – usually qualified in child care; may live with the family or live out

❧ **First name and family name.**

❧ **Personal details:** date of birth, full postal address and telephone number.

❧ **Education and qualifications:** include names of schools and colleges attended, with dates and qualifications obtained.

❧ **Employment history:** if you have not worked before, include babysitting experience, college work experience and Saturday and holiday jobs.

❧ **Other experience:** include any voluntary work, involvement in local organisations or groups, sport and leisure interests.

❧ **Referees:** give the names, positions and addresses of two people who are willing to provide references for you. Always ask them first.

CVs should be neatly typed and free from any mistakes.

Working as a nanny

A nanny is someone who makes a career out of caring for children. Responsibilities vary widely from post to post. Most jobs involve the nanny having full responsibility for all aspects of childcare. As a nanny, you might be responsible for:

❧ the children's health and welfare while they are under your supervision;

Guidelines for preparing for an interview

❧ **Dress smartly** and avoid lots of make-up and jewellery; first impressions are very important.

❧ **Check the address** and that you know how to get there. If possible, make the journey beforehand so that you can judge how long it will take.

❧ Ensure you **arrive in plenty of time**.

❧ **Facial expression:** you may be very nervous, but make an effort to smile and to appear cheerful and relaxed.

❧ Try to maintain **eye contact** when the interviewer is speaking to you and when you reply.

❧ **Shake hands** firmly with the interviewer and try not to fidget; clasp your hands loosely in your lap; never sit with your arms folded.

❧ Refer to your **own experiences**, giving examples (whenever they are relevant) to demonstrate your understanding.

❧ Take any **relevant material** with you: for example, certificates, portfolio of work with children.

❧ **Eat before the interview**, so that your stomach does not rumble.

❧ **Do not smoke**, even if the interviewer does. It is not acceptable to smoke during your working hours, even if the household has no objections.

❧ **Be realistic:** there may be many other applicants for the post; if you are not successful it does not reflect on you personally.

❧ their social, emotional and educational development;

❧ ensuring that the children always play in safety, in an environment free from danger and minor hazards;

❧ some light domestic duties, closely related to the care of the children.

Some employers place greater emphasis on experience and personality than on professional qualifications. Other parents will only employ someone with a recognised child care qualification.

FINDING EMPLOYMENT AS A NANNY

There are many nanny employment agencies, which usually offer qualified nannies:

❧ contact with a wide range of suitable employers within your chosen area of work;

❧ advice on matters of pay, tax and contractual obligations, such as hours of work, rates of pay and specific duties;

❧ a formal contract between a nanny and the employer (see page 596);

❧ a free follow-up service after the start of employment, with the aim of sorting out any teething problems that may arise.

THE INTERVIEW

Nanny agencies offer advice to parents on what to ask at interview to ensure that the person they employ suits their particular family's needs. Typical questions include:

1 Why do you wish to be a nanny?

Employers are looking for someone whose answers show a love of children. Taking care of children involves a very big commitment and is not a suitable career for anyone who is not enthusiastic or who is unsure about being a nanny.

2 What are your childcare experiences?

You should be prepared to give a brief account of your past jobs, your formal college training and other relevant experience, such as regular babysitting jobs, playgroup experience, and so on. Most employers will also ask for at least three references from people who can verify your experience and your suitability for child care work.

3 What are your child-rearing philosophies?

Employers may ask how you would react in a specific situation; for example, if a child refuses to put on her coat and throws a tantrum when you need to take her to nursery school. Always answer truthfully and try to expand on how you feel about dealing with difficult behaviour and any experiences and examples you can relate.

4 Why does this particular post interest you?

You should already be aware of the details of the post or job specification (i.e. the hours, responsibilities, days off, salary). The employer will want to know if there is any particular reason why you have chosen the post; this might be the ages of the children or the location of the position, for example.

5 What do you feel are your personal qualities that suit you for this job?

Many nannies feel uncomfortable when asked to list their personal strengths; they feel that they are boasting. However, an employer may have several candidates to interview and will need to know where you feel your special qualities lie, so try to speak honestly, without being embarrassed.

6 What domestic duties would you expect to be included in the job?

This area of work is one that is most often the subject of disagreement between a nanny and the family. Some nannies are willing to do all the family's ironing in addition to caring for the children's laundry; others may resent being asked to do any tasks that are not directly related to care of the children. Issues such as extra babysitting duties in the evenings also need to be discussed.

7 What are your hobbies and interests?

Most employers are trying to find out what sort of person you are, to see whether or not you will fit in with the family. For instance, some families will be looking for a nanny that wants to travel, or one who will encourage children's sporting interests.

Other typical questions if you are applying for a live-in nanny post are:

1 What qualities are you looking for in a family?

It is very important to you and to the family that the chemistry is right. Employers want a nanny whose personality meshes with their own. Some live-in nannies expect to be part of the family, while others view the relationship as strictly that of employer–employee. Ask relevant questions if they are not answered already; for example, will you be expected to eat with the family, and will you be expected to travel on holidays with the family?

2 Can you drive?

If you drive you will be asked if you have a clean driving licence. You may need to find out whether there is a car available for your day off and what your duties are in respect of driving the children to school, and so on.

3 Do you smoke?

The employer will probably describe the house rules about smoking. You should know if any members of the household smoke and exactly what the rules are concerning smoking in your time off in the house.

4 Do you have any special dietary needs or any medical problems?

If you have any allergies or special dietary needs or preferences, you should mention them at the interview. Some employers ask for a letter from your GP.

Caring for children outside the family home

DAY NURSERIES, CHILDREN'S CENTRES AND FAMILY CENTRES

Local authority day nurseries are funded by social services and offer full-time provision for children under school age. They are particularly important in working with families who may be facing many challenges. Staffing levels are high, the usual ratio being one staff member for every four children. Some local authority day nurseries also operate as family centres, providing advice, guidance and counselling to families with difficulties. They usually have a staff of trained nursery nurses, and sometimes trained teachers or social workers will work on the staff. Most day nurseries operate a system of

Table 14.2 A specimen contract for a nanny

Date of issue:
....
....

This is a contract between (employer's names) and (your name). (Your name) is contracted to work as a nanny by (employer's name) at (employer's address), starting on (starting date).

General Information
The employer is solely responsible for accounting for the employer's and employee's National Insurance and Income Tax contributions. Employer should ensure that they have employer's public liability insurance to cover them should the nanny be injured in the course of work.

Remuneration
The salary is .... per *week/month *before/after deduction of Income Tax and National Insurance payable on .... The employer will ensure that the employee is given a payslip on the day of payment, detailing gross payment, National Insurance and Income Tax deductions and net payment. Overtime will be paid at £.......... net per hour or part thereof.

Hours of work
The employee will be required to work (hours) .... (days of the week) .... and may be called upon for baby-sitting up to (nights per week) .... In addition, the employee may be required to work overtime provided that .... days' notice have been given and agreed in advance. Overtime will be paid in accordance with the overtime detailed in the paragraph above. In addition, the employee will be

entitled to .... *days/weeks paid holiday per year. In the first or final year of service, the employee will be entitled to holidays on a pro rata basis. Holidays may only be carried into next year with the express permission of the employer. Paid compensation is not normally given for holidays not actually taken. The employee will be free on all Bank Holidays or will receive a day off in lieu by agreement.

Duties (please specify) ....
....
....
....
....
....
....

The employee shall be entitled to:
a) Accommodation ❑
b) Bathroom *sole use/ shared ❑
c) Meals (please specify) ❑
d) Use of car *on duty/off duty ❑
e) Other benefits: ....

....

Sickness
The employer will pay Statutory Sick Pay (SSP) in accordance with current legislation. Any additional sick pay will be at the employer's discretion.

Termination
In the first four weeks of employment, one week's notice is required on either side. After four weeks' continuous service, either the employer or the employee may terminate the contract by giving .... weeks' notice.

Confidentiality
The employee shall keep all affairs and concerns of the employer, their household and business confidential, unless otherwise required by law.

Discipline
Reasons which might give rise to the need for disciplinary action include the following.
a) Causing a disruptive influence in the household.
b) Job incompetence.
c) Unsatisfactory standard of dress or appearance.
d) Conduct during or outside working hours prejudicial to the interest or reputation of the employer.
e) Unreliability in time-keeping or attendance.
f) Failure to comply with instructions and procedures.
g) Breach of confidentiality clause.
In the event of the need for disciplinary action, the procedure will be: firstly, an oral warning; secondly, a written warning, and thirdly, dismissal. Reasons which might give rise to summary dismissal include drunkenness, theft, illegal drug-taking, child abuse.

Signed by the employer
....
....
Date

....
Signed by the employee
....
....
Date
....

---

key workers. **Sure Start Children's Centres** are part of the government's strategy to provide integrated care and education to children under 5 years (see Chapter 15 for further information).

RESPONSIBILITIES OF THE KEY WORKER
A key worker is usually a trained early childhood practitioner who takes on responsibility for one or more particular children each day. By ensuring continuity of

care, the difficulty for the child of separation from his parent is minimised. Parents appreciate having a familiar worker with whom they can talk in confidence about any concerns they may have relating to their child's wellbeing. Responsibilities of a key worker will include:

* assessing the child's needs, often by visiting the family before admission to the nursery;

* sharing information with the parents on all aspects of their child's care;

* planning the child's daily routine;

* meeting all the child's needs when in the nursery, involving:

    1 physical needs: nappy changing, skincare and bottle-feeding;

    2 emotional needs: settling the child on arrival each session and comforting her when distressed;

    3 intellectual needs: planning a learning programme to promote development and to stimulate the child;

* observing and recording the child's development;

* returning the child to the care of his parents at the end of each session with a report.

PRIVATE DAY NURSERIES AND WORKPLACE CRÈCHES

An increase in the number of working mothers has led to the setting up of more private day nurseries and workplace crèches, which care for babies and young children during the normal working week. All child care providers must be registered by Ofsted and must meet the national standards published by the DfES.

CHILD-MINDING

Registered childminders are professional day carers who work in their own homes to provide care and learning opportunities for other people's children in a family setting.

By law, all childminders must:

* be registered by **Ofsted** if they live in England, or the **Care Standards Inspectorate for Wales** (CSIW) if they live in Wales;

* have their home inspected regularly to make sure it is safe and suitable for young children;

* be insured in case a child they are looking after has an accident or damages someone else's property;

* have first-aid training which covers first aid to babies and young children;

* be checked by the Criminal Records Bureau (CRB), as must everyone else aged over 16 who lives or works in the childminder's home;

* take introductory training within 6 months of registering as a childminder.

Childminders are usually registered to look after up to three children under 5 years and three children aged 5–8 years, including their own children. They may also look after older children up to the age of 14.

As well as induction training, many childminders undertake child care qualifications or attend workshops on subjects like nutrition, sign language or business management. CACHE has a specific course for childminders – CACHE Level 3 Certificate in Child-minding Practice. Many parents find child-minding an excellent choice of child care, for the following reasons:

* Childminders can pay particular attention to individual needs.

* They may be well set up to look after babies.

* They can form a stable, ongoing relationship with the child, from when

they are a baby through to when they need care around schooling.

❖ They may be able to look after siblings together.

❖ They can be flexible over the hours of care provided, and can pick up or deliver children to and from other forms of care.

❖ They can adapt readily to circumstances and the individual child's needs.

❖ They provide care in a home that can include involvement in activities such as cooking, shopping, gardening, and family mealtimes.

Childminders are allowed to fix their own charges and many early childhood practitioners choose this career option when they have children of their own.

WORKING WITH CHILDREN IN SCHOOLS

There are some opportunities for qualified child care staff to work alongside teachers in primary schools and special schools. There are recognised courses to take after completion of the basic child care qualification (see page 676).

CARING FOR CHILDREN IN HOSPITALS

Some health authorities employ trained early years workers to care for babies on maternity units and in special care baby units, but the opportunities are dwindling as the care of sick babies becomes more technically demanding. The hospital play specialist scheme provides training and career opportunities for nursery nurses wishing to work with children in a hospital environment.

Children's hospitals in the UK have large play departments employing hospital play specialists, play leaders and nursery nurses. In general hospitals' small teams of play staff work in different areas of the hospital, such as outpatient clinics, children's wards and adolescent units.

Hospital play specialists work as part of a multidisciplinary team; their role is to:

❖ organise daily play and art activities in the playroom or at the bedside;

❖ provide play to achieve developmental goals;

❖ help children to cope with anxieties and feelings;

❖ use play to prepare children for hospital procedures;

❖ support families and siblings;

❖ contribute to clinical judgements and diagnoses through their play-based observations;

❖ act as the child's advocate;

❖ teach the value of play for the sick child;

❖ encourage peer-group friendships to develop;

❖ organise parties and special events.

BABYSITTING AND CHILD-SITTING

When parents trust you to babysit, they are placing their child's safety in your hands. Babysitting is one of the biggest responsibilities you will ever accept. It is wise to take some precautions when accepting a new babysitting job:

❖ Know your employer; only accept jobs from people you already know or for whom you have reliable, personal references.

❖ Make sure that your own parent (or someone you live with) knows where you are babysitting. Leave them the name, address and telephone number of the people you are sitting for, and let them know what time to expect you home.

❖ Find out what time the parents expect to be home. Let them know if you have a curfew. Ask them to call if they are running late.

Compile a checklist and make sure you fill it in before the parents leave:

Babysitter's checklist

1 Address of the house.

2 Phone number at the house.

3 Name and phone number of GP.

4 Nearest hospital and number.

5 Where the parents will be.

6 Phone number where the parents can be reached.

7 What time the parents are expected home.

8 Name and phone number of neighbours.

9 Other contacts (e.g. grandparents).

10 Any allergies or special medical information for children.

NB This checklist is also useful to keep next to the phone if you are employed as a nanny.

Safety tips for nannies and babysitters

❖ Before the parents leave, ask for the information on the checklist above. Keep the list near the phone at all times.

❖ If the house has an electronic security system, learn how to use it.

❖ Do not open the door to strangers. Do not let anyone at the door or on the phone know that you are there alone. If asked, respond by saying that you are visiting, the children's parents cannot come to the door and you will deliver a message.

❖ If you plan to take the children out, make sure that you have a key to lock and unlock doors; do not forget window locks.

❖ When you get back to the house, do not go inside if anything seems unusual

---

(broken window, door open, etc.). Go to a neighbour and call the police.

❖ Make sure that you have an escort home if babysitting at night.

In an emergency:

❖ If there is a fire, get the children and yourself **OUT**! Go to a neighbour's and call the fire service – dial 999. If you can, call the parents and let them know where you and the children are, and what is happening.

❖ Try not to panic during an emergency. Not only will it prevent you from thinking clearly, but it will also frighten the children.

❖ If you suspect that a child has swallowed a poisonous substance, call 999 immediately. Be able to identify the poison and the amount taken.

CONDITIONS OF EMPLOYMENT

The law in the UK requires that any employee who works for more than 16 hours a week should have a **contract of employment**. This document must contain the following information:

❖ the names of the employer and employee;

❖ the title of the job;

❖ the date when employment commenced;

❖ the scale of pay;

❖ the hours of work;

❖ entitlement to holidays;

❖ the length of notice required from employer and employee;

❖ the procedures for disciplinary action or grievances;

❖ sick-pay provision;

❖ pensions and pension schemes.

Responsibility for paying income tax and National Insurance contributions will need to be decided; such payments are usually deducted from your gross pay. Those applying for jobs within the private sector may want to consider using a reputable nanny agency; such agencies are used to negotiating contracts designed to suit both employer and employee.

GRIEVANCE AND COMPLAINTS PROCEDURES

If a dispute arises in the workplace, either among employees or between employees and employers, it must be settled. Usually this is achieved at an early stage through discussion between colleagues or between the aggrieved person and his immediate superior. If the grievance is not easily settled, however, an official procedure is needed (see below).

PROFESSIONAL DEVELOPMENT

Working in the field of early years care and education can be physically and emotionally exhausting, and professionals will need to consolidate their skills and to develop the

Guidelines on complaints and grievances procedure

❖ All employees have a right to seek redress for grievances relating to their employment, and every employee must be told how to proceed on this matter.

❖ Except in very small establishments, there must be a formal procedure for settling grievances.

❖ The procedure should be in writing and should be simple and rapid in operation.

❖ The grievance should normally be discussed first between the employee and their immediate supervisor.

❖ The employee should be accompanied, at the next stage of the discussion with management, by their employee representative if they so wish.

❖ There should be a right of appeal.

Managers should always try to settle the grievance 'as near as possible to the point of origin', in the words of the Industrial Relations Code of Practice.

Case Study

Problem solving

Helen is a manager in a day nursery in an inner-city area. There are 6 full-time members of staff at the nursery, caring for 34 children. Two newly qualified nursery nurses have recently been employed and Helen has noticed new tensions within the nursery. One of the new workers, Sarah, has asked for 3 weeks' annual leave at Christmas so that she can visit her family in Australia. Darren, who has worked there for 8 years, always takes 2 weeks off at that time to visit Ireland. The other new staff member, Dianne, has suggested a more positive approach to equal opportunities, with more emphasis on multicultural provision, the observance of festivals and more variety in the daily menu, and so on. One of the more experienced members of staff claims that the nursery already offers equal opportunities and that any changes are

Case Study continued

both unnecessary and expensive; she also claims that parents are not in agreement with such plans.

In addition, another staff member, Pat, has had a great deal of time off work

because her father has recently died; the rest of the staff feel that her absences have gone on for an unreasonable length of time, and they are tired of having to take on extra work.

ACTIVITY: PROBLEM SOLVING

Divide into groups and discuss the following questions:

1 How should Helen deal with these issues?

2 Do you think they are all equally important, or should any one issue be addressed before the others?

3 Which management style works best in this care setting?

Feed back each group's answers into the whole group and summarise the strategies for solving the problems.

ability to be **reflective** in their practice. It is important to keep abreast of all the changes in child care practices by reading the relevant journals, such as *Nursery World*, *Early Years Educator* and *Infant Education*, and by being willing to attend in-service courses when available.

The need for qualified early childhood workers is increasing, and more courses are being developed. National Vocational Qualifications (NVQs) in Child Care and Education are offered at some colleges, and these enable child carers to achieve competencies in the workplace. Other courses which offer professional development after achieving the Level 3 CACHE Diploma are:

❖ NVQ Level 4 in Early Years Care and Education;

❖ BTEC Professional Diploma in Specialised Play for Sick Children and Young People;

❖ Early Childhood Curriculum 2.5–6 years (Montessori Centre International Examination Board);

❖ BTEC Advanced Practice in Work with Children and Families;

❖ Montessori Primary Teaching Diploma;

❖ Certificate in Managing Quality Standards in Children's Services;

❖ Level 4 Certificate in Early Years Practice (OU);

❖ Foundation Degree in Steiner Waldorf Early Years Education;

❖ Specialist Teacher Assistant (STA) course;

❖ Advanced Diploma in Child Care and Education;

- Certificate in Social Work (CSS);
- Certificate for Qualified Social Workers (CQSW);
- Hospital Play Specialist Examination Board;
- Advanced Certificate in Playgroup Practice;
- Advanced Certificate in Playwork;
- BTEC Higher National Certificate in Early Childhood Studies;
- BTEC Higher National Diploma in Early Childhood Studies;
- BTEC Professional Diploma in Specialised Play for Sick Children and Young People.

NB As these courses are constantly being revised and updated, you should visit the DfES website for further information (www.dfes.gov.uk).

ACTIVITY: EVALUATING YOUR CARING QUALITIES

1 Think about the qualities outlined on page 578. Do you feel you already possess these qualities? Do you think that *academic* knowledge is important for someone working with children?

2 Evaluate your own interpersonal skills. Can you empathise (i.e. put yourself in someone else's situation)? Think of someone you know who has a problem, and focus on viewing the world as that person sees it. Write a description of a 'day in the life' of the person you have chosen, told from their viewpoint.

ACTIVITY: ASSERTIVENESS AND COMMUNICATION

1 Construct an assertiveness self-assessment table.

2 In your work placement, analyse group communication: prepare a record sheet, a sociogram and an analysis grid, and record who communicates with whom and how often. (A sociogram is a representation in graphic form of the network of relationships between different individuals. It is a useful technique for observing children's behaviour in group settings.)

15

Provision of services and child protection

Contents

Section 1: Provision of services

Section 2: Child protection

Section 1: Provision of services

DEVELOPMENT AND STRUCTURE OF THE FAMILY IN SOCIETY

What is a family?

There are two commonly used definitions of a family:

1   A family is a social unit made up of people related to each other by blood, birth or marriage.

2   A family is a social unit made up of people who support each other in one or several ways (e.g. socially, economically, psychologically) or whose members identify with each other in a supportive unit.

There is no such thing as a 'standard' family. In different parts of the world, different cultures tend to have completely different family structures. Although in some parts of the world one type of family dominates, it is not possible to generalise.

The extended family

In some cultures the extended family is strong. This means that parents, children, grandparents, aunts, uncles and cousins live together in a close-knit community. It might mean, for example, that aunts bring up the children of their brothers and sisters. Or it might mean that grandmothers are the most important people in the family and do most of the child-rearing. There is a huge variety in the way that extended families live.

THE ADVANTAGE OF THE EXTENDED FAMILY
Arguments in favour of the extended family are usually that family members can help and support each other.

THE DISADVANTAGES OF EXTENDED FAMILIES
The disadvantages of extended families are usually that they are often hierarchical. This means that it is difficult for some members of the family (often women) to develop as fully as they might. Although these families are often much more stable and offer emotional support, it may be argued that they can hold people back in their personal development.

The nuclear family

In other cultures the nuclear family is strong. This means that parents and children live separately from other relatives, sometimes at a distance from the rest of the family. Children may meet grandparents, aunts, uncles and cousins much less often.

THE ADVANTAGES OF THE NUCLEAR FAMILY
Arguments in favour of the nuclear family are usually that families can change and keep up with the times much more rapidly. They are often better off economically because they are much more mobile and seek job opportunities and career development.

THE DISADVANTAGES OF NUCLEAR FAMILIES
Arguments against nuclear families are usually that they are mobile, go-getting and fragile, because if anything goes wrong between the parents, they disintegrate. This causes the parents and children a great deal of emotional pain. In the UK, between

Children in families

Percentage of children living in different family types, Great Britain			
	1981	1992	2002
Couple families			
I child	18	18	17
2 children	41	39	37
3 or more children	29	27	24
Lone mother families			
I child	3	4	6
2 children	4	5	7
3 or more children	3	4	6
Lone father families			
I child	I	I	I
2 or more children	I	I	I
All children	100	100	100

Source: General Household Survey and Labour Force Survey, ONS

Fig 15.1 Different family structures

one-third and one-half of nuclear families are experiencing this, and the divorce rate is rising all the time. It is argued that getting on in life is being put before the emotional wellbeing of the family. Researchers are beginning to study these new kinds of family in order to find out more about how children in these families feel and adjust.

Disrupted family structures

When a family moves from one cultural setting to another, the family structure may be disrupted. This was shown in the UK in the 1960s by Wilmott and Young, who studied families in the East End of London. These families were of the extended family type, living in close proximity, in back-to-back houses. Grandmothers were very important in helping daughters with advice on bringing up children. Some of the families were then rehoused in new high-rise flats some distance away, in another part of London. The daughters spent most of their time on the bus, going back to visit their mothers. Family life was seriously disrupted.

It is important that those working with young children are aware of different family structures and how changes can disrupt them. Moving from one part of a town to another is perhaps not as deep-seated a disruption as moving from one country to another, but different families may experience such changes in different ways.

Other kinds of family

Apart from the two main types of family discussed above, the nuclear and the extended family, there are other kinds of family.

FAMILIES HEADED BY MONOGAMOUS PARTNERS

Relationships might be monogamous (i.e. two partners stay together unless they decide to part). Partners may be married, and if they part they will divorce. Both marriage and divorce will be legal contracts. Alternatively, partners may cohabit.

Monogamous relationships can be:

❖ heterosexual (the partners are a man and a woman);

❖ homosexual (the partners are two men or two women in a gay or lesbian relationship).

As yet little is known about the effects on children of growing up with gay or lesbian parents. However, it seems likely that the experiences of these families are similar to those of other minorities, such as children growing up with parents of different religions, or children growing up in a family where the parents are wheelchair users.

FAMILIES HEADED BY POLYGAMOUS PARTNERS

Relationships can be polygamous. This means that one partner has several partners of the opposite sex – for example, the man may have several wives. In the UK, this is illegal and is called bigamy. In other cultures it is an acceptable or usual family set-up.

FAMILIES IN AGRICULTURAL SOCIETIES

In agricultural societies children often help with chores on the farm.

NOMADIC FAMILIES

These families have no permanent town or village. Children in these families usually help with the packing up and unpacking at each stopping point.

FAMILIES IN INDUSTRIAL SOCIETIES

In industrial societies, children are often set to work in factories (child labour), or they may attend formal schools. Some researchers argue that the latter are really another kind of child labour. Both types of child labour concentrate on what society finds it useful for the child to do. Neither approach looks at what the child needs during childhood in order to fulfil their long-term potential and to become a person who can contribute to their society.

FAMILY RELATIONSHIPS

Divorce, cohabitation and remarriage have become more usual in modern life in the UK. Many children now experience changes in their family life, and this might be through the death of the parent or divorce and the subsequent reordering of families. Children throughout history have always had to adapt to changes, so there is nothing new in this. However, the kinds of changes that modern children are now dealing with are different. This is because fewer parents now die when their children are young; today remarriage may follow separation of the parents. The following generalisations reflect the changes that we see in society.

Parents:

❖ generally have fewer children than they used to;

❖ are more likely both to be working, to share home tasks, and to share child care.

Children:

❖ are more likely to grow up with a lone parent;

❖ are more likely to grow up with parents who are in a homosexual relationship than in previous times;

❖ may live in two households, and move across from one to the other during holidays or at weekends;

❖ may grow up with full brothers and sisters, or with half-brothers and half-sisters; with parents who cohabit or have remarried after divorce;

❖ may grow up with parents, step-parents, aunts, and so on;

❖ are more likely to grow up with foster parents or adoptive parents.

Over the last 20 years there has been a decrease in the number of couple families and an increase in lone-mother families.

Cohabitation

This involves adults living together as if married but without a legally binding contract. There has been a marked increase in the number of cohabiting couples in the UK; this can take different forms, including:

❖ a trial period before marriage;

❖ raising children in long-term relationships;

❖ one or both parties divorced.

WHY IS MARRIAGE LESS POPULAR?
Sociologists put forward several ideas to try to explain the rise in cohabitation and the

decline in marriage; these include the following:

❖ Marriage is expensive.

❖ Secularisation: the process in modern societies in which religious ideas and organisations tend to lose influence when faced with science and other forms of knowledge.

❖ Economic independence of women.

❖ Insecurity of employment.

❖ Awareness of divorce.

Reconstituted families

These are families in which one or both partners has children from a former relationship. Over one-third of all marriages now involve at least one partner who has been married previously.

The pressures faced by some children and families

All children and their families need:

❖ good quality core **public services,** such as health and education;

❖ **safe places to play**;

❖ **decent housing**;

❖ **leisure opportunities**;

❖ an **inclusive community**, free of crime, antisocial behaviour and racial harassment.

While the majority of children and young people are well cared for, there are **vulnerable children** and young people in every community. This vulnerability may be due to:

❖ **poverty** and **social exclusion**;

❖ they (or their parents) being **disabled**;

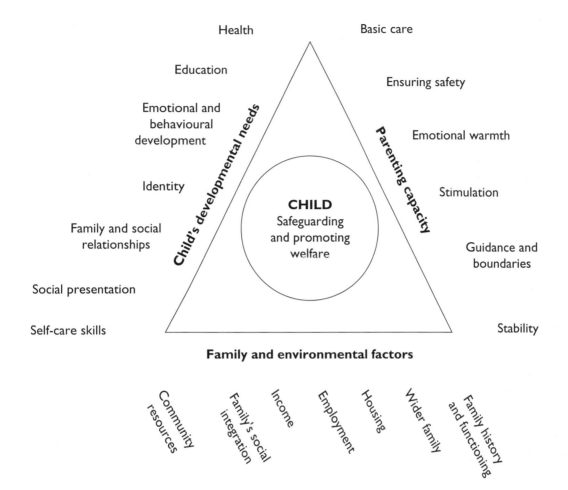

Fig 15.2 Framwork assessment triangle (from DoH, DfES and HO, 2000)

ACTIVITY: FAMILY STRUCTURES

Look at Figure 15.1 and answer the following questions:

1 What percentage of all children in Great Britain were living in lone-parent households in 1981?

2 What percentage of all children in Great Britain were living in lone-parent households in 2002?

3 Approximately what percentage increase has there been in 21 years?

Is one type of family structure best? There is no 'correct' model for a family structure. There is no 'best' way of bringing up children. However, some things do seem to be important for all families.

Always remember that each family is different from every other family.

> ## Guidelines for what all families need to give children
>
> ❧ Children need to be fed, clothed and sheltered, and to have sleep. This fulfils their **primary needs**.
>
> ❧ Children need to feel loved and to learn to love. This means they need some reliable people in their lives to show them affection and warmth, and who enjoy receiving their love and warmth in return. This is **nurture**.
>
> ❧ Families introduce children to their culture. This means that through their family children learn what people expect of them. The way this comes about varies in different parts of the world, and will be different in different families, even within one culture.

❧ **diminished parenting capacity** – some parents are isolated or inexperienced, or caught up with alcoholism or drug misuse, physical or mental illness;

❧ **parental conflict** or **violence**;

❧ **living away from their families**, excluded from school or with special educational needs.

THE EFFECTS OF SOCIAL AND ECONOMIC DEPRIVATION ON FAMILIES

During the nineteenth century, people were labelled as either the deserving or the undeserving poor, and the Poor Law of 1834 gave relief only to the deserving poor. The focus was on the relief of poverty, since it was not thought that poverty could be eradicated. It was during this period that the word **charity** was coined. During the twentieth century the emphasis changed, and the idea that poverty could be eradicated, given the political will, was taken seriously. The introduction of the **welfare state** aimed to eradicate poverty.

Poverty

Britain is currently near the bottom of the European league in **child poverty**. The only countries that have virtually no child poverty are mainly Nordic countries – Denmark, Sweden, Norway, Finland and Holland. One in three of Britain's children is born poor, according to the most recent figures and using the definition of relative poverty below. Poverty can be **absolute** or **relative**:

❧ **Absolute poverty** exists when people die from starvation and related diseases, for example in some countries in the developing world.

❧ **Relative poverty** exists when some people in a country are very rich compared with others. In the UK, a family is said to be living in poverty when its income is less than half the national average weekly wage.

There is also relative poverty between children growing up in poor and rich countries; this gap is widening.

In the UK in the twenty-first century there is most poverty among families with young children, disabled people and the elderly. A quarter of families with children under 5 years now live in poverty. Lack of employment is an important factor, together with the high cost of housing, nutritious food, clothing and transport.

Social exclusion

Poverty needs to be understood not just in terms of how little money some people have, but also in the **effects** that this has on several key aspects of life. **Social exclusion** describes how being poor severely limits people's ability to participate in the everyday life of their society. A child or young person experiencing social exclusion, for example, might be:

* living in poverty;
* experiencing life in a high-crime neighbourhood;
* living in poor housing conditions;
* experiencing higher incidences of accidents and ill health;
* attending a low-achieving school.

A **social exclusion approach** to tackling the causes of poverty focuses on the links between unemployment, poor work-related skills, educational underachievement, crime, ill health and substandard housing – all of which have a negative impact on people's lives. In some places whole communities are blighted by these interlinked problems.

The government has pledged to eradicate child poverty by 2020.

Children in need

The **Children Act 1989** defines '**children in need**' in broad and developmental terms as children:

* unlikely to achieve or maintain a reasonable standard of health and development without services;

* whose health and development will be significantly impaired without services;
* who are disabled.

In order to respond to the needs and aspirations of children in need, an assessment framework was developed which enables an increased understanding of what is happening to a child in relation to their parents and the wider context of family and community (Department of Health 2000). The interaction of the three areas – the child's **developmental needs**, the **parenting capacity** and the **family and environmental factors** – will have a direct impact on the current and long-term well-being of a child.

If a family has too little income to keep themselves, the Social Security Act 1986 provides a safety net and social security payments are made. Contributory benefits are available to those who have paid National Insurance during periods of employment. Non-contributory benefits are either:

* **available as of right:** Child Benefit is payable to all mothers, and Income Support is available to families provided there is no other source of income;

* **means tested:** family income is calculated and, if it is higher than a certain level, no benefit will be paid. Because the forms are complicated to fill in and people feel anxious about the process, these benefits are often not claimed. Examples of this type of benefit include help with rent for elderly people, or family tax credit for families where a parent is working full-time but the income falls below a certain level.

The Department for Work and Pensions is responsible for a range of benefits and

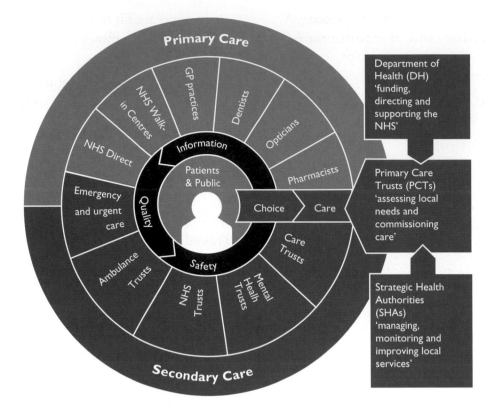

Fig 15.3 How the NHS works (in England)

services for families (the internet address is www.dwp.gov.uk).

Poverty causes a poor quality of life. It brings stress and sometimes also despair. These can affect social relationships and health.

Housing

The welfare state made cheap, rentable council housing a priority. During the market-forces approach of the 1980s, people were encouraged to buy their council houses, and local authorities have not been permitted to build more. This has meant that:

❧ government funding has supported **housing associations** (these are voluntary organisations) to develop alternatives to council housing (funding

for these has been reduced over recent years, however);

❧ there is less cheap **rented property** available;

❧ nearly two-thirds of people have **mortgages** and are buying their own homes; this has led to increased homelessness through evictions when people cannot keep up mortgage payments;

❧ some families rent in the **private sector**, but may also be evicted if they cannot keep up with payments;

❧ some families live with relatives in **overcrowded** circumstances;

❧ some families have to move into **temporary housing** – constant moves mean a lack of stability for children;

❖ some families are unsuitably placed in **bed-and-breakfast accommodation**, with inadequate space for basic cooking and washing facilities.

Different problems exist in rural and urban areas. In the UK fewer children live in the country, but the children of low-paid casual farm workers often grow up in poverty. They are also often lonely and isolated.

Children in urban settings (located in the inner city rather than in the suburbs) are more likely to experience poverty, a lack of facilities for play, fewer swimming pools and parks, and poor school buildings. Because of the difficult conditions in many urban areas, teachers, doctors and other professionals do not always stay in their jobs for long. Children experience a lack of continuity in their care.

Travellers

People who are travellers or nomads have always been viewed with suspicion by people who are settled in agricultural or industrial lifestyles. (Henry VIII banished travellers in the UK in the sixteenth century.)

❖ Since the Criminal Justice Act 1995 became law, travellers of all kinds (sometimes incorrectly all grouped together and called gypsies) are under threat in the UK. This is despite the fact that in July 1988 three Appeal Court Judges ruled that gypsies are a distinct racial group who have kept their identity within the meaning of the 1976 Race Relations Act. The Criminal Justice Act has drastically reduced stopping places for travellers.

❖ Because it is difficult for travellers to register with GPs, health care can be inconsistent. Education can also be fragmented. This is because most local authorities do not take account of the needs of travellers when planning services.

❖ Early childhood practitioners need to implement the **equal opportunities policy** and **code of practice** devised in their work setting. They can incorporate aspects of the traveller's way of life when setting up the home area (e.g. making a caravan). This helps children to focus on the positive aspects of the travelling life.

Traveller Education Services provide support for all groups of travellers – for example, Gypsies and Romanies, including English, Welsh and Scottish Romanies, and Irish and Scottish travellers; some Traveller Education Services work with European Romanies seeking asylum.

INTEGRATED SERVICES: EDUCATION AND CARE

Young children are not made up of separate parts: a child is a whole person. It is inappropriate to talk about either education of or caring for young children. Instead the term 'integrated early years settings' is used to describe places which provide education and care for young children. Children need good physical and health care as much as

---

The journey of life

Children should not be described as 'pre' or 'under'; they are not pre-linguistic, pre-reading, pre-number or pre-anything – this suggests that they are in some way deficient. It is much more useful to think of childhood as part of the continuum of life. Not all children reach the same point on the continuum in the same way or at the same age, but every child is moving on that continuum: starting life as a baby, becoming an 8-year-old, a teenager and an adult. Just as every life begins at birth, so it ends with death.

they need new, interesting and stimulating experiences.

THE ROLE OF THE STATUTORY SERVICES IN RELATION TO CHILDREN AND FAMILIES

A statutory service is one that is provided by the state. Some statutory services are provided by **central government** and funded from central taxation, such as the National Health Service (NHS). Others are provided by **local government** and funded by a combination of local and central taxation (education and social service departments).

The statutory sector
This sector comprises:

❖ **central government departments** in which policy is devised by a Secretary of State (who is an MP), helped by Ministers of State (also MPs) and managed by the Permanent Secretary (a civil servant);

❖ **executive agencies** (e.g. the Benefits Agency which issues social security payments) contracted by central government departments to deliver services;

❖ **local government departments** chaired by an elected member of the local council and administered by a paid officer (e.g. the Director of Education);

❖ **local health authorities and trusts** led by a chairperson and managed by a chief executive.

Statutory services are provided by the government. The services that are provided are set by laws passed in Parliament.

Health services for children and their families

The government's Department of Health is responsible for providing health care through the **National Health Service** (NHS), which was set up in 1948 to provide free health care

to the entire population. Since then there have been many changes and some services are no longer free – for example, dental care, prescriptions and ophthalmic services. However, there are exemptions to these charges, so that certain groups of people are not disadvantaged by being on low incomes. The following groups are exempt:

❖ children under 16 or in full-time education;

❖ pregnant women or women with a baby under 1 year;

❖ families receiving income support or family credit.

(Chapter 11 covers child health surveillance and the role of the primary care team.)

THE NATIONAL SERVICE FRAMEWORK FOR CHILDREN, YOUNG PEOPLE AND MATERNITY SERVICES

This Framework is one part of the government's overall strategy to tackle child poverty. It was set up by the Department of Health in 2004 and divides the services it covers into three types:

❖ **universal services:** used by all children, young people and their families, and those who are about to become parents;

❖ **targeted services:** services designed to encourage their use by people who usually do not use them;

❖ **specialist services:** for children and young people with difficulties or medical conditions which are identified as needing specialist care, treatment or support.

In **Part 1** of the Framework, there are five **standards** which cover services for *all* children, young people and parents or carers:

❖ Standard 1: Promoting health and wellbeing, identifying needs and intervening early (this includes the Child Health Promotion Programme, covered in Chapter 11).

✤ Standard 2: Supporting parenting.

✤ Standard 3: Child, young person and family-centred services.

✤ Standard 4: Growing up into adulthood.

✤ Standard 5: Safeguarding and promoting the welfare of children and young people.

In **Part 2**, there are five standards which cover services for children and young people who need specialist care, treatment or support:

✤ Standard 6: Children and young people who are ill.

✤ Standard 7: Children in hospital.

✤ Standard 8: Disabled children and young people and those with complex health needs.

✤ Standard 9: The mental health and psychological wellbeing of children and young people.

✤ Standard 10: Medicines for children and young people.

Part 3 sets out the standard for women expecting a baby and their partners and families, and for new parents:

✤ Standard 11: Maternity services.

This National Service Framework health promotion strategy must link to programmes to reduce the effect of **poverty** and the **environment** on children's health and wellbeing, in particular to:

✤ help parents find and stay in learning or work, including having **high-quality, affordable child care** for both preschool and school-age children) and child-friendly working practices;

✤ ensure that families are made aware of the **Healthy Start Scheme** and encouraged to apply for it if they qualify – Healthy Start will provide low-income pregnant women and young families with advice on diet and nutrition, local support to eat healthily and vouchers to buy healthy food;

✤ ensure families with low incomes are supported to claim all **benefits** to which they are entitled;

✤ **provide support** for groups especially likely to be living in poverty, for example teenage parents, families with disabled children, and those who are homeless;

✤ ensure as far as possible that **local authority accommodation** for families with children is not damp or cold (in line with the cross-government fuel poverty strategy), has adequate space for play and privacy, and at least one working smoke alarm and a carbon monoxide detector, where appropriate;

✤ minimise **environmental pollution** in residential areas and around nurseries and schools.

Social care services

Until recently children's social services have generally been provided jointly with services for adults, via social services departments within local authorities. However, structural changes in response to the **Children Act 2004** mean that, from April 2006, **education and social care services** for children will be brought together under a **director of children's services** in each local authority.

Social services provide a range of care and support for children and families, including:

* families where children are assessed as being **in need** (including disabled children);

* children who may be suffering '**significant harm**';

* children who require **looking after** by the local authority (through fostering or residential care);

* children who are placed for **adoption**.

Social workers with responsibilities for children and families may work in the following areas:

* **Safeguarding and promoting the welfare of children:** in the great majority of cases, children are safeguarded while remaining at home by social services working with their parents, family members and other significant adults in the child's life to make the child safe, and to promote his or her development within the family setting. For a small minority of children, where it is agreed at a child protection conference that a child is at continuing risk of significant harm, the child's name will be placed on a **child protection register**. Social services are then responsible for coordinating an inter-agency plan to safeguard the child, which sets out and draws upon the contribution of family members, professionals and other agencies. In a few cases, social services, in consultation with other agencies and professionals, may judge that a child's welfare cannot be adequately safeguarded if he or she remains at home. In these circumstances they may apply to the court for a **care order**, which commits the child to the care of the local authority. Where the child is thought to be in immediate danger, social services may apply to the court for an **emergency protection order**, which enables the child to be placed under the protection of the local authority for a maximum of 8 days.

* **Supporting disabled children:** social workers must provide a range of services to families with disabled children to minimise the impact of any disabilities and enable them to live as normal a life as possible. Typically they provide **short-term breaks** in foster families or residential units, **support services** in the home and, increasingly, assistance for disabled children to participate in out-of-school and leisure activities in the community alongside their non-disabled peers.

* **Supporting looked-after children:** where the local authority looks after a child following the imposition of a care order, or accommodates a child with the agreement of their parents, it is the role of the social worker to ensure that adequate arrangements are made for the child's care and that a plan is made, in partnership with the child, their parents and other agencies, so that the child's future is secure. Children are generally looked after in foster care. A minority will be cared for in children's homes and some by prospective adoptive parents. *All* looked-after children will have a social worker and carers (e.g. foster carers, residential care staff) responsible for their day-to-day care, who should be involved in making plans or decisions about the young person.

Early years provision: integrated care and education for children

Recent legislation has led to a number of reforms in the delivery of care and education to children. While the school system remains largely unchanged, the statutory services for children from **birth to 5 years** are becoming increasingly **integrated**. This involves a new structure for the delivery of an integrated service, to include:

❖ Children's trusts;

❖ The Early Years Foundation Stage;

❖ Sure Start programmes;

❖ Children's centres.

The role of local authorities

Local authorities must:

❖ improve the outcomes of all children under 5 years and close the gaps between those with the poorest outcomes and the rest, by ensuring that early childhood services are integrated, proactive and accessible;

❖ take the **lead role** in facilitating the child care market to ensure it meets the needs of **working parents**, in particular those on low incomes and with disabled children;

❖ ensure people have access to the full range of **information** they may need as a parent;

❖ introduce the **Early Years Foundation Stage** to support the delivery of quality integrated education and care for children from **birth to 5 years** (see below);

❖ work within a reformed, simplified, child care and early years regulation **framework** to reduce bureaucracy and focus on raising quality.

Local authorities in England have a statutory duty to improve the **Every Child Matters outcomes** for *all* children under 5 years and to reduce inequalities in achievements, through helping them to access integrated, proactive early childhood services. In discharging these duties, local authorities and their partners in the **NHS** and **Jobcentre Plus** work together and have regard to statutory guidance which will indicate how services will be delivered through **children's centres**. Local authorities must improve the wellbeing of young children and reduce inequalities in relation to the five outcomes laid out in Every Child Matters:

❖ **Be healthy – physical and mental health and emotional wellbeing:** sexually healthy; healthy lifestyles; choose not to take illegal drugs.

Parents, carers and families promote healthy choices.

❖ **Stay safe – protection from harm and neglect:** safe from maltreatment, neglect, violence and sexual exploitation; safe from accidental injury and death; safe from bullying and discrimination; safe from crime and antisocial behaviour in and out of school; have security, stability and be cared for.

Parents, carers and families provide safe homes and stability.

❖ **Enjoy and achieve – education, training and recreation:** ready for school; attend and enjoy school; achieve stretching national educational standards at primary school; achieve personal and social development and enjoy recreation; achieve stretching national educational standards at secondary school.

Parents, carers and families support learning.

- **Make a positive contribution to society – support for the vulnerable and positive outlooks:** engage in decision making and support the community and environment; engage in law-abiding and positive behaviour in and out of school; develop positive relationships and choose not to bully and discriminate; develop self-confidence and successfully deal with significant life changes and challenges; develop enterprising behaviour.

Parents, carers and families promote positive behaviour.

- **Social and economic wellbeing – parents in employment:** engage in further education, employment or training on leaving school, ready for employment; live in decent homes and sustainable communities; access to transport and material goods; live in households free from low income.

Parents, carers and families are supported to be economically active.

CHILDREN'S TRUSTS

Children's trusts are new organisations which bring together health, education and social services for children, young people and families. Some take on responsibility for *all* children's services, from child protection to speech therapy, while others will focus on particularly vulnerable children, such as those with disabilities. At first, most trusts will commission *local* children's services. The trusts will employ a range of professionals, for example:

- social workers;
- family support workers;
- health visitors;
- school nurses;
- educational psychologists;
- speech and language therapists;
- child and adolescent mental health professionals.
- educators, head teachers

Children's trusts are underpinned by the **Children Act 2004** duty to cooperate and to focus on improving outcomes for all children and young people. Trusts can also include **Sure Start** local programmes. Other local partners may include: housing, leisure services, the police, youth justice, independent sector organisations such as voluntary organisations, and community sector organisations such as churches. They will be led by local '**children's champions**', whose role is to **advocate** the interests of children across different services.

Ingegrated childhood services

Integrated early childhood services must include:

- **early years provision** (integrated childcare and early education);
- **social services**;
- relevant **health services** (e.g. health visitors, antenatal, post-natal care);
- services provided by **Jobcentre Plus** to assist parents to obtain work;
- **information services**.

THE EARLY YEARS FOUNDATION STAGE (EYFS)

This is the new, single, quality framework for children from birth to 5 years. All settings which offer provision for children from **birth** until the point when they begin **Key Stage 1** (subject to certain exceptions) will be required to deliver **integrated care and education** in line with the **EYFS**. The government has adopted the term '**early years provision**' to refer to integrated care and education. The free entitlement to nursery education will be recast as an entitlement to early years provision.

SURE START

Sure Start is an extensive government programme launched in the late 1990s as a cornerstone of the government's drive to eradicate child poverty in 20 years, and to halve it within a decade. The first Sure Start local programmes were established in 1999, with the aim of improving the health and wellbeing of families and children from before birth to 4 years, so that they can flourish at home and when they begin school. These programmes started in the most disadvantaged areas in the UK. Sure Start local programmes are delivered by local **partnerships** and work with parents-to-be, parents and children to promote the physical, intellectual and social development of babies and young children. All Sure Start local programmes are to become **Sure Start children's centres** by 2006.

Sure Start programmes have the following four key objectives:

1 **Improving social and emotional development:** in particular by supporting early bonding between parents and their children, helping families function and enabling early identification and support of children with emotional and behavioural difficulties.

2 **Improving health:** in particular by supporting parents in caring for their children to promote healthy development before and after birth.

3 **Improving children's ability to learn:** in particular by providing high-quality environments and child care that promote early learning and provide stimulating and enjoyable play, improving language skills and ensuring early identification of children with special needs.

4 **Strengthening families and communities:** in particular by involving families in building the community's capacity to sustain the programme and create pathways out of **social exclusion**.

The emphasis is on prevention in order to reduce social exclusion later on, and to improve the chances of younger children through early access to education, health services, family support and advice on nurturing. These projects include support for:

- ❖ special educational needs;
- ❖ outreach services and home visiting;
- ❖ families and parents;
- ❖ good-quality play, learning and child care;
- ❖ primary and community health care;
- ❖ advice about child health and development;
- ❖ advice about parent health.

CHILDREN'S CENTRES

The majority of children's centres will be developed from Sure Start local programmes, Neighbourhood Nurseries Early Excellence Centres and Maintained Nursery Schools. The government is committed to delivering a Sure Start children's centre for *every* community by 2010. Sure Start children's centres are places where children under 5 years and their families can receive seamless, holistic, integrated services and information, and where they can access help from multidisciplinary teams of professionals. They offer the following services:

- good-quality **early learning** combined with full day care provision for children (minimum 10 hours a day, 5 days a week, 48 weeks a year);

- good-quality **teacher input** to lead the development of learning within the centre;

- **child and family health services**, including antenatal services;

- **parental outreach**;

- **family support** services;

- a base for a **childminder network**;

- support for children and parents with **special needs**;

- effective links with **Jobcentre Plus** to support parents/carers who wish to consider training or employment.

In more advantaged areas, although local authorities will have flexibility in which services they provide to meet local needs, all Sure Start children's centres will have to provide a *minimum* range of services, including:

- appropriate support and outreach services for parents/carers and children who have been identified as in need of them;

- information and advice to parents/carers on a range of subjects, including: local child care, looking after babies and young children, local early years provision (child care and early learning), education services for children aged 3–4 years;

- support for childminders;

- drop-in sessions and other activities for children and carers at the centre;

- links to Jobcentre Plus services.

MAINTAINED NURSERY SCHOOLS

These are part of the provision made by some local education authorities. Maintained nursery schools, nursery classes and nursery units are all expected to become part of the Sure Start children's centres programme.

- Maintained nursery schools offer either full-time or part-time places for children of 3 years to the equivalent of the end of the Reception Year. Exceptionally, children may start at 2½ years, but only if there is a recommendation and joint decision by the education, health and social services departments.

- There is a head teacher who has specialist training in the age group, and there are graduate trained teachers working with qualified nursery nurses.

- Adult-to-child ratios are 1 to 10 in England and Wales, but 1 to 13 in Scotland.

NURSERY CLASSES AND NURSERY UNITS

- Nursery classes are attached to primary schools. The head teacher of the primary school may or may not be an expert in early years education.

- The class teacher will be a trained nursery teacher, who will work alongside a fully qualified nursery nurse.

- Nursery units are usually in a separate building, with a separate coordinator.

- They are larger than a nursery class, but will have the same adult-to-child ratio as the nursery class – which is 1 to 15. Like the nursery class, these units come under the management of the head teacher, who, again, may or may not be trained to work with this age group.

Extended services

In June 2005 the government published *Extended Schools: Access to Opportunities and Services for All*, a prospectus outlining the vision of extended schools. This vision is for all children to be able to access through schools by 2010:

- high-quality '**wraparound**' childcare provided by the school site or through other local providers, available 8 a.m. to 6 p.m. all year round;

- a varied **menu of activities** on offer, such as homework clubs and study support, sport, music tuition, special interest clubs and volunteering;

- **parenting support**, including information sessions for parents at key transition points, parenting programmes and family learning sessions;

- swift and easy referral to a wide range of **specialist support** services, such as speech and language therapy, family support services and behaviour support;

- providing wider community access to **ICT and sports and arts facilities**, including adult learning.

The voluntary sector

- This sector is made up of voluntary organisations. These tend to operate with a mixture of paid and volunteer workers.

- Voluntary organisations are often administered by a core of paid staff. Volunteers are then trained by the core staff to help the organisation in a variety of ways.

- There are both national voluntary organisations (e.g. Early Education, formerly called BAECE) and local voluntary

---

organisations. The local branches of an organisation are not necessarily closely linked with the national or head office branch of the organisation – for example, local groups of the Preschool Learning Alliance.

- Voluntary organisations often arise because:

  1 there is a gap in services (e.g. the Salvation Army provides hostels for homeless people);

  2 there is a need for a campaign both to alert the public to an issue and to push for action to be taken (e.g. Shelter, a pressure group for the homeless).

- Some charities receive government grants, but not all. In addition to donations, many have fee income from services they provide.

THE UK VOLUNTARY SECTOR

Community nurseries

- These are often funded by voluntary organisations, such as Barnardos, and function in similar ways to family centres.

- They sometimes offer full-time care, but more usually part-time care.

- Some charitable trusts offer integrated provision to children and their families, for instance Barnardos, the Royal National Institute of the Blind (RNIB), SENSE and SCOPE.

- These might be home-based or parent-and-toddler groups, community nurseries, day schools or residential special schools, or groups supporting children in mainstream education.

- The Preschool Learning Alliance was established in 1961, when there was concern from parents at the lack of nursery education available. Parents ran these playgroups, and the education and development of both parent and child were emphasised. (Not all playgroups, however, are affiliated to the Preschool Learning Alliance.)

✤ Preschools (these used to be called playgroups) are usually part-time, offering perhaps two or three half-day sessions a week, often in a church hall. This type of provision is often the only one available in rural areas.

The private sector

✤ This sector comprises businesses that make profits.

✤ In education, this includes private nurseries.

✤ In social services, the private sector includes old people's homes run by big chains and by individuals. In health there are private hospitals.

✤ Private nurseries, hospitals and schools are legally required to be registered and inspected, and to follow guidelines laid down in laws and by local authorities.

Private nursery schools and private day nurseries are still available for those parents who can afford them, although some financial support is available through government schemes. In addition, there are workplace nurseries, which subsidise places in order that staff and students in institutions can take up this form of care.

THE UK PRIVATE SECTOR

Private day nurseries, private nursery schools, preparatory schools and kindergartens

✤ These are required to appoint qualified staff and to meet the **National Day Care Standards**.

✤ The government is concerned that child care should be affordable for families, and has introduced a family tax credit to support the New Deal (an employment scheme).

Childminders, nannies and grandparents

✤ Children are looked after in their own homes by grandparents or nannies, or in the childminder's home.

✤ Childminders are offered training through the National Childminding Association and CACHE.

✤ Nannies sometimes live with a family, but not always. Sometimes they look after children from several different families.

(For more information on the roles of childminders and nannies, see Chapter 14.)

MULTIDISCIPLINARY WORK

Children gain when parents, midwives, health visitors, nurses, doctors, nursery teachers, social workers, play therapists, educational psychologists, hospital teachers, experts in special educational needs and members of voluntary organisations all work together. Mutual respect within the team is important: on a course for nursery nurses, 24 out of 28 said they felt deeply valued by the teachers and head teachers they worked with. However, they also said that other teaching staff in their primary and secondary schools did not always understand the depth of training they had received. Early childhood practitioners make an invaluable contribution because they work across the widest range of settings. Being a good networker will enable you to bring people together in the common cause of getting the best for young children and their families.

15

LEGAL ISSUES IN CHILD CARE PROVISION

Knowing the law relating to early years education and care

It is important for early childhood practitioners to be aware of those laws which relate to their work, both in the UK and internationally. It is illegal not to obey the law, of course. It is also important to understand the spirit and thinking that went into making the law.

NB The laws relating to equal opportunities and discrimination are described in Chapter 1.

How the laws are made in Britain

Britain is a **democracy**. This means it is governed by a body that is elected by the people. There are different types of democracy. For example, the USA, France and Germany are presidential democracies (an elected president heads an elected government). Sweden, Holland and the UK are constitutional monarchies (an unelected king or queen heads an elected government. In Britain, there are two ways to make a law:

1. **By statute law:** this is legislation which is passed by Parliament. A Bill goes through different stages in both the House of Commons and the House of Lords:

   ❖ First reading: the Bill is formally introduced to Parliament.

   ❖ Second reading: the general principles are debated and voted on.

   ❖ Committee stage: a committee debates every clause of the Bill and votes on it.

   ❖ Report stage: the Bill is debated again in Parliament and more amendments can be made.

   ❖ Third reading: the Bill is again debated and a final vote is taken.

   ❖ The monarch gives Royal Assent (usually a formality).

   ❖ The Bill becomes law as an Act of Parliament.

Following an Act of Parliament secondary legislation is required to show how the law is to be applied. This is written in two kinds of document:

   ❖ Rules of Court;

   ❖ Regulations.

2. **By case law:** this is legislation which results from rulings made in court. This is sometimes called common law. Judgement can be made in the:

   ❖ High Court;

   ❖ Court of Appeal;

   ❖ House of Lords.

Decisions made in these courts are binding on the decisions the lower courts can make.

Laws exist to protect people and to specify the ways in which we must all behave – someone who breaks the law acts illegally. Almost every aspect of our lives is in some way touched by laws.

   ❖ Private law concerns family relationships between children and their families.

   ❖ Public law is about the way the state provides services, for example child protection.

Laws that affect children

There is a checklist which the court must consider when making decisions about children:

1. The wishes and feelings of the child are considered.

2. The physical, emotional and educational needs of the child are considered.

3. The likely effects of changing the child's circumstances are thought through.

4. The child's age, sex, background and anything else that might be relevant are discussed.

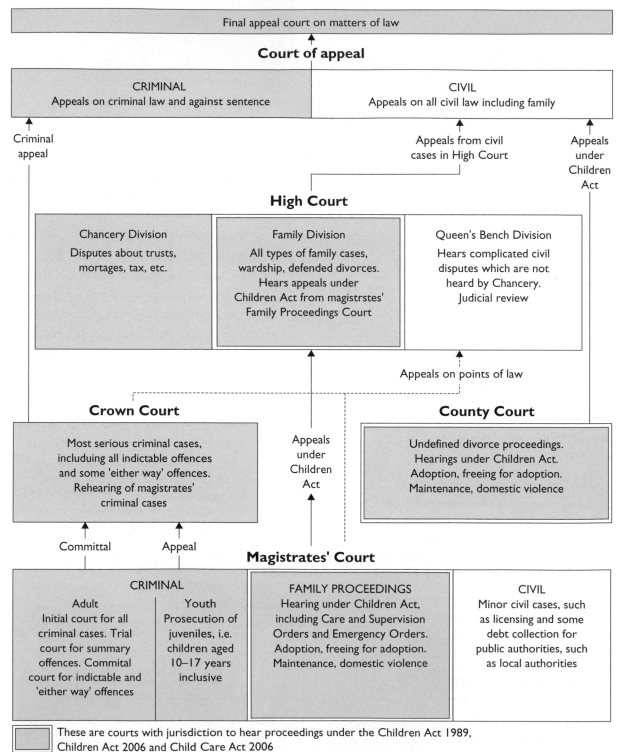

Fig 15.4 The UK Court system

5 Whether the child might come to significant harm or is at risk of harm is important.

6 There is discussion on whether the parents are able to meet the child's needs.

7 The court is required to discuss a range of powers that are available in making the decision.

Local government in the UK

No country can be governed entirely by central departments; some degree of decentralisation of power is required. This is why it is necessary for local government to exist. Local departments in local government are often called local authorities. In the UK, local authorities are divided into:

❖ **England and Wales:** district council; county council; unitary council;

❖ **Scotland:** district councils;

❖ **Northern Ireland:** boards.

In every local authority there are a council and councillors who are locally elected every 4 years. The power and influence of local government have been reduced since 1976. For example, state schools can now opt out of local authority control and become grant-maintained, obtaining their funding directly from central government.

Every local authority has a local education department and a social services department. In Scotland, social services are provided through social work departments. In Northern Ireland there are education and library boards, and health and social services departments.

How British democracy has developed in recent history

In the mid-1940s the major parts of the welfare state that we recognise today were introduced. The thinking behind this was that everyone should be entitled to free health care and treatment, free education and a minimum weekly income above the poverty line. By the 1970s there was anxiety about the ever-increasing financial demands that these entitlements made on the state. In 1979 the government of the day started to move away from the welfare-state approach. Margaret Thatcher, who was then prime minister, called the welfare state the 'nanny state', and she thought that people should take more responsibility for their own lives. There was a change towards policies based on market forces. The thinking behind this approach was that:

❖ people would be taxed at a low rate;

❖ public services should provide only a safety net;

❖ people should be given more choice;

❖ if services were forced to compete in the marketplace they could be made more streamlined and more efficient.

The following changes were brought in as a result:

❖ Eye tests were no longer free to all.

❖ Dental treatment and check-up charges were significantly increased.

❖ The school meals service was decreased.

❖ Private pensions were encouraged.

There are no simple answers as to whether a well-developed welfare state or a free market economy is the best option. Depending on someone's political persuasion, one approach would be favoured more than the other.

Government by consent

Sometimes laws are of historic importance just because they take a first and important step towards a goal. Laws work best when the spirit behind them is agreed by most people living in a democracy. This is called government by consent. As we have seen, by the mid-1970s most people agreed that discriminatory behaviour was unacceptable on the grounds of someone's sex or race. However, legislation on discriminatory behaviour towards people's disabilities has not yet assumed the same importance in the public consciousness.

Occasionally a law which is passed in Parliament does not carry the consent of the majority of people. This leads to demonstrations and even riots. Take, for example, the controversy concerning the introduction of the community charge (then called the poll tax) in 1990.

The Children Act 1989

When the welfare state was first set up in 1944 its services were quite separate from each other. The Seebohm Report (1968) found that some families were being visited by a whole range of professionals: for example, a social worker for the parents, a different social worker for an elderly relative and a speech therapist or a social worker to support the child with a hearing impairment. These professionals did not coordinate their work and often did not even know about each other! As a result, the Social Services Act 1970 set out to develop links between the different departments that have contact with children and their families. The Children Act 1989 took this further still and there have been far-reaching changes in the way young children are cared for and protected.

❖ **Private areas** covered by the Act involve parenthood matters and arrangements following parental separation.

❖ **Public areas** covered by the Act involve services provided for children and their families (e.g. child protection, care and supervision).

THE CHILDREN ACT: A NEW APPROACH TO PARENTHOOD

The Children Act introduced the phrase **'parental responsibility'**. As well as rights, parents now have responsibilities.

1   Sometimes people who are not the natural parents can be given parental responsibility.

2   Parenthood is seen as 'an enduring commitment'. Parents are encouraged to stay involved in bringing up their children, even if the children are not living with them.

3   Parental responsibility can be shared, for example between divorced parents or between biological parents and foster parents.

The Children Act aimed to strengthen the relationships within the many different kinds of family that exist.

STATUTORY SERVICES UNDER THE CHILDREN ACT

The spirit behind the Children Act is that families should be respected and given help in bringing up their children. The Act promotes the care and health of the child as paramount, while seeking to limit professional 'enforced intervention' in favour of partnership with parents. Like all other landmark legislation before it, the Children Act is only a beginning.

Under the Children Act, statutory services for children are based on five linked principles:

1 **Children in need.** Services may be provided for all children, but they must be provided for all 'children in need'. Parents, in addition, must be helped to demonstrate 'parental responsibility'. Children in need are:

   ❧ children with a disability;

   ❧ children whose health or development is likely to be significantly impaired, likely to be further impaired or unlikely to be maintained;

   ❧ children without the provision of services.

Disability, in this context, is defined as being blind, deaf or dumb, having a mental disorder or being handicapped by illness, injury, congenital deformity or any other disease or disorder as may be prescribed. It is important to appreciate the difference between 'children in need', as defined above, and 'children with special educational needs' (see Chapter 1). Children in need are given a degree of support that goes beyond that given by the education service.

2 **Partnership with parents.** Services must emphasise partnership by actively seeking participation, offering real choices and involving parents in decisions. For example, it should be usual for parents to join case conferences. Whenever possible, help should be given by the local authority on a voluntary basis (it should not be imposed or enforced). For example, the parent should be encouraged by the authority to decide when it is best for a child to go into a foster home.

3 **Race, culture, religion and language.** Services must link with children's experiences in relation to these areas. In work settings staff should not discriminate, and the whole setting should reflect a multicultural atmosphere (see Chapter 1). Foster parents, childminders and other service providers are required to show their support for this principle.

4 **The coordination of services.** Services are required to coordinate with each other in order to support a family. The idea is that families should not be passed from agency to agency. Instead one agency (e.g. the local education authority) should request the help of another department.

5 **Meeting the identified needs of an individual family.** Services must be geared to meet the identified needs of a particular family. Local authorities are therefore required to gather information and to plan services which are based on local needs. The aim is to produce a needs-led service: that is, to make the service fit the people, rather than making people fit the service.

The Children (Scotland) Act 1995

The Children (Scotland) Act 1995 has three fundamental child-centred principles, which are similar to those of the Children Act 1989:

1 **The welfare of the child is paramount:** the child's interests are always the most important factor, and will always be the deciding factor in any legal decision.

2 **The views of the child must be taken into account:** courts dealing

with any matters relating to children's welfare must take account of the child's views. This includes the child's right to attend their own hearing.

3 **No order principle:** courts and children's hearings need to be convinced that making an order is better than not making one.

The Children (Northern Ireland) Order 1995

The Children (Northern Ireland) Order 1995 came into force in October 1996 and is closely modelled on the Children Act 1989, but contains certain differences:

❖ Under the Order, those who provide day care and child-minding for children under 12 years are required to register.

❖ The Order does not provide for fees to be imposed on those providing child-minding and day care services.

❖ The Order requires all children's homes to be registered, irrespective of the number of children being accommodated.

❖ The Order removes most of the legal disadvantages of illegitimacy (in England and Wales these had been removed by the Family Law Reform Act 1987).

Adoption and Children Act 2002

This act aligns adoption law with the Children Act 1989 to make the child's welfare the paramount consideration in all decisions to do with adoption. It includes:

❖ Provisions to encourage more people to adopt **looked-after children** by helping to ensure that the support they need is available.

❖ A new, clear duty on local authorities to provide an **adoption support service** and a new right for people affected by adoption to request and receive an assessment of their needs for adoption support services.

❖ Provisions to enable **unmarried couples** to apply to adopt jointly, thereby widening the pool of potential adoptive parents.

❖ Stronger safeguards for adoption by improving the legal controls on inter-country adoption, arranging adoptions and advertising children for adoption.

❖ A new 'special guardianship' order to provide security and permanence for children who cannot return to their birth families, but for whom adoption is not the most suitable option.

❖ A duty on local authorities to arrange advocacy services for looked-after children and young people leaving care in the context of complaints.

The Children Act 2004

The Children Act 2004 does not replace or even amend much of the Children Act 1989. Instead it sets out the process for integrating services to children so that every child can achieve the five outcomes laid out in the Every Child Matters legislation (see page 615).

The Childcare Act 2006

The **Childcare Act 2006** enshrines in law parents' legitimate expectation of accessible, high-quality child care and services for children under 5 years and their families. The needs of children and their parents are at the heart of the Act, with local authorities as the *champions* of parents and children, ensuring that their views are heard in the planning and delivery of services which reflect the real needs of families.

INFORMATION FOR FAMILIES

Families need information about a wide range of topics. Much information can be gained from the media – radio, television and newspapers. The internet is also a valuable source of information, but not every family has easy access to computing and Internet connections. The sources of information generally available are outlined below:

* **Public library:** Usually with Internet services; local information about a wide range of services for children and families; also a reference section with books giving information on benefits and other government services.

* **Citizen's Advice Bureau:** Most towns have a CAB; rural areas may have to access one by telephone. They offer independent legal and financial support.

* **Childcare Information Service:** This service was set up by the government to provide information for parents about the range and costs of child care in their area. Their website (www.childcarelink.gov.uk) has links to all local authorities. Parents without Internet access could write directly to their local authority for printed information.

* **Benefit Agency:** Most large towns have a Benefits Agency office with a wide range of leaflets – often printed in different languages – and experienced staff to explain what is available.

* **Local authority or council:** Many local authorities have a separate department to provide support for children and families who are vulnerable

or need help with everyday living. They can be accessed directly or via the Internet.

* **Voluntary organisations:** Local charities often hold meetings and host events to publicise their work and to raise money; examples include: Gingerbread (a charity for the support of lone parents), The National Council for One Parent Families, The Daycare Trust (a national childcare charity) and Families Need Fathers.

Section 2: Child protection

HOW THE STATE HAS TREATED THE CHILD IN THE PAST AND IN MODERN TIMES

Although child protection is a fairly recent development, there has for many years been concern about the ways in which parents and schools physically ill-treat or abuse their children.

* The Poor Law (1834) tried to discourage what it saw as 'parental fecklessness' by removing children from some families. The state placed these children in institutions, believing that it was 'rescuing' them from the negligence, immorality and lawlessness of their families.

* In 1889 the NSPCC (National Society for the Prevention of Cruelty to Children) was founded and soon developed a national network of centres and inspectors. The first English Prevention of Cruelty to Children Act was passed in 1889 and created the

❖ When children do not have parents, or where their parents are not able to give adequate care, then high-quality substitute care must be provided.

❖ Children themselves must be consulted about their feelings and wishes. They must be able to take part in the decisions that are made about them.

❖ When a child lives away from home, this must be open to challenge in order to make sure that the best standards of care are maintained.

❖ Parents and the extended family should continue to play a major part in the child's life, even when the child is living apart from them. This means that everyone should be encouraged to stay in contact with the child, including foster parents.

(Based on Stainton-Rogers and Roche 1994)

REGULATING AND REGISTERING SERVICES

Anyone who looks after children for more than two hours a day, other than in the child's home, must register with their local authority. The local authority can refuse or cancel registration.

Services which must be registered are:

❖ day care;
❖ family centres;
❖ child-minding;
❖ private fostering.

The number of children in a given setting is always specified. The environment is inspected indoors and outdoors to check for health and safety compliance. A record must be kept, with the names and addresses of children attending. In addition to being registered themselves, childminders must also register other people living in the house or anyone who is likely to be working alongside them.

Everyone working with children is subject to a police check. A police check ensures that people working with children have no criminal record relating to child abuse.

THE RIGHTS OF CHILDREN

In order to understand the very complex issues surrounding child protection, it is necessary to know about children's rights. In December 1991, the UK government ratified the United Nations Convention on the Rights of the Child. These rights say something about how modern society believes children ought to be treated:

The rights of children

❖ The views of the child should be listened to and should carry weight.

❖ The child has a right to parental care and family life.

❖ Parents and guardians have the right to appropriate help to carry out their child-rearing responsibilities.

❖ Children have the right to protection.

❖ Children should be treated as individuals who have feelings and ideas, and they need to be listened to and respected.

❖ Children need to be with people who show them love and affection. This is usually their family.

❖ Children's developmental needs should be met and protected. Developmental needs

---

> are to do with: the physical care children receive; the way their ideas and play are encouraged, supported and extended; making certain they are shown love and made to feel secure so that their self-concept and self-esteem are strong; and encouraging positive social relationships.

WHY DO CHILDREN NEED PROTECTION?

You may think that at the beginning of the twenty-first century it should not be necessary to have an International Convention on the Rights of the Child, or to make UK Acts of Parliament and laws which protect children's rights. However, for many complex reasons, a minority of children are neglected or abused, which means that their rights and needs are being violated.

There are many different ways of bringing up children; the aim of UK legislation and international agreements on child protection is not to standardise the way children are brought up. However, there are certain aspects of growing up which do seem to be essential for children's wellbeing, and child protection focuses on these crucial elements: if they are missing, the child's development may suffer.

Keeping a sense of proportion

It is easy to imagine that child abuse and child neglect are present on a vast scale. This is because the media tend to sensationalise and focus on these cases. Also in the past, child abuse and neglect were not so frequently recorded or reported. In comparison, nowadays, with child protection registers in every local authority and a central register kept by the NSPCC, recording is much more vigorous. You should note that

abuse is found in all sections... None of the theories out... been found to be co... abuse and neglect... a wider range... these theori... difficult... areas... st...

...ous theories about why adults abuse or neglect children. Some of these are discussed in the box below.

> ### Theories about why people abuse children
>
> ❖ The cycle of abuse found in some families was called the '**battered child syndrome**' by Kempe and Kempe in 1962. This made it appear that abuse was something predictable, like an illness, which it is not.
>
> ❖ **Feminist views** about the sexual politics of relationships between men and women have been another approach to child protection. However, because both men and women abuse both boys and girls, this view has been criticised.
>
> ❖ **Dysfunctional families**, in which relationships break down, may lead to a child being scapegoated (blamed). This model sees **therapy** as the way forward, but scapegoating does not necessarily come as a result of the family breaking down.
>
> ❖ The poverty cycle, and other health and social factors, are thought to predispose some families to abuse.

Rich, poor, healthy and unhealthy people may all abuse and neglect children – child

... of society.
... lined above has
... fect. This is because
... have been found across
... of people than any of
... would suggest. It is always
... to develop a convincing theory in
... which are very complex and difficult to
... dy. Child protection is one of these areas.

The most positive approach we can take, until theory is better developed, is to prevent abuse by looking at what helps people to be 'confident parents'.

Factors which make child abuse more likely to occur

Child abuse is more likely to occur when people (often parents):

* have little knowledge about children's needs or how children develop;
* find it hard to use the knowledge they have about the way children develop;
* experience a great deal of stress in their lives;
* are poor decision makers;
* find it hard to take responsibility for things that they do;
* find it difficult to relate to or communicate with other people;
* are inconsistent;
* find it hard to change their ideas, to change what they have always done or to change what was done to them when they were children.

Certain factors within the family home can mean that children are at a higher risk of being abused:

* **Drug or alcohol abuse** by parents can lead to children being put at risk, even if the parents are not actually mistreating

them; such abuse is a familiar trigger for **violence** in the home and it can also lead to parents having a disordered lifestyle, which can leave children in danger.

* **Mental illness:** although this does not prevent individuals from being good parents, it can sometimes move a child up the scale from being one in need to one at significant risk of harm.

Some facts about child abuse

* All sections of society produce adults who abuse or neglect children. It is very dangerous to form stereotypes about the kind of people who might violate a child's rights or about the situations which could lead to child abuse or neglect.

* As evidence grows on the subject of child protection, it is becoming apparent that the abusive or neglectful person is almost always known to the child (e.g. parent, family member, friend of the family, carer or cohabitee).

* Premature babies and children of 0–4 years are most likely to be abused or neglected.

* Separation of the mother and the baby for a period of time after birth can be associated with child abuse or neglect.

* Children who cry a great deal are much more likely to be abused or neglected.

* Children who do not enjoy eating are more likely to be abused or neglected.

* Stepchildren are vulnerable.

* Children with disabilities are more likely to be abused or neglected.

* Children who are boys when parents wanted girls, or girls when parents wanted boys, are more likely to be neglected.

ENABLING CHILDREN TO PROTECT THEMSELVES

Kidscape is a national charity committed to preventing bullying and child abuse. It has produced a pack that aims to empower children and to help to keep them safe from abuse. The Kidscape Kit covers the following areas:

*   general rules about feeling and keeping safe – telling an adult if you are frightened, saying NO;

*   how to deal with bullies;

*   how to recognise and deal with approaches from strangers (stranger danger);

*   strategies for what to do if you get lost;

*   saying NO when someone (even someone you know) tries to touch you in a confusing, unsafe or frightening way;

*   body awareness and self-protection;

*   refusing to keep secrets of any kind;

*   knowing the difference between safe and unsafe secrets (for example, secrets about surprises, parties or presents are okay, but secrets about touching, hugging or kissing are not);

*   yelling and telling – learning to shout and run away in a frightening situation, telling an adult.

Your role in enabling children to protect themselves

You have an important role to play in safeguarding children from abuse. You should always:

*   **listen to children** and take their concerns seriously; often when a child has been bullied or abused in another way, he or she will try to put into words what has happened – they need to know that you are there to listen and, most importantly, that you will believe what they tell you;

*   encourage children to think about their own **personal safety**; for example, never allow them to leave the setting with anyone other than the person designated to collect them;

*   create opportunities for children to **express their feelings**; they need to know that it is okay to feel sad or afraid;

*   aim to **increase children's confidence** by praising them for any achievements and showing a genuine interest in what they have to say;

*   **observe children** and keep regular records of their behaviour – you are in a strong position to note any changes of behaviour or signs of insecurity which could be a result of child abuse.

FORMS OF ABUSE AND EFFECTS ON CHILD, FAMILY AND WORKERS

There are various types of child abuse and neglect:

*   physical abuse;

*   physical neglect;

*   emotional abuse;

*   emotional neglect;

*   intellectual abuse;

*   intellectual neglect;

*   sexual abuse;

*   grave concern (faltering growth or failure to thrive).

Physical abuse

A child who has been physically abused may present various signs and symptoms (as shown in Figure 15.5).

NON-ACCIDENTAL INJURY

Non-accidental injury (NAI) involves someone deliberately harming a child. This may take the form of:

❖ bruising – from being slapped, shaken, squeezed or punched;

❖ cuts, scratches, bite marks, a torn frenulum (the web of skin inside the upper lip);

❖ burns and scalds;

❖ fractures;

❖ poisoning.

It is vital that all people working in early years settings be aware of the indicators of child abuse, although it is important not to jump to conclusions. Any concerns that you may have about the nature of an injury should be dealt with according to the procedures outlined on page 639. Any injury to a *baby* is considered suspicious, as babies have a limited capacity to move about and injure themselves. In non-accidental injury the explanation of the parent or carer as to how the injury occurred is usually inadequate, and their attitude may even seem bizarre. The parents may have delayed seeking medical help, or may only have done so when prompted by others.

Indicators of physical abuse and neglect
Physical indicators of physical neglect

❖ The child may be underweight and show other signs of failure to thrive (see page 369).

❖ Clothing may be inappropriate for the weather, and be smelly and dirty.

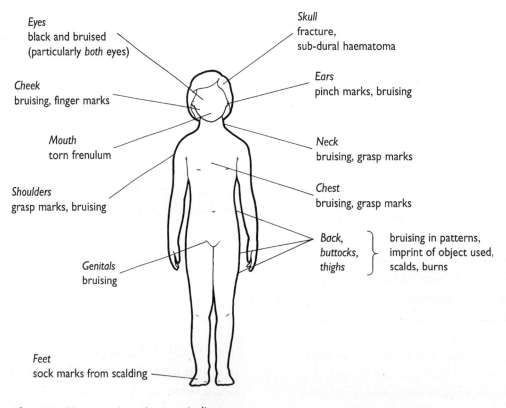

Eyes
black and bruised
(particularly *both* eyes)

Cheek
bruising, finger marks

Mouth
torn frenulum

Shoulders
grasp marks, bruising

Genitals
bruising

Feet
sock marks from scalding

Skull
fracture,
sub-dural haematoma

Ears
pinch marks, bruising

Neck
bruising, grasp marks

Chest
bruising, grasp marks

Back,
buttocks,
thighs
} bruising in patterns,
imprint of object used,
scalds, burns

Fig 15.5 Non-accidental injury indicators

- The child may have poor skin tone and dull, matted hair; a baby may have a persistent rash from infrequent nappy changing.
- The child may be constantly hungry, tired and listless.
- The child has frequent health problems and is prone to accidents.

Behavioural indicators of physical abuse and neglect

Changes in behaviour may include:

- being sad, listless, preoccupied or withdrawn;
- being extra vigilant about what is going on around them (sometimes referred to as an expression of 'frozen watchfulness');
- showing signs of poor self-esteem;
- being aggressive towards other children;
- showing signs of false independence or offering indiscriminate attention to any adult who shows an interest;
- improbable excuses or refusal to explain injuries;
- wearing clothes to cover injuries, even in hot weather – refusal to undress for gym;
- self-destructive tendencies;
- fear of physical contact – shrinking back if touched;
- admitting that they are punished, but the punishment is excessive (such as a child being beaten every night to 'make him study');
- bedwetting, bizarre behaviour or eating problems;
- lacking concentration.

Physical neglect

The adult fails to give the child what they need in order to develop physically.

- Frequently the child is left alone and unattended.
- The child may not have adequate food, sleep, clothing, a clean environment or medical care.
- The child may suddenly change from thriving to not thriving.

The causes of child neglect are very complex, but most children who are physically neglected are often left unsupervised at home. Children who are neglected in this way are frequently injured in accidents, both in their own homes and on the roads where they play.

None of the behavioural indicators listed above are exclusive to abused children, nor are they exhibited by all children who suffer abuse. How children react depends on several factors:

- the child's personality and stage of development;
- particular family circumstances and relationships;
- the nature and severity of the abuse inflicted;
- the duration of the abuse.

Emotional abuse

In cases of emotional abuse children are threatened by the adult. They are insulted and undermined, shouted at and constantly ridiculed. It is not known how common this form of neglect is, because it is not as easy to detect as physical abuse or neglect.

Emotional neglect

In this case children do not receive love and affection from the adult. They are often left alone, without the support and company of someone who loves them.

Behavioural indicators of emotional abuse and neglect

Some children become withdrawn and will not play or take an active part in things. Life does not seem to be fun for them. Their self-esteem might be low, showing itself in a lack of confidence and reluctance to have a go at doing things. Other children react by constantly seeking attention: they seize upon any adult in an attempt to gain their attention. Tantrums might continue to a later age than usual and speech disorders might emerge. The child might tell lies and even steal. Emotional abuse or neglect is not easy to detect.

There may be:

* withdrawn movements, or signs of frustration;
* anger and sadness in the form of temper tantrums;
* sudden speech disorders;
* continual self-deprecation (I'm stupid, ugly, useless, etc.);
* overreaction to mistakes;
* extreme fear of any new situation;
* inappropriate response to pain (I deserve this);
* neurotic behaviour (rocking, hair-twisting, self-mutilation).

Intellectual abuse

Some adults may 'force' children into doing so-called 'academic' work for much of their waking lives. Children are pushed to achieve intellectually and can suffer severe stress.

Intellectual neglect

At the opposite extreme of intellectual abuse is intellectual neglect. Children are left with little or no intellectual stimulation and cannot develop their own ideas and thinking. Sometimes children are wrongly thought to have learning difficulties when in fact they are suffering from a severe lack of intellectual stimulation.

Sexual abuse

The adult uses the child in order to gratify their sexual desires. This could involve sexual intercourse or anal intercourse; it may involve watching pornographic material with the child. Children may be forced to engage in sexually explicit behaviour or oral sex, masturbation or the fondling of sexual parts. Most sexual abusers are men; 10 per cent are women. Children who are sexually abused can be boys or girls. Sexual abuse can continue undetected for some years. It is in the child's interest to recognise it as early as possible, so that the abuse does not escalate over time. It is difficult to know how many children are sexually abused, but it is quite likely, on the basis of existing evidence, that about 1 in 5 girls and 1 in 10 boys have had this experience.

Indicators of sexual abuse
Physical indicators of sexual abuse

* Children may have bruises or scratches, as in an accidental injury.
* There may be itching, or even pain, in the genital area. This might make walking or sitting uncomfortable for the child.
* It might lead to bedwetting and poor sleeping and eating patterns.
* Underclothes might be bloody or torn, and there may be discharge from the penis or vagina.

Behavioural indicators of sexual abuse

The child may:

* become rather withdrawn from other children or from adults;
* seem to be lacking in self-confidence and wanting to be 'babied';

- have poor self-esteem and feelings of being dirty or bad;
- not eat or sleep well;
- show an unusual knowledge of sexual behaviour, demonstrated by the things that they say, play with (often in the home area) or draw;
- seem fascinated by sexual behaviour and may flirt with adults, as if trying to please;
- show other extreme reactions, such as depression, self-mutilation, running away, overdoses, anorexia;
- become insecure or clinging;
- regress to younger behaviour patterns, such as thumb-sucking or bringing out discarded cuddly toys;
- show an inability to concentrate;
- show a lack of trust or even fear of someone they know well, such as not wanting to be alone with a babysitter or childminder;
- start to wet again, day or night, and have nightmares;
- become worried about clothing being removed;
- try to be 'ultra-good' or perfect and overreact to criticism.

Cause for grave concern (failure to thrive)

When a child does not develop physically, even though there may seem to be no apparent reason for this, it is a matter of grave concern which needs to be investigated by a multi–professional team.

The abuse of disabled children

Disabled children can be more vulnerable to abuse because their disability can make them dependent on parents or carers for help in everyday matters like toileting, washing, feeding and getting dressed. Although one of the indicators that a child has been abused is

Case Study

Failure to thrive

An interesting study in Mexico in the 1960s looked at children who were failing to thrive. The children were taken to hospital, where they put on weight before returning to their families. The failure to thrive then recurred. Instead of readmission to hospital, a team of workers visited the homes and found that the families never came together around a table to share a meal. When the families were encouraged to do this, the children gained weight and began to thrive. Eating is about the food that is eaten, but it is also about enjoying good company and conversations. Eating is an emotional and social activity; an opportunity to share thoughts and ideas.

a change in their behaviour, with disabled children any such change can be mistaken as being a result of their disability. Children with a physical or learning disability are especially vulnerable to all kinds of abuse; they might have communication difficulties which make it hard for them to reveal what has happened. Some children are abused by the people who care for them, while others are victims of society's view of disabled people as an 'inferior' minority group.

CHILD PROTECTION PROCEDURES

Your role in protecting children from abuse

If you are working in an early years setting other than the child's home, you should develop the good practice of keeping accurate and detailed records of children's development. These observations can be very important when assessing any changes in a child's behaviour; if you work alone – as a childminder or a nanny – you should also keep short observations of a child – in order to help you to build up a picture of their progress.

If you work in an early years setting you will be required to follow the **policies and procedures** of the setting; among many others, these include settling-in, safety at home-times and child protection policies. You also need to be able to:

❖ recognise the **signs and symptoms of abuse**;

❖ know **how to respond** to a child who tells you that he or she has been abused (**disclosure**);

❖ **report your suspicions**;

❖ maintain **confidentiality** according to the guidelines in the setting's policy.

WHAT TO DO IF A CHILD TELLS YOU THEY HAVE BEEN ABUSED

When a child tells an adult that they have been abused, this is called a **disclosure interview**. It is very important not to be judgemental about a person who has abused a child – although it can be very hard not to, especially if you are committed to children and their rights. There are many reasons why

an adult might abuse a child, and you should not try to second-guess someone's motivation.

The modern approach to child protection is to help the child by *preventing* further abuse or neglect. In the past, this was often done by removing the abusing person or the child from the family. However, even in cases of abuse, separating a child from their parents is not necessarily best for the child – under the Children Act this is a principle that is paramount. Separation might result in the child feeling punished for telling about what happened.

There are now programmes whereby families are supported through a family centre, a day nursery or a special therapeutic centre. These enable families to stay together, but to be supported and supervised by health visitors, educational welfare officers, psychologists, social workers and early childhood practitioners.

PROCEDURES FOR REPORTING SUSPICIONS OF ABUSE AND DISCLOSURES

If child abuse or neglect is suspected, it is very important that procedures be followed which are regarded as good practice and which fulfil the legal requirements. The NSPCC and, in Scotland, the RSSPCC

Guidelines for dealing with disclosure

❖ Reassure the child, saying that you are glad they have told you about this.

♣ Believe the child. Tell the child that you will do your best to protect them, but do not promise that you can keep them safe.

♣ Remember that the child is not to blame. It is important that you make the child understand this.

♣ Do a lot of listening. Do not ask questions.

♣ Report your conversation with the child to your senior designated manager.

(Royal Scottish Society for the Prevention of Cruelty to Children) are the only voluntary organisations with **statutory** powers to apply to a court for protection orders for a child.

RECORDING SUSPICIONS OF ABUSE AND DISCLOSURES

You should make a record of:

❖ the child's name;

❖ the child's address;

❖ the age of the child;

❖ the date and time of the observation or the disclosure;

❖ an objective record of the observation or disclosure;

❖ the exact words spoken by the child;

❖ the name of the person to whom the concern was reported, with date and time;

❖ the names of any other person present at the time.

These records must be signed and dated and kept in a separate confidential file.

CONFIDENTIALITY

As a general rule, information about a child protection issue should only be shared with people on a **need-to-know** basis. This means that only staff working directly with the child or the parents will have access to any information about a disclosure or investigation. Gossip must be avoided; names and identities must never be disclosed outside the group designated as having a need to know.

Procedures involved in cases of child abuse

POLICE PROTECTION ORDER

Specially trained police officers can remove a child who is in danger into foster care for 72 hours. This is to make sure that the child is safe. This officer is required to inform:

❖ the child;

❖ the parent or carer;

❖ the local authority.

EMERGENCY PROTECTION ORDER

1   A concerned adult (who may be a teacher) can apply, in an emergency, to a court or to an individual magistrate for an emergency protection order which lasts for up to 8 days. (This can be extended for another 7 days.)

2   The child is then taken to a safe place, such as a foster home. After 8 days, if the situation is safe, the emergency protection order can be discharged.

CHILD ASSESSMENT ORDER

Either the local authority or the NSPCC can apply for a child assessment order, giving 7 days during which the child can be assessed. This might be used in a situation in which the parents will not cooperate but where there is not an emergency.

CHILD PROTECTION CONFERENCE

When it has been established that there is evidence suggesting child abuse or neglect, a child protection conference is arranged.

❖ Professionals involved with the child or family join together in a multi-professional discussion of written evidence.

❖ The early years worker may also be asked to attend.

❖ The chairperson decides whether it is appropriate to invite the parents to attend. In any case, the parents must be informed that the conference is taking place.

❖ It is a requirement that local authorities work towards parents attending at part, if not the whole, of the ʿerence.

action plan called the **child protection plan** is made.

❖ The child may be placed on the child protection register.

CHILD PROTECTION PLAN

1 **Assessment:** the first stage in putting together a plan is to initiate an assessment. This will involve assessing both the child and the family situation.

2 **Protection of the child:** this would be achieved by either:

❖ **a care order** – the child will be taken into the care of the local authority's social services department (in a foster home or community children's home);

❖ **a supervision order** – the local authority will support and supervise the family and the child in the home setting for 1 year.

3 **Regular review:** the child protection plan is reviewed regularly in a review conference attended by the multi-professional team involved with the family, and perhaps also by the parents. These conferences take place at least every 6 months. The child may be deregistered if the situation changes and the child no longer requires support or supervised protection.

Child protection and schools

When a child starts or is already attending a nursery school, nursery class or primary school, social services are required to notify

Guidelines for reporting child abuse or neglect

❖ Clarify your own thinking. Is this a situation which demands instant action – for example, if a child is injured and needs immediate medical attention? Put the child's feelings and physical care first. Be calm, reassuring and warm. This will help the child to have as high self-esteem as possible.

❖ Usually evidence about child abuse or neglect emerges in a much less sudden way. Report the indicators which have led you to suspect child abuse or neglect to your designated senior manager. You will need to supply written evidence within 24 hours, and it is particularly helpful if you make observations of the child on that day. If there is already a well-established record-keeping system in the work setting, this will be easier to manage.

❖ Your line manager will help you to follow the correct procedures, but you should know them too. They will be written down in every work setting (this is legally required under the Children Act).

❖ You will need to continue to keep carefully written observations. This is because you will be required to make a report, and for this you must have written evidence.

❖ The police, social services and perhaps the NSPCC will be involved, and will consult each other in order to be sure there is evidence and decide whether to issue a police protection order, an emergency protection order or a child assessment order (see above).

the head teacher if a child's name is put on the child protection register. The register states:

* whether the child is subject to a care order;
* the name of the key worker on the case;
* what information may be known to the parents.

The school is required to monitor how the child is getting along, especially in terms of their development. The school's observations should be shared with the social services department should any concern arise.

WORKING TOGETHER UNDER THE CHILDREN ACT 1989

* Every school is required to appoint a teacher who is responsible for linking with the social services department.
* Every school is required to have a written policy on child protection procedures, making clear the lines of reporting to social services, and sometimes to the NSPCC.
* Registers of named staff taking on this role are kept by the local education authority. Regular training and support are given to these teachers.

Case Study

Child abuse

Late one Saturday night the police are called out by neighbours to a flat where it is reported that a child is screaming and no one will answer the door. The police try to gain entrance by the front door, but end up forcing their way through a window. In the main living room a child of about 4 years is strapped to a chair watching television; she appears not to notice her surroundings. The screams have stopped, but slight whimpering sounds are coming from the bedroom. The two police officers enter the bedroom and find a thin baby of about 10 months in a filthy nappy, with tobacco and ash over his hands and mouth; his eyes look dull and he is moaning softly. The officers

notice an open pack of cigarettes and an upturned ashtray on the chair next to the baby's cot. The children are taken to hospital and the baby is kept in overnight for observation; the duty social workers are contacted and the 4-year-old girl is taken to emergency foster parents for the night. The children's parents arrive home at 2 a.m., drunk and high on drugs, having been to a party. The father finds out from neighbours that the police have been and is furious. He demands the return of his children and claims that they had never left the children on their own before – the mother claimed that a friend had promised to stop by and look after the children at 10 p.m.

ACTIVITY: CHILD ABUSE

1 Divide into groups and list the indicators of neglect and abuse in the case study.

2 What do you think will happen to the children now? Discuss the alternatives.

❖ Schools, as well as care settings, are encouraged to develop curriculum plans which help children to develop skills and practices which protect them from abuse.

SUPPORTING CHILDREN

The use of play therapy

Play therapy is a mode of therapy that helps children to explore their feelings, to express themselves and to make sense of their life experiences. It is appropriate for children of all ages, but is most often used for children aged 3–12 years. Play therapists generally work with individual children, but many have experience of working with groups and with siblings. Play therapy is particularly effective in supporting children who have experienced abuse. Play therapy can help children by offering:

❖ **play** – children's natural medium to learn, communicate and explore their world;

❖ **freedom of expression** in a safe and trusting environment;

❖ a space in which the feelings their experiences generate can be expressed and contained – this cannot change what has happened, but it can promote resilience within each child to enable him or her to discover a more hopeful view of the world;

❖ the opportunity to explore and understand these feelings – it can enable them to shift their perspective of abuse or difficulty so that they are less likely to internalise blame; the resulting empowerment and increased self-esteem can be the springboard to help the child to cope with difficulties in the real world.

Consistency is also important, so play therapy sessions usually take place once a week at the same time. This may be at the child's home, school or clinic.

Play therapists take a specialist course; it is usual for trainees to hold a first qualification in either teaching, social work, occupational therapy or another related field and to have extensive experience of working with children. Personal therapy and supervised practice are essential elements of the training. For further information on all aspects of play therapy, contact The British Association of Play Therapists (www.bapt.info).

Working with voluntary organisations to prevent abuse

❖ **Kidscape** works with schools and other early years settings to devise assertiveness training programmes, which give young children protection from abuse.

❖ **Childline** is a voluntary organisation which operates a 24-hour free telephone line for children. They can call in to discuss with trained counsellors situations which place them under stress for one reason or another.

Many early years settings now have a transitions initiative, linking to Primary Schools to ensure children have high wellbeing when starting their Primary education.

HELPING CHILDREN AND FAMILIES TO DEAL WITH THE EFFECTS OF CHILD ABUSE OR NEGLECT

Children are best helped when early childhood practitioners are not judgemental about the child's family and, in particular, about the person who has abused the child.

Building self-esteem

❖ It is important to build the self-esteem of both the child and the family.

❖ Low self-esteem is associated with children who have been abused or neglected, and also with adults who abuse or neglect children.

❖ Improving self-esteem can be difficult when parents who are required to bring their children, under a child protection order, to a family centre, day nursery or children's centre do not appear responsive or positive to staff or to the child.

❖ It takes time to build self-esteem.

❖ Staff who give messages of warmth, who respect other people's dignity and who value people, although they may reject what they have done, are more likely to help parents in this way. Feeling valued as an individual, whatever you have done, builds self-esteem.

Guidelines for helping children deal with abuse and neglect

❖ Encourage children to play.

❖ Some children will need to be supported by trained play therapists or psychologists. Where there has been sexual abuse, anatomically correct dolls are sometimes used with the child. With help from these professionals, you might be able to use the dolls with the child. These can help children to play, acting out their experiences and expressing how they feel about what has happened to them.

❖ Be warm – just be there for the child. Do not ask questions.

❖ Encourage the child to try to enjoy activities with you.

❖ Remember that children who have been abused or neglected are often challenging. Remind yourself about ways of helping children who boundary-push and challenge (see Chapter 9).

❖ Help parents to feel confident in their parenting.

❖ Do not undermine parents with remarks such as, 'He doesn't do that here!' Instead tackle problems together. Try saying to parents, 'Let's both try the same approach. When she does it next time, either at home or in the nursery, shall we both make sure we have the same reaction?'

❖ The aim is to get parents and children relating well to each other.

❖ Remember that many people who work with young children were themselves abused as children. It is important to manage feelings about this subject in a professional way.

Case Study

John

One early years worker had enjoyed telling stories to John (3 years), who had been referred to the nursery under a child protection order. One day she went to tell him a story and found that his mother had arrived early. She was in the book area with John, reading him a story. They were completely involved. The early years worker felt a pang of disappointment, but it did not last, as she knew it was more important for the parent and child to enjoy stories together than it was for her to do so. She also knew that she had helped to bring about this situation. She began to realise that working with children who have been hurt in some way can bring a different kind of satisfaction, even though it can also be distressing sometimes.

ACTIVITY: WHAT KIND OF PROVISION?

Research the early years provision made by your local authority. What proportion of 4-year-olds are in reception classes?

What kind of provision are most 3-year-olds and their families offered?

ACTIVITY: INVESTIGATING LEGAL AND POLITICAL ISSUES IN CHILD CARE PROVISION

1   Under the following three headings, discuss how people can find solutions to poor housing:

    * statutory sector;
    * voluntary sector;
    * private sector.

2   In a group of five, play the game 'balloons'. In this game, each person takes a different Parliamentary Act (see below) and argues that all other Parliamentary Acts should be thrown out of the balloon basket; there is only room for one Parliamentary Act in the basket.

3   Each player should research one of the following Acts of Parliament, writing down their reasons for it remaining in the basket:

    * The Sex Discrimination Act 1975
    * The Race Relations Act 1976
    * The Employment Act 1982
    * The Health and Safety Act 1982
    * The Children Act 1989.

4   Over 3 days you are going to analyse programming and reporting in different media.

Day 1: Look at the way the news is reported on the early evening news and on the 10 o'clock news. Then watch a news analysis programme that is on television late at night (after 10.30 p.m.).

+ How were the programmes different?

+ Did they have the same main headlines?

+ Did they cover the same subjects in the same way?

Day 2: Listen to a pop music radio programme. Then listen to Radio 4 in the early evening and to the 10 o'clock news. Compare these with the World Service at any time of the day or night. Is presentation of the radio news similar to the news presented on television?

Day 3: Read a selection of Sunday papers, for example *The Observer*, *The Sunday Times* and a tabloid newspaper. Compare them.

+ Do they choose the same headlines?

+ Do they write about news items in the same way?

If a group of you do this activity you could make your findings into a chart (using a computer to display your data).

5 Tom is made redundant from work 2 weeks before Christmas. He has borrowed money at a very high interest rate in order to buy some expensive toys that his children (Karen, 4 years, and Jason, 6 years) have asked for in their letters to Father Christmas. His wife has recently been ill with stress and is on antidepressant tablets. Tom collects his benefit from the DSS each week, but he is not allowed to earn extra or he loses it. He cannot pay back the loan. Whom can he go to for advice?

6 Look up the Children Act 1989 in the index of this book. Find all the references to the Act and read them again so that you are thoroughly

informed about it. Write down any key messages that you need to know.

7 Try to visit the Houses of Parliament – consult your MP for information on how to do this. If you cannot do this, watch *Today in Parliament* on television when there is a debate. Summarise the arguments of the different political parties. How do they compare?

8 Write down the names of ten voluntary organisations (charities) that come into your mind – the fact that you remember them is called 'unprompted awareness'. Research what these organisations do.

Now find ten voluntary organisations that you have not heard of before. Find out what these organisations do. Write down reasons why some voluntary organisations are better-known to the public than others.

9 Set out a scenario which results in a child being taken into the care of the local authority. Who has parental responsibility? What kind of care order is made?

10 Imagine you want to register as a childminder. What must you do? Research this and make a plan.

11 Plan a debate on this topic: 'Should prisoners or people who are mentally ill be allowed the right to vote in a democracy?' Research whether prisoners, the royal family, peers or compulsorily detained psychiatric patients may vote at the current time, before you take part in the debate. Remember that you will need representatives to argue each side of the debate.

16

Working in partnership with parents

Contents

THE ROLES OF PARENTS

Parents have a central role in their children's lives. Parents:

* are the first and most enduring carers and educators of their children;

* know and understand their own child best;

* have responsibilities towards their children (see page 650);

* give their children a strong sense of identity and belonging;

* have skills and experience which can be of value to the early years setting;

* are partners with early childhood practitioners in the care and education of their children.

Different parenting styles and attitudes

Early childhood practitioners need to bear in mind the following facts:

* Every family is different, with different needs and traditions.

* The great majority of parents are concerned to do their best for their children, even if they are not always sure what this might be.

* Each one of us only really knows what it is like to grow up in our own family. Parents almost always like some of the things about their own family and the way they were brought up; but they will just as certainly wish that other aspects of their upbringing had been different.

* Parents usually welcome help when trying out some alternative ways of doing things. They will not want to change too much, though, and they will not want rapid changes forced on them by other people. Early childhood practitioners need to respect parents' wishes.

Why do parents choose child care?

Parents choose child care for many different reasons:

* Many parents need personal space away from their child for part of the day. This

Guidelines for working with parents

❖ **Supporting parents:** begin by seeing yourself as a resource and support that can be used by parents to further their children's best interests.

❖ **Respect all parents:** the vast majority of parents, including those who abuse their children, love them. It is important not to judge parents, and to respect their good intentions. Almost every parent, even if on the surface they do not seem to be interested or loving, want to do the job well.

❖ **Recognise the good intentions of parents:** work positively, with this aim as a central focus. Concentrating on the good intentions of parents helps to give them a positive self-image. Just as children need positive images reflected about themselves, so do parents. The attitude of the staff must therefore be to show parents respect; it is hard bringing up a child.

❖ **Reinforce the parents' sense of dignity and self-esteem:** showing parents respect and reinforcing their dignity demonstrates to them that the child also needs respect and a sense of dignity.

❖ **Using your experience:** if you are not a parent, you will not have experienced some of the things that parents have. If you are a parent, you will only know about being a parent of your own children; you will not know what it is like to be a parent of other people's children.

Case Study

Melissa and her mother

The mother of a 3-year-old in a day care centre said to her daughter's key worker, 'When I was little I was always hit when I did wrong. I don't want to do that to Melissa, but I don't know what to do instead.'

By coming to the early years setting, the child and her mother are meeting other people. This inevitably means that they are meeting other ways of doing things. Melissa's mother can learn about other ways – instead of hitting – of dealing with unacceptable behaviour. She can then decide whether she wants to use some of these other methods, and this will give her more choice about the way she can bring up Melissa.

may be while the family adjusts to a new baby, or while the parent catches up with chores or simply relaxes.

❖ It is sometimes thought that all parents want full-time nursery places for their children so that they can work. This is almost certainly not the case. Some

parents do want full-time nursery places so that they can work, because they positively want to work. Other parents want full-time nursery places because they have to work, for economic reasons.

❖ Some parents will be required to bring their child to the nursery as a matter of child protection – they will have no choice in the matter.

✤ Other parents only want part-time nursery places. They may want their child to move in a wider social circle and to have new and interesting experiences.

✤ Some parents think it is important for their child to have some experiences away from them. Other parents will want to join in with their child – perhaps not every day, but regularly.

THE RIGHTS AND RESPONSIBILITIES OF PARENTS

The Children Act 1989 replaced the term 'parental rights' with 'parental responsibility'. Parents have responsibility for all aspects of a child's upbringing and welfare. The box sets out the most significant of the powers, rights, duties and responsibilities that parents have in relation to their children.

Parents' powers, rights, duties and responsibilities

1 A responsibility for the physical care and control of the child.

2 A responsibility to ensure that the child receives an efficient, full-time education suited to his or her needs and abilities.

3 A responsibility to maintain the child.

4 The authority to discipline the child.

5 The authority to consent to the child being medically examined or receiving medical treatment.

6 The authority to appoint a guardian (although a guardian will not acquire parental responsibility unless both parents are dead).

Some aspects of parental responsibility require the consent of both parents of the child. These include:

1 The authority to agree to the child being adopted.

2 The authority to remove the child from the UK.

How parental responsibility is acquired

1 The mother always has automatic parental responsibility.

2 The father only has automatic parental responsibility if married to the mother at the time of the birth of the child.

3 An 'unmarried' father has to acquire parental responsibility either by agreement with the mother or by court order.

4 The Children Act 1989 does not create any rights of consultation between a child's parents before action is taken in respect of a child. On the contrary, the Act says that each person with parental responsibility may act independently in meeting that responsibility, except where the law requires consent (e.g. adoption).

Because of this, parental responsibility is no guarantee of cooperation. If the child is living with the mother, for example, a father with parental responsibility may find it very frustrating that he does not have to be involved in decisions regarding the child. If he disagrees very strongly with what the mother is doing, he has to apply to the court for either a 'prohibited steps order' or a 'specific issue order'.

Can parental responsibility be lost or given away?

❖ Parental responsibility cannot be surrendered or transferred. It can, however, be temporarily delegated or entrusted to someone else.

❖ Parental responsibility is not lost when another person acquires it. Rather parental responsibility is then shared. This is so even when a local authority acquires parental responsibility under a care order.

❖ Parental responsibility is lost when an adoption order is made; otherwise, it is lost only in exceptional circumstances.

PARTNERSHIPS BETWEEN PARENTS AND STAFF

The differences between parents and staff

The parent is a deeply important person to the child, and the relationship between parent and child is always very emotional. Emotional relationships can be a source of great strength, but they can also be very unreasonable at times. It is important to recognise that parents and staff have different kinds of relationships with the children in their care.

Staff need to develop consistent, warm and affectionate relationships with children, especially babies, but they do not seek to replace the parents. Babies need to be with the same people each day to develop social relationships. This is why, with the new Day Care Standards, settings are expected to use a **key worker** system – one member of staff becomes a child's key person and links with the family.

Parents and staff have one thing in common which is very important: they all want the

best for the child. The roles involved are not the same, but they are complementary:

❖ Staff have knowledge of general child development.

❖ Parents know their own child the best.

If the partnership between parents, staff and child is going to develop well, each needs to be able to trust and respect the other. The self-esteem and wellbeing of the people in the partnership – the parents, the staff members and the child – are important when they are working together. How we feel about ourselves influences how we relate to other people.

Parents may have had bad experiences at school, and when their child joins a group setting all those past feelings may come rushing back to the surface. Parents will then be anxious and not feel good about themselves. They might expect your setting to be like the one they went to, and this will make them fear for their child. This is often so when parents are required to bring their child to the early years setting under a child protection order. Staff will need to be sensitive to the feelings of parents in this sort of situation.

The history of working in partnership

In the 1960s, work with parents concentrated on home–school links. Parents and staff kept a respectful distance, but at least it was acknowledged that links were a good thing. Staff thought links would help them to tell parents about what they expected of families. There was little emphasis on parents telling staff what they expected of the early years setting.

In the 1970s there was an emphasis on what was called compensatory education (see Chapter 6). Some families were thought to lack the ability to help their children through school. Staff talked of 'problem families', 'disadvantaged families' and 'inadequate families'. These negative labels did not respect the parents.

From the 1980s to the present day there has been a shift towards emphasising partnership with parents. Early childhood practitioners see parents as both the primary carer and the primary educator of the child.

Researchers, such as Judy Dunn, have found that children have richer conversations at home than at school because their parents, and their brothers and sisters, understand and help them. In an early years setting children are often in an unfamiliar situation. Therefore, it is more difficult for them to talk at a deep level in conversations. If staff are rather busy they may not be able to take time for a one-to-one conversation such as the child has at home.

Researchers have shown how staff can undermine the confidence of parents by showing off their knowledge and using jargon. Some staff even talk about 'my children'. Children in a setting do not belong to the staff: children belong to their families. Staff are there to help, but not to take over.

Early childhood practitioners need to be mindful of the balance between the parent's self-esteem, the child's self-esteem and the staff's self-esteem.

Beginning the partnership – home visits

In some early years settings home visits are set up as soon as the child's name is registered. This means that parents meet staff on the parents' own territory. It is important that parents do not feel forced into accepting

> ### Building self-esteem within the partnership
>
> ❖ Staff who are well trained will be able to use their knowledge sensitively and to appreciate the family background, culture, language, physical surroundings and economic background of each child.
>
> ❖ Staff must be confident enough to work together with parents, and to share rather than show off what they know about each child's development and learning.
>
> ❖ This does not mean that parents must do things the way staff do things. There are many ways of working with children. Exchanging ideas and respecting others' ideas about children are important when working with parents.

a home visit from staff. Usually, however, parents do welcome an opportunity to get to know the early childhood practitioner, the childminder or the nanny.

A home visit allows for sharing of ideas and feelings about the child. For a child who is just about to start in an early years setting it is important to find out:

❖ what the parents are expecting;

❖ what the parents hope for.

Are the parents expecting the nursery to be like the schools that they went to? Do they want their child to learn to read at 2 or 3 years of age? Do they think that mathematics is another word for numbers? Do they think children should play?

Sharing information

The home visit is an opportunity to clear up any misunderstandings. Staff can explain to parents what to expect and will also be able to reassure the child about what will happen.

Guidelines for conducting home visits

❖ Do not go alone for your own safety, especially in the evenings. Tell colleagues where you are and the time of the home visit.

❖ Make an appointment, as the parent may not want to open the door to a stranger.

❖ Staff usually find that if one key worker concentrates on the parent(s) and the other worker gets to know the child, everyone enjoys the visit. The child has the full attention of one adult, with a bag of carefully chosen books and toys. The parents and staff are free to get to know each other, and can fill in the basic information records together, without the pressure of being in a busy setting.

❖ Parents should not feel judged or tested. They need to be sure that their home is not being inspected to see if it is clean, tidy, fashionable or tasteful.

❖ Not all parents will accept the invitation to be visited. Parents' wishes should be treated with respect.

Staff may discuss:

❖ the routines of the day;

❖ what equipment the children use;

❖ the key worker or family worker system, if there is one in place;

❖ outings and permissions for them;

❖ photographs, videoing the children, ethics and parental permission.

AIDS TO SHARING INFORMATION

This kind of information can be shared with parents by going through a 'brochure' together. This may take the form of a photograph album, for example, which shows in a very practical way the philosophy, activities and timetabling of the day. Photographs are enhanced by brief notes. For example, there might be pictures of children playing with sand, the home area with boys and girls playing, the book area stocked with books in different languages. The pictures show the setting's approach to reading, writing, mathematics and science.

These brochures can be changed and updated as required, and can be borrowed by parents to look through at home. Children enjoy browsing through this type of photographic record.

Some photograph books can be very general, while others might focus on one aspect of the work with children, for example play, mealtimes or the approach to reading.

THE PARENTS' BOOKLET

Parents appreciate having a booklet of their own to keep. This can be given at the first meeting with the key worker, teacher, childminder or nanny. The parents' booklet should contain:

❖ the address and telephone number of the early years setting;

❖ the name of the child's key worker or teacher;

❖ a chart showing the names of all the staff, what they do and their qualifications;

❖ information about the opening and closing times;

Fig 16.1 Parents' noticeboard

* details of other services, such as parent-and-toddler groups, drop-ins, toy library, and so on;

* information about how the children are admitted, and about fees if appropriate;

* information about what to do if the child is to leave the setting;

* information about the age range of the children;

* information about what the parent needs to provide – nappies, spare clothes, snacks;

* information about the rules and boundaries that are adopted in the early years setting.

The basic information record

During the home visit the parents usually help the key worker or teacher to fill in the basic information record. All parents should

be reassured that this record will be treated with **confidentiality** and that it will be stored safely. The record will then be reviewed regularly and kept up-to-date with the parents' help.

The key worker or teacher collects all this information by chatting with the parent(s). If the family speaks a different language, it may be possible to have a translator present. If not, proceed sensitively and remember that:

* eye contact helps;

* gesture is a very powerful way of communicating with people;

* you can use photographs – those in the brochure will be a great help;

* the toys and books that you have taken to use with the child will also be a big help.

Other things which may be discussed during the home visit include:

1 **Admission procedures:** the parent will probably appreciate as much information and discussion as possible on this point. Make sure that the parent understands all the admission procedures, especially that they need to stay with the child before leaving them in the nursery (see point 2 below).

2 **Settling-in policy:** sometimes parents have difficulty taking time off work because of an unsympathetic employer. In this case the parent will not be able to settle their children in for a full fortnight – which might be the policy of the nursery. The situation will need to be discussed and an alternative arrangement made. Perhaps another relative, for example a grandparent, could help to settle a child.

3 **Separation anxiety:** the parent may be anxious about how their child will cope when they are left. You need to reassure the parent and discuss the ways in which you plan to ease the child's transition (see Chapter 9).

4 **Home-time arrangements:** parents should understand, even before their child joins the group, that the staff will not be able to let their child go home with anybody but those adults agreed in the negotiations. Staff need to know exactly who can collect the child. Furthermore, staff will not be able to let the child go home with any child under 12 years of age.

Most parents tend to enjoy chatting, so at the beginning of your meeting together set a time limit – half an hour to an hour is usual. This is important, or your home-visiting procedures will break down and parents may feel that some are being given much longer visits than others.

DETAILS INCLUDED ON THE BASIC INFORMATION RECORD

- the child's name, address and date of birth;
- emergency contact addresses and telephone numbers;
- the child's doctor's name, address and telephone number;
- any medical details which are important (e.g. in relation to diet, allergies, medicine);
- information about social workers or other professionals working with the child (e.g. a speech therapist);
- the names of people who are allowed to collect the child, bearing in mind that other children may not fetch the child;

- details about the child's interests, fears, favourite toys and comforters, and about any special words the child uses.

Building trust

UNDERSTANDING THE VIEWS OF PARENTS

An advantage of home visits is that professionals can ask parents about their views of education and care. It is only by understanding how parents feel that professionals can share effectively what they know and have learnt in their own training. This is especially important when working with families from different cultural backgrounds. The assumptions on both sides about what education is and how it should be carried out are often different. Through mutual respect, trust is established. This brings a deep commitment on both sides to working together for the child.

RESPECTING DIFFERENCES OF OPINION

The parents may hope that their child will learn to read early and might already have taught the alphabet to their 3-year-old. Do not reject their ideas about how children learn to read, even though your own point of view might be very different as a result of your training. Try asking the parent if they would like to know some of the other 12 or so things children need to know in order to read. Stress that learning each of these things is valuable in itself and that there is no hurry to learn to read. It is more important that children learn at their own pace, and they are more likely to become avid readers as a result. This does not reject the fact that the parent has taught their child the alphabet, but it does open up all sorts of other possibilities for what the parent can do to help their child to read. The messages to the parent are that the staff also value reading, that they respect the intentions of the parent and that they can be a helpful resource for a family that is teaching a child to read.

Parents keeping records

Staff may ask parents to take an observation sheet and to complete it at home. Parents can draw or write about interesting things that their child does. Drawing helps parents and staff to have a dialogue without the need for words or skilled writing. It can involve, with sensitivity, parents who use a different language or who are not confident about writing. Until recently many staff thought that parents would not want to be involved in record keeping. However, Chris Athey found that parents (several of whom spoke Urdu but not English) loved to keep observation notes as part of the Froebel Research Project – they drew in order that staff and parents could communicate with each other. Older brothers and sisters often enjoy filling in these observation sheets too. In many settings parents are encouraged to fill in observation sheets and meet with staff to discuss them.

Visits to the early years setting

Not all early years staff make home visits. This may be for a variety of reasons; for example, children in a workplace nursery may come from a very wide catchment area, making home visits impractical. If there is no home-visiting policy in your early years setting, the same procedures can be followed when the family first visits the setting. This initial visit usually takes place before the child starts to attend regularly. Some settings encourage families to visit several times before the child starts.

FIRST IMPRESSIONS ARE IMPORTANT
Ask yourself:

❖ Do parents feel welcomed by the staff?

❖ Does the building itself feel welcoming?

The following suggestions make a setting seem more welcoming:

❖ Notices with arrows to the reception office help. These might be in different languages.

❖ An attractive display in the entrance area, showing some of the recent activities that children have been involved in, can be useful.

❖ Information showing the names of staff, with their photographs, should be on display.

❖ Photograph albums containing brief notes explaining the setting's philosophy and activities are very informative.

❖ A menu of the week's meals highlights a multicultural approach.

❖ Something for children to do is helpful. One nursery school has a beautiful rocking horse in the entrance hall and this is very popular

Fig 16.2 A welcoming setting

with the children. One family centre has an aquarium to look at and an interest table with baskets full of shells.

Establishing and maintaining a professional relationship

Hopefully an atmosphere of trust is initiated during the first meeting with parents. Remember that you are not trying to make *friends* with parents: this is a professional relationship only. Friendships are about choosing each other; they are based on being interested in the same things, for example the same sort of food, dancing or football. A professional relationship is one in which people do not choose each other. They come together because of the work they do together. Early childhood practitioners and parents come together because they each spend time with and work with the child. You do not have to like someone to have a good professional relationship with them.

ADDRESSING STAFF AND PARENTS

Some people like to use first names, others do not. There will be a policy about this in your setting. Again, calling each other by first names does not mean being friends. But it can help to create a relaxed, warm and inviting atmosphere. Either all staff should be called by their first names or all by their surnames. Staff must make sure that they address parents correctly and as they wish to be addressed. This is particularly important where names are used differently in different cultural traditions.

ADDITIONAL SERVICES THAT SETTINGS MAY OFFER TO PARENTS

When settings are able to offer additional benefits and services to parents the working partnership is enhanced. Children also benefit as they become familiar with the setting in a number of different ways.

Parent-and-baby and parent-and-toddler groups

These groups introduce parents and children to settings in a very informal way. Parents might bring their toddler to the group once a week. There will be drinks and healthy snacks for parents and children, together with activities appropriate for toddlers. Adults can talk, exchanging ideas and feelings. Babies can also be brought to the group.

TOY LIBRARIES

Many early childhood settings now have toy libraries where families can borrow toys:

- Families can see if the interest in a particular toy is short-lived.
- Families can save money.
- It broadens the play experience for the child.
- It helps parents to see how pre-structured toys are less interesting to children than toys which can be used in a variety of ways. So-called educational toys, generally quite expensive, are often narrowly pre-structured.
- Toy libraries are particularly useful for children with disabilities, as it can be much more difficult to predict what the child will enjoy. Parents can experiment.

BOOK LIBRARIES AND ACTIVITY PACKS

These help parents to provide opportunities for early language and literacy, and maths and science experiences in the family home, at no or low cost. They encourage parents to enjoy books and educational activities with their children. Children can begin to learn mathematics and science in a very natural way. Eastwood Nursery School in London has developed an exciting set of mathematical packs for families to borrow. Southway Nursery School in Bedford has developed multicultural recipe packs for its resource centre.

SETTLING CHILDREN INTO THE SETTING

Probably the most important thing an early childhood practitioner does is to settle a child into an early years group, in partnership with the parent(s). Many settings have a very clear policy on admissions and settling-in. This helps all adults – staff and parents – to adopt a common approach. For example, after a home visit or first meeting, the key worker will be well enough informed to plan something the child knows and likes. For example, if the child has a much-loved teddy bear at home, the key worker might organise a basket of different teddies and a picnic set. If the child loves putting things in and out of boxes, there might be a table with boxes and objects on it. Good practice for settling children includes the following:

❖ Every child and parent should be greeted as they arrive, and goodbyes must be said as they leave – meetings and partings are important to human beings.

❖ The parent is usually encouraged to stay with the child during the settling-in period, which often lasts for the first fortnight. For the sake of the child, there need to be very firm, clear boundaries about this period.

The way a child settles into a group situation can have a lasting impact on their later life. Parents may need help to understand this. Occasionally they may not realise the significance of this period to the child's development. You will need to communicate confidently so that parents understand the reasoning behind your settling-in policy.

Guidelines for helping the child to settle into an early years setting – transitions

❖ Prepare the child for what will happen.

❖ Prepare the staff for the individual needs of the child.

❖ Arrange a home visit by the key worker who will relate to this child and family.

❖ Arrange a preliminary visit(s) to the early years setting.

❖ Arrange for the parents and child to look at books or videos about starting at the setting.

❖ Make sure that all the staff know about the child's cultural background, diet and any health-related issues.

❖ Together with the parents, use the setting's policy in such a way as to find the best way of settling the child. The policy needs to cater for the fact that each child will be different.

Fig 16.3 Settling-in

Advise parents on how to behave during the settling-in period. It is best that parents do not join in too actively with their child, but sit back quietly as a 'safe person' for the child to return to. Staff usually invite the child to join an activity such as the sand tray. The parent sits next to the sand tray, smiling and looking encouraging. Staff gradually begin to join in with the child more and more. Eventually the child will turn to the key worker for help as often as to the parent.

Children use social referencing (see page 000) as they settle in. If the parent is obviously anxious, the child will sense this. Try to help parents to relax. If you are warm and interesting to be with, this helps both the parent and the child to settle (see Chapter 9).

A typical schedule for a 2-week settling-in period

❖ Best practice is to ask a parent or other family member to stay with the child for 2 weeks.

❖ During the first week, the parent stays with the child most of the time. The child

and parent will go home after an hour or so, perhaps just before story-time, especially if this is at the end of the morning. Then the child will be in a frame of mind in which they cannot wait to return the next time. Often children leave protesting that they want to stay!

❖ The parent gradually begins to leave the child for 10-minute coffee breaks. However, they might leave a bag with their shopping, (but with no money) or something else which clearly signals to the child that they are returning.

❖ Most children like their parents to tell them that they are leaving for a short time. As they are with their key worker when the parent goes, and as long as the key worker quickly involves them in something that they enjoy, children are not usually disturbed.

❖ Some children cannot bear 'the parting'. These children are, however, a minority. The parent will know how best to leave their child – whether to tell them in advance or not. Agree in advance with the parent how you are going to proceed.

❖ Throughout our lives it is hard to part from the people we love. Some people like to wave goodbye as the train leaves the platform. Others prefer to say goodbye and leave the platform before the train goes. When children as young as 2 or 3 years are asked what is best, they are often able to say what they would prefer. Do not forget to ask for the child's view.

❖ As the parent leaves, getting the child involved in something that they enjoy is essential. Distraction only works for a few moments. Unless the child is really involved in what they are doing, feelings about being left alone without the parent will rise to the surface. Popular activities for children who are settling in are playing with rocking-horses and sand. Children can watch what is going on around them while they do these things.

Reassuring the parent

Some parents find it hard to leave and fear the key worker might compete for or even replace them in their child's affections. Try to say things which parents will find reassuring; for example, 'Marne keeps telling me that you don't spread the butter like I do. She prefers the way you do it!'

COMMUNICATION SKILLS

We have already looked at some instances where it is important that you pass information to parents clearly, but parents will want to talk, as well as listen, to you. You will need to develop listening skills. Try to set a particular time for parents so that they do not take your attention when you are involved with the children. For some parents this can be very difficult to arrange, especially if they are working.

Dealing with an angry parent

Most early years settings have a policy on how a member of staff can get help from a senior colleague if there is an emergency of any kind. Make sure that you know about this in advance! Call on your manager if you are not sure how to handle a situation.

Remember that when parents become upset it is almost always because they are under emotional stress of some kind. The paint spilt on the child's clothing may not seem serious to you, but it might be the last straw for a parent after a stressful day. Try to remain calm and polite. Your line manager will encourage the parent to move away from the public area, and will help by offering a quiet place to talk.

Case Study

Janie

Parents worry deep-down about whether staff like their child. When they ask, 'Has she been good?' they often mean, 'Do you like my child?' Staff can reassure parents by what they say. Emphasise something positive, even if you have to tell the parent that the child has not behaved well. 'I had to stop Janie from hitting Sean today. She wanted the spoon he had. It's a favourite because it has got a bit bent in its handle. She is so determined – I really respect it. I told her that she could have a turn with that spoon tomorrow. She seemed to think that was all right.' The parent is receiving the message that this key worker likes the child, respects what she wants and is helping the child to be assertive rather than aggressive. Janie has made two very positive steps in her learning:

1   recognising that a bent spoon is different from a straight one (a mathematical concept);

2   accepting that she will have to take a turn, and being able to wait a whole day to do so.

Janie's mother may appreciate being told about these advances and will not be so concerned about any naughtiness.

Maintaining confidentiality

It is your duty to keep confidential information about parents and children that you discover in the course of your partnership. Confidentiality is one of the bedrocks of trust.

Guidelines for communicating well with parents

❖ Maintaining eye contact helps you to give your full attention to a parent.

❖ Remember that your body language shows how you really feel.

❖ Try not to interrupt when someone is talking to you. Nod and smile instead.

❖ Every so often summarise the main points of a discussion, so that you are both clear about what has been said.

❖ If you do not know the answer to a parent's question, say so, and say that you will find out. Do not forget to do this!

❖ Remember that different cultures have different traditions. Touching and certain gestures might be seen as insulting by some parents, so be careful.

❖ If the parent speaks a different language from you, use photographs and visual aids. Talk slowly and clearly.

❖ If the parent has a hearing impairment, use sign language or visual aids.

❖ When you are talking together, bear in mind whether this is the parent's first child or whether they have had other children already.

❖ Remember that if the parents have a child with a disability, they may need to see you more often to discuss the child's progress.

❖ If the parent has a disability, make sure that when you sit together you are at the same level.

❖ Occasionally parents might become upset and will shout at you. If this happens do not shout back. Simply talk quietly and calmly and show that you are listening to them.

❖ Never gossip.

CONSOLIDATING AND EXTENDING THE PARTNERSHIP WITH PARENTS

There is no *one* way to have a partnership with parents. There needs to be a whole range of ways for parents to access partnership so that they can find the one that is most suitable for them. Some parents like to have regular home visits and to collect their child quickly, without waiting about for a long chat with the key worker. Some parents prefer to use a diary to communicate. In an ideal situation diaries are updated daily, but more usually they are updated weekly or even monthly. The diary is sent home with the child; parents can add to it and send it back. This is particularly helpful in monitoring the child's progress. Some parents like to come in to the nursery setting to talk to the key worker. Staff may be very tired, however, if they have worked a long shift. Some parents prefer to come to morning or afternoon sessions in the parents' or staff room. Many early years settings now make provision for this. Parents come in to sit with one another and their babies, or to attend a session led by the local health visitor.

Table 16.1 An example of a wall chart from Eastwood Nursery School.

Making and using the sensory garden

LANGUAGE AND LITERACY
There are many stories, picture books, rhymes, poems and videos to support the focus of making and using the
Sensory Garden, e.g. stories about gardens and growing
Solomon's Secret   Mr Plum's Paradise
Peter Rabbit   Jasper's Beanstalk
Titch   Worm's Eye View
Links to the senses, e.g. Makaton Nursery Rhymes video
Talking about our own gardens at home, window boxes, etc.
Development of small-world play
Naming parts of plants, trees – link to use of non-fiction books

DESIGN TECHNOLOGY
Miniature gardens – planning
Using the same material in different ways, e.g. concrete, clay
Tools for the job
Designing tools, e.g. a wheelbarrow
Weather vane

MUSIC AND MOVEMENT
Wind chimes – listening and making
Musical instruments made from natural materials,
e.g. bean pod or gourd
Listening to sounds in the garden

ART
Looking at beautiful gardens in paintings and drawings
Dyeing using natural materials, e.g. dye from plants
Pressed flowers
Children's drawings and paintings of the environment
Using clay, sand
Rubbings

MORAL AND SPIRITUAL
Appreciating life processes
Awe and wonder
Caring for nature
Creating a joint project – involvement and responsibility
Sense of achievement
Care and maintenance of the garden
Links to the local community
Care of minibeasts and discussion of why they are important to the garden
Sensitive use of the garden – behaviour
Gardens – what people use them for

SCIENCE
The senses – sight, hearing, smell, taste and touch
Using a feely box
Investigating materials – soil, stones, gravel, bark, wooden sleepers, clay, concrete
Effect of light on growth – link to use of the membrane
Soil as food – looking at minibeasts
Making a wormery
Cooking food from other countries
Edible flowers and herbs
Making perfume from petals

I.T.
Using colour magic – drawing and making plans
Using photocopier colour enlargements for a shared display
Use of the camera to record progress and make comparisons
Recording noises made on different surfaces and textures

MATHS
Sundial – telling the time
Measuring, matching, sorting, comparing, estimating, tessellation
Puzzles – growing, sequence, etc.
Recording, e.g. number of butterflies seen
Shapes of flowers, leaves, stones

HISTORY
Developing the garden – various stages
Sharing ideas
Old songs, e.g. Lavender Blue …, Mary, Mary …, I had a little nut tree …
Posters and paintings which convey a sense of history
Looking at old implements

GEOGRAPHY
Maps and plans
Talking about places where there are different sorts of gardens
Japanese gardens
Weather and its effects
Soil and water
Stones – where they come from
Growing food in other countries

- Children, parents and staff each select some of the things they think are important to include in the book. They do this at regular intervals.
- Many settings now use an edited video of the child's time in the nursery, which becomes a parent-held record.
- Through these books, parents, staff and children are able to share in the life of the setting.

Some examples of projects to involve parents

- At Pen Green Centre the projects, 'Involving parents in their children's learning' (3–5 years) and 'Growing together' (0–3 years), are helping staff to develop their work with parents. The projects are proving particularly successful with parents who have not come to meetings in the past, and they are encouraging much greater participation by fathers. This is especially so in families where there has been a divorce.
- Sure Start programmes are aimed at helping families with very young children in areas of need. The success of such projects depends on the partnerships formed with parents.

Some projects use a **transmission model** of teaching parents to bring up their children. This means the staff show parents examples of what to do, hoping the parents will copy 'good models'. Sometimes the approach is very **laissez-faire**. This means that parents are left to get on with it, perhaps being told of local groups they might like to join. However, probably the most effective approach is an **interactionist** or **social constructivist** approach to working in a close partnership with parents. In this approach staff:

- work alongside parents;
- do not try to tell parents how to bring up their children;
- find out what the parents think and feel, and respect their views;
- help parents to build on what they already know about and want for their children, offering knowledge, information and discussion;
- respect the different ways children can be brought up.

The Haringey Early Years Excellence Network uses this approach.

Change for children

The Sure Start Change for Children programme aims to ensure that support for parents becomes routine, particularly at key points in a child or young person's life. This includes information, advice and support provided through universal services, as well as targeted and more specialist support for parents of children who need it.

Measures to ensure that *all* children can benefit from confident, positive and resilient parenting include:

- **good-quality universal support:** information, advice and signposting to other services are available to all parents – both mothers and fathers. It is important that access to support can be found in places and in ways that make parents and carers feel comfortable, such as early years settings, schools, primary healthcare services and through child care information services, telephone helplines and web-based information.
- **more specialised targeted support:** for example, structured parenting education groups, couple support, home

visiting and employment or training advice – all available at the local level to meet the needs of families and communities facing additional difficulties.

❖ **a coherent set of services:** children's centres and extended schools develop both to support parents and to involve them properly at all stages of a child's learning and development.

ACTIVITY: PLANNING BROCHURES

1 Plan a brochure which will introduce parents to an early years setting. Use photographs or drawings, with brief notes, to make a booklet which shows the philosophy of the setting. The brochure will need to illustrate the range of activities, the daily timetable of events and the rationale behind the organisation.

2 Plan further booklets which show particular and specific aspects of the setting in action (e.g. the importance of the water tray and what children learn from this mathematically and socially).

3 Evaluate this activity.

ACTIVITY: PLANNING A DISPLAY

1 Plan a display for the entrance hall of the setting. What do you wish a visitor's first impression to be?

2 If possible, set up the display and observe how the area is used by parents and children.

3 Evaluate the activity.

ACTIVITY: PLANNING, IMPLEMENTING AND EVALUATING A POLICY

1 Plan a policy for settling a new child into the setting. Give the aims of the policy and reasons for certain actions.

2 Implement your plan and then evaluate it.

ACTIVITY: PLANNING AND EVALUATING A WORKSHOP

1 Plan a workshop for parents which will help them to understand how children learn through activities such as cooking, sand play and painting, for example. Plan the materials you would use for a demonstration, and make instruction cards with diagrams to help parents experiment with the materials.

2 Rehearse what you might say in a presentation to parents about one of the activities.

3 Evaluate how successful your workshop is.

ACTIVITY: PLANNING AN ACHIEVEMENT BOOK FOR THE CHILD

1 Plan a book which celebrates a child's achievements and which you and the child can share with the child's family. Discuss with the child what should be included.

2 Choose some drawings and photographs yourself. Write notes which will help the parents understand why you and the child want to celebrate the items chosen.

3 Evaluate the activity.

ACTIVITY: MODELS FOR PARENTS' LEARNING

Make a chart with these three headings:

❖ Transmission model of parental learning;

❖ Laissez-faire or 'leave it to nature' model of learning;

❖ Interactionist or social constructivist model of learning.

Which of the following sentences go under which heading?

1 Staff in an early years setting need to educate parents about how their children learn. Staff need to explain because parents do not know.

2 Parents are their child's first educator. They are the experts on their child, not the staff, and no one should interfere.

3 Parents are full of interesting knowledge about their children, but they need staff

to talk it through with them so that it begins to make sense.

4   Staff are experts who should tell parents what to do because they are trained.

5   Parents mean well, but they often do all the wrong things, so the child behaves better in the nursery than at home. Parents need to be educated.

6   Trained experts know best.

7   Parents never come to meetings, so I need to find out why. I am obviously not getting it right for some parents. I need to get better at including parents because otherwise I cannot discuss every child's progress. It is up to me as a trained member of staff to get better at my work.

8   Parents know intuitively how to bring up their children.

9   Staff need to find out how parents think and feel about their children and what they want from the setting. Otherwise they will not be able to tune in to that family and be helpful to them.

Glossary

Adult-led activities: the adult decides what the child should do

Ageism: discriminatory behaviour relating to someone's age

Allergy: a hypersensitivity to certain antigens called allergens

Ambience: the general atmosphere of a place

Amenorrhoea: the absence of menstrual periods

Anaemia: a condition in which the concentration of the oxygen-carrying pigment, haemoglobin, in the blood is below normal

Analyse: to examine closely, or consider, information looking at all the various components (parts)

Anencephaly: a condition in which most of the brain and skull are absent. Stillbirth or death shortly after delivery is inevitable

Anorexia nervosa: A recognised eating disorder, characterised by severe weight loss, wilful avoidance of food, and intense fear of being fat

Anterior fontanelle: a diamond-shaped soft area at the front of the head, just above the brow. It is covered by a tough membrane; you can often see the baby's pulse beating there under the skin. The fontanelle closes between 12 and 18 months of age

Articulation: the ability to speak clearly

Attention deficit disorder: a disorder of childhood characterised by marked failure of attention, impulsiveness and increased motor activity

Bias: prejudice or preconceived notion.

Bibliography: detailed list of written source material – usually now to include other media such as videos, TV programmes and website information

Bilingual: speaking two languages

Biological path of development: brain, physical and genetic aspects of development

Blood pressure: the pressure exerted by the flow of blood through the main arteries

Blood transfusion: the infusion of large volumes of blood or blood components directly into the bloodstream

Bone marrow: the soft fatty tissue found in bone cavities

Bone marrow biopsy: a procedure to obtain a sample of cells from the bone marrow; it is usually taken from the sternum (breastbone) or the iliac crests (upper part of the hip-bones)

Book language: the formal language that is found in books – 'And they lived happily ever after'

Bovine spongiform encephalopathy (BSE): A disorder contracted by cows from infected sheep or cattle tissue in their feed. BSE causes degeneration of the infected cow's brain and is fatal

Brochure: a book giving information about the aims and philosophy in action of the early childhood work setting

Campylobacter enteritis: An acute infection of the stomach and intestines caused by the Campylobacter bacterium

Care orders: these are issued when intervention is necessary if there is a situation where 'significant harm' to the child could result

Case law (common law): legislation by rulings in the highest courts

Cataract: loss of transparency of the cystalline lens of the eye

Central nervous system: the brain and spinal cord – the control centres of the body

Cervical smear test: a test to detect abnormal changes in the cervix (the neck of the womb) and so prevent the development of cervical cancer

Children in need: children whose health or development is likely to be significantly impaired without the provision of services, and children with disabilities

Cholera: An infection of the small intestine caused by swallowing food or water contaminated with the bacterium vibrio cholerae. It is a notifiable disease.

Christmas disease: a rare type of bleeding disorder caused by a defect in the blood-clotting system

Chromosome: a threadlike structure in the cell nucleus that carries genetic information in the form of genes

Chromosome analysis: the study of the chromosomal material in an adult's, child's or unborn baby's cells to discover whether a chromosomal abnormality is present, or to establish its nature

Cochlear implant: a device for treating severe deafness that consists of one or more electrodes surgically implanted inside or outside the cochlea in the inner ear

Code of practice for equal opportunities: document stating how the equal opportunities policy is to be put into practice

Communication: facial expressions, body language, gestures and verbal or sign languages – language involves reception (understanding) and expression. Talking about feelings, ideas and relationships through signs or words

Comprehensible input: using actions and gestures to make what is said understandable

Concept: being able to link past, present and future ideas which share some properties or attributes. A child may sit on a variety of chairs, but a concept of a chair is an idea the child has in the mind

Conforming bandage: a fabric bandage used to secure dressings and to provide light support to injuries

Conservation: linking past, present and future ideas (concepts) but being able to hold in mind several aspects of an idea at the same time (decentrating)

Content: what the child knows and understands, wants to know more about and needs to know according to the culture and society in which the child grows up

Context: this is made up of people and provision. It creates both the access to learning and the ethos in which the child learns

Contextual sensitivities: the child is not seen in isolation from the people, culture and experiences which influence development and learning

Creativity: making something of the idea you imagined, for example a dance, model, poem, mathematical equation – i.e. making something through an act of creativity

Cultural artefacts: the objects which are familiar to the child because they relate to the child's culture

Cultural identity: feeling part of a culture

Cultural path of development: social, cultural, intellectual, linguistics, representational and play aspects of development

Curriculum: this is a balance between the knowledge and understanding of the child's development, contextual sensitivities and what the child learns and understands

Development: the general sequence in the way that the child functions in terms of movement, language, thinking, feelings, etc. Development continues from birth to death and can be linked to a web or network

Developmentally appropriate curriculum: this is a curriculum appropriate for most children at the particular age and stage of development for which the curriculum is designed. The term was developed in the USA by the National Association for the Education of Young Children (NAEYC)

Diabetes mellitus: a disorder caused by insufficient production of the hormone insulin by the pancreas

Diagnosis: the determination by a doctor of the nature and cause of a person's problem

Differentiated curriculum: this helps individual children to learn in ways which are suitable for their stage of development, personality, linguistic needs, cultural background, interests and needs

Diphtheria: An acute bacterial illness that causes a sore throat and fever; it was responsible for many childhood deaths until mass immunisation against the bacillus was introduced

Disability: see Chapter 15

Display rules: culturally acquired patterns of behaviour which hide how the child feels from other people

Divorce: a legal contract separating husband and wife

Dysgenesis: defective development or malformation

Dyslexia: a specific reading disability characterised by difficulty in coping with written symbols

Ectopic pregnancy: a pregnancy that develops outside the uterus, most usually in the fallopian tube

Empowerment: helping people to believe in themselves, so that they feel able to attempt something they might not previously have thought they could do

Encephalocoele: a rare condition with the brain protruding through a defect in the skull

Encopresis: incontinence of faeces (soiling) not due to any physical defect or illness

Enuresis: the medical term for bed-wetting

Epistaxis: the medical term for a nosebleed

Equal opportunities policy: a statement of non-discriminatory aims and values

Ethnic group: a traditional way to describe a group of people who share the same culture, language, physical features or religion

Ethos: the characteristic spirit of a group of people or community, e.g. a happy ethos or a caring ethos.

Evaluation: an appraisal or assessment based on available information which is analysed

Exacerbation: a worsening of the condition as shown by the signs and symptoms

Family: a group of people living together or apart who have strong emotional relationships and who are significant to each other through blood or other links

Fatherese: when men (often fathers) talk to babies in a high-pitched tone about what is happening

First Nation Family: e.g. a Hopi family living in Arizona, USA. The Hopi Indians were settled in Arizona long before the white settlers arrived. They were the First Nation in this part of the USA. The Aborigines in Australia and the Maori people in New Zealand are other examples

Fragile X syndrome: an inherited defect in the X-chromosome that causes mental retardation

Gastro-enteritis: inflammation of the stomach and intestines, often causing sudden and violent upsets – diarrhoea, cramps, nausea and vomiting are common symptoms

Gender role: the way that boys learn to be male and girls learn to be female in the culture they grow up in. The gender role might be narrow or broad according to the culture.

Genetic counselling: guidance given (usually by a doctor with experience in genetics) to individuals who are considering having a child but who are concerned because there is a blood relative with an inherited disorder

Goodness of fit: the match between a child's temperament and a parent's way of bringing up the child. This influences the child's social development

Graphic representation: making marks on paper which relate to prior or future experiences

GUM clinic: genito-urinary medicine clinic where sexually transmitted infections (STIs) and other genito-urinary conditions are treated

Haemophilia: an inherited bleeding disorder caused by a deficiency of a particular blood protein

Hepatitis B: inflammation of the liver, caused by a virus. A mother can unknowingly pass the infection to the child she carries in her womb

Heritage, myths and legends: stories, poems, dances, songs which have been handed down across time; many contain a shred of original truth which has since been embroidered out of recognition

Holistic: seeing a child in the round as a whole person, emotionally, intellectually, socially, physically, morally, healthily, culturally and spiritually

Homophobic: fear of gay or lesbian homosexual people

Human immuno-deficiency virus (HIV): A virus which causes AIDS

Hydrocephalus: an excessive accumulation of cerebrospinal fluid under increased pressure within the skull. Commonly known as 'water on the brain', hydrocephalus occurs in more than 80% of babies born with spina bifida

Hyperactivity: abnormally increased activity

Hypoglycaemia: an abnormally low level of glucose (sugar) in the blood

Hypogonadism: underactivity of the gonads (testes or ovaries)

Hypothesis: making a prediction that if you do one thing, something else will happen as a result

Illiteracy: when someone cannot write or read

Imagination: having a new idea which has emerged from your first-hand experiences of life

Immunisation: The process of inducing immunity as a preventative measure against certain infectious diseases

Intellectual/cognitive: these words both refer to the ideas and thinking of the child. Cognition emphasises that children are aware, active learners, and that understanding is an important part of intellectual life.

Intelligence is about the ability to profit from experience

IQ: a measurement of some aspects of intelligence, through an intelligence quotient which gives a score. An IQ of 100 is the average

Jaundice: yellowing of the skin and the whites of the eyes caused by an accumulation of the pigment bilirubin in the blood

Key Stage 1: in England, years 1 and 2 in an infant, lower or primary school when child is 5+ to 7+ years old

Laissez-faire: leaving learning to nature: the idea is that if the environment and relationships are good, the child will learn naturally (nature)

Learning skills in context: children learn to master things and become competent when they are doing something that really needs doing, rather than an exercise that is removed from meaningful situations

Legionnaire's disease: A form of pneumonia (infection of the lungs) caused by a bacterium often found in contaminated water systems

Lines of reporting: procedures for ensuring child protection

Listeria: A bacterial infection resulting from eating chilled foods, particularly soft cheeses, meat pâté. It causes a 'flu-like' illness, can also cause miscarriages, and is sometimes fatal in babies and elderly people

Literacy: when spoken language is put into code, it is written. When written codes are decoded, they are read

Longitudinal: over a length of time

Marriage: a legal contract between husband and wife

Material provisions: play dough, paint, paper, pencils, home area, etc

Membranes: tough membranes which surround the amniotic fluid in which the baby floats in the womb.

Meninges: the covering of the brain and spinal cord. In meningitis, they become inflamed because of infection by bacteria or a virus

Micturition: a term for passing urine

Motherese: when women (often mothers) talk to babies in a high-pitched tone about what is happening

Multicultural: drawing on the rich variety of cultural influences

Multilingual: speaking many languages

Muscular dystrophy: an inherited muscle disorder of unknown cause in which there is slow but progressive degeneration of muscle fibres

Neonate: a newly born infant (under the age of one month)

The network for learning: this involves children in first-hand experiences, games, representation and play

Neural tube defects: The term includes anencephaly, encephalocoele and spina bifida. These conditions occur if the brain and/or spinal cord, together with its protecting skull and spinal column, fail to develop properly during the first month of embryonic life

Neuroscience: studies of the brain which are providing evidence that helps early childhood specialists to work with young children.

Nutrient: essential dietary factors, such as carbohydrates, proteins, certain fats, vitamins and minerals

Objectivity: impartiality, detachment

Oedema: an abnormal accumulation of fluid in the body tissues; in pregnancy, oedema is often shown as swollen ankles and fingers

Open-ended materials: there are many possible ways to use the material, for example clay, wooden blocks

Operations: linking past, present and future ideas (concepts) but concentrating on one aspect of an idea at a time (centrating)

Ophthalmologist: a doctor who specialises in care of the eyes

Optimum period: the best time for the child to learn something

Optometry: the practice of assessing vision and deciding whether glasses are needed to correct any visual defect

Orthopaedic traction: a procedure in which part of the body is placed under tension to correct the alignment of two adjoining structures or to hold them in position

Parental responsibility: parents should have responsibility to bring up their own children but may need support in order to do so

Perception: making sense, understanding and getting feedback through the senses and movements of your own body

Peripatetic: travelling about

Personality: the experiences children have of life and of other people influence this, as well as the child's own natural temperament. It thus involves both nature and nurture

Placenta: the organ that develops in the uterus during pregnancy and links the blood supplies of mother and baby; often referred to as the 'afterbirth'

Plaque: a rough, sticky coating on the teeth that consists of saliva, bacteria and food debris

Play-tutoring: the adult teaches the child what is involved in play

Possetting: the regurgitation (or bringing back) of small amounts of milk by infants after they have been fed

Posterior fontanelle: a small triangular-shaped soft area near the crown of the head; it is much smaller and less noticeable than the anterior fontanelle

Pre-eclampsia: a serious condition in which hypertension, oedema and protein in the urine develop in the latter part of the pregnancy

Prescription drugs: medicines that are only available on the authorization of a doctor because they may dangerous, habit-forming, or used to treat a disease that needs to be monitored

Pre-structured materials: where there are only a few narrow ways to use the material 'correctly', for example stacking toys

Principle of paramountcy: the welfare of the child is paramount

Private sector: profit-making services – e.g. a private nursery

Prognosis: a medical assessment of the probable course and outcome of a disease

Provision: the way in which time, space and materials are structured in the curriculum

Psoriasis: A common skin disease characterized by thickened patches of inflamed, red skin, often covered by silvery scales

Racism: discriminatory behaviour relating to someone's race

Rationale: reasoned explanation/statement of reasons

Representation: ways of keeping hold of first-hand experiences – drawing or models, dances, music, etc.

Rules of court: how the law is to be applied

Salmonellosis: An infection caused by the Salmonella group of bacteria, generally by ingesting infected food; the organisms can be found in raw meats, raw poultry, eggs and dairy products

Schemas: patterns of linked actions and behaviours which the child can generalise and use in a whole variety of different situations, for example up and down, in and out, round and round

Self-esteem: the way you feel about yourself – good or bad – leads to high or low self-esteem

Self-identification or self-labelling: choosing how you would like to be described

Self-identity: a sense of who you are; liking yourself, respecting yourself and

developing the skills and care to look after yourself

Self-image/self-concept: how you see yourself and how you think others see you

Sensation: being aware that you are having an experience through seeing, smelling, hearing, touching, tasting, moving (kinaesthetic)

Sensori-motor: using the senses and your own movement/actions

Sexual orientation: whether someone is heterosexual, bisexual, transsexual or homosexual

Social constructivist: using nature and nurture to help the child learn through people and provision offered

Social referencing: babies and young children look at adults to see how they react, as a guide to how they should react to a situation themselves

Special educational needs: It has been estimated that, nationally, twenty per cent of children will have special educational needs at some point during their time at school. These range from a temporary need to a more permanent need. Special educational needs are covered in more detail in Chapter 15.

Spina bifida: this occurs when the spinal canal in the vertebral columns is not closed (although it may be covered with skin). Individuals with spina bifida can have a wide range of physical disabilities. In the more severe forms the spinal cord bulges out of the back, the legs and bladder may be paralysed, and obstruction to the fluid surrounding the brain causes hydrocephalus

Statute law: legislation which is passed by an Act of Parliament

Statutory service: any service provided and managed by the state or government – e.g. the NHS or a local authority day nursery

Statutory services: central government services and local government services – e.g. social services

STI or Sexually Transmitted Infection: infection transmitted primarily, but not exclusively, by sexual intercourse

Stereotype: a limited image of someone and what they can do or be

Structured/guided play: the adult decides what the play is to be about and helps the child to carry this out, for example stacking toys, building a tower of wooden blocks, acting out a scene such as going shopping

Sudden Infant Death Syndrome (SIDS): Often termed 'cot death', Sudden Infant Death Syndrome is the sudden and unexpected death of a baby for no obvious reason

Summarise: review or recap the main points

Symbolic behaviour: making something stand for something else

Temperament: this is the style of behaviour which comes naturally to you, for example relaxed

Teratogen: an agent or influence (e.g. a drug) that causes physical defects in the developing embryo

Tetanus (lockjaw): a bacterial infection in which the muscles of the jaw and neck go into spasm. Rarely seen in the UK now because of the effective immunisation campaign

Theory: a prediction about how something will be. This can then be tested out

Tinnitus: a ringing, buzzing, whistling, hissing or other kind of noise heard in the ear in the absence of a noise in the environment

Tokenist: a stereotyped symbol which is like a short-hand code for a culture. It gives a superficial and often inaccurate introduction to a culture, people with disabilities or of different genders

Transitional bilingualism: using the first language in order to learn English (or the main language)

Transmission: shaping the child's behaviour so that the child has the knowledge the adult wants to transmit (or send) to him or her (nurture)

Tuberculosis (TB): An infectious disease, caused by the tubercle bacillus, which commonly affects the lungs. It used to be a major killer in childhood and early adult life

Uterus: another name for the womb

Vaccination: A type of immunisation in which killed or weakened micro-organisms are introduced into the body, usually by injection

Varicose veins: enlarged or twisted superficial veins, usually in the legs (varicose veins of the anus are called haemorrhoids or piles)

Visualisation technique: thinking positive images about how you would like things to be

Voluntary organisation: an association or society which has been created by its members rather than being created by the state, for example a charity

The N/SVQs and the **National Occupational Standards** on which they are based are now called **Children's Care, Learning & Development**. This reflects the fact that these awards now apply to people who are working with children from **0–16 years**. Previously the Early Years Care & Education awards applied to people working with children from **0–8 years**.

CCLD203, CCLD303 and **CCLD403** are the only units requiring evidence **across the entire age range** (the rest of the units assess the learner's knowledge against the age range in which they are working).

Child Care and Education (4th edn)

Chapter	Level 3 CCLD NVQ/SVQ Unit	Element	Level 4 CCLD NVQ/SVQ Unit	Element
1. Anti-discriminatory/anti-bias practice	**CCLD 305:** Protect and promote children's rights **CCLD 321:** Support children with disabilities or special educational needs and their families	305.1,2 321.1	**CCLD 402:** Support policies, procedures and practice to safeguard children and ensure their inclusion and well-being	402.1
2. Observation and assessment	**CCLD 303:** Promote children's development *(NB Birth to 8 years only)*	303.1 303.2	**CCLD 403:** Support programmes for the promotion of children's development *(NB Birth to 8 years only)*	403.1,3
3. Working with young children	**CCLD 301:** Develop and promote positive relationships **CCLD 303:** Promote children's development *(NB Birth to 8 years only)* **CCLD 309:** Plan and implement curriculum frameworks for early education	301.all 303.3 303.4 309.1 309.2	**CCLD 403:** Support programmes for the promotion of children's development *(NB Birth to 8 years only)*	403.2
4. Caring for young children – the essential foundations	**CCLD 302:** Develop and maintain a healthy, safe and secure environment for children **CCLD 306:** Plan and organise environments for children and families **CCLD 307:** Promote the health and physical development of children **CCLD 312:** Plan and implement positive environments for babies and children under 3 years **CCLD 314:** Provide physical care that promotes the health and development of babies and children under 3 years	302.1,2 306.all 307.all 312.all 314.all	**CCLD 403:** Support programmes for the promotion of children's development *(NB Birth to 8 years only)*	403.2
5. Holistic child development	**CCLD 303:** Promote children's development *(NB Birth to 8 years only)*	303.all	**CCLD 403:** Support programmes for the promotion of children's development *(NB Birth to 8 years only)*	403.2,3

Topic	Unit	Code	Unit	Code
6. Cognitive development	**CCLD 303:** Promote children's development (*NB Birth to 8 years only*)	303.all	**CCLD 403:** Support programmes for the promotion of children's development (*NB Birth to 8 years only*)	403.2,3
			CCLD 408: Evaluate, assess and support the physical, intellectual, emotional and social development of children	408.2
7. Communication, including language development	**CCLD 301:** Develop and promote positive relationships	301.all	**CCLD 403:** Support programmes for the promotion of children's development (*NB Birth to 8 years only*)	403.2,3
	CCLD 303: Promote children's development (*NB Birth to 8 years only*)	303.all	**CCLD 408:** Evaluate, assess and support the physical, intellectual, emotional and social development of children	408.3
			CCLD 409: Evaluate, assess and support children's communication	409.1 409.2
8. Physical development	**CCLD 303:** Promote children's development (*NB Birth to 8 years only*)	303.all	**CCLD 403:** Support programmes for the promotion of children's development (*NB Birth to 8 years only*)	403.2,3
			CCLD 408: Evaluate, assess and support the physical, intellectual, emotional and social development of children	408.1
9. Emotional and social development	**CCLD 303:** Promote children's development (*NB Birth to 8 years only*)	303.all	**CCLD 403:** Support programmes for the promotion of children's development	401.1 403.2
	CCLD 308: Promote children's well-being and resilience			
10. Understanding the behaviour of children	**CCLD 321:** Support children with disabilities or special educational needs and their families	321.2	**CCLD 403:** Support programmes for the promotion of children's development	403.3
11. Health and community care	**CCLD 302:** Develop and maintain a healthy, safe and secure environment for children	302.3		
	CCLD 319: Promote healthy living for children and families	319.1 319.2		

Appendix (Continued)

Child Care and Education (4th edn)

Chapter	Level 3 CCLD NVQ/SVQ Unit	Element	Level 4 CCLD NVQ/SVQ Unit	Element
12. Play, curriculum and early learning	**CCLD 309:** Plan and implement curriculum frameworks for early education	309.1 309.2	**CCLD 407 :** Support and evaluate the curriculum for children's early learning	407.1,2
	CCLD 318: Plan for and support self-directed play	318.1,2,3	**CCLD 419:** Contribute to the enhancement of early education for children	419
13. Caring for babies in the first year of life	**CCLD 312:** Plan and implement positive environments for babies and children under 3 years	312.all		
	CCLD 314: Provide physical care that promotes the health and development of babies and children under 3 years	314.all		
14. Preparation for employment	**CCLD 304:** Reflect on and develop practice	304.1 304.2	**CCLD 401:** Establish and develop working relationships	401.1 401.2
			CCLD 404: Reflect on, review and develop own practice	404.3
15. Provision of services and child protection	**CCLD 305:** Protect and promote children's rights	305.3	**CCLD 402:** Support policies, procedures and practice to safeguard children and ensure their inclusion and well-being	402.2
16. Working in partnership with parents	**CCLD 301:** Develop and promote positive relationships	301.4	**CCLD 405:** Co-ordinate provision for babies and children under 3 years in partnership with their families	405.1 405.2 405.3

Index